Caligari trueSpace2™ Bible

Caligari trueSpace2™ Bible

by Peter M. Plantec

IDG BOOKS WORLDWIDE

IDG Books Worldwide, Inc.
An International Data Group Company
Foster City, CA ✦ Chicago, IL ✦ Indianapolis, IN ✦ Braintree, MA ✦ Dallas, TX

Caligari trueSpace2™ Bible

Published by
IDG Books Worldwide, Inc.
An International Data Group Company
919 E. Hillsdale Blvd.
Suite 400
Foster City, CA 94404

Library of Congress Catalog Card No.: 96-75410

ISBN: 1-56884-841-2

Printed in the United States of America

10 9 8 7 6 5 4 3 2 1

1B/RV/QV/ZW/FC

Distributed in the United States by IDG Books Worldwide, Inc.

Distributed by Macmillan Canada for Canada; by Computer and Technical Books for the Caribbean Basin; by Contemporanea de Ediciones for Venezuela; by Distribuidora Cuspide for Argentina; by CITEC for Brazil; by Ediciones ZETA S.C.R. Ltda. for Peru; by Editorial Limusa SA for Mexico; by Transworld Publishers Limited in the United Kingdom and Europe; by Al-Maiman Publishers & Distributors for Saudi Arabia; by Simron Pty. Ltd. for South Africa; by IDG Communications (HK) Ltd. for Hong Kong; by Toppan Company Ltd. for Japan; by Addison Wesley Publishing Company for Korea; by Longman Singapore Publishers Ltd. for Singapore, Malaysia, Thailand, and Indonesia; by Unalis Corporation for Taiwan; by WS Computer Publishing Company, Inc. for the Philippines; by WoodsLane Pty. Ltd. for Australia; by WoodsLane Enterprises Ltd. for New Zealand.

For general information on IDG Books Worldwide's books in the U.S., please call our Consumer Customer Service department at 800-762-2974. For reseller information, including discounts and premium sales, please call our Reseller Customer Service department at 800-434-3422.

For information on where to purchase IDG Books Worldwide's books outside the U.S., contact IDG Books Worldwide at 415-655-3021 or fax 415-655-3295.

For information on translations, contact Marc Jeffrey Mikulich, Director, Foreign & Subsidiary Rights, at IDG Books Worldwide, 415-655-3018 or fax 415-655-3295.

For sales inquiries and special prices for bulk quantities, write to the address above or call IDG Books Worldwide at 415-655-3200.

For information on using IDG Books Worldwide's books in the classroom, or ordering examination copies, contact the Education Office at 800-434-2086 or fax 817-251-8174.

For authorization to photocopy items for corporate, personal, or educational use, please contact Copyright Clearance Center, 222 Rosewood Drive, Danvers, MA 01923, or fax 508-750-4470.

About the Author

In addition to being an animator, Peter Plantec is also a clinical psychologist, former Aspen ski shop owner, European clothing designer, and a screenwriter and columnist. Currently he's contributing editor of *MultimediaToday*, and a columnist in *Animation Magazine* and *3D Design*. He has also authored many feature articles on 3D animation and special effects. He's a member AMC SIGGRAPH Hollywood, ASIFA (The International Animated Film Society), and Women In Film.

He is currently head of DreamScape Productions, an entertainment think-tank specializing in advanced game concepts, and pioneering entertainment uses for artificial agents and procedural animation. The author is teaching a seminar entitled "Becoming a Great Animator" at Silicon Studios in Santa Monica, California, and has taught more than 20 different seminars at Colorado Mountain College in Aspen and Glenwood Springs, Colorado.

Mr. Plantec is also a psychologist who has written and taught numerous courses in motivation and creativity. He shares some of his secrets to unleashing your inner creative genius in the *Caligari trueSpace2 Bible*.

He's been an animator since the age of six when his first-grade teacher sent him to the principal's office for constantly flipping the corners of his note book. Though he has little time for his passion these days, Peter *did* animate the opening to the Virtual Reality show at Comdex in 1995. He is a frequent writer, public speaker, and consultant on entertainment uses of technology.

Peter lives in Beverly Hills with his wife, one of his daughters, two dogs, and a flock of cockatoos.

ABOUT IDG BOOKS WORLDWIDE

Welcome to the world of IDG Books Worldwide.

IDG Books Worldwide, Inc., is a subsidiary of International Data Group, the world's largest publisher of computer-related information and the leading global provider of information services on information technology. IDG was founded more than 25 years ago and now employs more than 7,700 people worldwide. IDG publishes more than 250 computer publications in 67 countries (see listing below). More than 70 million people read one or more IDG publications each month.

Launched in 1990, IDG Books Worldwide is today the #1 publisher of best-selling computer books in the United States. We are proud to have received 8 awards from the Computer Press Association in recognition of editorial excellence and three from Computer Currents' First Annual Readers' Choice Awards, and our best-selling *...For Dummies®* series has more than 19 million copies in print with translations in 28 languages. IDG Books Worldwide, through a joint venture with IDG's Hi-Tech Beijing, became the first U.S. publisher to publish a computer book in the People's Republic of China. In record time, IDG Books Worldwide has become the first choice for millions of readers around the world who want to learn how to better manage their businesses.

Our mission is simple: Every one of our books is designed to bring extra value and skill-building instructions to the reader. Our books are written by experts who understand and care about our readers. The knowledge base of our editorial staff comes from years of experience in publishing, education, and journalism — experience which we use to produce books for the '90s. In short, we care about books, so we attract the best people. We devote special attention to details such as audience, interior design, use of icons, and illustrations. And because we use an efficient process of authoring, editing, and desktop publishing our books electronically, we can spend more time ensuring superior content and spend less time on the technicalities of making books.

You can count on our commitment to deliver high-quality books at competitive prices on topics you want to read about. At IDG Books Worldwide, we continue in the IDG tradition of delivering quality for more than 25 years. You'll find no better book on a subject than one from IDG Books Worldwide.

John Kilcullen
President and CEO
IDG Books Worldwide, Inc.

VIII
WINNER
Eighth Annual Computer Press Awards 1992

IX
WINNER
Ninth Annual Computer Press Awards 1993

IDG Books Worldwide, Inc., is a subsidiary of International Data Group, the world's largest publisher of computer-related information and the leading global provider of information services on information technology. International Data Group publishes over 250 computer publications in 67 countries. Seventy million people read one or more International Data Group publications each month. International Data Group's publications include: **ARGENTINA**: Computerworld Argentina, GamePro, Infoworld, PC World Argentina; **AUSTRALIA**: Australian Macworld, Client/Server Journal, Computer Living, Computerworld, Digital News, Network World, PC World, Publishing Essentials, Reseller; **AUSTRIA**: Computerwelt, PC TEST; **BELARUS**: PC World Belarus; **BELGIUM**: Data News; **BRAZIL**: Annuário de Informática, Computerworld Brazil, Connections, Super Game Power, Macworld, PC World Brazil, Publish Brazil, SUPERGAME; **BULGARIA**: Computerworld Bulgaria, Networkworld/Bulgaria, PC & MacWorld Bulgaria; **CANADA**: CIO Canada, ComputerWorld Canada, InfoCanada, Network World Canada, Reseller World; **CHILE**: Computerworld Chile, GamePro, PC World Chile; **COLUMBIA**: Computerworld Colombia, GamePro, PC World Colombia; **COSTA RICA**: PC World Costa Rica/Nicaragua; **THE CZECH AND SLOVAK REPUBLICS**: Computerworld Czechoslovakia, Elektronika Czechoslovakia, PC World Czechoslovakia; **DENMARK**: Communications World, Computerworld Danmark, Macworld Danmark, PC World Danmark, PC World Danmark Supplements, TECH World; **DOMINICAN REPUBLIC**: PC World Republica Dominicana; **ECUADOR**: PC World Ecuador, GamePro; **EGYPT**: Computerworld Middle East, PC World Middle East; **EL SALVADOR**: PC World Centro America; **FINLAND**: MikroPC, Tietoverkko, Tietoviikko; **FRANCE**: Distributique, Golden, Info PC, Le Guide du Monde Informatique, Le Monde Informatique, Reseaux & Telecoms; **GERMANY**: Computer Business, Computerwoche, Computerwoche Extra, Computerwoche Focus, Electronic Entertainment, GamePro, I/M Information Management, Macwelt, PC Welt; **GREECE**: GamePro, Macworld & Publish; **GUATEMALA**: PC World Centro America; **HONDURAS**: PC World Centro America; **HONG KONG**: Computerworld Hong Kong, PCWorld Hong Kong, Publish in Asia; **HUNGARY**: ABCD CD-ROM, Computerworld Szamitastechnika, PC & Mac World Hungary, PC-X Magazine; **INDIA**: Computerworld India, PC World India, Publish in Asia; **INDONESIA**: InfoKomputer PC World, Komputek Computerworld, Publish in Asia; **IRELAND**: ComputerScope, PC Live!; **ISRAEL**: PC World 32 BIT, People & Computers; **ITALY**: Computerworld Italia, Computerworld Italia Special Editions, Lotus Italia, Macworld Italia, Networking Italia, PC Shopping, PC World Italia, PC World/Walt Disney; **JAPAN**: Macworld Japan, Nikkei Personal Computing, SunWorld Japan, Windows World Japan; **KENYA**: East African Computer News; **KOREA**: Hi-Tech Information/Computerworld, Macworld Korea, PC World Korea; **MACEDONIA**: PC World Macedonia; **MALAYSIA**: Computerworld Malaysia, PC World Malaysia, Publish in Asia; **MEXICO**: Computerworld Mexico, GamePro, Macworld, PC World Mexico; **MYANMAR**: PC World Myanmar; **NETHERLANDS**: Computable, Computer! Totaal, LAN Magazine, Macworld, Net Magazine; **NEW ZEALAND**: Computer Buyer, Computerworld New Zealand, MTB, Network World, PC World New Zealand; **NICARAGUA**: PC World Costa Rica/Nicaragua; **NIGERIA**: PC World Africa; **NORWAY**: Computerworld Norge, Computerworld Privat, CW Rapport Klient/Tjener, CW Rapport Nettverk & Telecom, CW Rapport Offentlig Sektor, IDG's KURSGUIDE, Macworld Norge, Multimedia World, PC World Ekspress, PC World Nettverk, PC World Norge, PC World's Produktguide, Windows Spesial; **PAKISTAN**: Computerworld Pakistan, PC World Pakistan; **PANAMA**: GamePro, PC World Panama; **PARAGUAY**: PC World Paraguay; **P. R. OF CHINA**: China Computerworld, China Infoworld, Computer & Communication, Electronic Product World, Electronics Today, Game Camp, PC World China, Popular Computer Week, Software World, Telecom Product World; **PERU**: Computerworld Peru, GamePro, PC World Profesional Peru, PC World Peru; **POLAND**: Computerworld Poland, Computerworld Special Report, Macworld, Networld, PC World Komputer; **PHILIPPINES**: Computerworld Philippines, PC Digest, Publish in Asia; **PORTUGAL**: Cerebro/PC World, Correio Informático/Computerworld, Mac•In/PC•In Portugal; **PUERTO RICO**: PC World Puerto Rico; **ROMANIA**: Computerworld Romania, PC World Romania, Telecom Romania; **RUSSIA**: Computerworld Rossiya, Network World Russia, PC World Russia; **SINGAPORE**: Computerworld Singapore, PC World Singapore, Publish in Asia; **SLOVENIA**: MONITOR; **SOUTH AFRICA**: Computing S.A., Network World S.A., Software World; **SPAIN**: Computerworld España, COMUNICACIONES WORLD, Dealer World, Macworld España, PC World España; **SWEDEN**: CAP&Design, Computer Sweden, Corporate Computing, MacWorld, Maxi Data, MikroDatorn, Nätverk & Kommunikation, PC/Aktiv, PC World, Windows World; **SWITZERLAND**: Computerworld Schweiz, Macworld Schweiz, PCtip; **TAIWAN**: Computerworld Taiwan, Macworld Taiwan, PC World Taiwan, Publish Taiwan, Windows World; **THAILAND**: Thai Computerworld, Publish in Asia; **TURKEY**: Computerworld Monitör, MACWORLD Turkiye, PC WORLD Turkiye; **UKRAINE**: Computerworld Kiev, Computers & Software Magazine, PC World Ukraine; **UNITED KINGDOM**: Acorn User, Amiga Action, Amiga Computing, Amiga, Appletalk, CD Powerplay, CD-ROM Now, Computing, Connexion, GamePro, Lotus Magazine, Macaction, Macworld, Open Computing, Parents and Computers, PC Home, PC Works, The WEB; **UNITED STATES**: Cable in the Classroom, CD Review, CIO Magazine, Computerworld, Computerworld Client/Server Journal, Digital Video Magazine, DOS World, Electronic, InfoWorld, I-Way, Macworld, Maximize, MULTIMEDIA WORLD, Network World, PC World, PUBLISH, SWATPro Magazine, Video Event, WebMaster; **URUGUAY**: PC World Uruguay; **VENEZUELA**: Computerworld Venezuela, GamePro, PC World Venezuela; and **VIETNAM**: PC World Vietnam 10/17/95a

IDG BOOKS WORLDWIDE™

This one is for Adele, my wife, who makes it possible for me to get all the glory while she does dishes, pays bills, and cheers me up on bad days. She's also the real brains of the outfit.

Credits

Senior Vice President and Group Publisher
Brenda McLaughlin

Acquisitions Manager
Gregory Croy

Brand Manager
Melisa Duffy

Managing Editor
Andy Cummings

Development Editor
Kenyon Brown

Editorial Assistants
Jean Leitner
Laura Moss
Dan Hilldale

Copy Editors
Diane Eagle Kataoka
Michael D. Welch

Production Director
Andrew Walker

Supervisor of Page Layout
Craig A. Harrison

Project Coordinator
Phyllis Beaty

Production Staff
Vince Burns
Laura Carpenter
Renée Dunn
Sharon Harrison
Mary Ellen Moran
Steven Noetzel
Chris Pimentel
Andreas Schueller
Elsie Yim

Proofreaders
Christine Sabooni
Michael D. Welch

Indexer
Ty Koontz

Book Design
Drew R. Moore
Stephen Noetzel
Elsie Yim

Cover Design
Kent Tayenaka

Foreword

I first arrived in the United States on a cold but sunny February morning in 1982. Like many other refugees before me, I had no possessions but an enormous hope for the future. I moved to New York City and when I first saw a bunch of kids breakdance on Fifth Avenue I knew I was in the right place. Soon I landed a job in the shipping department of a suitcase factory. It may not sound like much but we were making suitcases for Apple IIs. I was in the "computer" business.

Three years later I saved enough money to fly to San Francisco — the second time in my life I flew in an airplane. The reason for my trip was the SIGGRAPH conference, an annual gathering of artists, scientists, businessmen, and free spirits dedicated to 3D computer graphics. This event changed my life.

Three weeks later I purchased one of the first Amiga computers. Three months after that I got my hands on a prototype of what became Caligari, one of the first 3D modeling and animation programs for Amiga. After six more years and three generations on the Amiga we completely redesigned the product. In April of 1994 we released the fourth generation under the name of trueSpace, on the Microsoft Windows platform. We liked the Caligari name so much that we renamed the company after it.

The rest, as they say, is history. A week before its release trueSpace was named the best software application at Cebit94 in Hannover, the world's largest computer show. *PC Magazine* named trueSpace a product of the year in the graphics category. A year later *InfoWorld* gave the same award to trueSpace2. Altogether trueSpace has received close to 20 major industry awards.

trueSpace offers a powerful tool set, yet it remains easy to use. It is the only 3D program with direct manipulation, perspective space-based editing with real-time feedback, and a modeless interface. It is designed entirely to accommodate human perception as well as the interactive aspect of personal computers. trueSpace pays no respect to the way 2D design is taught in traditional educational establishments.

At Caligari we believe that 3D computer graphics is a new art form. And now, in conjunction with the Internet, trueSpace is a new communication medium too. Our mission is to deliver this new medium to you, but it is up to you to decide what the meaning of the this new medium should be. trueSpace is a very good tool but it is just a tool. Mr. Plantec's book breathes life into this tool and creates meaning through the power of his imagination. For us at Caligari this is the highest reward we can get.

For you, this book is an opportunity to become an artist and to help define this new art form. We will be adding many new capabilities to trueSpace and will always improve its interface, yet you will be able to apply what you learn here for a very long time.

In addition to guiding you in how to use trueSpace2, this book teaches you the professional approach to 3D graphics. It takes you beyond simple animation and teaches you how to create your own excellent entertainment products — and market them as well. I particularly like the many exercises designed to stimulate your creativity and self-confidence.

I hope, after you read this book, that you will carry the torch for 3D computer graphics and create stuff no one has ever even dreamed of. Whether you're new to this art form, or you've been at it for awhile, I like to think that we're all like I was when I first arrived in the United States, on the cutting edge of a new frontier. Come and help us make new worlds!

Roman Ormandy
President, Caligari Corporation

Preface

Reading computer graphics books twists my brain into a pretzel. So aside from sharing my trueSpace2 knowledge with you, I've written this book so even I might understand trueSpace. However, I don't mean to give you the impression that the book is simple.

If you really want to create your own gorgeous images, this book is for you. Even if you fail miserably at ordinary brush- and pen-oriented artistic pursuits, you can still learn to create images that will even get you excited. All you need to supply is artistic passion and vision.

A Book Is Born

I'm a bit of a maverick. When I first proposed this book I went to three other publishers with the concept. Each offered me a contract, but I passed for various reasons that I won't bore you with.

Then I approached Greg Croy at IDG Books, and found a home. Mind you, I'm a little ornery and spoiled. As a columnist I get to call my own shots most of the time, and I wanted to write this book in my own style. I warned IDG about me, but they went forward with the project anyway. I was assigned a saint of an editor, Kenyon Brown, who put up with a lot of my nonsense with patience, and provided excellent guidance. All of the staff at IDG got me through a very long tunnel, and I thank all of them.

My purpose in writing this book transcends the usual fare that's available in animation and 3D. I care more about the art of animation, 3D graphics, and entertainment than about a single suite of animation programs. trueSpace2 is probably the best program to help you learn about animation and creating 3D worlds.

3D is a combination of visualization and virtual sculpture that you combine with interactive surfacing and backgrounding. 3D lets you achieve your vision from many new directions. I encourage you to break rules and experiment to attain your private dream.

In addition to all the tutorials and instructions, I also share with you some of Hollywood's most interesting secrets. My guess is that some of you harbor deep yet maybe unformed desires to make a living as professional animators. I want this book to titillate your interest.

The first chapter of this book is called "From Beginner to Broadcast Pro." To make that leap, you need to know a lot more than how to make chrome balls reflect clouds (which is an old animation technique).

I know people who hire new animators, and I know what they're looking for. In fact, I just moderated a panel on the subject at ASIFA, the International Animated Film Society's annual job expo at Universal City, Hollywood. This business pays well and demands a lot. Just to get your head in the door you need to have animation skills, modeling skills, lighting skills, and a portfolio that includes stills, clay sculptures, and your animation demo tape. The personnel director at one of the largest houses told me they hire four lighters for every modeler. He also told me they accumulated 2,700 applications and hired only 21 people. There has to be a better way. There is. If you have talent and a great demo tape, this book tells you how to parlay that into a career.

You also need to understand how to tell a story. This book helps you put together the best demo tape you can. The digital animator who has a grasp of story stands a better chance of rising to a position of leadership. Though no book can actually guarantee that you'll be a pro when you finish; if you follow the tutorials and apply the techniques discussed in this book, cover to cover, you'll be prepared to begin a professional career in digital animation.

Who Should Read This Book

My book is aimed at everyone who ever dreamed of becoming an animator, but hasn't yet found the way. That includes children, teachers, house people, cartoonists, Web page builders, multimedia producers, would-be digital film makers, TV producers, film students, 3D Web browsers, and entertainment executives. I include the latter because they're responsible for the creation of wonderful works, but never get the hands-on satisfaction of creation.

Between these covers is everything you need to launch yourself as a professional animator, including the techniques, the software, some inspiration and a lot of professional secrets. Just add a computer, your inspiration, and a little perspiration.

But there is *another* vast group that I hope to reach. It's all of you frustrated artists who can see things — you just can't paint them. For once in your life you'd like to create a work of art you can be proud of. I'm both pen and brush challenged, but with Caligari trueSpace2, I produce works of art and animation that I am actually *proud* of. This may be the first time in your life that you look at your final rendering and say "Wow, did I do that!?" And of course, you did — from scratch.

This book has everything you need. All you need to supply is a speedy multimedia PC with at least 8 megs of RAM, some time, and a modicum of courage.

New technology tools change the way we visualize and create. If you're a precise person, the tools take care of all that precision; if you're a wild artistic type, they give you space, materials, and tools to work with in a natural way. trueSpace does this well.

In addition to the nuts and bolts of digital animation, you'll learn about such things as character design, writing short animation, how to make a killer demo tape, and how to market yourself in the industry. You'll even learn how build your own digital animation studio and market your capability on the Web.

My experience in Hollywood helps this book transcend its genre by addressing classical and aesthetic issues such as lighting, art direction, and digital cinematography. I also address issues such as judging your own talent and overcoming emotional barriers to success in the field.

How This Book Is Organized

I've divided the book into eight logical parts so you can work through them one at a time and reach closure on each. Attacking a book this size is a daunting task both from your perspective and mine, so take it part by part.

Part I: So You Want to Work in 3D

Here is where we check you out. I introduce the general concept of working in 3D, look into possibilities, and throw you right in the middle of everything with a fast tutorial. You actually render your first digital movie in Chapter 2. Then I back off a tad and we talk about what the heck are you going to animate once you know how? I've found that the greatest motivation in the business is having a great concept to animate. Chapter 3 gives you a short, intense course in animation writing, complete with non-bogocious creativity tips from the shrink himself.

Chapter 1: trueSpace2: From Beginner to Broadcast Pro

This introductory chapter makes a good argument for why the beginner should start with tS2 and stick with it all the way to the professional level. It also talks about the computer power now available to virtually anyone who wants it.

Chapter 2: Animation Jump-Start

You probably want to get your feet wet without having to read a lot of boring description. Chapter 2 launches you directly into the world of animation through the use of prebuilt scenes and objects. You actually load the elements and assign the animation paths to objects.

Chapter 3: A Brief Course in Animation Story Concepts

You need something to animate and it ought to have a story to it. One of the glaring signs of amateur animation is the mission story. Objects are animated and special effects flash by, but it doesn't hang together. Animation is way more about entertainment than about technique. This chapter teaches the basics of story writing and helps the stuck reader with creativity skills.

Part II: You Can Build Absolutely Anything in trueSpace2

Here you get five intense chapters on the nuts and bolts of building 3D objects. And in Chapter 8 I tell you how to cheat and use other people's objects in your project. Hey, why not save yourself some time?

Chapter 4: The X, Y, and Zs of the trueSpace2 Interface

3D space has three directions: side to side (X), up and down (Y), and in and out, or depth (Z). In this chapter you learn about working on a 3D Cartesian plane, and you place objects and navigate the view too. Here, I introduce all the basic tS2 tools and concepts used to create a traditional pile of chrome balls reflecting the sky and each other.

Chapter 5: The Universe from Scratch

Here you use Primitives to create a reasonably sophisticated space tanker. In assembling the ship, you'll use tools and learning techniques for creating all sorts of component shapes and objects. I also introduce you to backgrounds and shading concepts.

Chapter 6: There's Magic in your Tools

Building an industrial flashlight may not sound like fun, but when it starts to look like a photo of the real thing, you get the picture. Here you learn more advanced object construction and manipulation techniques including 3D Boolean operations, spline polygons, complex sweeps, and text object manipulation.

Chapter 7: Sculpture In Space

One of the big new interests in animation is organic modeling and movement. tS2 is ready for both. Here you learn about tools for sculpting organic forms, character creation, deformation tools, and objects. You create a lifelike shark and place him in a believable underwater environment for later organic animation.

Chapter 8: Object Hierarchies

Objects in 3D are usually constructed as a series of assembled parts. There is a logic and order to this structure called the Object Hierarchy. Ordinarily the object acts as a single entity, but through Object Hierarchy navigation, you can select and manipulate individual sub-objects. In this chapter you learn different ways of gluing objects together to create hierarchies that make sense to you. Understanding this concept is critical to building complex articulated characters with dependent motion as in walking robots or animals, and so on.

Part III: The Art of Surface Design

This is one of my favorites. I'm still amazed at how photo-real you can make your images if you know the tips and tricks I give you here. I've brought in a great colleague for advice: Kathy White from Rhythm & Hues. She knows more about surfaces than I'll ever know and she shares a lot of tips with us. It's a complex subject and I take six chapters — from tools to animated materials — to cover it. It's exciting reading.

Chapter 9: Foreign Objects in Your System

Sometimes you won't want to sculpt or construct your own geometry. It's then that you'll want to import objects into tS2. trueSpace2 makes the process an absolute snap compared to such expensive packages as SoftImage — where you don't have a universal import filter. trueSpace2 directly imports files from most of the big suites such as WaveFront, LightWave, 3D Studio, and many more. This chapter explains what all the little adjustments are about and how to get the best results importing images for other formats. It also reveals some great sources for thousands of free quality models.

Chapter 10: Even More Neat Tools

I wouldn't want to cover all the tools in tS2 in only one chapter. Here you can indulge in the finer points of sweeping, beveling, and extruding, and get introduced to some handy utility tools, such as the Mirror tool and the Divide series of tools. Mirror reverses an object's geometry to create a mirror image. The divide tools help you manage the density of polygons in your mesh and the smoothness of your object. I also discuss and use other tools such as the measuring tape and the flip normal tools.

Chapter 11: Surface is a Verb – in trueSpace2

Chapter 11 covers all you need to know about trueSpace's wonderful collection of easy-to-use brushes. One paints single polygons, one paints on a gradient, one paints individual polygons, and another paints only over old paint. You learn to mix the virtual paint that creates the illusion of reality: liquid golds, cloth your mind can feel, glowing marble floors, even glass. You learn to use the interactive shading interface to create exactly the look you want while viewing at a real-time 3D rendering of the surface. You learn all about texture mapping too and using the libraries to save those unique textures you create.

Chapter 12: Shader Techniques

In this short chapter you'll have a love affair with light. The shaders in tS2 enable you to add such enhancements as highlights, surface texture, transparency, refraction, and ambient light to your creations. Here you learn to create a variety of surfaces from rusty metal through wood to fine crystal glass. (Now if only it could create spendable gold...)

Chapter 13: Images That Go Bump in the Light

Here you learn all about how to create suspension of disbelief through the magic of textures with bumpmaps, transparency maps, and the like. Kathy White, digital effects supervisor at Rhythm & Hues, with credits from *Batman Forever* to Japan's amazing underwater SeaFari ride, shares many professional secrets here. These are the kinds of tips you could take years to learn. Here you quickly learn about creating your own texture maps and get an introduction to the best image preparation tools available.

Chapter 14: Animated Materials

One major advance in tS2 over tS1 is the use of animated textures. This is like using live paint. You paint a moving picture onto a TV screen, or moving clouds on a sky. You find lots of places to scrounge for animated textures and even how to make your own. If you can't imagine how you might use them, read the whole chapter.

Part IV: Setting the Cosmos... er, Stage

Three very rare, important chapters you should not miss. They're all about art directing your project and lighting it for maximum impact. Again I got help from two of the most talented in their field. Sharon Calahan, technical lighting director for PIXAR, and Ed Lee, a top art director at Rhythm & Hues. You won't find this kind of essential information in most application books and I think you're going to enjoy it.

Chapter 15: The Art of Production Design

Production design can be child's play. By that I mean it takes a child-like ability to see things in new and unusual ways. Here you learn where to find inspiration, how to use storyboards in your design process, and how to think like a production designer considering the camera all the time. You learn to integrate your conceptual ideas with the dramatic needs of the story to create a beautiful and synergistic whole.

Chapter 16: The Magic of Great Lighting

Light is the most critical single element in 3D. In this chapter you learn about the psychology and symbolism of light, and how it's been used down through the history of film making. You'll learn how to enhance the dramatic mood of your images with light. I've also included a description of the different kinds of lighting you can use from a Key light to an Obie. We're lucky to have one of the most accomplished digital lighting experts in the world, Sharon Calahan, giving you advice and tips throughout this chapter.

Chapter 17: Creating Atmospheric Effects

One of the frequent questions coming over the Internet is, "How do I create such and such an atmosphere?" In trueSpace2 you have many tools and techniques for creating interesting atmospheres. The best ones are not automatic, like fog. They require you to do some creative engineering to achieve them. In this chapter I show you how to come up with nifty atmospheric effects and how to think them up on your own. Here you learn atmospheric effects ranging from light mist to dense, layered smog.

Part V: Action!

Animation is all about movement. This is the biggest section of the book with plenty of exciting things to learn over ten chapters. I think you'll find it a moving experience. I cover everything from tools to the final rendering of your animation. In between you learn how to control complex, articulated movements, how to install motion paths, and how to create Hollywood special effects and character animation. I got help on the digital cinematography from Steve Katz, author of two of my favorite books on directing and cinematography.

The way your camera and actors move is far more important than you may realize. It really separates the players from the Players. For example, the easiest way to track a moving spaceship with a moving camera is to lock the camera eye to the ship's axis. This causes the camera to *always* look exactly at the ship's center.

This is also a dead giveaway of amateur cinematography. Cameras and objects do not naturally suffer from continuous synchronized axis realignment, so it looks cheesy if you use too much of it.

In these chapters you also learn all about organic movement. This software is particularly powerful for creating smooth and natural-looking movements. We'll animate a shark swimming along the sea bottom, for grins.

You also learn how to achieve some of Hollywood's most spectacular special effects using tS2 and Exploder, a standalone special-effects generator you'll find on the CD-ROM.

Chapter 18: The Tools of Motion

Creating a believable model is only one third the story. You can give it real life through complex, realistic motion. Then your space ships can dodge chunky asteroids, your suns can explode, and your robots can walk (and maybe even chew gum at the same time). Even your characters can talk with facial expression.

Chapter 19: Relational Animation: Hierarchies

Celestial choreography is how I think of planetary motion. Moons around planets around suns. It's a dance with a clear hierarchy. In this chapter you learn how to build a solar system with hierarchical orbits. You learn one method of giving articulated movement to the Robie robot that comes with trueSpace2 and perhaps how to make the wheels on the bus go round and round; round and round... all day long.

Chapter 20: The Animation Project Window

The project window is an enormously powerful tool that is often overlooked by casual trueSpace2 users. In this chapter you learn to use it to automatically change the length of your animation sequence, rearrange movements with in your sequence, duplicate or loop behaviors, and in general tweak your movement timing. This chapter explains the use of each tool with examples.

Chapter 21: Keyframe Techniques

Cool moves are essential to professional animation. They require a knowledge of how keyframes are used to sketch in movement that is interpolated by the tS2 engine. You only have to create the frames where movement changes, like the two ends of the sweep of s fish's tail. The in-between frames are created automatically. You also learn how to keyframe the movement of such things as lights and cameras to achieve sophisticated sequences for your demo tape.

Chapter 22: Choreographing Movement

As a cinematographer you are concerned about two kinds of movement: movement within the scene and camera moves. I discuss both kinds of movement here with examples. Cool camera moves are a sign of the professional. When your demo tape shows that you know your moves, you move up one notch in the competition. In this chapter you also learn how to use the camera to tell the story better, and how to move it and cut to different angles to achieve your desired cinematic look.

Chapter 23: Organic Motion

Until recently the most difficult motion to create digitally was smooth, lifelike, organic motion, like that of a jellyfish or even the ocean. With new animated deformation and sculpting tools in tS2 it's actually fun. In this chapter you learn the methods used to make a Porsche jump through a keyhole, or have a shark swim the way a shark swims. Ocean waves, a cow turning its head. After reading this chapter you'll be able to orchestrate all of these organic movements — with no preservatives added. You even learn how to use the undocumented animation capability of the object sculpt tool.

Chapter 24: Character Animation

This chapter is about creating human-like characters appealing to your audience. You learn things like how to give your character a consistent personality, how to give him or her or it charm. Here you learn a few animator's secrets to imbuing your characters with believable movement and personality. You also learn that cute movements can lend personality to a talking head or a block of wood.

Chapter 25: Camera Work

Digital cinematography is an art. Done well it makes you look like a professional. Done poorly and it can detract from excellent modeling and story. This chapter shows how to plan your shots to enhance dramatic impact, and focus the viewer's attention from scene to scene. You learn how to use the camera to transfer the viewer from space to space. You learn about the concept of coverage and how easy it is in tS2. You learn how to use the various camera constraints and controls in tS2 to achieve professional results.

Chapter 26: Hollywood-Style Special Effects

Here you get an introduction to the kinds of special effects you see in film and on television including particles, gravity, and collision effects, how they put those amazing explosions in outer space, and compositing live action with 3D and more. You learn many tricks of the trade and gain an understanding of how they were done and how you can do them. You'll never watch an effects film again without saying "I know how they did that," or "How the heck did they do that? I'm going to try it myself."

Chapter 27: Rendering Your Animation

Time for a short but important chapter that takes you beyond the physical aspects of rendering to the artistic ones. It considers the practical side of rendering for time's sake as well. Here you learn about video compression, render parameters, raytracing, file formats, and all the stuff you need to know to make rendering decisions including the impact your choices have on total render time.

Part VI: Post-Production: The Professional Touch

Three more important little chapters about ladling that professional touch onto your work. A pro can spot pro work a mile away, amateur work, three miles away. What do they look for? Sometimes they don't even know, they just recognize undeniable pro quality. In many cases that quality comes from perfectly synched sound, perfect color balance, seamless composites, and no messy spots.

Here I introduce you to such things as adding sound to your productions, and using post-production software and plug-ins to achieve clean effects and transitions. I also go into special-effect post processing as used on films such as *The Abyss* and *Death Becomes Her*, and discuss how it relates to 3D animation. Sometimes the last 5 percent of the work takes 95 percent of the effort — yet that last 5 percent is what separates the pros from wannabes.

Chapter 28: Silence Is Deafening – Creating a Winning Soundtrack

Play a soundless demo next to one with a well-planned, well-synched audio track — the difference is astounding. You forget all about the silent one. This chapter introduces you to sound editing and enhancement. You also learn about multitrack composition where you combine music, sound effects, ambient or wild tracks, dialog, and emphasis tracks into a single synchronized sound track. You learn about affordable tools for creating your own sound enhancement and effects as well as multitrack sound/video software you need to do professional work. You also learn how you *can* afford the equipment to do professional sound work in your home studio.

Chapter 29: Plug-in Filter Effects

A relatively new concept, plug-ins are modular pieces of software that enhance the capability of your existing application. For example, Kai's Power Tools bring a wealth of texture filters and texture engines into Photoshop. These plug-ins can also be used to create animated textures not possible in Photoshop alone. Strata's MEDIAPaint uses plug-in special effects such as lightning, bubbles, and glowing pixie dust that you can add to your rendering in post-production. You learn about video filters for Premiere and Razor Pro that you can change over time, such as lens flares that can become supernovas. Many Photoshop compliant plug-ins can be used directly in tS2 to achieve interesting background effects and textures.

Chapter 30: Post-Production Software

This chapter reveals the tip of an iceberg — the vast field of new post-production software you can save up to buy. They include image editors, video editors, sound editors, special-effects post-production suites, morph editors, and a raft of texture creation tools. You learn my opinions on various packages, and what you can do with them (the packages, not my opinions).

Chapter 31: Post-Production Techniques

Here you learn some nifty tricks and techniques for using the various film editing, painting, and special effects doodads. The purpose of the chapter is to show you some of the ways you can use these packages to add special qualities to your finished presentations. You also hear about how easy it is to overdo post-production and ruin the original material.

Part VII: Now Do Something with It!

This section is about self-promotion. I'll show you how to create a killer demo tape that will reach out of that monitor, grab 'em by the nose hairs, and pull those bleary-eyed reviewers to the screen. You have to do that to overcome the fact that they've just seen a hundred other demo tapes. Your advantage is that most of those tapes all looked the same. Yours will not.

Personal Web home pages and links to the right feeder sites can also make a big difference in your career. I have two chapters in this section that teach you how to create 3D environments on the Web; this alone can become a full-time, fun occupation. The CD-ROM includes a special form of trueSpace Fountain in beta for you to experiment with. You can even get updates via the Web at `http://www.caligari.com`.

Chapter 32: Creating Your Own Demo Real

This is probably what you secretly wanted to know about from the beginning. Here you learn how to spell out what it is you want your tape to accomplish, how long to make it, How to come up with killer ideas and how to get it out of your computer onto video tape.

Getting a career started in CGI takes a few quirks and characteristics all rolled into one person. Some of it is natural ability, but most of it comes from the creative application of persistence and determination. Here you learn how to out-stride the competition by building a smart and beautiful sales tool — your demo.

Chapter 33: Creating a 3D Web Site with VRML

This is an introduction to Fountain, Caligari's 3D Web browser/authoring package based on the tS2 interface. I introduce many dandy concepts here to give you a grounding in VRML, the language of the 3D Web. You learn about In-lining objects, what LODs are, and how to use Fountain's innovative new help interface.

Chapter 34: Using Fountain

Once you're well-grounded in the concepts and principles of the 3D Web, you get to learn the details of how to construct interactive 3D worlds using Fountain. Most of your skills translate directly, so you'll be up and running in a very short time. You learn how to install Fountain, all about its two interfaces (authoring and browsing), and you get a set of extensive tutorials to carry you through the whole operation.

Part VIII: Career Opportunities in 3D Animation

Finding the right job is your most important life quest next to finding the right mate. For some people it *is* the most important thing in life, forget the mate. Most really good ways to get yourself hired in this business are not totally obvious. If you try looking in the news papers for a job as a digital animator, good luck. It's not going to happen. But you *will* find what you want when you understand the dynamics of the industry.

I'll show you how to meet people working in 3D animation — your future colleagues. You don't have to be just some face off the street, walking into the employment office with a demo reel. If you have some personal credibility and talent, let people know, and spend time with your future peers. They might support your bid for a job, and it's the only way you'll know if these are the kind of dudes you'd like to spend your days with.

These four chapters tell you all about places to look for employment. The Web has provided a stage to carry self-promotion to high art — literally. You learn about exploiting this link to the world to promote yourself and your work.

As your talents grow you may want to start your own digital studio. Chapter 37 goes into some depth on building a high-end digital studio on a shoestring. I spill some secrets here such as building a DEC Alpha graphics workstation from parts, finding high-end software at low-end prices, and guerrilla marketing your business.

The last chapter is a look at where this industry is headed. My company, DreamScape Productions, is an entertainment think-tank; we help develop advanced entertainment experiences such as fully immersive environments with real-time animated characters controlled by artificial intelligence. I'll tell you about it and about other areas of future growth in the industry.

Chapter 35: How to Find a Job in the 3D Industry

Here I get specific about finding a job in the industry, looking at such things as what fields now offer opportunities, where to find the companies you'd most like to work for, how to conduct your interviews, how to schmooze your way to a job, and what organizations can help you meet the right people.

Chapter 36: Animation Resources on the World Wide Web

Digital animators need to be Web-wise. This chapter sets you well on your way to accomplishing that goal. It shows you where to look for job opportunities, to post your availability as a freelance animator, how to do guerrilla marketing for yourself, where to list yourself, and how to find useful goodies online. Some neat stuff here.

Chapter 37: Building Your Own Digital Animation Studio

If you want to freelance you have to be competitive. In this chapter I give details on how to start your own digital animation studio on a bare-bones budget. I give specifics on how to market and finance your studio, build your own equipment, what software to consider, what kind of space you'll need, and how to charge for your services — the whole ball of wax.

Chapter 38: The Future of Digital Animation

My company looks to the future of entertainment and communications. In this chapter I share with you some of what I see on the horizon. These visions imply future occupations in digital animation that will be needed to fill a growing demand for quality material. I reveal DreamScape concept games of the future where your opponent and all the other characters are artificial intelligence agents controlling procedurally animated avatars. If you've paid attention and done your exercises, you'll be ready for that future before it gets here.

Appendixes

The book includes five appendixes, covering the CD-ROM, offering tips and techniques on using trueSpace, sharing a primer on character development, listing resources and organizations, and providing information on tS2 file formats. I also whipped up a collection of bad surgical jokes... but the publisher had that appendix removed.

Appendix A: Using the Companion CD-ROM

I provide a guided tour of the CD-ROM that is packaged with the book. The CD contains much useful material, animations, stills and textures, and many models, as well as shareware and demos you can use with tS2. You will also find full functional versions of tS2 and Fountain on the disk. This appendix gives you complete installation instructions. Every computer book seems to have a CD-ROM these days, but this onc is better — it's not a bunch of shovelware. So many toys! You'll think it's your birthday.

Appendix B: trueSpace2 Tips and Techniques

Want all the low-down on things you won't find in the trueSpace documentation? This appendix doles out just such tips and techniques to help make you a trueSpace2 whiz. This information derives from the trueSpace Mailing List, so these tips and techniques are straight from the trenches — real advice from real experts. (By the way, the CD-ROM contains a hypertext version of this appendix.)

Appendix C: The Dynamics of Character Development

This is perhaps the strangest appendix, yet it may be the key to your animation success. After interviewing many of the people who hire in this field I'm convinced that the way to their hearts is to develop animated characters with a truly human manner. This appendix prepared by Dr. Anthony Gregorc, a noted psychologist and expert on character traits, gives you a wealth of ideas for character development. If you pay attention, you'll never have another dull animation. Also, you'll gain a lot of insight in to your friends and family.

Appendix D: Media Resources and Organizations

If you want to succeed, you need to get connected. This appendix lists resources and organizations that can help you build your competitive edge in the job market. The more you know, the better chance you stand at making a positive impression in your next job interview. You might want to put a sticky note in this appendix.

Appendix E: trueSpace2 File Formats

Chunks and headers. You learn about such beasts in this appendix, which provides details on the geometry and material information stored in Caligari object (*.cob) files. It helps enable you to read, manipulate, and write such files. If you like programming, this appendix is an invaluable reference for creating your own engines for the complex manipulation of objects. Impress your friends (and maybe potential clients) — learn about tS2 file formats here.

Conventions Used in This Book

This book looks pretty much like all the other bibles from IDG. First, e-mail addresses and things you type into your computer are usually given in `monospace font`. In addition, I've used some funky icons in the left margin to bring your attention to things of note. Some of them are neat ways of doing things that aren't in the manual and some point out pitfall areas.

TAKE NOTE POWER TIP These icons highlight text written to give you some professional insight or methodology that saves you time and effort.

WEB CONNECTION With the explosive growth of the Internet recently, Web connections are hot stuff. This icon emphasizes these connections, which are particularly hot in the world of 3D animation.

CAUTION This icon indicates some little pitfall that you better step over. These are things I fell smack into during my many hours of learning tS2. I wish I'd had this book.

Off and Running

Ready to get started? Computer graphics, trueSpace2, and the universe of 3D animation is an amazing realm. It's populated by creative, fun, and stimulating people who produce top-notch work of innovative artistry. What these people hold in common is enthusiasm, a dash of discipline, and unbounded imagination. The cool thing about trueSpace2 is that it won't hold you back. Let's go!

Acknowledgments

You don't write a book like this without a little help. In my case, it was a lot of help. Some of the most talented and knowledgeable digital filmmakers in the business have shared their insight and creative approaches with me in this book. Altogether, people in more than a dozen countries — from Zaire to Sri Lanka — contributed in one way or another.

The Californians

Thank you to Hollywood, that virtual entertainment mecca that exists only in dreams of California. It's real, yes, but it's not in any one physical place. Here are some of the Hollywood's denizens that helped me in a big way.

First I'd like to thank Sharon Calahan of PIXAR for your time and invaluable contributions to the chapter on lighting. Your deep knowledge has added richness to this book.

Kathy White of Rhythm & Hues, thanks for your insights into texture, lighting, and your general philosophy as well as images for my color section (and your occasional moral support too). Also at R&H, Ed Lee, the wildly talented art director, thanks for sharing your insight into the process of art direction and production design and for your killer story boards. And thanks to Suzanne Datz in public relations at R&H for being the lubricant that made things go so well, especially in obtaining permissions to publish R&H artwork.

My appreciation to Jim Hillin at Disney Feature Animation — thanks for sharing your deep wisdom about light, and how to study and make use of it. To Academy Award nominee Christopher Landreth of Alias/WaveFront, thanks for clueing me in to what good animation is, and how to have fun creating it. Independent animator Allen Coulter, your "Balls and Blocks" convinced me that marbles do live — thanks for your many words of wisdom, Allen. You also showed me that "professional" has nothing to do with the cost of your equipment or your software — it's all in your attitude.

Caligari animator I-Wei Huang actually flew down to my studio from Northern California to teach me how to animate articulated motion. Thanx I-Wei. Also at Caligari, I want to thank Roman Ormandy, Bibanna Gasparik, Stan Ziel, and Konstantine Guericke, all of whom helped me stay on top of tS2 from early beta to shipping product and beyond.

At Visual Concepts Entertainment (VCE), I want to thank Kim Terhorst for keeping me supplied with special effects material, and thanks to Peter Kuran, top man/ optical FX wizard at VCE, for helping me better understand film FX and professional pyrotechnics.

The tSML

I also have to thank the generous members of the tSML, the trueSpace Mailing List. Started in December of 1994 by Shane Davison at the University of Regina in Canada, It quickly grew into a major resource for tS fans. Shane's insights helped me to learn tS2 from early on. Thank you to all the folks at netnet.net, especially Bill Ehrendreich, who managed the original unofficial trueSpace FTP site. This site helped us all share our brilliant animations and techniques from the early days.

And all the trueSpace animators from more than a half dozen countries, who have contributed ideas, opinions, and tips that influenced my thinking as I wrote this book. They include but are not limited to (forgive me if I forgot to list you): Josh Andersen, David Campbell, Chng Ching Huei, Terry Cotant, Sean Cunningham, Shane Davison, David Duberman, Ian Firth, Dale Gass, Adam Glassman, Serge Golikov, Brian Hickey, Aaron Hill, Ulrich Haessler, Ulrich Kliegis, Eric Knisley, Nontajit Lertworachon, James Eric Mason, Mark E. Marshall, Mark Menger, Michael Mills, Dave Moller, Nigel, Bjørn-Kåre Nillsen, Dean Oliver, Walter Reed, Robert Stephen Rodgers, David Sieks, Larry E. Touchette, Todd Tucker, Mike Vanderlaan, Bruce G. Vryenhoek, Kon Wilms, Ernest Yanarella, Mike Zemina, and everyone else who contributed along the way.

The Staff

I'm severely dyslexic and my editors can vouch for it. Thank you Diane Eagle Kataoka, my friend and trusted copy editor, for making me look literate. Thank you, Mauricio Baiocchi, my tech editor, for catching my major blunders.

Most of all, Kenyon Brown, development editor, you are a saint of patience. No one else could have handled me as well. And Michael Welch, thank you for your punctilious copy editing.

Thank you, Tracy Cramer, for your TLC in getting permissions, and Jean Leitner for more permissions, Shelley Lea for your spectacular art direction on the color section, Kent Tayenaka for art directing the cover, and brand manager Melisa Duffy for your enthusiasm in marketing my book.

Thanks to all the companies that contributed materials for the CD-ROM and the people who assisted at each company. I can't list them all or the whole book would be thank-yous.

The Family

Finally, it's obligatory to thank one's family. But in my case they truly were my support team. They now accept that, for me, staring out the window means I'm working. Thanks Adele, Dani, and Michelle.

And thank you dear reader. If you had the patience to read this list you will surely make it to the end of this tome in good spirits.

The Folks from Elsewhere

At Iguana Entertainment way down Austin way (there's only one), the very cool and talented Cyrus Lumm — thanks for letting me use your now-famous shark animation sequence and that great dragon piece to demonstrate organic movement. More importantly, thanks for helping me better understand what makes organic movement look the way it should.

Mid-country we find Rob Bryerton, author of Exploder. Thanks Rob, for the tutorials, the suggestions, and the great fun Exploder has given me. David Duberman of Morph's Outpost, I'd have been lost without your nice work on the Fountain tutorials and frequent tSML contributions. Ed Swan, thank you very much for designing the special effects objects included on the CD-ROM.

On the East Coast, my thanks go to Steve Katz, well-known author, director, and head of the digital animation and effects division at Curious Pictures in New York. Your wisdom on camera work, production design, and film direction have been invaluable, Steven.

The Artists

Many artists from around the world contributed animations and images for the beautiful color section in this book. Thank you for helping me add a little eye candy: Todd Barnes, David Campbell, Ian Firth, I-Wei Huang, Mark Jeffers, Tom Marlin, Bjørn-Kåre Nillsen, Arie Sztajnworc, Devon Taylor, Glen Tittermary, Jonno Winchester, and Oliver Zeller.

Contents at a Glance

Table of Contents

Chapter 17: Creating Atmospheric Effects 281

Part 5: Action! 289

Chapter 18: The Tools of Motion........... 291

Chapter 19: Relational Animation: Hierarchies 307

Chapter 20: The Animation Project Window 325

Chapter 21: Keyframe Techniques 331

Chapter 22: Choreographing Movement 353

Chapter 23: Organic Motion 363

Chapter 24: Character Animation 377

Chapter 25: Camera Work 389

Chapter 26: Hollywood-Style Special Effects 401

Chapter 37: Building Your Own Digital Animation Studio 601

Chapter 38: The Future of Digital Animation 613

Appendixes 621

Appendix A: What's On the CD-ROM 623

Appendix C: The Dynamics of Character Development 705

Appendix D: Media Resources and Organizations 713

PART I

So You Want to Work in 3D

I hope the cover of this book caught your eye. I bet you're curious about 3D and you'd like to know what goes into creating such images. Well, fellow traveler, I'm betting you can create the photorealistic scene on the cover from scratch in about a week's time. Most of that time you'll spend learning the tools of 3D. They are not strange, esoteric, or difficult to use. With trueSpace2, you can easily learn 3D animation techniques.

trueSpace2 actually makes it easy for you to create professional-looking work. I suspect more than one person will finish this book and try to make a living in the exciting, rewarding, and exploding field of 3D. The challenge is to make enough money in order to buy all the equipment and software you'll need to open your own studio. If you do it, let me know.

✦ ✦ ✦ ✦

In This Part

✦ ✦ ✦ ✦

CHAPTER 1

trueSpace2: From Beginner to Broadcast Pro

In This Chapter

Introducing the world of 3D graphics

Enabling hardware

Why *you* want to learn trueSpace2

Why trueSpace2 appeals to traditional artists

trueSpace2 concepts and tools

Every once in a purple moon a new technology comes surging down the rails of change and knocks the entertainment world on its behind. Remember celluloid? Talkies? TV? It's happening again, and you can be right smack in the middle of it.

You have some fascination with 3D animation or you wouldn't have laid down cash for this book. Good. Grab hold and get ready for a wild ride as you learn all about trueSpace2, an affordable, artist-oriented 3D software solution that will get you up to speed quickly. trueSpace2 is no toy; it's a professional suite of tools capable of anything from small multimedia animations all the way up to feature film special effects.

The Hardware Revolution

As silicon horsepower rises through the roof, PC prices fall like lead rain. DEC's new 21164 CPU, dubbed the BIPS chip, has nearly a billion (not million) transistors and can execute a billion instructions per second. It runs so fast it can almost push itself from behind. Pentium Power is everywhere and PowerPC is nudging from across the way. PCs already come in speeds of 120 to 333 megahertz (MHz), with commonplace parallel processing around the corner. In addition to straight speed increases, floating point calculation, important in 3D work, has jumped from 486pcs at 15 SPEC a few years ago to 790 SPEC on latest Alpha (see sidebar).

The Specifics on SPEC

SPEC is the most reliable and respected set of performance benchmarks for computer performance. Floating Point (fp) SPEC is critical to 3D work. To show you just how competitive you can be on a hot home computer, compare these numbers supplied by Virtual Construction Technology, an Alpha Workstation manufacturer in Montana:

SGI Indy – SPEC 73 fp[1] (this is a CGI Workstation used by some studios)

Pentium 100 – SPEC 81.8 fp[1]

PowerPC (604 chip) SPEC 149 fp[1]

Pentium Pro (P6) SPEC 215[2]

*DEC Alpha AXP 21064A SPEC 290[3]

PowerPC 620 SPEC 300[2]

HP PA 8000 SPEC 550[2]

Sun UltraSparc SPEC 600 fp[2]

Alpha 21164 SPEC 590[2]

DEC Alpha 21164A SPEC[2] 700[2]

*The DEC Alpha AXP 21064A workstations outperform many professional CG workstations costing 2–3 times as much. They run Windows NT or Unix. tS2 will run on Windows NT.

As reported by: [1] *NewMedia* February 1995; [2] *Byte Magazine* November 1995; [3] Digital Equipment Corporation.

All this is good news to the 3D enthusiast. You can have a graphics supercomputer on your desk, whipping out high resolution animation faster than Ron whips out chocolate linguine — fast enough for professional work.

This cheap power has ignited a frenzy of 3D software development. The competition is fierce, forcing PC applications to include even more features in their low-end packages. It has gotten to the point where the difference between a company's $250.00 product and its $2000.00 product is virtually in the packaging. Martin Hash, of Animation Master, justifies his unprecedented pricing of Animation Master's little sister, Martin Hash's 3D Animation, at $199.00, by saying, "There's only one big market left for this software — new users and they don't start at the top of the market." You'll learn this suite makes a perfect companion to trueSpace2.

The searingly complex calculations inherent in 3D manipulation brought 386/486 PCs to their virtual knees, taking hours to render a single frame. Useless to a professional. With the new equipment, PCs burn out these frames in minutes or even seconds.

Until recently, creating fully shaded, textured 3D animations on the fly was possible only on supercomputers. The thought of doing it on a PC where each frame took minutes to render was ludicrous. No longer.

The introduction of APIs (Application Programming Interfaces), proprietary code engines that handle the most complex computer processes with stunningly efficient code, has brought real-time 3D rendering to the Pentium PC. When coupled with API-friendly hardware like Glint or Nvidia-powered boards, the accelerated 3D processing yields real-time animation, real-time texture-mapped solid modeling, and interactive lighting at 30 frames per minute or better. These boards can output hundreds of thousands of fully textured, filled polygons per second. Truly an astounding feat. trueSpace2 uses Intel's 3DR API for real-time solid modeling, even *without* hardware acceleration. In a later chapter, I'll tell you how to match up 3DR with an inexpensive hardware accelerator for blazing performance.

Empowered by these husky render engines, a new breed of digital cel jockey is arising from Waukegan to Secaucas. Setting up in old garages and back bedrooms, they have brought energy, innovation and a new high standard to the field. They may have sold their cars to get started, but it's cheap entrée to owning a digital studio — many are walking all the way to the bank. Judging from my trueSpace2 e-mail queries, it's happening from Chiang Mai to Oslo; Zaire to Moscow. Digital animation is literally exploding everywhere.

Many of today's runaway bestseller games, amazing movie effects, and most local TV flying logos originate at small companies like Diversions Software, Denver.

Ian Firth, Diversions' digital animator, is author of Void Pirates (see Plate 1-1), a shoot-em-up space game with lots of great action sequences and cosmic scenery. He can tell you, "money and computer power aren't the big barriers any more, it's brain power. You have to be sharp, know your market, have talent, and push hard when you can't even afford lunch." Check out the demo of Void Pirates on the CD-ROM.

3D Is Everywhere You Look

Spreading faster than good news on a bad day, digital artistry has become an integral part of our culture. Look at TV, film, or magazine ads and you'll see 3D rendering everywhere; it's so photorealistic you'll miss much of it. This wild world of infinite possibilities is raging out of Hollywood's back streets from such unpretentious places as MetroLight Studios, Boss Film, Rhythm & Hues, Rez.N.8 Productions, and ILM. It's reaching out across the world via the Internet where job postings in many countries already outnumber resume postings.

WEB CONNECTION

Although most digital animators today learned on the job or are self-taught, increasing numbers of schools are offering courses, even degrees, in advanced digital graphics. Some already have interactive course catalogs on the World Wide Web. You can get to them via 3D Site at `http:// www.lightside.com:80/~dani/`

A Stunning Leap in Affordability

Professional animation features like rotoscoping, particle physics, and motion blur were until very recently found only on high-end animation suites costing from $12,000.00 to upwards of $70,000.00. Now you can have these professional capabilities with trueSpace2 and the utilities included on the CD-ROM attached to this book. Later, when you've got your feet wet, you may want to buy Martin Hash's Three Dimensional Animation (MHA). It's complementary to trueSpace2, giving you a complete suite of high-end tools by adding motion capture, inverse kinematics (IK), spline patch modeling, and muscle animation to your repertory. Though they are very different applications, tS2 and MHA make a splendid pair for the serious animator because they cover each other's areas of weakness almost perfectly.

You Did This! Really?

Even if you can't draw a straight line, you can now create worlds in the digital domain. You can get a quick start by using 3D clip art — pull together an original animation from libraries of models, textures, animated backgrounds, and even movements. Those nasty straight lines are drawn perfectly at your command, as are circles and squares. Their 3D equivalents, cones, spheres, donuts, planes, and boxes — called Primitives — are the bricks and blocks of 3D. They too are generated at the click of your mouse (see Figure 1-1).

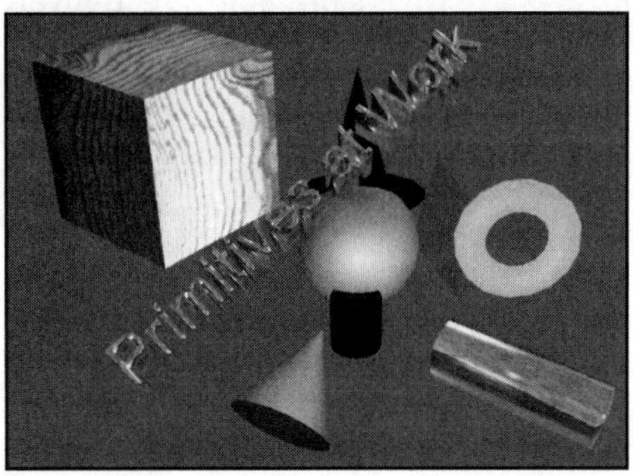

Figure 1-1: You can build all sorts of things by reshaping and gluing Primitives together.

You'll learn to build complex objects from Primitives through Boolean addition and subtraction of their volumes. It's a little like blocks and Legos, only a lot more flexible. You can put one block halfway in the middle of another one and join them as a single complex block. Similarly you can subtract a small block from a large one, leaving a missing chunk where the small block was. As you go through the book you'll discover ways to build just about anything in trueSpace2, from a spaceship to a cloud.

From Technology to Artistry

3D tools allow you to realize any concept you can visualize. But in the past, the complexity of using 3D technology often kept traditional artists at bay. The first artists in 3D tended to be from technical fields like programming, engineering, and architecture. Some of the best migrated from CAD fields. They strongly influenced the early look of 3D graphics with a lot of shiny chrome and glass balls, checkerboard floors, and red plastic blobs. There were also architectural renderings and walk-throughs. Lawyers found they could use 3D in courtrooms to recreate crime scenes. These tended to be very primitive looking. Chemists started visualizing 3D molecules, and mathematicians could now see abstract concepts vividly in 3D. These were the people who felt comfortable within the arcane technical matrix that gave birth to 3D. Slowly a new breed of explorers discovered this emerging graphic medium. These were artists with a rare combination of technical training and artistic sensibility. They brought a new vision to digital graphics, and new demands for software developers.

Natural media software began to sprout up — Matisse, Fractal Design Painter, Photo-Paint, and Photoshop. Pressure-sensitive digital tablets gave digital artistry the feel of traditional media and added the flex of natural brush strokes. Each innovation made it easier for non-technical artists to relate. The complexity and abstruse interfaces still kept most artists away from 3D. But the demand for 3D product began to grow. It was clear that the field needed people with superb artistic talent.

Dr. Anthony Gregorc, a psychology professor at the University of Connecticut, discovered that traditional artists and technical types view the world very differently. He dubbed this different Cognitive Styles. The technical artist tends to be more precise, detailed, and photorealistic. The traditional artist tends to be more symbolic, emotional, and stylistic.

There was a need for a 3D interface with a natural, intuitive feel. I believe that Caligari's trueSpace 1.0 was the first real success in this arena. As the focus continues to shift away from technology and toward creativity, trueSpace2 gives the artist remarkably powerful tools to work with.Tools he can relate to. With this book (software included), a decent computer system, and a little imagination, you'll be producing stunning animations in a few hours, and polished work in a month. With a street price under $500.00, trueSpace2 will connect you to a new world of employment possibilities whether you're a teckie or a graphic type. If you work at it, you'll be in business before you know it, and you might not have to hock your car.

Caligari and I have arranged to lend you a fullbore copy of trueSpace2 for 30 days (that's 30 sessions in any number of days) to see if you've got what it takes. It'll pay for itself in no time. If you already own trueSpace2, a copy of this book will help you see what it can do.

In addition, I've gathered trueSpace2 special effects software to help you impress friends and family right off the bat. This is all new stuff, no shovelware, and much of it is exclusive to this book. I think you'll be pleased. To help you purchase the essentials of your digital studio, I've also put together a batch of coupons for things you'll need, at deeply discounted prices.

Why trueSpace2?

trueSpace2 is the vehicle for this book because, IMHO (Web talk: In My Humble Opinion), it is the best place to learn 3D animation, yet has the depth to carry you from beginner to broadcast pro.

Not the most powerful, versatile, or even the fastest application, it simply has the best designed modeless interface I've worked with. That means you don't have to jump from 2D shape program to 3D model program to materials program to animation program, and then assemble all the pieces. It's all right there in front of you. The procedures, for the most part, make intuitive sense to a graphics person, rather than architects (3D Studio), programmers (Real3D), or rich people (Alias/WaveFront, SoftImage, and Prisms). tS2 (as it will be abbreviated from now on) runs on Windows 3.1 or Windows 95, the most common platforms. tS2 also has new brothers and sisters (with substantially the same interface) that are the official development tools for Sony PlayStation, Microsoft Internet Studio, and Fountain, which are commercial VRML authoring packages for 3D Web sites.

Okay, so you're getting bored, and want to start burning out animations. We're almost there. Pay attention throughout the book and I'll reveal professional secrets, things you need to know to make your demo tape stand out like a rose in a cabbage patch. There are a lot of demo tapes out there, but only about one in a hundred pops out at you. I'll show you what to include and what to leave out, how long to make it, and what reviewers are likely to be looking for.

Along the way, I'll let you in on all sorts of undocumented goodies buried in tS2 to make your demo look like it was done on an SGI.

A Few Concepts to Start You Rolling

The basic plan in tS2 is to figure out what you're going to animate, sketch out your storyboards, then grab the tools you need to do the job. tS2 has more tools than a Lamborghini mechanic. Here's a brief overview with more detail in chapters down the line.

The Tool Panel

Caligari puts its tool icons across the bottom of the screen. The interface has been optimized for a screen ratio of 1024 × 756. At that resolution the tools spread in a single line, as in Figure 1-2. At lower resolution they form a double line, covering too much screen space.

Figure 1-2: Opening screen of tS2. The logo disappears and in a few seconds you're ready to dig in.

To select a tool simply left-click on it — I don't have to teach you Windows, right? If the icon has a little triangle in the *upper left* corner, click and hold the *left* mouse button to see a menu of tool variants (see Figure 1-3 for an example). Simply slide your pointer up to the tool you want and let go. That tool replaces the original one on the work bar and is ready for use. The Help Bar explains what each tool is used for, as your mouse pointer runs over it. Once you select a tool, the Help bar may give suggestions on how to use it.

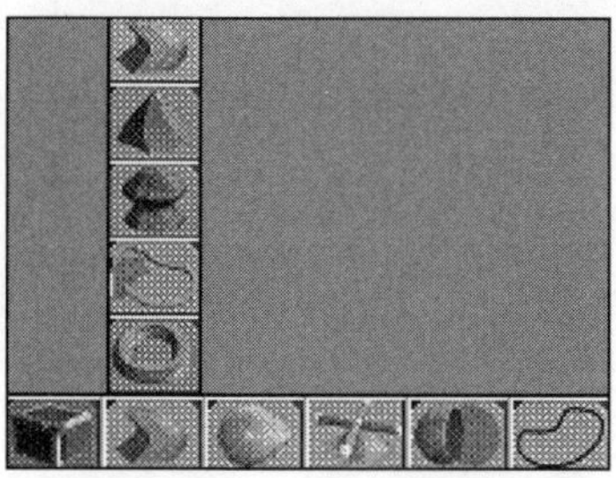

Figure 1-3: A typical tool icon with triangles in the upper corners indicating further depth. Inset shows tool variants.

If there's a triangle in the *upper right* corner of a tool you simply *right* click to reveal one or more property panels. Here you select options and adjust various parameters with numeric input or sliders. If a property window pops up in the middle of your work, grab it with your pointer and drag to a better position.

Sometimes you'll select a tool by mistake, like the render tool that could take ten minutes. Move your pointer off the tool before letting go. If it's too late, and you've already started the long process, hit escape to stop the render and move on.

You can see which buttons are active by their depressed position and blue shading (in Figure 1-2 you can see that the selection arrow is active, and so are the X, Y, and Z coordinates). Sometimes tools are not available because there's no object selected or for whatever reason they will be grayed out and you'll have to think a minute to figure out why. I still do. So you'll feel a little dense and move on.

Tool Overview

Everything is arranged in logical groups. Well, logical to the people at Caligari. They put the cameras and lights on the Primitives panel. I only vaguely see their logic. I'd have put them elsewhere. But most things are easy to find and work with. There are eight groups. Including all variants, you have more than 60 tools to work with. You'll learn about each one of them. Don't freak. The ones you'll use all the time are easy to learn, convenient to reach, and easy to remember.

The View Group

Twenty tools for setting up your view of the work space. They include all sorts of view navigation tools like Zoom and Move and Rotate, as well as solid/wireframe views, view render setup, tool arrangements, and extra view ports.

Object Navigation

Here are five tools to select things, move them in space, rotate them, and scale or size them. Because objects may be made up of a hierarchy of sub-objects glued together, there's also a tool to let you navigate the tree to select individual sub-objects.

Modeling Group

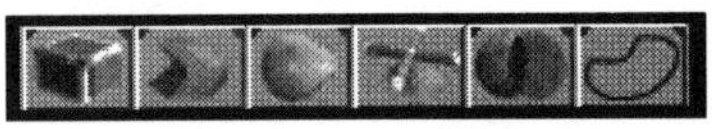

Here we have a total of 19 tools to perform such operations as selecting parts of an object to edit, surface sculpting, extrusion of 2D shapes, lathing of shapes around an axis, volume deformation, beveling, Boolean operations, and 2D polygon drawing.

Surfacing (Rendering) Group

Caligari refers to these as rendering tools, but they all have to do with putting surfaces on objects. This is a very strong and easy-to-use group. It's one of the strong points that puts trueSpace2 in a league of its own. There are interactive tools for painting, surface mapping, vertex painting, decaling and manipulating material rectangles, selecting surface projection strategies, and even for using PhotoShop standard plug-ins to create textures. The eight basic tools open many panels that will be explained later.

Editing Group

Six tools here allow you to undo mistakes, redo things you undid, glue objects together to form hierarchies, unglue them, and either copy or erase them.

Libraries Group

There are three libraries containing pre-built stuff you can use to construct your scenes.

Primitives Library

Here you can simply click, and basic objects appear on the screen. It contains lights, cameras, text tools, and deformation objects as well as Primitives like the Sphere, Cone, Cube, and Planar.

Materials Library

This is preloaded with several libraries of surface materials; you create new favorites, and save them for fast retrieval later.

Paths Library

Here you save all sorts of spline paths: animation paths, macro sweeps, and spline shapes. You can retrieve them to duplicate movement, sweeps, or polygon shapes.

Animation Group

Here we have the five tools you need to control animation sequences. They include a VCR-type control for exploring animations and setting keyframes, a tool to apply a spline path to an object to define its movement, and tools to constrain an object's orientation while moving. The *Animation Project Window* gives you an overview of the project, all objects, and their associate actions. It also contains a sub-set of tools for setting up, repeating, and localizing actions.

Utilities Group

Fourteen utilities set up the work space the way you want it and do routine operations on objects. They include tools for setting snap constraints, axes, parameter normalization, and a number of utilities related to modeling. For example, the smooth quad divide tool increases polygons to give a smoother appearance. Another tool fixes bad geometry. There's a mirror tool and so forth.

A Few Tools to Get You Started

In the next chapter we will set the stage for a neat animation using these tools. As you go through the book, you'll pick up the techniques you need to create your own animations like this one.

Object Select Tool

Click on this tool to enter the object selection mode or to exit other modes such as point editing or animation. This tool works in concert with the Move, Rotate, and Scale tools. By right clicking on the object tool, you will get the Object Information panel. This will give you details of the object's position, rotation, and scale, and a place to type in its name. I recommend giving every object an evocative, unique name. This becomes particularly important in complex hierarchies. You may also select units of measurement here to give the object relative scale.

Object Move

With this tool selected you can click on an object or glued group of objects and move them. When selected in wireframe, the group turns white. This tool behaves differently for each observation window (such as top, side, perspective, and so on). In the perspective window, the right button controls movement in the Z direction while the left button controls X and Y.

Object Rotate

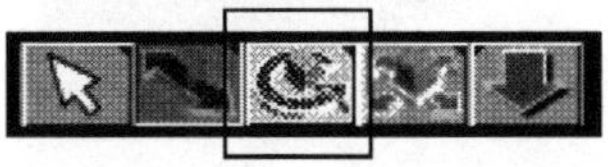

In 3D you can rotate objects in three-space. That means left-right, up-down and back-forth, or in the X, Y, and Z dimensions. When selected, the right button controls rotation along the X and Y axes. Move the mouse parallel to an axis while holding the button — the object will rotate.

Object Scale

Objects can be stretched or shrunk at will, either symmetrically or asymmetrically with this tool. Symmetrical scaling is scaling equally on all three axes: a cube goes from small to large. Asymmetrical scaling disproportionately scales one or more axes: the cube becomes an oblong box. For symmetrical scaling, depress both buttons and move your mouse. You'll get instant feedback, so you don't have to remember which way to move. For asymmetrical scaling, the left button controls X and Y axis scaling while, predictably, Z scaling is controlled by the right.

CAUTION If the three navigation modes above do not seem to be working as advertised, check OrthoNav and Tablet in the trueSpace2 Setup panel. Each affects the behavorial characteristics of one or more modes.

Coordinates Panel

Located on the right side of the Help Bar, it lets you lock out movement for one or more axes. This will be very handy when we begin to set the stage for your first animation. There is more to this tool, but let's not complicate matters until you're comfortable.

With these tools you can set your virtual stage by positioning objects where you want them. It's a good way to get a feel for 3D space. Pretend you're the director and you are positioning your props and actors. Go ahead, feel important.

Working in Virtual Three Space

trueSpace2 gives you three different coordinate systems: World, Object, and Screen. For now, we'll focus on the default, World system, with X running along the floor grid from top right to bottom left, and Y running from top left to bottom right. Z runs at a 90-degree angle to them. That makes it straight up and down. Figure 1-4 will help you visualize what I'm saying.

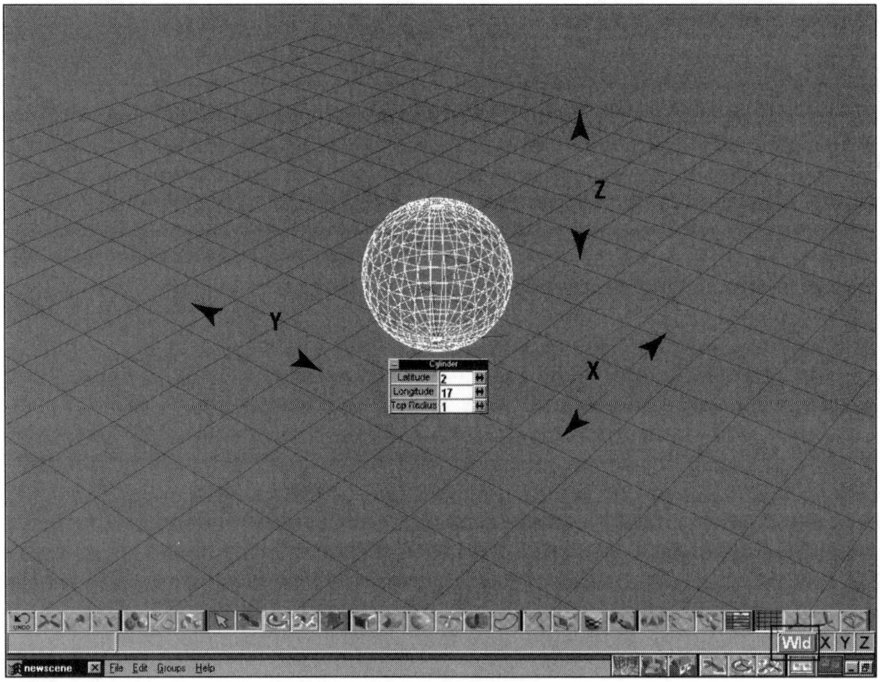

Figure 1-4: Arrows indicate how the World Coordinate Axes run.

This may be confusing if you're used to thinking of a traditional Cartesian plane with X running horizontally and Y vertically, with Z reaching back into the screen. In trueSpace2 this arrangement is called Screen Coordinates, and you can elect to work in them, but for the moment let's continue in World.

By default, a click on the left mouse button gets you moving in the X/Y plane. To move in the Z plane, depress your right button. Moving in X and Y at the same time can be tricky, so for now try moving in one direction at a time by disengaging either the X or Y vectors on the coordinates panel.

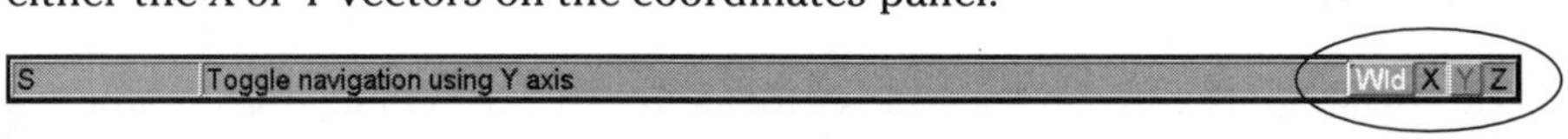

In the example, movement in the Y direction has been disabled. We can see that the S key is a hot key to toggle Y movement on and off. Switching between X and Y will make positioning way more predictable.

POWER TIP

The X axis lock is toggled with the A key and the Z axis by the D key. Using them in concert with the mouse, you can develop a personal style of positioning objects very rapidly and precisely. Practice this throughout the exercises.

You can tell what coordinate system you're using by looking on the left side of the panel. Here it indicates Wld for world. You can switch systems by left clicking and selecting the variant.

I recommend developing a routine for placing objects. First, position an object in space; next, rotate the object to the desired position; and finally, scale to the proper size. Having a routine helps establish a work pattern that eases things when you're doing this for a living and they needed it yesterday. It happens.

Now fire up tS2 in the default Perspective View, and pop a sphere on the screen using the Primitives panel. Select it.

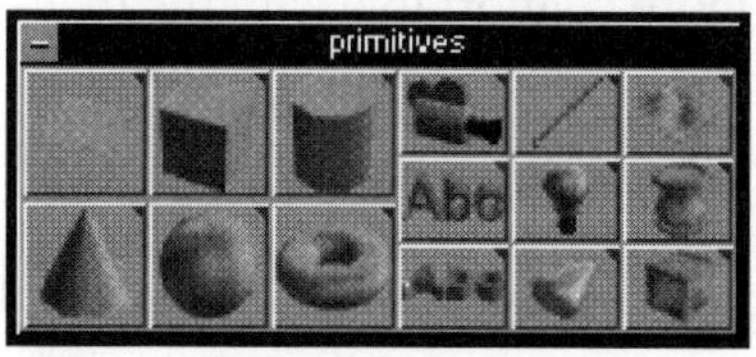

Make sure the Object Select arrow is depressed. Object Move should engage automatically. Good. Left click on the sphere and, holding down your left mouse button, move it deep into the background. It will get smaller as you go deeper. Move it forward for practice. Keep pulling forward until it goes off the bottom of your screen. Switching to the Z axis (right click), pull it back up into view by moving your mouse away from you. The sphere will rise into view and be quite large because it's so close.

POWER TIP: If you're having trouble grabbing and moving objects, check the Preferences panel under Files and see if Dynapick is selected. This will cause your selection to cycle if you have other objects on the screen. Work with it deselected at the moment.

Now rotate the sphere. You'll see the wireframe lines rotating nicely. Pop up a cube for a more graphic demo of Rotate. Next we'll scale the ball down to a pinpoint. Click on the Scale tool, select the sphere, and press *both* mouse buttons. Pull in different directions to get a feel for your instrument. Now, by depressing only one button and moving the mouse, you can make the ball all lopsided. Amazing, isn't it.

Pop up four more balls and place them different distances from you, at different altitudes (Z), locations, and sizes. Click up an alternate view with the New View button.

Select the variant that looks like the roof of a house, looking down. Do this by left clicking and moving the pointer up the selection list to the house roof. This is called Top View. Notice where you placed the balls front to back. Try the Left View window to check out the various altitudes. Good. Now you're ready for some BIG time. In the next chapter we'll assemble an animation using these tools and for fun we'll render and play it.

Summary

In this chapter you were introduced to the world of 3D and learned about some of the latest trends:

- ✦ New hardware is turning home computers into practical 3D engines.
- ✦ New software is making graphic artists more comfortable with the technology, attracting them to the field.
- ✦ trueSpace2 is becoming a new standard in 3D interfaces, both for professional animation and 3D Web authoring.
- ✦ trueSpace2 has the tools you need for creative expression and world building.
- ✦ You can move, rotate, and scale 3D objects in real-time.

✦ ✦ ✦

CHAPTER 2

Animation Jump-Start

In This Chapter

A story to animate

Setting up a scene for animation

Placing models

Setting up an animation render

Video compression

When I was a kid, special effects guys were a different breed. They used to glue plastic model parts onto wooden hulls to build their spaceships. They'd run the things down piano wire and crash them into plaster landscapes — I loved it. I'd sneak parts out of older cousin Jimmy's battleship kits to glue them onto my latest dreadnought-of-the-void. He always wondered where they had gotten to. Then for realism, I'd shove a sparkler up the exhaust tube and set the thing off. It would slide halfway down the wire and hang, never allowing for suspension of disbelief.

Then I got my Gilbert chemistry set and made flash powder from powdered magnesium and potassium nitrate. I put that up the rocket tube, thinking it would look more like "real" spaceship exhaust flames. That's when I discovered the joy of blowing up spaceships. Though this gave me hours of perilous pleasure and my mother a nervous breakdown, it never produced a truly believable image.

I'm still building space vehicles, but now they're virtually real. With 3D animation you can create believable universes and run them according to your own rules. It's a way of playing God without hurting anyone. Now when I build a hyperspace tanker, she looks like the real thing, moves like one, and sometimes even dies like one. Just as important, she flies through "real" space with a depth of stars and planets, no more lights behind pinholes for me (see Plate 2-1, Space Tanker in Orion sector). I'm still a kid at heart and I've aimed this book at that part of you.

Naturally, we'll start with a deep space animation. To get a fast jump-start, I've come up with a story and saved part of the scene in a trueSpace2 .scn file. You'll use the .scn file format to save work in progress.

Putting this animation together, you'll get a taste of tS2's interface.You'll start as a stage manager and work your way up to director. This is a substantial animation sequence and may take all night to render, but it'll give you an idea of what your computer can do.

The Story

StarFalcon, our A-Life, nanomolecular recon vehicle, is running point at the edge of Keltorian territory without crew. Recent intelligence indicates Keltorians, an aggressive technoid species, have been moving massive numbers of their people to an M-Class planet in Gamma quadrant. Ordinarily we wouldn't pay much attention, but this planet is located in the neutral sector, outside their sovereign territory. In addition, our sensors have picked up intense, regular bursts of Gamma-radiation from deep in their home territory, as if some unimaginably powerful weapon were being tested. This is all very unusual and must be investigated. The NeuronScout will cautiously scour the sector, sending back data via inter-dimensional phase matrix. We have only a few seconds of screen time, and we have to get the drone's story across.

Through Space with trueSpace2

I've made a few sketches of how I see the stage. One from the top looking down, to locate major props and players, and a few sketches of camera angles I'm considering.

POWER TIP

No matter how badly you draw, sketch out your storyboard; stick figures are fine. Some famous directors draw worse than you do. I can't emphasize this enough. "Pencil before screen gives you more in between." Unless, of course, you just can't work that way. If you try storyboarding and hate it, do your own thing... and good luck.

Just to give you an idea of how it goes, Figure 2-1 exposes my extraordinary sketching talent, while showing the actual scene as it rendered. Hardly any difference, right?

Figure 2-1: My storyboard sketch and the corresponding rendering

Let's Fly This Thing

It's time to see what you and trueSpace2 can do. Launch it now. As soon as the logo disappears, go to File ➪ Scene ➪ Load.

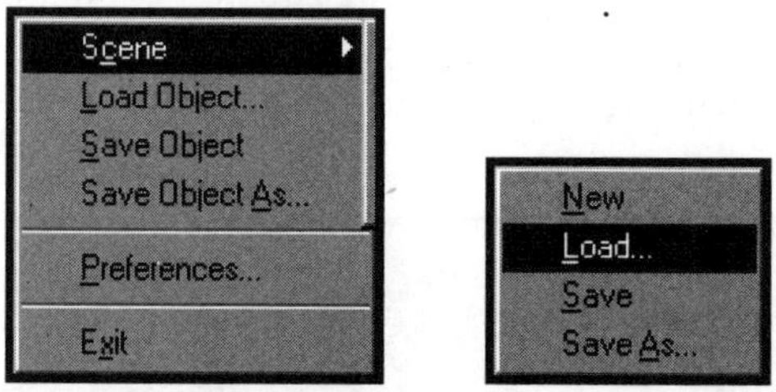

Go to your CD-ROM drive: \scenes subdirectory and choose probe.scn. It'll load in a few minutes or less. I've worked on studio sets as an associate production designer and I can tell you, point and click is the coolest way to set a stage. A real sound stage can take days or weeks, and I'd bet dressing the cosmos would take forever.

Let There Be Light

The warnings you get mean that textures aren't where tS2 expects them to be. This happens a lot if you use textures on removable media. Don't fret. Notice that one star is bright white. That means it's selected. Hit the Delete key — bam, it's gone. Now select the planet and hit Delete — ultimate destruction. It's that easy to get rid of planetary bodies in tS2.

Let's play creator and add a few cosmic goodies. Click File ➪ Load Object. The dialog box appears, probably still on your CD at: \scenes. Change to the \geometry\dreamscp\space directory. Double-click on `Lclastar.cob`. She'll load reluctantly as old stars sometimes do. Be patient, it's all an act. There she is, bright white (already selected at X=0 Y=0 Z=1). Right-click the Selection arrow on the toolbar to bring up an Object Info panel something like this one:

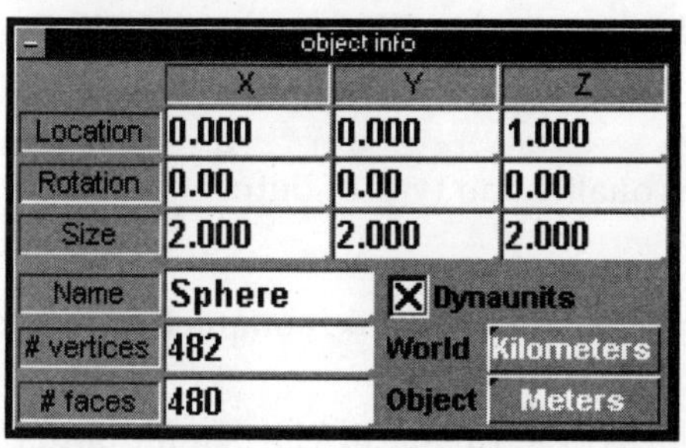

Under Name you'll see Exploder. Highlight that with your mouse and rename it `L Class Star`. It just fits. Click on Dynaunits and ignore the rest. Now type in the following coordinates: X=-5 Y=-8 Z=-2. These coordinates position the star in the upper left quadrant.

Now load the object gplan2.cob and ignore the warning. It's an artifact caused by tS2 loading the spotlight portion of the object before the target. Scary though, right? This is a planet with its own atmosphere and sun (a spotlight glued on and pointed back at the planet). The atmosphere and surface textures are done with procedural texture tricks you'll learn later. Rename it in the Object Parameters box to `G Class Planet`. Too many letters — but the box scrolls to accept them. Move the planet to X=-11 Y=0 Z=0. Depending on your screen resolution it should look something like Figure 2.2.

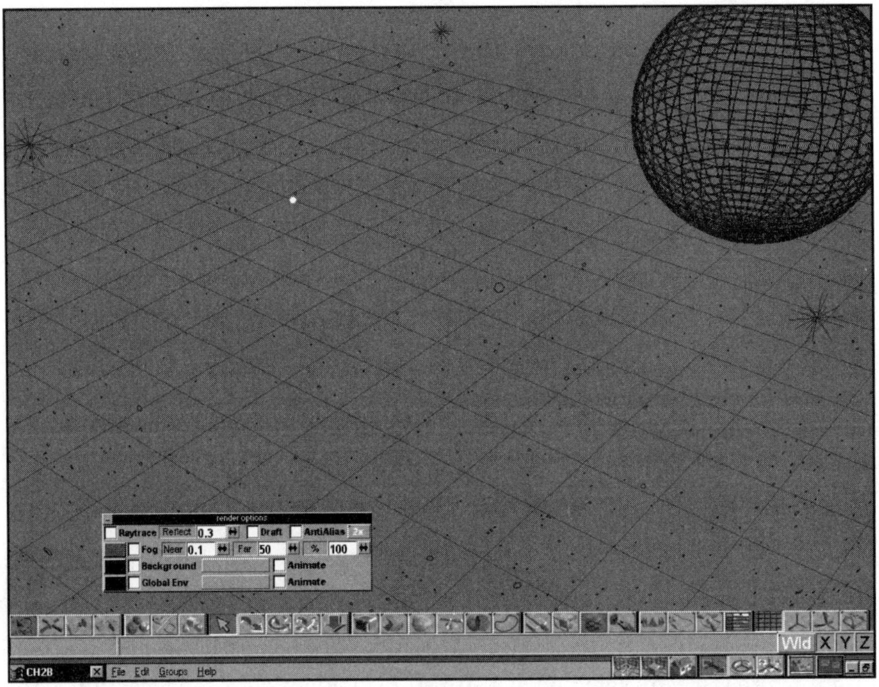

Figure 2-2: Before rendering, your work space should look something like this.

Setting Up the Render

You have to tell the render engine what quality and type of output you want. There are many options:

- ✦ You can render a series of high quality .tga files to be compiled into video by another program.
- ✦ You can compile directly to Autodesk FLIC (.fli or .flc) format for both DOS or Windows applications.

- ✦ You can compile to a compressed .avi file for Windows (strongly recommended).
- ✦ You can render in various qualities from raytraced down to draft.
- ✦ You have a wide choice of custom or preset render sizes.
- ✦ There are other parameters, but we'll leave them alone for now.

The higher your image resolution, the more data your computer has to handle. If you don't have a 2D accelerator for desktop video, use the 320 × 240 or MPEG 1 standard NTSC presets. This will allow you to easily convert to MPEG later for full-screen, full-speed performance.

You can set up your render as follows:

1. Right-click on the Render Current Object icon to get the Render Options panel.

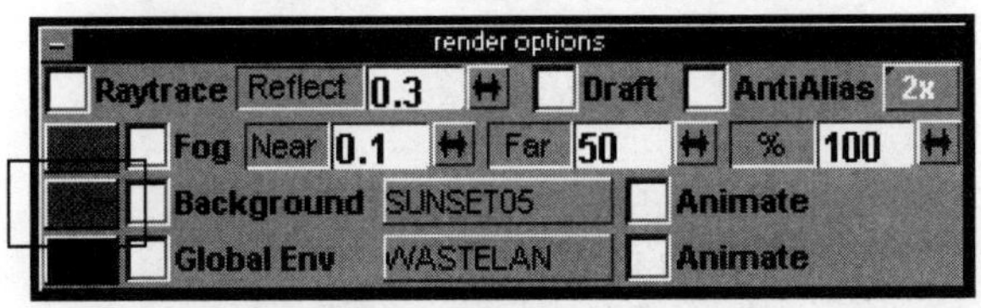

2. Leave everything deselected.
3. Click the black rectangle to the far left of Background to bring up an RGB (Red/Green/Blue) color selection panel. Make sure Background is black by sliding each color control all the way to the left, to read 0, 0, 0.

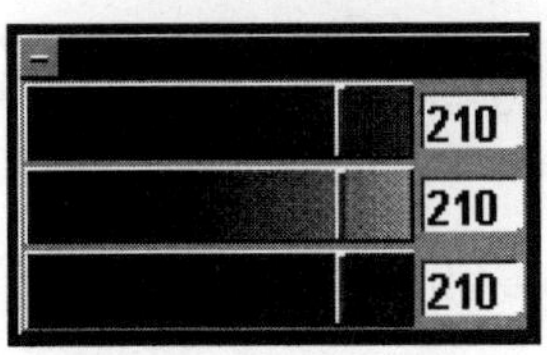

4. Click and hold the Render Current Object icon, slide up to the Render to File icon, and then let go. You'll get the Render to File dialog box:

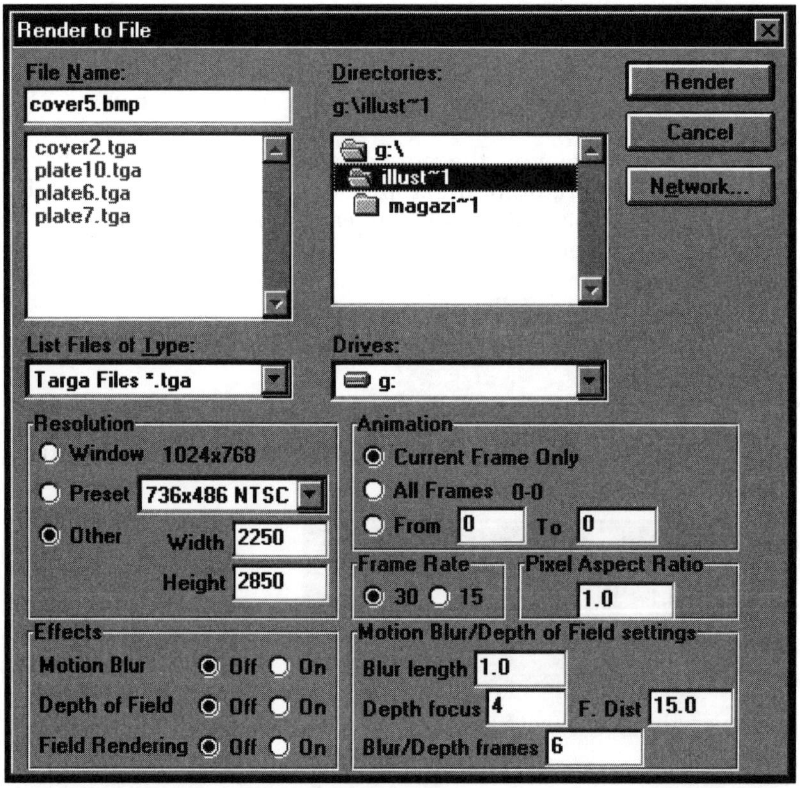

5. Type in a file name, such as probe.avi.

You have to specify the .avi extension. The default is .tga, even when you have the .avi filter on. This is unusual and you could easily type the file name and not the extension — you'll end up with a drive full of comparatively huge .tga files.

6. Select the Resolution Preset ➪ MPEG -1 352 × 240. This allows you to later convert to MPEG for full-screen play.

7. Make sure all the Effects settings are off.

8. Check the Directory and make sure you are sending your file to the drive with plenty of space.

9. Check All Frames in the Animation section.

10. Let's keep it at 30fps and a 1:1 pixel ratio.

11. You can ignore the rest because it's shut off.

12. You'll hit the Render button and get the .avi Compression panel.

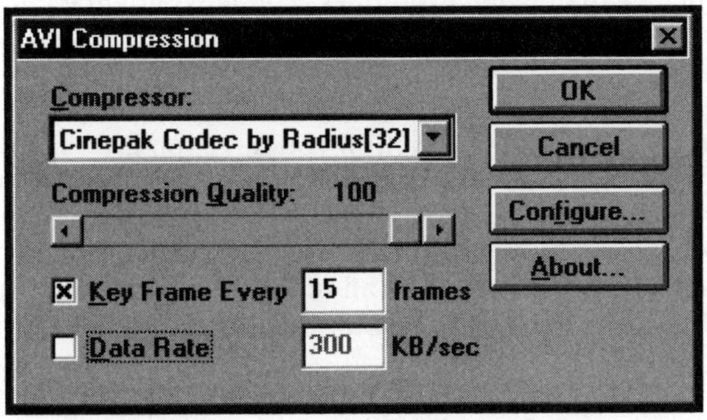

If you get the Targa settings panel abort the render and start again, making sure you type in .avi after your file name.

Set up your animation render as follows:

✦ Compressor: CinePak Codec by Radius. It's by far the best performer for most clips. It's smoother with fewer motion artifacts.

✦ Compression quality: 100%.

✦ Data Rate: de-select.

✦ Leave Key Frame Every... alone.

If you have slow equipment, an .avi compressed at 100% may be jumpy. You can try re-rendering at 50%, or set the Data Rate to 200K. If that doesn't work you should consider getting one of the new 2D/3D acceleration video cards from Diamond or Creative Labs. Look for boards built around chips like Nvidia, Glint, Rendition, or 3DFX.

I avoid Microsoft Codecs; they're pretty lame, IMHO. Better ones are on their way, but don't hold your breath. Indio Codecs aren't much better.

If you plan to do a lot of editing, set Compression ⇨ None for high quality source pictures. You won't be able to play .avi files with no compression — the files contain too much data for real-time. Compress after you edit. The idea is to edit with high-quality originals to avoid the GIGO effect: Garbage In ⇨ Garbage Out. Using compressed originals leads to recompression which ⇨ garbage.

When you hit OK there will be a pause while your machine gathers resources for the render. You can follow by reading the changing messages on your Information Bar. When the render begins, your screen will clear and a small window in the center will display the birth of each frame. You'll probably want to watch a few, but it gets old fast.

POWER TIP: If you're not raytracing, have a lot of RAM, and a fast machine, you *may* be able to minimize trueSpace2 and check e-mail while it renders. You'll experience minor catches. If it bogs down too much, shut down all but trueSpace2 and go take a siesta.

CAUTION: Your rendering may blow in the middle of the night if you have too little memory. 8 megs is tighter than cheap pants, 16 is better, I have 32 for good measure, and I dream of 64. The other most common source of glitches is video card incompatibility. Users have experienced strange errors with some of the most popular video boards. It helps to have the latest drivers at all times. Internet is your route to instant driver updates; if you don't have access, try the company BBS.

Here's a thought to ponder: you didn't have to set up the action in this animation, but you will when you build your own. That's where we can really tell the amateurs from the pros. The action you design can be a dead giveaway, one way or the other. Be thinking about that as we move on.

Summary

In this short chapter you've had an opportunity to:

- ✦ Think about story and how important it is.
- ✦ Get a feel for storyboarding animation.
- ✦ Load a scene.
- ✦ Load and place objects.
- ✦ Set up a render.
- ✦ Set up an .avi compression session.
- ✦ Be patient while the damn thing renders.
- ✦ And think about action.

✦ ✦ ✦

CHAPTER 3

A Brief Course in Animation Story Concepts

In This Chapter

Animation story ideas

Importance of themes

How to overcome your moments of creativity deficit

Writing your animation story

How to find interesting themes

First steps toward your demo tape

Okay, let's start with the *story*. Assignments often have a script, but an understanding of story will absolutely give you a professional edge. It gives you something worth animating. Even when there's a script, you'll do a more professional job if you understand the story between the boards.

You Need Something Interesting to Animate

I've seen enough boring footage of robots walking and shooting, or cars careering down some road, or spaceships cruising through space, or surfaces warping, or disconnected scenes, to sour me on digital animation. But I'm not sour; I've also seen the good stuff.

With all the new animation software, nearly anyone can do animation tricks. Thousands of demos with this simple, dull stuff are floating around. Some are even put out by big-name companies. It does not impress — well it does, but not the way you'd like.

Story?

Newbie digital animators tend to bypass story in their mad rush to build pretty chrome balls. Well, I promise you all the balls you want, but the story comes first, by a long shot. If you find yourself frustrated by this — and want to skip ahead — don't. I've counseled a lot of young animators on putting demos together. When I suggest they sketch out a little yarn for their presentation, their response might be:

NEWBIE: "Knitting, it's not about knitting... what?"

ME: "Think up a little story... a narrative that puts your sequences together in a logical, meaningful order... a story."

NEWBIE: "I don't get it... you mean like... organize it? I'm an artist, I don't organize things, I answer only to my muse."

I've heard it, you probably have too. I don't know a single talented/successful artist who buys that garbage. I sometimes teach a Success Motivation seminar at Colorado Mountain College, where one thing becomes clear: creative brilliance by itself is about as useful as a sieve without holes. There are millions of creative, talented people out there, going nowhere. You're not going to be one of them.

When you team up with technology like trueSpace2, animation becomes a relative snap. Story is what makes animation fun. It'll give your work an unmistakable professional quality and give your pride a kick in the petunias to boot. Trust me.

What Is a Story?

I've read a lot of definitions of story and not one is completely adequate. Traditionally a story is the telling of events in a way that grabs your interest, builds your involvement, and resolves the action in the final act or chapter. But some stories, like book one of a trilogy, may not resolve everything in the last chapter. They are complete unto themselves, yet part of a larger tale. We need to narrow the range.[1]

For the purposes of this book, a classic story has three parts: beginning, middle, and end, and at a minimum:

✦ Part one introduces the main character(s), sets the place and mood, and introduces an event that sets off the story's main action. It rocks the main character's boat.

✦ Part two begins with the situation caused by the event. Throw a lot of apples at your main character as he tries to regain an even keel. You can build this middle section to a mid-point reversal; say things are going along too well and suddenly comes a seemingly insurmountable barrier. It builds tension.

✦ In part three the main character either overcomes the last obstacle or he rallies forces to help him do so, or he makes peace with his new situation. In any case, the story is resolved and the main character did the main resolving.

There are other story structures, but they're not the main focus of this book.

[1] This is one approach to story. For a fuller discussion, read *Making a Good Script Great*, by Linda Seger. Her *Creating Unforgettable Characters* is also excellent.

A Case in Point

The best digital animation story I've seen in years is titled *the end* and it was produced by Chris Landreth by Alias/WaveFront, for the 1995 SIGGRAPH Electronic Theater. Chris, an animator at Alias, worked with friend Robin Barger at the North Carolina Supercomputing Center (Robin did the experimental sound track). Chris calls *the end* "…a lighthearted, hellish frolic on the buffalo chips of cyber-profundity." It contains a lot of references to graphic types who take themselves a little too seriously, "…and that includes me," he admits. Chris worked on the storyboard sketches for nearly seven weeks before he even thought about the animation. "We worked out story independent of software. You have to be careful not to incorporate effects and stuff just because you can. In professional film animation, you really have to work out the details before you shoot, whereas in regular film you make a lot of the decisions afterwards in editing."

The animation starts out with a disembodied man and a woman with long flowing hair, supported only by flowing, swirling ribbons and tubes of some sort. They seem to be practicing a dance or play that involves a pretentious pseudo-intellectual conversation about the meaning of life. Something innocent about their conversation makes you like them despite the hyperbole. Their performance comes to an abrupt end and the stage lights go out. They appear somewhat disoriented… kind of, "what do we do now?" Then they hear someone in phone conversation, who stops to tell them they are only animated characters fulfilling his creative fantasy. The female takes umbrage at this, claiming she is conscious and self-aware, that he has been created by her. We see the life-like animator on the phone as he works his storyboard. He's negotiating the ending with someone on the phone. The voice suggests that this is really an animation about him, the animator who is himself an animation. He's told to dump the disembodied characters. I won't reveal the final end, but it's very interesting and brilliantly animated. As this book goes to press, *the end* has been nominated for an Academy Award.

This story has several interwoven themes, but the important thing is that there is an engaging story, well told and beautifully animated, with characters you can relate to. Chris is a professional; his work leaves no doubt about that. That's what you'll want people to think about your work.

Coming up with Your Theme

Think up an interesting, unique theme, right now, before you read the next sentence. If you're like most people, a big garage door just rolled down over your brain. I call it MBP syndrome (see sidebar). I'm asking you to pull something unique out of thin air and make it good. That's serious pressure. Some people can do it at the drop of a hat. Most cannot.

Overcoming MBP Syndrome

Momentary Brain Phart Syndrome can have a variety of root causes. Most commonly, it's brought on by panic at having to be creative. This actually causes blood pressure in your cerebral cortex to plummet, which impedes high order thinking. Try this exercise to bring the pressure up and your brain back on line. This technique has been tested on hundreds of college students with excellent results.

Start by taking a deep breath through your nose. Hold it. Picture autumn leaves floating down a river (closeup). Notice how peaceful they look. Any peaceful image will work here, so insert your own if you like. Breathe out slowly, picturing air passing out through your ears as well as your mouth.

Another deep breath. Hold. Picture yourself uptight. Find the humor in that. As you breathe out through your mouth, imagine your body getting warm all over. As your breath finishes, smile affectionately at your silly uptightness. Good.

Now relax for a moment before you go back to the creative process. This time don't judge the quality of your ideas. Write your concepts down without evaluating them; it can be done. It seems most people have learned to be prejudiced against their own creative efforts. You have to get past that by deselecting the harsh judgment icon.

But, there's good news in all this. People who can't come up with ideas off the top of their heads often come up with the best ideas, given time. The process is one of creativity, technique, and patience. It happens best when you let your mind go, yet guide its general course toward your story.

An engineer, a painter, a writer, an animator — each approaches creativity from a unique perspective and cognitive style, no two alike. Consider your personality and work within it. If you're a Spielberg, create Spielberg stuff, not Picasso stuff… but don't do Spielberg, he's been done. You'll know you're on the right track when you start to enjoy this part of animation.

Children are way more freely creative because they're least constrained by hard-shell identity. Still forming a selfview, they tend to experiment more. If you really get stuck, sit down with a bunch of kids and get some help. I'm serious.

Stretching Exercises

These are Peter's half dozen plus, non-fast, general rules for animation story development:

- ✦ Everything's been done, so pick a theme and do it differently.
- ✦ Pick a main character and follow him/her/it.
- ✦ The main dilemma must be faced/resolved by the main character.

- Give him/her/it an empathetic personality.
- Start with an ordinary situation.
- Have something unusual or unexpected happen.
- Resolve it in a way your audience doesn't expect. Surprise is good.
- Avoid the *Deus ex machina* solution, where an insoluable problem is solved by an act of God in form of machine, for example, the hero finds a magic weapon and blows the bad guys all away in the nick of time.

It's an Old Story

It really has all been told before, so don't let that hold you back. If you think of a neat idea and know it's been done, find a new twist. In fact, this can be a good way to exercise your creativity. Start with a theme you've seen before, and make it your own. The Alias film had many themes. For grins, let's use the "realization that I'm an animation" theme. As an example, I'll make a reasonably unique story based on it. After we go through the process, you do the same — your way.

How to be Creative

Here are some ideas for making a creative story your own.

- **Place.** Every animation has a place and you have infinite choice of settings. Pick an interesting juxtaposition of character and place: a cockatoo in a barnyard.
- **Personality.** You can keep a theme, but give your characters different personalities. Again, surprise your audience. Give that mouse a very deep voice and a miniature pipe.
- **Gender.** Often a theme will work as well with sex role switching — play with it.
- **Species.** Sometimes you can transfer a human theme to turtles or anthropomorphic toy blocks and have it work even better.
- **Dialogue.** The words or dearth of them can be your very own. In animation it's better to rely on business (action) than on words, but well-chosen words have their place.
- **Humor.** Add your own vision to the situation to spark it up. Be gentle though. Overdoing it can blow the whole bit.
- **Button.** Add a little twist or something special at the very end to leave people with a grin or a thought. This is the way commercial actors nail down jobs. The good ones always throw in a button at the end of an audition. The really good ones come up with it on the spot.

My Attempt at Writing an Instant Story

Title: (I don't know, I haven't written it yet)

Characters: Two male blue-collar humanoid robots, George and Larry.

Place: Industrial. Hallway to restrooms.

Time: Quitting time.

Notes: The two male robots with human-like personalities.

Scene: George and Larry stride along an industrial hallway, talking like two human buddies after a hard day's work. They pass a big mirror and George stops dead in his tracks. He's upset by what he sees, doesn't say anything, just stares, steel jaw dropped.

Larry: "What's up George?"

George: "What's going on here Larry?"

Larry: "Whaddaya mean?"

George: "This robot thing in the mirror… some kind of trick or what?"

Larry: "Yeah."

George begins rotating his robot arm 360 degrees.

George: "I knew *you* were a Bot, but…"

Larry: "I'm not a Bot, George."

George: "Right, Larry, look at yourself."

We see both robots reflected in the mirror.

George: (cont.) "Exactly what you look like in real life, Larry."

Larry: "Think of it this way George – you and me, we're not limited by predetermined carcasses the way real humans are. Being animated characters has its advantages.

George turns away from the mirror, rolls his eye cameras as if Larry is crazy – starts to walk away.

George: "Yeah, right, Larry, and I'm a purple cow."

George becomes an upright purple cow robot, but doesn't seem to notice.

Larry: "Come 'ere, I'll prove it to yah."

George returns to robot form as...

Larry leads the way to foreground. Their heads fill the screen and Larry knocks on it. We hear the hollow sound of a knuckle on a heavy glass monitor.

Larry: "See, dis here is glass, George. Take a gander."

They cup hands over eye cameras to look out at the AUDIENCE.

CAMERA: Dollies back and we see a family in living room watching them on TV.

George: "Jeezus Larry, there's people out there lookin' at us."

Larry: "That's kinda the point George."

George jerks away and stares at the floor, clearly pondering something uncomfortable.

Larry: "George??"

George: "I gotta go to the John now, Larry. (beat) I can't do nothing with these people watchin' my every movement."

Larry: "They don't animate that kinda stuff, George."

George looks relieved.

CAMERA: Dollies back into scene as...

They turn and walk into the distance. George turns philosopher.

George: "So I'm a cartoon, huh?"

Larry: "Yup, me too. It's a great life, ain't it."

They take a few more steps, come to a door labeled restrooms, step in.

George: "Well… if they don't animate it… How the hell am I gonna do it, Larry?"

Restroom door closes to FILL SCREEN.

Begin Credit Roll over door.

(A beat. We hear a flush.)

George (v.o.): "Aw Jeezuz, that's a relief Larry."

Larry (v.o.): "I guess dese newfangled cel jockeys'll animate anything, Georgie."

Fade to BLACK.

Complete credit roll.

THE END.

This little story illustrates my rules in the following way:

- ✦ It's been done before, but not quite this way.
- ✦ George is the main character. (He's facing a problem.)
- ✦ Despite the strange circumstances, we can empathize with George's confusion and questions.
- ✦ We started with a seemingly ordinary cartoon situation: two robots walking along, and we gave it a human touch to start the empathy.
- ✦ Something unexpected happens: George's reaction to the mirror.
- ✦ George resolves the conflict by adjusting to the situation.
- ✦ I added a little of my own bizarre sense of humor.
- ✦ The situation is resolved in an unexpected way with a little twist at the end. Actually two twists.

I made it up just now, starting with the theme of realizing you are an animated character. It took 22 minutes. All I did was follow the rules and add a little creativity. I've had experience at this, which probably helped, but you can do it too. It may take you twice as long… big deal. Hey, I just thought of a title, *The Audience*.

Practice by starting with this or some other familiar theme. Make up your own story to it. You'll learn more effectively if you write it all down using the arbitrary format above. Your main character can be a chicken, a gear, or a marble, a flying logo or a space vehicle. It doesn't matter — this is animation — do what you think is cool. There's creativity in applying the rules. When you get to the level of wanting to animate complex, humanoid characters with fancy coordinated limb movements, you'll use Animation Master or MHA. But for now, apply your story to simple characters: a fish, a head, a potato.

When you get a story you really like, set it aside and congratulate yourself. You now have strong motivation to learn all about animation so you can tell it. Here are a few ideas on how to come up with themes for your stories.

How to Find a Theme

Make a list of ten interesting themes. If this sounds impossible, you're pretty normal. For most people, blankness descends upon the brain at moments like this. But no mercy. We're separating the wheat from the chaff. Here are some things you can do to come up with themes. They all involve behavior observation. Get yourself a note pad and a felt-tip pen and start taking notes:

- Go to a playground and watch children being kids. There are lots of themes here. Look for the positive ones, like, smallest kid can't reach the swing bar. Friend tries to boost him up and can't. A bunch of bigger kids see this and they form a pyramid. The friend helps kid climb to bar. Exercise: Apply this theme to toy blocks.
- Go to a party and observe how people interact. Take good notes. People will ask what you're doing. Tell them you're a writer researching a book. Look for themes like: The interest people show in you because you are a writer who might put them in your book. Observe the geeks who shrink away — make up a story about what they have to hide. Try introducing yourself as a psychiatrist. Watch the conversation flip and die. Find the themes.
- Watch animals playing. Baby animals are full of lovely themes. Observe some kittens and then apply the themes and movements to baby spaceships or marbles or octopi.

You're starting to get the idea. Empathy is the key. You can establish it in a few seconds in your short sequences. You'll build it in your long ones.

Now that I've put you through all of this, I need to tell you that character animation is one of the more advanced parts of animation. It takes a lot of patience and hard work to learn it. My theory is that you'll be more motivated if you have this great original story to tell. Later, we'll start you animating things. Since no one knows what a humanoid robot is *supposed* to look like, you can get away with plenty. It's when you do a human face that you start to get in trouble with the critics, everybody's an expert on them

Though it's technically easier to animate objects, it requires a very creative application of the empathy rule. Done right, it can be very charming; done wrong....

It's time to learn how to put your ideas on that screen. Let's step back and learn the nuts and bolts of trueSpace2 animation. We begin with the interface in Chapter 4.

Summary

In this chapter you had an opportunity to learn what motivates real animators:

✦ You learned that story is king, it motivates both the animator and the audience.

✦ You learned that a good story has a logical structure.

✦ You now understand that it's all been done before but you can do it better, or at least uniquely.

✦ You learned about themes, where to find them and how to use them.

✦ You learned what MBP syndrome is and how to overcome it.

✦ You learned beyond a doubt that no matter what you animate, an understanding of story will give the professional edge to be a big success.

✦ ✦ ✦

PART II

You Can Build Absolutely Anything in trueSpace2

You can construct photorealistic images in trueSpace — from guitars to nebulae, bones to bananas — using the tools and techniques discussed in this section. Furthermore, you can produce photographic "evidence" of places and things that don't exist (and never will) except in your mind. So let your creativity and imagination guide you as you start creating 3D worlds.

In This Part

CHAPTER 4

The X, Y, and Zs of the trueSpace2 Interface

In This Chapter

Setting up your 3D work space

3D Coordinate Systems and how they work

Navigating 3D Space

Using the Solid Render and Wireframe options

You got an exterior overview of the trueSpace2 interface in Chapter 1. You've had some cockpit time, so let's take her a little higher. trueSpace2 is eminently customizable, so let's get right to it: setting up trueSpace2 to work the way you do.

The Menu Bar

Here are a few things you should understand about the Menu Bar.

Context-Sensitive Help

Make life easy. Keep your eye on the Help Bar for messages about tools under the mouse pointer; it's on by default. If it's off for some reason, go to the Help item and enable Help Bar. If there's a Keyboard Shortcut assigned, you'll see it too. If you select a tool, then run the mouse pointer over neutral territory (not over a tool), you may even get suggestions on how to use it.

Keyboard Shortcuts

Hot Keys are called Keyboard Shortcuts in tS2. Not all tools have one assigned. You can assign a shortcut key to any tool or change existing assignments yourself, which can really speed up production. You concentrate mouse moves in the View windows while selecting tools very rapidly with keys.

Don't assign a lot of keys right now, wait until you get a feel for how you'll be using the tools. Try one or two to get the idea, then come back next week and add a few more.

To assign a tool to a shortcut, place the mouse pointer over that tool. Check the Help Bar to see if it already has one. If not, do a <Ctrl> F1 to get the Shortcuts dialog box. Click on the New Key button and input the keystroke you want. You can use any combo of <Alt> <Ctrl>, or <Shift>, plus an alphanumeric or punctuation key.

The Find button will scan for preassigned shortcuts. You might want to use unusual key combos to avoid screwing up existing ones. I discovered by accident that you can assign a previously assigned shortcut to a new tool. It automatically unsets the original tool and reassigns the key to the new tool. It's easy to do by mistake. You might want to make a list of key assignments and learn them. They do save time.

Preference Settings

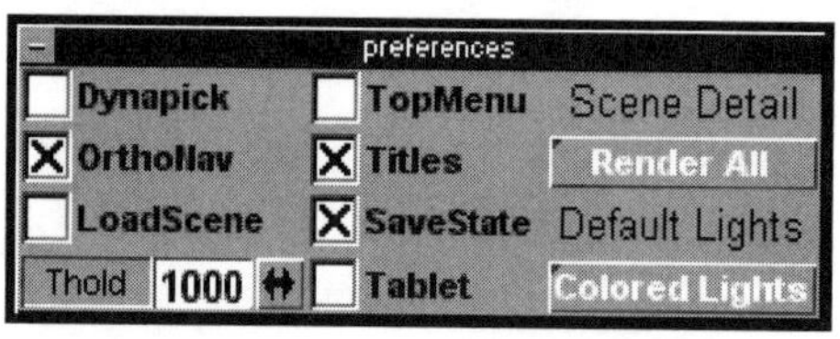

You get to the Preferences panel via the File menu. It's used to set up some of trueSpace2's behavioral characteristics.

Dynapick

In default mode, you manipulate objects (Move, Scale, Rotate), by placing the mouse pointer over them and clicking to select. Then you click again and hold to execute the operation. This is the general procedure for most manipulations.

Once an object is selected, you don't have to have the mouse pointer over it to click and move.

With Dynapick enabled this system changes. You can use any current tool to select and manipulate an object with a single click or click/hold. This means if you want to select a face on an inactive object you can do it directly with the Face Select tool.

If you have layers of objects, the selection will alternate among them with each successive click. It can become confusing. Don't use the paint tool with Dynapick and object stacks because it will both select and paint the object at the same time, often the wrong one.

I'm never exactly sure which object will be selected, probably something to do with my dyslexia, or perhaps Dynapick selects objects like a blind circus monkey. I usually work with it off, especially in complex scenes where it inevitably grabs the wrong thing and causes a gnashing of teeth. In simple scenes I sometimes leave it on. It's useful when you have a lot of paint-overs or other manipulations on objects in plain sight: just point/click/paint. Otherwise you have to select with the arrow tool then manipulate. A pain.

OrthoNav

This is one of those words designed to make you appear totally wizard-like when you use it in casual conversation. OrthoNav refers to navigating in orthogonal windows; that is, straight-on windows like Front View and Left View.

It's simple; when OrthoNav is engaged, your left mouse button controls navigation (movement) in both the horizontal and vertical directions, depending on how you move your mouse. Holding down your right button does nothing. With OrthoNav disengaged, the left button controls horizontal movement and the right one controls vertical.

Positioning is more precise with OrthoNav off. You can take two legs to get to a spot, like Etch-a-sketch®, or you can press both buttons and move on the diagonal. Try both ways, but I usually keep OrthoNav off.

LoadScene

Just click here before shutting down for the day and your scene will reload next time you open trueSpace2.

Engage LoadScene and SaveState to get right back to work where you left off, without having to set things up each session.

Thold (Threshold Time)

Strong visual feedback is a key to trueSpace2's charm. But moving and rotating and painting objects in real-time requires a lot of screen updating. This can slow things worse than an octogenarian on the freeway. With Thold, you set the maximum amount of redraw time you're willing to wait before objects are manipulated in bounding boxes. It's in milliseconds. Bounding boxes symbolically represent objects and their individual parts being manipulated, but chew up few resources, thus faster updates. As soon as you stop moving an object, each bounding box reverts to its rendered form. This really helps in rotating or positioning huge models.

POWER TIP: For complicated scenes, such as those with particle effects, lower this setting to force bounding box mode early on, speeding things along.

Top Menu

This puts all the controls across the top. Try it once. If you have a big monitor, it'll give you a kink in the neck to look up all the time. I prefer the default, with menus on the bottom. The interface was designed to be used that way. The Top Menu option was put in for people who don't like change. If you prefer it, we'll accept you into the club anyway, but loosen up, there're a lot of newfangled things coming at you in this book.

Titles

Figure 4-1 shows the Preferences panels. Selecting the Titles option puts standard Windows title bars on all program panels. They close with a single click. Easy. I leave Titles on. Some people turn them off to make the panels a little smaller. If you do this, close panels by right clicking on the panel in an inactive gray area and then drag the pointer outside the box. You'll get a big X and the box will disappear. If you have a small screen, this may make some sense.

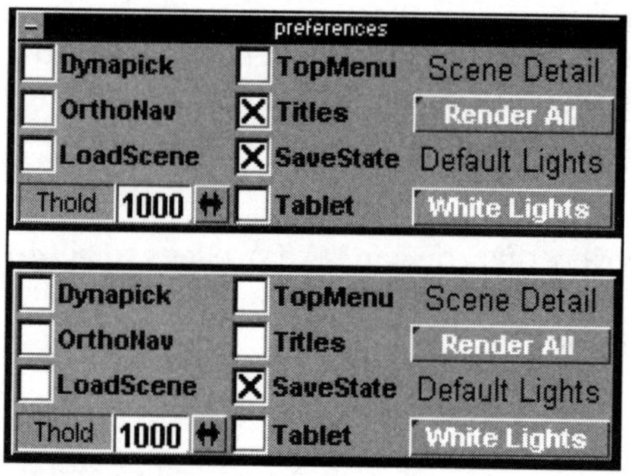

Figure 4-1: Note the state of the Titles box in each of these Preferences panels.

SaveState

With this box checked, trueSpace2 will save the interface status quo when you shut it off and return you to the same tools and windows, etc. next time.

Tablet

If you have a graphics tablet, you can use it like a mouse. trueSpace2 doesn't actually have much support for tablets. A trackball works better. I got a cheap one with a large ball, and I love it. Enabled, Tablet sets the trackball/mouse/tablet to proportional scaling on all three axes when you depress the left button. This has its uses; try it.

Use your Tablet in Fractal Design Painter and Photoshop to build texture maps. It's of limited help in tS2. I find that scaling and rotating are easier with it, but other things are slowed down a bit. I keep both my mouse and my pen connected at all times which works well if you avoid IRQ conflicts. Do this by connecting them to adjacent serial ports, such as Com 1 and Com 2, or 3 and 4. If you do 1 and 3, you'll have both on the same IRQ and will likely experience problems.

Scene Detail

In 3DR (solid render), scenes are refreshed constantly. The level of detail updated is set here in cahoots with the Render Quality panel of the 3DR option. Your choices here can have a major impact on screen refresh rate, especially with complex scenes and slow machines. I'm listing choices in order of speed:

- **Always Boxes.** All objects that are not selected will be shown as bounding boxes. The selected object will be rendered fully.
- **Boxes.** All objects that are not selected are displayed as bounding boxes while the selected object is being manipulated. They are rendered during moments when the selected object is not being fiddled with.
- **Always Wireframe.** All selected objects are locked into wireframe mode for quick rendering. They aren't solid rendered until chosen.
- **Wireframe.** All unsolicited objects will switch to wireframe while the selected object is being manipulated, then back to solid render when there is time. This is handy when you have to align things, but still need speed.
- **Render All.** Self-explanatory.

You want to start with as much feedback as you can get, so start in Render All and work your way down as necessary to accommodate your equipment.

Default Lights

There are three possible default light scenarios:

- **White Light.** This is a very bland overall lighting scheme that uses four infinite lights pointing to center stage and providing even lighting. Okay for setup, but don't stick with it as it is very boring.
- **Colored Lights.** Designed for use with solid render Mode, three colored local lights are arranged in a big triangle above the stage. It's supposed to give a better sense of depth. It does. You can change the light colors if they bug you.
- **No Lights.** I hardly use this one. I can't see a reason. It erases all lights. It would be useful if it just removed default lights. That way you could place your lights and then remove just the defaults. But it zaps all the lights. I delete the default lights one by one.

We'll learn a lot more about lighting later on from Sharon Calahan, Creative Lighting Supervisor on the Disney/PIXAR film *Toy Story.* She has designed more fancy lighting for a single digital presentation than anybody in history. Here's the general plan: start with default lights, build your scene, dump the default lights, and put in cool lighting. You have to get rid of the default lights because they wash out the effect of shadows and highlights from your key light.

Making the Interface Work for You

The View Group

There are nearly four dozen settings and adjustments you can use to customize your view of 3D space. You'll find them nested directly below the main Help Bar to the right side.

Trust me, you will use these tools constantly, so take time now and pay close attention.

Object Mode

Object Mode has two icons in its flyout:

- ✦ **Render Wire.** With this engaged all objects are rendered in wireframe. Select this option to disable the Solid Render Mode. When objects are selected they turn white, while unselected wire is rendered in blue. This is a fast choice.
- ✦ **Solid Render.** This engages the 3DR solid render API. This makes it much easier for artists to visualize the final output.

Figure 4-2 shows how you can open up to four View windows at a time, the main and three smaller ones. Each has its own control bar with a separate Object Mode icon to control how that window is rendered while you're working.

This arrangement allows you to have the main window rendered in wireframe, a smaller window of the same view in 3DR, and two other windows in wire or 3DR, showing different views of your work space.

Extra windows and detailed rendering require substantial update juice. Speed is always an issue in 3D, because it takes massive processor power to continuously update 3D worlds. Along the way I'll point out the speed impact of various choices.

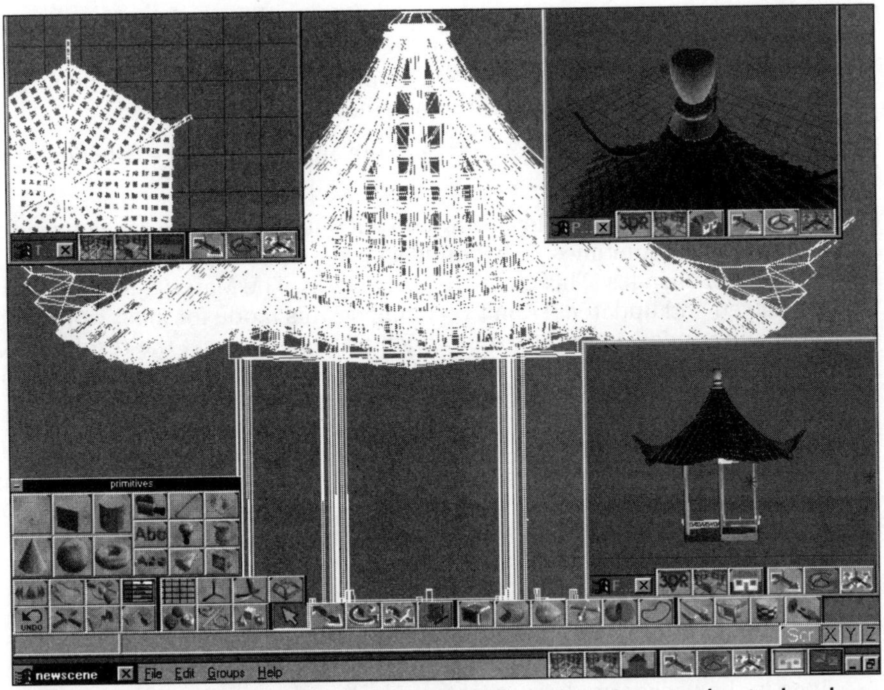

Figure 4-2: A screen shows four different windows in various modes. It also shows crowding at lower resolutions.

You only get an approximation to the final render quality, which will have far greater detail. You'll have several options for setting up the depth of solid rendering in the Render Quality panel pop-up. You know which object is selected because a funky 3D arrow points to it. If you drop down in the object hierarchy, the arrow turns into an axis marker (not to be, but can be easily confused with the object's real axis). The axis marker identifies the individual axis of the individual part, indicating that it can be manipulated as an individual object for the moment. The axis marker follows the active sub-objects down the hierarchy. It's hard for me to navigate this way. I use wireframe. Using solid mode can also slow you down if you don't have hardware acceleration.

Right-clicking on the Object Mode icon brings up the Render Quality panel.

It has five parameters:

- ✦ **Faceted render.** Each face is shaded, but no smoothing is done between polygons. It's the quickest solid shade mode.
- ✦ **Smooth.** Object faces are shaded, and the angular interface between polygons is smoothed over.
- ✦ **Textures.** This one will slow things down, but it's handy to see your models fully clothed sometimes. As a bonus you get instant updates on any UV projection changes. This can help align things. The Material Rectangle is also displayed and updated. I don't recommend this mode for most work. There's a pop-up window under textures which allows you to set the resolution of any textures you apply. Higher resolutions are slower, but who cares, you'll only use this for special circumstances — experiment.
- ✦ **Solid Grid.** The trueSpace2 View window has grid lines to help with modeling. It can also represent the "floor" of your space. With this option engaged, the floor will look like blue and white linoleum tile. It too slows things down considerably. I use it when I have no floor and want to move my lights around and see how they'll affect the scene.
- ✦ **Show Background.** This check box enables a faded version of the background image or color to show behind your work. It helps to align things. It's also a great way to trace a picture with the draw poly tools. You can put a logo in the background, trace it, extrude it, and you have a 3D logo. Easy.

Render Tools

This innocent looking set of tools opens a labyrinth of options, but don't panic, they're all easy to use when you understand what they do.

Render Options Panel

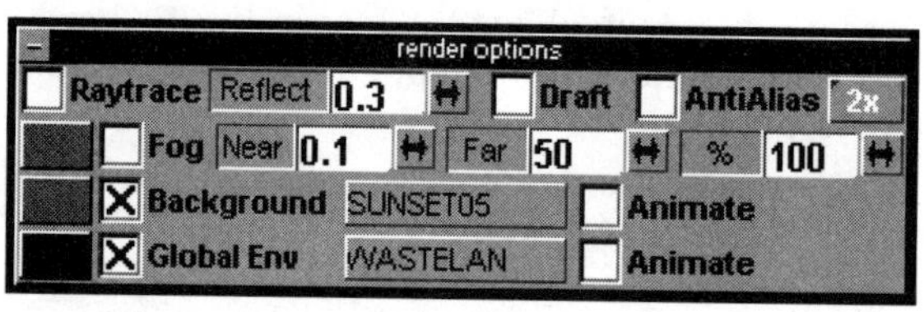

This opens by right clicking on any render tool.

- ✦ **Raytrace.** This engages the most sophisticated render engine. It actually follows the trajectory of virtual light beams, calculating reflections, shadows, and refraction.

Raytracing gobbles time and computer resources like a turkey on steroids. So use it mostly for final renders where you must show true reflections and glass refraction effects. If your render chokes due to lack of memory, deselect this option and try again. When raytrace is disengaged trueSpace2 uses its excellent scan-line engine for faster rendering.

- ✦ **Reflect.** Used with above, it relates to the shine value in the object's surface material, which is set by using a shade slider. Objects with shine set below this value will not have their reflections raytraced. This can save a lot of time.
- ✦ **Draft.** This is a real time saver. It renders the scene at quarter screen size then interpolates it back to full screen. You get a fast approximation with big jaggies.
- ✦ **AntiAlias.** This is one of those words bandied all about the graphics kingdom. It's simply the process of reducing the jaggies along edges by sampling the surrounding colors and blending them along the edge. When selected, AntiAlias produces a time-consuming series of re-sampling passes. The number of AntiAlias passes can be set from x1 to x4 being progressively more smooth and time consuming.
- ✦ **Fog.** This simulates a foggy atmosphere by adjusting the color saturation of objects and background.

You can do some nifty special effects with fog. It makes a good underwater effect and you can keyframe changes for its various parameters.

- ✦ **Fog Color.** Gray is the default color, but by using black, you can simulate distance attenuation. Blue-green makes for the underwater effect.
- ✦ **Fog Maximum Percentage.** This is just the maximum density beyond the far point boundary set in below.
- ✦ **Fog Extents.** There are three zones: the initial clear zone in front of the camera, the near point where the fog begins (thinnest fog), and the far point where the fog reaches maximum. Maximum Percentage starts here and extends on backwards, forever.

AntiAlias Tricks of the Trade

Fast scan-line rendering uses a different kind of antialiasing called supersampling. It's pretty slow. So avoid it where you can. In multimedia animation you don't need AntiAlias, because movement obscures the jaggies.

If you find you need a smoother render, but don't have time, here's a little trick. Engage Raytrace, but set reflection up to 1.0. That will effectively cancel the raytracing, but will engage adaptive antialiasing which is far superior and faster.

Don't use AntiAlias with Draft, they work against each other. Use it for high resolution raytraced pictures, the adaptive antialiasing takes little extra time and gives your images a stunning quality.

If you are using a background image and fog, you won't see it unless you set the far point density below 100%.

✦ **Background.** You can set a background color, bitmap, or animation here. To set the color just click on the color square and you'll get an RGB dialog box. Set the sliders until the color looks right. You can also input exact color values. Color morphs can be keyframe animated for interesting effects.

✦ **Background Image.** Click on the requester box following Background and you'll get an image file dialog. You can load in just about any image file you have that seems appropriate. Select and trueSpace2 automatically scales it to the right size and puts into the background full screen. A very nice feature.

✦ **Animate.** You can use animated backgrounds too. Video .avi and .fli files as well as sequentially numbered image files can all be used. When Animate is engaged, trueSpace2 lines up the images and inputs them one at time, frame by frame. tS2 automatically loops the animation if it's too short for the sequence, so try to use loops that don't show.

Use videos recorded at 30 fps, otherwise, trueSpace2 repeats each frame twice. It's a little strange when your animation is updating at 30 fps and the background at half that. Most people don't notice it. (See the Trek video on the CD-ROM.)

✦ **Global Environment.** This is for reflection maps that affect all the shiny objects in your scene. You get global reflections in scan-line rendering as well as raytrace. Raytracing will reflect the global environment according to the shine of each object, but they will reflect things around them as well. You can use straight color or an image. It's animatable too.

✦ **Global Environment Image.** You can set global environment to an image map using this option. A desert scene can really sell a shiny metal object.

You can create special cubic images with the image utilities. These accurately simulate reflections and render very quickly. Each is made up of six shots from a selected object's points of view.

✦ **Animate.** Same as for Background. You can create some wicked special effects using animated global environments on shiny stuff. Picture a silver sphere reflecting swiftly moving clouds or better yet, blue flames reflected in a purple Testarossa.

Render Mode

The Render Mode icon allows you to select the manner and location where the render takes place. Each window can be rendered in its own way. Here are your options:

✦ **Render Current Object.** If you want to see how the current object will look fully rendered, click this tool. Only the selected object will render.

If you are in raytrace mode, the object will be raytraced, but the engine will ignore shadows and the rest of the scene. Therefore, you will see only reflections of the global environment and of itself. This can be misleading. Do a full scene raytrace in a small alternate window to get a better feel.

If you have a light, camera, or deformation Primitive selected, nothing will render. I do it all the time and wait like a fool for something to happen.

✦ **Render to Screen.** Self-explanatory. It uses the Render Options panel to set render quality and renders to the active screen.

✦ **Render to File.** Use this to make a movie or still shot. It'll pop up Render Properties panel. Here you instruct the render engine on how you want the work done. There are enough settings here to scare you, but they all make sense when you know what they do.

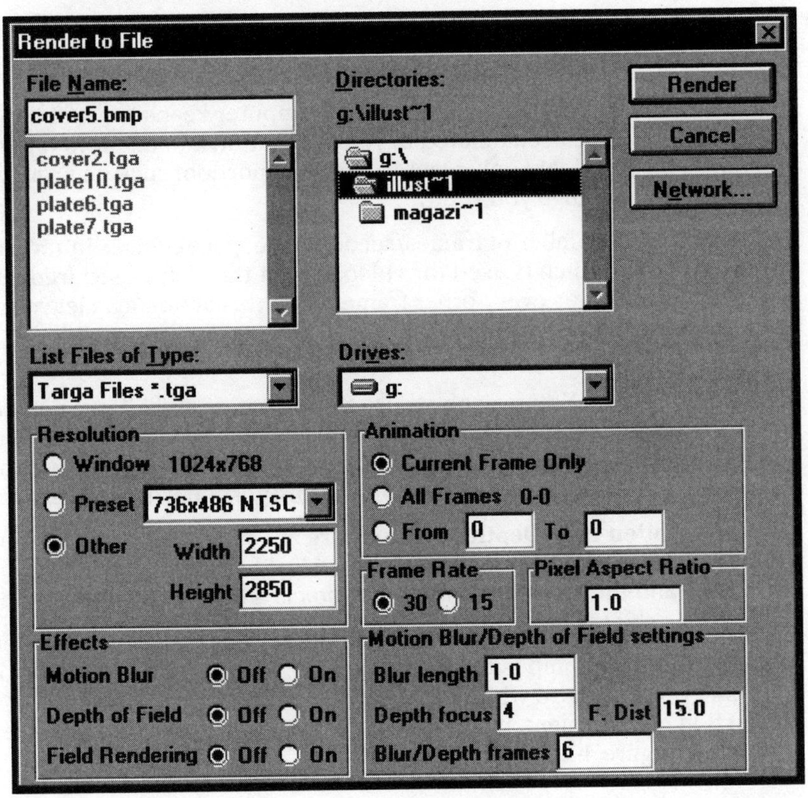

- **File Name.** Self-explanatory, but it works differently from most programs. You actually have to type in the extension of the file type you'll use. It doesn't matter if you have clicked a certain type in the List Files Type window. trueSpace2 will save three still image types: .tga, .jpg, and .bmp (also .dib, but this is the same as .bmp). It will save both .flc and .avi files as well.

CAUTION

It's easy to screw up and just type in the file name, leaving off an extension. Most graphics dialog boxes assume the extension of the type of file you're filtering for. Not so with trueSpace2. You could end up with a huge number of .tga files instead of a single .avi file. So type in the whole file name and extension.

- **List Files of Type.** Displays specific graphics file types in the File: name window.
- **Resolution.** This is where you set the size of the rendering. There's a useful smattering of presets, or you can set your own.

POWER TIP

You can render odd sizes: a long thin (400 × 30) title for the top of a page or full motion picture resolution of 2,000 × 3,000 pixels, all the way up to a huge wall poster at 8,192 × 8,192.

Render times increase exponentially as the very large formats and storage requirements become prodigious. Fear not, you'll never come close to these giant sizes.

- **Animation.** Pretty easy to figure out. The computer keeps track of how many frames you've accumulated in your animation and displays it in the All Frames option. If you only want to render a portion, click on From and type in the frame range you want.
- **Frame Rate.** The number of frames/second. trueSpace2 thinks in terms of 30 fps internally, which is used for video. To get the 15 fps used frequently in multimedia, it skips every other frame. I find this annoying. I leave it at 30 fps and have a hardware accelerator to play it at full speed. It looks smoother and I hate choppy movement.
- **Pixel Aspect Ratio.** You may never use this, but it's handy if you need it. If you're exporting animation to a multimedia software package you can run into lopsided pixels. Spheres will look like eggs. You can adjust the aspect ratio here so the picture appears in proper proportion when you export it.
- **Effects — Motion Blur/Depth of Field.** Here are some of the professional touches I mentioned: Motion Blur, Depth of Field (Z-focus), and Field Rendering, and their settings (the dialog box is a bit confusing).
  - **Motion Blur.** This is a major time muncher. trueSpace2 renders several frames and then composites them together. The result is a frame with all the still objects sharp while the objects in motion are blurred in the direction of movement. It simulates the blur a real camera would see, as shown in Figure 4-3.

Figure 4-3: Note the effect of Z-focus blur at default setting.

- **Blur Length**. This is the length of time (in frames) the blur spans. You set the number of frames in the little input box. A value of 1 would mean little blur because it extends over the time one frame to the next. The Frames field controls quality of the blur blending. (I should have worked blue berries in there too.) If you have fast movement and a long blur but few frames, you'll get a line of transparent images. If you increase the frame count you get increasingly smooth blurs. But the more frames, the more render time. Longer blur lengths require more frames. You need to work these two in cahoots.

POWER TIP: You can get some interesting special effects by rendering long sequences in a single frame. For example, render a 60-frame animation, but first set the blur length to 30 frames. Your results depend on the speed of action in the piece and your frame count, but can look cool, especially with steady movement and a low frame count. Be prepared for this to take way more than all night. trueSpace2 will actually have to render 1,800 frames! I've never actually finished one.

- **Depth of Field.** This is like lens focus. You set a focal point with the F. Dist window. It looks down the Z axis in World coordinates.
- **Depth Focus.** Adjusts the strength of focus effect. Larger values yield more blurring with distance from the focal point.
- **F. Dist (focal distance).** Set the distance to the center of focus in whatever units of measurement your scene is set to (if you use the Look At icon, this distance is set automatically).

POWER TIP: When used with the Look At tool, focal point is automatically set to the axis of that object in view.

- **Blur/Depth frames.** The number of frames rendered to calculate the amount of blur.
- **Field Rendering.** This is used when recording interlaced NTSC video. It forces the program to render two separate frames for each actual frame; each one has half the information (every other line). When shown on U.S. TV, you get a very smooth, professional-quality animation.

✦ **Render.** This button sets off the render engine once you've set the parameters in the Render Options panel. Depending on the file format you've chosen, you may get a dialog box asking for compression or color depth information.

✦ AVI Compression panel (this dialog box appears when you click on the Render button):

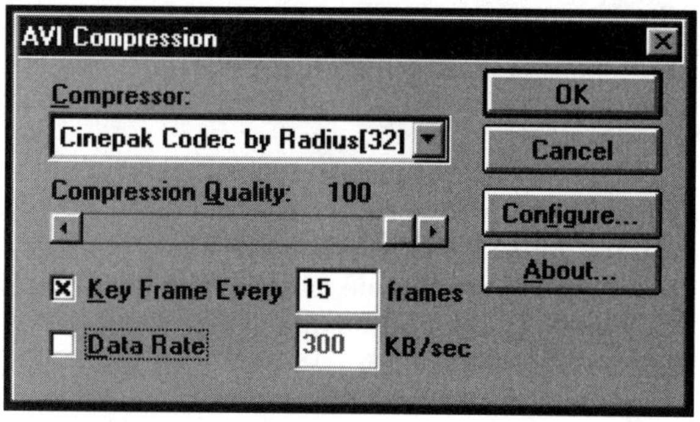

- **Compressor.** You can have any number of compression schemes installed. They're called Codecs. Different ones are supposed to be good under different circumstances. Some may bomb in trueSpace2 because they haven't been tested. The choice looks complicated, but it's not. There's only one that works well every time, CinePack Codec by Radius. *Not* CinePack Codec by SuperMac. The former is newer and does a better job.

If you're planning to edit your animation in another program, choose None as your compressor. You probably won't be able to play the resulting, rather large .avi smoothly, but you'll get high quality original frames for your edit. Compress it with CinePak from your video editor before playing. If you forget, don't panic; CinePack compressed .avi files edit reasonably well.

- **Compression Quality.** Quality and file size are inversely proportional. If you're not worried about file size, set this between 75–100%.
- **Key Frame Every.** Inserting keyframes lets the compression program "tween" frames, where it estimates movement between frames, only recording the change from frame to frame. This vastly reduces the amount of data recorded, but also the quality of image.

If you intend to edit the clip, deselect the Key Frame option. Otherwise set it at every 5 to 7 frames.

- **Data Rate.** This allows you to set a data rate to tune your animation to specific hardware, like CD-ROM. The trade-off is that when you clip the data rate, more complex frames are encoded at a lower quality in order to stay at or below your limit.

When using a fast hard drive, deselect Data Rate. If you need to use it, render animations at 352 × 240 (MPEG-1) or smaller.

Each file type that you select has its own set of parameters, such as TGA, JPEG, or Flic, as follows:

✦ **TGA.** Targa files gives you two settings:

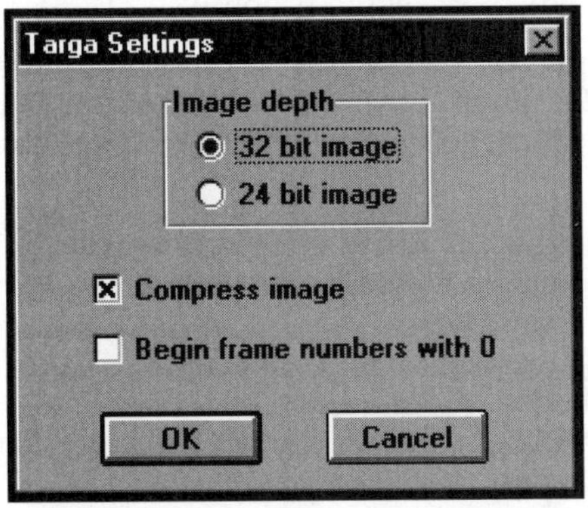

- **Image depth — 24 or 32 bits.** The latter records an 8-bit alpha channel with transparency information for compositing and special effects.

If you don't need 32 bits, don't use it, 24 bits should be adequate for most things because, as you undoubtedly know, it's 16 million colors deep.

- **Compress Image.** This is a lossless compression option.

Use lossless image compression wherever you can. It slows down your load, but only by a trivial amount in most cases. Targa files are big and you'll be accumulating scads of them during animation work.

✦ **JPEG.** This is a very good lossy compression method you can use when you need large numbers of files. It has one setting, Quality, which goes from 0–100. Pictures used on the World Wide Web are often stored in this format because of the excellent compression. The lower you set Quality, the tighter the compression will be.

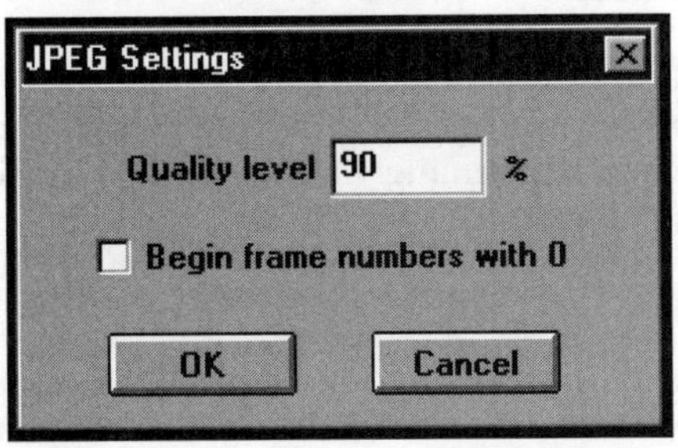

Set JPEG between 80–100 and you won't notice much lossage, but the file will be nicely compressed. I set it at around 50 to upload to the Web. This gives a very compact file.

✦ **Flic (.fli).** This is an aging 8-bit file format from Autodesk. Because it's been around, there's a lot of material available in it. It also works in both DOS and Windows. On its way out, it is being replaced by .avi, quick time, and MPEG.

- **Universal Color Palette.** Uses a standard color palette.

- **Create palette on first frame.** Dangerous. If you introduce new colors later in the animation, they won't be represented properly.
- **Create palette for each frame.** Quality but quirky, creates palettes that can't be displayed on an 8-bit display. Use it with a 16-bit DOS display to get full-screen video. This way you can record to videotape using a cheap scan converter.
- **Dither Frames.** The limited color palette of the .fli format causes annoying color bands in gradations. This is a feeble attempt to fix that. It often causes artifacts of its own.

POWER TIP: Use the standard color palette and don't dither for the most consistent results in this limited format. Its main use is to import the vast array of textures already recorded in .fli for Autodesk's 3D studio.

Navigating through trueSpace2

One of the great joys of 3D is the ability to move around in your world. trueSpace2 has excellent view tools with Eye navigation.

The View Navigation tools are located on each window bar. Each window can be set to a different view mode. The tool also allows you to set up cameras anywhere in your world and have simultaneous views presented in different windows.

Preset Views

✦ **Perspective View.** The default view for the main window gives a feeling of depth. Many graphic artists prefer to work here, but it can be difficult to position objects accurately. You can seemingly attach one object to another in this view, only to discover, in an orthogonal window, the parts are separated by meters. Perspective can be Zoomed (Scale), Tracked (Move), or Panned/Tilted (Rotate).

✦ **Orthogonal Views.** These World Coordinate Views look at the work space head-on along each axis. They can be moved and scaled, but not rotated. OrthoNav affects these windows. They are:

- **Front View.**

In this window, you look straight down the Y axis. Your eye is just above the origin plane.

- **Left View.**

Looking down the X axis just above the origin plane.

- **Top View.**

Looking straight down on your world, along the Z axis.

✦ **Camera Views.**

This is more than the name implies. You can place cameras anywhere in your world and look through them. These are the most versatile views, as they can be rotated, scaled, positioned exactly where you want them. Importantly, cameras can be tracked along complex spline paths for sophisticated animation shots.

POWER TIP: A spotlight can serve as a camera. Look through its lens to view exactly what part of the scene its light covers. You'll even see the hot spot as a green circle and adjust it from that view with the Object Move tool. Other objects can be cameras as well, though most are useless, because the axis is deep inside. You can put the axis of a jet in the cockpit, and get a pilot's-eye view without having to install a camera.

Eye Navigation

Each view is like a robotic eye that can be tracked, tilted, rotated, and panned.

✦ **Eye Move.** Eye can be moved in any of the three Coordinate Systems.

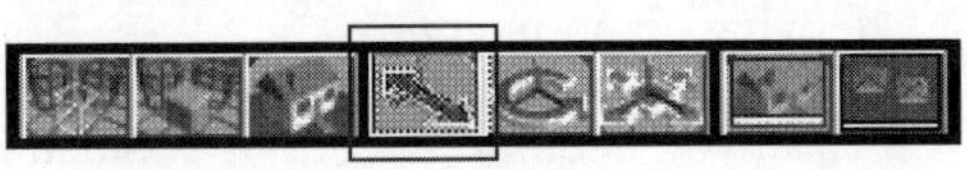

- In WORLD Coordinates, left clicking moves it over the X/Y grid like a bird flying. You can change altitude (Z axis) by right clicking and dragging.
- In SCREEN Coordinates, left clicking moves the view up or down (X) the screen, and left or right (Y); while the right moves the view in and out of the screen (Z).
- In OBJECT Coordinates, the eye behavior is similar to the setting for World Coordinates except it follows the local axes of the current object.

✦ **Eye Rotate.**

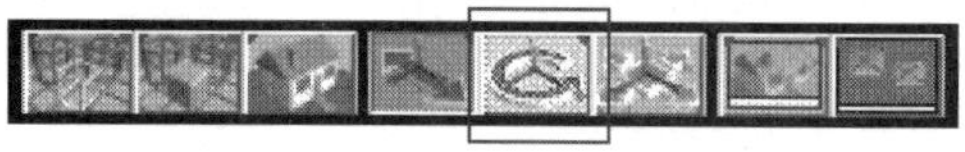

All eye rotation is done in reference to SCREEN Coordinates, but the center of rotation or tilt is determined by the Coordinate System engaged.

✦ **Eye Scale (Zoom).**

This is the same as using a Zoom lens to change the focal length of the eye. In the Perspective View, Zoom can go from the Fish Eye lens to Super telephoto but you'll see the same kinds of distortions as you would with a camera lens. This is a feature, not a bug. For non-distorted Zooming, use the orthogonal views.

If your eye is a camera view and you discover you can't rotate it, you've got the Look At icon engaged.

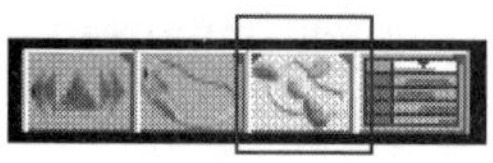

This constrains the camera to look at only one spot (axis). Deselect it to rotate the eye.

- **WORLD.** Eye will orbit the center of the World regardless of where it is pointed.
- **OBJECT.** Eye will orbit the selected (active) object's local axis regardless of the direction it is pointed.
- **SCREEN.** Eye will not orbit, but will pan and tilt around its own axes, which are the same as the SCREEN axes.

You really don't get an exact picture from my words, and static illustrations would be pointless. Like flying a plane, you ain't gonna know what it's like until you do it. In fact, navigation in 3D *is* a lot like flying. Experiment.

Zoom has limits in Perspective View. If you need to pull out or zoom in further than you can, switch to the Move tool and SCREEN coordinates to do it.

It's undocumented, but you can keyframe animate the Zoom eye for some interesting effects.

✦ **New Window Tool.**

Located on the main window bar, it looks like the View Select tool, only a lighter shade. It has the same variants as View Select, but opens a small alternate View window in the view selected.

Each new window has a bar with Viewpoint Navigation, View Select, and Render tools unique to that window. Each works the same way as the main window. You can size these windows, with maximum size being a third to a quarter of the screen, depending on the resolution you're running. I suggest using smaller than maximum windows; it preserves resources and gives you more work space.

POWER TIP: You can open up to three new windows simultaneously, but each one uses system resources; 3DR windows use the most, so apply the rule of parsimony.

✦ **Close All Panels.**

Even better. Get rid of all those panels by closing them all in one swell foop. This is so handy you'll want to give it a keyboard shortcut.

• **Reset View.**

A very important tool. It returns to your Default View settings for the active window (the ones in which trueSpace2 fires up). I use it a lot because I'll zoom and move around in a view to check things out, but when I'm ready to render, it's usually from the original settings.

• **Look At Object.**

This is useful when you have an object selected in one window and can't find it in your active window. It will focus your view on the selected object. It's also the easiest way to center an object to work on it.

• **Dock All Panels.**

When invoked, this tool lines up all the open panels in a nice row or rows along the bottom of the work space. It's handy when you've been madly working and find your screen all cluttered with stray panels.

POWER TIP: I close all panels before a screen render so I can see the darn thing. It's frustrating to render a scene only to find a panel right over the spot you want to check out.

Now that you have a pretty good idea how to move around in trueSpace2, let's look at the view rendering options.

Working in Wireframe and Solid Render Modes

trueSpace2 is one of the first 3D suites to offer a solid mode with real-time lighting. Even some of the most advanced high-end 3D software is only now developing interactive lighting. Sharon Calahan revealed, "Lighting is one of the most difficult and important parts of digital animation. We didn't have a real-time interactive lighting system for *Toy Story*, we're developing one now." Well, you are fortunate to have a very good real-time interactive lighting system in trueSpace2, now. When you engage Intel's 3DR API (Applications Programming Interface) your window shows nearly everything in solid shapes, including the effect of lighting changes — as you make them.

Both wireframe and 3DR modes are useful and I generally work in both at the same time. Being an old-timer, I'm comfortable working in wireframe, but you'll also learn that some things are just plain easier in wireframe. I nearly always have a 3DR window open as a visual reference. It helps me understand what I'm seeing in wireframe. By the same token, complex object hierarchies are way easier to understand and navigate in wireframe. The convention of brightening the selected portion in wireframe works better for me.

On the other hand, I get very confused when rotating objects in wireframe mode. I can almost never visualize them perfectly. Being dyslexic, I'm usually 180 degrees off. I think the face is pointed at me — I render it and get the back side of a mask. Referencing a small 3DR window has saved me a lot of agony here.

Caligari optimized the trueSpace2 interface for solid render operation and they encourage you to use it almost exclusively. It's up to you. I think you'll find that the combination is better.

Advantages of Wireframe Mode

- ✦ It's faster... a lot faster. If you don't have an accelerator, even a single solid window will slow everything down — forget three.
- ✦ Wireframe lets you see things behind the object, and even select them.
- ✦ It's easier to manipulate axes.
- ✦ Complex hierarchies are much easier to comprehend and navigate.
- ✦ You can see internal structure and move items inside others.
- ✦ And there's more, but this will do for now.

Advantages of Solid Render Mode

- You can see the impact of lighting in real-time.
- You can more easily determine object orientation.
- You have a better feel for surface appearance.
- It's easier to sculpt solid objects.

Acceleration

To render a constantly refreshed 3D scene takes a lot of horsepower. If you have a 486 or older machine, 3DR will slow it to a belly crawl. But if you install one of several new 3D accelerator cards coming onto the market, you can get very smooth, real-time performance from 3DR, especially in Windows 95.

Accelerator cards do the hideously complex floating point math required by object translation, rotation, and scaling as well as handling textures and lighting and other housekeeping duties. They remove these burdens from your CPU and handle them in super-optimized hardware at blinding speeds. This accelerates performance in other areas of trueSpace2 as well. The net effect is a miracle of smooth perfection.

Some accelerators don't fully support 3DR. You might find that the card will not support real-time texture mapping or animated materials. Check the specs before you buy.

Better yet, check with Caligari via your Web browser at `www.caligari.com`. You should be able to download the latest 3DR data library here as well. If you have problems with the accelerator you have, it may be your driver. Check with the manufacturer for latest driver versions. In this field it pays to regularly update your graphics drivers as they improve constantly.

To keep up with the latest information on accelerator boards on the Web, check out the 3D accelerator FAQ at `http://www.cs.tu-berlin.de/~ki/engines.html`. URLs change frequently, so if the address is not available, do an InfoSeek search on *3D accelerat*.

Object Navigation

When you fire up your trueSpace2 interface, most tools are grayed out because there are no objects. Don't worry, all the tools you need to create or retrieve objects are active. I'll explain more about building worlds later in our journey, but it's time now for a few basics.

You start a project by either popping up a Primitive or drawing a 2D shape and sweeping it into 3D or, alternatively, by loading a prebuilt object. Let's pop a Primitive and play with it to get a feel for moving objects around in space. In Chapter 6, you'll use these techniques to build a nifty space vehicle.

Accelerator Recommendations

Matrox

There are many boards in development as I write this. I'm currently using a 4M Matrox Impression-Plus. This has already been superseded by the faster Matrox Millennium which uses a new kind of ram optimized for video, called Windows Ram. Matrox has been slow in developing drivers for 3DR. Recent e-mail indicates that we won't see 3DR drivers for the Impression-Plus board. However, I understand they are shipping 3DR drivers for the Millennium board.

Matrox has always been kind of a high-end line, but prices are dropping rapidly. I believe the 4M Millennium will be just over $450.00 US by the time you read this. Get a 4M board; you'll need the extra memory to handle textures, lighting, and fast object manipulation.

Diamond Multimedia

Diamond Multimedia has recently announced the Diamond Edge card. This amazing card should have a street price of around $275.00 and will feature the Nvidia chip, with both 2D and 3D acceleration as well as automatic perspective control and enhanced texture mapping which can simulate curved surfaces. The 2D acceleration is for video and animated textures. You'll also be able to preview your animations in real-time. 3DR is scheduled for support. The edge is optimized for games so it also includes a sound card featuring really good wavetable sound.

Creative Labs

Creative Labs, makers of the Sound Blaster series, bought 18 percent of 3D Labs. I suspect they did it to get dibs on 3D Labs' amazing Glint technology. This 0.5 micron chip (actually built by IBM) is said to render 300,000 polygons/second. Just so you know, that's astounding. An unaccelerated SGI Indigo using B-render can only put out about 80,000 polys per second. The 3D Blaster version fully supports the major 3D APIs except OpenGL.

Fortunately, Creative Labs says their board, 3D Blaster, will be affordable. It uses a game-optimized version of the Glint that should be extremely snappy. You'll need 4M of VRAM, so expect it to be around $349.00. IMHO, 3D Blaster, with its potentially stunning performance, should be the best price/performance trade-off. By the time you read this, a second generation chip from 3D Labs will be providing a pervasive 3D solution at an even lower price. Look for it.

It Takes Balls to Start an Evolution

The following project is a raytrace exercise that results in the creation of silver balls that reflect the sky and each other — a classic raytrace theme. My daughter Dani, a creative type, followed this lesson and changed things around (as artists do). I've included her results in the color section (see Plate 4-1).

Raytracing pretty much started with displaying shiny balls that reflect everything in sight. They are fascinating to look at and easy to create, as the following steps illustrate. Don't get hung up on them, they've been done.

1. Start by opening an extra little window in the upper right–hand corner. Make it Top View, looking smack down on the grid. Now pop up the Primitives panel and click on the Sphere.

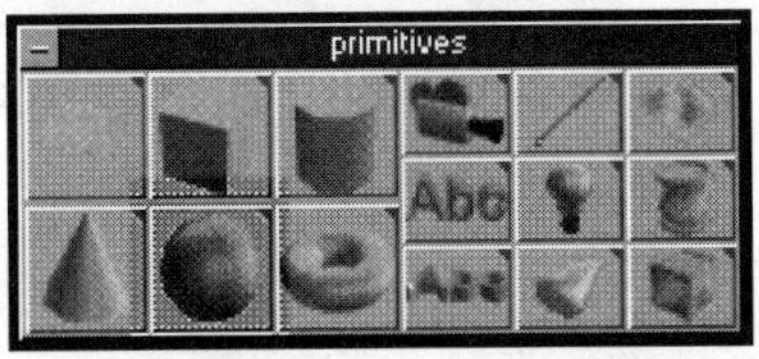

You get a sphere in the middle of the grid. Measured against the grid, it's exactly two meters in diameter. We set the grid to a one-meter interval when we set the World and Object Units in the Object Properties panel. Handy deal.

2. Go to the tool bar and find Smooth Quad Divide.

   It's on the right-hand side if you're in 1024 × 756.

3. Click and the sphere magically subdivides into a smoother surface.

For close-ups you may have to subdivide again to avoid seeing polys. This is also useful if you want to build an exploder object with lots of polygons to blow apart.

4. Now, run your mouse pointer along the left side of the tool bar until you come to Copy. Click on it. I'll repeat this several times throughout the book — *nothing* seems to happen — but it does.
5. Click on the visible sphere and move it to the left, centering it on the grid so the two spheres are just touching as in Figure 4-4. Note that the original sphere remains in place.
6. Now produce two more balls and set them into a quadrant cluster as in Figure 4-5.

It's much faster to glue the first two balls together, copy them, and move the new pair to form a tight four-ball cluster, rather than producing individual spheres.

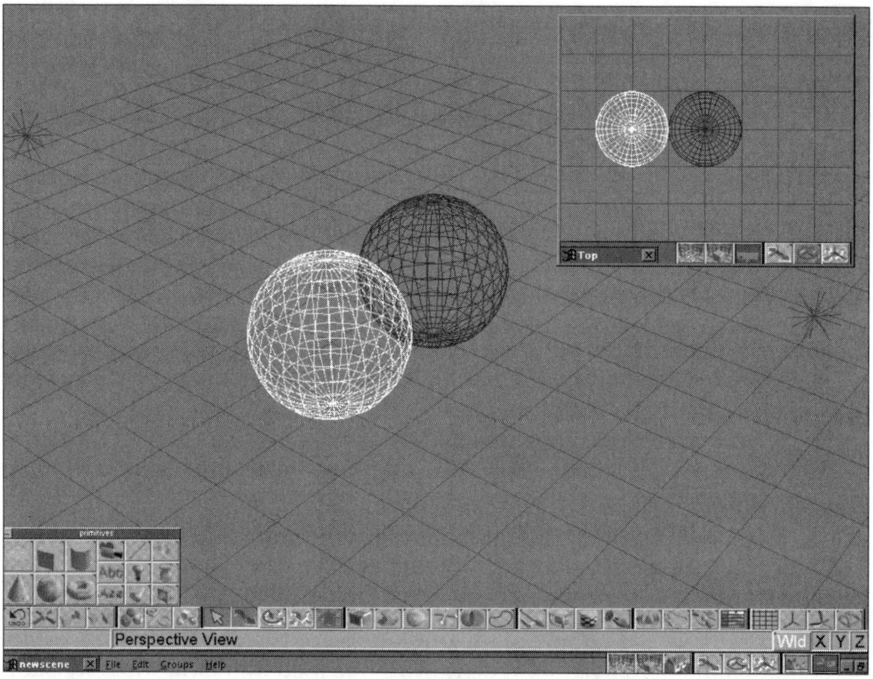

Figure 4-4: At the beginning of a pyramid, the original ball has been copied to form a pair.

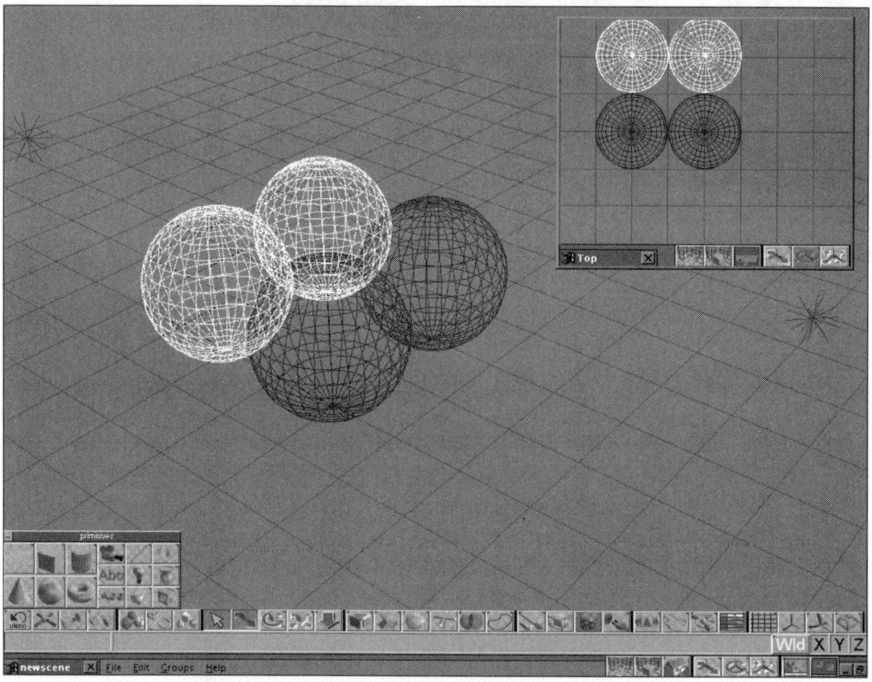

Figure 4-5: Four balls in a quadrant cluster nest wait for the egg.

Smooth Moves

Here's where object navigation gets interesting.

7. Pop up a fifth ball. Defying the laws of physics, it materializes in the exact space as your original ball — no worries — everything pops up here. It's called the Origin. Smooth Quad subdivide it.

We want to nest this ball on top of the other four. Here's a suggestion to make it go perfectly.

8. Open another window to a Front View and right click on the ball in the main Perspective View.
9. Watching the little window, lift the ball until it's above the others. Good.
10. Now, still referencing the Front View, left click and move the ball to the center of the cluster, as shown in Figure 4-6. It looks like it's in position. But the additional windows show it's not.

Extra windows are necessary in 3D because positioning requires more information than it did in 2D. Two more moves will nail it. Make sure you have a Left View window, and a Top View open. You can see clearly what needs to be done.

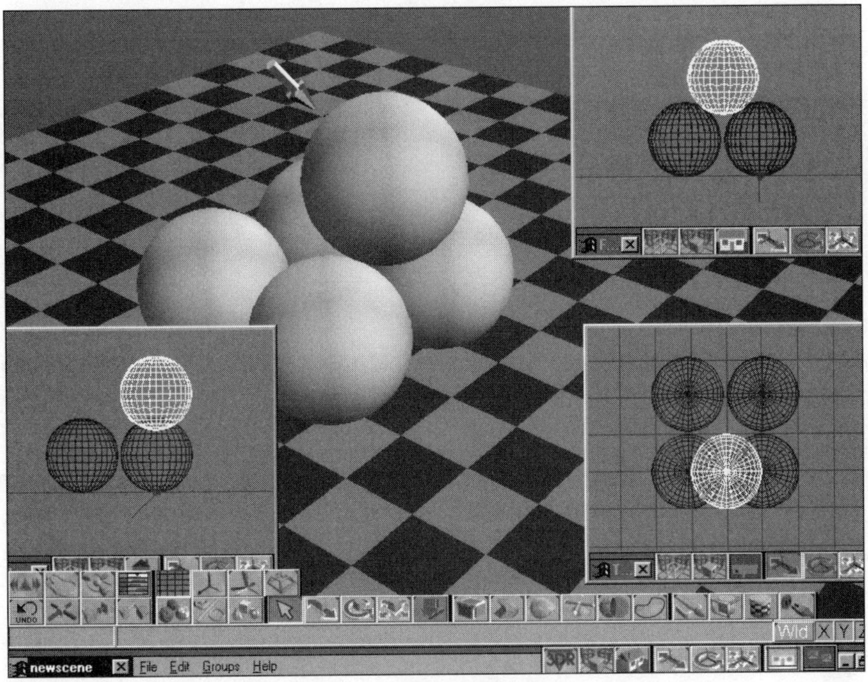

Figure 4-6: The last ball is about to be centered above cluster.

11. Center the ball above the other four. Set up 3DR mode in Perspective View, to drop the ball in the nest. Right click on the Wireframe Icon and select the 3DR mode. You can see relative positions now.

12. Right click on the ball, lower it gently in place until it looks right.

Congratulations!!! You now qualify as an object navigator. Nearly everything you have to position will roughly follow this pattern. We'll build something a lot more complicated in Chapter 6, when I'll tell you about an easy way to position objects precisely on the grid, using the Grid Snap tool. But first, let's have a little fun. Glue all the balls together into a single object.

Adding a Little Sheen

We might as well try out the paint tool. Lots more on this later, but this'll be a quick shot to get your feet damp.

13. Left click/hold the paint tool (it looks more like a Q-tip than a paint brush) to pop up the Paint Tool variant list. Good.

14. Now move up and select the brush that looks like a paint roller.

It becomes the active paintbrush.

15. Go to the Tool Bar and find the Materials Library icon and click it. This brings up the Materials Library selection window.

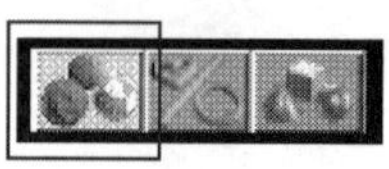

16. Select the polished chrome material. It will be automatically created and displayed in a Material Preview window. Later I'll show you how to make all sorts of neat surfaces.

17. Use the paint roller and click on any ball. They all turn black, but that's a shortcoming of 3DR. Do a quick scan-line render; you'll see simulated reflections from a reflection map.

Adding a Floor

Now we need some kind of floor for the balls to sit on.

18. Go back to wireframe in the main window, and pop up the Planar Object.

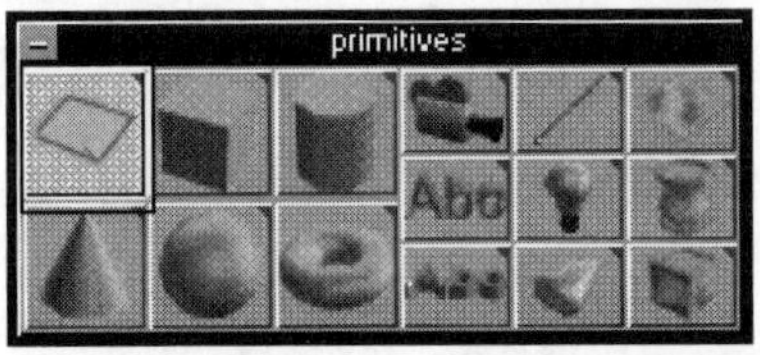

19. Scale it up, holding down *both* mouse buttons, until it covers most of the grid.

20. If you don't see the floor, it's because it is slightly below the solid render checkerboard floor. Raise it slightly, or go to Wireframe. Go to the default Materials Library and select the ash wood texture and apply it to the floor... er, table top.

Let's render and see what we get:

21. Pop up the Render Options panel, set Raytrace and AntiAlias on, and Draft should definitely be off. Leave the Reflect setting alone.

22. Click on Global Env and enter `Wastlan` as the environment map. That's it. Now render to screen or a file. The image appears in Figure 4-7.

If you're in a hurry, select the little window and render it, using its own render icon on its mini work bar.

Pretty decent, huh? Okay, so I did a few extra things, like adding a skydome with fractal clouds and I made the top ball partly transparent. But yours should look pretty amazing too. Your rendering required more than a billion calculations as your CPU and FPU traced light beams back and forth, and up and down. Notice the balls reflecting themselves like infinite mirrors. Chrome balls have been way overdone, but they still look neat to me.

Now for grins, turn off Raytrace and re-render this very same scene. You'll see what a fine render engine trueSpace2 has. It's much faster, but it can simulate reflections and shadows. Using a custom cubic map from the Image Utilities panel would be even more convincing. More on this later.

If you're confused about any of this, go back and fiddle with it on your own. It's smart to have basics well in hand before moving on.

Figure 4-7: Here's the finished product. (See color Plate 4-1.)

Summary

Okay, let's look at the most important things you learned in this chapter:

- You can find the interface setup controls by looking at icons and the help bar.
- You can set up the 3D workspace the way you like it including views, scale, and coordinate system.
- You can set up your render engine to produce the quality of output image you want.
- You can set up and control your views of the work space in alternate windows where the view can be customized.
- You can use 3DR and wireframe views for lighting feedback and for previewing your work.
- You can pop up Primitives from the Primitives panel to start your projects.
- 3D accelerator boards can significantly increase the performance of real-time 3D rendering needed for 3DR windows.
- You can position objects exactly where you want them by using the Object Navigation tools to move, rotate, and scale an item.
- You can surface objects by using the Materials Library to bring up prefabricated materials that come with tS2 or that you've saved in your own library.
- You can render a scene with raytracing to bring out shadows and reflections.

✦ ✦ ✦

CHAPTER 5

The Universe from Scratch

✦ ✦ ✦ ✦

In This Chapter

Using Primitives to build complex objects

Tweaking Primitives to your liking

Gluing objects into a hierarchy

Navigating hierarchies

3D Boolean Union

Adjusting your views

Space vehicle construction techniques

✦ ✦ ✦ ✦

You never really know what you can do until you lay yourself on the line. Some people — many people — quit before testing their range. They'll tell you they're 3D artists, but they've never built a model. I think you have to build something first — just one thing. We might as well do that now. A space tanker, built from a bunch of object Primitives. We'll pop them up, manipulate them, glue them and even Boolean them together. I designed this vehicle to give you practice in construction techniques you'll use over and over again. It's a simple design; feel free to embellish or change it as you like after you build the basic model. In later chapters, I'll show you ways to create intricate parts and add details.

Considerations

Space vehicles are popular models on AOL, CIS, and the Web. The problem is that most models uploaded aren't exactly what I'm looking for. When I get a picture in my mind of a tanker or star cruiser, I just have to build it myself. You can actually become famous if you upload a slick enough starship. Just attach a text file that explains it and give yourself credit. Often you can see how many times it's been downloaded. You'll be amazed at how fast and how far a good-looking model can go.

Folks also upload rendered scenes and .avi files. Many are wonderful, while others fall short for lack of balance or detail and/or believable textures. Common mistakes appear as mighty star cruisers that look like plastic models, or have inappropriate proportions, and bad or missing detail. I can't help with your personal aesthetics, but if you have a sense of balance and a little time, you can win contests and even make your living at 3D by getting it right.

They say there is no one right way to do it. Actually there are lots of right ways, and even more wrong ways. But right sells. It sells if people like it. Tune into this, and you just might build a career displaying your wares on the Web. Oh the blessed freedom, but more on this in the Internet chapter.

Important thing to remember in 3D animation: light is your best buddy. Use it to create the illusion of reality by letting it reflect off ship details as it rotates in space. Understand that bump mapping may look very convincing, but it's a cheat. Bump maps don't glint in the harsh light of space. 3D detail does, but you have to *model* it. Lighting is the subject of another chapter, but it pervades everything, so start thinking about it now. Fire up your tS2 engine and we'll play a little.

A Space Tanker – The Primitive Approach

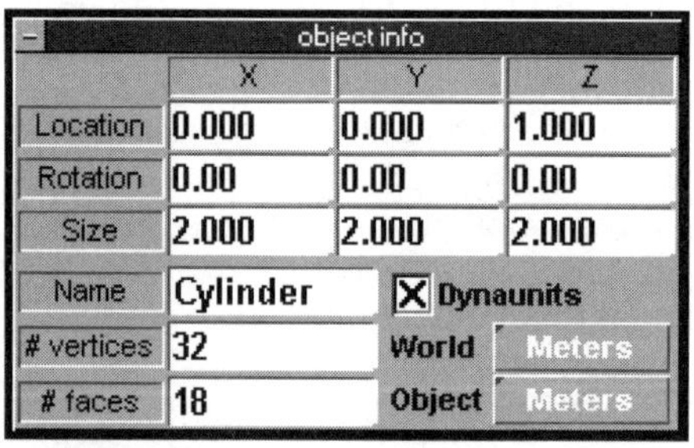

Pop up a cylinder Primitive. Make sure DynaUnits is checked. Next, set your view to wireframe mode.

Good, your cylinder should look like a pipe-shaped wire matrix, two meters in each dimension.

If the cylinder is more like a cone, right click on the cylinder icon and check the properties box. You can see an example of it later in Figure 5-7. The Top Radius should be set at one meter. If not, correct it. Note that you can also adjust the number of latitude and longitude segments. This controls the complexity and accuracy of the cylinder. It can go from a triangular block (Lat. ➪ 2, Long. ➪ 3) to a very fine cylinder (Long. ➪ 12). Latitude becomes important later, when you learn object deformation.

Your cylinder should be more or less in the center of the screen aligned with the Z axis (pointing up and down). We need to elongate it for the project. This can be done by mouse or by direct input. Because this is an architectural/engineering project, access the OPP, Size window, Set Z ➪ 6.0 (Z=6 meters). This elongates the cylinder up and down the Z axis from the origin.

The Setup

Open a new Front View window and drag it to the upper right of your screen. Set it to 3DR mode.

You will use this window for visual reference as we build the tanker. Now switch the default Perspective View in the main window to a Front View as well. Now and then you'll have to Zoom in or out for a full screen view of the tanker, using the Zoom tool:

To move objects predictably, you'll want to constrain movement to one axis at a time and turn on Snap-to-Grid. You can disable the X axis or Y axis, back and forth, but it gets tedious. I prefer to disengage OrthoNav in the Files ➪ Preferences panel. This effectively constrains movement to World X axis on left button, Y axis on right button, but only in orthogonal windows like Front View or Top View.

Next, click the Snap-to-Grid icon:

This wonderful item is a double-edged sword. It's fabulous for aligning stuff as we are doing now. When you move things, they jump to discrete grid locations with great precision. Same with rotating things, by default they rotate in 45° increments.

POWER TIP

If you forget to turn grid off, it will prevent any fine positional adjustments. So when you find objects not moving at all, then making a big jump, you know the Snap-to-Grid function is engaged. You can't change the grid display size, but you can adjust the snap increments via numeric input in the grid control panel (right-click on the grid icon).

Pop up a sphere primitive. A two-meter sphere will materialize smack in the middle of your cylinder, as shown in Figure 5-1.

Make sure your Object Select and Object Move icons are depressed, then grab the sphere in the main window with a *right* click, and drag. Simply move it to the top until it fills the end of the tube. A right click constrains your sphere to move only in the vertical or Z direction.

It's easy to align the center of the sphere with the top of the tube as shown in Figure 5-1; the grid pops it to exactly the right place. Notice how the sphere and cylinder polygons line up perfectly. This will make a nice clean Boolean union in a few minutes.

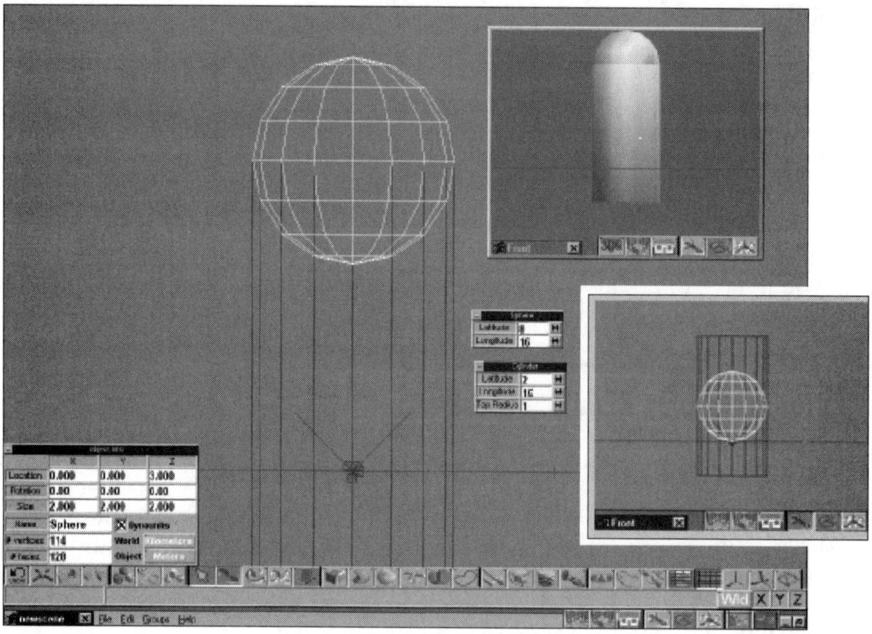

Figure 5-1: Sphere positioned at head of cylinder with inset sphere at origin

If you screwed up and left-clicked, the sphere may have gotten all misaligned. (It must be perfectly aligned for this operation.) Fear not, you can start again by clicking the Normalize Location icon. This moves the axis back to the origin. The Undo icon will effectively do the same thing by backing you up one operation. But learn to use the Normalize icons, they come in handy often.

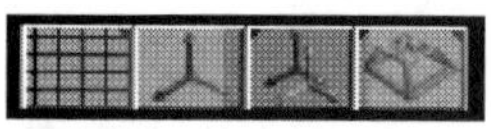

This will realign the sphere in the center of the tube. *Right* click this time. With the sphere still selected, go to the Copy Icon

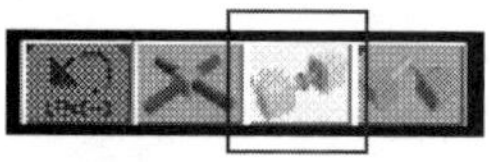

and click. Nothing seems to happen, as in Chapter 4. Grab the ball, *right* click, and drag it to the bottom of the tube. Notice that a copy remains at the top. Or maybe that's the original. Align the midpoint line of the ball as before. Good work.

Detail

You now have a simple tanker that needs some detail to make it interesting. We don't have to know what the detail actually does. It just has to look as if it might function. Let's add some reinforcing ribs around the fuselage, like some liquid nitrogen trucks have. The torus Primitive is a natural choice. We don't want the fat default torus, so right-click on the torus icon and increase the inner radius ➪ 0.8.

This will make a very skinny bagel shape or ring. Set Lat. ➪ 12 Long. ➪ 16, and pop one up. Bam, right in the middle of the tank. Easy.

Next we'll symmetrically scale the ring up

by pressing both buttons at once and moving the mouse. Expand the ring, watching your 3DR window, until it looks right. Oops, we forgot to release the grid. Click on the grid icon. Now things will move smoothly.

Keep these ribs reasonably subtle. (See Figure 5-2.) Mine ended up at Object Size X=2.115 and Y=2.115. With the torus selected, re-engage the grid. Right click and set the X=1, Y=1, Z=0.22. This will cause movement in the vertical direction to jump 0.22 meters at a time, a little more than the exposed torus. Using the Copy icon, make successive copies (I used eight), positioning each in the upper half of the tanker one click apart.

We don't want ribs on the whole tanker, that would be boring, so let's try a new Primitive act. Copy the original torus once again and move it down Z close to the bottom of the tanker. Let's stretch it out to look like there's some business going on down here — maybe this is where the reactor core is located. (See Figure 5-3.) Here's what I came up with: Scale to X=2.3, Y=2.3, Z=2.0. This looks more like what I'm trying for.

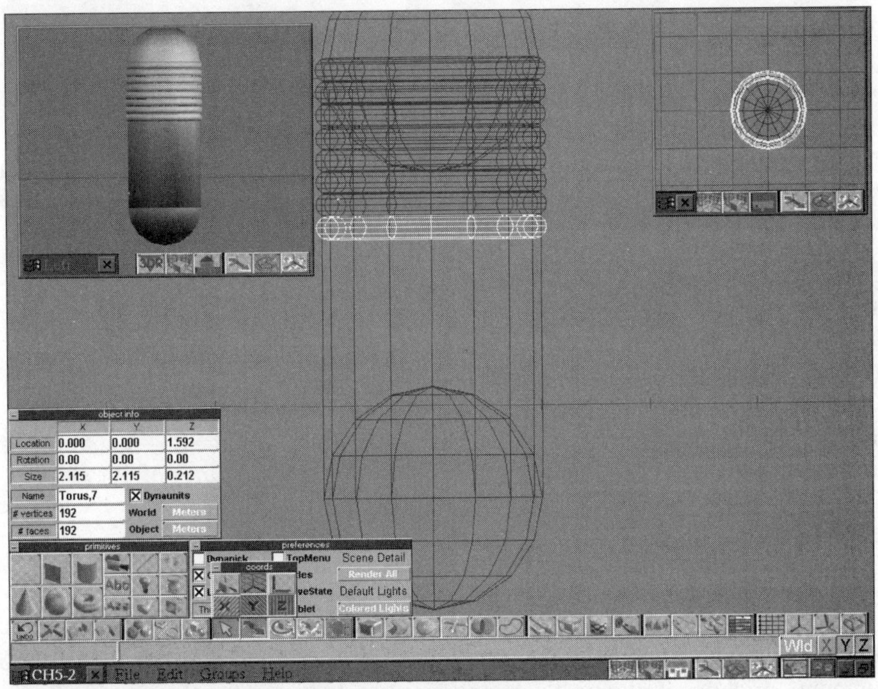

Figure 5-2: Tanker structure with reinforcing ribs

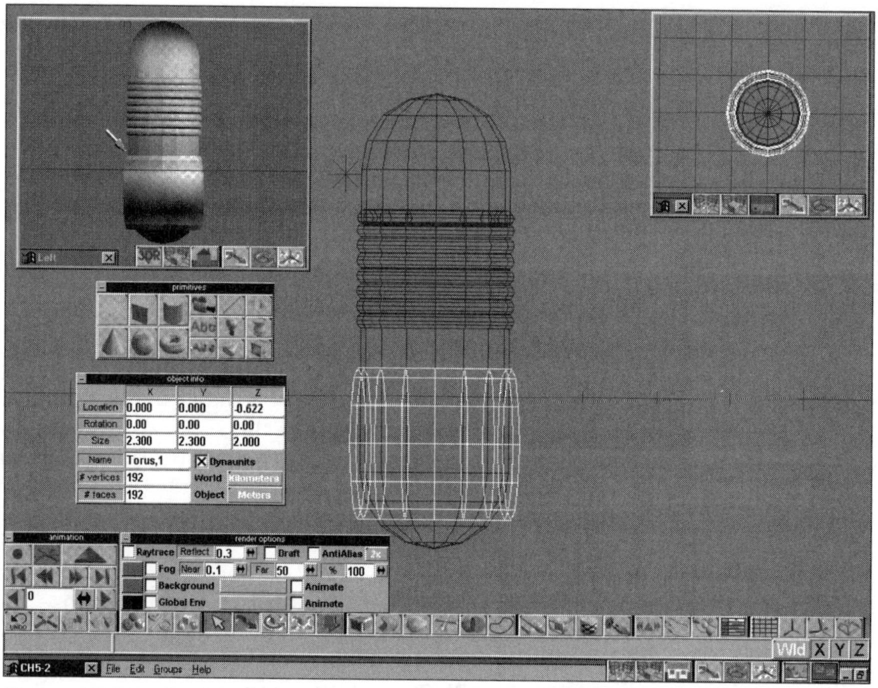

Figure 5-3: Tanker fuselage with reactor shield in place

I located it at X=0, Y=0, Z=-0.8. Good. Now let's Boolean the whole thing together.

The Whole is Less than the Sum of its Parts

We could leave the tank this way, but it has way more polygons than we need. Remember each polygon you render eats up resources. We can kill several buzzards with one rock here by joining the parts together into a solid whole. This is accomplished through Boolean Union.

Select the main fuselage tube and then click on the Union icon. When you get the little glue bottle cursor, select each part of the tanker in sequence. Begin with the sphere on top, then each ring, and then the bottom sphere. Note how the complexity disappears, the contour smoothes out, and you now have one solid object. Neat. Save this object as tank.cob. We'll use it for several parts of our ship.

Take a Good Look

Before we move on, let's look at this thing from different angles. Select it with the Object Rotate tool and turn it in different directions.

Only the selected object will rotate. If you had tried to rotate the tanker *before* unioning or gluing it, the part selected would rotate, leaving the rest in place, a mess. Hit Undo and glue.

This will expose your goofs, so do it periodically. It also gives you a feel for the object's dimension.

Try Zooming in and out or moving

the view around or even rotating it.

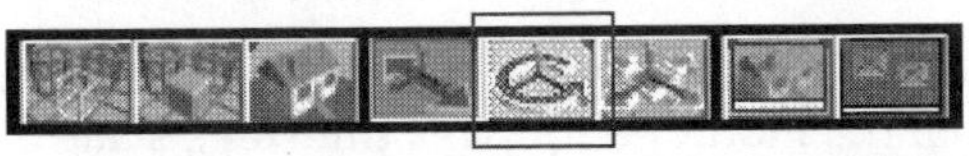

Remember, Rotate View operates differently in each Axis scheme. Once you've had a good look at your work, return it to the vertically aligned work position.

How do you get it back into position? You can play around for 20 minutes with the mouse, but you won't get it unless you remember to engage Snap-to-Grid. Better, zero all the location coordinates in the OPP, but best and easiest is just to hit the Normalize Rotation icon.

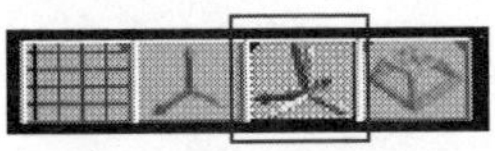

I don't like the way this thing looks — it's way too stubby. Let's increase the Z length to 12 and see how it looks. No more calls, we have a winner. Figure 5-4 shows what I had in mind.

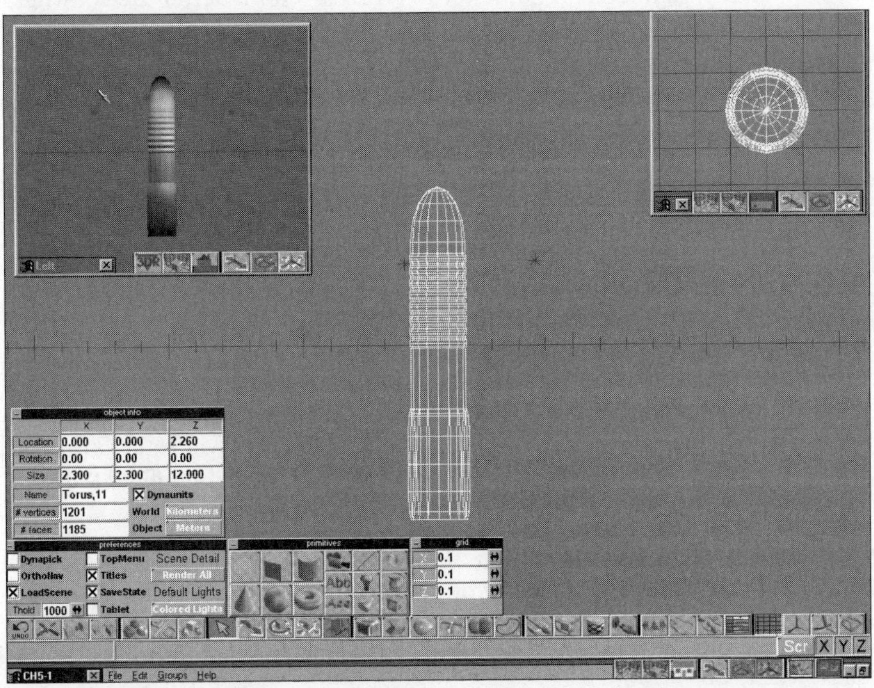

Figure 5-4: Tanker has been unioned and stretched to 12 meters

More Details

My story says this old freighter is propelled by an ancient hydroreactor using nuclear fuel to superheat water, which it injects into an ion stream for propulsion. We need some fuel pods for the water. Use the rule of parsimony; see if there is a way to clone and reuse parts you already have. In this case, the entire tanker can be copied and rescaled to make fuel pods.

Click on your Snap-to-Grid and Copy the tanker. In your Top View window (shown in Figure 5-5), separate the copy from the mother ship. This time let's scale it with straight numeric input. Go to the OPP and enter Object Size X=1, Y=1, Z=8.

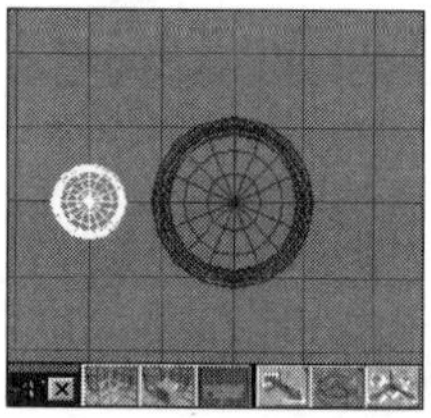

Figure 5-5: Top view of fuel pod rescaled and separated from main tanker assembly

This should yield a ribbed hot-dog-shaped pod you need. (This kind of symbolism has been around space travel since the V-2 rocket. It has something to do with the cosmos being fertile ground for self-expression.) Now move the pod to the right of the main tank until it looks right. Refer to Figure 5-5 for a better idea of what I did.

Remember this Technique

Here comes a great trick that you'll use often to create radial detail. While the pod is selected, click on the Axis icon to reveal the axes.

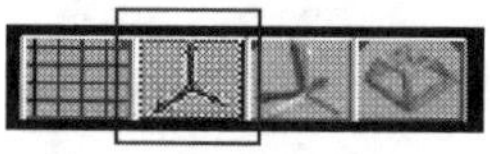

In wireframe, the pod will turn orange with yellow 3D axes somewhere in the middle. Now click on the Normalize Location icon. I wouldn't try this in 3DR because I find Solid Mode confusing when working with axes.

The axis will jump out of the pod and zip to the exact center of the tanker fuselage. Now click the Axis icon again to lock it in place. This is great because now when you use the Rotate icon in the Top View window, the pod will rotate around the new axis location, orbit the tank in a circular orbit, equidistant at all points. (See Figure 5-6.) Try it.

Here's why this motion is important. When you copy the pod, each copy will be born with its axis also in the center of the ship. Make a copy, rotate it two snaps or 90° and, bam, you have two pods in place. Copy the copy and repeat. Copy another two and set them each 90° apart. Your space tanker is really starting to take form.

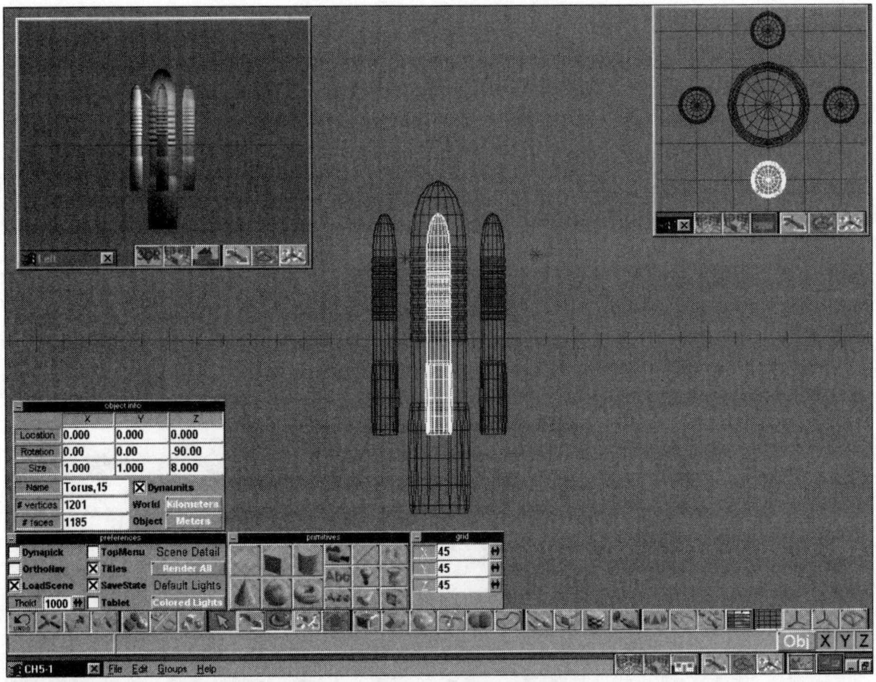

Figure 5-6: Four fuel pods in place around the main tanker assembly

You can glue the pods to the mother ship in different ways. You'll learn more about this in hierarchies. For now, select one of the pods ➪ Glue As Sibling ➪ Click on the other four pods ➪ Select Object (cancels glue) ➪ Select Tanker ➪ Glue as Sibling ➪ Select the Pod object. Now all the pieces should be white.

Flatten that Cylinder

Now we need to connect pods to tanker. I like the idea of a wing-like strut narrowing as it reaches out to the pods. This will give a bit of aerodynamic rake. Though this tanker will never see atmosphere, it looks better this way. We need an easy way to build a neat looking strut and the cylinder Primitive will give it to us. Always think of how you can rescale or deform Primitives to get what you want.

POWER TIP

Remember, in laying out your ship you don't have to follow physics completely. Use logic combined with a sense of design. Your audience will forgive certain unlikely but believable bits of license. Look at the opening of *Star Trek Voyager*, a magnificent piece of animation; they actually created volumetric light and shadows as Voyager passes through some kind of mist cloud in space. Not bloody likely, but it looks fabulous. I bought it.

Here's how we turn a cylinder into an airfoil. Select one face on the end of a cylinder and scale it down to about half its current size. Select the whole cylinder and scale (flatten) it into an airfoil. Navigate it into position. We'll need four copies, one for each pod.

Airfoil Details

Pop up the cylinder. With the Point Edit Faces tool, select an end face.

This is not easy because the ends are not facing you in this window. One solution is to open a Perspective View window, or to rotate the cylinder and then normalize it after you select the face. Zoom in if it helps. You'll notice that a Point Edit control panel appears, supplying you with move, rotate, and scale options.

Select the scale option and pull down the diameter of your end face to about half its present size. In Figure 5-7, the Point Control panel Scale icon is depressed, and the right face is selected and scaled. This setting gives you a truncated cone.

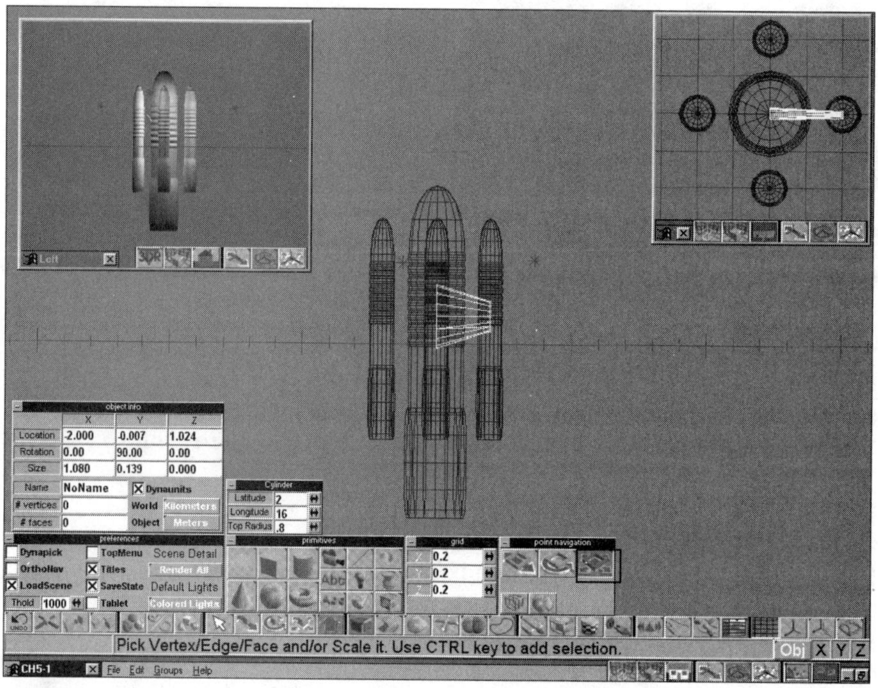

Figure 5-7: One pod strut is now in place and ready to have three copies rotated into position.

You could have designed a similar Primitive by right clicking on the Cylinder icon and adjusting Cylinder control panel parameters. I find it easier to use the Point ➪ Click ➪ Scale methodology. It's up to you.

Now we flatten and position the object into an airfoil. Easiest way is to input the numbers directly into the OPP. I flatten it to about .3 meters on the Y axis and rotate 90° on same. It's easy, input Size Y ➪ 0.3 leaving the X and Z alone, and

Rotation Y ➪ 90. That's it. Now I snap off the grid and position the strut, referencing all windows, until it looks right.

To align the struts with the fuel pods, line the first one up as previously shown in Figure 5-7. Repeat the radial detail technique of exposing the strut's axis, normalizing and locking it as with the pods. Make four copies and rotate them into position. Remember: use Axis icon to reveal axes ➪ Normalize Location ➪ Axis icon to lock axes at origin ➪ Grid on ➪ Copy ➪ rotate 90° (two snaps) ➪ Copy ➪ Rotate, continuing until all four are in place. Rotate in the Top View window with the *right* mouse button; the strut will click in 45° jumps around the main fuselage. When the final strut is in place, you're ready to glue all of them. Follow the same pattern as for the pods. Select one strut ➪ Glue As Sibling ➪ Select other three struts ➪ Object Select tool ➪ Select Tanker ➪ Glue As Sibling ➪ Select Strut object. Now your ship should be all glued together.

Catch the Light

Now we get to that beveled detail I mentioned earlier. Glints contribute handsomely to disbelief suspension, especially in space scenes. Sticking with Primitives, we'll add more radial detail on the main tank. Pop up a cube Primitive, and rescale it in the OPP to Size X ➪ 0.4 Y ➪ 0.4 Z ➪ 4.0 a rectangular box. To bevel this, select the face to be beveled. Point Edit ➪ Select Faces tool, then click on the center of your long rectangular front face. The edges of the face will turn green when they're selected. Now *right* click on the Extrude tool to bring up the variants menu. Select the Bevel tool

and click on the selected face. You'll get an instant default bevel. It's probably just enough, but you can hold the button and play with it to get a feel for bevel possibilities.

CAUTION

Bevel is an overly sensitive tool, unnecessarily difficult to use. But if you're careful, you can lift the face and a bevel will form around the edges. Move your mouse only a miniscule amount to get a feel. Don't overdo it, you might criss-cross lines (check in the Top View). If this happens the bevel won't render properly.

Pull the bevel carefully up as shown in Figure 5-8, and render the box to see what it looks like. Fool with it until you like it.

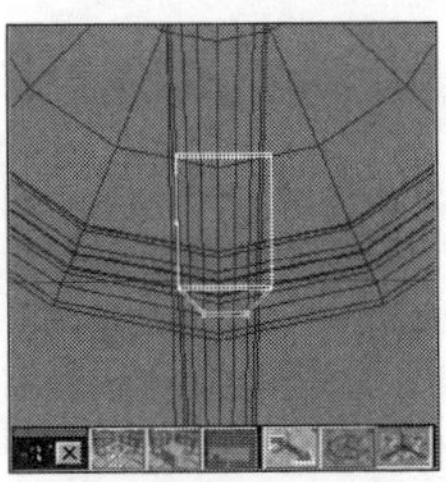

Figure 5-8: One of eight pieces of beveled radial detail, wireframe close up.

Building Radial Detail

We'll use the Top View again to copy and rotate the detail as we have done before. Select the bevel object, and do the: Axis tool ➪ Normalize Location ➪ Axis (locks it) ➪ Grid ON ➪ Copy ➪ Rotate 90° ➪ Copy ➪ etc., routine. This time we'll lay in eight radial copies to create an interesting detail.

This thing is going to serve double duty. Glue each of the eight pieces together as siblings and, in the Front View window, right click and pull the whole shebang down the Z axis until it penetrates the radiation shield. Keep going south until only about a quarter of the length is still visible. Excellent. Look inside the shield; these bits of detail form a nice radial engine mount. (See Figure 5-9 for details.)

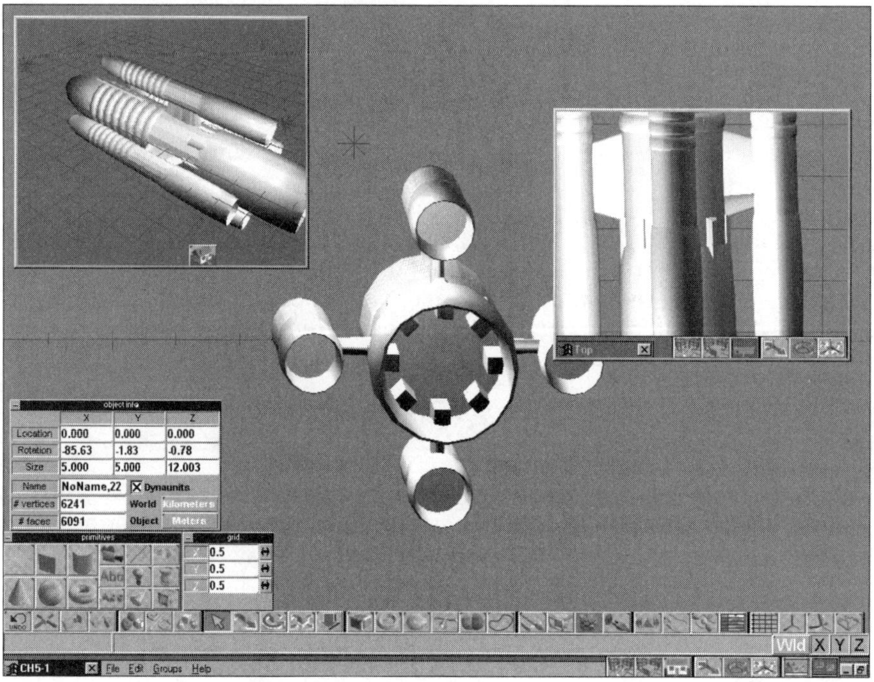

Figure 5-9: Radial detail serving double duty on fuselage surface and as internal engine support

The Engine

This is yet another distorted torus. Set the torus' inner radius to .5 and pop one in the middle of the ship. In Front View, elongate it along the ship and drag it down the Z axis (*right* click) to an aft position. Looking Top down, center it inside the radial detail. The dimensions I ended up with were X=1.7, Y=1.7, Z=3.5. Select the main tanker and glue the engine as a sibling. As I work, I feel this thing is starting to look like a space vehicle. That's important. It has to look right to you. I like a big ol' klunky impulse engine like this. I see it all dirty from exhaust carbon, which no space engine would have, but that's how I see it. I think plasma blackens duratanium hulls, right?

I suggest rendering a Perspective View with some texture and a background. If you don't know how to do it, skip around in the book and figure it out. I used dirtyhull.bmp for texture and NGC1976.bmp as background as shown in Figure 5-10. Both are on the CD-ROM. Notice I have the 3DR set up to not render textures — it's faster.

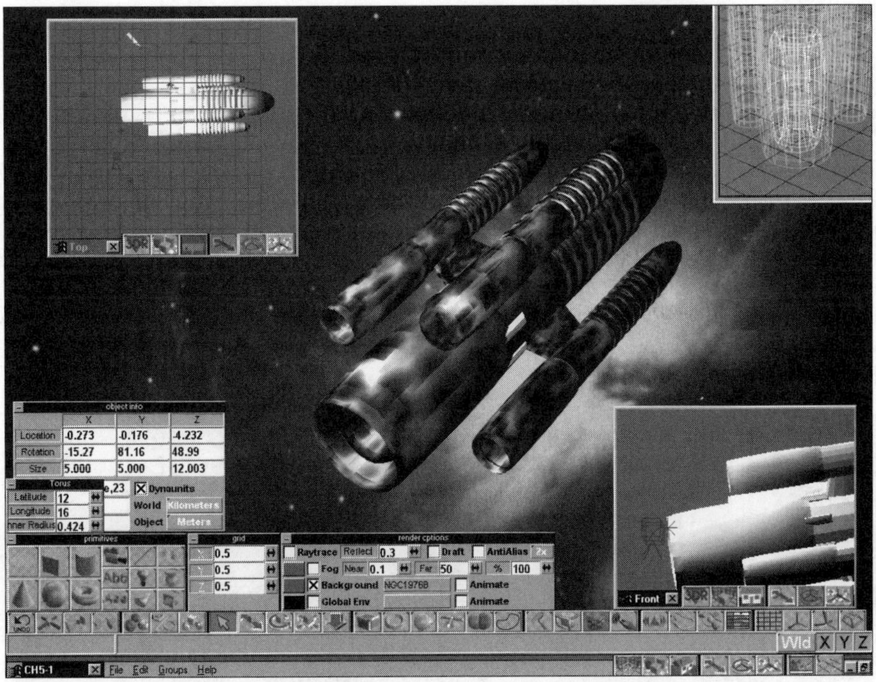

Figure 5-10: Space tanker, engine in place, rendered with sample texture and background to judge appearance

By now you're getting a feel for this 3D work space. Let's move off center and do something nonsymmetrical: curved pipes. This is tricky since there is no pipe Primitive, but I'm going to stretch the definition and use the letter O, which *is* a Primitive. By extruding it, we can make some nice tubing to carry the fuel into the nuclear ion furnace.

Begin in a Top View, click on the horizontal text icon.

Click on the intersection of two grid lines and type a capital O — this is a 2D object of the letter O — and click the Extrude button. You'll see the green circle of the

selected face. Now open a Front View window. You see white lines reaching out with the green face at the end of them. Click Extrude two more times. With each click you get a short length of hollow pipe. To make the curve, select the Point Rotate icon in the Point Navigation control panel, then follow these moves:

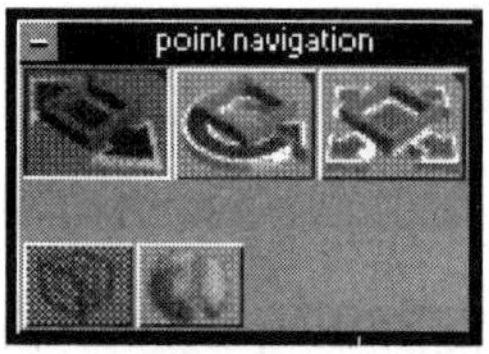

Point Rotate ➪ *right* click Grid icon ➪ Grid Control Panel ➪ change Grid Rotation 22.5° ➪ Grid ON ➪ Disable Y and Z axes on the Help Bar. Rotate the pipe one snap in the X direction and extrude. Notice that the new section comes off at a 22.5° angle. Click/extrude three more times. Each time the new section bends further until you have a nice 90° curve. To now get a straight length you have to snap the O back one grid mark so that it will be perpendicular to its original position. Now when you extrude you'll get a straight piece of pipe parallel to the floor. Use Figure 5-11 as a reference.

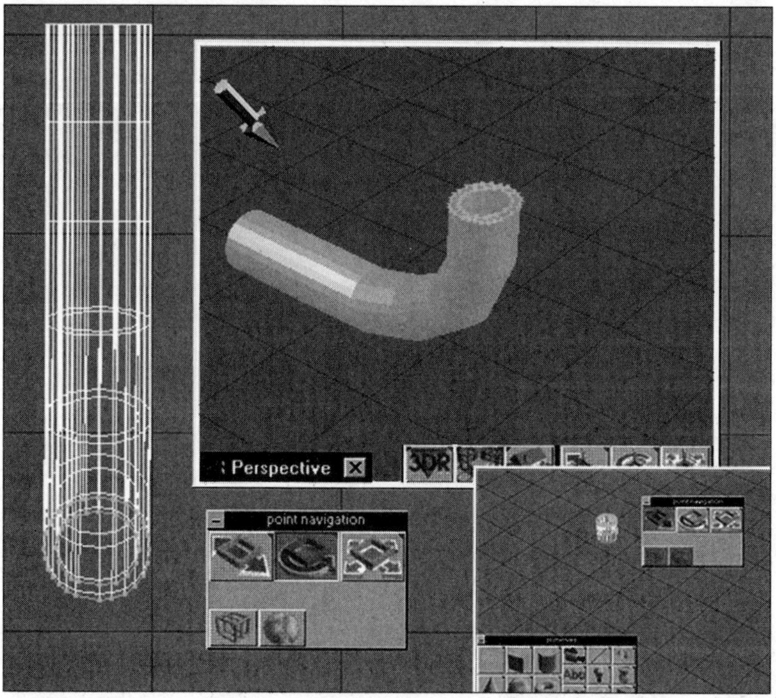

Figure 5-11: Curved pipe made by extruding a Primitive, the letter O (inset)

CAUTION

If you rotate the O's face without the grid, you can go too far and flatten the pipe. Take in at least four bends. If you lose the face of the O as your selection, it's difficult to reselect it. Zoom can help, change windows, or switch to 3DR mode and nail the face with ease.

POWER TIP

You can make some interesting pieces of detail with extruded letters. Try the V but instead of the Extrude tool, try the Tip tool, which extrudes from the letter to a zero point. The V becomes an angled piece of detail to stick inside the engine or clone and use for radial detail. A long strip of B makes a nice detailed edging. Be creative.

You've Got to Have Connections

We're going to put the curved pipe between the fuel pods and the engine. The curved part actually goes inside the pod end as a piece of detail seen from the rear of the craft. We can't just leave the bare pipe sticking in the engine. I tried it and it looks tacky. Let's pop a simple box, scale and bevel it. Using default bevel, click once and it's just right. Scale the beveled box face a little wider than the pipe diameter. Now mount the box on the end of the pipe, nonbeveled end toward the engine. Take a look at Figure 5-12 for an idea of how it should look.

You're on your own to get the pipe in position. Once there, readjust the axes to the ship's center, and rotate three copies of the pipe into position within each pod. You're getting good at this. Glue the four pipes together and then glue the pipe object to mother.

POWER TIP

Don't sweat the small stuff. If you can't get the angle exactly the way you want, check the OPP settings. If Rotation is at X=82, try upping it to 90° and it might straighten out. Otherwise get it close and move on. Often a small angular deficit on a bit of detail isn't visible. If you are a precision personality, use your head, the Grid, and the OPP to align things exactly.

A Place for the Crew

So far this space tanker is a straight drone with no place for people. Naturally, I have a story to help finish the design. This old nuclear class freighter was designed with human quarters removed from main hull and fusion core because of potential radiation leaks. The entire crew pod can be jettisoned in case of emergency and it has a small engine of its own for such emergencies. I placed it forward, off center, to allow for visual front docking control if necessary. I know, there's no front docking bay... yet.

Pop up a sphere and, on your own, scale it until it looks right. I stretched mine out to X=0.77, Y=0.77, Z=2.44. I suppose you could pop a cube, scale and bevel it for a rectangular crew pod. Not me, but it's your ship. Good, now select it in the Top View and drag it, centered between two fuel pods, to a good position. Your call. In a Front View window, drag the crew pod up the Z axis until it's a little forward of the front of the ship.

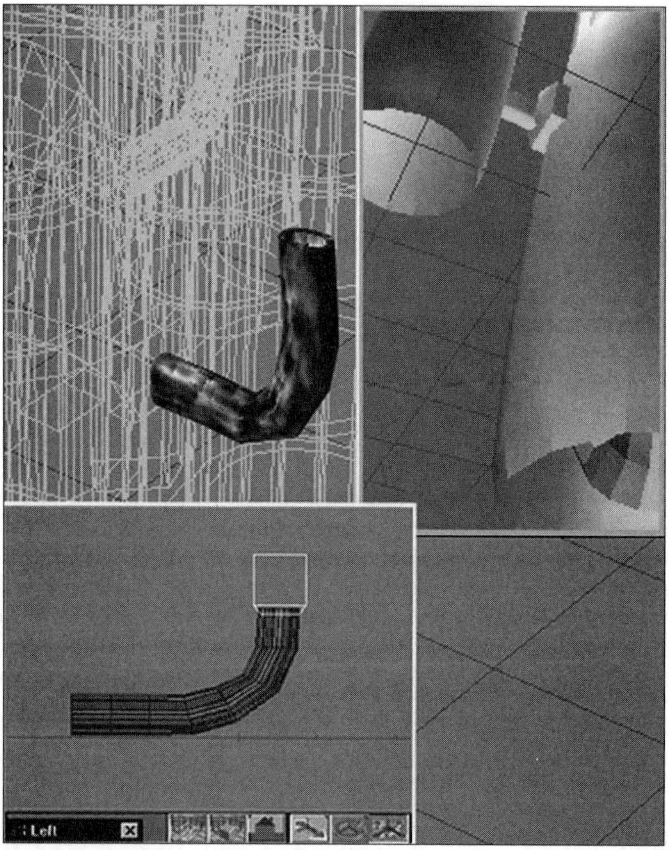

Figure 5-12: Detail of fuel pipe and (detail) junction box arrangement

Now for a sexy way to attach it to the ship. I tried several ideas using only Primitives, and my favorite is a flattened cone, rotated and positioned so that the bulk is hidden inside the tanker. Give it a rakish jut out of the tank and into the crew pod. Use Figure 5-13 as a reference.

Select the pod and glue it to the support as a sibling. Select the mother and glue the whole thing to her.

A Docking Bay

A tanker needs to dock with space stations in order to transfer goods. We'll build a simple docking port that you can further embellish as you pick up skills. Decide how large you want your bay to be. Pop a cylinder in the center of your ship and scale it to the diameter you want your forward dock to be. Move the cylinder up the Z axis until it pokes out the top of the ship. When it's about halfway out, check in the Top View to make sure it's perfectly centered on the ship's nose. Next, select Tanker ➪ Boolean Subtract ➪ Cylinder. Voilà. You have a docking bay without any decoration.

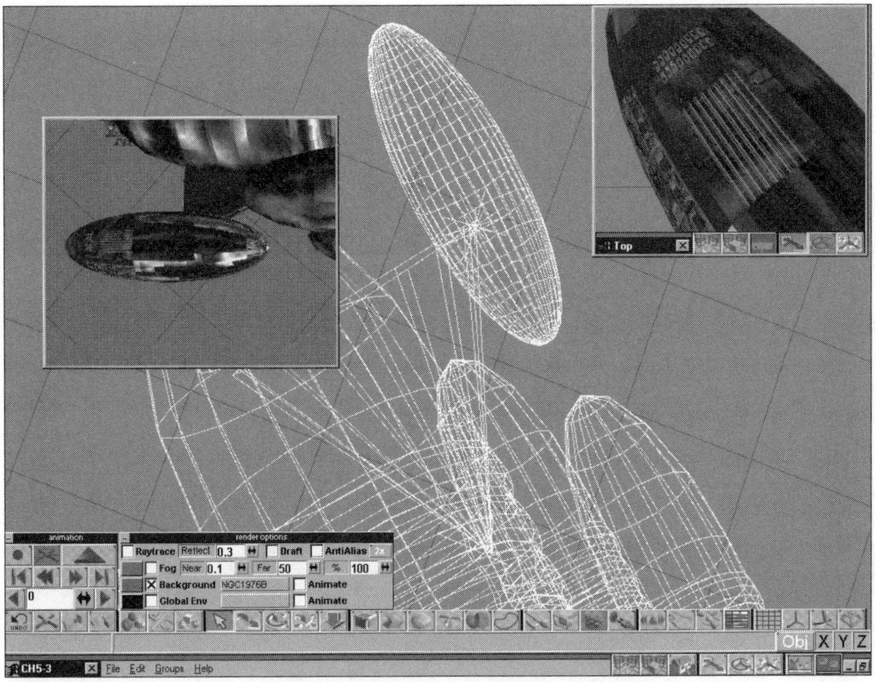

Figure 5-13: Crew pod in place with flattened cone support

Always make a copy of your main objects before Boolean operations because they can blow up on you. In most cases you can hit Undo and retry it, but sometimes your computer will freeze. If you hit Ctrl+Alt+Del you could lose your latest main object.

You can decorate the interior with mechanical textures and bump maps to make it look technical. Figure 5-14 shows what I did inside. Most of the texture comes from a bump map I made from a photo of a building with lots of windows that I stretched out. To make a finished edge on the bay, pop up a skinny torus and fit it around the rim. If you have patience, you can copy a bunch of tiny boxes and place them around the torus like bolts. In Figure 5-14 I added some nernies from the Nernie subdirectory on my CD. Build your own and use them. The one I used doesn't really look much like a docking clamp. I'm sure you could do a way better job. Nernies are generic spaceship parts that can be clustered and placed to make useful-looking detail. I put the docking feet every 22.5° around the edge of the port using the radial detail method. You'll learn how to make such simple parts using 2D Boolean technique in Chapter 6. The textures are all very simple, using mostly color and bump maps or a generic hull map that you'll learn to make in the chapter on textures. Experiment. On the crew pod, I used the Q-tip Tip tool (polygon painter) to give alternate polys different shine, reflection, and ambient light. Just use very small differences. It will give your surface a constructed, imperfect, worn look.

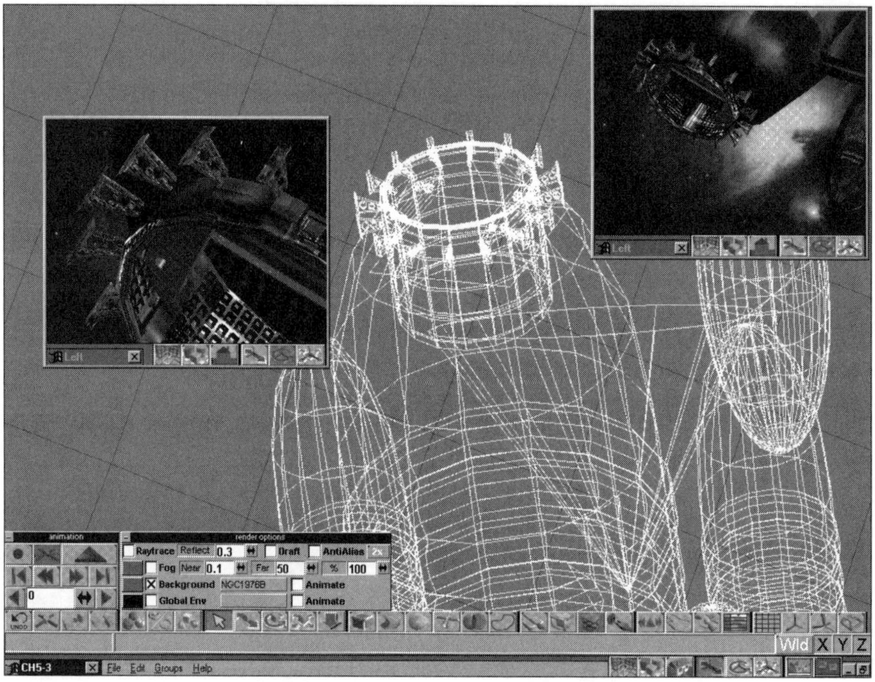

Figure 5-14: Docking Bay structure showing Boolean interior and nernie detail

It's time to rotate this mighty dreadnought of the void to a jaunty angle and render it. Make sure it's all glued together properly, then right click on the Render icon.

Click on the background window and select NGC1976.bmp from the CD-ROM as your background. Click draft mode *OFF* if you want a clean render. Build a single Targa (.tga) or .bmp file any size you like and enjoy the lovely fruits of your early labor. You still have a lot to learn about maps and textures and compositing before it will look like the cover of this book, but you're getting there. It's all fun stuff. We'll cover the hows as we work through the book. Save the scene with a File/Scene/Save command.

Now it's getting interesting. You're well on your way to being a digital frame jockey. I know you're anxious to learn animation, but it's a bad idea to put the caboose in front of the cow catcher. Look at how far you've come.

You deserve a break. Stretch, have a cup of coffee, and stay away as long as you can stand it, but not more than a day. Good stuff coming up, like sharks and nernie teeth.

Summary

- ✦ You've learned a bunch of construction shortcuts using Primitives to construct a whole space vehicle in every detail.
- ✦ You've learned some pretty tricky ways to use the Axis tool to create radial detail, like pulling the detail's axis of rotation to the center of the model and using the grid to perform precise rotations, placing copies around the ship.
- ✦ You've learned to navigate around in the view using the various Eye navigation controls.
- ✦ You've gotten a taste of realistic surfacing by loading pre-done textures from the library and using them on your fuselage.
- ✦ You've done a really cool rendering of your project to show your friends.
- ✦ You've learned to use Boolean operations to join your model's separate parts into one, reducing your poly count and simplifying your object. This gives faster render times.
- ✦ You've extruded the letter O into a curved pipe by navigating it around a 90° curve. That calls for some kind of celebration.
- ✦ And you've learned how designing with virtual light in mind can give you realistic glints off modeled details.

✦ ✦ ✦

CHAPTER 6

There's Magic in Your Tools

In This Chapter

Selecting object parts for manipulation

Flashlights and lens making

Boolean operations

Splines and Flat polygons

Extrusion tools

The Text tool

The quality of your output will be a function of your cleverness, your patience, your talent, and your tools. Before we go into organic modeling, which is both wonderful and terrifying, I want you to be well-grounded in basic tools. You've already used some of them, but there are variants and myriad uses.

3D construction constantly requires the selection of a vertex, line, face, or object to work on. Selecting a whole object is a breeze and you already know how to do it. You've also had some experience selecting faces. So here is the story of the Point Edit tools.

Point Edit Tools

When you select a Point Edit tool, the Point Navigation Options panel

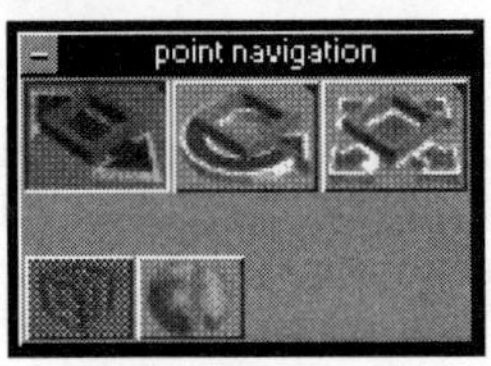

pops up with buttons to perform moves, rotations, and scaling on the selected portion of the object. Right clicking on the Move, Rotate, or Scale tool pops up the Coordinates property panel.

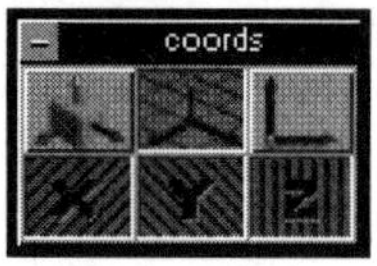

This is similar to the Object Navigation Coordinates panel and can be accessed by right clicking on most tools. With it you can reset to an alternate Coordinate system and/or set up Axis Navigation constraints.

CAUTION

In the Object Coordinates system, each edge, face, and vertex, when selected, has its own axis that you can't see. You can guess about the face; its Z axis is parallel with the surface normal. That's a line pointing perpendicular to the surface plane. I find it very difficult to manipulate these objects predictably as it's difficult to know their orientation. It's better to use the Screen or World Coordinates systems when working with them.

On the bottom left of the Point Navigation panel, you'll find two more icons, one for Slice and one for Separate. Slice lets you subdivide an object into sections, while Separate allows you to detach parts of an object that have been sliced or selected with hierarchy navigation. These aren't relevant to the current project, so we'll look at them more closely later.

Selection Modes

Using the default Context selection tool, you can select multiple entities — faces, edges and vertices — all at the same time by holding down the <Ctrl> key and clicking on them in turn. The restriction is that they can't be contiguous. Once selected the entities can be jointly manipulated.

POWER TIP

You can actually select contiguous entities by using the <Shift> key instead of the <Ctrl> key, but it disables dimensional promotion.

The Tools

✦ **Face Selection.**

This is the one I use most. It will only select faces as the name implies. Just click in the center of a face, as we did in the space tanker tutorial; the edges turn green indicating it's selected. Select the navigation you want and manipulate with care. It's easy to be rough-handed and pull a mesh out of shape, forcing you to Undo and try again.

✦ **Edge Selection.**

Click on an edge between vertices and it will be selected. Holding down the Control key allows you to select multiple edges.

✦ **Vertex Selection.**

Click on the intersection of two or more lines and the vertex will be selected. You can also create a new vertex with this tool. Simply hold down Shift while you click in the middle of a line and, Shazam, a new vertex is born. You can also create a face by selecting one vertex, then with the Shift key down, select another vertex. You get the face.

✦ **Context Selection.**

In this mode you can select faces, edges, and points. To select a face, click near its center, away from any edges; to pick an edge, just click on the middle of it; and for a point or vertex, click on the intersection of two or more lines. You'll probably prefer this tool for much of your work. If you're dyslexic like me you may have a problem selecting the wrong thing much of the time. In that case, use the individual selection tools.

Dimensional Promotion

This is a fancy handle for a simple concept. In dimensional promotion you use the Shift key with mouse clicks to move from a point to a line to a face with progressive clicks. Select a vertex or point (no dimension), an edge (one dimension), or a face (two dimensions) with Context tool. You can even select a whole chunk of an object (a three-dimensional section). It saves a lot of fine motor coordination and time.

In this chapter we'll build an industrial flashlight. Even if you're not interested in industrial flashlights, don't skip this section; it demonstrates dimensional promotion and other neat techniques you need to know. Save the flashlight for later use.

Flashlight

Start a new scene with File ⇨ Scene ⇨ New. Right click on the cylinder Primitive in the Primitives panel. You'll get the Properties panel. Set: Latitude ⇨ 16 Longitude ⇨16 and Top Radius ⇨ 1. This will divide the cylinder into fine sections for manipulation. Pop up a cylinder — it's subdivided by 16 vertical and 16 horizontal lines. You'll only see this in your wireframe windows. 3DR doesn't display subdivisions, another reason we use both kinds of windows.

Shift to Front View, where you can see the side of the cylinder clearly. Select the Vertex tool and click on a vertex eight lines down from the top, toward the right side of the cylinder. You'll see a green dot. Shift and select another vertex in that same line. You'll get a line. With Shift still down select a third point *at least one vertex removed from the green line*, and the entire circle will turn green.

There will be times when the vertex you want to select is behind or around the curve from you. In that case you can simply move or rotate the camera eye until you can see the spot you want to select. Select a floor — it's a face — in the middle of the object. Holding the <Shift> key down, click anywhere in the bottom half of the cylinder and the whole bottom section will turn green. You have a cubic selection to play with. Click the Point Scale tool:

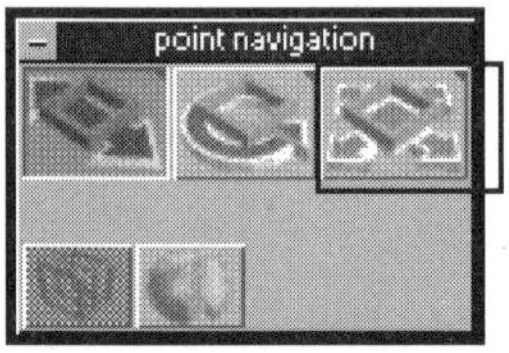

Then, pressing *both* mouse buttons, scale the bottom section down. Keep an eye on the OPP scale readout and bring it down to about 0.8 for both X and Y.

The Object Properties panel gives direct scaling feedback. If you watch it while scaling, rotating, or moving, you'll see the numbers changing. This will help you make fast, accurate manipulations.

Figure 6-1 already looks a lot like the head of a flashlight.

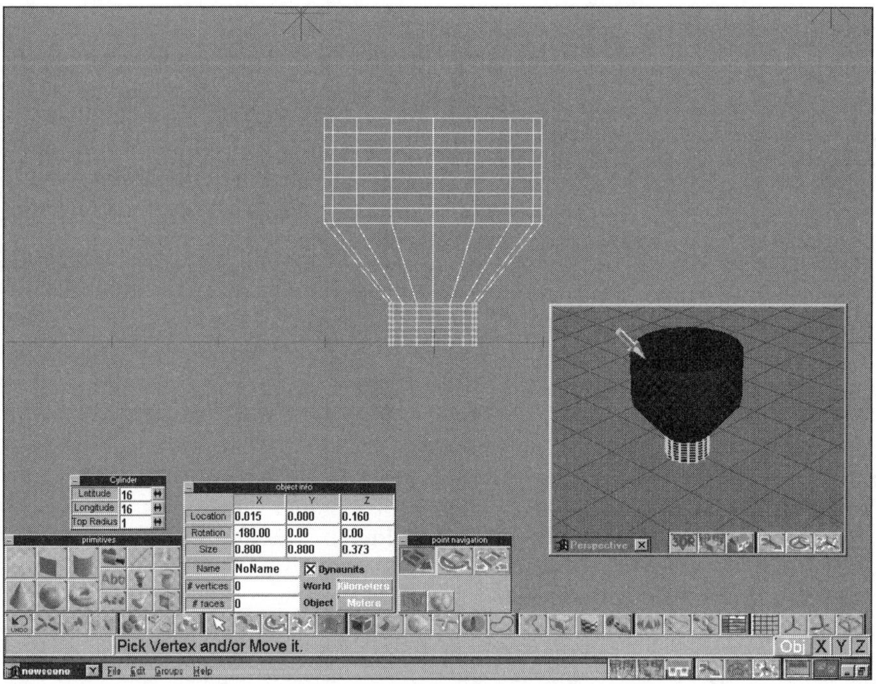

Figure 6-1: The beginnings of an industrial flashlight

We need to give some detail to it by selecting the floor two down from the top. Use dimensional promotion. Scale this down just a tad and you'll get a nice clean groove around the head. Skip two faces down and repeat on the third, skip two more and repeat on the sixth. Be light-handed and it'll look better.

CAUTION Depending on the window and the angle you're working at, it's easy to get confused and create a strange cross section, with new edges at an angle to the others. If this happens, hit Undo immediately, otherwise those edges are created permanently.

Now we make the barrel of the flashlight by popping up another cylinder and scaling the whole thing down to a diameter of 0.8 meters. (See Figure 6-2.) Lengthen the cylinder along Z until it looks right to you, then glue it to the head using the Glue As Sibling tool. Just select the barrel ➪ Glue tool ➪ Head, in that order. Or reverse order is good too.

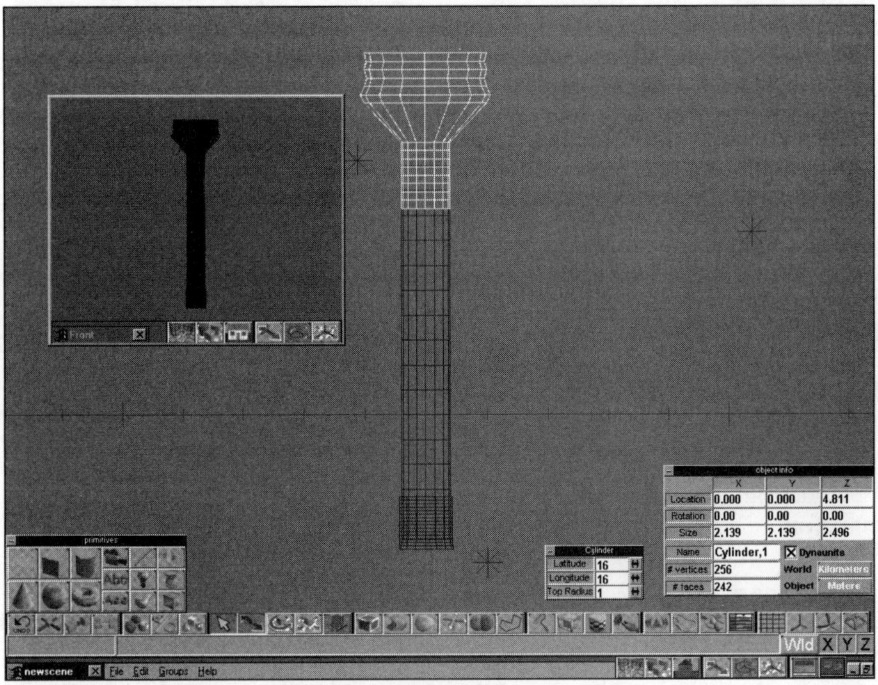

Figure 6-2: Battery barrel added to flashlight head

On your own, scale some cubes into flat rectangles, and embed them in the flashlight body to make a switch. I made one long one for the base of the switch and a small block for the part your thumb pushes. Make an end cap from a short cylinder, slightly larger than the body, and put some grooves in it, as shown in Figure 6-3. When you learn about 3D Booleans, you'll be able to emboss a logo into the end cap. Just make sure you have it in the right direction. I tend to make it read backwards and have to re-do. No biggie.

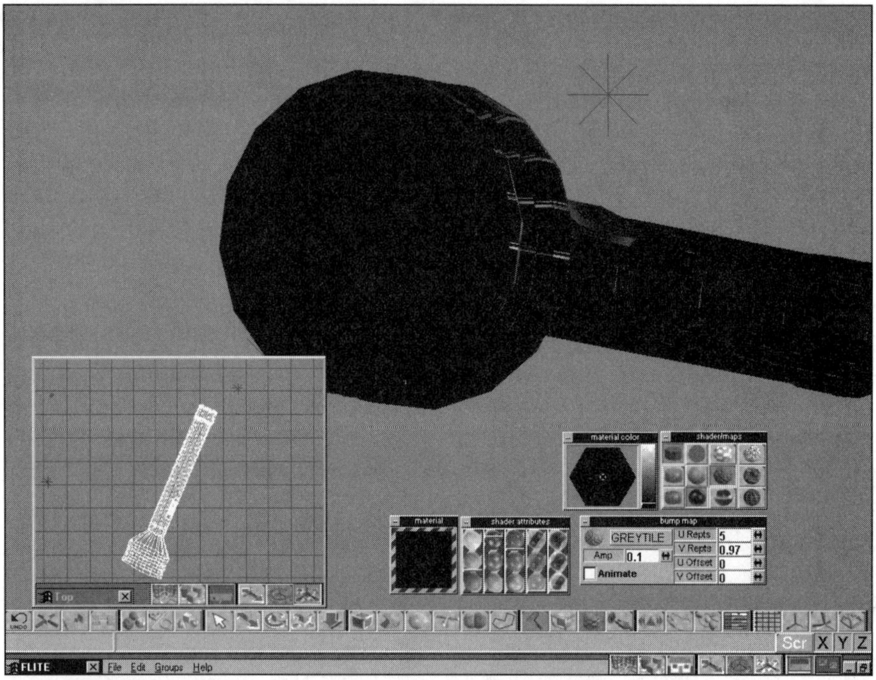

Figure 6-3: The flashlight up to this point, rendered with texture.

Boolean Construction — Learning to Add and Subtract All Over Again

You can build amazingly complex items in short order with boolean operations. There are three boolean operators: Subtraction; Union; Intersection. You can do boolean operations on either 2D or 3D objects to cut construction time to a minimum.

3D Booleans

Here's how they work. Overlap two objects. Select one of them, then pick one of the boolean operators by left clicking and sliding the pointer to the one you want. Now click on the other object. Shazam, a little internal mathematical magic and you end up with a single object based on the first two. What it looks like depends on the operation you chose.

Boolean Subtraction

This is great for adding detail to objects. It subtracts the volume of one object from another. You can use it to drill holes in things, create niches and odd shapes, as well as to carve letters into a gravestone or a logo into a flashlight's end cap. One of the nice things about subtraction is that the object subtracted leaves its surface qualities behind in the niche it created. We'll use Boolean Subtraction to form the reflector for our flashlight.

The order in which the objects are selected determines the final outcome. Be careful. The first part selected remains and the second part is subtracted.

Boolean operations transfer most surface qualities, but try to avoid doing it with a material rectangle. It's better to do the Boolean and apply the rectangle later.

Boolean Union

Here the resultant object has the exterior shape and dimensions of the combined objects. All the interior parts are gone and it's one object. A little later we'll use this to union our flashlight head to the battery tube, making a single object.

Boolean Intersection

In this operation, everything disappears except the overlapped portion of the two objects. This takes a little more creative visualization, but it's very handy.

For fun let's make a convex lens by intersecting two spheres, as shown in Figure 6-4.

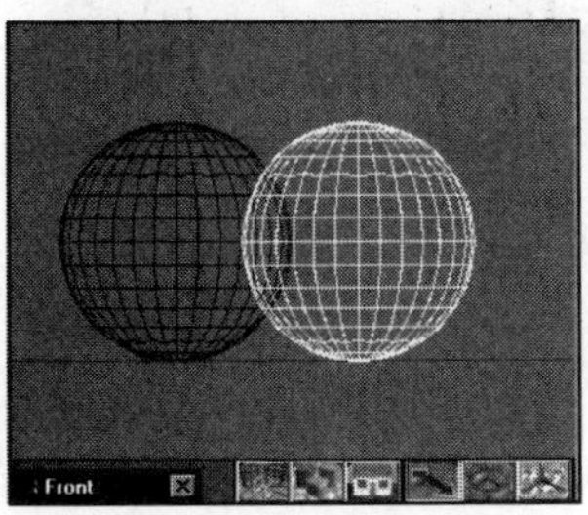

Figure 6-4: Two spheres with their intersection forming a convex lens.

Select either sphere and click on the Boolean Intersection icon. As soon as you click on the other sphere, they both disappear, leaving behind a lens shape where they overlapped. (See Figure 6-5.)

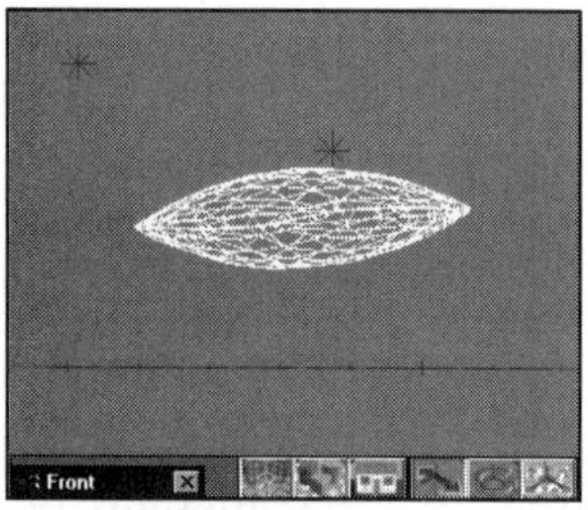

Figure 6-5: The lens remaining after Boolean Intersection of two spheres.

This shape will actually act like a lens if you make it out of glass and raytrace it with a moderate-to-high refraction index.

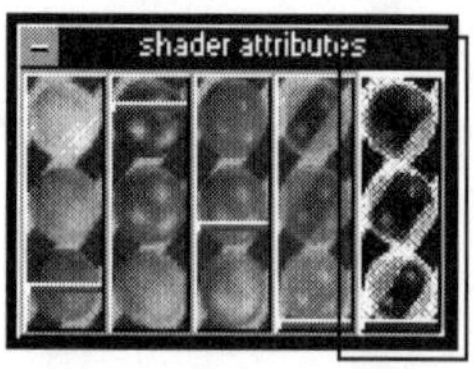

Pretty cool bit of pseudo-reality. Figure 6-6 shows what this particular lens looks like when raytraced as clear glass with a moderate refraction index. You can scale it and glue it to the flashlight face if you like.

Figure 6-6: The raytraced lens shows refraction effect.

I've used Boolean Intersection to make parts fit nicely within other parts, especially transparent objects where you can see if it's a good fit or not. Picture a large glass sphere with a sculptural array of wires or tubes fitted inside it. You can build an array of wires out of long thin cylinders. Glue or boolean them together to form a wild sculpture. It must be larger than the sphere. Now pop up a sphere around it and scale it to a pixel or so smaller than your glass sphere will be. Select the array of wires and do a Boolean Intersection with the sphere. The sphere will clip off everything outside, leaving a sculpture the same shape as the inside of the glass sphere. Now pop up another sphere, smooth quad divide it and make it glass (from the library). The sculpture should already be in place. Glue it and rotate to make sure the sculpture isn't sticking out anywhere. It looks cool and any other way of doing this would be murder. For an example of this kind of fitting, check out Plate 21-1 titled "Once Was a Weapon." It's a battle knife that's been cut by a glass sphere. To make it, I duplicated the knife. For the inside portion I boolean intersected the knife with a sphere as above. To get the outside I selected the knife and did a Boolean Subtract operation and was left with two ends. I simply popped a sphere in the middle, scaled it, and painted it gold glass. It looks really symbolic, but I don't know what it means; I just enjoyed creating it.

More Flash

Okay, so a flashlight isn't very exciting… unless you can make it so real people think it's a photograph. We'll need that reflector to make the light look authentic. It's easy with Boolean Subtraction. Return to tS2 with your flashlight in place. Pop up a sphere. The Default is too grossly faceted for a reflector, so Smooth Quad Divide it.

This process increases the sphere's polygon count in a way that smoothes the surface. Before you subtract the sphere, paint it with shiny polished chrome metal from the library, or make your own. When we subtract, this shiny coating will be deposited on the surface of the reflector inside the flashlight.

It's easy, select the Paint tool that looks like a cheap roller from the pop-up Paint Variants menu.

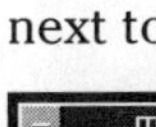

Notice that several Material Creation windows pop up. More on them later. I'll just show you how to create polished chrome for now. Later you'll learn fine points of surface design.

Go to the Material Color cube and make sure it is set to white. The intensity slider next to the cube should be up to the top, which is bright white.

Then go to the Shader/Maps panel, and click the three bottom buttons: Smooth facet ⇨ Metal shader ⇨ Reflection Map. *Right* click on Reflection Map to select a new map. Replace rainbow with Day or wastlan. This will give your reflector something to reflect. Good. Go to Shader Attributes and pull the first one (Ambient Glow) halfway up, and the next two all the way to the top. The last two (Transparency and Refraction) should be at the bottom. Now paint the sphere with this texture using the Paint Object tool (little tornado). It should make a nice silver ball.

Move the ball up the Z axis (*right* click) until its center line is just above the flashlight's top rim, as shown in Figure 6-7. A 3DR window helps here.

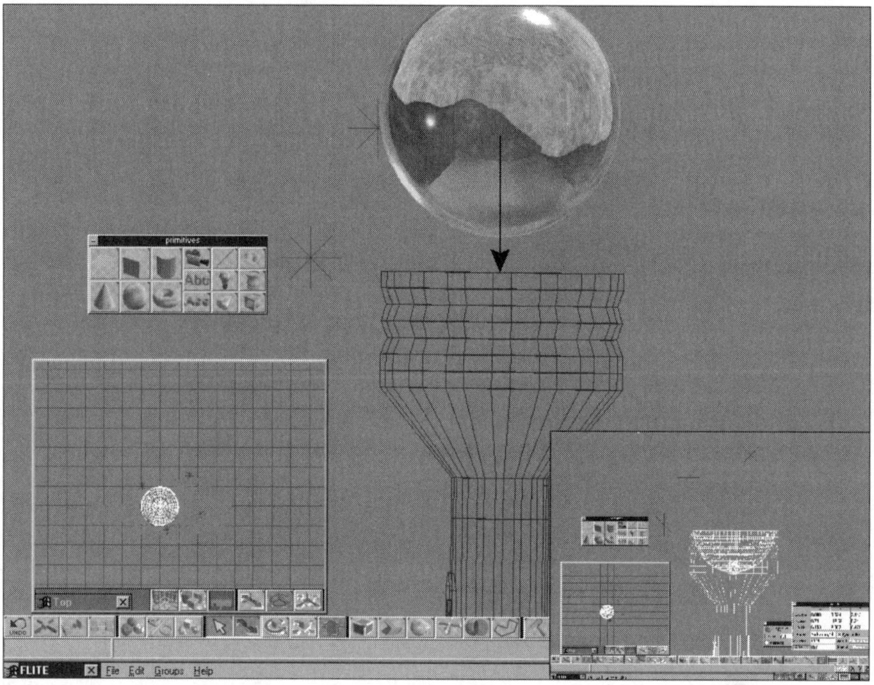

Figure 6-7: Flashlight with silvered ball in place ready to be boolean subtracted to form reflector. (Inset shows the flashlight after the operation.)

This should leave a little less than half the sphere dishing out a reflector. Click: Flashlight ⇨ Boolean Subtract ⇨ Sphere, and bam, your flashlight has a polished chrome reflector. Almost too easy, right? Make a bulb out of a little glass sphere. If you like you can also add the glass lens here. It'll give the light an authentic look from side angles, as shown in Figure 6-8.

POWER TIP

If everything but half the sphere disappeared, you selected objects in reverse order. Undo and try again, selecting the body of the flashlight first. The rule of thumb is the part you pick first remains.

Figure 6-8: The industrial flashlight with reflector and bulb is ready for spelunking. You can add the lens to see what it will look like.

The boolean process automatically went through the flashlight hierarchy, unioning everything before subtracting the sphere. You now should have one solid flashlight object. Good job, save it.

Later in the book we'll assign the rest of the materials needed to make the flashlight believable.

POWER TIP: You can even glue a spotlight where the bulb should be and use it like a real flashlight.

Nernies from 2D Polys

You can quickly build complex 3D shapes by creating 2D shapes and extruding them. I use this technique to make nernies for my space vehicles. It's fun, easy, and a pleasure to do. There are three Polygon tools:

- ✦ Freehand Polygon
- ✦ Regular Polygon
- ✦ Spline Polygon

The Freehand tool creates irregular polygons out of straight lines. These have uneven legs and angles. The Regular tool is similar except that it creates even polygons like pentagons, hexagons, and that sort of thing.

Spline polygons are a different story. They are flat polygons bounded by spline curves. You'll find out more about these segmented, curved lines when we talk about paths.

Using the first two Polygon tool variants you can overlap and subtract, union or intersect flat surfaces. All polygon drawing must be done in either the Perspective or Top Views.

POWER TIP

Spline polygons are not directly set up for Boolean operations, but once you draw a spline poly and exit from it, you can go back and use it in a Boolean operation.

Freehand Polygon Tool

When you click this tool you also get a Polygon Control panel that becomes active when you finish your poly. Set or define vertices by left clicking anywhere on the grid. The first click starts the irregular poly. After adding as many sides as you like, finish by right clicking and the first and last vertex will be connected by a line and the Control panel will give you boolean options. The finished polygon can then be further shaped through Boolean operations or used in an extrusion.

Regular Polygon Tool

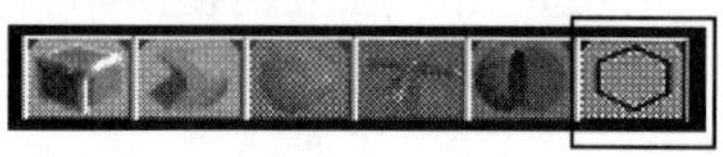

When you select this tool you again pop-up the polygon Control panel. Check and adjust the number of sides before pulling a poly. To start your poly, click on the grid approximately where you want the center of your regular poly to be. Hold down the clicker and drag the mouse from that point to the size poly you want. You'll see the poly resizing as you move. When you let go it becomes fixed at that size.

2D Boolean Operations

I love 2D Booleans. At first I didn't understand the power in them — hardly ever built one. Big mistake. As a space craftsman, I need to build lots of little intricate-looking parts and this makes it easy. I'll show you in two sections. Here we'll make a few little shapes.

Shape one is a universal nernie bit. I used it to make the docking cleats on my version of the space tanker. We'll make the basic two shapes using Freehand and Regular poly tools. Draw a flange shape like the one in Figure 6-9 on the base grid. Don't worry about the size, you can adjust it later.

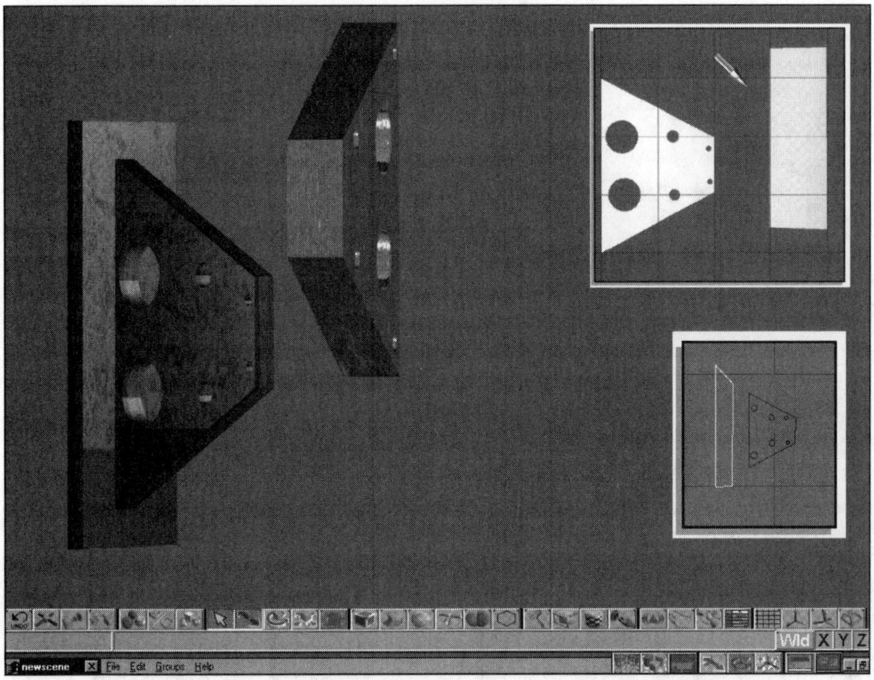

Figure 6-9: Detail of nernie flat polys, extrusion, and assembled flange parts.

Next we punch some nice official-looking circular holes in it. We do this by creating a circle polygon. That's an oxymoron; it can't be a circle if it's a polygon, circles don't have sides. In this case it's a regular polygon with so many straight sides it looks like a circle — somewhere between 15 and 20 will do nicely. It's a little tricky to get the circle exactly where you want it, so just undo and try again if you screw up. After you set the number of sides you want, then enable Boolean Subtract in the Poly Modes selection panel.

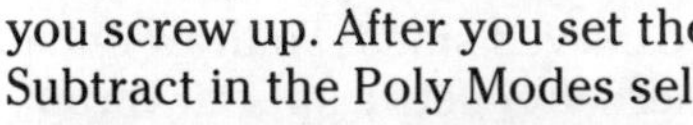

Draw a circle on the flat flange shape. When you let go of your mouse button, the circle will be subtracted. Do several of them in a pattern (as shown previously in Figure 6-9).

I got so deep into making nernies, I built a whole batch in about fifteen minutes. Here they are in Figure 6-10 and in Plate 6-1 as well. You can see that texture is a good way to make them look even more complex than they are. Note that the pipe with radial detail on top is exactly the same as the one on the bottom, just rescaled and repainted. I suggest keeping an object subdirectory just for these handy building parts. Just to get you started, I included a few of mine on the CD-ROM in the nernies subdirectory (\geometry\dreamscp\nernies).

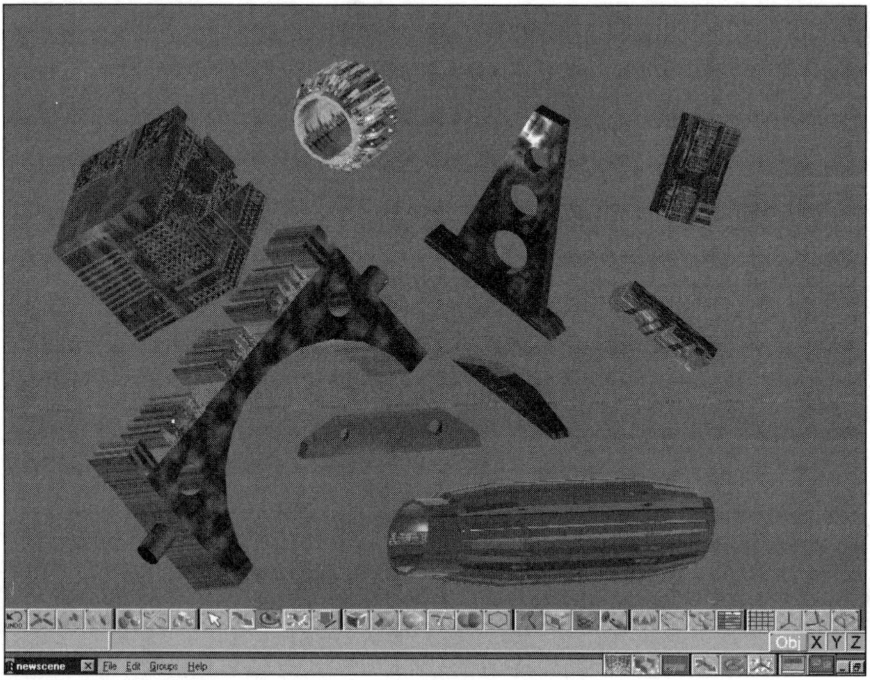

Figure 6-10: A collection of nernies assembled from flat extrusions.

Spline Polygon Tool

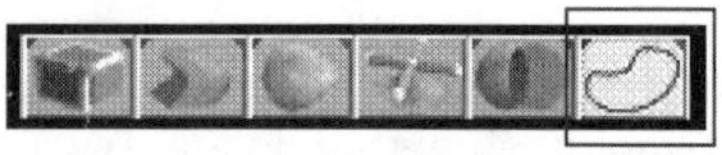

Spline polys start out like regular polys but have curved sides. To draw one just left click to place a starting vertex. Each click thereafter sets a special vertex known as a spline node. Between the nodes there are a defined number of segments. These are actually little arcs separated by interpolated vertices. I think you'll find it easiest to work with spline polys in the Top View window, looking straight down on the drawing grid. If you want to use a spline poly again you must save it in a path library, because once you finish editing it, the spline that defines the perimeter of the polygon disappears, leaving a normal polygon behind. If you've saved the spline, you can recall it for use again.

Editing Splines (In Brief)

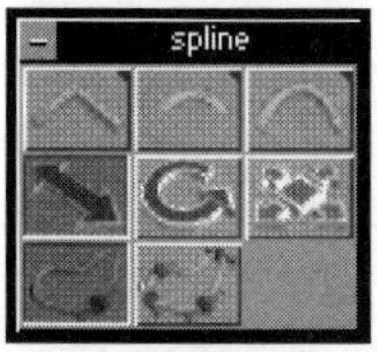

The Spline Control panel has the standard set of editing tools, so you can make fine adjustments to the splines as you plot them, switching back and forth between the Add Points and Edit Points modes. Again, you close a spline poly with a right click of the mouse. At that point you can play with the poly by moving nodes around and adjusting the shape. There are four things about a spline you can play with:

- **Position.** Moving any node in relation to its neighboring nodes will change the overall shape of the polygon. Try it.
- **Tension.** This controls the sharpness of the bend at each node. When you select a node you can see a control handle. Change the tension value of the node by left or right clicking the handle while holding down the Shift key and dragging from left to right. You can also bring up a Spline Settings panel by right clicking on any of the three interpolation presets in the Spline Control panel. Negative values can be input, but that's another story....
- **Continuity.** This parameter indicates the angle at which curves approach the node. A minus value has the two curves approaching the node like an arrowhead, while a positive value causes them to overshoot and return to the node, looking a little like a baby's behind. Zero is for linear interpolation, where there's neither under nor overshoot. You change continuity by *right* clicking on the control handle and holding down the Control key while dragging vertically.
- **Bias.** This is related to continuity in that it causes an imbalance in the continuity between the two sides of the node. A negative bias will cause the left spline to overshoot the node, while a positive one causes the right side to overshoot. You change bias by selecting the control handle, holding down the Control key and *left* clicking as you drag vertically.

Applying Node Characteristics

By default, spline curves are smooth. Across the top of the Spline Control panel you'll see three presets. These control the sharpness and shape of how lines meet at spline nodes. The three presets from left to right are: Sharp Point, Smooth (default), and Very Smooth. Across the bottom of the Control panel you'll see two icons. One applies characteristics to single nodes while the other applies them globally. I'll explain these controls in more detail when we talk about spline paths later in the book. Figure 6-11 shows characteristics of spline paths with different parameter settings.

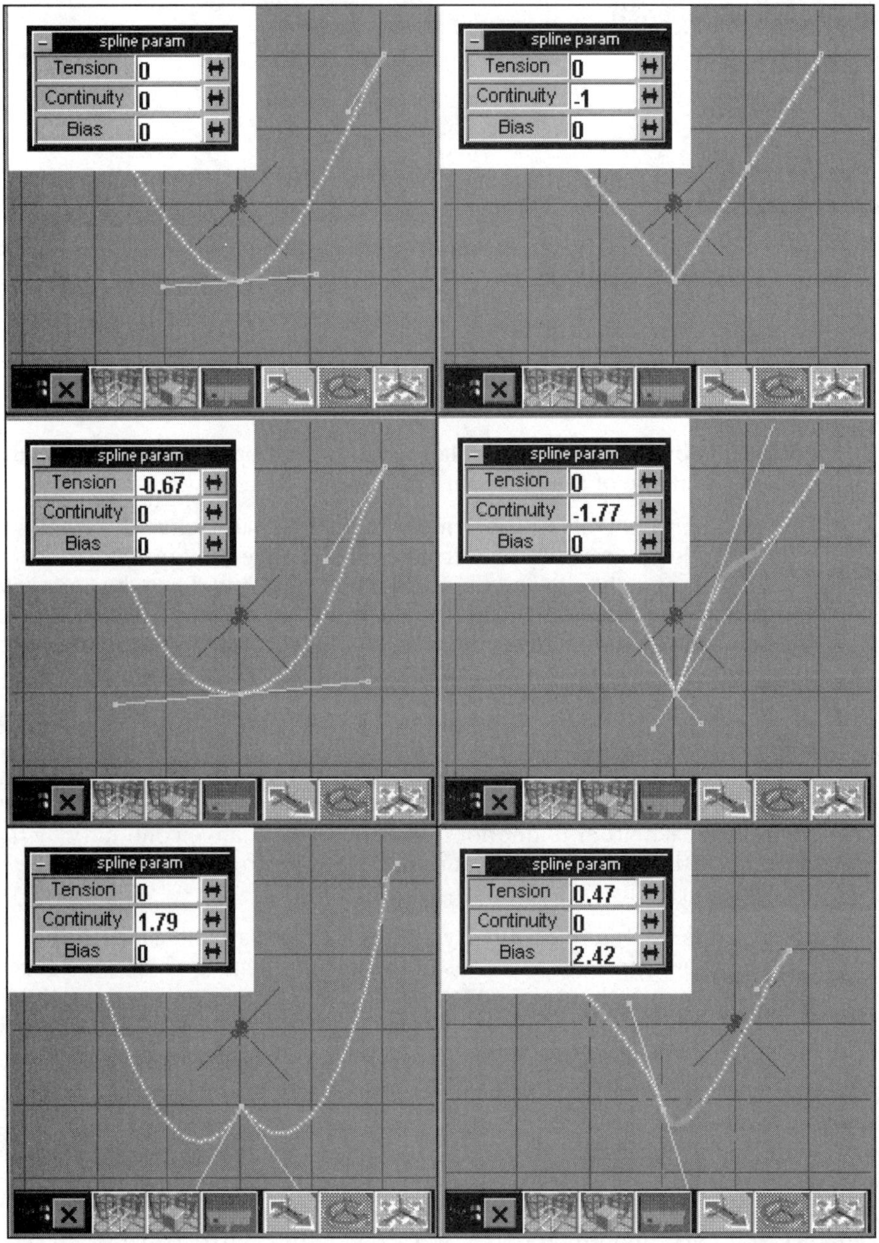

Figure 6-11: Examples of how parameter changes affect spline shape at nodes.

A Tree Grows in Beverly Hills

I think Beverly Hills has more trees than any town has a right to grow. It takes five full-time crews just to keep them trimmed. Live trees are easy, but I'm going to show you how to grow a dead tree. This one's been through a forest fire and retains only a nub of its former glory. It's an example of what you can do with a spline polygon and a little imagination. Here's where you learn the art of manipulated extrusion. This seemingly simple tool, when properly directed, can help you create some pretty awesome organic as well as mechanical shapes. Moreover, you can use the Macro tool to save your artistic manipulations so they can be repeated using different basic shapes.

Start by drawing a spline polygon something like the one in Figure 6-12.

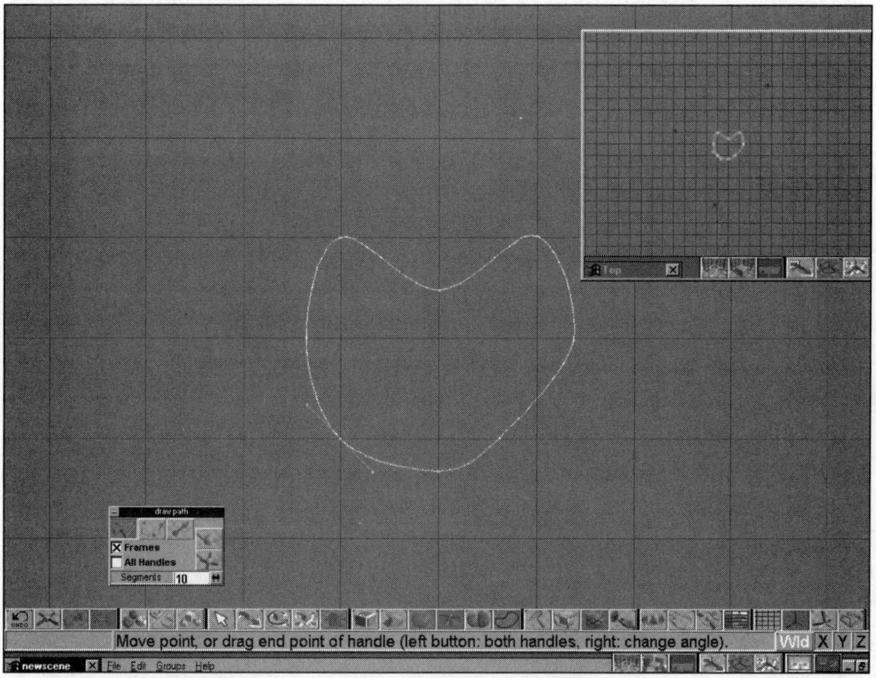

Figure 6-12: A spline polygon is the root of a dead tree.

Don't mess with the tension, bias, and other parameters; leave them at default. Select the Extrude tool,

and click once with your polygon's face selected (that's automatic as you create it). Good. Here's where the alchemy comes in. Select the Face Scale tool from the Point Nav panel,

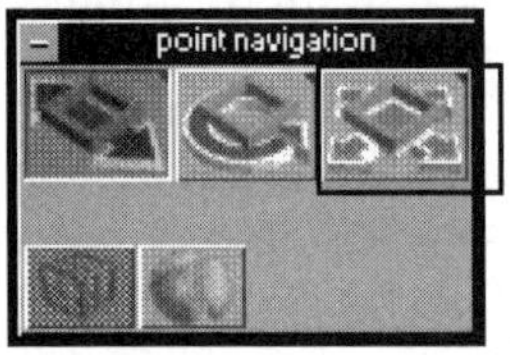

and scale the face down slightly. Be very gentle here because each time you click the Extrude tool, your face will scale down by this same amount (percentage), so you get a cumulative effect. Select the Face Rotate tool from the panel and rotate the face just a tiny bit in the X, Y, and Z planes, or just one if you like. Extrude again. Now open an extra window or two to check your tree from several angles. It should be growing reasonably straight. By scaling and rotating you can make a very gnarly tree. Scale up and back down for a massive knot to which you can attach branches.

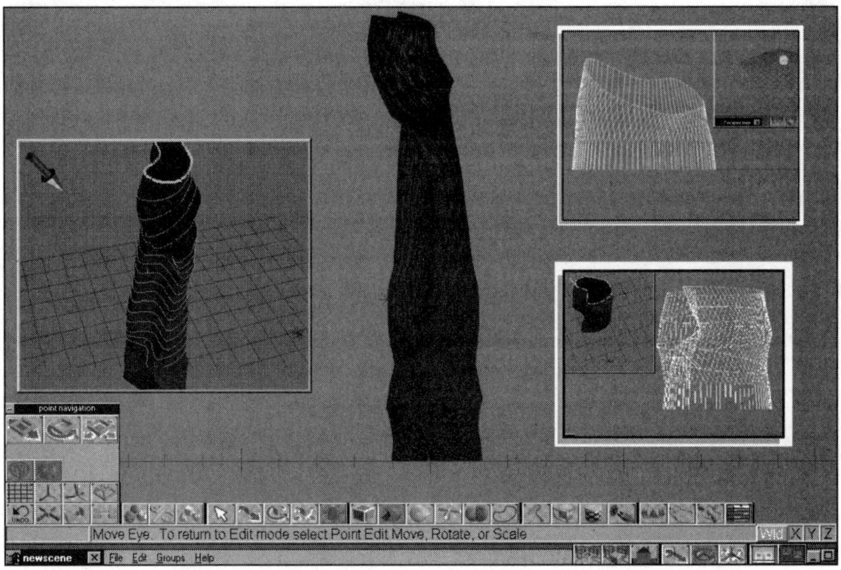

Figure 6-13: A dead tree takes shape from a single polygon extrusion.

The one twisty, turny branch was made the same way as the trunk. If you want more branches, don't make them one by one. Duplicate the original one and change its shape by stretching (scale) and otherwise manipulating each one to make it a little different.

When you have your branch(es), move (navigate) them into position. Again you'll need several windows to line up the branch with its base inside the tree trunk. You've got enough experience by now to do this without detailed instruction. The second branch is a clone of the first. I scaled and rotated it. You'd never know it's the same branch. Make this your own tree, using my efforts as an example. You could make a whole dead forest this way. Just clone a trunk, scale and twist and add branches, over and over again, but I suspect it would be depressing to look at.

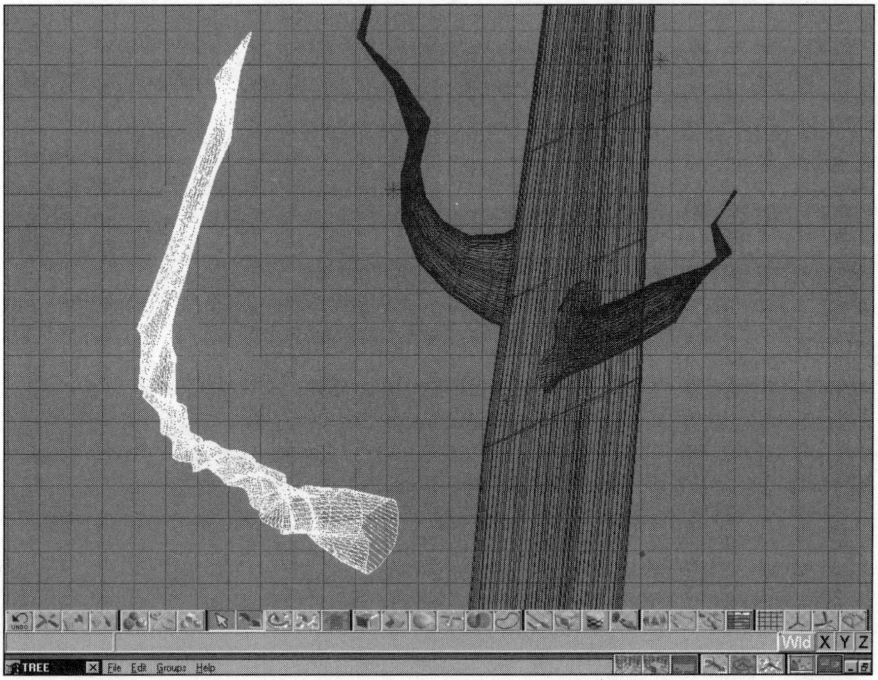

Figure 6-14: You can copy, rotate, and stretch a single extruded branch to make a whole tree or forest.

You can make the bark out of nearly any rough bump map. I used the one called blacktop, which should be on the CD-ROM in the \textures\misc subdirectory. A friend of mine made an excellent bark from a scanned photo of bat droppings that she scaled vertically with the repeat option. Try increasing the repeats in one direction to get the elongated bark-like lines. I simply applied a uniform brown color from the color cube to the tree and added the bump map after altering the default settings to U ➪ 3.39 V ➪ .69, AMP ➪ -0.04, but these are arbitrary. They looked good to me. You'll learn more about this when we get to surface techniques.

Once I had a trunk and some branches, I Boolean unioned the whole shebang together forming a single tree with a reduced number of vertices. If you are patient and really want a neat looking tree, I recommend distorting a sphere and inserting it where the branch enters the tree to give a rounded, more organic junction. I'm not patient. To see a color rendering of the tree against a sunset in a forest, see Plate 6-1.

Figure 6-15: Sunset on a deceased paragon of the forest.

Quick Nernies

Now you know how to extrude. Let's finish our nernies, started several headings ago. To make the example flange, extrude it once to get a piece of steel with round holes in it as previously shown in Figure 6-9.

Extrude the rectangle and use it as a base. Glue or Boolean the things together (as previously shown in the Figure 6-9 inset). That's it. You can make all sorts of simple gizmos this way to put inside your vehicles, so when you look through glass it looks like something's going on inside. Every time you think of one, build and save it in a gizmo library for recycling.

Text Objects for Fun and Profit

One of the most common ways people make money with 3D animation is by creating flying logos for individuals and companies. In trueSpace2 the Text tool is particularly easy to use. Text objects are fun to build out of truetype faces. If you can get your hands on CorelDraw 6 or even one of the earlier versions, you get hundreds of typefaces. You'll have more variety than you'll ever be able to use. There are also hundreds of TrueType fonts available on the Internet as well. Find them by scanning for *truetype shareware* on any of the information search indexes like Lycos or Yahoo. Other combinations may also help.

Here's how it works. Select one of the two Text tools from your Primitives panel.

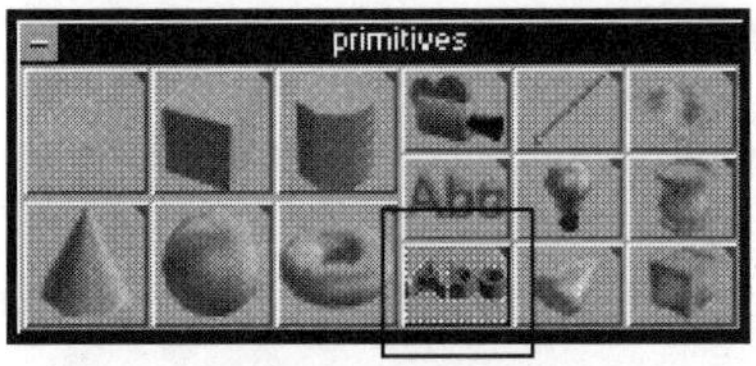

One produces horizontal text, the other vertical.

Right-click to get the Typeface Properties panel.

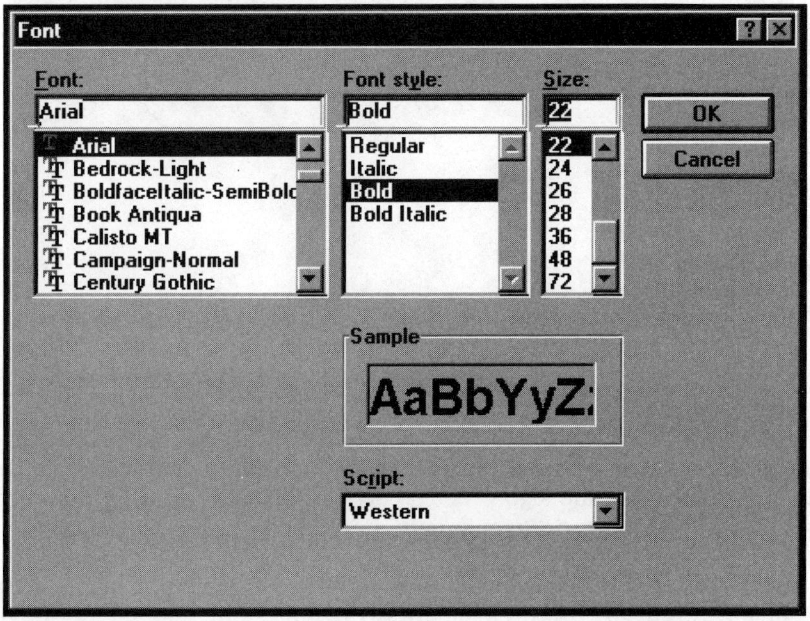

Pick out the typeface, size, and style you want and type a few words. Sweep (extrude) them, then bevel the face gently. That's it. Later you'll learn to make letters into actors. I'll even show you how to shape your text logo from a swirling cloud of particles. You can build text out of just about any material you can visualize (and a few you can't). All you need is that story and a little creativity, and you can add your contribution to the annals of flying logo history.

Have Text Will Show

Let's start by displaying your name in large, solid gold text. Clear your scene and then pop up the Primitives panel. Right-click on one of the Text tools to bring up the Text Properties panel. Select a bold typeface. Arial is a good one to choose. Select Vertical Text and click anywhere in the work space. Type your name. As you type, trueSpace2 automatically converts TrueType letter shapes into 2D polygons and lines them up perpendicular to the ground plane, as shown in Figure 6-16.

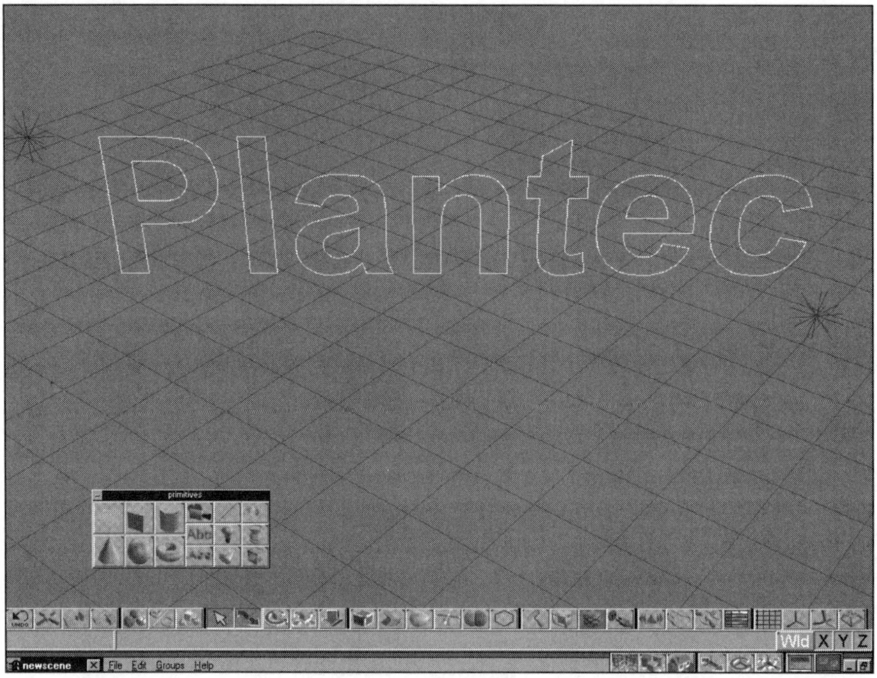

Figure 6-16: Flat text needs to be extruded before it becomes a 3D logo.

Notice the face is already selected because tS2 anticipates our desire to extrude them into 3D objects. Select the Extrude icon. One click and your name is a solid object. If you click again, the logo gets deeper. With the letter faces selected you can scale, bevel, and otherwise manipulate them.

POWER TIP

Here's an interesting, undocumented goodie. tS2 places the letters of a word as siblings in a hierarchical object. This allows you to navigate to them for individual adjustments. This will be handy later on when you learn how to do localized animation. You'll easily be able to have each letter doing something different.

I weep when I remember how I suffered trying to build letters in POV, the fabulous public domain raytrace program. This was a few years ago before it had decent (a relative term) front ends. You had to build objects by writing lines of code. To create my name took weeks of trial and lots of error. The results were pitiful, but then I'm no great programmer. Trust me, this is a dream.

Now we need to bevel the name logo so it catches light as it rotates in the sun. You've done this before, so click on the Bevel tool, click on the still selected face, and bevel ever so slightly. I hope Caligari tones this tool down a lot.

Be extra careful about criss-crossed polys. The inside top parts of Ms are a good place to check for this. There are a few typefaces you simply cannot bevel, especially the very thin ones like Architectura. If you have trouble, try a thicker typeface.

Your logo needs a floor. Pop up a Planar object. It's just a flat polygon you can paint with marble. Scale it larger than your name. Now, a new tool: the Material Library.

Whenever you create an interesting material, no matter how complex, you can save it in a Material Library. Pop it up and click on the left name block (the name of the library) and an options box appears. Select load ➪ Book.lbr from the CD-ROM's /matlib subdirectory. Here you'll find a nice shiny gold I made for the occasion. It already has reflections built in. Select it and hit the Paint Object icon.

Your name is painted in liquid gold. It's not very thrilling though. You need the floor and a lot of lights to reflect in the gold, and you'll need to raytrace the whole thing for maximum effect. Another trick we'll use is to turn off the default lights which provide a uniform light. We'll use more dramatic lighting.

Select the floor object, click on the marble texture in the library, and Paint it on. Now for lights. Go to the Primitives panel and pop up a local light.

It behaves like a lightbulb, sending out light uniformly in all directions. Open a Solid Render window if you haven't already and move the light close to your name. Repeat this six to eight more times, locating lights around the name object. If you want to be adventurous, you can also play with some shadow-casting spotlights.

You'll get a rough idea of how the various lights hit the logo from the Solid Render window. You'll notice that each time you pop up a light, the Lights panel opens.

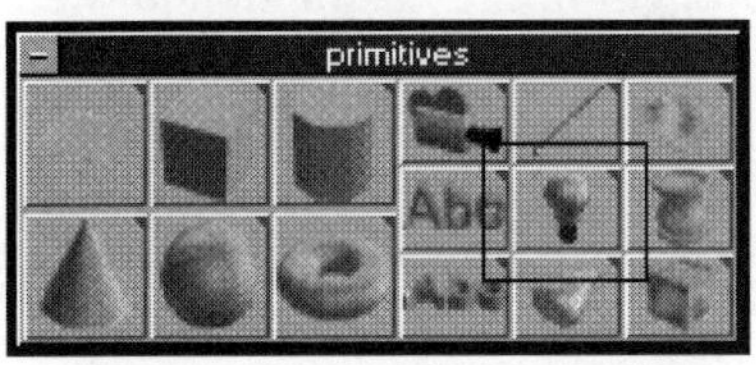

Here you can select different light parameters. Make some lights brighter than others and vary the colors a little. Later you'll learn more about lights and what you can do with them.

If you right click on the light intensity slider, you'll get a Numeric Input panel that will allow you to enter negative values to make shadows and very high positive values for extremely bright conditions. For this example, play with values up to 2 or 3 intensity.

Right click on the Render tool to get the Render Control panel. Select Raytrace ➪ 2X AntiAlias ➪ Draft OFF (unselected). Now render a full screen .bmp file in truecolor. This will take a while, so get yourself some coffee.

Figure 6-17: My logo is textured, lighted, and rendered.

You Can Really Use This Stuff!

Wow, check out those reflections. You can use this as wallpaper if you like. Keep your eyes peeled for flying logos on TV to get ideas for how to use this stuff. Later, when you learn about lighting, we'll glue a spotlight in the flashlight and then place it in the scene to shine on your logo.

Here are a few ideas:

- ✦ Build a fabulous opening sequence for your demo tape using flying logos instead of traditional text roll.
- ✦ Provide color slides to local business for presentations. You can whip up any title slides they'll need quickly. Send your files by modem to a local service bureau to be made into slides, and deliver them by the next day.

- ✦ Create flying logo ads and station breaks for your local television stations. Sure there's a lot of competition, but you're creative. Go for it.
- ✦ Cable TV channels are becoming a good market for this kind of thing. Check with your local cable company.
- ✦ Electronic greetings can be fun. Send the family a video opening with a personalized flying logo. They're sure to be impressed. After all, they didn't know you could do this kind of thing, right?

You keep adding to this list. Next it's time to build a few things with chicken wire. Like the Pasadena Rose Parade floats, nearly anything can be constructed with meshes made from joined polygons.

Summary

In this chapter, you should have learned:

- ✦ How to select critical parts of an object by engaging the Point Navigation tools to isolate specific sections of an object.
- ✦ Dimensional Promotion is a way of moving from point to line to polygon to 3D section.
- ✦ Flashlight construction using selective object scaling to create the head and boolean technique to dish out the reflector. Boolean intersection was used to create a glass lens.
- ✦ Boolean techniques of combining and subtracting both 2D and 3D objects to build configurations that would be very difficult any other way.
- ✦ A little about painting, transparency, bump and reflection maps so you could give the flashlight a lens and realistic exterior.
- ✦ About Polygons and how to build them using various polygon tools and 2D boolean operations to shape them.
- ✦ How to grow digital dead trees by repeatedly extruding a polygon while twisting and scaling it to create a complex trunk object and branches.
- ✦ How to extrude 2D shapes into 3D nernies, the odd little bits of detail that make space vehicles more believable. Nernies can be reshaped through uneven scaling to create a variety of detail effects.
- ✦ How to become rich and famous creating 3D text logos that you can sell to local television stations and elsewhere.

✦ ✦ ✦

CHAPTER 7

Sculpture in Space

✦ ✦ ✦ ✦

In This Chapter

Tools for sculpting organic forms

How to sculpt a character

Deformation tools

Create a lifelike shark using a clip model

Deformation Objects

Dancing Pickles

✦ ✦ ✦ ✦

Some of the most sophisticated 3D packages allow you to shape objects interactively by grabbing and pulling or pushing them into new shapes. It's called Object Deformation and it's one of the most exciting innovations to come down from high-end modeling. In trueSpace2, you get two types of deformation, Surface and Volume.

Surface Sculpt

It's like playing with the abundant wrinkles on a Shar-pei pup. With this tool and a *well-subdivided* surface you can generally mold the skin any way you like. You could deform a flat ground plane to make neat terrain, pulling up mountains and pushing down valleys. With animation you have ocean surf. It's perfect if you need to keyframe a crater after an explosion. Simply start with terrain, have your explosion, and keyframe the depression to form in synchrony with the blast. You'll know how when you learn about empty keyframes later in the book.

POWER TIP

Surface sculptures are not supposed to be animated. In fact, it requires you to remove any animated deformations before applying the sculpt deformation. You *can* animate sculpt operations. It's great for oceans. I believe it's undocumented because it can be unreliable. Nevertheless, certain things are easier to animate with sculpt. All you do is keyframe the different sculpted manipulations and it will work 9 times out of 10. If you want to go back and make changes after you change modes, you can't. It will require you to again remove all animated deformations, even though they are sculpts.

When you pop up the Surface Sculpt tool you get a typical control panel with six selections and adjustments.

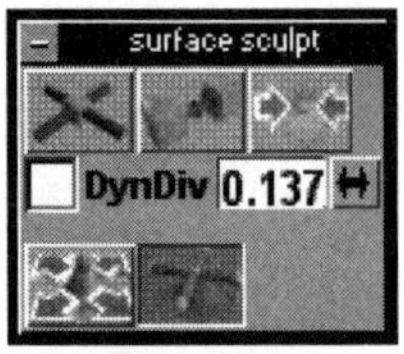

- **Deformation Erase.** Clicking this will delete the active deformation from the surface.

Once you start a new deformation, you can't go back and delete the previous one, so make sure you want it, or you'll have to start all over again.

- **Deformation Copy.** This is useful if you're building a surface with a lot of repeated deformations, say an egg carton. You just set your Grid tool, sink one egg pocket, then copy the rest to their respective locations. All you do is click on Copy, then select the spot to drop it and, bam, it's in place. If it's not exactly right, just delete and do it again.
- **New Deformation.** You have to click on this and then on the surface to start a new point of deformation.
- **DynDiv.** Dynamic Quadrangle Division automatically subdivides your new surface to maintain planarity. You can set the slider from 0 to 1.0, the higher the number, the more division and the smoother the curves.
- **Scope.** Click to enter Scope Mode wherein you can change the surface range of your instrument by manipulating the special set of blue handles which appear. Grab the blue bar to extend the scope.
- **Sharpness.** Puts you back in Sculpt Mode with green handles.

Be careful with high DynDiv settings, or you'll end up with a tight web of little polygons that will slow down your whole project. Use it, but keep the subdivide fairly low.

Sculpting a Zany Face

You can build yourself a simple character face using only Surface Sculpt and one Boolean operation for the mouth. We'll use nernie technology for the teeth. Start in Front View, with a Top View 3DR window in the upper right corner of your screen. This will help you judge the depth of your sculpting. Pop up a sphere and Smooth Quad Subdivide it. We'll start by gently pushing in eye sockets. Set your first sculpt node two lines to the left of center and push in gingerly. Repeat symmetrically on the right side of the sphere as shown in Figure 7-1 and push in with the *right* button down. This also starts to form the nose.

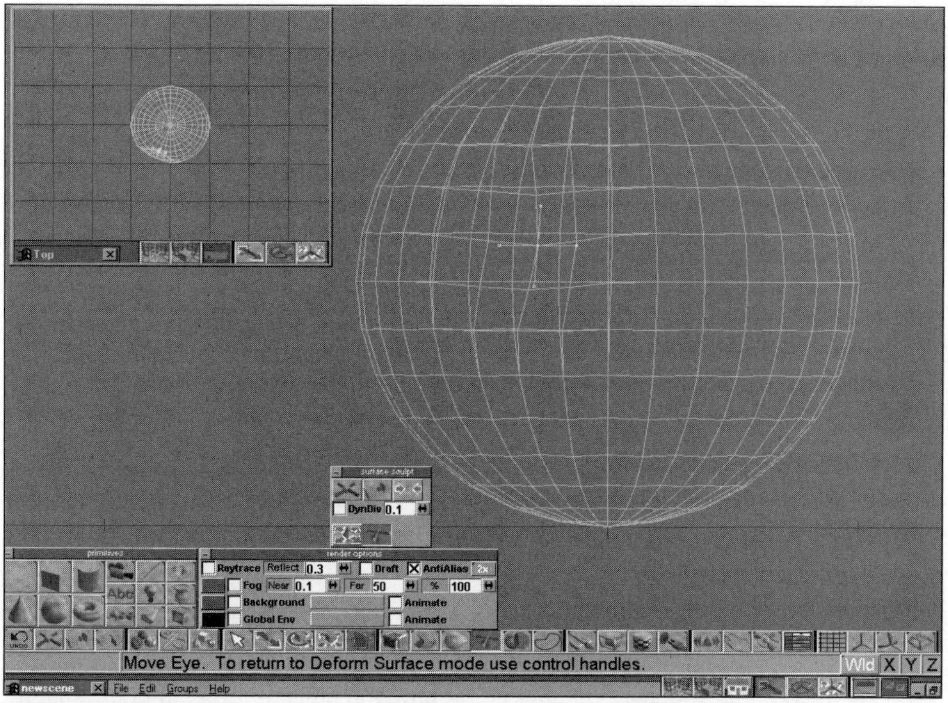

Figure 7-1: The start of a face, a simple sphere with eye sockets pushed in

Locate where you think the tip of the nose should be and plant a sculpt node there. With a *right* click, gently pull out, referencing the Top View window.

You can see in Figure 7-2 that the nose is a bit pointy. You can adjust this with the handles. I liked it that way so I left it. This guy is real sharp, but he continues to poke his nose into other people's business.

Pop up a sphere and scale it down for an eyeball. Drag it into position, again referencing the Top View window. You want to position it so that the sphere is slightly sunken into the head as shown in Figure 7-3.

Now figure out where you want your mouth to go. Center the sculpt node below the nose and engage Scope Mode by grabbing the horizontal bar in the middle of one side and stretching it out to influence a wider portion of the mouth area. Now gently push in. If you want you can pull out a little on the chin. This will give you the mouth area. We'll Boolean cut the mouth out, leaving a mouth interior for teeth.

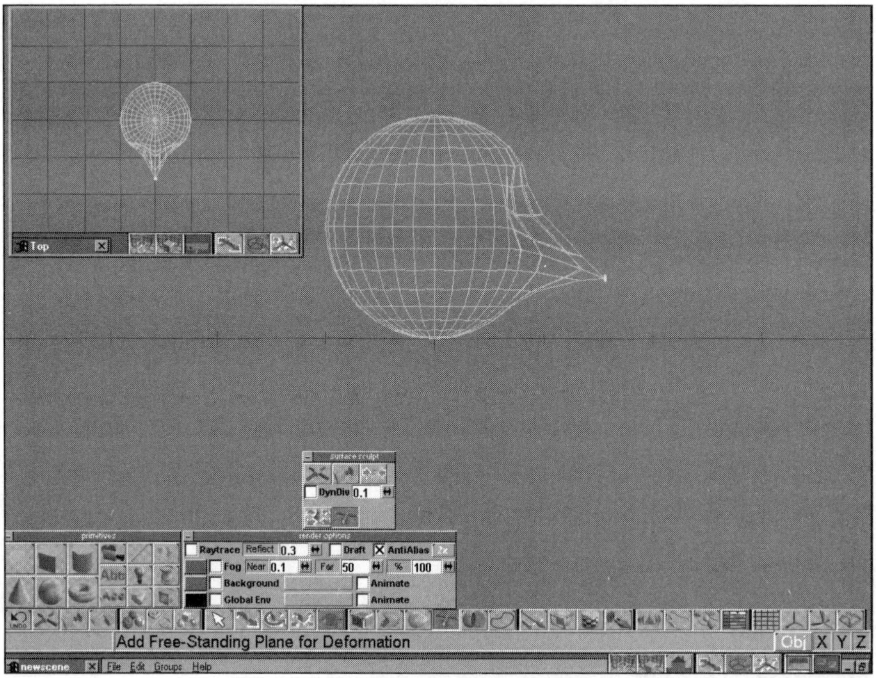

Figure 7-2: The Top View window shows how you pull the nose out of the sphere to form the character's face.

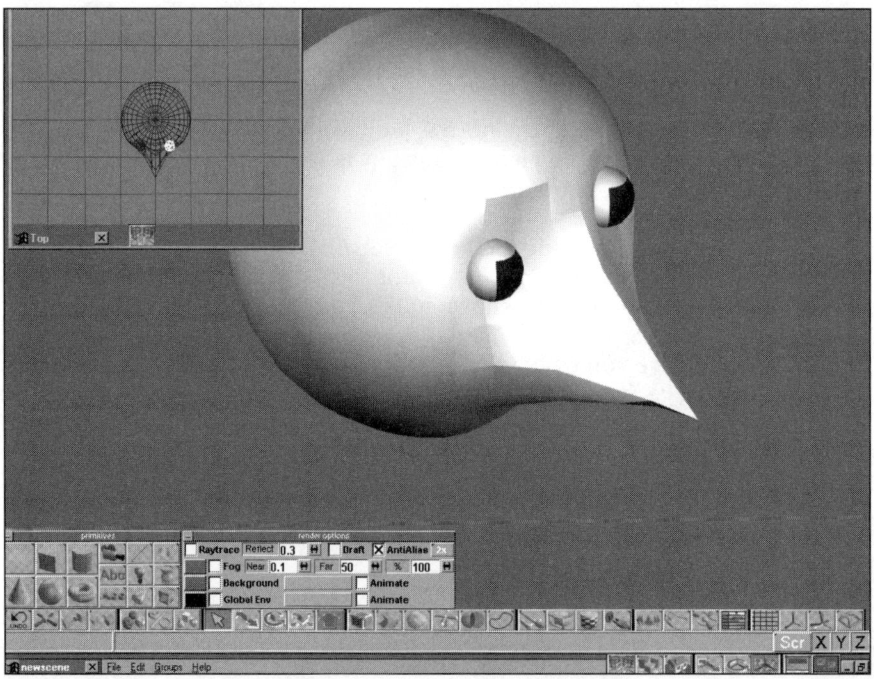

Figure 7-3: The face takes shape with the eyes in place.

Change your main work space to a Top View and, using the Spline or Freehand Poly tool, draw a mouth shape as shown in Figure 7-4.

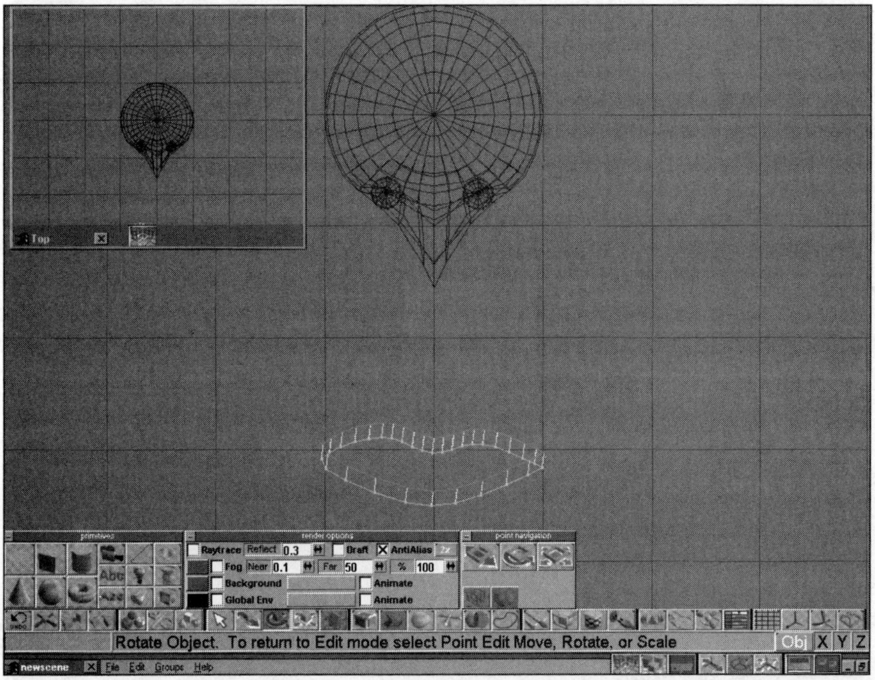

Figure 7-4: You draw a mouth-shaped flat polygon and extrude for the mouth's opening.

Then extrude it a few times until it looks a little like a lip-shaped cookie cutter. Good, now position this by rotating 90° into mouth position. Switch your work window to a Front View, and with an eye on the Top View, slide the lip cutter into the head exactly where you want the mouth to be. Not very difficult.

Here's the hard part. As you recall, Booleans can be a little touchy. Make sure you've set the Boolean control to delete edges by right clicking on the 3D Boolean tool and checking the delete edges box. Then select Head ⇨ Boolean Subtract ⇨ Lips. The lips should cut a mouth-like hole in the head (see Figure 7-5). But I'll almost bet you get a message to reposition the lips because the Boolean failed. No worries. Just move it about a smidgen, maybe change the angle of entry slightly. After a couple of tries, you'll get it.

My head definitely needs teeth in its mouth, and maybe a tongue as well. Teeth are really people nernies. So I made a simple 2D teeth-shaped polygon, extruded it and placed it in the mouth cavity. I then copied the teeth, inverted and placed a set in the upper mouth. Of course I painted them with a nice glossy white (see Figure 7-6).

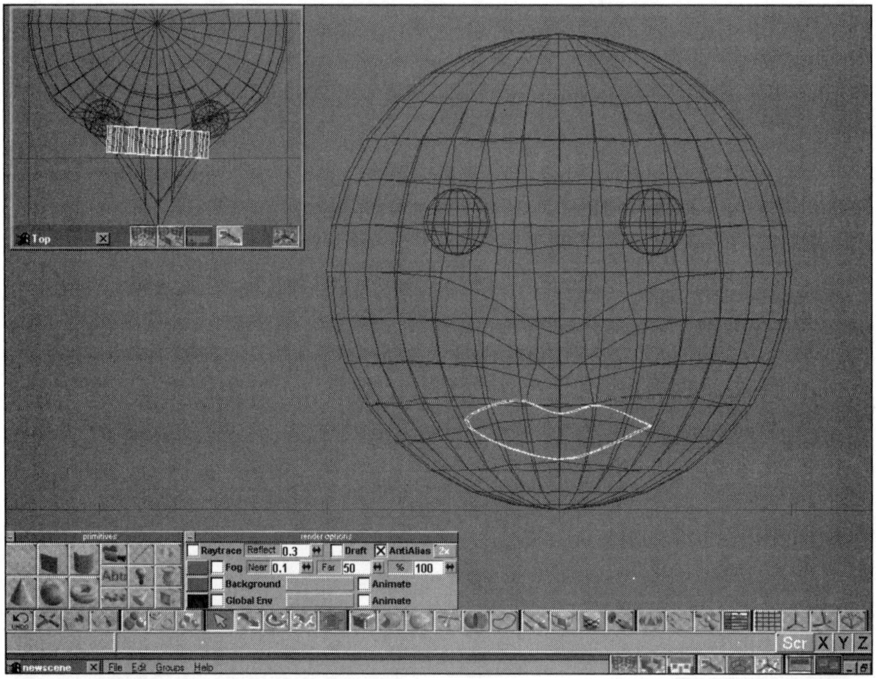

Figure 7-5: The character's head with its mouth cut in, ready for teeth.

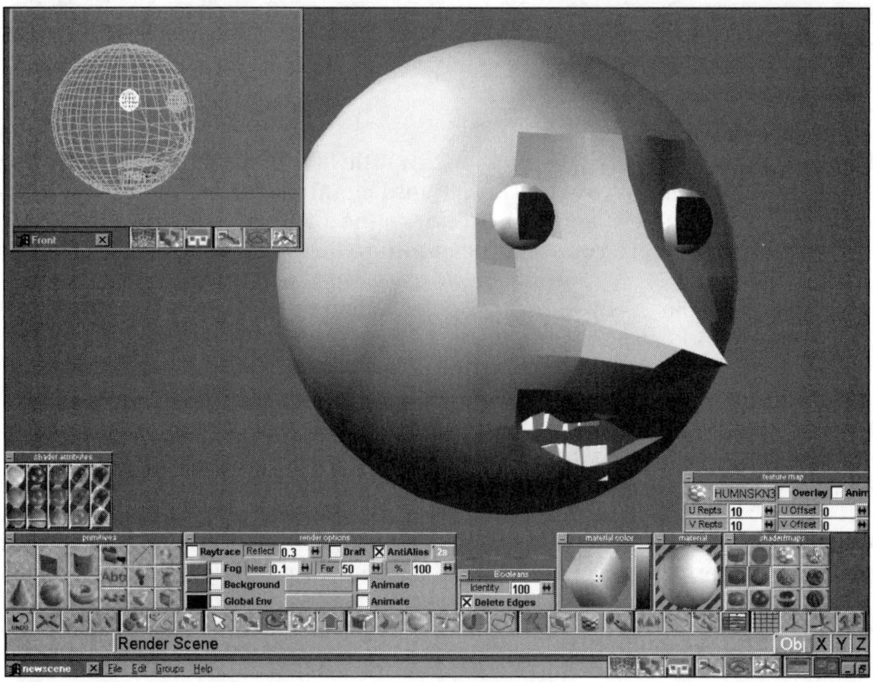

Figure 7-6: The head shows the nernie teeth in place.

Let's put in a tongue so later we can make him talk. The tongue is an organic nernie. There are probably lots of ways to come up with one, but here's mine. Simply pop up a sphere, reduce it in size and flatten it with uneven scaling. Select the Volume Deform tool, and pull the tongue into shape as shown in Figure 7-7. I know you've not received proper instruction in this tool, but what the heck. Go for it, or wait till after you learn to use it in the next section.

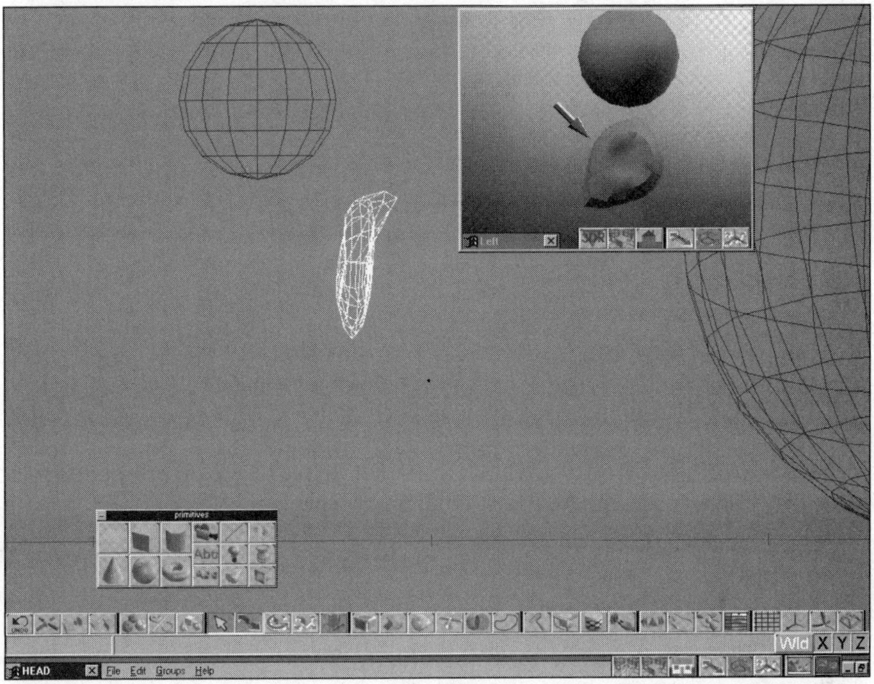

Figure 7-7: You can shape the character's tongue from a sphere using the Deform Object tool.

Navigate the tongue into position in the mouth. This is a little tricky, so take your time. The 3DR window is essential here. Set up a good view of the mouth and move the teeth and tongue around until they look right to you. In character design, I find it best to avoid rules and play with the design until you like it. This character will win no prizes (see Figure 7-8) but he's a good fellow whose mouth detail will help us when he learns to talk later in the book.

During character animation, you'll be able to apply something called a Deformation Object to the head to animate changes in its shape, giving a feeling of expression and muscles moving. You'll also be able to move his mouth to simulate talking.

Enough said, you get the idea. There's nothing stopping you from reshaping the entire head, coming up with a creative hair solution, and making the nose bulbous. Go for it, it's your mind.

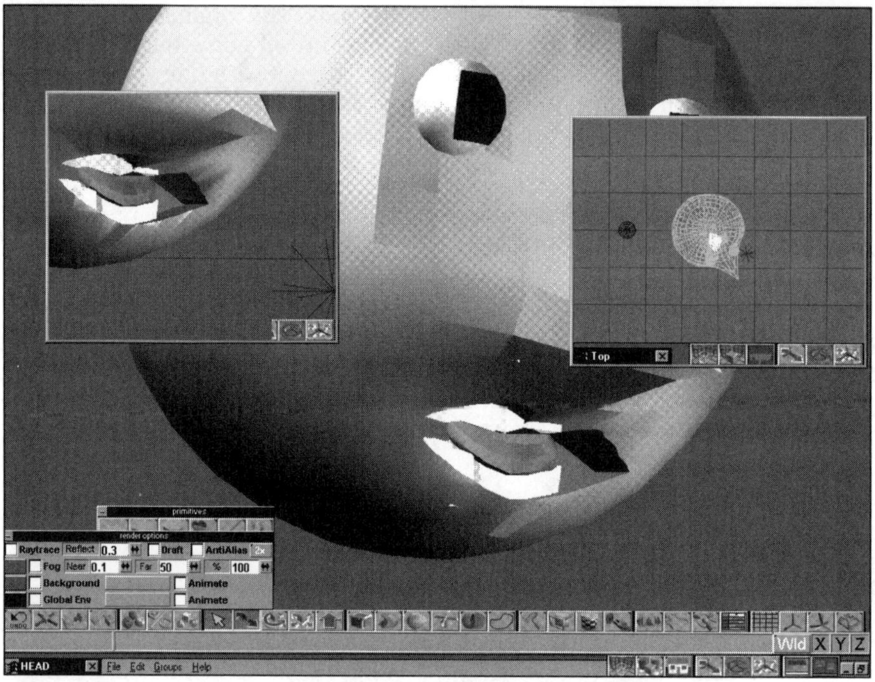

Figure 7-8: The fellow is ready to talk and possibly even eat. It's a start.

Volume Deformation

I slipped a new tool in on you with the tongue. Whenever you need to bend, twist, or otherwise deform an object, particularly when you plan to animate that deformation, use the Object Deformation tools.

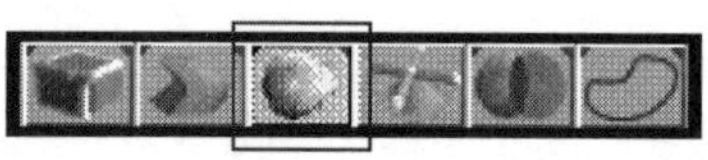

You can achieve natural organic movement with these tools because they can bend and stretch surfaces smoothly, and you can animate those moves. Use them to change one shape to another over time.

Save your head and clear your work space (good advice for all endeavors). It's a good idea to experiment a little and develop a feel for this tool. Avoid seriousness — don't get discouraged when you can't do exactly what you want right away. It's a bit unwieldy until you get used to it. Practice. Caligari claims this tool makes object deformation like working with clay. That's stretching it a bit, but with hardware acceleration, it comes close. Start out in Solid Render Mode and select the Object Deform icon. You'll get an Object Deformation Navigation panel.

Deform Navigation Panel

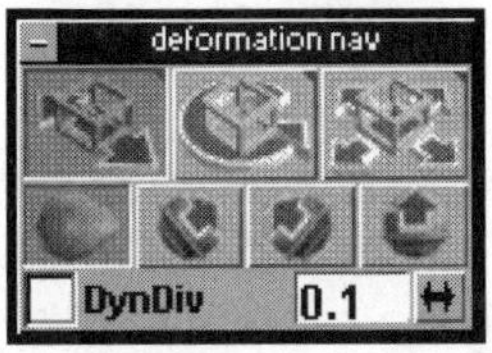

We'll go over this entry point in detail because you'll be using it frequently. Across the top of the DNP, you'll see the standard navigation tools for Move, Rotate, and Scale. In this case, the operations affect the selected control node or outline, and all points under its influence. By this I mean the node is like a magnet with strong influence on polygons close, with decreasing influence farther away. The more polygons you have and the smaller they are, the more focused the area of effect will be.

POWER TIP

It's often useful to switch back and forth between manipulating the object and its deformation. With the Deform Navigation panel open, you can instantly switch to manipulating the whole object simply by clicking the appropriate navigation icon in the main Tool Bar. You don't have to click on the arrow first. This saves a lot of time, as clicking the arrow takes you out of the Deform tools entirely.

The Push/Pull Tool

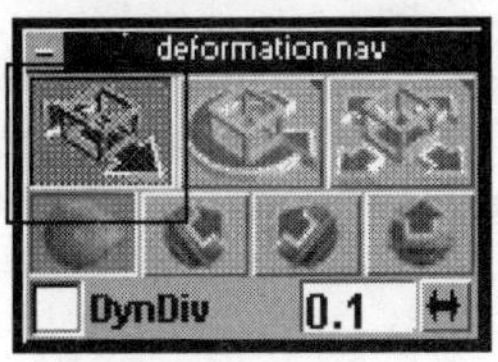

This will move the control node or outline, within the active Coordinate system. It's easy to change Coordinate systems simply by right clicking on any top row tools to get an Axes and Coordinate panel.

I usually prefer to work in the World system, but you pick the one that works the way your brain works. One will be more comfortable for you. With the Push/Pull tool selected, your left mouse button controls movement parallel to the X and Y axes, while the right controls movement parallel to the Z axis. You could have guessed this by now.

The Twist Tool

With this tool you twist the node or outline in the desired direction. We'll use this to give fluid motion to our shark later on. To figure out in which direction the thing is going to move, think perpendicular: Rotate around the X axis by moving perpendicular to the X axis, around the Y axis by moving perpendicular to the Y axis. Good. To rotate around the Z axis you just click the *right* button and move.

The Stretch Tool

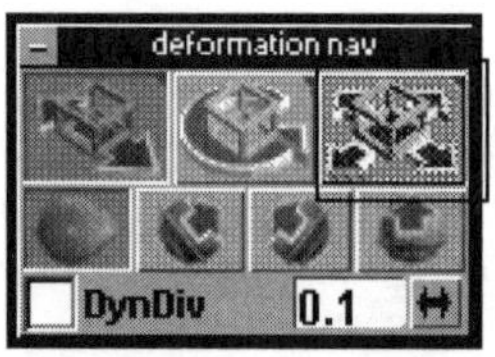

This is the scale tool of the deform system. With it you can scale the points under the influence of the control node or outline. (I hate saying that over and over again, so every time I say node, I mean both from now on.) This time think parallel. You scale along the X axis with movement parallel to it and along the Y axis with movement parallel to it. I hope that's clear. Experiment; you'll see what I mean. Pop a sphere and stretch parts, change nodes and shrink it. This is actually very useful, especially in animation. Imagine having a flower grow in front of your eyes using the Stretch tool across keyframes.

Local Deformation

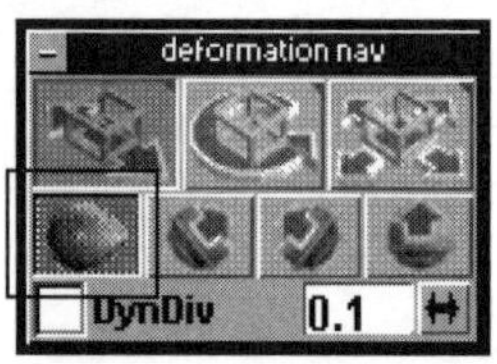

You know this one pretty well by now. You click, setting a control node, then use the above tools to deform as you will. To deform another section of the object, just click on it to move the control node. Easy.

Outline Deformation

There are three Outline Deformation tools. Each performs outline deformation perpendicular to a specific axis.

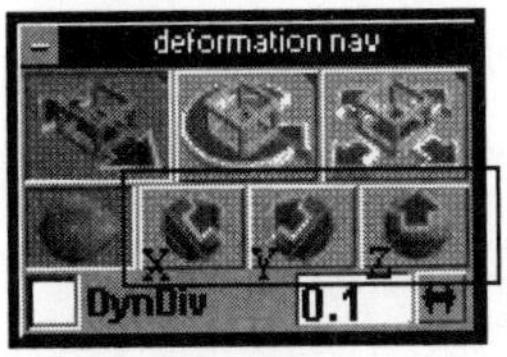

When you choose one of these tools, the selected object instantly develops a sparse set of outlines favoring movement along the axis chosen. With the outlines set up, click on a cross section and drag — slowly so you can see what's happening. Six times out of ten, it won't be what you want — in the beginning. Later you get good at it. Play with it until you get the feel of your instrument. These tools allow you to breathe life into your objects.

If you want to work on a small area of the object, you need to increase the number of control lines. Do this by clicking and dragging outside the object *before* doing any deformation and dragging. This is important because you can't do it once you've started deforming. As usual the left mouse affects the accumulation of control outlines on the X and Y coordinates while a right click affects outlines on the Z axis.

Getting the Feel of Your Instrument

Start a new scene and pop up a sphere. Right click on the Deform Object icon to get the Deformation Properties panel.

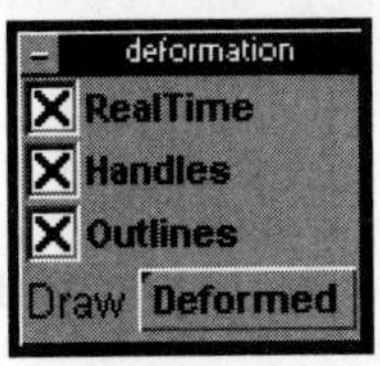

Make sure the Outlines option is enabled in the Deform Property panel so you can see the green lines at all times. Make sure Handles is also selected so you can see and use the control handles for real-time interactive manipulations.

Select the Deform tool and look at the sphere. The green outlines form floors and vertices where they cross. The actual Deform tool is represented by a cluster of control handles, usually five. Four form a cross with the fifth perpendicular to the surface being manipulated, in the center of the crosshairs. Sometimes the array of handles will be slightly different depending on where you click.

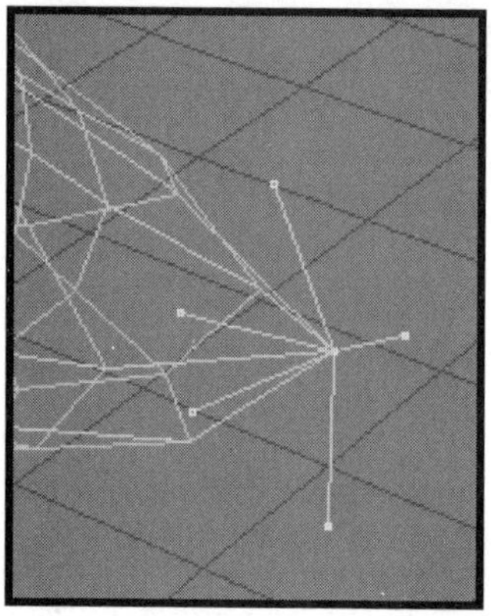

When you select an Outline Mode, there will be two handles (more or less) tangential to the surface.

Pop up a Front View window, and drag it to the upper right corner of your screen and make sure you still have the Top View, upper left.

Before you do anything with your sphere, experiment with increasing the number of control floors. Click alongside the object and drag, first horizontally and then vertically. You can create floors proportionately by holding down both buttons at the same time and moving your mouse. Outlines are created in orientation with the object's *Local* axes.

POWER TIP: Keep the number of control lines to approximately 1/3 to 1/4 the number of subdivisions in the object. Otherwise you won't get reliable deformation. Use even more on planar deformations or you could pull holes in the floor.

Now click on a vertex, any vertex, while in Local Mode. Click on each of the control handles and move it to examine the effect it has on the sphere. Try clicking away from the handles and moving your mouse. Note how the control node moves.

It's not as intuitively predictable as I would like, but as you use it, it becomes second nature. Here's what it appears to be doing[1]:

- ✦ Each handle controls an area on the object surface beneath it. That area isn't marked, but you can see roughly where it is when you manipulate the handles, because the control lines move.
- ✦ The control influence diminishes as you move away from the center of influence.

[1] I'm told that this isn't exactly what's happening, but it helps in visualizing what to expect.

✦ The control point's range of influence is determined by the number and distribution of control intersections, and the length of the tool's green handles.

✦ The greater the number of control intersections the more localized the influence of each manipulation.

✦ The Mode selected, Push/Pull, Twister, or Scale, determines the kind of manipulation the area will recieve.

✦ The distance you move your mouse determines the magnitude of that influence.

POWER TIP Use the fewest number of control lines you can get away with. This makes object deformation easier and smoother.

I had to read that three times to understand it — and I wrote it. In 3D work, words are often inadequate to describe what's going on. That's why an interactive interface is so important in learning the art. You really have to try this stuff hands on, so let's do it.

The Shark Project

Outline deformation is more useful than a vegematic, and not nearly so dangerous. I love it. That fluid motion I told you about has the look of Bones movements in LightWave and 3D Studio, only it's a lot easier. If you have a cow, you can have it turn its head and look at you very naturally. We happen to have a hammerhead shark from the folks at ViewPoint Data Labs. They're the fine folks who run Avalon, the Internet repository for 3D objects. In live, the shark is special. It moves with grace.

I chose this project in honor of Cyrus Lum, one of the great pioneers of organic 3D animation, who was probably the first person to animate a shark with such fluid motion that it could fool the casual onlooker. As I write, Cyrus is at Iguana Entertainment in Austin, Texas. He's also known for his remarkably realistic 3D dragons with wings that billow with air on the down stroke. Check out dragon.mpg on the CD-ROM for a taste, and before beginning this project, also review shark.avi, Lum's original piece created with 3D Studio (both files are in the \movies\cyruslum subdirectory). It was a lot harder to get results like this when he did it.
I think it will give you an idea of what to shoot for in this project.

The Model

Commercial models are very useful, and you can find collections of them on CD-ROM. I'm going to work with a prebuilt, low-resolution model of a shark (see Figure 7-9). You can find it on the CD-ROM.

Go to Files ➪ Load Object ➪ Shark.cob.

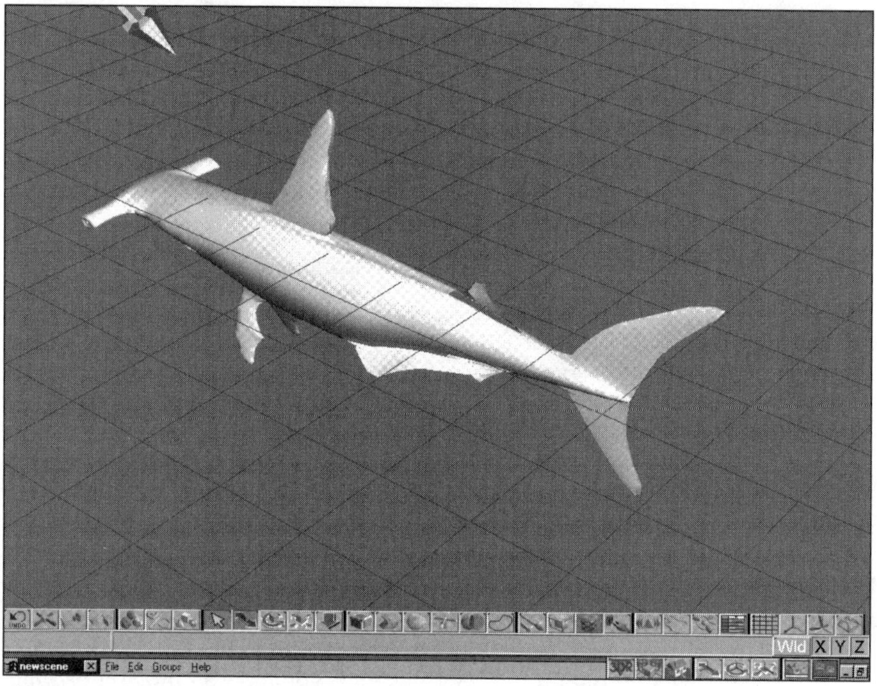

Figure 7-9: This hammerhead shark model is on the CD.

It will pop up aligned with the Y axis. Don't worry that it looks like a carved chunk of Styrofoam. We're going to use Outline Deformation to give it some life and a simple texture map to simulate skin. Examining Cyrus's shark you can see what painstaking texture mapping can do for a fish. Because I needed to create a lot of illustrations for this book, I took a shortcut and created a fractal cloud pattern in Fractal Design Painter 3.1. The pattern is located on the CD-ROM (under \textures\space) as frac2.bmp. Feel free to use it too.

You want the minimum number of control outlines. One line produces the most organic and predictable movement. Click the Deform Object ➪ Outline/Y axis tool ➪ Shark's tail. You'll notice a vertical floor segment turn white around the shark's midsection. This will be the pivot point for his tail sweep. We'll experiment with Push/Pull and Twister, pulling the shark into various natural positions for practice. Later, when you learn more about animation, we'll create an underwater scene and have him swim by with fluid, natural motion. This is sophisticated stuff. When you're done, I think you'll agree the movement you produce is as good or better than a lot of professional work on TV.

When you selected the shark's tail you also planted a deformation control node. Look for the little whiskers sticking out. Select the Push/Pull tool and move the tail to one side. Try different windows to see which angle works best for you. Manipulate the tail slowly to get a feel for how it bends, and keep checking Top View for alignment. The tail should move slowly and organically.

It's sometimes hard to see the control handles, but they are there, so look closely.

There's a bug in trueSpace2 that causes Outline Deformation to become wildly erratic at times. You can't miss it when it hits, often after running through a wireframe animation. If this happens, just click Undo, go to a different Deform tool and then back to the one you were using. It should be reset and back to predictable movements. Your model should also be back to where it was before the zanies hit.

After you've moved the fish's tail around a bit, switch to the Twister tool and slowly adjust the tilt and sweep of the tail (see Figure 7-10). Experiment, there's no exactly correct way to do this as long as it looks reasonably natural. Check out Plate 7-1 in the color section to see what a good pose, texture, and a background can do for Styrofoam.

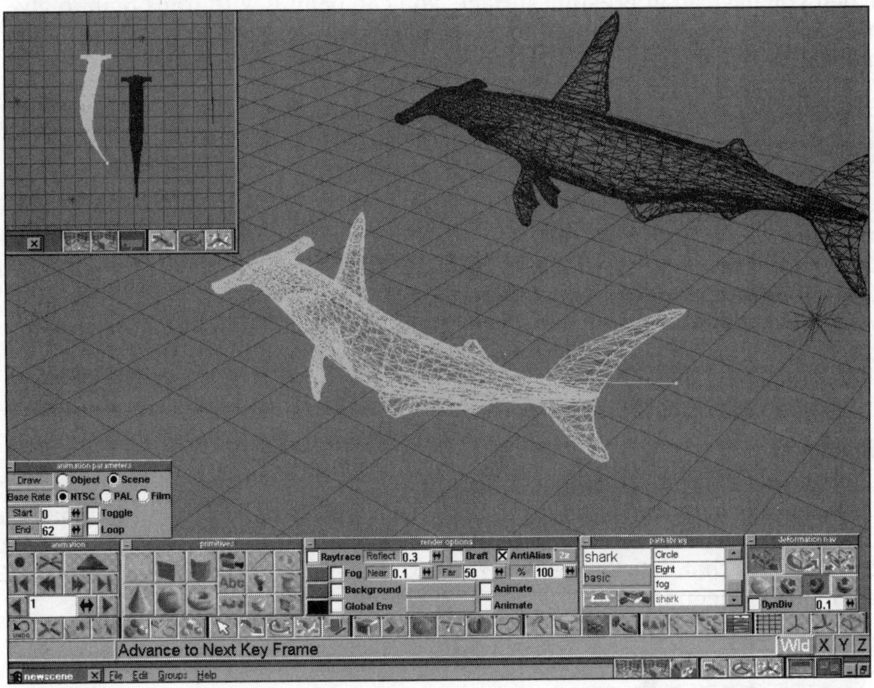

Figure 7-10: The shark is positioned in a more natural pose.

The Setting

We have to give this shark a nice underwater place to live. We start by popping up a flat Primitive, but first right click the planar object in the Primitives panel, and

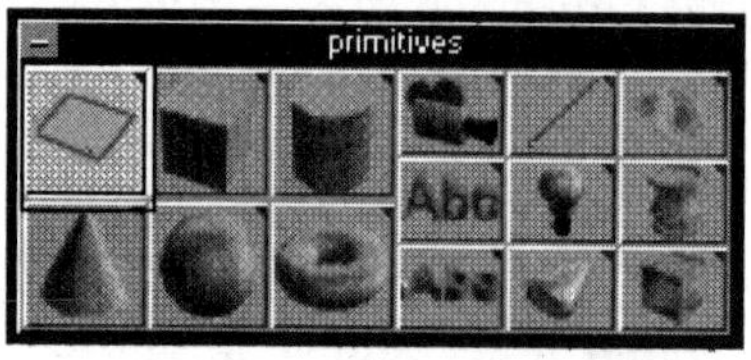

set the resolution to about 60 or a little more. Pop the plane and Scale it up to cover the entire grid or more. Before sculpting a sea bed, go to the utilities group ➪ SmoothQuad ➪ hold and ➪ Triangulate Object tool. When you click this tool the seabed will divide into triangles. This will make it more flexible for sculpting. Invoke the Surface Sculpt tool and and check the DynDiv option. This will keep the sea bed from tearing. Slowly begin pulling up and pushing down the sea floor. Don't make mountains, just soft sandy mounds like you might see while scuba diving. Experiment by elongating the handles to expand the area of influence. Play with it.

When you have an interesting surface, you can paint it with frac2.bmp to give it a mottled appearence. Before rendering, make sure your shark is above the bottom in clear water.

Prepare to render by turning off Raytrace and Draft. Turn on AntiAlias, and Fog. Set the Fog parameters as follows: Color ➪ deep blue green, Near ➪ 12, Far ➪ 34, % ➪ 100.

You can paint both the sea bed and shark with frac2.bmp, yet achieve very different looks. Do this by clicking on the paint roller, which brings up the texture tools. Right click on the Texture Map icon and select frac2.tga as your map. If you want a slightly different effect use the same map as a bump map by right clicking on the Bumpmap icon and selecting it. Leave the U and V repetitions at 1 and paint the sea floor. You should get a nice mottled appearence.

Sharkskin

Click off the bump map and paint the shark with the same texture map. Notice that you only get a uniform gray look to the shark. This model was not made in trueSpace2, so it has no texture map coordinates. Picture these as an anchor grid on the object that determines how the texture will wrap around the surface. Click on the UV Projection tool,

and select one of the three projections: Planar, Cylindrical, Spherical. You don't have to go with the closest match to your object, each looks different, so pick the one you like. To make things more interesting, you can play around with the pattern repeat parameters in the Texture Options panel. By increasing repeats in one direction, you'll create a striated pattern that may look good on a fish. Also, try bringing one of the repeats below 1.0 for interesting effects. Go for it and have some fun.

The shark that appears in Figure 7-11 looks pretty good, but if you look closely, his position isn't really natural. If you study the way sharks move, you'll notice that the head would look better turning to the other side. Look at Cyrus Lumm's shark again. He studied the way sharks move and it's obvious in his work. It really pays to study life if you want to copy it. Observing details like this will help you become a respected professional.

Figure 7-11: The shark appears in comfortable surroundings that you created.

Later, when you learn keyframing, I'll show you how to observe fish and create a natural looking shark animation using this same model.

Stand-Alone Deformation Objects

These are neat, state-of-the-art tools. Deformation Objects are special, invisible Primitives that you can shape. You can then deform regular objects by attaching them to a Deformation Object. As the regular object passes through the Deform Object, its shape is distorted to conform with the Deformation Object. To see that concept, you need to look at some pictures. This approach is useful in animation for applying a specific kind of motion to several different objects. I'm just going to introduce you for now. Later you'll learn to use these tools for special effects that would otherwise be enormously difficult — like driving your Porsche up to a door and jumping it through a keyhole. I mean it.

Deform Primitives

The process starts with the primitives panel. Along the right-hand side are some strange looking Deform Primitives: A plane, a cylinder, a cube. These unique objects do not render, but in every other way they are identical to an object selected with the Volume Deform tool mentioned above. You can click outside and draw your mouse to increase the number of outlines, and so on. In fact, when you pop one up, you automatically get the Deformation Navigation panel you already know about. There is an interesting and useful difference though. As you increase the number of control outlines, the object automatically subdivides optimally to keep it flexible. Remember you can jump back and forth between the whole object navigation controls on the main bar and the similar object deformation controls in the panel (Twist, Stretch, and Push/Pull) for fast modeling.

You associate the Deform Object with a standard object using an icon with the formidable name Start Deforming by Stand-Alone Deform Primitive. From then on, whenever the standard object is placed within the bounds of the Deform Object, its shape will be appropriately deformed as well — if you have subdivided the standard object appropriately.

If you pop up a single polygon plane and try to make waves in it by attaching it to a Deformation Plane shaped like waves, it's not going to happen. Single polygons do not bend. You can only bend objects at the junction of polygons. First set the resolution (right click), on the Plane tool to, say, 80–100. This will give you a finely divided plane with thousands of polygons. The plane can then bend at each polygon to conform to the Deformation Object. This is particularly important because Dynamic Divide is not available in Stand-Alone Mode.

You might wonder why not just deform the original object. There are several advantages to the Stand-Alone Deform Object approach. One, you can save a deform object with its animation sequence for use with other objects. In character animation this can save you a lot of time. It's often useful in character animation to give your lead character a few signature moves. Let's say your character has a special nose wiggle; you can save it and apply it over and over again and get exactly the right movement every time.

This is a simple experiment to give you a visual on what the heck I'm talking about. You'll pop up a Deformation Pipe, deform it, pop a sphere, and run it through the pipe. Simple, but you'll see how powerful this can be.

Start a new Scene in Front View, World Coordinates. Select Primitives Library ➪ Deformation Pipe ➪ Sphere ➪ Smooth Quad Divide. Move the sphere up away from the Pipe by left clicking.

Select Deform Nav panel ➪ Stretch ➪ Green line in the center of the pipe. Reduce the pipe's central diameter to about one-fourth original size so it looks a little like an egg holder, as shown in Figure 7-12.

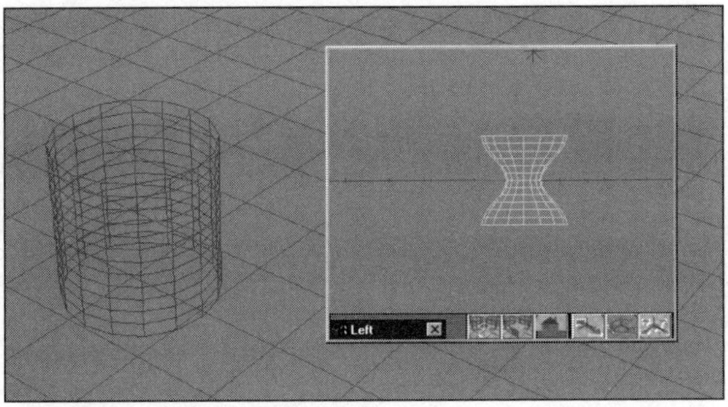

Figure 7-12: The Deformation Pipe is ready to be shaped and shows the center cinched (inset).

Switch to the Main Tool Bar's Object Scale tool and scale up the pipe a smidgen. You want it to be just slightly larger than the ball because if any portion of the ball is outside the pipe, it will tear and look goofy. Good. Now for grins, move the ball down through the object. Nothing happens. That's proper, because we have not yet established a relationship between the ball and the pipe. Do that as follows:

Select the ball ➪ Local Deformation Icon on the control bar ➪ Hold Slide up to the now famous Start Deforming by Stand-Alone Deformation Object icon.

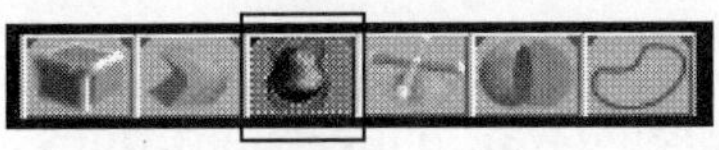

Now let go. Now click on the egg cup. Nothing appears to happen, but it does. Repeat your previous move. As the ball approaches the pipe all is as it was. But as soon as it starts to enter the pipe, the ball turns into silly putty and squeezes down through the tight center and reconstitutes itself on the bottom side. (See Figure 7-13.) Kuel, eh?

POWER TIP

You can use this same technique on complex objects — a spaceship going through a space warp, Rubber Man exiting his car through the air vent, or simulating a blob of liquid gold dripping into your name logo. Remember, you can stretch the Deformation Object into a long, curved pipe if you like. You can even put the Deform Pipe inside a semitransparent glass pipe to make an interesting flowing liquid or gas display.

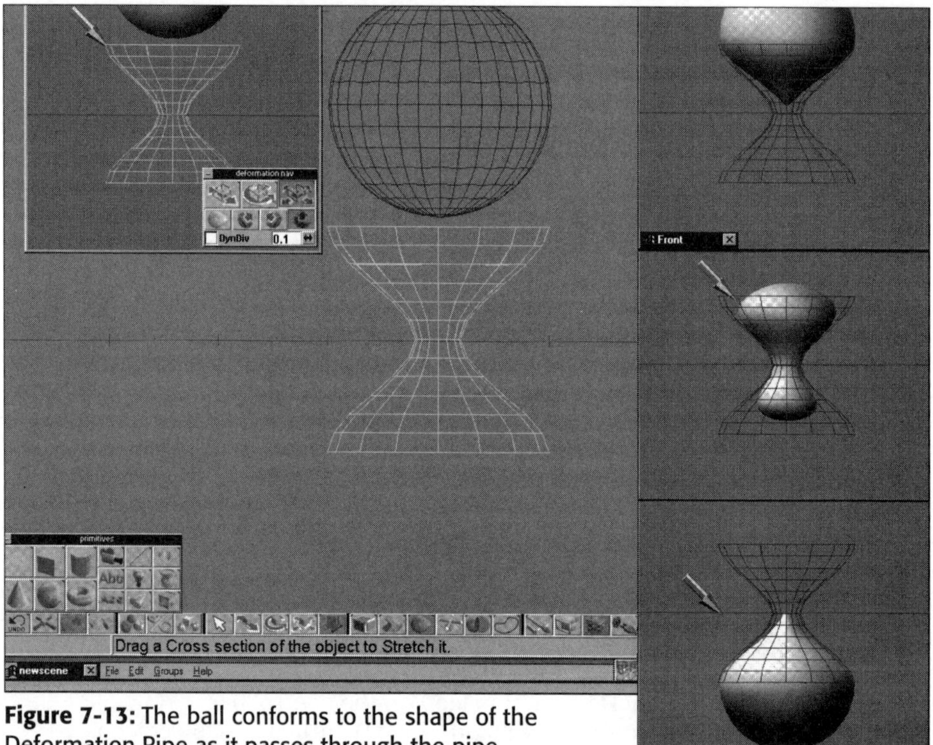

Figure 7-13: The ball conforms to the shape of the Deformation Pipe as it passes through the pipe.

Each of the three Deform Objects works in the same way, but each provides a different range of shapes. Remember that the deformations are animatable so you can have a pipe with waves pulsing down its length or a cube changing shape to music. Copy it several times, offset the timing by a frame or two, and have a whole stage full of dancing pickles. In fact, you can make many different standard objects dance using the same Deformation Object. Can motion capture be far away, Caligari?

Summary

If your imagination didn't distract you too much while reading this chapter, you learned:

✦ How to sculpt a crazy animatable character using just three spheres, the object deform tool, and a 3D Boolean. We even gave him nernie teeth made by creating a 2D polygon in the shape of teeth and then extruding it.

✦ How to give a stiff wireframe model a life-like shape by deforming it using the Object Deform tool. In this case it was a Styrofoam-looking shark that we molded into a life-like position. This will help you later when you animate smooth, life-like organic movements.

✦ How to twist a shark's tail while keeping your fingers intact. Cozumel is not the place to twist a shark's tail, tS2 is. With the Object Deform tool you can twist as well as bend.

✦ How to create an underwater scene effect. Using green fog and a sandy sea bottom you can make a credible environment for your shark.

✦ How to squeeze a big ball through a little opening using stand-alone deformation. The invisible objects make your object conform to their shape as it passes through. In the example, we push a golf ball down through an hourglass' narrow neck.

✦ And of course, how to make a pickle dance by putting a pickle object inside an object deformation cylinder that has the dance animation attached to it.

✦ ✦ ✦

CHAPTER 8

Object Hierarchies

✦ ✦ ✦ ✦

In This Chapter

The anatomy of complex objects

The joys of virtual glue, by brand

Hierarchy navigation

Manipulating sub-objects within a hierarchy

✦ ✦ ✦ ✦

Complex 3D models, like your typical government, are arranged in hierarchies that no one really understands. They can be made up of sub-objects glued in all sorts of arrangements. Sub-objects can be glued into clusters and clusters can be glued together to form a meta-hierarchy. Yet each sub-object can be handled as a unique object *if you can get to it*. There's the trick — navigating through a complex hierarchy in tS2 can be like climbing the Alps at midnight knee deep in mud. I'll try to clarify the process as much as possible, but if you remain confused, you're not alone. Fortunately the system works reasonably well even if you don't understand the underpinnings.

POWER TIP

By the time this book is published, Rob Bryerton (Exploder) should have an application written that will, among other things, show you what the hierarchy looks like. The information on how to contact him is packed with Exploder on the CD-ROM.

You need to learn these basics; they're essential to building complex object animations. Animation behavior of sub-objects is determined by three things: the brand of glue (there are only two), position in hierarchy, and location of axis. You can have an object physically separated from the main object and still be within its hierarchy. This is useful in animating the complex orbits of moons, for example. Visualize the planet orbiting its star while the moon orbits the planet *and* the star. Without hierarchies this would be pretty tough to animate. It looks cool. I'll show you how a little later in the book, so keep reading.

To be redundant, the hierarchy model is definitely one of the klunkier aspects of trueSpace2. Rumor has it that an Eastern European programmer from a dysfunctional family is responsible. It amazes me that Caligari conceptualized the much-emulated and best, by far, 3D interface I've seen, then put in a confusing hierarchy navigation system. Phew, that's out of my system. You'll use it often, so learn it. You'll forgive Caligari because this is one of only a few minor klunkers in a mighty fine machine.

Complex Objects and Their Substructure

✦ That space tanker you built a few days ago is an example of a complex object. It's made up of clusters of items glued together and then glued to the whole at different levels. That is a reasonably haphazard example. Try to navigate around in it and see what I mean. The Glue tool has three components:

- Glue as Sibling

- Glue as Child

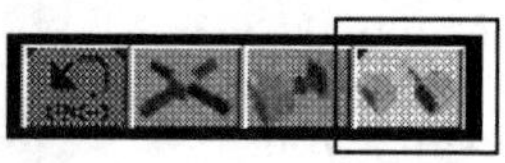

- Unglue

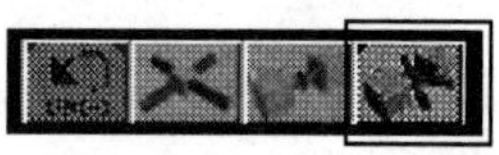

A number of trueSpace2 Frequently Asked Questions (FAQs) have to do with what this all means. The manual gives an abstruse discussion of symbolic nodes which I never did understand. I don't know what a symbolic node is — well, it's a placeholder, but I don't know what that is either. So forget the manual for the time being. trueSpace2 hierarchies are complicated by the terminology of Child and Sibling. It's a close analogy but different enough to confuse. To really understand hierarchy navigation, you have to experiment.

A Practical Guide to Gluing

I use Glue-as-Sibling nearly all the time. I still don't fully understand the Parent-Child relationship, but I find the sibling relationships, properly established, more cooperative.

You'll learn more about gluing for articulated animation later. I-Wei Huang, chief animator at Caligari, shows us how to use Parent-Child glue to articulate and animate the neat I-Wei robot provided by Caligari on the CD-ROM. Also check out I-Wei's remarkable animations of a robot race, karate guys, and two chameleons trying to shag a fly (\movies\optic\ani.avi). This is all in the way of motivating you to keep reading this tome. There is much fantastic stuff to come.

Cooperative is a relative term. When gluing items or clusters together, it is assumed the axis of the unit was active at the time of gluing. Bear this in mind when positioning complex objects. If the two axes were far apart, the object losing its axis may behave in unexpected ways because of its now distant axis. To remedy this, isolate the sub-object and engage the Move-Axis-to-Center-of-Object tool variant of the Axis tools. This centers the axis between the two sub-objects, yielding symmetrical rotation and animation behaviors.

Let's glue some balls together as siblings, then navigate to each in turn. With only four balls, it can get confusing if you glue them together randomly. So four it is. Carefully pop up balls one at a time and glue them into a cluster. Be sure you *always* have the main cluster active when gluing a newcomer to the pack. We do *not* want the newcomer active when you invoke Glue-as-Sibling. This will keep the order simple and the axis centered in the main cluster. Whichever object is selected first in the glue operation (and this bears repeating) retains the overall axis.

Pop up two balls, separate them, and glue one to the other. Both turn white, indicating that we now have a single complex object. Pop another ball. It is selected, so click on the double ball to switch the selection to it. Easy so far. Now glue the new ball to the cluster as a sibling. Pop up a fourth ball ➪ select the cluster ➪ glue new ball as sibling. You now have a cluster to navigate. There is no parent here, only brothers and sisters. All equal. So to get to each in turn you can enter the hierarchy by clicking the down arrow on the Main Bar (alternatively the down arrow key).

All the balls turn orange except for the very first kid. She's selected, as shown in Figure 8-1. Since they're all on the same level, you access them by traversing the group laterally, that is, by using the *left or right* keyboard arrows. This will make each ball active in turn. There are only two levels in this example: whole object and the siblings level.

It's undocumented, but you can pop up four balls at once by clicking the Sphere Primitive four times. Move each copy to the left or right to expose the underlying ball. The trick is that the last two are invisible. Fear not, they are there. Simply click in the empty space at the origin and the next ball will appear. Move it aside and repeat. This way you can glue them all as siblings in one operation.

When you reach a specific object in a cluster, you can manipulate it as if it were a separate item. For grins, navigate to a sibling ball, rescale, and paint it a different color. Use your keyboard up arrow to get to the top. Click Render Object and notice your complex object is whole again with the scaled ball still scaled and a different color. Easy.

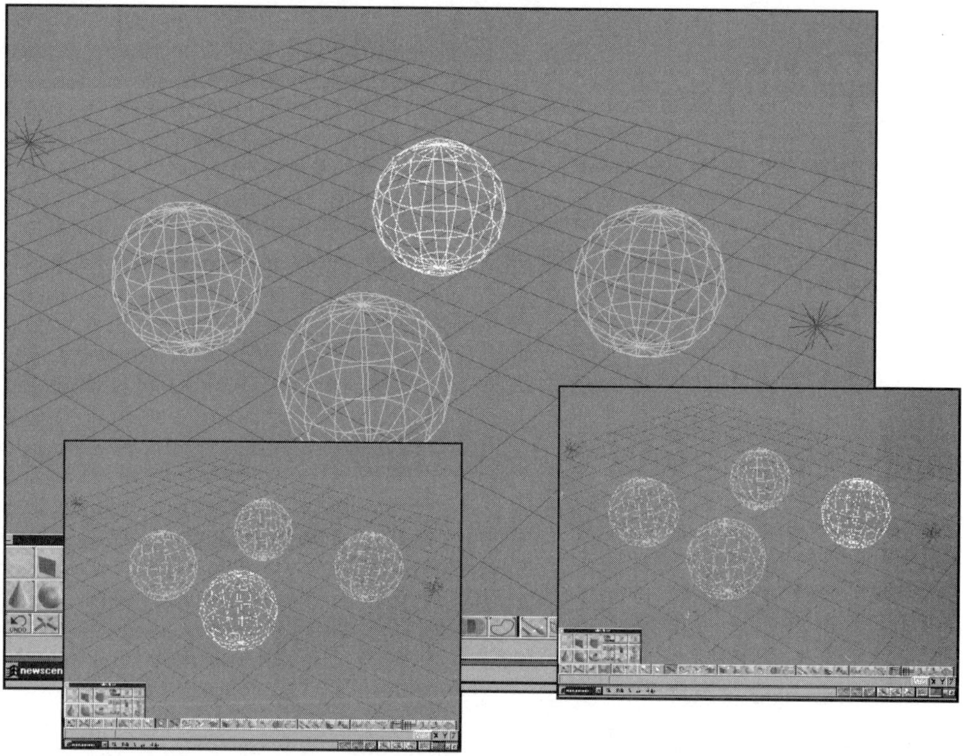

Figure 8-1: Down arrow was pressed, hierarchy entered, and one ball selected. Insets show effect of successive right arrow clicks.

Here's the beginning of confusion. New balls pop up selected. It's easy to forget to reselect the cluster before gluing. Let's see what happens in this case. Clear your work space and pop up two fresh balls. Glue them together. Now pop up a third ball. It comes up selected, so just glue the other two to it. Repeat with the fourth ball, again gluing the three-cluster to it. Theoretically, since they are all glued as siblings, they should all be at the same level. No such luck.

When you hit the down arrow, it looks okay, three orange balls and one selected. But when you try to reach the other individual balls, using left and right arrow keys, it's no go. You get either the three selected or the single. It turns out this is more of a parental arrangement, or certainly sibling rivalry. You can get to other siblings, but you have to hit the down arrow and then move right or left, then hit the down arrow again. In this arrangement, one ball is at the top, each of the others is situated one level down from the last. The first ball ends up on the bottom. (See Figure 8-2, right.)

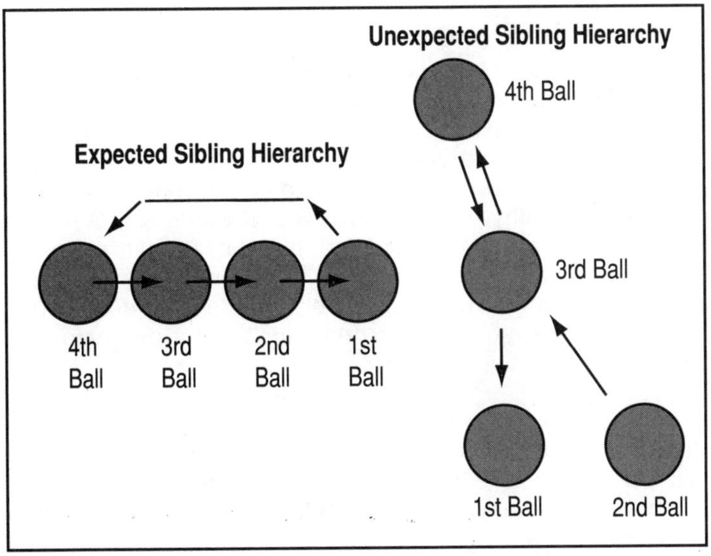

Figure 8-2: Expected Sibling Hierarchy is derived by always selecting the cluster before gluing a new sibling. Unexpected Sibling Hierarchy is derived by selecting the new sibling before gluing to cluster.

CAUTION

This is not the hierarchy you should get as advertised in the manual, so be careful. Always select the cluster object before gluing if you want good sibling relationships.

POWER TIP

It's easier to join items at the same level if you have them all laid out and just select them each in order — like we did with the radial detail in the space tanker. That way when you navigate to a cluster of radial detail, you go around the circle of parts easily with the left/right arrow keys.

Glue-as-Child

Let's repeat the experiment using your Glue-as-Child tool. Pop up two balls and glue one to the other as a child. Pop up another ball, select the cluster, and glue the new ball to it. Repeat. You'll have a cluster of four balls as before. Click the down arrow icon to enter the hierarchy. It all looks the same as before — one ball selected, the others orange. But now when you try to select the next ball with the right arrow key, you get three. Right arrow key will toggle you back and forth between one and three balls selected instead of going around to each in turn. To progress you must use right arrow to select the cluster of three, hit the down arrow or icon to select one of them. Now you'll have a new ball selected and the other three orange. To get to the next ball you again select the cluster (now two) with a lateral arrow, then down again to the bottom. A lot of work to say the least. Unlike with Glue-as-Sibling, reversing the process seems to make no difference. This Parent-Child relationship is useful when you articulate robots and other objects.

Glue Cluster-to-Cluster

You now have two clusters of four balls (words are so confusing so follow the pictures). Select the sibling cluster ➪ down arrow ➪ right arrow ➪ right arrow. You'll have one of the balls selected and the other three orange. Glue the entire parental cluster to this ball as a child. Now we get to navigate a really complex object. Click the up arrow to the top and all balls should be white. Now click the down arrow to enter the hierarchy. You are actually in the sibling group as before and you can navigate around from ball to ball with just the lateral arrows. When you get to the second ball on the right, you find it is selected along with all of its children. You can go right past it to the next ball or you can drop down into that hierarchy branch. I'm sure you know what to do at this point. Down arrow ➪ right arrow ➪ down arrow ➪ right arrow and so on.

So when you glue one hierarchy to another, they remain intact. You just have to remember to drop down into the new branch and check it out. Try the right arrow thing and if you get nowhere, you're in a parental array. Continue on by alternating down and lateral moves. At each level, test for siblings with the right arrow key.

POWER TIP

If you have diagonal arrows on your keyboard, they make navigation easier. Each diagonal arrow represents one vertical and one lateral arrow. Thus, using the lower right arrow moves you right around the cluster. The down click is ignored after the first one. The upper right arrow will take you back to the top.

This all seems complicated and confusing as hell, but in actual practice, you can pretty much use the two interchangeably. I know one successful professional who does just that. You have to pay attention though, if you want to animate a sub-part in relation to the whole. It seems that in the child role, an object moves independently of the parent, whereas siblings move in relationship to each other. More on this in Animation.

Detaching an Object From a Group

Now that you can navigate through a complex object, you are empowered to disassemble it. Sounds dangerous. As soon as you have isolated a part you want you can treat it as a separate item. You can save it as an individual object, for example, or paint it or move it. You can also remove it by invoking the Unglue tool.

You can remove clusters of objects as well. This is handy for revising very complex structures that you don't want to rebuild from scratch. Install new windows, rebuild the plasma generator. Replace the tires with snow treads.

Plantec's Rules for 3D Hierarchical Mucilaginy

These rules are hard and fast and therefore shatter when they hit the exception. But for most things they ride pretty well.

- When gluing two objects together, select the one with the most desirable axis as the principal (active) object. The axis remains with the active object after gluing.
- You cannot move an axis after you animate an object, so adjust all sub-object axes *before* animating!
- Always glue a sibling to the larger group, never the other way around.
- Cluster related parts as siblings on the same level of the hierarchy so you can reach them with left/right arrow keys.
- Rotate individual sub-objects by isolating them in the hierarchy and rotating on their local axes.
- If you isolate a cluster of sub-objects, the local axis will be the one owned by the active object when the cluster was assembled.
- To get more predictable rotation for the whole, you can relocate a group's axis to the center using the Normalize Location tool (which should have been called the Move-Axis-to-Origin tool). Individual local axes will not be affected.
- Sibling groups are easier to navigate than Parent-Child groups (it's been that way since the dawn of time).
- Cluster related items in sibling groups and attach them to the main object in a logical manner — for example, attach motor parts to the motor, not the fuselage. That way, you navigate to the part cluster and then just move laterally to get the part you want.
- You can attach two or more groups of siblings as siblings. This allows more lateral (read easier) navigation.
- Glue as siblings when you want to animate one sub-object with motion relative to the whole — for example, a torpedo moving through water with its propeller spinning. The prop is spinning on its local axis, while moving relative to the torpedo's axis.
- The main reason to worry about which brand of glue to use and in which order you glue pieces has mostly to do with the ease of moving around inside the hierarchy. If you screw up, it probably only means you have to hit the down arrow a few extra times. Big deal.

With these concepts in mind you'll do fine most of the time. Don't forget to check out I-Wei's robot later in the book. The way he explains it, Parent-Child relationships can work out after all.

Summary

In this chapter you learned that Caligari had a lapse of brilliance while designing its methodology for dealing with hierarchies, but it all works in its fashion. Key issues were:

- There are two types of glue, Sibling and Parent-Child. They are interchangeable for the most part except when creating articulated motion.
- You use glue to join objects together into a complex object and the two glues connect the objects differently.
- The axis of a glued object stays with the first object selected
- Each sub-object in a complex hierarchy retains its own axis, hidden until you navigate to it and expose it with the Axis tool. You can rearrange individual sub-axes within a complex object this way.
- Clusters can be glued to clusters at different levels in the hierarchy, forming their own little sub-hierarchies.
- You learned how to navigate hierarchies using the keyboard arrows.
- You learned that gluing is a pain, but you're going to figure it out because it's important and worth the time.
- Last, but not least, you learned my fragile rules of gluing to guide you through the lonely hours when there's nobody online to tell you how to do it.

✦ ✦ ✦

P A R T

III

The Art of Surface Design

You can give images a 3D look and photorealistic — or surrealistic — quality by wrapping shaded or lighted textures around objects. Texture maps are simply photos or drawings of surfaces that you map onto virtual surfaces. Designing 3D surfaces is an exciting new art form. In this section, you learn the process of designing surfaces, and get some special tips and techniques from experts in the field.

✦ ✦ ✦ ✦

In This Part

✦ ✦ ✦ ✦

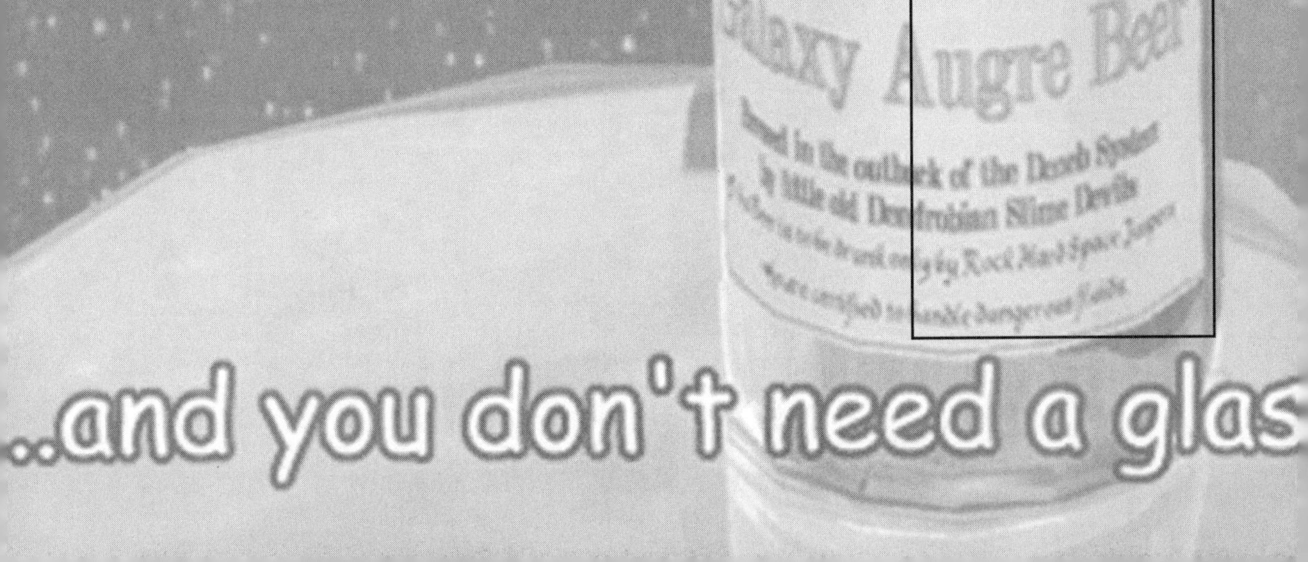

CHAPTER 9

Foreign Objects in Your System

✦ ✦ ✦ ✦

In This Chapter

How to import files using universal DXF format

Importing files from the major suites: WaveFront, LightWave, 3D Studio, and others

Importing PostScript files for extrusion

Where to find hundreds of usable 3D models on the Internet

Using online services and resources

✦ ✦ ✦ ✦

Some say it's cheating. I say it's legitimate unless you're just being toad lazy. Collecting and recycling objects built by others can become an obsession like typefaces or comic books.

Objects from Elsewhere

There are probably thousands of free objects around, but you can spend up to thousands of dollars for a single one. Depends on your situation. If you're in production and you don't have the time to build it, by all means buy or borrow it. I find importing prebuilt objects is particularly helpful when I'm building a complex scene but I don't feel like modeling every little detail like the desk lamp or the computer, and so on. These are common items, and many are on the trueClips CD-ROM that's included with the complete packaged tS2 product.

The problem is that not all models are created equal and they import differently. The trueClip models that ship with trueSpace2 were actually made in an entirely different format and you may experience problems with them. For example, some whole rooms are a single object with no logical subdivision. Some people have tried slicing off sub-objects with poor results.

Nevertheless, trueSpace2 can use a remarkable variety of object formats with a little tweaking. I'm going to clarify and simplify the process as much as I can for you.

Popular File Formats

There are a number of common 3D object formats, each containing the information needed by trueSpace2 to import the object intact. There are also public domain conversion programs you can convert some of the more esoteric formats with — into a format trueSpace2 can read. Let's begin with the formats trueSpace2 imports directly.

.DXF

Unfortunately the universal cross-platform 3D object transport format is DXF. It's a powerful format originally designed by AutoDesk for 2D CAD objects and later updated to handle 3D objects. The unfortunate part is that it's an antique from the old days of AutoCad. DXF is cumbersome, and complex objects require huge files. trueSpace2 can take all lunchtime to parse them. The good news is that almost every 3D program in the cosmos can import DXF files and many including trueSpace2 can export them. This means you can build an object with tS2's excellent modeler, save it in DXF, then transfer it into LightWave or even Alias/WaveFront modules as part of a high-end project.

A number of standard DXF conventions and options are not supported under trueSpace 2.0, including text, zero width lines, extrusion vectors, bulges in polylines, polyarcs, 3D lines, traces, shapes, and types. Don't worry if you don't know what these are, I don't either. If it imports okay — and most will — fine. If not, look for a 3DS file of the same name or try a public domain converter.

When you import a DXF file you get a DXF Import Settings panel in which you set up the way trueSpace2 will handle the incoming file.

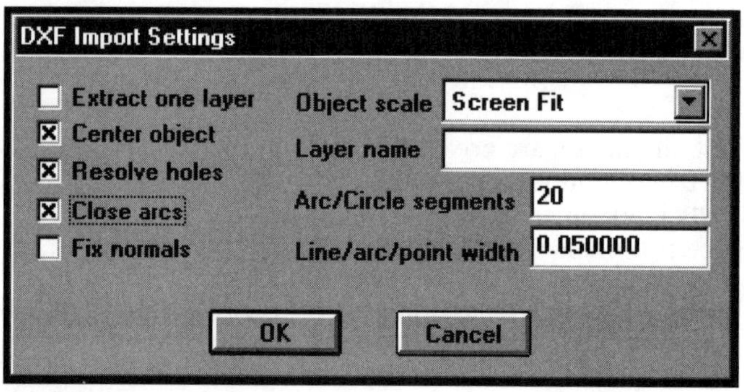

Extract One Layer

If you are familiar with the DXF file of choice, you can import only a portion of it via layers. You have to know the layer name and type it into the Layer Name field. There are usually objects which are not layer-specific. These are always imported, which works out well most of the time. Each layer is imported as a single object.

Center Object

If you don't check this, your object is likely to materialize out of sight and you have to find it with the Look-at-Current-Object tool, then you have to navigate it to the origin. Always check this one. I don't even think it should be an option, straight automatic. But then I may not know something the big boys know about esoteric uses for noncentered DXF files. What it actually does is center an incoming object's axis at coordinates 0, 0, 0, as you might expect.

Resolve Holes

This applies to CorelDraw 2D DXFs where a filled white polygon is defined as a hole. If you are importing such, by all means use it.

Close Arcs

trueSpace2 is not happy with straight lines. In fact, all unconnected lines in tS2 are actually long skinny polygons. Some 3D formats like LightWave's .obj files support open arcs, single lines, and other unacceptable entities. Close Arcs, when invoked, will neatly draw a skinny filled polygon along the outside edge of the arc and return down its center. You'll never know it's a poly.

So if you get messages, or it's pretty clear that lines and arcs are lurking about, select Close Arcs. I usually do, because I never know what the heck I'm importing until I see it.

Fix Normals

You have to know what normals are if you want them fixed. The Normal vector is an imaginary line perpendicular to the face of each polygon, *pointing outwards*. If you get an object with reversed normals it appears inside out when rendered or in 3DR. Also, if a polygon is only painted on its face, reversing it hides the surface texture.

That said, Fix Normals reverses all the polygons in an object as it is imported. I never use this unless the object clearly looks inverted.

Object Scale

DXF objects are often very large in comparison to your screen. If you don't scale them you could end up looking at the corner of a doorknob. You get an options field from which to select one of nine different measuring systems (millimeters, centimeters, meters, kilometers, inches, feet, yards, miles, points), and Fit-to-Screen or None. I have not tried None — nor will I ever try it. I'm afraid of the potentially ensuing chaos.

If you are familiar with a DXF file, you might as well set the scale to your work space. Just check the OPP for it. I personally leave this option on Fit to Screen. That way I can see what it looks like and resize if I need to. It's an individual preference.

Arc/Circle Segments

This applies to something called polycine entities found in some DXF files. They have to be parsed. I'm no expert on them. I understand the default setting of 20 rarely needs to be changed and that it sets the resolution of circles and arcs. I suspect this means a circle will be simulated by a 20-sided polygon. Don't quote me on it, and don't mess with the setting.

Line/Arc/Point Width

Coming from an art background I find this one a bit abstruse. The manual says it has something to do with converting from 2D to 3D. I suspect it really assigns 3D thickness to 2D polygons used to simulate lines, arcs, and points. I leave it at default all the time and have never had a problem. Play with it if you want to know more.

That's it. When you select a DXF file, trueSpace2 automatically brings up the panel, you don't even have to go looking for it. In most cases all you do is click on Fit-to-Screen and then go have a cup of coffee while the file dribbles in. At least once you'll think your machine has hung (indeed that *is* possible) but it's just aggravating over the DXF file. It brings the file in bit by byte and parses it into understandable format. You'll get messages on the information panel as it progresses. But you could literally spend 20 minutes or more parsing the quarter megabyte ncc1701.dxf, available from Avalon. Check your drive light, it should be blipping on about once every 30 seconds or so. Don't blink, or you'll never see it.

.3DS Files

Autodesk has donated many wonderful gifts into the public domain. This is one — an excellent binary 3D file format. Autodesk also provides us with useful mini-apps like Flic players and Flic editor for windows, gratis. As parents of 3D Studio, AutoDesk brought the first serious professional 3D suite to the PC. That's a controversial statement, but it's my opinion. 3DS files are the format used by 3D Studio and many other programs. IMHO, 3DS files are far more efficient than DXF. They load faster and carry more relevant information.

When you load a 3DS file you'll get the universal Object Import Settings panel, where there are only three settings:

Object Unit Scale

This is identical to the Scale in DXF. I leave it set at Fit-to-Screen.

Center Object

Again, the same as DXF. It puts the object at the origin. Leave this box checked as well.

Fix Normals

Don't click this one unless you need it. Remember, if an object renders inside out, delete it and reimport it invoking Fix-Normals. Alternatively, try using the Flip Normals icon.

When trueSpace2 parses the 3DS file, it separates objects into sub-objects of a single parent. 3DS files have all sorts of inherent additional information, like lighting, camera angles and paths, animation, and so on. In addition, 3DS objects have their own hierarchies, which may include information that trueSpace2 simply doesn't understand. No problem. The original hierarchies are not maintained, cameras, lights, and paths are not imported, as they would likely screw up your existing work space anyway. The assumption is, you want only the object, not its entire history, of which you know nothing. I mean it could have been anywhere, done anything. You don't need to get involved.

One thing trueSpace2 does do, is give you an idea of the color scheme of this object. It interprets the Diffuse color channel for each poly and applies it with an autofaceted surface. Texture map coordinates are preserved and, if the texture map is around, either in the subdirectory where the 3DS is located, or pointed to by your 3DS.set file, it is applied. Unless you have 3D Studio installed, you don't have a 3DS.set file. I didn't know that and searched my 3 gigs of cluttered disk real estate in vain for a long time. Then, I actually installed 3D Studio and suddenly textures were being found and applied. It's nice.

.ASC Files

As with trueSpace2, 3D Studio has both binary and ASCII file formats. By nature ASCII formats are more cumbersome, but far more accessible. You can actually print them out and figure out what they do. If you ever played with the POV raytracer, you are familiar with ASCII files. Unlike the tS2 ASCII format, this one carries less information than the binary. For example it does not preserve specific material information, just the names. The import filter randomly applies different shades of gray to these names and it's up to you to figure out what to put here. No big deal. Although it keeps track of separate objects, it has no hierarchy info, but apparently Caligari would not have converted it anyway (they didn't in 3DS, which does have it). Again, texture map coordinates are preserved, but you can change them once the object is in your work space.

.SOB Files

I've always been curious as to the *real* origin of that suffix. These are old Caligari 3D files from Amiga days. They are similar to .cob files. Object, hierarchy, and mapping coordinates are imported.

.LWB and .LWO Files

LightWave has several file extensions depending on the version in which it was created. I've discovered that, though it's not documented, tS2 can recognize and import LightWave 4.0 (.lwo) files as well as .iob files, even though they are not listed in the selection box. These files are all imported nicely, including information on smoothing, secularity, and color. Certain surface details and one or two point polygons are not imported. These are usually associated with special effects like hair and particle animation that tS2 can't use anyway.

LightWave files are important to you, because lots of high quality models are available on the Web. LightWave users are a fanatical bunch (I'm one myself), who have invested a lot of time learning their engine. They tend to be serious modelers who put out interesting space stuff as well as just about everything else you can think of. You can find everything from a Vorlon battle cruiser to Voyager out there. In addition there are CD-ROMs filled with LightWave objects available at reasonable prices. I scanned the LightWave Pro forum to keep my eyes open. It's a forum where top professional animators share their most interesting secrets. Reading it will help you start thinking like a pro. It also has great ideas that often translate well to tS2. Though you may eventually want to buy LightWave for its fabulous rendering engine, I find building things in tS2 is a lot easier, and less convoluted than building the same thing in LightWave.

.OBJ Files

One of the premiere high-end 3D suites — I'm talking mega expensive — is WaveFront, now Alias/WaveFront. This is strictly a professional, government, or student deal because nobody could afford it for home use. It runs on an SGI (Silicon Graphics) machine and has always been super-cumbersome to learn and use. The trade-off is that it's always been extremely powerful. Most of the neat special effects you'll be learning were invented by the WaveFront people. Consequently, many of the .obj files out there are very professional. Not all, mind you, but most. There are a lot of military related objects on the Internet and a good assortment of space, terrain, and general objects as well. As a side note, the merger of Alias and WaveFront with SGI has produced an interface that's much easier to use... kinda reminds me of trueSpace2. You'll notice Studio Max from Autodesk looks familiar as well.

LightWave files are very different from tS2 files, but with a little import filter magic you get to have the essential models in your workspace. One of the problems is that WaveFront uses an object grouping scheme that can run afoul of the hierarchy system. Thus, grouping information is not preserved in the translation. Also, color information in WaveFront is translated by name. Since the WaveFront artist could have his own set of colors, rather than a standard set, you could get strange colors on your model. Fortunately there are some conventional names. trueSpace2 parses the color names and tries to match them up with common color names and applies the appropriate hue where possible. It also attempts to convert transparency information.

I find that tS2 doesn't preserve the texture coordinates of WaveFront files. This is not a large problem as you can easily assign coordinates of choice once the object is imported.

.IOB Files

Imagine is probably the best DOS-based 3D program in an affordable price range. It comes with all sorts of powerful special effects, etc. I don't use it, though, because I'm strictly a Windows kinda guy. I'm not saying I even like Windows all that much, it's just that I prefer software available on Windows. And I like the interface. I just don't like the frequent crashes (yes, even in Windows 95).

I've found a lot of files in this format that aren't available in more common ones. I do have Imagine 3.0 and it comes with some neat models. They import well in the same manner as 3DS files. Again, Caligari ignores the hierarchy information and imports all sub-models as children under a single parent.

PostScript Files

PostScript is a 2D page description language developed by Adobe and it handles several flavors of file format. trueSpace2 can import most .ps .eps and .ai variations. Adobe Illustrator 88 format (.ai) has become a standard for vector file transport. If you use Adobe Illustrator, CorelDraw, Smart Sketch, or any of the Bezier/vector-oriented drawing programs, it probably can output an .ai file. While many programs import this format, it is capable of extremely accurate description of complex curves using mathematical vectors rather than bitmaps. Standard PostScript and Extended PostScript files are also widely available and are similar in structure to the ai files.

PostScript Settings

Caligari included PostScript import in this version because it's useful for transferring designs and logos for extrusion. In fact, it opens up the vast Corel clip art archives with nearly every logo known to man, immediately available to you for extrusion as a demo of your commercial viability. Think about doing a great Nike Swosh ad in 3D. 3D life suddenly got a lot easier with PS import, however, there is a problem, IMHO. I've yet to successfully import an .ai file. At first it wouldn't work because I'd removed Adobe Type Manager from my system, then it wouldn't load because it required unavailable resources, then just because there was an error. I suspect this part of the Import is not very useful as it looks like it imports an older version of .ai files. I admit I didn't try very hard to make it work; I don't have the time to mess with it and you probably don't either.

When you select a PS file you will get a special PostScript Settings panel automatically.

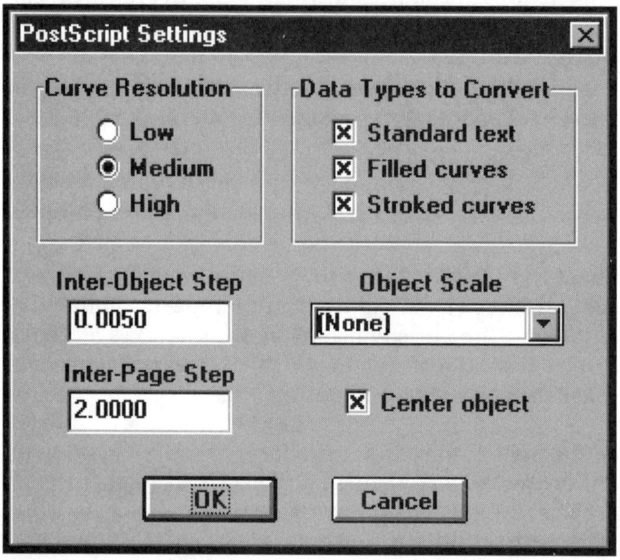

Curve Resolution

This sets the quality the filter will use when converting PS curves to tS2 polys. It's set up in three ranges, and with 95 percent of your work, leave it Low. This is more accurate than the name implies and uses less memory, manipulates, and renders more quickly. If you have to import small text or symbols at twelve points or less, increase the resolution.

Data Types to Convert

PostScript is a complex language as well as file format. It was designed to communicate directly with printers. It therefore may have all sorts of information you don't need. This option gives you an opportunity to specify:

- ✦ **Standard Text.** Many PostScript pages will have a lot of standard text that you're not interested in and a graphic that you are. Deselect this option and tS2 will ignore the text and import only the graphic. Of course if you want the text converted, by all means leave this option selected.
- ✦ **Filled Curves.** These are graphic elements that correspond to filled polygons or solid polys. Generally you do want these converted, so leave it clicked.
- ✦ **Stroked Curves.** This would be the equivalent of an arc segment, a line, or a closed line curve. These are imported by converting them to long, thin, curved polygons which run down the outside edge and return down the center of the curve. It works.

Inter-Object Step

This is kind of a neat deal. When set above zero, this option allows trueSpace2 to import each set of curves, characters, text, and such, in unique 3D layers (at different heights). The setting indicates the distance between layers. Bigger values exaggerate the distance between layers, which can create some cool special effects. Try importing a fancy brochure page with this setting at 0.5 and see what happens.

Inter-Page Step

PostScript documents are usually multi-page affairs. If you try to import a multi-page document, tS2 will attempt to separate inter-page elements. This setting determines how much space is inserted between elements of different pages. Each page will be encoded as a separate tS2 object as well. I admit I haven't fooled around with this so far, I don't see much use for importing several pages of PostScript into tS2. It must be my point of observation.

Center Object

This one's a little obvious. tS2 calculates where the center is for the PS objects and then places this spot at the origin. Use it to avoid chaos.

Public Domain Utilities

I won't go into detail here because it's likely to change as I type, but you can readily find many conversion utilities on the Internet. Look at the URLs (addresses) I've included in this chapter. Avalon in particular has a large collection of conversion utilities. Every once in a while you'll find an object, like a dragon, that only exists in some esoteric format. You may have to convert it to some less esoteric format and perhaps even convert that one, but eventually you'll be able to get most things to a format that trueSpace2 will accept. The one exception I've found is NURBS — Non-Uniform-Rational-B-Splines. This high-end format seems inconvertible to polygons at the moment. It's a shame, because that's where the dragons are. Look for files with names like asc2rib.exe (3DS ASCII file to RenderMan.rib files) or iob23ds.exe (Imagine to 3DS), they are usually pretty self-explanatory.

Web Resources

The World Wide Web is a stunning resource for 3D frame jockeys. Last time I scanned there were over 7,000 pages that had something to do with digital animation, most of it 3D. The Internet has always been a generous place where people share resources to create a more powerful whole. Even with the invasion of commercial interests, the Internet retains some of this kinder, gentler philosophy of public domain sharing.

trueSpace2 Home Pages

Hop on over to `http://www.caligari.com` for the Caligari trueSpace2 home pages. Here you'll find all sorts of goodies including the free upgrade patch to trueSpace2.01 which fixes more than 40 minor glitches, speeds up raytracing for a factor of 2 while decreasing memory requirements. It also makes modeling and animation more stable, fixing some of my complaints in the text. According to the latest, trueSpace2.5 will be released about the time this book is. It is a fully Windows 95 compatible (not compliant), 32-bit application. It will add many of the VRML goodies being developed for Fountain, including browsing, as well as some new and powerful modeling tools. trueSpace3 is scheduled for late 1996.

While you're visiting the Caligari Web site (`http://www.caligari.com`), check out the Inner Circle for software file and patches, or download Fountain, a Virtual Reality Modeling Language (VRML) authoring tool. Chapter 34 describes how to use Fountain.

Avalon

For many years, China Lake Naval Station was the kindly custodian of *Avalon*, the Internet repository for 3D objects (see Figure 9-1). The *Avalon* FTP site maintained donated items from all over the globe. You could find nearly everything from a LightWave nebula to a 3DS ankle bone. You still can. ViewPoint Datalabs, the world's major supplier of 3D geometry, has taken over administration of *Avalon*. They've spruced it up, and converted it to snazzy Web pages. The site is now much easier to navigate (see Figure 9-2). ViewPoint also has commercial props available that they charge for. Some can be expensive, but if it's what you need and you don't have the ability to model it yourself, it can keep you in business.

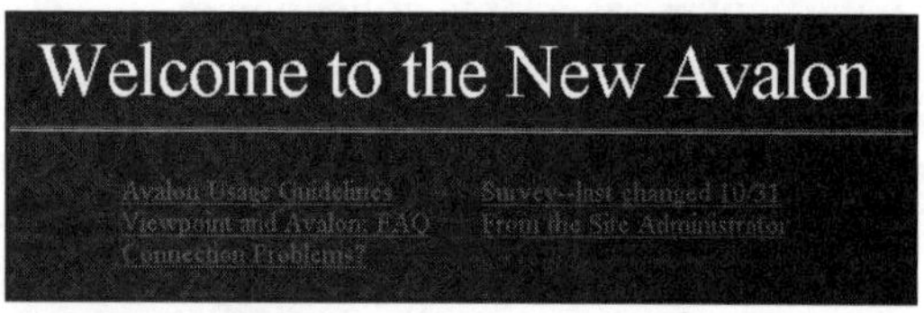

Figure 9-1: The *Avalon* Web pages link you to hundreds of free models.

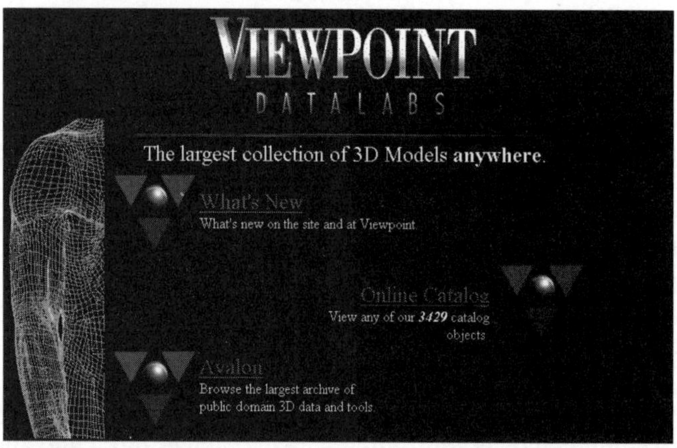

Figure 9-2: ViewPoint Datalabs home page, gateway to *Avalon*.

Actually ViewPoint has a great home page for 3D fans. It contains links to many other sites of interest, as well as their massive online catalog of 3D objects. ViewPoint is one of the key places Hollywood gets its 3D models from to create special effects, commercials, and so on. It's also one of the primary motion-capture studios in tinsel town.

Avalon will post your models as well. So if you have neat textures and/or models that you'd share with us, upload them to Avalon and become world famous within a fortnight.

Model Masters

Model Masters also has a Web page or two, as shown in Figure 9-3. Drop by some of these pages and give a howdy-thanks for donating models to our project.

Figure 9-3: Model Master's Web page

UK VR-SIG

From ViewPoint Datalabs Link page you can jump to a number of interesting places. Distance no longer is a factor, so check out the DFX models at UK VR-SIG (see Figure 9-4). This is a Web site whose main purpose is to collect and collate models that are polygon-limited specifically for Virtual Reality applications. They tend to have simple yet good looking structures.

Figure 9-4: You can download efficient DXF models from England at UK VR-SIG.

Polygon-limited models are not only useful for Virtual Reality, they make excellent items for distant placement in your scenes. For example, simple people, cars, or buildings in the background give you smaller, faster scene files that look absolutely as good as if you had used complex (read slow) models there.

If you take a Poly-limited model and apply the Smooth Quad Divide, you're likely to get a beautifully detailed complex model. A chunky lightbulb will become smooth and rounded. Try it.

Later on I'll tell you about Caligari's sister products to trueSpace2, such as Fountain and Pioneer, which use the tS2 interface you're becoming an expert in, to produce VRML worlds on the World Wide Web. VRML is the 3D language of the Web that allows you to build interactive multi-user worlds. It's pretty exciting. You actually enter real-time 3D environments, explore them, and meet fellow Web travelers along the way. Very Kuel. UK VR-SIG also has many objects which are specifically designed for VRML authoring suites as well as a range of interesting textures. Check it out.

Lycos

My favorite service is the Lycos index at Carnegie Tech, as shown in Figure 9-5. Developed by Michael Mauldin, an artificial intelligence wizard, it constantly scans the Web for new sites. When it finds one, it abstracts the content, puts it into a database, and will yield this information after a key word search. All you do is type in the subject of interest and let 'er rip. You'll most likely get the first ten of several thousand hits. If you used more than one key word, the first ten will be the most likely ones of interest. Lycos offers a search option that allows you to increase the number of hits displayed. I don't usually need it, but it's there.

Figure 9-5: The Lycos home page, where you can find the pages you want.

By now you are familiar with the Web, a hyperdimensional virtual environment with instant tele-transport to any of ten million locations around the world. It works via hyperlinks. These are sensitive color text or pictures called hot spots. When you click on a hot spot you're instantly transported to the page it's linked to. It could be anywhere in the world. The Web pages shown in this chapter are only a starting point for your 3D scavenger hunt. Each of them is hyperlinked to other pages which are in turn linked to even more pages. That's why it's called the Web. You could lose a lot of sleep in your quest for the end of these V-Space threads but it's worth the trip.

One constant about the Web is change. Most pages have a warning that they are under perpetual reconstruction. Pages come and pages go, mostly come. The number of 3D-oriented pages seems to be growing disproportionately on the high side. Fortunately there are several free services that can help you keep up.

The Lycos Web address is www.lycos.com. It's also on the Netscape Net Search page, which offers automatic access at the touch of an icon in Netscape. There are other search indexes there as well, including WebCrawler, InfoSeek, Yahoo, and CUSI in the UK.

CompuServe and AOL

CompuServe has an active trueSpace2 SIG (special interest group). That's where I met Rob Bryerton, author of Exploder. America Online used to have one, but it's been absorbed by the graphics group. In both cases, you can get a lot of help when you get stuck, and you'll find plenty of objects that you can download.

tSML

The trueSpace Mailing List (tSML) is a very active and helpful place for learning the fine points of tS2 as well as keeping up with the latest scoops on sister applications. It's generally a comfortable place where newbies are not only tolerated, but welcomed. I've watched people go from asking really dumb questions that were already in the FAQ section to giving spectacular advice and suggestions for creative new uses in a matter of weeks. To subscribe or unsubscribe, send a message with no subject or signature to truespace-request@caligari.com. That is, just e-mail with only the word "subscribe" in the body of the message. You'll start getting missives shortly. If you are a busy person who wants the digest version, you can check the Caligari home page to see how to get it. The digest version is easier to delete than 30 messages, which is fairly common. At times the message load gets pretty heavy. I understand the membership at the time of writing is now over 800 users.

Summary

It's always handy be in a multi-source situation. Since you were a kid, they've warned you about foreign objects. Keep them out of your body, they said. But foreign objects are handy in 3D. In this chapter we've talked about a bunch of ways to find and use foreign objects:

- ✦ Direct object importation via trueSpace2's built-in import filters gives you access to objects in 13 formats including: 3DStudio, LightWave, WaveFront, VideoScape, Imagine, AutoCad, and others.
- ✦ Use of public domain utilities to convert alien objects into one of tS2's loadable formats opens possibilities for importing just about any format.
- ✦ Sources of free foreign objects on the Internet include such places as *Avalon*, the trueSpace home page at Caligari, and others.
- ✦ You can use the Internet to find vast catalogs of commercial objects as well including places like ViewPoint Labs and ModelMasters.
- ✦ Ways to find new resources on the World Wide Web using search engines, especially Lycos, the engine that gives you an annotated menu of sites by key word.
- ✦ You learned how to become a member of the tSML (trueSpace Mailing List) family sharing your ideas with 800 other tS2 enthusiasts, and getting help in a relative instant for free.

✦ ✦ ✦

CHAPTER 10

Even More Neat Tools

✦ ✦ ✦ ✦

In This Chapter

The Tip tool

Macro Sweep

Lathe

Mirror

The Divide tool

Dimension markers

✦ ✦ ✦ ✦

If you're going to build universes, you need a lot of great tools. Here are some that will make life a lot easier when you're building complex items.

Sweeping Up

There are three more sweep tools related to the Extrude and Bevel tools you've been using. Tip, Macro Sweep, and Lathe are each useful for creating otherwise difficult shapes.

The Tip Tool

The Tip Tool is pretty simple. It does one thing, and does it very well. Using the same Properties panel as the Extrude tool, it extrudes to a point. If you have a flat circular polygon and extrude it with the Tip tool, you'll get a cone. Chapters ago I mentioned you can even make nernies by tip-extruding certain letters. I find that one way to use, say the letter Z, as a nernie is to tip-extrude it and set the point into another surface, as in Figure 10-1.

Experiment with the panel settings. Use your imagination to use this tool in creative ways.

Figure 10-1: This three-minute satellite uses one sphere, one cylinder, and eight Z nernies.

Macro Sweep

Macro Sweep extrudes a 2D shape along a path. It's called a Macro because you can record all sorts of movements along that path and apply them to other shapes at other times by saving the macro in your paths library. I mentioned that you could record the extrusion of a dead tree trunk — this is the tool that you'd use.

This is one of the less used, more powerful tools in tS2. Don't skimp on it, because it's going to save you a lot of time and effort. That means more money per person/effort/unit over time. Not a bad return for a few hours' experimentation. It can be frustrating to work with at first, because it doesn't always behave as advertised. But if you watch your axes and paths, you should do well.

Pipes

Remember when we made the fuel transfer pipes for the space tanker? We should have used Macro Sweep to make it — woulda been a lot easier. But then you wouldn't have learned about face manipulation. Following the procedure outlined in the manual, you'll get strange, unusable results with letters. For example, the O is likely to flip a 360 in the middle of the bend, turning the tube inside out. This has something arcane to do with the letter's axis.

Here's the procedure to save hours of trial and error. Pop up an O and use the Center Axis tool to pop the axis to the center of the letter.

There's a tool for almost everything in trueSpace2. You'll notice that the axis is visible and centered. The Expose Axis icon will hide it.

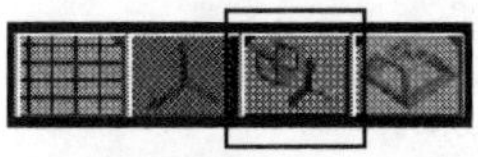

You need a sweep path, so, with any object selected (it doesn't matter what, we only want the path), create an open path using the Animation Path tool, in the shape you want the pipe to bend in. Pop up the Path Library tool,

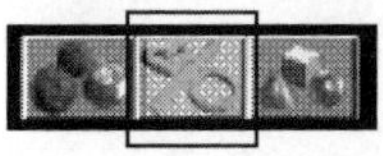

and save the path. It'll be entered into the library as anim. Rename it by typing `pipe1` in the upper left name window. Now click on the O with Macro Sweep and you'll see your new path attached to it along the Z axis. If not, just click pipe1 in the library. Right click the Path Sweep tool to get the Path Sweep options panel.

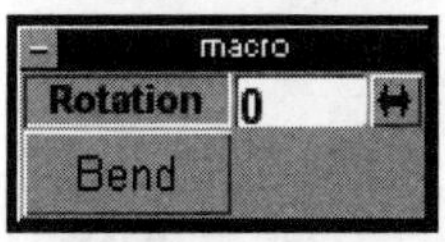

Engage Bend. Click a second time on the Path Sweep tool. It'll pause a beat, then sweep the O along the path, Z axis parallel to the path line. Bend rotates the O in bends, keeping its Z axis parallel with the path. This keeps your pipe from collapsing.

Save a few interesting lengths of bent pipe in your spaceship nernie library. They come in handy when adding detail. Remember, you can still stretch and scale these pipes to fit, using the Object Scale tool, so you only need a few basic shapes.

If you forget to use Bend, the O will be extruded along the path without rotating to stay perpendicular. This will give you a pipe with a flat mashed end as in Figure 10-2.

If you use vertical letters, the Z axis is different than if you use horizontal letters. This can lead to confusion, so always use one or the other to prevent headaches. Just make sure the Z axis of the letter is perpendicular to the direction you want it extruded.

You may have seen video shot from a camera rushing through a pipe, like through a blood vessel or subway tunnel. You can simulate this by saving the macro path and applying it to a camera so it can run down the pipe, exactly following the curves. Glue a light just ahead of the camera to light the way.

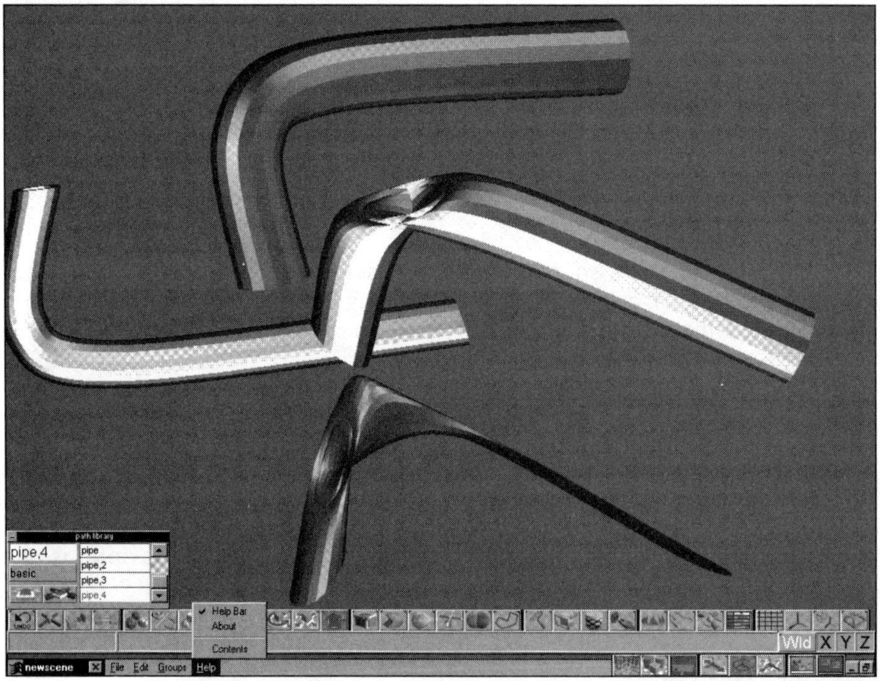

Figure 10-2: These examples show extruding the letter O along a curve to make a pipe.

Creating a Complex Macro

Here's another secret. You could have saved a macro when you built that complicated tree trunk. That way you could have built other trees, no two alike, because you started each with a different polygon. In fact, with as few as three different tree macros, you could build an entire forest in a half hour and nobody would know.

If you wanted to take the time, you could extrude a neat space vehicle fuselage and later make slightly different vehicles by macro-ing a different starting poly.

Lathe Tool

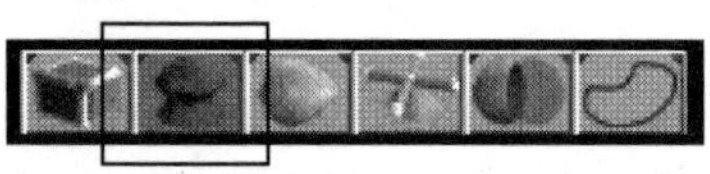

I used to love using the lathe in shop class. My teacher Mr. Hart had us turn all sorts of things from bowling pins to lamps and bowls. I'm glad I had that class because it gave me a feel for this electronic tool. It's almost exactly the same as the wood lathe. Mr. Hart would have us draw out a profile template of an object before turning. We'd constantly check our work against the template until it was perfect. Of course if you took off too much, there was nothing to do but revise your template or start over.

No such problems in 3D lathing. This is a standard tool in nearly all 3D packages, but trueSpace2 gives you a few fancy extras like a 3D spiral jig and very fast 3D setup controls. Lathe has five parameters you can manipulate:

- Segments
- Angle
- Radius
- Rotation
- Helix

Each of these parameters can cause wild differences in how the final object will look. We need a credible space station for our Universe, and this is the tool we'll use to build it in a flash. But first, the essentials.

Segments

Unlike turning on a wood lathe, 3D is done in segments. If you have few segments, they show as faceted surfaces (picture an octagonal donut). If you want this effect, highlight it by surfacing your object with faceted material. This gives a crisp edge to each segment. If you want a smooth look, increase segments to 20–40 or even more, depending on how close the camera will come. Then surface with smooth material. It will actively attempt to hide whatever segments might show.

It's Interactive

You can vary the number of segments interactively once you've selected a polygon to lathe. The tool sets up some green and white lines with a cross bar. Grab the white one and drag left or right. Right adds segments (you can watch it) and left removes them. Easy, otherwise you can just input number of segments in the options panel.

Angle

With the Lathe tool, you can turn less than a full circle. You can turn only part of an arc by setting an Angle of less than 360°, or more if you're making a helix. If you want to lathe a fancy arch for the top of a doorway, set Angle to 180° and sweep half a circle. You can make some pretty fancy architectural pieces this way. For a space station we'll want a full 360° rotation. Normally you can only set this option between 0 and 360°. When you engage the Helix option you can set it as high as you need. Each 360° equals one rotation of the helix and there is a helix offset amount. If you need a three inch long helix, simply divide the helix offset in inches into the three inches and multiply the result by 360 to get the rotation angle you need.

Radius

This option sets the radius of the circle made by the outer edge of the polygon and the center of rotation. If the radius is very small, the piece rotates as a solid, if it is larger than the diameter of the piece, you get a torus-like extrusion.

Radius can be set interactively in an instant by grabbing the crossbeam center point and pulling. You can adjust both radius and rotation at the same time by grabbing the middle of the crossbar and moving your mouse around. It's pretty obvious what's happening. (See Figure 10-3.)

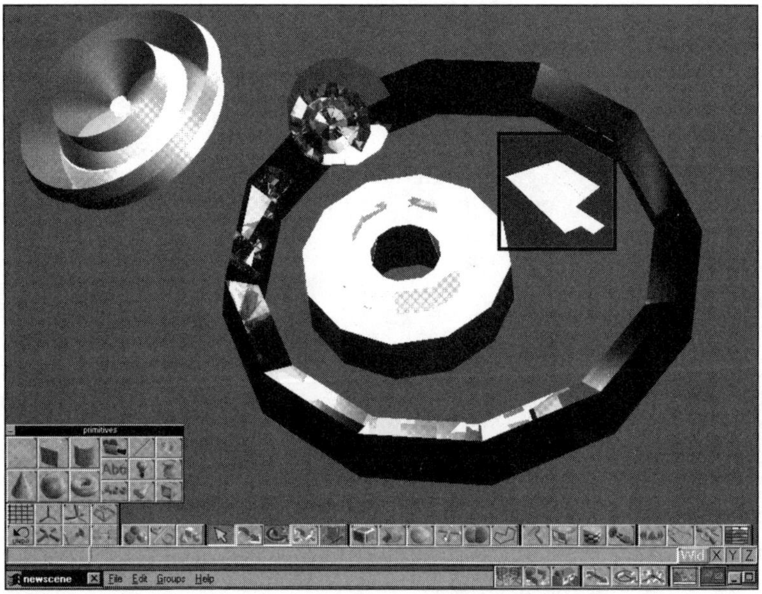

Figure 10-3: Each of these shapes was lathed from the flat poly on the floor, changing only the radius and the angle of rotation.

Rotation

A little tricky to explain, Rotation changes the angle of the path to the polygon from the center of rotation. This means you can take an oddly shaped poly and lathe it from different angles to get a variety of shapes. Picture it this way: You glue a polygon to the table and tack a string to the center of its axes. Pull the string taught over your thumbnail, and rotate it around the polygon, parallel with the table. Now imagine that when it's lathed it will be rotated perpendicular to the table. You can let out more string or pull in to make it shorter and change the radius of rotation. Imagine what that polygon would look like as a solid turning. I hope that helps.

In any case, experiment. Make an irregular polygon, click the Lathe tool, and grab the crossbar. As you move it around you'll see what I mean. You are actually setting angle and rotation at the same time. Pretty nifty.

Helix

A helix is a spiral 3D path — as in DNA, for instance. The groove in a threaded bolt follows a helix pattern. The Lathe tool will create a helix out of a polygon. If you ever wondered how to make a screw or bolt in 3D, this is the tool to do it. Just pop a cylindrical shaft and boolean out a sharp helix for the thread. Put on a head and you have a bolt.

You'll usually want to set your angle at way more than 360° if you make a helix, so it can keep rotating beyond the start point, angling up as it rotates. Do this interactively by dragging the perpendicular green bar at the end of the curve. This is called the helix handle. Figure 10-4 shows something called a Helicoil. It's used by ski mechanics to reinforce binding screws. To make it, I simply fabricated a polygon in the shape of the Helicoil's thread cross section and swept it in a helix. It looks pretty much like the real thing. Guess what my job was in Aspen.

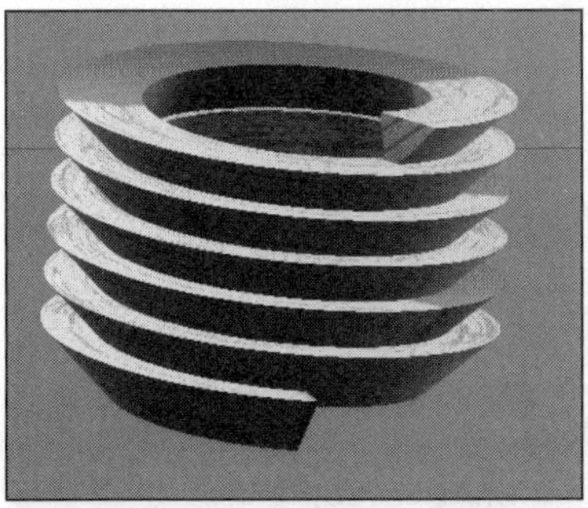

Figure 10-4: A good example of a helix is the HeliCoil, which used to reinforce ski binding screws for racers.

There's an interesting little deal about the way lathe installs UV mapping. This invisible coordinate system wraps texture maps around the surface of an object. When you lathe 360°, without helix, trueSpace2 installs a default mapping that's shaped like a torus. It's a continuous form of cylindrical mapping that's applied along the extrusion path and bent around to the shape of the extrusion. If you build a helix, it has ends. In this case you get special mapping with flat or planar mapping applied to end surfaces. This gives a believable surface.

Space Station

This station is designed to be seen at near distance. If you want closeups, add more polygons by increasing the number of nodes in your swept poly and segments in the Lathe tool options. Also, add more nernie detail. Design your space station with pencil and paper. For the example we'll go with a familiar torus design. I'm giving you less specific detail for this project; it's time to use your personal judgment in size, texture, and so on. Later on you'll probably want to design an entirely new concept in space stations, but for now we want to lathe one.

Begin by drawing a polygon of the cross section of the main torus-shaped section of the space station. Lathe it 360°. Inset A in Figure 10-5 gives you an idea what my cross section looked like. Give it a little character, some grooves. I projected a rim toward the center — maybe a walkway. Add a few nernies. Figure 10-5, inset B, is a detail of nernie clusters I added on the top surface of the station. I simply copied and glued a nernie into cluster, exposed and normalized its axis, then placed and rotated 12 copies around the top.

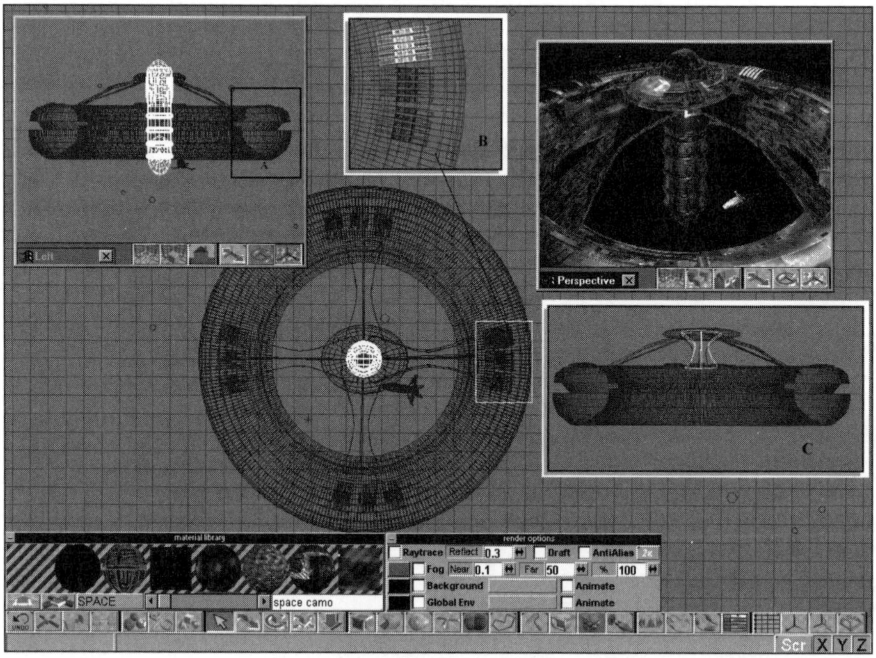

Figure 10-5: This composite of a space station shows construction details.

The central control pod on top is nothing more than a flattened sphere. Just scale a fresh sphere down its Z axis. The central tower spokes (see Figure 10-5, inset C) were made by drawing the basic shape on the floor grid with the Spline tool, and extruding to a thin (0.01), flat shape. I gave it a little form using Volume Deform, and rotated copies into place. This piece sits at an angle, so when you center its axis on the origin, also lift it to the center of the flattened sphere. Then align the Z axis to vertical by hitting the Normalize Rotation icon, then lock it. Rotate four copies into position using the *right* button.

POWER TIP

If the struts rotate at a strange angle, make sure you've normalized both the location and the rotation of the axis point before rotating copies into position.

The central docking tower was easy. Use the main fuselage of the ribbed tanker we built earlier. When you normalize its rotation and position, it will be in the center of the space station in vertical alignment. Move it up the Z axis until the engine portion pokes through the sphere to form a central roof detail. You could paint individual faces on the top with a transparent glass material. I'd make it gold to simulate solar protection glass. I also advise placing some nernies inside so it looks like something is going on in there. If you like you can scale the tank section a little shorter and fatter to make it less recognizable.

Building the whole station took about a half hour, but texturing it was a different story. I fooled around for almost an hour, tried space textures I already have, and played with surface qualities and bump maps until it looked right to me. I rendered a small window shown previously in Figure 10-5 to give you an idea of how it might look. The final rendering is Plate 10-1 in the color insert. Note that I also loaded a small vehicle and some stars against a black background, to give it a spacey feeling. These Sweep tools put all kinds of creation into your hands. Play with them and you'll discover as yet unthought of ways to use them.

Reusing parts is one of the ways professionals save a lot of time. They also use the same parts over and over again in the same picture, merely rescaling and retexturing them, and you'd never notice.

Utilities

I haven't used all the utilities in construction tutorials so far. I could have, but I didn't want to pile it on too heavy. This is supposed to be fun. Here are a few tools you'll use often, especially the first one, Mirror.

Mirror Tool

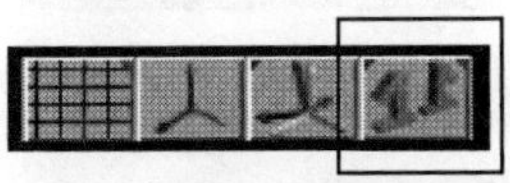

When you build symmetrical objects you'll find lots of uses for this tool. If it's a complex object, why build the whole thing. Since it's symmetrical, you should only have to build half of it, right? Use this tool with the copy command to instantly clone a mirror image. By setting the object axis to the center point of the *finished* object, the mirror image will flip into place, where you can glue or boolean it to the original. Cake. It's great for wings on spacecraft. I know wings don't work in space, but they look good, so why not. Besides, some of these things can land in atmospheres.

I spent a lot of time trying to figure out why the Mirror tool didn't seem to work right. Mirror reverses an object's geometry along the World X/Z plane. Remember this or you'll spend hours trying to get it to work and probably give up and never use it. So to make a clone, open a Top Down window, line up your object with the grid so the top half is in the top half of the screen. When you mirror, the reverse geometry will flip down. Before you flip, expose the axis, align it where you want the center of the *final* object to be. That is, drop it down to the lower edge of the object to be mirrored. Then Copy ➪ Mirror ➪ Glue-as-Sibling.

We need a small space vehicle for our stable — a good opportunity to demonstrate Mirror and practice other skills.

The Drone

As the story goes, this is an unmanned instrument probe carrying no weapons. It's fast and highly maneuverable. It's also capable of flying through most atmospheres to gather data. Therefore, it has wings and control surfaces.

The Fuselage

We'll create the fuselage using the Lathe tool to turn a smooth aerodynamic body. Open a Top View window and use the Spline tool to draw a flat polygon shaped like half the longitudinal cross section of the drone. See Figure 10-6A for an idea of what I mean.

Expose and move the polygon's axis to the center line and lock it (Figure10-6B). Right click on the Lathe tool, set the angle to 360°, then invoke it with the fuselage poly selected (Figure 10-6C). Grab the crossbar and rotate the control cross to the center line of the ship. Make sure the crossbar is parallel with the axis (Figure 10-6D), then hit the Lathe icon again and bam, you have a 3D fuselage mesh. See Figure 10-6E and 10-6F.

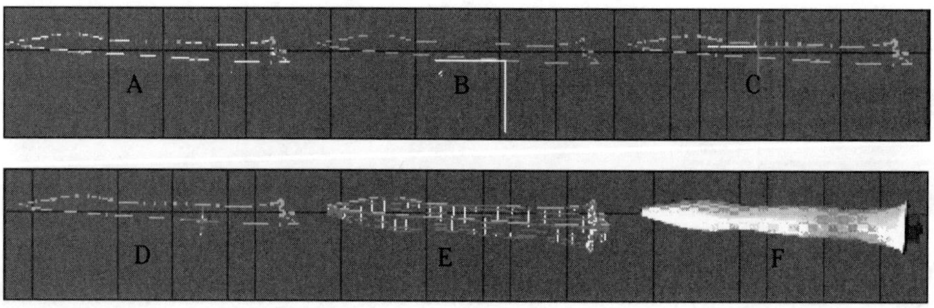

Figure 10-6: Sequence of details (A–F) shows steps in turning a smooth fuselage

POWER TIP

You can make an efficient shape by managing the number of nodes in each spline segment. For long sections use about 10, for very short ones use 3. This will keep them from bunching up in short segments, making a cumbersome model. I used only three for each line on the rear engine.

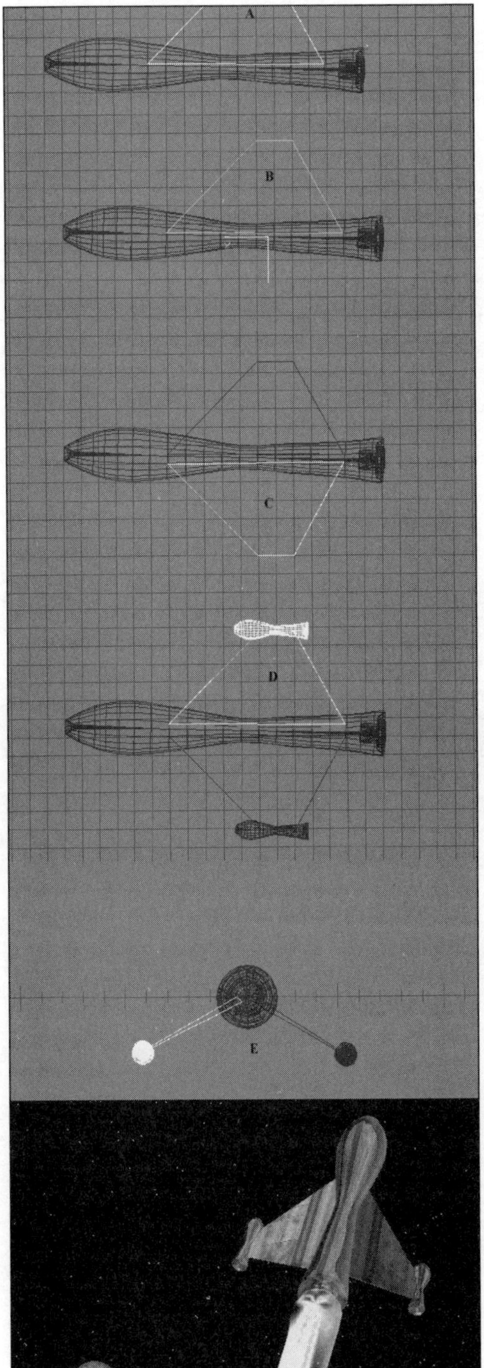

Figure 10-7: Sequence of details (A-F) shows how to build and mirror a wing

Still in Top View, draw a wing for the top half of the fuselage as in Figure 10-7A. Give it a little shape — extrude it. First reset the extrude Z thickness down to 0.01. With the top surface selected, as it always is after an extrude, select the Stretch or Scale icon in the Point Nav panel (it came up automatically when you extruded). Scale the top surface to about 2/3 of the bottom. This gives the wing a long sharp bevel. It'll be centered on the fuselage. Switch to the Point Nav Move icon and drag it even with the center (fuselage) edge of the wing and slightly back to give the front of the wing a longer bevel. Good work. It's time to Mirror.

Expose the wing axis and move it to the center of the fuselage, as in Figure 10-7B, then lock down. Good, you know what you're doing now. Next, Copy ➪ Mirror as in Figure 10-7C. This sequence reverses the wing's geometry and flips into place on the opposite half of the vehicle. If it doesn't, go back and try again, following instructions carefully.

Next we need wing tanks. Select the main fuselage ➪ Copy ➪ Scale it way down and drag this new object to one wing tip, as shown in Figure 10-7D. If you like you can make it a little shorter and stubbier. You could mirror and flip it, but since it doesn't need reverse geometry, just copy and move it. Glue each one as a sibling to its wing.

I'm not partial to flat wings. I used to prefer a dihedral rake to them, like an eagle going in for the strike, but the current vogue is an anhedral tilt. I credit the trend to Ron Thornton and Foundation Imaging, they popularized it in *Babylon 5*.

Anhedral means angled down and back from the fuselage. Open a Left View window, grab, and rotate one of the wings downward slightly as in Figure 10-7E. I set the grid to a fine interval, ten degrees, and counted two clicks to rotate both wings exactly 20° down. Glue it all together, give it your favorite texture, and render, as shown in Figure 10-7F. Check out color Plate 10-2 to see how mine came out. The flame tail is a trick using a deformed sphere and vertex painting, something you'll learn about in the next part of the book.

Divide Tools

Smooth Quad Divide

You're already familiar with Smooth Quad Divide; here's how it works. It attempts to smooth the surfaces of the object it's applied to by physically subdividing the surface and bending to a smoother angle. These surfaces tend toward a sphere shape. You set the degree of smoothing by right clicking and setting the smoothing angle. This represents the interior angle between two polygons at the time of subdividing. If that angle is less than the angle you set in the options box, smoothing will take place. The higher you set the angle, the more smoothing will take place. I use the default of 40 percent most of the time because I don't think in degrees. It seems to work fine. You can play around with different shapes and see what happens at different angle settings. You'll get it a lot faster that way than reading about it.

Quad Divide

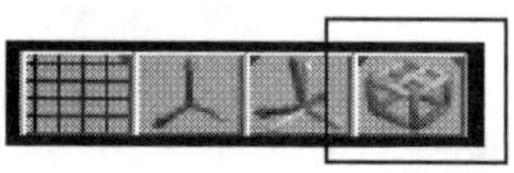

This one is a little different. It simply divides a polygon into quarters. Not all polygons can be quartered — depends on shape. I use this mostly in concert with the Face Select tool. If I want to add some detail to a section of a surface, I'll select one polygon and Quad Divide it several times, then use the Surface Sculpt or some other tool on this now usable spot. Note that when you use this tool, the object looks the same afterwards as opposed to the Smooth tool which changes the object's shape.

Triangulate

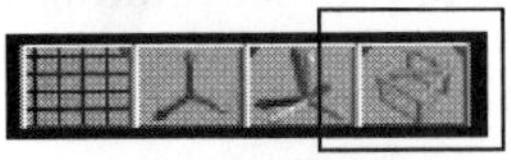

If your polygons are out of whack, you'll get a lot of rendering artifacts, like holes. Try triangulating them. This divides certain polygons into triangles so they can follow contours easier. Use this and other subdivide tools with parsimony. Remember that you only want to build what you need. Every extra polygon takes up resources and measurable time.

Dimensioning Tool

Though I don't use this much, many people do. It's a nifty tool that displays the distance between two points on an object. Remember early on when you set World and Object measuring units? Well, this tool remembers and uses that scale to read out distances.

To use Dimensioning, select the Dimensioning icon.

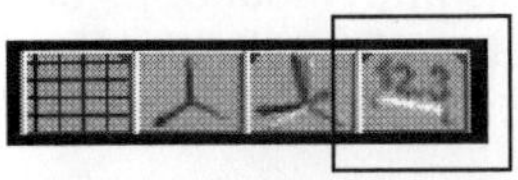

Click a vertex on the surface of an object. You can't put dimension marks directly on glued objects. If it's a complex object, hit the down arrow and navigate to the sub-object of interest. When you click on that first vertex, you get a yellow marker line. Click on the second and you get a second marker line with a dimension arrow between them, as shown in Figure 10-8.

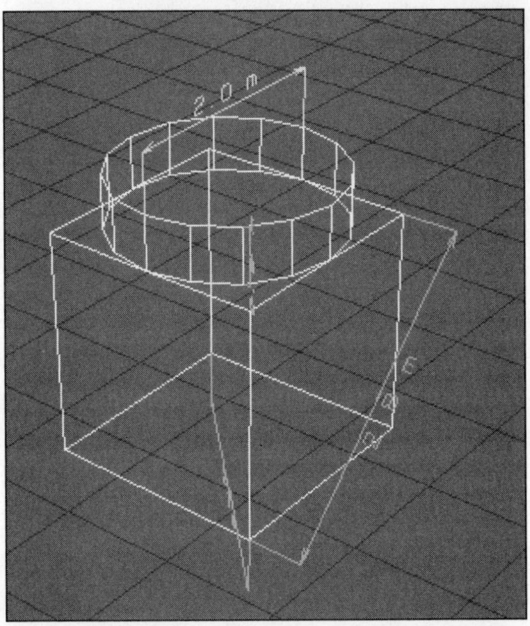

Figure 10-8: An example of an object with dimension call-outs in place

Very cool actually. They are placed three-dimensionally, right above the object in three space. That means you may not be able to read some without rotating your view of the object. Unfortunately you can't measure the distance between objects this way, which would be handy.

POWER TIP

You don't have to select an object to use the Dimension tool Simply click on any vertex in your work space and it will be selected automatically. This saves a lot of clicks.

Decompose

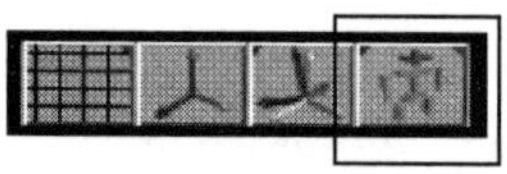

When this tool was added in beta, I didn't know what to do with it. It turns out that you may often import an object with no hierarchy. You can tell by looking at the hierarchy Nav down arrow on the control panel. It'll be grayed out, meaning there's no place to go down to. With your object selected, hit Decompose and the original elements should be discovered and separated as individual objects, then grouped as siblings. You can then go down and manipulate the individual parts. I seem to use this a lot with DXF files.

Flip Normals

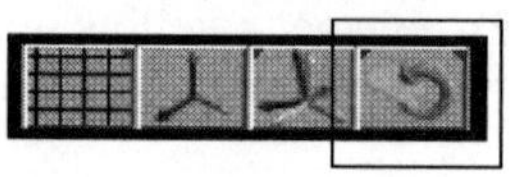

Sometimes when you render an import, it's all inside out because the normals are facing inward. This tool simply flips all normals 180°, so you don't have to re-import it.

Summary

If you haven't taken a break for a while, now is a good time. Come back refreshed and we'll start designing surfaces. In this chapter you've learned a heap of useful stuff:

✦ Use the Tip tool to quickly build pointy objects for use in detailing your larger objects.

✦ Extrude polygons along complex paths to make cool things like pipes and trees.

✦ Build things with the lathe, like a space station and a space vehicle fuselage.

✦ Build symmetrical objects, using the Mirror tool to create a mirror copy which can be glued to the original to form a whole.

✦ Use the Divide utilities to prepare objects and surfaces for further manipulation.

✦ Use the Dimension tool to map out your object's surface distances for building precise models.

✦ Break down a solid imported object into its component objects using the Decompose Surfaces tool.

✦ Flip all normals in an object using the Flip All Normals tool.

✦ ✦ ✦

CHAPTER 11

Surface is a Verb – in trueSpace2

✦ ✦ ✦ ✦

In This Chapter

trueSpace2's wonderful brushes

The Materials Design Interface with all its amazing tools

The elements of shading

Magical material mapping

How to capture and save material after you build it

✦ ✦ ✦ ✦

By now you've noticed that your objects render as plain white plastic. That's the default material. Like default lighting, it's rarely used. I've already shown you a few snippets of texturing to whet your appetite. Now you'll learn the tools of surfacing. trueSpace2 has a bunch of them and each has its own charm. In this chapter I'll give you a quick rundown of the tools and follow with chapters suggesting neat ways to use them.

Your Palette

Fortunately, what could have been a nightmare of complexity is laid out in a simple, intuitive, interactive interface. It's pretty much WYSIWYG. What you see in the Materials window is what gets painted on your object.

The surprise comes when you first see it rendered.... Three-D colors have a life of their own. That's because lighting, shadows, and object shapes all contribute to each pixel's final values. Lighting is so critical to the look you render, I've devoted an entire chapter to it. In addition, I've brought in a few top industry experts to share their special knowledge with you. As we design materials, keep in mind each will look unique when you wrap it around your object.

The general approach is to decide what materials the various parts of the object need, figure some creative way to build that material, then assign it to the proper surfaces. There is a lot of serendipity here because of the lavish trial and error you'll engage in. I've met people who have been so taken by material creation that's all they do.

Materials are made up of a base material and surface characteristics. The base can be a color or a texture map. If you need to add a decal to the surface, like the label on a Bud bottle, you have a Material Rectangle tool that'll wrap it right where you want it. That said, let's look at some tools.

The Basics

Brushes

You apply surfaces using various brushes built into trueSpace2.

Paint Object Brush

This one paints the entire object with the same material, regardless of what design or material was there originally.

Paint Over Brush

Paint over an existing surface only, leaving the rest of the object alone. That is, if part of an object is green, and you use this tool on it, only the green parts will be replaced. I use this one most. Pressing the Control key turns the Paint Over Brush into an inspection tool. You can copy surfaces from one area to another by inspecting the source and painting over the target. This is also the tool you use to *keyframe* texture and color changes.

If you find your colors are not changing the way you want in an animation, you probably didn't use the Paint Over tool to create the surface changes. If you use the Paint Object tool, you don't get a keyframe, so the texture goes all the way back to frame 0. This is a common frustration FAQ.

Paint Faces Brush

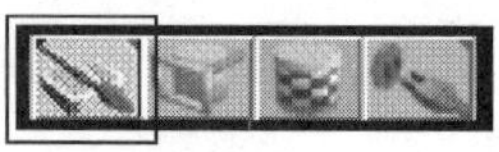

This one isn't for painting character faces — no, polygon faces. Sometimes you only want to touch up a poly or two. With this brush you can create detail using the polygon pattern substructure of an object. The finer your polygon structure, the finer you can paint with this brush. (See Figure 11-1.) You can use the Control key to jump back and forth between Inspect and Paint Faces to rapidly create interesting surfaces, as shown in Figure 11-1. It's very useful for making hulls look repaired. You pick a slightly lighter hull section with the Inspection tool and then paint a single hull face with it in a darker section. This looks like a newer panel.

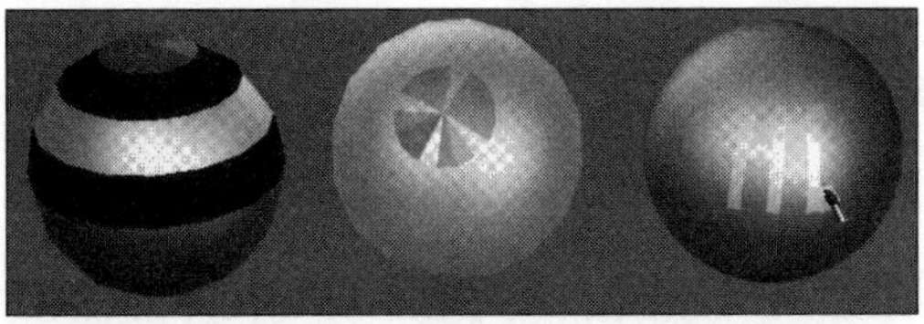

Figure 11-1: The Paint Faces tool in action, using the polygon substructure of the object.

Paint Vertex Brush

The last one is a little tricky and a little buggy, but it's a lot of fun. It's called Vertex Paint and it's a strange device. When you touch a vertex with it, you get the base color, with all maps and procedurals removed. It's applied as a radial gradient from the vertex out, as shown in Figure 11-2. Since most faces share vertices, you can expect the effect on all faces associated with that vertex.

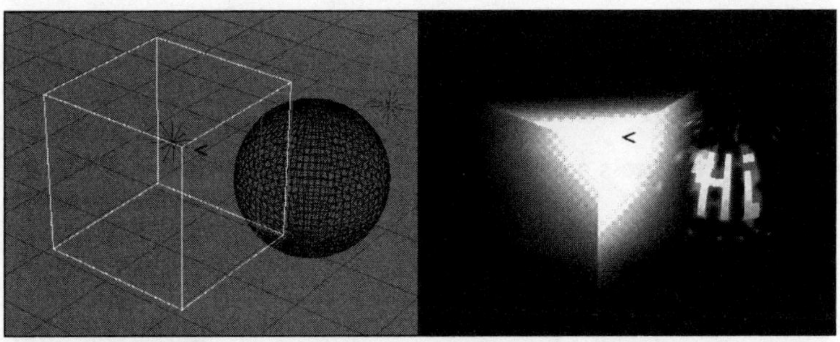

Figure 11-2: The Vertex Paint Tool in action: the carat points to a single vertex painted on the cube. The sphere shows the flame effect of many small, painted vertices. Notice the transparency.

The only way to remove the Vertex paint effect is to hit either <Ctrl> or <Shift> and reclick on the vertex you want cleaned.

POWER TIP: This tool works best in 3DR mode. In wireframe it seems very hard to hit the vertices you want to paint. Not so in 3DR.

Here's the cool part. As the gradient spreads out from the vertex, color fades into the object's base material. This gives a soft feathering out to the edge of the polygon. You can create a soft glow effect by making underlying material transparent. It works perfectly against a black background, but as soon as you have color or texture behind, you can see the bug. Instead of being fully transparent, the edges retain a gel of the base color. This should be fixed. It wasn't in the latest (at this writing) repair patch available from `www.caligari.com`. Experiment with visible light sources, glow effects, and neon lettering using the vertex tool.

Brushes make life simple. When you click on an object or part of it, the surface material you've chosen is immediately deposited and rendered so you can see results. Experiment on your own for a bit. You'll learn more, faster than my paper words can explain.

If you don't want to wait for the object to render after painting it (usually you won't), just hit escape and you'll be right back in work mode.

Inspection Brush

This isn't really a brush, but a nifty way to capture a complex surface to the Materials Design Interface for use or modification. To use it you simply click on the surface material you want to capture and, zap, it's in the Material Preview window ready to apply or modify.

Material Design Interface

This is one of my favorite tools and another brilliant design by Caligari. It comes in four separate windows:

✦ Material Preview window

✦ Color Cube window

✦ Shader/Map/Procedural Selection window

✦ Shader Attribute window

I love to mix up textures from virtually nothing. I made the realistic black rubber for the industrial flashlight in a few seconds. Actually I chose a cross between flat black rubber and shiny plastic to give it some character and reveal the texture. The grooves were added using a bump map made from a bitmap of gray floor tiles. I stretched it out with V repeats and wrapped it around the flashlight with cylindrical mapping. Easy as pie.

Every time you hit one of the surfacing tools tS2 reacts with a question: At your service, what surface would you like to paint with today? It does this by presenting you with the Materials Design Interface. Let's take a look at its parts.

Material Preview Window

Real-time material preview is one of the most valuable innovations Caligari put into the trueSpace line. It allows you to see the impact of every little adjustment you make to your material and its shaders — in 3D. When you first see the material window it has a fully rendered sphere with the current material under default white lighting. It's mapped to the ball by spherical UV projection.

Remember the Mercator projection maps of the world when you were a kid? They flattened the globe into a bunch of pointy globs, all connected in the middle. If you cut out that projected map, you could wrap the pieces around a globe and they would fit perfectly, no creases. Projection is the way the computer decides how to fit a texture map on a flat or curved surface, stretching and squeezing in different places.

POWER TIP

Remember, your lighting will probably differ, but it gives the designer in you a good idea of what she's working with. If you want to see the material on a flat plane, just click the window and it'll go flat. You can toggle back and forth with alternate clicks. The difference can be dramatic.

Color Property Cube

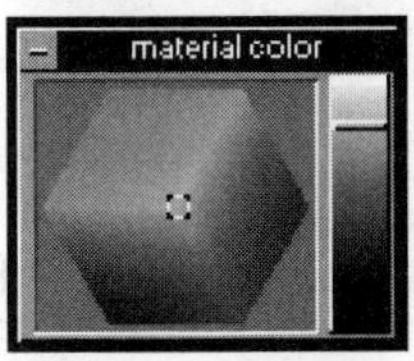

Caligari chose to use the HSB, or Hue/Saturation/Brightness model for color selection. A good choice. The colors are laid out on a hexagon with white smack in the center. As you head for the outer edges, saturation increases. This gives it the look of a cube. There is a separate slider for brightness to its right. An intelligent associate of mine, new to CGI, remarked "This damn cube has every color but gray. I want to make plain old steel. I can't do it with this stupid system."

Nonsense. Gray is just a darker form of white or a brighter form of black; just slide the brightness control to the gray you want.

When you select a color, it's immediately reflected in the brightness selector. You can go from the base color/saturation up a few notches in brightness, or all the way down to black. If you want a yellow lightbulb, you'll naturally run up the brightness to the top along with a few other things like ambient glow, which we'll discuss in a moment.

You can *right* click on the Color Property Cube to access a different system — the RGB slide bars.

I like this color selection method less, because it's cumbersome and takes much longer for me to use. It's just there if you're a dyed-in-the-wool RGB person, or you have to input RGB values to match a color. It consists of three color bars, one each for red, green, and blue. Each bar has a brightness/saturation slider attached. You build a color by changing the amount of each color in the mix. As you move the sliders to the right you get white, as you move the sliders to the left you get black. You do this interactively, watching the Material Preview.

The Shader/Map/Procedural Window

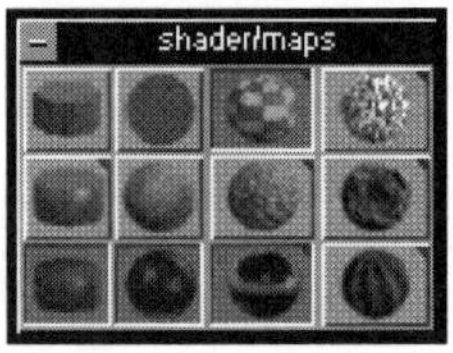

Here you'll find twelve magic push buttons. Each one affects the way your surface material will look. We'll examine each control and its panels; they're stacked in four distinct groups, from left to right:

- ✦ Surface Contour Selection
- ✦ Shading Model Selection
- ✦ Texture Map Selection
- ✦ Procedural Texture Selection

By invoking various combinations of these attributes, you can create a near infinite number of surfaces. Some selections preclude others, like a radio button, while others are additive. For example, you can't have both faceted and smooth shading, but you can have texture, reflection, and bump maps at the same time. Let's look closer.

Surface Contour Selection

Reading left to right, the Contour Select tool is the first stack. They go from top to bottom, starting with:

Faceted Faces

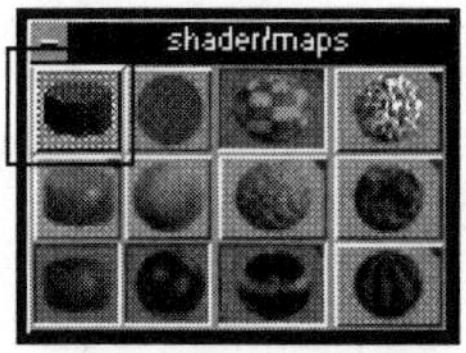

If you create a gemstone, you'll want to use this. It produces clean break lines at polygon junctions. They catch light as the object rotates. You can experiment using it when you have vehicle panels aligned with the polygon substructure. Visualize painting each polygon on a dodecahedron with a textured surface and you want the crease between panels to show cleanly. You engage Faceted and paint each face separately. If you have a single texture map for the whole surface, just use the Paint Object tool and the facets will show through the map.

Auto Facet

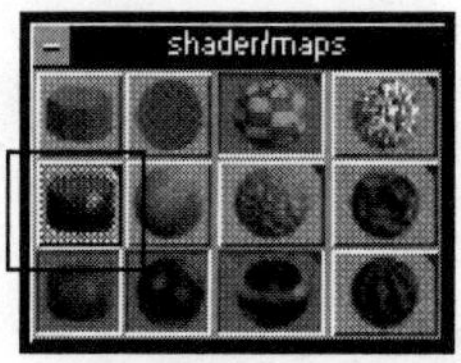

This is the selection I use most often. It gives a modified/adjustable smoothing that takes the polygon structure into account. You adjust it by setting the angle between two polygons below which smoothing takes place. It's really hard for me to picture this, so I frequently use the default and it just seems to work out. Where I find this very useful is when I'm doing a vehicle that has smooth panels and then some pretty angled panels. Recall that even the smooth panels on a curved surface have facets. So let's say I want the panels with a small angle of intercept to show as smooth and the other to have sharp edges. If I right click on the Auto Facet tool,

and set the threshold to an angle larger than the one on my smooth panels (I guess at this), it will hide the facets on the smooth panels and show the others. Neat trick.

Smooth Surface

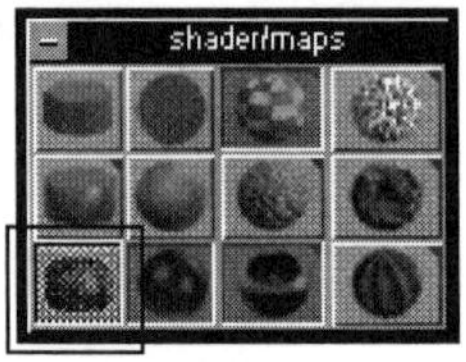

I don't use this tool much because it smoothes too much for most purposes. You can take a really choppy faceted torus, apply this tool, and come out with a reasonably smooth donut, as shown in Figure 11-3.

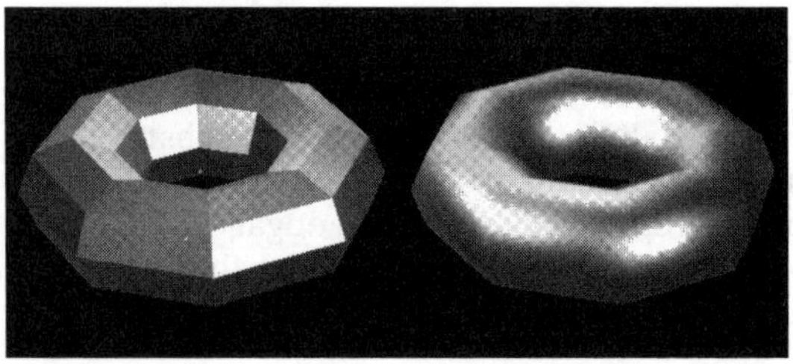

Figure 11-3: The same hexagonal torus shows a Left = Faceted surface and a Right = Smooth surface. Notice how the smooth torus still has a choppy outline, but a smooth surface.

Shading Model Selection

The way light plays with a surface in real life can be simulated using various shading algorithms. Caligari gives you a choice of three:

- ✦ Flat Shading
- ✦ Phong Shading
- ✦ Metal Shading

Each has its own uses. Generally I think of the Phong and Metal shading as the more sophisticated — not one better than the other, just different.

Flat Shading

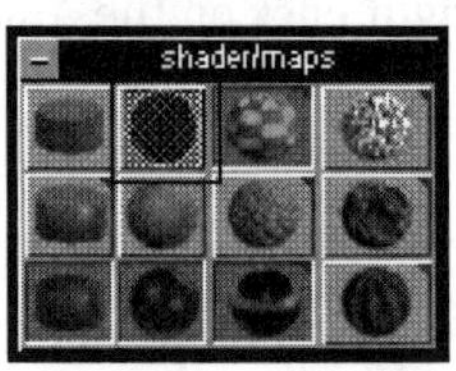

The simplest and least interesting for 3D is flat shading. This yields comic book colors: flat, no shading. The left-most torus in Figure 11-4 is a good example.

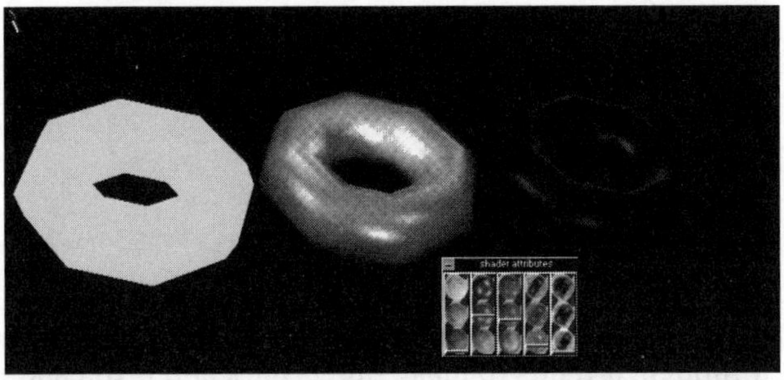

Figure 11-4: A flat, shaded chunky torus looks more like a paper cut-out without shadows or highlights. Compare it with Phong and Metal shaded tori, each rendered at the Shader settings shown in the Shader Attributes window.

I use flat shading to mark shapes for further processing. For example, if I want to create a special Material Rectangle in the exact shape of an object, I paint that object bright flat red and shoot it from a distance to get the profile with no shading. Later in Photoshop, I select the red for masking purposes and then paint in my material map the exact size and shape I need to decal it on the object's surface. Other than this, I never use it. Just me I guess. Disney uses the tool to blend 3D into the backgrounds for its films.

Notice, when you select flat shading, the Shading Attributes panel blanks out everything but transparency, which is the only parameter besides color you get. If you need a non-reflective transparent panel, this is the way to go.

Phong Shading

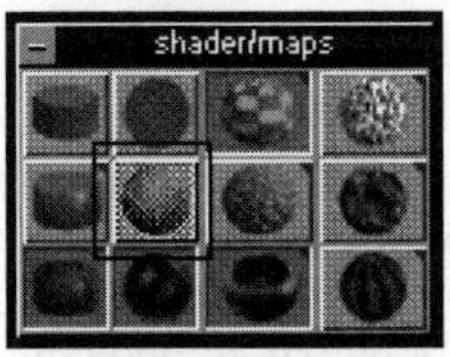

I love Phong Shading. It produces nice specular highlights on a surface depending on settings in the Shader Attributes panel (as previously shown in Figure 11-4) and can show true reflections when raytraced. This is the most-used shader in trueSpace2. It's good for creating most surfaces from paint to plastic to tree bark to space vehicle hulls. The results you get with Phong are highly interdependent with your mapping selections. For example, if you pick a reflection map or a bump map, they will greatly influence the look you get. More on this in a few minutes.

Metal Shading

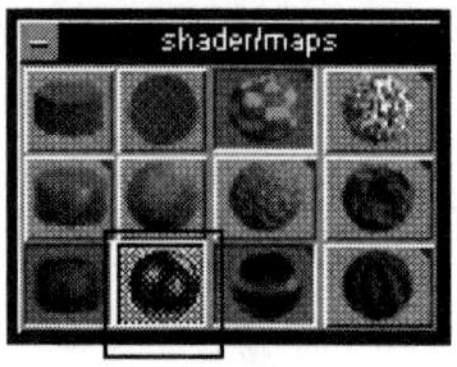

This one is very cool. I use it far more than I should because I love it. You have to be careful how you use it though. It tends to make things dark and if you slide the ambient light up to compensate, you screw up the whole effect. The answer is to add more light; try spotlights on the surface. Adding a reflection map to your metal can make all the difference in credibility, but only if you reduce the roughness (increase polish). Of course if you render metal with raytrace on, it will reflect the things around it (providing you give it some shininess attribute). The best shiny metals are made with just a color (say gold) and a reflection map, with this shader selected. It's a snap. Rusty metal is actually more complex and made with Phong shading.

This is also the shader you use to make glass. You can get some really awesome looks with this one, but don't forget it requires a lot of light.

Map Selection

Maps are *the* great addition to 3D graphics. I don't think anything has done more to create the photorealistic qualities of 3D than mapping. It's not just mapping a picture onto the surface of an object. That would be too easy and not good enough. trueSpace2 has three different mapping modes:

- ✦ Texture Mapping
- ✦ Bump Mapping
- ✦ Reflection Mapping

Other packages may let you map such things as shininess (specularity), roughness (diffusion), or transparency (alpha channel). I hope additional mapping channels are added because, from a professional point of view, you can make things look even more real, like the uneven shininess of rusty metal. As is, trueSpace2 gives you plenty to work with to achieve a high level of realism without unnecessary complication. There are ways of achieving the others if you absolutely crave them… but that won't be often.

Texture Maps

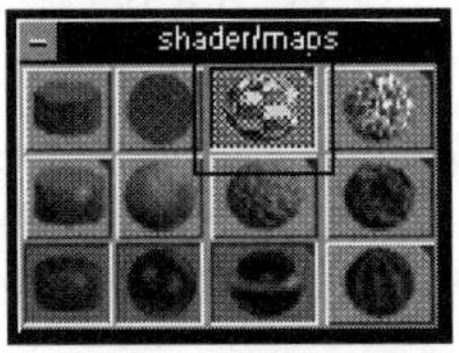

Any picture file you have can be a texture map. In fact, if you have a scanner, any picture you can get your hands on can be a texture map. There are CD-ROMs full of textures. They come in two major flavors, seamless and nonseamless.

The seamless variety are like the wallpaper icons you tile in Windows to make a uniform background wallpaper. Use them with caution, most have a repeating signature that gives them away. Really good ones are so symmetrical you can't see the pattern, but most are reasonably bad in my experience. Fractal Design Painter 3.1 and 4.0 have tools for making seamless textures. Check out the Image Hose if you want to make some neat ones involving vegetation.

The trueSpace family of programs allows you to set vertical and horizontal repeats within an object's UV space, by right clicking on the Texture Map icon and inputting the number of repeats. You can create special effects by using values more or less than one in combination.

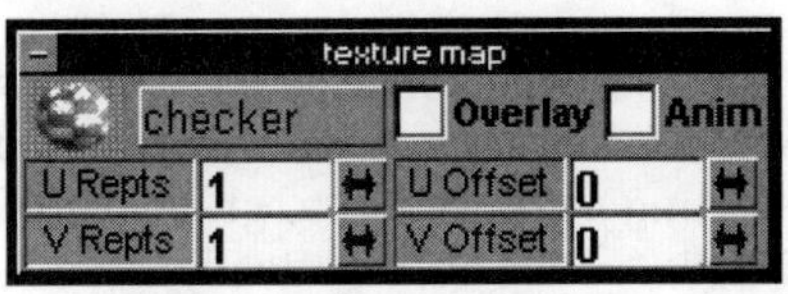

- ✦ **Map window.** Left click on the default Map (Checker) to select a new map of your choice. Almost any bitmap will do.
- ✦ **Overlay.** If you use bitmaps with transparency (alpha channel) information, Overlay engaged will make those portions of the map transparent, revealing the underlying surface. With it off, the underlying surface is treated as if it isn't even there. Transparent areas are completely transparent.
- ✦ **Anim(ate).** Click this if you are using an animated texture. It will apply the texture frame by frame, matching your render. When it comes to the end of the sequence it will start over again This is great for flame loops, water shadows, sky effects, and loop rotoscoping in general.

POWER TIP

If you use an .avi file for a texture, try to use one at the same base frame rate as your rendering. Otherwise, trueSpace2 will make adjustments. If you're doing a 30 fps rendering and using a 15 fps .avi file as a texture, tS2 will apply each .avi frame to two frames in a row to make up the difference. Not always cool.

✦ **U Repts.** This sets the number of times the image is repeated in the horizontal direction. (Shouldn't it be H Repts? No, because it doesn't always coincide with the horizontal and vertical on screen. It's tied to the UV coordinates of the object, which can be rotated.) I used this to stretch out the tiles map to make long grooves for the flashlight. I dropped it below 1.0 to stretch it out. I think I also increased the V Repts too. There is madness to the method of using U instead of H — I just don't remember what it is at the moment.

✦ **V Repts.** Pretty obvious, this is vertical repeats, but it is also tied to the object's rotatable UV coordinates. Both U and V repeats can be increased up to 100.

✦ **U Offset.** Use this one to adjust the way the pattern fits on the object. It's a little tricky, usually requiring a lot of trial and error. The setting is how far the image is offset horizontally from the start of the UV mapping space — 0 starts the image at the left edge, 1 starts it at the right edge. In between is in between.

✦ **V Offset.** Need I say more?

Bump Maps

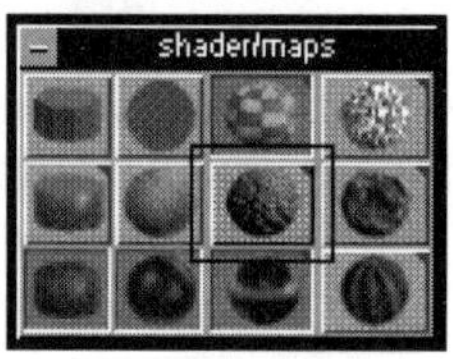

Bump maps are more fun than a flock of cockatoos. Many 3D suites require you to use grayscale bump maps. This can be a pain; you have to create them in an image edit program either from scratch or by converting a color map to gray scale. In trueSpace2 you don't worry about conversion, it's done automatically, so you can use color maps directly. By using the same map for texture and bumps you can achieve excellent results.

Here's how it works. tS2 uses the brightness of each pixel in the map as a height reference. The brighter the pixel, the higher relief it will be assigned. Thus, the higher the apparent bumps will be. You set the range of offsets by right clicking on the tool to get the Bump Map Setup panel.

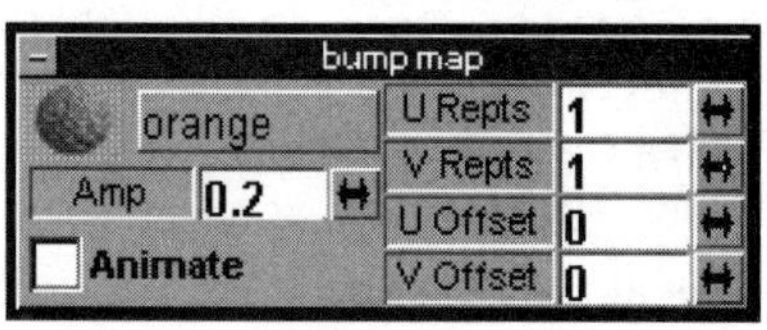

✦ **Map Selection.** The default bump map is orange. This gives a skin texture similar to a Valencia orange. You can change this any time by merely clicking the map name and selecting a different bitmap. It's fun to see what various maps produce.

Diffusion Mapping

Mauricio Baiocchi, a trueSpace2 expert in Mountain View, California, shares one of his discoveries – a way to create the effect of diffusion mapping on a surface using the material rectangle projection system. Because the Material Rectangle allows you to place several layers on top of each other, it's possible to create some interesting surface effects. For example, you can have a surface that you want to show variable reflectivity in a certain area. It's possible to create a dirty looking fractal .tga file with an alpha channel. If you use Photoshop to replace the original alpha channel with a different dark, grayscale fractal pattern, the .tga will have variable transparency. Placing it over a shiny surface will create areas where the shine comes through (the black alpha) and areas that are dulled (lighter alpha). This simulates specular mapping as you might see in LightWave. Try experimenting with several layers to create different effects.

✦ **Amp(litude).** The height of apparent bumps. Negative values can be input to reverse the effect, making black high and white low. Zero is the same as no effect. I keep the value between .1 and .3 for most work.

✦ **Animate.** This is the same as for other textures. You can use an animation to simulate moving surface texture. It's great for water and wind effects.

The U and V repeats and offsets are the same as for other textures.

Reflection Maps

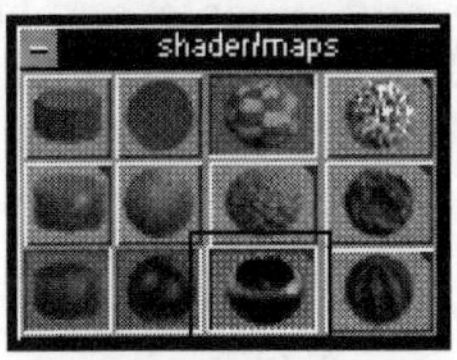

In trueSpace2 Reflection Maps are called Environment Maps. If you assign a shininess value to your object, it will appear to reflect the bitmap you apply here. This is particularly handy if you need reflections and don't intend to raytrace the scene. Raytracing generates real reflections in addition to the environment map. One neat thing about this tool: the reflections actually move or change perspective as the object moves. This seriously improves the illusion. The setup is simple.

Simply select your reflection map and notify tS2 if it's an animation.

You can get really believable reflections using Cubic reflection maps. These are created with the Image utilities found under the Files menu. It has several uses, which we'll look at more later.

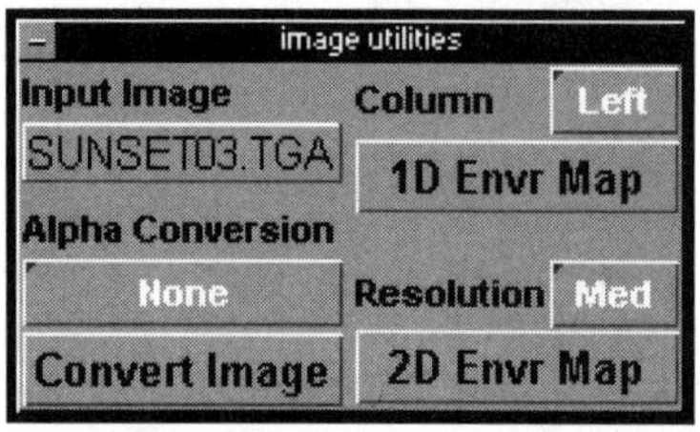

Cubic maps accurately simulate raytrace reflections for a given object. The utility creates the cubic map (2D Envr Map) by taking six pictures from the point of view of the selected object — four shots, 90° apart for a panorama, plus one each, top and bottom. Applied as a reflection map, this is a convincing substitute for the time-consuming raytrace approach. The drawback is if you have a lot of shiny objects, each one needs its own cubic map. This can become tedious, especially if you have limited ram.

The utility also creates a 1D map also, but I never use it. It's like a horizon color gradient based on a color column sampled from your image. It may have uses, but not for my style of work.

The default reflection map is Rainbow. I don't use this much, but it's handy for a number of special effects. I tend to use the desert scene, wastlan, because it simulates chrome-like reflections nicely. I've collected about a hundred reflection maps that I've made from some Corel Photo CDs of scenes and sunsets, and I use maps that came with suites like 3D Studio, and Visual Reality. Animated reflections using .avi and .flc files can create some interesting special effects.

Now we move on to another interesting innovation in 3D: Procedural textures.

Procedural Selection

Procedural textures are created mathematically and simulate solid texture. That is, you can slice through a procedural log and find internal rings consistent with the surface pattern. The names of tS2 procedurals are somewhat arbitrary. They can produce their namesake texture quite nicely, but each has a settings panel to vastly increase the realm of possibilities. The major drawback to procedurals is that they take a while to render. So use them only when you need their special qualities.

Granite

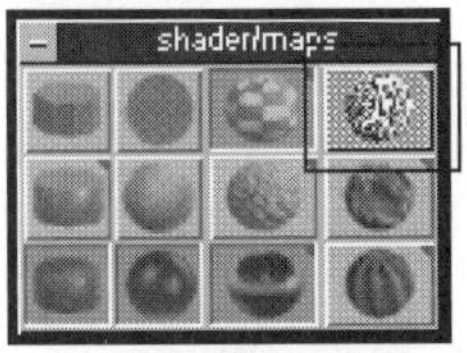

The Granite default setting looks a lot like granite. When you apply it, it overrides any texture map you may have in place. Right click on the Granite icon and bring up the settings panel.

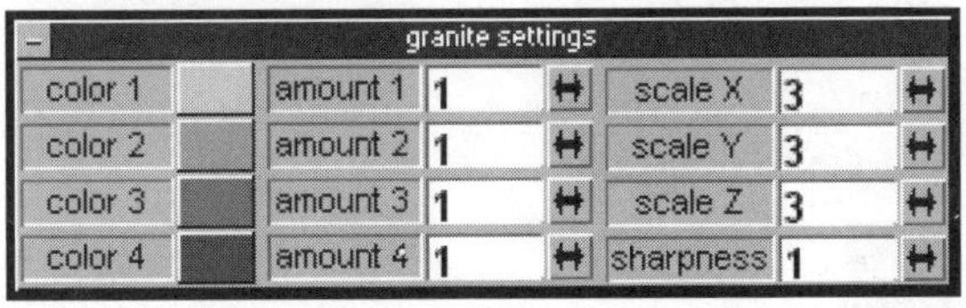

Here's where you get to play. The interactive nature of tS2 makes this a breeze. There are five different kinds of settings to fiddle with.

- ✦ **Color.** Four or fewer colors make up the granite texture. You can use fewer by making two or three the same, but you won't do it very often. In Granite, colors are combined randomly to form a blobby, mottled surface. The default is a set of four grays going from light to dark. By changing colors and shaders, you can do some neat special effects which I'll cover in an upcoming chapter. Each of the four colors has a color setup panel with variable transparency. If you're creative, you'll find plenty of interesting uses for these — play around with them.
- ✦ **Amount.** You can seriously affect the appearance of Granite by fiddling with amount. There is one setting for each color and it can range between zero and one. The four seem to interact in a weighting scheme that may take a little time to get used to. Take the time because you'll use this control a lot. In general, the higher your amount setting for a given color, the greater predominance it will have in the pattern. I find that you can increase this effect by lowering the values of the other colors.
- ✦ **Scale.** You get one setting here for each axis. The range is from 10 to 0; yes, strangely, zero is the *maximum.* The larger the number, the smaller the color blotches will be along that vector. They operate independently.
- ✦ **Seed.** This is a random start point for generating the texture. I change it every once in a while to keep a fresh look. I don't see much difference — random is kinda random, period.
- ✦ **Sharpness.** This is a useful control that is hard to define. When you set it to zero you get kind of an average color useless texture. At the maximum (default) you get the grainy granite look. In between you get a blending of the colors that can be useful for special effects.

Marble

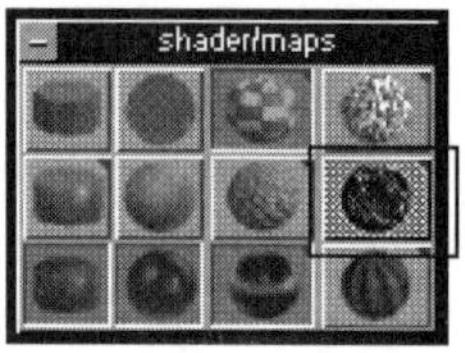

Marble is a really cool texture, my favorite. It uses fractal noise to create the typical marble look of stone and grain. Grain is the lines running through the marble and Stone is the bulk of the material with a subtly variegated color scheme. Right click to bring up the settings panel.

This may not look like much, but it's a powerful panel. You'll use Marble to create all sorts of special effects from smoke to lightning.

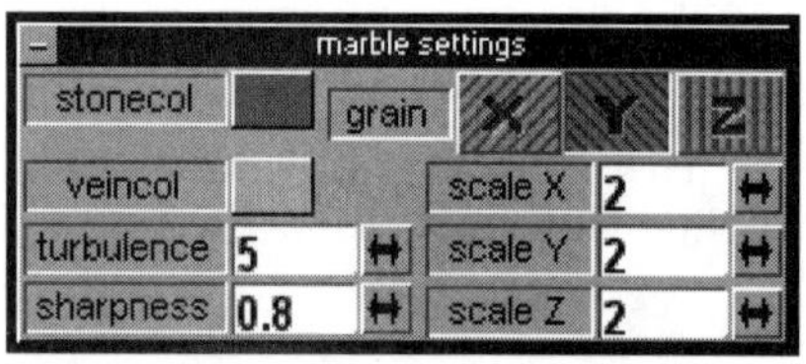

- ✦ **Color.** Stonecol is stone color and Veincol is vein color (like I really had to tell you that), with defaults of dark pink and light pink, respectively. Big deal. I never use the defaults. You change color and transparency by clicking on each color window and getting the color setting panel that looks the same as the one for Granite. By fooling with color and transparency you can create some terrific effects.
- ✦ **Turbulence.** Fractal noise is introduced into the veins in proportion to this setting. That means at zero you get no noise or a pretty smooth vein. At 1 you get a lot of noise that makes the vein twist and swirl a lot.
- ✦ **Sharpness.** You control the density and spread of the veins with this. At zero, you get a diffuse fractal cloud, like steam. At 1 you get a very tight, narrow vein you can hardly see.
- ✦ **Grain.** Marble texture is developed along a predominant vector called the vein. It can be along any of the three object axes. Experiment with this one to see the impact of each on your object. It can be surprising.
- ✦ **Scale.** You control the number of veins and zagginess of the zigs with these. Play with it to see what it does, then paint your material on a big sphere to check it out.

All five controls work in concert with each other. If you set the grain to X, you'll get more veins by increasing Y. Why? Because grain runs along the X and the number of veins is distributed along the Y vector. It makes sense if you take a second to ponder it.

Wood

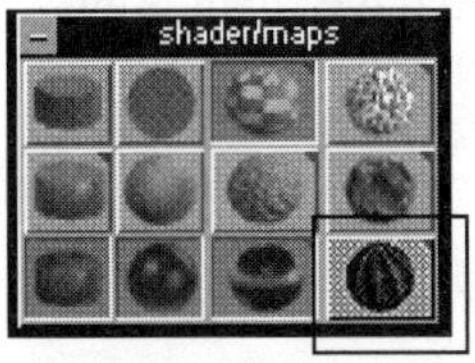

With eight different adjustments, you'd think wood would give you the greatest variety of textures. Wrong. It almost all looks like wood. Wood grain has a very distinctive look no matter what you do to it. But in the special effects section I'll show you some interesting, far out uses for wood. Pop up the settings panel and let's take a look.

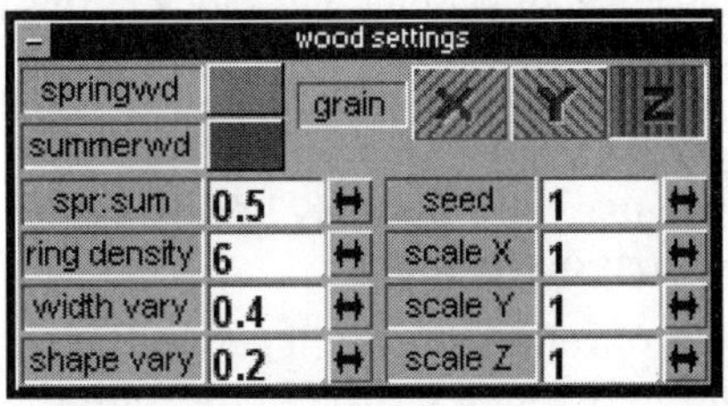

✦ **Color.** Like Marble you get to choose two colors:

- **Springwd.** I'm not going to tell you what it stands for either. This one defaults to light brown; and
- **Summerwd.** This defaults to dark brown. Big news, right?

✦ **Spr:Sum.** This is the ratio of relative weights for each wood color in the texture design. The lower the number here, the more summerwd and vice versa.

✦ **Ring Density.** This ranges from 0 to 10. The higher the value, the more rings in the design.

✦ **Width Vary.** This introduces a random width factor into the rings. At 0 all the rings appear the same width, while at 1, they vary pretty widely.

✦ **Shape Vary.** The basic shape of rings is circular (amazing information, you'll agree); this tool introduces random variance from circular. Zero yields circles while 1 gives you wood from a nasty environment.

✦ **Seed.** Random seed gives you different patterns.

✦ **Grain.** Determines which object axis the grain is developed along. It's like which way the saw cut through the wood.

✦ **Scale.** You can further distort rings by scaling them independently along each of the three object axes. Range is 0 to 10. You get more but smaller rings the higher you go.

That's it for procedurals. We come back to them later in special effects. Now you need to understand how you can polish textures once you have them built.

The Shader Attribute Panel

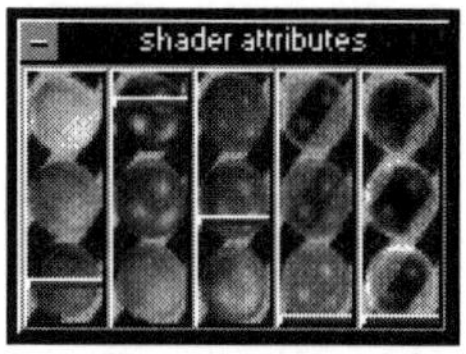

Phong and Metal shaders have five attributes or parameters you can control in trueSpace2. These are relatively few but make life a lot simpler. Let's look at this tool:

- **Ambient Glow.** To the far left, the first slider controls the amount of self-generating light the object has. If there is ambient glow, the object will render with no lights at all. You want to use this sparingly because it washes out other lighting effects. Keep it low most of the time.
- **Shininess.** This determines the amount of reflection you'll get off the surface. If you're using a reflection map you'll see the map clearly in the Material Preview, when shininess is set all the way to the top. You won't see it at all if you pull this one down to the bottom.
- **Roughness.** This determines the size of specular highlights, those bright spots on shiny surfaces. At the top you get the look of highly polished glass or metal, tight little highlights because the micro surface is very fine and doesn't break up the light. As you slide this one down, it simulates a progressively rougher micro surface structure, giving ever larger highlights.
- **Transparency.** You know what this is. You can see through the object when the slider is at the top; you can't when it's at the bottom. This is great for all kinds of special effects. It doesn't work with texture maps. You can put it all the way to transparent and it won't affect them. To get transparency in texture maps you need to use the image alpha chanel. More on that later.
- **Refraction.** When you look through a thick piece of glass, it distorts the view behind it. That's refraction, the bending of light. Earlier you saw the lens we built rendered with Refraction to show you what it does. You can set the refraction index exactly, and by knowing the index of water, glass, and diamond, you can get a pretty good simulation of same.

The infinite variety you can produce with textures and shaders is truly astounding. No one can reveal all the secrets, you just have to play with them and see what you get. Keep your eye out for a sidebar in the Hollywood Special Effects section in Chapter 26 that reveals a few secrets. After a while you'll develop a feel for the tools and find yourself creating the texture you want in a matter of seconds. Your range will increase along with your collection of texture maps. I currently have several thousand — can't keep track of them anymore.

UV Projection Schemes

It's easy to put a material on a 2D object, but in 3D things get complicated. Calculations must be made to bend the texture around the object in a believable way. tS2 gives you three different ways to project your material.

Figure 11-5: Here the checker design UV is projected from left to right three ways, Spherical, Planar, and Cylindrical. (When you select the UV Projection icon, you automatically get the settings panel.)

Figure 11-5 compares the appearance of the same map when it's projected three different ways.

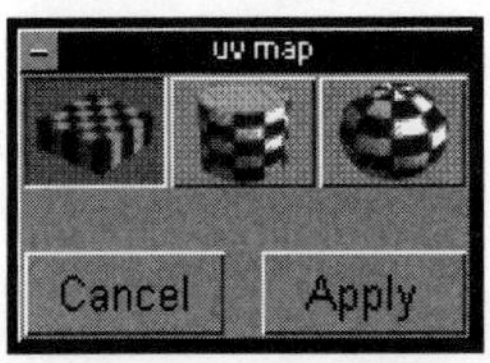

Objects created in tS2 have a UV space assigned to them. You may want to change it. Further, imported objects often have no UV projection attached to them. You can tell when you try to apply a nice texture and all you get is some average color over the whole surface. UV space is a mathematical term that describes a 3D system capable of describing any point on an object's surface. U is the horizontal distance around the object's surface from an arbitrary starting point. V is the vertical distance around the object at that point.

When you engage UV projection with an object selected, a wireframe depiction of the UV space is assigned to the object.

CAUTION

The wireframe depiction you see is not the default assigned to the object. You can't see that once it's assigned. I find it's safer to not reassign UV mapping to objects I've made in tS2. I used to think that everything gets a planar map so I'd change it to one of the others but could never get back to the original, which usually looked best.

You can see where the texture's seam will be (the brown line) and will want to rotate the seam out of view using the Object Rotate tool. You can also make adjustments to the spherical and cylindrical projections with the Object Move tool.

When you get the UV space the way you want it, click on Apply and whatever maps are already assigned will be remapped and you'll be put back to work mode. Let's take a closer look at the three types of projection.

Planar

Specifies a rectangular mapping. The image is projected through the object and displayed on front and back, stretched along the sides. The center object (previously shown in Figure 11-5) shows how the image is distorted around the sphere. You can rotate your image to reposition its mapping plane. When you do this, visualize the image being stretched and compressed to match the object's changing cross section. I use this one a lot, especially on square-ish space vehicles. Some other 3D packages offer Cubic mapping which applies the image from each of the six sides of a cube. It's very useful and I hope Caligari includes it in the next edition of tS.

Cylindrical

This one wraps the image around the object like the label on a dog food can, as previously shown in Figure 11-5, right. Remember to rotate the seam out of view.

Spherical

Like the Mercator projection map, this one calculates and scales the image around a sphere. (See Figure 11-5, left.)

Default Mapping

When you build an object in trueSpace2 it receives an appropriate and sometimes irreplaceable map space. The Helix, for example gets cylindrical mapping along its axis of rotation, while the ends get planar mapping. You can't do that yourself. Also the Cube gets cubic mapping which I was complaining about above. The torus gets toroidal mapping which is like a cylinder wrapped around the torus with no end.

The Material Rectangle Tool

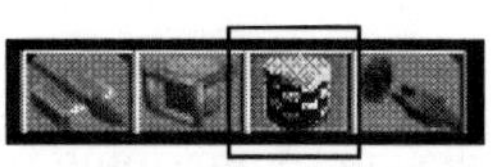

I think of this as the Decal tool. It lets you place an image on the surface of an object. It even lets you stack up to eight images to create interesting effects. It uses whatever material is showing in the Material Preview window. The decal actually sticks to the surface of the object, so as you deform it with various tools, the image is likewise deformed to conform with the new surface. Bump maps on the original surface affect the decal as well. Figure 11-6 shows a bitmap that's wrapped around a wine bottle. Check out the Galaxy Bee ad in the color section.

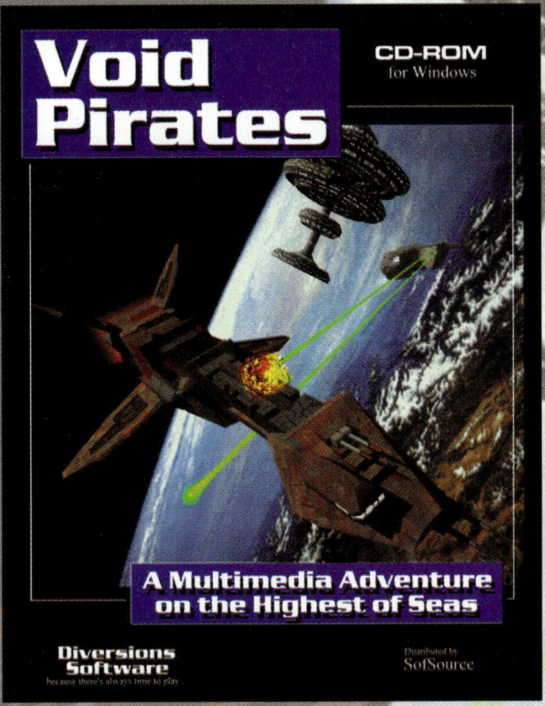

Plate 1-1: This is the CD-ROM cover for Ian Firth's *Void Pirates*, a game that was completely designed and rendered in trueSpace2. Ian's games are known for their dynamic graphics and challenging plays.

Plate 2-1: *Attack in Orion Sector*. These images demonstrate how you can liven up an image by adding composited elements. This is often done in post-production. You can create truly believable effects.

Plate 4-1: I promised you chrome balls. Here are some chrome and glass balls on a mirror. This is my daughter Dani's very first rendering. I like it.

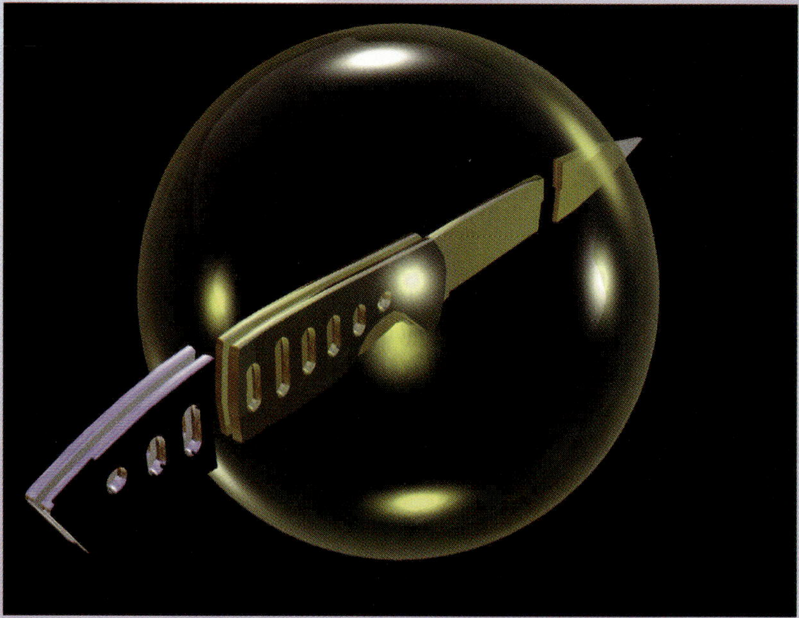

Plate 6-1: I call this *Once Was a Weapon*. This piece demonstrates the use of both boolean intersection and boolean subtract. It uses two knives and three spheres. The center section of the knife is made by a boolean intersecting a whole knife with the first sphere. The outside sections are created by a boolean subtracting a second sphere from the second knife. The remaining pieces are separated slightly. The third sphere is placed, and the glass is textured.

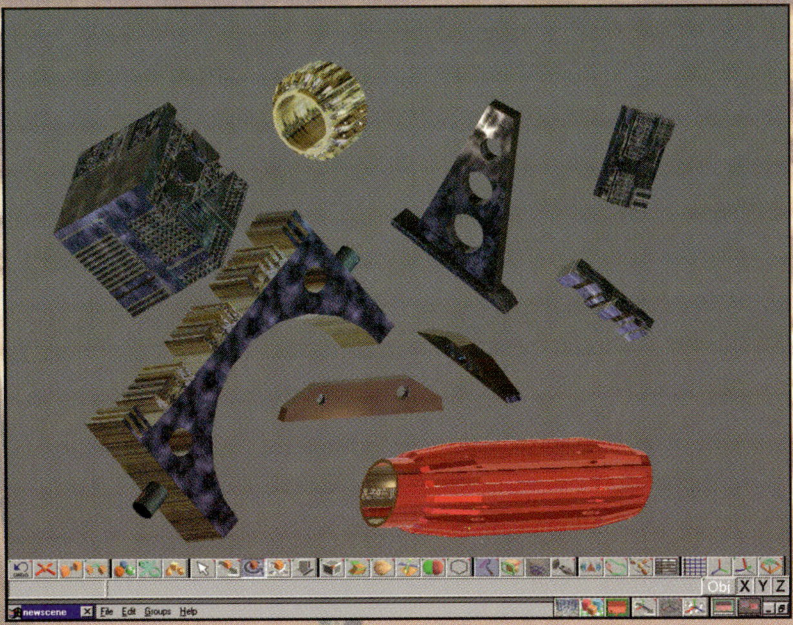

Plate 6-2: Nernies! This is a collection of pieces and parts that can be used in a thousand ways to add detail to your models. I keep a library of them and add to it regularly. You can stretch them and texture them in different ways to achieve many different looks. The gold-finned tube is the same nernie as the red exhaust pipe.

Plate 6-3: *Sunset on a Dead Tree.* This 12-minute project was rendered by extruding a polygon and then shaping it with the scale command along the way. The tree's branches were rendered by creating one branch and then making two copies of the branch, which were scaled and rotated.

Plate 7-1: The shark model looks like a Styrofoam cutout when we first open it. There's no life to it at all. By adding a simple fractal texture, some shader magic, and deformation of the model, we achieve a realistic shark. Place him in a simple sea setting, with a few underwater plants and a floor of sculpted planar objects that are covered with the same rescaled fractal texture, and we have a believable scene.

Plate 10-1: Ah, the loneliness of outer space. This image uses the intergalactic tanker, space station, and drone ship that you can construct in the tutorials in this book.

Plate 10-2: Here is a detail of the drone ship. This handy pilotless unit is used for delivering supplies to small outlying stations and for conducting reconnaissance.

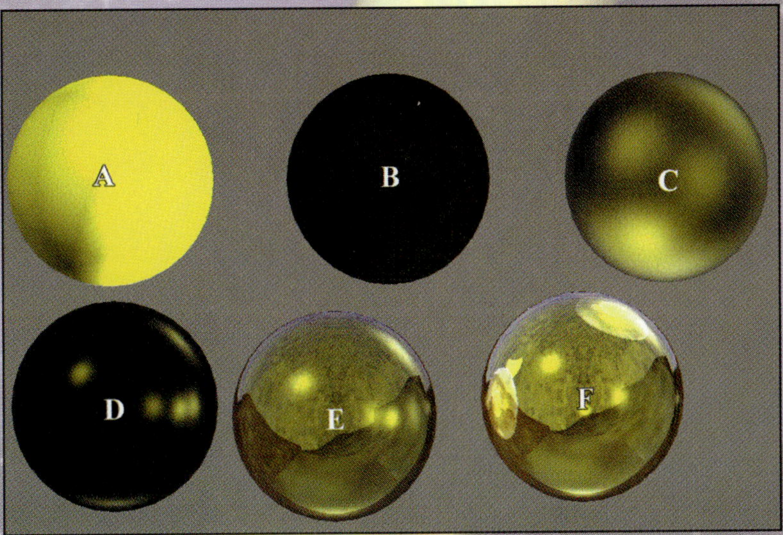

Plate 12-1: How about a little digital alchemy? Here are the six stages of creating gold in trueSpace2:

A. Start with a flat-shaded, yellow sphere.
B. Rework the same sphere in Phong shading so it shows all the shaders at the bottom.
C. Increase the shininess and roughness shaders to get a dull brass look.
D. Click the Metal shader.
E. Add the Wastlan reflection map.
F. Raytrace the sphere. Notice how the raytraced sphere reflects the other balls, and displays both simulated and real reflections.

Plate 12-2: These cloth samples were created by using a number of techniques. Some started out as a photo image of a piece of cloth and then used the same image as a bump map. Others, like the white terry cloth, were actually made. The terry was created by using a white paper texture with a sand bump map. See Chapter 12 for details.

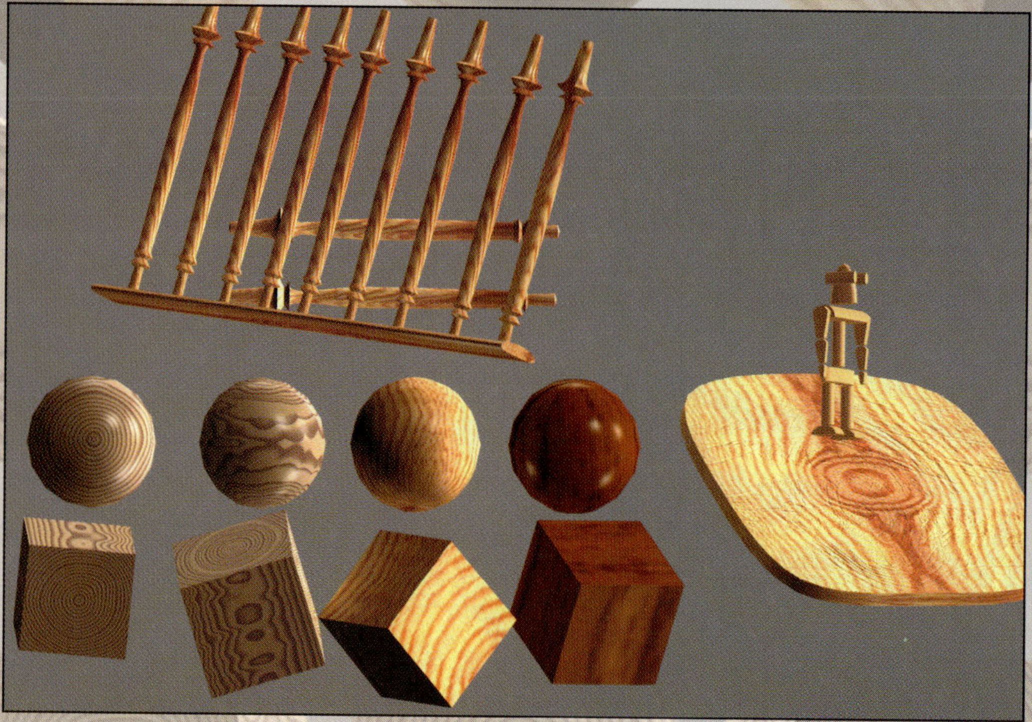

Plate 12-3: This 3D image shows different kinds of wood. Can you identify the oak? The Hemfir? The procedural and the mapped pieces? Try. The spindles are actually copies of one piece that was lathed in less than a minute. You can create fancy wood work quickly in trueSpace2. Consider using bump maps to make the lightly carved detail.

Plate 12-4: The industrial flashlight you've built can be used to light up a logo. Here a spot light was placed inside the reflector and aimed at the DreamScape Logo. Note that it's a shadow caster, which adds realism to the image.

Plate 12-5: By using the Material projection method, you can wrap labels around 3D surfaces. This example shows a beer bottle from Deneb Prime, where they use only the finest Denebian slime fungus.

Plate 13-1: This scene from *SeaFari* illustrates a virtual reality ride in Japan that was designed by Rhythm & Hues. Kate White was in charge of the project. This plate and Plate 13-2 give you an idea of her work. ©1996 Rhythm & Hues.

Plate 13-2: This illustration by Kate White shows a detail from an underwater wreck. Notice the fish, bubbles, and bits of stuff moving realistically in the water. ©1996 Rhythm & Hues

Plate 13-3: This background was made with the gradient tool in Photoshop. It's been swirled with the polar coordinate filter. I used a series of long and short strokes with the linear setting and then switched to a radial gradient. The difference setting was used to create the unusual color effects.

Plate 13-4: This is the same background, which I tweaked and added some lens flares. My intent here is to convey the feeling of a quantum singularity threshold vortex. Since I've never seen one, nor have you, who's to argue with me about how it looks?

Plate 15-1: A shuttle as it appears in deep space. This animation still shows the Starfire shuttle approaching Trilon station. Here she's out a ways in the harsh, cold environs of the cosmos. The picture also demonstrates some Hollywood-style post-effects you can use to create the star flares. Black Box plug-in filters from Alien Skin are useful in creating image effects in post-production. Check this image against the ones in Plate 31-1 and you'll see how each filter affected the image.

Plate 15-2: Here is the pilot's view of Trilon Station. I used the Z axis of the Starfire model as the camera for this view.

Plate 15-3: This is the view of Trilon as the pilot prepares to dock.

Plate 15-4: This is how Starfire appears when it's locked down in the service bay after the flight. The mechanical arms are articulated in the animation. The vacuum doors are also animated in this scene. Notice how the spot lights help to play down the emphasis on the vacuum door and highlight its texture.

Plate 16-1: Using key lighting is critical for achieving a mood for your illustration or animation. It determines the main shadows and highlights in the scene. Here the key light shines from the high-front left, effectively highlighting the foliage, and casting shadows backwards.

Plate 16-2: The key light from the high-left creates a little more mood, and casts dark shadows on the leaves and across the sand.

Plate 16-3: Using the backlight key is a special case. You can only use it when you have a light background, because the key light silhouettes the foreground objects. A black background leaves you with shadows. Using a backlight key can be a very effective way to create a romantic mood. Here I've used the same spot as it appears in the previous two examples.

Plate 16-4: Backlighting a scene with a shadow that casts infinite light can be used to simulate the setting sun. Here I've added refraction to the glass ball and then raytraced the scene to show how refraction can affect the look of glass objects.

Plate 17-1: Here I've created a rough set with boxes, nernies, and odd models that I had around. I created this simple cityscape and illuminated it with default light. I didn't want the scene to look "finished" because the point is to create a mood and to mask the simplicity of the set by effectively using atmosphere and lighting.

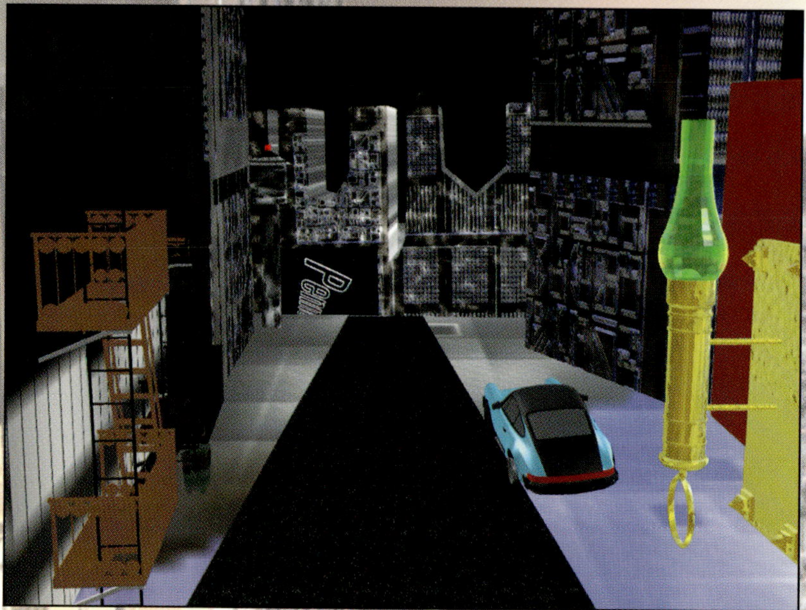

Plate 17-2: Here I've omitted the default light and added some light elements of my own. Note the splotches of light on the ground and on the fire escapes. I've also placed a bright local light behind the rear cityscape buildings to achieve the background gradient. The buildings were created by scaling and stretching a nernie I had in my library. I've also used it on many space ships.

Plate 17-3: Here I've overdone the atmosphere of patchy fog by placing a semi-transparent marble filter in front of the camera. I shined some spots on the filter to bring out the fog. You would normally shine less light on the filter to get a more realistic effect.

Plate 17-4: Here's the full effect. I've used set lighting, particle snow, fog, density filtering, and even a lens flare that I made by placing a local light between the camera and the marble filter plane. Then I added a shiny shader.

Plate 23-1: I've always liked the water pod in the movie, *The Abyss*. You can build one, too. This shot is part of an animation where the pod lifts out of the water and takes shape using the Sculpt Tool. To make it more realistic, you would add things like ripples around the base and a background image.

Plate 24-1: Your characters need to have expressive faces. This is the simplest kind of face: A sphere with some eyes, a nose pulled out, and a mouth with nernie teeth and a tongue. By using the Object Deform tool, you can create an infinite variety of expressions and even do lip-synching.

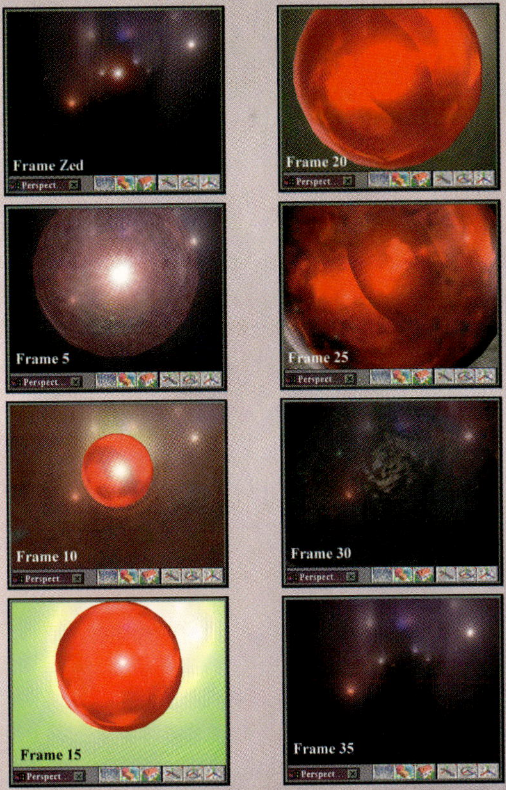

Plate 26-1: This is a series of screen shots of a cosmic gas explosion. The effect is created by nesting two transparent, reflection-textured spheres with a light in the center. You keyframe the scale of the balls, from very tiny to larger than the screen, in a series of frames. At the same time, you keyframe the light intensity from zed to about 16. As the explosion peaks, you keyframe the reduced light and increase the transparency of the spheres until all is as it was.

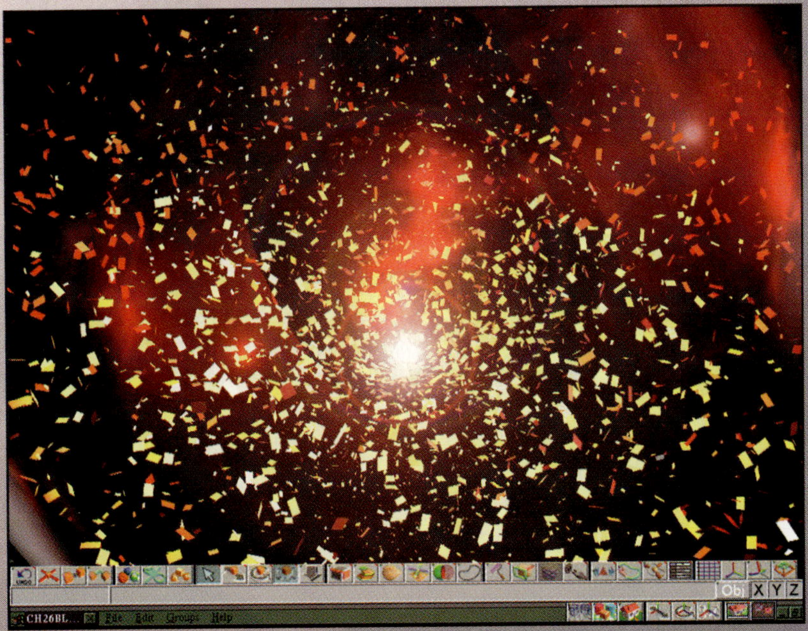

Plate 26-2: For a really impressive blast, combine the cosmic gas explosion with a particle explosion. Here I've used Rob Bryerton's *Exploder* to create two dense exploder spheres, which I scaled down to near invisibility. Next, I timed the particles to explode after the gas peaked, figuring the particles would travel slower than light. As you can see, it looks cool (I mean hot) as a still. Wait until you animate it.

Plate 26-3: This is how the intergalactic tanker appears after it is attacked by hostile aliens as it comes out of a transdimensional space warp. The effect was created by compositing 32-bit tga images of real explosions with laser fire on the trueSpace image, using the Alpha transparency channel. You can also use 24-bit files and the lighten option on the Paste as Layer pull down menu.

Plate 29-1: You can create wild special effects using Plug-in filters with trueSpace2. Here I've used Kai's Power Tools to add some color to a rendering of a light bulb. This composite shows the image before and after rendering.

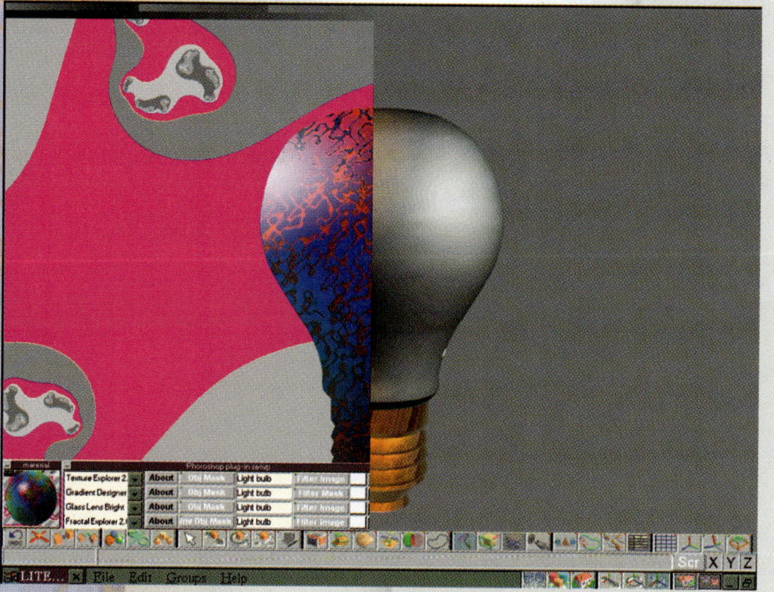

Plate 31-1: This large triptych shows the stages of producing a digital special effect in post-production. Here the bright star that you see cresting the planet was added to the original image, but it bleeds all over the planet. A copy of the planet was composited over the original image to make the star appear behind the planet.

trueSpace2 Gallery

The Work of BjØrn Kåre Nillsen

Bjorn is a young professional illustrator in Norway, whose beautiful work covers a wide range of styles and subject matter. He's been an active member of the trueSpace Mailing List (TSML) for a long time and is always ready to help new animators learn advanced techniques. His advice and encouragement have helped hundreds of digital artists around the globe. Bjorn describes his work in Plates 1-10.

Plate 1: *Kitchen*. This a typical after-supper kitchen scene in Norway. It was modeled and then raytraced in trueSpace2.

Plate 2: *Some / no· body*. What's inside? Perhaps a diamond in the rough? It's kind of up to you to figure it out.

Plate 3: *Bank Vault.* This is a detail from a larger fly-through animation that I created. The image shows a room with a vaulted ceiling that I made by using boolean functions to shape the roof and then depositing the texture. It was modeled and rendered in trueSpace2. Note the visible beams of light. This effect was achieved by adding semitransparent cones to the light shafts.

Plate 4: *Horsepower.* This whimsical toy was modeled and raytraced in trueSpace1, which is now called trueSpace S/E. The image shows the power of this entry-level version of trueSpace.

Plate 9: *Glessa*. This is another fanciful illustration that shows glass textures and refraction.

Plate 5: *Cathedral*. This is my futuristic vision of a cathedral in the sky. It was modeled and rendered in trueSpace2, and demonstrates lathing, boolean texturing, and extrusion along a path. The 28 columns are actually copies of just one column.

Plate 6: *Cyberhead*. I am fascinated by the Internet. I modeled Cyberhead and then rendered it in trueSpace2, using scanned and manipulated photos.

Plate 7: *CyberPort 5*. This is another series of illustrations that depict the interconnectedness that we experience online.

Plate 8: *Dice*. This image demonstrates using boolean subtraction for the dots and then depositing color. I used strong refraction and raytracing to give the cubes a solid look.

Plate 10: *Internet*. This Internet logo was designed and modeled by me and then rendered in trueSpace2 using the Z focus effect.

The Work of Tom Marlin

Tom Marlin is an award winning game developer. His most recent work can be seen in *Rings of the Magi* by MVP Software, which was given a five-star rating (highest rating) by Ziff-Davis Net. His 3D artwork has also been awarded first and second place in national competitions. His company, Marlin Studios, is developing several projects, including a 3D graphic mystery game called *The Roswell Omen*. The three illustrations shown here are from *The Roswell Omen*.

Plate 11: *The Sphinx*. In this illustration, texture and bump mapping helps to keep the polygon count way down.

Plate 12: *The Mine.* Here you see how shadows are created by casting light through a Cookie filter.

Plate 13: *The Lost City of Machu Picchu in the Andes.* This illustration shows how you can create an effective scene by using a very low polygon count and incorporating textures, bumps, and background maps.

The Work of Optic Edge Nerve

Optic Edge Nerve is a new animation company that's comprised of former trueSpace animators. (Each of the talented principals got their start with trueSpace.) Although they use other 3D rendering tools, they still use trueSpace2 extensively in their professional animation work. You can access samples of their video work in the Optic subdirectory on the CD-ROM. The three Principles are: I-Wai Huang, Arie Sztajnworc and Devon Taylor.

I-Wei Huang's Work

Plate 15: *Dinoray*. This is one of I-Wei's many unique robot characters. Dino is fully articulated and capable of complex movements. The limbs are joined by using the parent/child glue method.

Plate 16: *The Kick*. This is a nice example of compositing live action with animated film. The kicker looks an awful lot like I-Wei himself.

Plate 19: *I-Bot*. Caligari's famous running robots were designed, modeled, and animated by I-Wei. You can find this rendering on the CD-ROM.

Plate 14: *The Ant.* The ant was modeled in trueSpace2, and has articulated legs. The texture was created by using the wood procedural.

Plate 18: *The Shell.* This meticulous rendering of a sea shell shows an example of extruding along a path. The textured image looks very close to the real thing.

Plate 17: *The Log Cabin.* In this illustration of a mountain cabin, I-Wei saved a lot of modeling time by using multiple copies of many elements, such as the logs and structural members. The fireplace emits a flickering shadow, casting a warm glow that helps to create the inviting mood.

Arie Sztajnworc's Work

Plate 20: *Lunar Lander*. Arie is known for his detailed modeling. This example of an articulated model shows remarkable detail. Note the many workings of the legs. The moon's surface is also modeled and textured to perfection. Note the moody lighting and the interesting way the lights were enhanced in Photoshop. Arie didn't use a straight lens flare here. Can you figure out how he did it?

Plate 21: *The Caligari Logo*. Arie's logos are works of art. The dynamic quality of his designs sets them apart from ordinary work. Take a look at his number count down for the Optic Edge demo, which you'll find on the CD-ROM.

Devon Taylor's Work

Here's a special piece from Devon Taylor. I bet you've never seen the interior of a Roman temple done in such grand detail.

Plate 22: *The Temple*. This temple interior evokes a somber mood and a little awe. Note the water in the long pools and the gold vase in the case at the far end. The torches were enhanced with Photoshop. By using lens flares, Devon gives the torches a realistic finishing touch. Who says you need radiosity to achieve realistic interior lighting? I think Devon created this lighting effect in trueSpace2.

The Web Plates

This is a small sample of renderings that I found on the Web from sites like `www.caligari.com`. You'll find links to other sites that contain all sorts of wonderful images that you can download. The following images will give you ideas of what can be achieved in trueSpace2.

Oliver Zeller's Work

Plate 23: *Microcassette*. This is an older example of Oliver's work, but I like it. This piece is an excellent example of how a product image can be created. Oliver used PhotoPaint 5 to create the texture maps, which give the microcassette its authentic appearance. Note the side panel views as well. He modeled the piece in trueSpace2. You can use similar techniques to visualize new products very quickly. With a good die sublimation printer, you can actually produce photo-like images of yet-to-be-built products.

Glen Tittermary's Work

Glen's piece is a wonderfully detailed view of the Apollo 11 Moon lander.

Plate 24: *Apollo 11*. The moon's surface looks remarkably real. It's actually a photo of the real surface that was mapped onto a plane. The footprints are booleaned out one by one using a duplicate of the astronaut's boot. The time to model and texture the lunar lander came close to 100 hours. The whole scene, including the astronaut, equipment and flag, were all built in trueSpace2 and took about 150 hours to complete. Glen hasn't modified the image in any way. It looks exactly the same as when it came out of trueSpace2. Note the excellent use of a shadow-casting infinite light.

The Web Guitar Gallery

Guitars are a favorite subject of 3D types. Here are two guitars from two excellent artists. These fellows are known for their stunning photorealism and composition. Both David and Todd have helped countless new animators, answering all sorts of questions they receive. Getting help is one of the wonderful perk's of being part of this community of digital artists. They're always willing to share ideas and techniques.

Todd Barnes' Work

Todd owns a small company called Infinite Designs, where he creates Web pages and images for advertising. He's also a gifted animator and works in both LightWave and trueSpace.

Plate 25: *My Guitar.* This illustration of Todd's electric guitar was a successful early effort using trueSpace2. Despite moving to the powerful LightWave 4.0, Todd still uses trueSpace2 because of its superior modeling interface.

David Campbell's Work

David possesses the perfect skills for a digital artist: He's a Unix programmer by day and a talented 3D artist by night. You've already seen his remarkable *Hammer.*

Plate 26: *The Red Stratocaster.* Here is David's red Stratocaster. It was created and rendered in trueSpace2.

Figure 11-6: You can easily wrap a label around a bottle with the Material Rectangle tool.

If you want to use a Material Rectangle on an object you expect to use in a boolean operation, wait until *after* the boolean to place a decal. If you boolean one or two objects with Material Rectangles in place, you'll get unpredictable, usually destructive results. Put that on your rule of thumb list. It's a good general rule whether you're using tS2 or Alias/Wavefront.

CAUTION

The Material Rectangle will follow the UV Projection associated with the object as you rotate it. When it comes to the seam, it will slide behind it and disappear. I couldn't figure out where it went, so be forewarned. Also, if you are using planar UV mapping, you'll get the image on both sides of the object.

Let's take a closer look at the Selection panel.

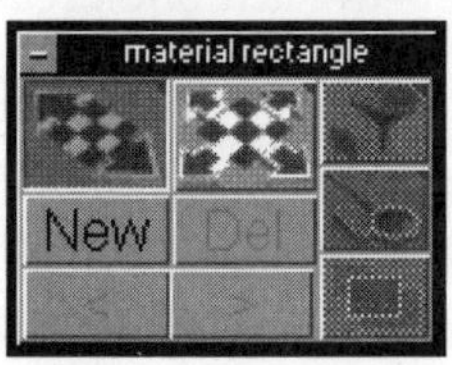

New

This option creates a new Material Rectangle and displays its location on the object's surface. If you are in 3DR mode and have selected a render quality that includes texture maps, you'll get a nice representation of the map in place. This makes it easier to work with. If you have 3D acceleration, this mode is the way to go when working with Material Rectangles.

Del

Deletes the current Material Rectangle. If you have a stack of them, it deletes the one on top.

Move

Allows you to interactively place the rectangle where you want it. It moves the thing around the object's surface.

Scale

Changes the rectangle's size and aspect ratio interactively. Horizontal and Vertical mouse movements control U and V scaling, respectively.

</>

These are the Cycle Materials buttons. When you have a stack of rectangles you can bring them successively to the top with this tool. The 3DR window updates, but the Material Preview window does not.

Paint

The little tornado-shaped tool paints the current material onto your object's rectangle.

Inspect

The little magnifying glass works the same way as the Inspection Brush does. Place it over a material in the work space and click. It will make that material current in the Material Preview window, ready for use. A right click on this tool will open the Material Design panels so you can modify the material.

To the Front

The lower right corner has an icon I call: To the Front. It brings the current material to the top of the stack. Normally the top material is the last one created.

Material Library

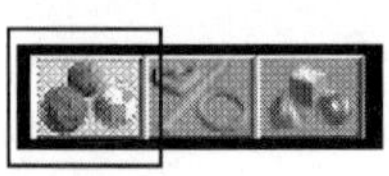

You've already used the Material Library. I'll be brief: This is a great innovation. When you click on the Material Library icon, you get a visual material selection window.

It comes with a nice selection of materials and you can add new ones at will. I suggest you create several libraries of like materials — construction, space, organic, special effects, glass, metal, and so on. The default library is called Simple. You can delete it if you like and name a different library Simple. The new simple.lib will load as the default (unless you've engaged Save State, in which case the library in that state will come up).

The library window displays eight materials at a time, with a scroll bar to bring more into view. The material is displayed on either a sphere or a plane, depending on how you had it in the Material Preview window at the time of saving. To choose a material click on it and it's set up automatically in the Material Preview window, ready for use. A red line under a material in the library indicates it is selected for use.

To save a new material to the library, just click the in arrow on the lower right of the library window. Then give it a name in the Material Name panel on the right side. Simple as that. Just remember to do it. I keep forgetting and you absolutely cannot reproduce some great textures ever again. Next to the Add button is a Delete arrow (with a red X through it) for library maintenance. Use it to remove unused materials.

POWER TIP

Don't save textures from removable media in the libraries. You can't retrieve them unless you have the CD-ROM or syquest or floppy in place. Always move a texture you intend to put in a library onto your permanent hard drive.

Next to the Delete arrow is your Current Library indicator. Click on it to bring up a typical file functions window to choose a new library or to create a new one or even delete one.

Libraries are extremely handy for keeping track of those special textures you could never get back again. Use them to organize your textures in a logical way to speed up your production capability. In Chapter 12 I'll be introducing a lot of ideas on how to create nifty textures using different types of maps. Way up in Chapter 26 you'll learn how to use the alpha channel to create maps with transparent backgrounds for use in rotoscoping.

This was long for a quick and dirty overview of tools, but you needed it. Now we move on to the even more interesting part: how to use them.

Summary

In this chapter you've been introduced to all the basic surfacing tools, including:

- ✦ All the brushes that are used to apply surfaces to the whole object, object sections, and individual polygons or vertices.
- ✦ Material Preview, which gives you instant, interactive 3D feedback on the material you are creating, either on a plane or a sphere.
- ✦ Mapping of textures, bumps, and reflections to create photorealistic surfaces. Maps simulate natural looking textures on plain surfaces.
- ✦ Shaders, which interactively provide different surface microstructure and transparency characteristics to your surfaces.
- ✦ UV mapping to create different looks by applying mapping coordinates for the object in planar, spherical, or cylindrical formats.
- ✦ Material Rectangles, the decals of tS2. They allow you to build up complex surface treatments (up to eight layers) or apply images to specific spots on an object.
- ✦ Material Libraries wherein you save interesting textures you've discovered. They allow instant recall of any texture/shader combination and help organize large collections of textures into individual libraries.

✦ ✦ ✦

CHAPTER 12

Shader Techniques

In This Chapter

Using Gloss and Shininess

Creating metals from rust to shiny gold

Creating glass with Transparency and Refraction

Implying natural surfaces like cloth and wood

Uses of Ambient Light

Simulating surface texture with bump's specular highlights

There is something about light glinting off a shiny surface that I love. When I was a teenager I was fascinated by those glitter balls at high school dances. I'm a sucker for a good airbrush painting depicting a shiny Harley or even a glossy patent leather shoe. I think all artists have a love affair with light. It's one of the things that drew me to the CGI world.

Interactive Alchemy

Come play with me as we shed a little light on surfaces, starting with gold and working our way up to rusty iron. In 3D, a good rusty iron is a more sophisticated and challenging material than gold. Shiny gold balls look cool, so pop up a sphere and smooth it way out. Because this is color stuff, I'm putting some illustrations as plates in the color section. Check them out.

In Figure 12-1 (Plate 12-1 as well) I've painted six spheres illustrating progressive steps in the creation of shiny gold effects.

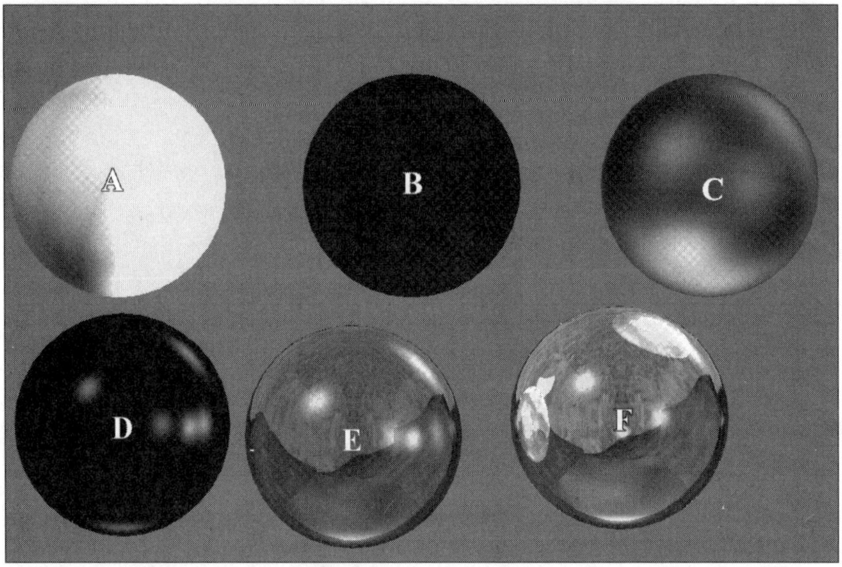

Figure 12-1: Six stages of creating gold: plain yellow phong ➪ plain yellow metal ➪ increase shine ➪ add highlights ➪ add reflections ➪ add raytrace reflections

A. Upper left is the Default Phong shader with Ambient Glow, Shininess, Roughness, Transparency, and Refraction all set at minimum.

B. Moving to the right, I've engaged the Metal shader. Notice how black ball two got. We'll need some reflection and specular highlights.

C. Moving top right, I've increased the shininess (reflectivity) to 80%. Remember you can right click on the Shader Attribute panel to access direct numeric input. It still doesn't look much like polished gold… Florentine gold or brass maybe. Gold should have a really fine, polished surface.

D. I've increased specular highlights on the bottom left ball to harden and polish up the surface. It's still not gold — the real thing reflects stuff.

E. At bottom center I've added reflections by simply selecting Use Environment Map and opting for the wastlan environment map that comes with tS2. Now this looks pretty much like gold. The reflections really make it nice, but these are pseudo reflections. We need some real ones for believability.

F. I've raytraced this ball at bottom right to give it genuine reflections. Look closely and you'll see the first, third, and fifth balls reflected accurately. This adds a lot more when you have 3D gold letters because each letter reflects the one next to it in a very convincing way. Lights will also be reflected, adding appropriate highlights.

Until It Looks Right

You'll work this way a lot, adding and adjusting surface characteristics until it looks right. Some professionals call it "tricking out" the scene. There are an infinite variety of golds you can make. Try adding a little green or a bump map. The default bump map, orange, makes a nice primitive gold. Play around with different reflection maps as well. I find those with colorful contrast and a bright sun spot work best. Vary the plan a little by decreasing reflectivity and specularity (giving larger highlights) a little and adding a bit of red to the metal color. You'll make a nice brass. Use strange colors and make up metals that don't exist in nature.

Textures Happen

Serendipity is a big factor in creating the right textures. Like a great chef, you spend time playing with oddball ingredient combinations. In time you develop a feel for texture and what elements will give you what you want.

Iron

On our journey to rust we have to visit iron. What is it about iron that gives it the look of iron? It's difficult to pin down. To me polished iron has a waxy look to its surface and there is usually some microstructure. Iron has character — a faint hammer mark, a worn scratch, that sort of thing. If you take a lot of time and create the right bump maps you can make very realistic polished iron.

Scrounging Materials

But in this case I'm going to show you something more important. How to scrounge up a good iron texture from common rendering ingredients. So let's use this as a general methodology for creating metal with an interesting yet believable surface. I cut and swept a nernie on which to try out different textures. I'm going to give you some specific recipes for materials I discovered along my journey to cheap steel (see Figure 12-2). Let it be the last time you use a formula from someone else. Creating materials is a personal journey with plenty of productive side trips. Along my way to iron I discovered a neat stone texture and a radical way to make rusty iron.

Stone

The stone happened when I was using a granite bitmap texture as a bump map and I accidentally clicked one of my texture maps called gldfoil as the reflection map. My point here is not to show you how to make this specific material, but how materials happen. Again, I forgot to save this one and I can't quite get it back. I remember playing around with the roughness channel, bringing the slider down quite a bit to increase the size of the highlights. Oh yes, I also remember turning down the relief parameter on bumps to somewhere around .02. Textures happen.

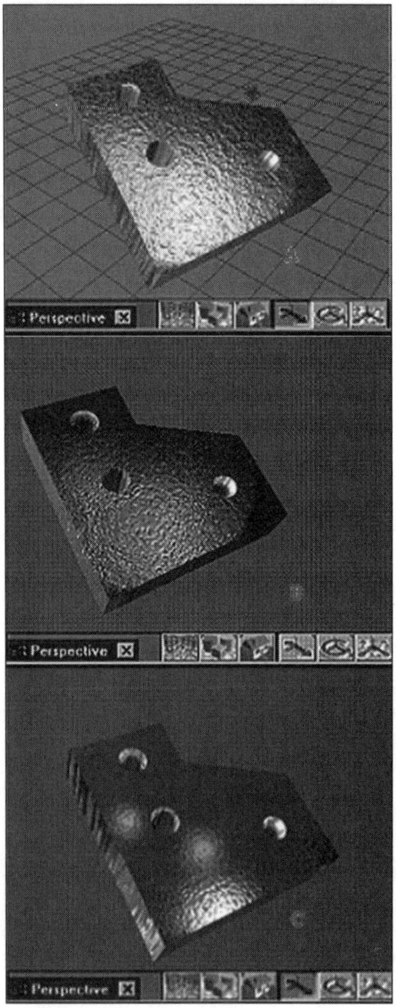

Figure 12-2: Textures I ran into on the way to cheap steel: Stone, Rusty Iron, Cheap Steel.

Rusty Iron

The middle example is a very nice replica of worn rusty iron. This too happened by accident. I was going to do rusty iron for you in a different way, but I liked this one. Here's the recipe:

1. Take one dark marble bump map and turn down the relief to near zero (I used .04). Experiment with different marble and granite bump maps.
2. Increase the specular highlight size by increasing roughness (ironically, this means *decreasing* the roughness setting to around 25%. It should have been called smoothness or specularity).
3. Take one NASA Nebula bitmap, ngc224c.bmp, from the CD-ROM (\textures\space) and use it as a reflection map. It has a reddish cast and highlights. Don't ask me why it works, it just does — that's why you experiment.
4. Set the reflection up to about 90%.
5. Select Phong Shader (also try Metal Shader for a polished rust look).
6. Select Auto Facet.
7. Select a rust base color and decrease the brightness to just below half.
8. Check it out and adjust until it feels right.

Cheap Steel

This is polished rough iron. Not as oxymoronic as it may sound, the rough metal has been polished by time and use. The texture is still there, just rounded and smoothed out. Here's the recipe:

1. Take one dark marble bitmap and use it as a bump map.
2. Set the bump relief to about .02.
3. Set roughness somewhere in the middle.
4. Set reflectivity somewhere in the middle.

5. Put some more lights in, close to the metal.
6. Use the wastlan reflection map.
7. Pick a neutral gray base color from the Cube, that would be whitish with a mid-brightness level.
8. Choose the Metal shader and Auto Facet.
9. Nudge controls until done.

Test your concoctions on various shaped objects. Since much of the surface quality comes from the bumps, reflections, and specularity, you incorporate a texture map to enhance the effect. For example, try making a texture map in Corel Draw or Fractal Design Painter that looks like distressed metal, and use it with above. If you're lazy or unskilled at painting texture maps, try a photograph of iron. I'll give you some tips on collecting texture photos in the next chapter.

Transparency Effects

Some of the coolest effects are done with transparency. Since particle effects with more than a few thousand pieces will bog down a computer, I use transparency to simulate gas clouds, vapor, and steam. It's easy; your transparency slider works by progressively making your texture more transparent. It doesn't work on procedural textures because they have special transparency sliders accessed via their own settings panel. Nor does it work on texture maps because their characteristics are cast in stone.

Glass

Glass has both transparency and refraction. Since I'm an artist, I'm not very concerned about accuracy of refraction. If it looks right, save it — my motto on glass. It's amazing how every bit of life's experience helps an artist. One summer vacation, I worked as a glass cutter in a window factory in Plainfield, New Jersey. I remember three things about it:

- I lost a lot of blood.
- Somebody misspelled "You're on Candid Camara" on the men's room door and it annoyed me on a daily basis.
- Clear glass comes in an amazing variety of colors when you look through its edges.

Glass from Sweden had a definite blue tinge, the glass that came from Japan tended toward deep green, and U.S. glass was somewhere in the middle. Every once in a while I'd get a piece of glass with a green/gold cast I particularly liked. I never found a neutral gray/white glass.

When I make glass, I often put in a little green/gold. In space vehicles, I use gold glass to simulate solar coatings. Another thing I noticed about glass that summer: only plate glass appears perfect. Most glass derives character from the microstructure of its surface.

Here are a few tips for making glass:

- ✦ If you have more than one type of glass in a scene, vary the color, surface texture, and transparency of each slightly.
- ✦ Bump map some of your glass for interesting specular highlights. Sometimes I use the default orange map repeated a few times to scale the detail smaller. Be creative, mess with the UV repeats, and keep your relief way down. Use the smallest Amp you can get.
- ✦ Glass without refraction is glass without soul. Don't forget to slide this one up halfway or more. You can see a comparison of glass with and without refraction under a palm tree in the color section.
- ✦ Refraction gives the illusion of thickness to your glass object; play with it.

CAUTION

You won't see any refraction when you scan-line render, the usual way to check your image. You'll probably forget and push up the refraction setting, looking for effect. *The only time you actually see the impact of Refraction settings is after you raytrace the image*. Since refraction depends on what's behind your object, put a texture there and render the whole scene to get an idea of how it will look.

- ✦ Not all glass is the same transparency. Vary it slightly for different effects.
- ✦ Make different kinds of stained glass by giving a little color to the glass and shining a spot light through to get colored shadows.
- ✦ Make some milky stained glass using marble procedural texture.
- ✦ Experiment with the Material Rectangle tool using semi-transparent designs.

POWER TIP

Study the way glass objects are made, and make yours that way. Notice the thick bottoms of bottles, embossed lettering, etched markings. Spend a few days doing nothing but glass projects. In tS2 you can teach yourself to build photo-perfect glass.

Half the fun of 3D is discovering how to simulate reality in a delicious way that will give your audience a little thrill at being deceived. They want to be cleverly deceived. They want to suspend disbelief. It's how we all cross the virtuality dimension.

Transparent Coatings

You can achieve spectacularly believable materials by overlaying a texture-mapped surface with a clear color coat. The guitar (see Plate 12-3) is a perfect example. Dave Campbell couldn't get the effect he wanted any other way. He duplicated the guitar body, surfaced on in a flattish natural wood. He upsized the duplicate body by a tiny fraction and made it a transparent lacquer color. When the two bodies are perfectly aligned (Normalize Location) they render as wood-through-clear-lacquer. Sweet trick. It's interesting to read his notes on how he achieved the wonderfully authentic spruce face of the guitar as well. Thanks Campbell.

Natural Textures

Essential to the establishment of a believable world is natural texture. Perhaps not as exciting in themselves as the metals and glasses, natural textures provide a contrast that emphasizes the spectacular nature of the other surfaces.

Wood

Probably the most used natural texture is wood. Polished wood, dull wood, cross cut wood, you name it. I've been a wood sculptor for 20 years and have an intimate relationship with wood. My particular affection for Brazilian Rosewood, the queen of all woods, leads me to overuse it. Every time I look at wood, I check out the grain and color to identify the tree it came from. So wood isn't just wood to me, it's Cocabola, Purple Heart, Oak, Birch, Zebra wood, and Gabon Ebony. I love the feel of wood, the way knots distort the grain, the way sap wood and heart wood fight for dominance. Take the time to look at wood — learn it.

There are two basic ways to make wood in tS2. Each yields excellent results.

- **Procedural Wood.** The easiest wood is made by selecting the procedural wood texture and applying it to a planar surface or object. This is a generic clear variety which can simulate everything from fir to birch. Practice by lathing some wood spindles and applying the procedurals with different parameter settings. Then set the surface gloss, etc. to your liking. It's quick and easy, but it takes a while to render as your CPU calculates where to put all those rings.
- **Mapped wood.** I use this more often. Most people don't care, but when I look at a 3D rendering, I try to identify wood species. Ergo, procedural wood annoys me — no character. I prefer to take a photo of real wood and wrap it around the object, hiding the seam. Use this approach for furniture/guitars/veneers, etc. Simply a texture map applied to an object with the surface qualities adjusted to your liking. If you have the time and courage, try using a subtle bump map to create raised grain on the wood.

POWER TIP

Bitmapped wood works best if you don't have a lot of cross grain in your image. If you do, use a separate map on the ends to get a realistic look. Procedural wood is a true 3D texture and takes end grain into account, simulating the rings along the axis you choose.

Authentic wood texture photos populate every texture CD-ROM known to man. They come with most 3D suites including trueSpace2 and SE. Experiment with some wood tabletops. Build one or use a prebuilt model of a wood table. Use gentle bump mapping to install years of wear, nail and hammer marks, grain relief, and cracks. Figure 12-3 shows examples of both bitmapped and procedural types of wood.

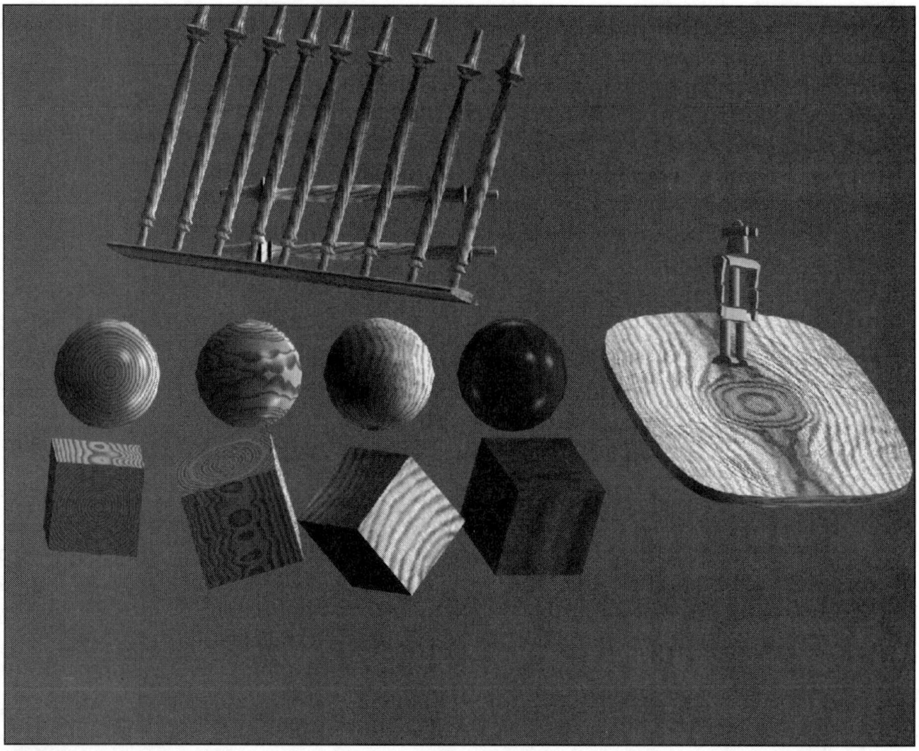

Figure 12-3: Wood objects made using either bitmapped images or procedural wood. Can you tell which is which? Identify the oak, mahogany, and fir.

Cloth

Cloth is something I don't use very much and probably should. But my experience with it is pretty much wearing it. Done properly, cloth can be impressive. Use cloth techniques for rugs, clothing, tablecloths, and even wallpaper. Develop a cloth texture library and you'll use it more often.

Patterned cloth can be made by applying bump texture to a seamless pattern. I find this is one place where I actually use my seamless texture collection. I've made up a sampler of cloth items that's shown in Figure 12- 4. This might give you some ideas, but remember this is not my forte. (See also color Plate 12-2.)

I made the various cloths in different ways. All had low reflectivity and bump maps about as low as I could make them (0.01–0.02). Ambient light was kept close to zero so the natural light could play with the texture.

POWER TIP

If your cloth looks a little too hard, set transparency to 5–10% to diffuse any glints that normal cloth wouldn't have.

Figure 12-4: A sampling of cloth ideas from someone who doesn't sew. You can do better.

I used default white light so you can compare what you get. These will all look much better under custom lighting at a low angle to emphasize the surface texture. Most samples here were made using both a texture and bump map from a photo of real cloth. I get a bigger kick out of making realistic cloth out of unrelated items, as in the terry facecloth.

A. A rough weave place mat made from a photo texture used as both the texture map and the bump map.

B. Denim made from photo, as above, but here I have a reasonably high specularity, which tends to darken since there's no reflection.

C. My favorite. Look closely, it's a terry facecloth. No cloth photos were used. The texture map is white paper and the bump map is a green noise bitmap I found. I got a reasonably good facsimile using a photo of white sand as a bump map too.

D. White percale. I built it from the white paper in C and no bump map. I fiddled with the reflection and specularity channels until it looked right. Paper texture maps are as handy as bump maps, and you get a bunch with Fractal Design Painter.

E. Woven rattan rug material. Again I used a photo and the same photo as a bump map. The ability to do this is trueSpace2 is a big time saver.

F. Look at the example photo I used for the background. I made the 3D cloth in F, as above. I'm not sure how it will look in print, but on my screen it's a winner.

G. Light fleece blanket. I made it with a simple color pattern as a texture map and bump map I found called weave8 on the Pixar Classic Textures CD-ROM.

H. A simple Native American wool blanket.

I. A heavy-textured bedspread in two colors.

The variety of textures you can create in 3D is astounding and motivating. Start out after dinner and you may see the sun rise. Remember to save them.

Ambient Light

I dislike this parameter; it's silly. Ambient light has its uses. But it's usually pretty ugly. Use it to build bright objects that do not take shadows. This is a self-generating light that emanates evenly from the object. It's not actual light in that it can't illuminate other objects or cast a shadow. I often use it with a real light source to simulate visible light sources. The bulb in the industrial flashlight we made earlier was done this way.

- ✦ Size and deform a small sphere to a bulb shape.
- ✦ Place it in the center of the reflector and glue.
- ✦ Surface it with a semi-transparent, highly ambient surface.
- ✦ Glue a high wattage spotlight (set intensity about 5–6 by right clicking on the intensity slider in the Light Properties panel) to bulb pointing out the front of the flashlight (Z axis).

This flashlight looks like it has a real light source in it, as shown in Figure 12-5.

Figure 12-5: Our virtual flashlight shines virtual light on our virtual logo.

The light on the logo does not come from the ambient light setting of the bulb, but rather from the spotlight within. If you look into the light, the bulb will appear reasonably bright.

Often with a spaceship, you'll need some kind of strobing, xenon-type light. Ambient is way inadequate for this kind of effect. Nevertheless, you can combine a flashing ambient light level with a flashing light source to create most of the illusions you'll need. Post processing with a flashing lens flare (Adobe Photoshop or Premiere) is also a possibility. I wish Caligari had incorporated some sort of lens flare like the one in LightWave; it makes doing credible light sources that much easier.

Art is about visual ideas and creatively applied technique. Don't feel badly if you don't immediately grasp some of these concepts, you're not alone. 3D is one of the most complex art forms ever devised. The added dimension requires a quantum leap in visualization. If you find yourself looking at wireframes and getting all confused, give it time. You have to train your mind/eye system to see 3D. That's why we have 3DR.

When you feel your cocky confidence fading, you're really becoming one of us. It usually happens when you know enough to glimpse how much there is to learn. One symptom: you ask people for exact Material Formulas. Drained of testicular integrity, you've resorted to the digital equivalent of paint by numbers. Everybody resorts to this kind of linear thinking at one time or another. When a student asks me, I suggest they go off and study that surface in real life and tell me all about its color, reflection specularity, and texture characteristics. After about ten minutes of that they usually get it. Force yourself to go back to your tools. Use them interactively to produce this clearer vision step, by side step, by step. Never in the history of art has there been a more accessible medium capable of such lifelike images. 3D opens to anyone willing to learn it, the ability to create illusions beyond the wildest dreams.

Summary

- ✦ You learned a little about using shaders in concert with maps to create some pretty believable textures for your objects.
- ✦ You learned that ambient light can destroy your texture effects by killing shadows.
- ✦ You also learned how to work interactively with shaders to create new looks.
- ✦ You learned that cloth and other natural materials can be effectively simulated by a wide range of techniques, and that they provide a realistic touch.
- ✦ You learned how to make your industrial flashlight shine, by imbedding a spot light in it.
- ✦ You probably have learned that I'm piling on a lot of complex stuff that doesn't seem much like art.

✦ ✦ ✦

CHAPTER 13

Images That Go Bump in the Light

✦ ✦ ✦ ✦

In This Chapter

Building your media collection database

How to create and use texture maps for your projects

Introduction to image prep programs

Tricks of the Hollywood experts in how to make a spaceship look real

Sources for photo images you can use in your work

More materials, real and otherwise

Background maps

Some fun projects, as usual

✦ ✦ ✦ ✦

This is an important chapter, so I've brought in an especially knowledgeable tipster for the inserts. Kathy White is technical lighting director at Rhythm & Hues, one of the premiere effects houses in Hollywood. She's had rich experience in all phases of digital effects and animation, including Digital Effects Supervisor for R&H on *Batman Forever*, and Technical Director for the EuroDisney Circle Vision project that involved a digital recreation of Paris. She was also CGI Supervisor on the spectacular SeaFari effects ride in Japan. Kate, as she's known in the Biz, is passionate about texture and lighting. She's a professional with soul; you can see it in her work.

Building Your Map Collection

Like a painter dabbing into his ultramarine and mixing it with burnt umber, you'll dip into your maps and materials and mix them with bumps and surface qualities.

Few things will speed up your productivity like a well-organized collection of texture maps. You may not have many now, but you soon will. My collection approaches 24,000, counting my CorelDraw Photo CD collection. No, I don't use them all, but they're there in case I need something I can't make myself.

Fortunately the Corel collection came with a thumbnail/keyword database to help locate specific images. I still have to keep track of close to 4,000 textures, both commercial and home grown, if I intend to use them. Until I found a good visual database, I simply couldn't find and use the textures I had.

An Image Database

You'll need a good multimedia database. Write your own in Access or some other multimedia database package or — a better idea — buy one. There are two excellent suites already set up for you.

✦ **Ulead MediaStudio Pro 2.5.** A complete and beautifully designed media studio with a module called Album. Album, a sophisticated media database, generates a thumbnail library; not just textures, but all images, animations, and audio tracks as well. (See Figure 13-1 for a view of the interface.) It comes with truly excellent interlinked modules for image editing, sound editing, 32-bit video editing and CD-browsing. In addition you get a CD-ROM full of great media to play with.

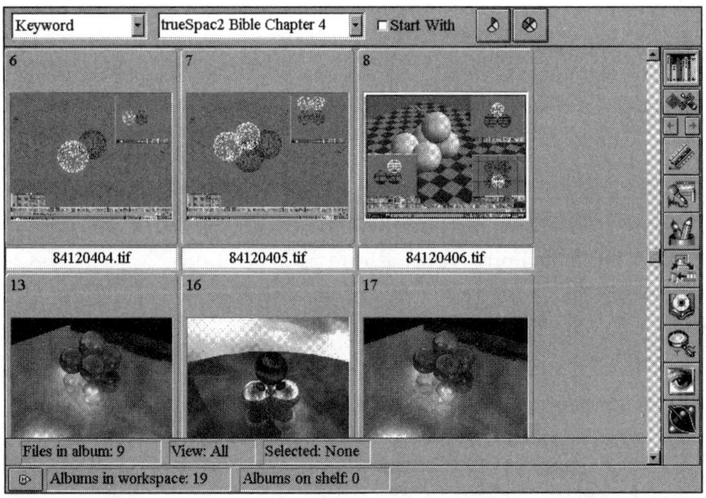

Figure 13-1: Ulead's Album displays some of my book illustrations. To the right is a drag-and-drop bar for your edit and utility programs.

✦ **JASC Media Center.** This is a shareware package you can start using today. It's included on the CD-ROM with this book. Similar to Album, Media Center is a standalone application to organize all your media. To view a thumbnail full size in Media Center, just double click on it, or you can set up slide shows. It's pretty intuitive. Remember, if you continue to use Media Center, send in your $39.00. It's well worth the price. (See Figure 13-2.)

Both packages help you maintain your files: rename, delete, copy, or move them. Album has a nice drag and drop tool bar with icons of your favorite media editors. You simply drag a thumbnail into Photoshop, Image Editor, Sound Edit, or any program you set up on the bar. trueSpace2 can't accept images this way, but I put it on the bar anyway. Just click on the logo to start the program.

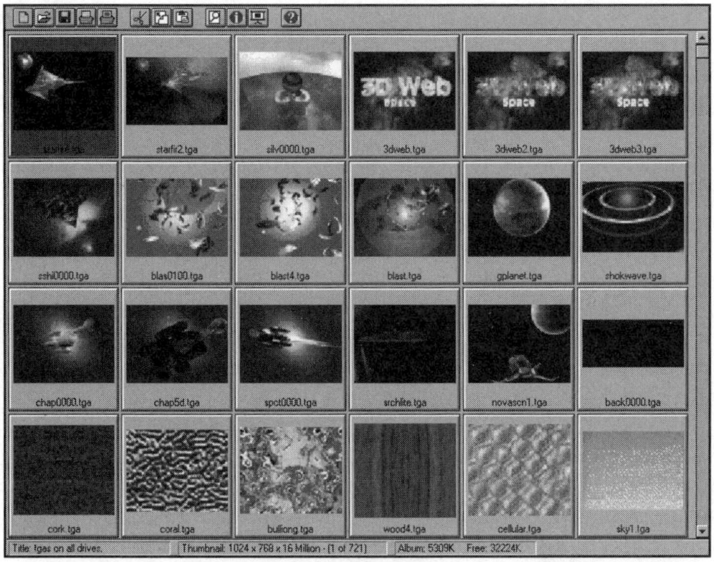

Figure 13-2: MediaCenter Screen Capture is a shareware program.

Whichever suite you use, set up separate albums for reflection, bump, texture maps, and backgrounds. I even further divvied them into space and nonspace elements. You can have the same image in more than one album if you like. After you accumulate a fair number, you'll remember what only a few look like. Worse, many image files are named with esoteric numbering systems. I recommend you rename them something you can relate to — like rdsunset.tif instead of 8412011.tif. Spend less on Prozac.

Finding Image Maps

Nowadays you can find image maps for free or a little more. If you count the Internet, there're about a million places. First, the World Wide Web is filled with pictures you can capture. I'm no lawyer (life has been good) but it stands to reason that you don't use someone else's images in a commercial venture without a license from them. You can buy CD-ROMs of pictures and music that come with a specific license. Read the licenses, as they are rarely blanket. Some prohibit republishing the material in a commercial venture.

Bitmap Collections

Since I need a range of backgrounds for various projects, I got Corel's First Professional Photos CD-ROM Library. Now a second one's been released. It's the best buy in image media. Though not all the photos are top drawer, most are excellent and you can't beat the license price of about four cents each. All twenty thousand images in either collection can be purchased for under $700.00 street price. In addition, you get an extra CD with superb, prize-winning photos and, most important, a prebuilt thumbnail database to help you locate the images you want quickly and efficiently. Mostly for backgrounds, you will find a few texture disks included. One disk has hand-drawn fantasy cartoon backgrounds you can use. It's easy to convert the Photo-CD format to just about any format/size/resolution you need with included utilities.

I also have PIXAR's famous PIXAR 128 collection of textures and their Classic Textures album (which are no longer available). Along the way I also picked up Textures for Professionals from Visual Software and their Textures and Materials CD-ROM, both included with Visual Reality 2.0. On the World Wide Web, I found Cameo Graphics' best buy CD-ROM with 3,000 300 × 300 seamless textures for under twenty bucks. Many of them are really pretty and they make interesting tiled backgrounds for Web pages, fantasy backgrounds, and unearthly materials. These are not just a bunch of default Kai's tiles (which I'm getting tired of); they are creative, painstakingly made, and interesting.

I've also created hundreds of bitmap textures in the various image programs I own. My daughter, Dani, is in charge of neat background gradients. She makes them in Photoshop, using the Gradient tool. Experiment (see Background Plates in the color section for examples).

You'd think that would be enough textures for anybody. But I frequently find myself looking for something I don't have. As you become more professional you find plenty of occasions when only a custom map will do. That's when you'll find new use for programs like Fractal Design Painter 4.0 and Photoshop. The two work well together. I also find the Ulead Image Editor very useful. You need a good Image editor for creating maps as well as compositing special effects. And for a really fast (32-bit) powerful program that's a little bit different, look at QFX from Ron Scott, Inc. CorelDraw also comes in handy, and I just got a copy of MacroMedia Freehand 5.0 for Windows. Now this is a nice drawing program that will help you create all sorts of neat maps. It's a personal choice.

The Web

I'm not going to give you specific places to find texture maps here. That would be foolish; they change daily. The way to go is to scan with one of the great Web search indexes like Yahoo, Lycos, WebCrawler, or InfoSeek. You don't need the addresses for these as they are part of the Netscape and Windows 95 Internet access interfaces. Just click on the search buttons and you'll see them. New search engines seem to emerge monthly. I use all of them and others as well.

When I did a Lycos scan just on textures, it found more than 5,000 pages. Many weren't very useful, many were. But using WebCrawler, I got about 900 pages. I only looked at about 20, but most were relevant. At other times you'll get better results on a different engine. I suspect there are thousands of textures you can nab for free. I found whole libraries of them. The one at Media Lab at MIT was over 225MB, but it was all encoded in UNIX stuff, which I avoid, but if you know what you're doing, you could probably use these in tS2. You have to look around, but there are loads of freebies out there.

Creating Your Own Textures

The most exciting way to collect textures is to make them yourself. You'll need an image edit/drawing program that takes plug-ins. Heck, you can use plug-ins like Kai's powertools right in trueSpace2. But to do real texture map development you need something like PhotoPaint 6 from Corel, Photoshop from Adobe, Fractal Design Painter from Fractal Design Corp., MediaStudio Image Edit, or QFX. I use Photoshop most because I'm used to it and it's handy for publishing. The others are great too, and Fractal Design Painter offers the most options for developing both seamless and regular textures. It has all sorts of gimmicks like fractal noise and image hose. In version 4.0 you can even go online and work on an image with a friend in France, or anyplace, in real-time.

POWER TIP

Kate White: "Give a lot of thought to *each* of your objects. Try to look at references in real life and think about each of the material components you have control over. This may sound obvious, but you can't take *anything* for granted. Things look real because of a million subtleties."

The Hull Maps

To make your spacecraft look like the real thing, you need to give it believable skin. I'm going to reveal a few trade secrets here, so listen up. First, I assume you have some kind of paint program. This is an essential investment. The general approach I use can be translated across suites. Here are a few rules of thumb for current mode spaceship hull maps.

✦ Make up some logic to the design. Rivets are not placed randomly on space vehicles, they follow the understructure. Sketch out a logical pattern or if you're good at it, fake it.

✦ Old technology hulls are the vogue right now. These are made of recognizable materials like steel or aluminum, riveted, aged, and maybe stained with oil. People can relate to them.

✦ There is also a trend toward creative sentient ships with hull textures made of living material. Lots of room for experiment here.

✦ Avoid the glossy look on conventional hulls — too much like plastic models.

✦ Detail the surface character. A uniform surface is the sign of a quick and dirty job, or worse — no skill.

✦ Use a combination of texture and bump maps to give the hull authenticity — interest.

✦ Avoid bright primary colors, preferring instead muted, uneven washes.

✦ Space vehicles have logos on them. Make one up or lift one from the CorelDraw collections and modify to your liking. Corel 6 even has a number of U.S. and European space insignia you can use.

✦ If you'll have close-ups of the hull, put in more detail like cool caution signs: Danger: Plasma Exhaust; or Caution: Vacuum Containment Door, Deep Breath Required Before Opening; or Security Area, Trespassers Will Be Violated. Few people will read them, but they look authentic and you can have fun with your audience. Use the classic sign templates in Corel and change the wording.

✦ The hull map gives your audience lots of clues as to the size of the ship. Keep your texture details in proportion. If it's a very large ship, details will be small and vice versa. You can usually use tS2's U/V repeat feature to change the scale of the map.

✦ Detail leading edges to make them appear a little worn.

✦ Dirty-down surfaces with semitransparent airbrush or fractal noise maps you make in Fractal Design Painter 3 or 4. If you can do it in your application, spray a semitransparent fractal noise pattern over the fuselage.

✦ Blacken areas around plasma exhaust ports.

✦ Key your texture to the hull's surface detail. That is, align hatch texture details with the hatch sub-object.

✦ Use the Material Rectangle to place detail exactly where you want it.

Let's Do It

For this exercise I'm using Photoshop. I realize it's a tad expensive and you may not have it, so you'll find a demo and a Shareware package called PaintShop Pro on the CD-ROM. It's reasonably priced if less powerful. If you decide to do this kind of work you'll just have to find a way to get the software and equipment you need. Don't do the bandit copy thing, these publishers put a lot into their products and deserve to be paid for them. Do scrounge around for the best street price you can find. I've seen Photoshop seriously discounted at computer shows, Kai's Tools as well.

Thoughts About Scale

Kate: "Texture map *everything* – but be very careful to maintain the proper *scale* of the map and avoid aliasing and chattering. Scale can mean two different things, both important. First, there is the resolution of the map itself. If you make it too high, you'll get all kinds of chattering (interference patterns) from too much detail; if it's too lo-res, it'll appear blurry. Secondly, there's the scale of the texture as it relates to the object wearing it; you may have found the perfect map to apply, but if you don't tile it right, it will never read as real.

"For instance, suppose you have the perfect texture to use for the cement on a road, but the details are too large. You can throw off the scale of the whole scene if the details are mapped on too large."

Thoughts About Texture Maps

Kate: "When designing texture maps, think about your objects standing on their own. Think about what they are and what their surfaces should look like regardless of a particular lighting situation. Of course you need to take into account where it'll ultimately be, so you don't waste time tricking out what is never seen. I find it helps to think and plan your objects with a lot of their own integrity. Then you map them and put them in the scene and *light* them."

In tS2 I tend to use two different kinds of image maps for objects. Most often I use a generic map that violates my own rules about keying the map to the object details. I'm right about doing it that way, but I'm also pretty lazy and often in a hurry. I want to get an idea what the ship will look like, so I slap on a generic map, fiddle with the scale and shader values. Often I end up liking it enough to leave it that way. For fine broadcast work you won't get away with it. Let's start by building a cool generic map for your collection.

Generic Hull Map

Fire up your paint program and we shall play. Photoshop has a nice ability to create masks in any shape you like. You can then apply texture just within the mask. Recall the rule about nonuniform surfaces. I do that by subtly using Image Adjust ⇨ Brightness and Contrast of various panels in a random pattern.

Just select the area of a single hull plate with the rectangular (or other) Marquee tool, then adjust values. They will only be applied to the selected area. You don't want a radical shift between adjacent hull plates.

This method gives a nice uneven look to the ship's surface. If you overdo it, it looks bleeding awful. You can apply all sorts of adjustments to each panel to give a slightly unique look. As with all things in 3D, don't overdo it in your excitement to use the tool. I begin by laying out a panel structure that makes sense to me.

Laying Out the Panel

I'm going to lay out a panel that has barrier strips between regular panels. I don't know why, I've never used a design like this before, but that's the nature of this gig. It just struck me as an interesting thing to try, and it illustrates the general approach. Remember, I'm using Photoshop. Read the manual of your application to do equivalent operations. Begin laying out a grid of rectangles with the Marquee tool as in the top of Figure 13-3. Hold down the Shift key to keep adding, otherwise the first one will disappear when you start the second. The rectangles are your work areas. The areas outside the selected area are protected and will not be affected by your work.

POWER TIP

Kate: "Create maps that incorporate *color washes* and apply to surfaces to break up (subtly) that CGI-looking solid block of color. Create *dirt* maps to scuff-up surface. Sometimes, just a slight dither map can take something quickly out of the CGI-look and into a more gritty, real look."

Next, use the Color Fill tool to give the major panels some color. I picked a dull green — wonder what that says about my personality. For variation try spray painting a slightly lighter or darker green to break up the monotony. Next, I inverted the mask: Selection ➪ Invert. I got even more dull and filled it with a depressing gray. Must be the weather. Inverting back to make the larger panels active, I selected the Airbrush tool. I made a bunch of different length custom brushes with a long skinny shape and feathered edges. These let me easily paint the dirt streaks coming off leading edges (see Figure 13.3).

I pop the mouse button rapidly up and down as I move across the top edge of each panel. This gives that streaky look. The blotchy look comes next.

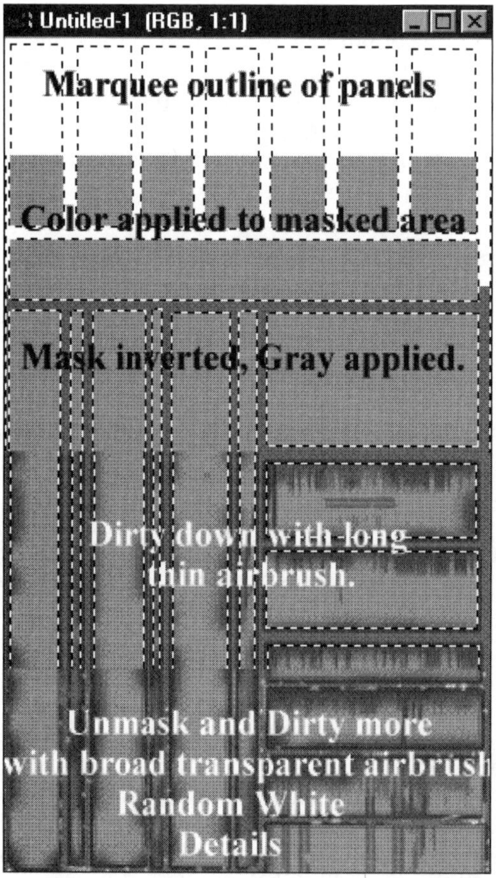

Figure 13-3: A typical sequence of steps to prepare a generic hull texture map

Remove the masks by selecting the entire image (or by clicking once with the Marquee tool, on the image). Then selecting an airbrush with a large, round, soft brush, set transparency down around 50% ➪ Black and carefully nudge color where I think it should be. Look at a real airplane wing and see where the streaks are for ideas.

I finish up the map with a fine brush that I use to dab semitransparent white paint around leading edges here and there to enhance the worn/uneven look. I find this is a good way to keep a vehicle from looking like a plastic model. Take a look at the different stages in Figure 13-3. It may not be the best looking hull in the world, but you get the idea. You probably ought to make up a bunch of different size and pattern hull maps. I often use three or four on a single vehicle, applying different shader values to each. If you want you can even paint individual faces around detail with the Face Paint tool, changing hull maps as you go.

When you finish your texture map you'll want to apply it to your hull to test it out. I like to experiment with different shininess, reflectivity, and ambient settings. Mostly I keep them pretty low unless I want a glossy or metallic section. I keep facet set on auto and stick to Phong shading for most work.

I've found that if I put four or five small cubes painted with various hull materials in the work space, I can speedily change among them using the Control key with the Paint Over or Paint Faces tools. All you do is hit <Ctrl>, the paint tool changes to Inspect, click on the material you want, let go of <Ctrl> and you're ready to paint with it. You'll find this handy when you need a lot of different materials, like when doing fancy vertex painting. When you're done, just delete the sample boxes. It's a lot like using an artist's palette.

The Bump Map

Bump maps in tS2 work as follows: The lighter the color of the pixel, the higher the bump. White sets the highest point which is limited by your Amplitude setting. Gradients of gray to black indicate relief height between the bottom (black) and top. If you want a sharp line, as between panels, you use a black line. For a beveled look, use gradients. For the panel above, I chose to stroke (put a dark line around) the original rectangles. Figure 13-4 shows that I also darkened each large panel slightly to have it inset slightly. The gray that I used is dithered; it's a shade created from tiny gray and white dots. This will give the surface a rough patterned texture. Play with it. Use a pure color if you want a very flat surface. If you make the panels lighter, they'll look slightly projected (see Figure 13-5).

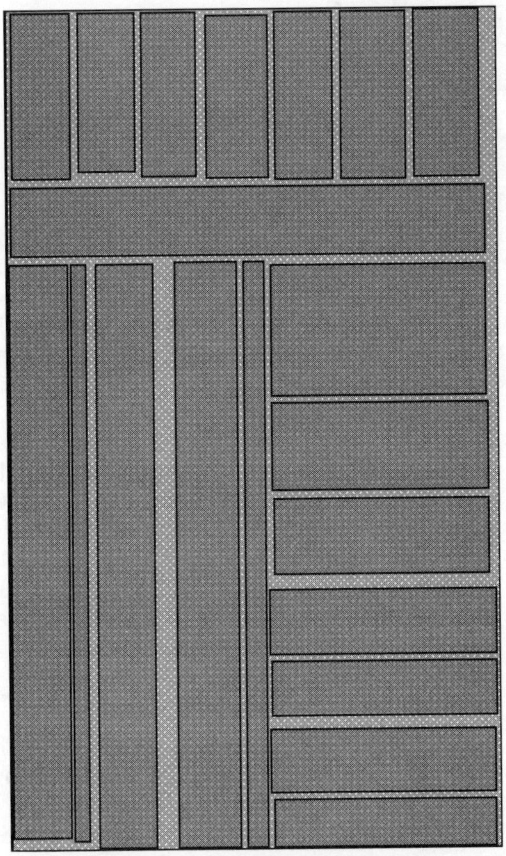

Figure 13-4: A simple bump map made by stroking the mask outline in Photoshop and darkening the large panels

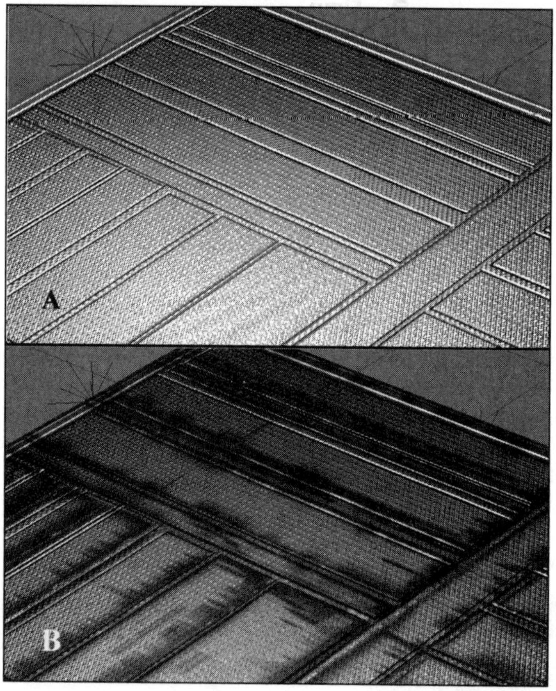

Figure 13-5: Here are two versions of a bump map: (A) alone (no texture map) and (B) combined with hull texture.

Corroding Your Hull

If you want your hull to really look old, you can make a bump map from the texture map by duplicating it, converting to grayscale (Image Mode), and adjusting the curves: Image ➪ Adjust ➪ Curves, to get the effect you want. You adjust curves on a graph with a line going from top right to bottom left. You can pull the line to the bottom from the center, pull up spikes. It's interactive in Photoshop, so play with it until the bump map looks the way you want. Remember, the darker the deeper, the lighter the higher (see Figure 13-6).

If you test render and find the bumps are too deep or obvious, try using Image ➪ Adjust ➪ Contrast, in Photoshop or your equivalent to reduce the contrast. The smaller the distance between the darkest and lightest part of the map, the lower your bumps will be. Of course you can reverse the process if you want higher bumps. It's always fun to make some changes and see how they affect the look. All of this is within the range you set in amplitude. Sometimes a small change will make your surface look just right, or totally screwed up. Don't feel bad, just keep working on it.

A Quick Example

The first illustration (Figure 13-7A) shows a generic tanker hull with default white surface. The second illustration (Figure 13-7B) uses the same lighting and shows the generic tanker sporting the generic hull surface we just made. It has been applied with slightly different shader qualities to different surfaces. I went down in

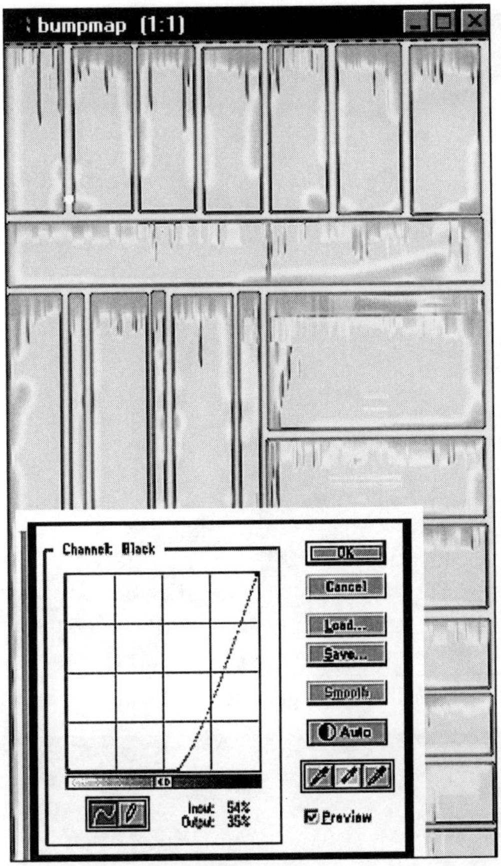

Figure 13-6: A bump map made by adjusting curves on grayscale image of hull map.

the object's hierarchy to reach the different surfaces. I also changed the texture repeats value. On the main hull I set U repeats to 8 and left V at 1. Using these variations on a hull map can have near infinite variety.

POWER TIP

Make sure you match up your bump map repeats and offsets with your texture map. Sometimes it looks good if they are slightly different, depends on the pattern

Creating an Insignia Decal

You can give a nice nudge toward reality by adding a cool beatup logo or two. For this example I'm using the EuroSpace insignia on page B-466 of the CorelDraw 6 Libraries Catalog. Use any insignia you want, the steps are easy. Load insignia into Corel (or any similar program) ⇨ save as .bmp file ⇨ load trueSpace2 ⇨ Edit ⇨ Image Utilities ⇨ Input Image=eurospce.bmp ⇨ Alpha Conversion=Top Left ⇨ Convert Image. You'll get a file window asking where you want your new .txr file. Name and save it with your textures. Remember to add it to your space textures album, and to your Materials Library, if you plan to use it a lot.

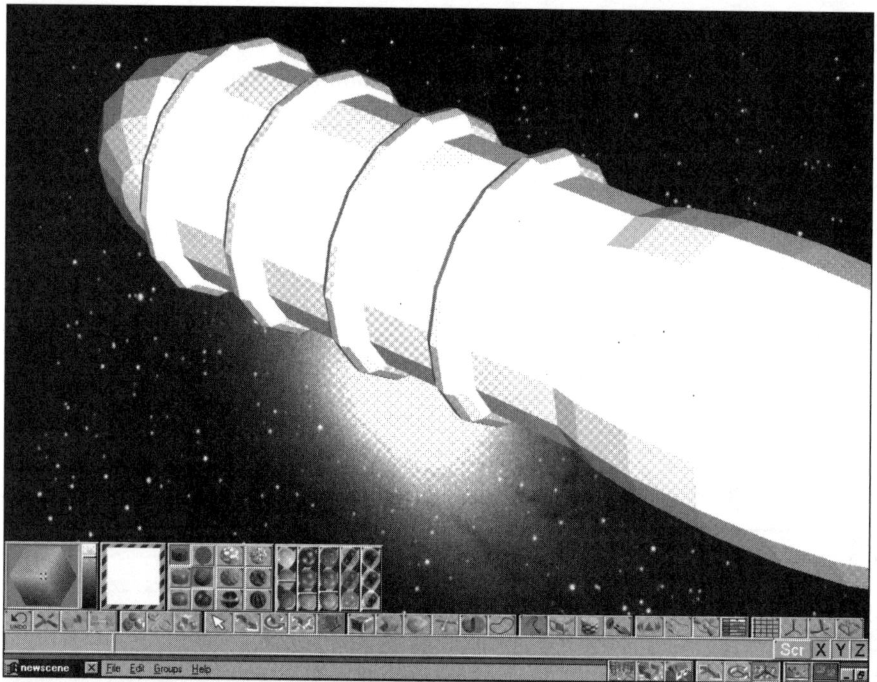

Figure 13-7A: Here's how the tanker looks without the generic hull texture.

Figure 13-7B: Here's how the tanker appears after the generic hull texture has been applied. Adjustments were made to shaders and scaling to achieve a varied look.

As you get more expert, you'll add a step — dirty down the logo but not the white, by using the Magic Wand tool in your image program. Each one works a little differently, but the idea is to make a mask around the logo area. In Photoshop the easiest way is to go: Select ➪ Color Range, and then click on the white background. This will create the exact opposite of the mask you want. Next: Select ➪ Inverse. This gives you dotted lines around your logo. Now when you dirty down, the white stays white and the logo tarnishes nicely. If you get dirt on the white, the trueSpace2 image utility will do a blotchy job of alpha conversion — not what you want.

In any other program, use the tools you have to select white, then invert the selection so you have a mask for just the logo. Use your own dirty down techniques to make the logo look a little time worn.

The Utility has converted your Insignia-on-White .bmp image file to an Insignia-on-transparent .txr texture file, as shown in Figure 13-8. When you selected Top Left the program looked at the top left pixel, saw it was white, then made all white pixels transparent. You get a clean logo to plaster on your ship. Bump textures under your logo show through, keeping it tight to the virtual surface.

Figure 13-8: The insignia file before and after alpha conversion includes background showing where the white was. The ship texture will show here.

The .txr contains alpha channel information trueSpace2 uses to composite the insignia cleanly, wherever you want it. .tga images can also contain an alpha channel. You'll learn more about this when we cover compositing in the Hollywood Special Effects chapter. For now, don't worry about understanding alpha channels. It's just a way of controlling transparency.

Placing the Decal

Bring up tS2 and load an object you want to decal. I've loaded an old fuselage that has too many polygons to be practical, but gives a nice smooth surface. Create the material for the decal using the standard materials interface. That means engage the texture map and select the insignia .txr file you just made. Or, you can use the one on the CD-ROM under \textures\space. Select the Material Rectangle tool,

to bring up a projected rectangle on the surface of the hull and the setup window.

Move and scale the rectangle to where you want it, then hit the Paint icon on the control window. The rectangle will wrap the current material in the Preview window around the hull of the ship, within the rectangle you've set up (see Figure 13-9). Experiment with different mapping schemes. Sometimes cylindrical is better than planar. It depends what you're looking for.

Figure 13-9: EuroSpace logo is decaled onto a hull using Material Rectangle tool.

CAUTION

It's not documented, but the Material Rectangle tool will be grayed out unless you've selected a unique object. If you select a complex object, you have to go down the hierarchy until you've reached the surface you want to decal. This is a royal pain. I'm hoping Caligari will change this to allow you to simply paint any object, as is.

POWER TIP

Kate: "Don't be afraid to *cheat*. It's all a cheat anyway. I've gotten a lot of mileage out of simple techniques like mapping a grad onto a box so it looks like it is getting shadow at the bottom. Software has gotten pretty sophisticated, but it can box you (no pun intended) into corners if you try to be too literal. A lot of time can be wasted trying to exactly *simulate* when you have much more control (and fun) if you know when to cheat."

Backgrounds

Backgrounds are essential to good animation. In tS2 you can have background color, image or animation. But background doesn't have to be a bit map you assign in the Render Options panel. It can be, but you'll rarely use it except in still images. You want to build backgrounds into the scene for a more professional look

Here's the problem: When you assign a background map, it tracks with the camera. No matter what angle you're shooting, it's always smack in front of your camera. This can be a serious pain. You render a complex, moving camera animation sequence only to find the camera looks stationary with the object moving in front of it. The whole sense of movement in the clip is lost.

Pros build *live* backgrounds into scenes. There are several ways to do it:

- ✦ The diorama
- ✦ Sky dome
- ✦ Atmosphere
- ✦ Projection panels
- ✦ Star Sphere

You'll find other creative ways too and you can combine these for different effects. Just remember that when you have the background built into the scene, bright spotlights can cause shading artifacts. So try to aim them so they don't hit the background elements. Flat shading these elements will also eliminate any lighting artifacts, if you don't need phong or metal effects.

Diorama

You've been to the museum and looked at all the diorama scenes with the wide screen backgrounds. In 3D you simply place a very large cylinder around your scene and paint your background on it. Use scenery images.

You can use this with a background color and semitransparent paint for interesting effects. For example, put a black background and paint stars on a transparent ground. Putting gas clouds on transparent planes behind the diorama will give you a nice depth effect. Or you could use a fractal cloud reflection map on a transparent diorama with blue background for a sky effect.

Place your camera inside the cylinder and as it moves the background will stay put, enhancing the visual cues of camera movement.

Check out I-Wei Huang's *Sure Shot* Animation for a terrific example of a built in background. He created a diorama and then created matching objects to give a 3D look as you move around in the jungle. It's a lot of work, but it's impressive.

You can make a double-long background map for your diorama by flipping the original and duplicating it in your image processing application. Join the original and the mirror image side by side. This works very well for cloud maps. Because it's a flip image, you get a seamless joint between the two. If there is a lot of pattern, you may get a kaleidoscope effect, so pick your images accordingly.

Sky Dome

Similar to the Diorama, this one is used a lot in space footage because it gives a background in every direction. Pop up a sphere, Smooth Quad Divide it twice, and scale it up until it completely surrounds your scene with room to spare. (See Figure 13-10.) Again place your camera inside. The special transparency effects above hold here as well. It's smart to check out your coordinates and rotate the seam to beneath the floor of your stage. You can also use an animated Material Rectangle on the Sky Dome for interesting effects, like a far off explosion or a balloon floating by.

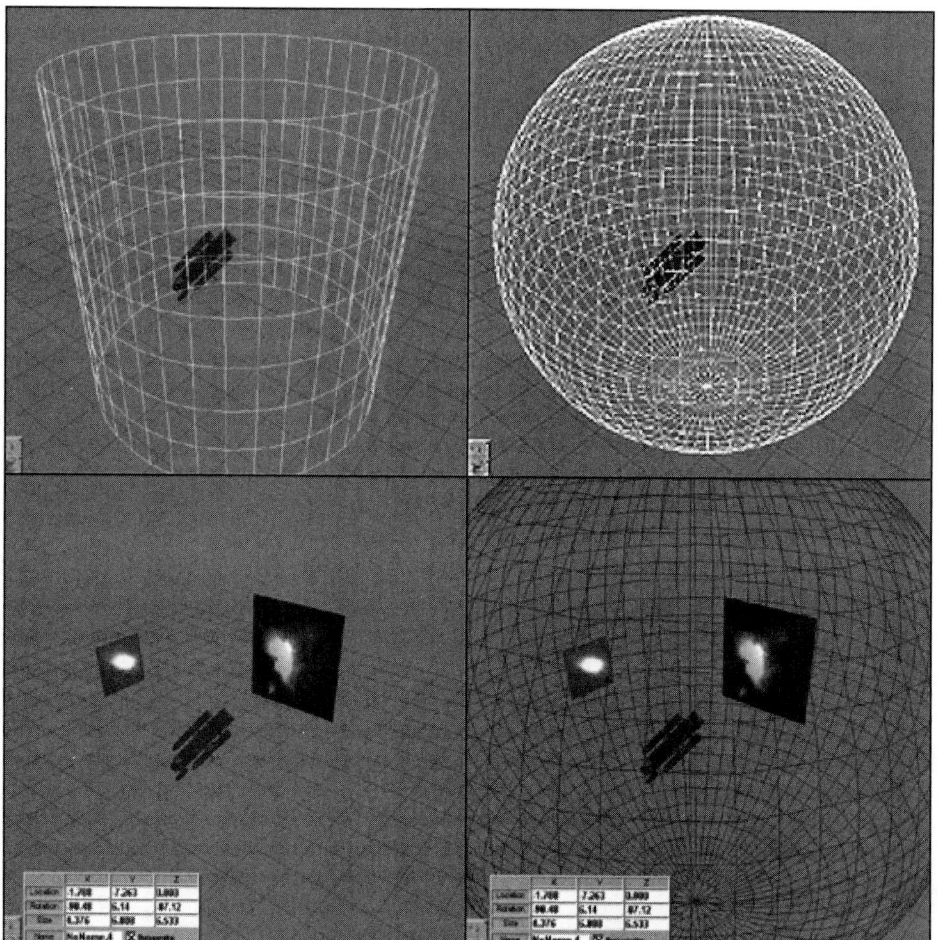

Figure 13-10: Diorama, sky dome, projection panels, and combo illustrated.

Atmosphere

The Fog tool can be used to create a murky background that partly engulfs your scene. By making the far point density 100%, the scene will fade off into gloom. By placing a few indistinct objects, trees, buildings, or terrain in the depths you reinforce the feeling of eerie depth. You can use any color you like for fog. You've already played with the blue-green for underwater. Try a brownish red for pollution, or purple for an otherworldly atmosphere.

Projection Panels

I use this one a lot because it gives nice freedom of expression. You pop up as many Planar Object Primitives as you need, scale, and paint them with the image you want. Make sure each is sized to look right at the distance you place it. Try to use an image that is surrounded by black. That way you won't get a squared off look at the edges of the planar object. You can adjust this in your paint application with the Vignette tool. It places a clear center to black edge gradient around your picture. This works best with a black background. You can use these panels with some of the other techniques, as well, to create complex backgrounds.

POWER TIP

If you use fog with any of these background approaches make sure you reduce the final density to under 100% or the background elements will disappear in the fog.

Starfield

This is a lot of work to build, so I've included one on the CD-ROM (\geometry\dreamscp\space\starfld.cob). A starfield is a carefully constructed cluster of star objects filling a 3D sphere. You can expand it, position it, and rotate it. You have to be careful, the illusion is killed if you get a star in front of your forground objects. I expand the field and move it into the background. If you rotate it slowly it gives an interesting effect.

The real advantage of a starfield is that as your camera moves through it, you get a serious feeling of deep space. Since each star is a different distance from the camera, each angle is different. Thus the apparent movement of each star enhances the depth effect

There's been a lot of debate about this on the Internet. The most ardent opposition feels that you could never see stars move like this in reality. They offer all sorts of scientific reasoning as to why we shouldn't use a star sphere. Then someone pointed out that the Enterprise has a tendency to *whoosh* through the vacuum of space and nobody seems to mind. Someone else pointed out that stars do have relative motion when you rotate your head.

So, in reality stars wouldn't appear to move as they do with the star sphere, but this isn't reality, it's entertainment, and it works. Try it.

Fantasy Backgrounds

Gradient tools are the greatest invention for building interesting backgrounds for space as well as conventional illustration and animation. I'm going to let you in on a little Photoshop secret. You can design the most beautiful and fantastic backgrounds in a few minutes using the gradient tool in Photoshop. I'd like to thank my daughter Dani, who is a CGI intern, for showing me this stuff.

Open up a new file about 640 × 480 or a little bigger. trueSpace2 will scale it automatically to the full background size. But if it scales up too much you naturally lose detail. Select the Gradient tool from the tool box and set it up as follows: In the Gradient tool options box, set: difference ➪ Foreground to Background ➪ Linear. Make sure the mode is RGB. Now when you drag a line across your new image, Photoshop will create a linear color gradient from Foreground to Background color. I picked magenta and aqua. You can also change mid-stream. Draw a few straight lines in different directions and at different lengths to see what you get. Short strokes give you a tight gradient, long strokes a broad one. Notice how your colors reverse with each stroke. That's caused by using the difference mode. I like it because it gives me the most interesting and unexpected designs. I could do this for hours.

Now change the type of gradient to Radial. You can make stars and nebulae by pulling a tiny radial gradient, one to three pixels long. It takes a little practice, but you can create some bizarre outer space backgrounds, stellar gas effects, even a nova. If you keep intersecting circles you can get some interesting glass effects as well. Once you have something interesting, try some of the filters on it. Put in a lens flare, twirl it, or set up wave motion. I have Alien Skin's Black Box set of filters and find it very useful. Experiment. That's really what this book is all about, experimenting with this fantastic medium. Look at some of the effects in color plates under Backgrounds, in the color section.

In Plate 13-1 I got the swirly effect by using the polar coordinates filter after having made a lot of little radials. Then in 13-2 I twisted it a tad with the twist filter, ran a few large gradients over the whole thing to get colors it liked, then gave it two lens flares. No two will ever be the same.

For a truly bizarre effect, make both a color and a grayscale bitmap of one of your designs. It's easy in Photoshop, save your color background, then go to Mode ➪ Grayscale. You'll have an instant bump map. Use them together in a surface paint on a large planar polygon and render in trueSpace2. You'll get some pretty amazing effects that you can save and use as backgrounds to animations. I've used this little trick to make terrain maps quickly as well as undersea floor effects. Set your mind free, your options are not limited.

Summary

In this chapter you learned how to experiment with textures and backgrounds, including:

✦ Using a database to organize your collection of texture maps saves time and gives you better access.

✦ Finding images to use as texture maps in lots of unexpected places like on CD-ROMs as parts of a presentation, and so on.

✦ About the World Wide Web and how to use it to search for textures by using Yahoo and other search engines.

✦ How to create your own texture maps using your image editor.

✦ How to create your own bump maps to nail down the surface details you want.

✦ How to create and use decals to place logos and other effects exactly where you want them on any surface.

✦ How to create backgrounds that stay put in animations using various diorama techniques to create surrounding backgrounds.

✦ How to create fantastic gradient backgrounds in Photoshop using only the Gradient tool and image filters.

✦ ✦ ✦

CHAPTER 14

Animated Materials

In This Chapter

- Using animations as textures
- Where to find useful animated textures
- How to make useful animated textures
- Some neat ways to use moving textures

A new addition to trueSpace2 is rotoscoping, or putting moving pictures into your animation. It can be done with both textures and the background, which opens vast opportunities for special effects. We're working our way toward the chapter on Hollywood Special Effects and this is an important prerequisite.

What Are Animated Textures?

An animated texture is simply a numbered series of bitmap files, or an .avi or .flc file that you use as a texture. You have to check the Animated box next to the file name in the Texture Selection panel. That's all there is to it. As I mentioned in the tools chapter, tS2 will match the video file frame by frame to your animation. Also recall that if your animation base rate is different from the base rate of the texture, tS2 will interpolate. That means if the texture runs at 15fps and your animation at 30fps, tS2 will insert each texture frame for two animation frames. So keep them matched if you can.

At first you might wonder how to use animated textures — it's kind of a strange concept — moving paint. Just a few examples to give you an idea, then more as we go along. Imagine that you have a TV set in your animation and it's tuned to the Simpsons. You could make a tape (remembering all about getting permissions), digitize it with a cheap capture board, and paint the screen with it. You get a sophisticated effect that's as easy as falling off a greased pig.

If you have a video camera — and statistically you do — plug it into the capture board and record whatever you want as a texture, following the instructions that came with the board. If you have MediaStudio, it's all set up to capture and edit your home videos. Just make sure you have a big drive since these files are not tiny.

Moving backgrounds can also be cool. Take a live shot of storm clouds building up. Develop an eerie look by speeding up cloud movement. Increase contrast in your video edit program, maybe add an evil color to enhance the effect. Make an .avi file and use it as the background to a scene of a haunted house with its door creaking open all on its own. Sure it's trite, but at least you know how it's done.

Where You Can Find Animated Textures

Animated textures are everywhere you look. Sometimes they aren't obvious, like on CD-ROMs where .avi files are kept in a directory and used by the presentation but not mentioned. Just do a directory scan for the various video file types. Let your computer do the walking. BBSs are loaded with .avi files; some aren't even XXX-rated. There are sites that specialize in video files, check your local computer magazines or Computer Shopper.

As your collection grows you'll be glad you have a multimedia database like Album or MediaCenter. You can keep all your animations in the thumbnail libraries for easy access.

On the Web

Animated textures are easy to find on the Web. Just fire up your Web browser and go to a search engine, like Lycos. Scan key words: animation, .avi, .flc, .fli, QuickTime, videos, movies, and so on. For the latest film trailers, visit the various studio Web pages by inputting the studio name: MGM, Warner, Viacom, Disney, and more, have pages with downloadable images and videos. Use your head and you'll find more than you'll ever need.

Buy a Collection

If you're not online, you can buy some animated textures. They come on just about all CD-ROMs with any video:

- ✦ Loads of video clips of old films (often public domain, but check first) can be found on Cinemania and other movie database ROMs.
- ✦ All sorts of NASA flicks hide on the Explorer Series from Virtual Reality Labs, including Mars Explorer, Venus Explorer, and Distant Suns (805-545-8515).

- If you have Premiere or MediaStudio Pro, you can convert QuickTime videos from the Mac world into .avi files easily.
- Walnut Creek CD-ROM Clips for QuickTime has more than 200 video clips all organized in categories: airplanes, motorcycles, space, morphs, animations, and so forth (510-674-0783).
- For a professional ROM used to rotoscope explosions into battle scenes on *Babylon 5,* get Movie Effects Studio — Pyromania for PC Volumes 1 and 2 (Playing with fire on CD-ROM) from Visual Concepts Engineering (VCE). They have all sorts of explosions, firewipes, shock waves, and flames you can use to enhance your battle scenes. I've included one of their great zero G explosions on the CD-ROM and highly recommend their product. It's a bit more expensive because it's not a mass consumer product (800-843-9497).
- Nearly every game CD-ROM has video files on it. Some are encoded and you can't use them, but most are usable as is. Get all the free demo ROMs you can get your hands on and save out the video files. Don't use them for commercial purposes, but they're great for your personal stuff and for demo tapes.

Bumps That Move

Think of things you can do with moving bumps. Turn a flat plane into a rippling brook or an ocean. Make a living space vehicle from a far-off galaxy with a skin that changes surface shape before your eyes. How about raindrops running down glass. By combining animated bumps with animated reflections you can get interesting water effects, like a setting sun reflected in rippling water (see Figure 23-4). Very buyable illusion.

Rippling Reflections

So many good ideas, so little time. I've experimented with animated reflections only briefly. It's pregnant with possibilities. I've done some interesting water and I've been able to show an explosion reflecting off an object. Try it. Rotoscope an explosion onto a flat plate attached to one of your vehicles as it passes a space station. Use an animated reflection of the same explosion as a material rectangle on the space station. Use either Phong or Metal shading with shininess set pretty high. For Metal you'll have to put transparency at 0%. With Phong you have more control, but it may not look as convincing. I use an underlying color as dark as I can get away with. Put the material rectangle on a dark part of the station so you can't see the edges. You can experiment with muting colors, and so on, to get a realistic reflection. There are trunkloads of ideas you'll think of to enhance scene reality using animated textures, bumps, reflections, or combinations.

Let's Do It

Load up your space tanker and leave the background black; main view is Perspective. Open a top down alternate window and pop a planar object. Navigate the object to a position on the far side of the tanker just beyond the fuel pod facing the perspective camera. Glue it in place, so you can see it clearly, but partially hide it so the flame comes from the far side of the ship, enhancing the 3D effect. I used Sibling. We're going to paint an explosion sequence on it.

The explosion .fli was supplied by VCE and has been used on such TV shows as *Babylon 5* and *SeaQuest.* It has a black background instead of transparent, so you need a plain black background to obscure the edges of the planar object.

To give the look of space, put a projection panel with nebula where it won't be overlapped by the moving explosion panel. It's possible to extract each frame using VidEdit, a free utility from Microsoft, so you can use the tS2 transparency utility, but that would be tedious. This is just an experiment anyway. To mix the paint, open the Texture file selection panel ➪ Explode.avi from the CD-ROM \VCE subdirectory. Next, click Anim. Next set your material attributes ➪ flat shading ➪ Zero-out the Shaders except for Ambient ➪ 75%.

Navigate down the hierarchy to the planar object and paint it with this moving picture. Return the ship to the top of its hierarchy. It's time for animation.

Add a Path

Pop up the Animation tool; you'll need it for reference and for moving through the animation.

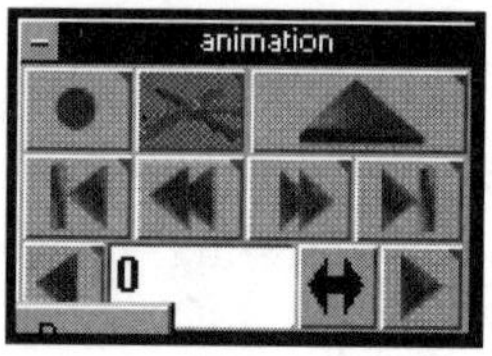

Click on the Animation Path tool. This will allow you to attach an animation path to the selected object (the tanker). You'll see the Animation Settings panel pop up. An animation path is a special form of spline curve. Each node point stands for the point on the path where the tanker will be for any given frame. Set the number of nodes to 80. This should give reasonably smooth movement and the explosion has 79 frames in it. If the end looks quirky you can cut off two frames. Be careful not to make changes on any frame but frame zero, otherwise you'll end up with extraneous keys placed by AutoRecord. Perhaps you'd better disable it for this exercise by right clicking on the Record button and deselecting it.

In the Perspective view be aware that, in World Coordinates, the higher on the screen you click, the farther back the starting point will be. If you want the ship to move from top left to bottom right (not a bad idea since the ancients used left to right for evil or tragic entries), click a little below mid-point, screen right, for your first mark. Then click about the same level on the left side for your end point. Next move the start point up by right clicking on it and moving it up the screen.

I'm jumping ahead here, so if you get stuck doing paths, check Chapter 18 or 22 for answers. When you give the object a path, it'll jump to the starting point as soon as you place it. If your ship has its object Z axis pointing out the nose (as it should), you can select the Look Ahead icon. If not, your tanker will go down the path cockeyed. Remember that the Z axis always points ahead or at the object selected by the Look At icon. Z is the pointer axis.

TAKE NOTE

Right click on the Play button on the Animation Control panel and change from the default Object setting to Scene. Now when you click the Play button the entire scene will animate, as opposed to just the selected object. You have only one path at the moment, but it's a good habit. I think they should have made Scene the default. In Object mode you animate only the selected object. Click the Play button and check out your action. The ship should snap along from the upper right to the lower left of the screen. If you haven't already, paint the ship with a nice material like the generic hull map.

Check It Out

Set your animation to frame 10 by typing `10` in the Animation Control panel frame field.

POWER TIP

Remember, you find these buttons by placing the mouse button over the various options in the panel until the Help Bar reads out what you're looking for.

Render a test frame to the screen to see what it looks like. If the explosion is not bright enough you can glue a light near it as a sibling and it will travel along lighting the screen.

POWER TIP

Don't place the light too close to the explosion projection panel because it may highlight the edges. If this happens, either turn down the brightness or move it farther away by navigating down the new hierarchy to the light, move it, and return to the top of the hierarchy.

Render again and if all is good, proceed to Render Scene to File. Select the Animate to File icon from the render variants menu. You'll get the Render to File setup panel. Set the following: Name ➪ shipblo.avi, List of files ➪ .avi, Preset ➪ MPEG, Animation ➪ Render all frames. Hit return and when the Compression panel comes up, select CinePak Codec. Accept the default settings and render your animation. This isn't totally new to you at this point.

CAUTION

If your animation comes out all strange with jumps and changes, etc., you undoubtedly have stray keyframes in it. The best thing to do at this point is start again by hitting the Start New Spline icon and replacing your path. Repeat, *don't* make *any* changes on frames other than 0 and 80. That includes moving things, painting things, or changing lights. If you change *anything* on a middle frame it could screw up the gears. Wait until you know more about how it all works before getting fancy.

Go have dinner while tS2 compiles an animation for you. When you come back, play it and you should be mildly astounded by your own work.

It All Seems Familiar

By now you've noticed a pattern to things in tS2. Once you learn a general principle you can use it within many tools. Naturally, working with animated bumps and reflections follows the same operation conventions as texture maps. With reflection maps and bumps you'll need to watch your lighting and shader settings a bit more, but you have a feel for it by now. If you don't, experiment until you do; it's the best way. This is a great big book, but it's only going to get you started. You'll learn more once you have the courage to explore.

Before you go any further, it's time to learn the secrets of designing your overall digital production. In Chapter 15 you'll learn about stage setting the cosmos and giving it a professional look.

Summary

In this lovely short chapter you learned that, in tS2, paint can move. You also learned:

✦ Where to look for animated textures on the Internet, on CD-ROMs, and under your pillow.

✦ Where to find free animated textures and to uncover some you already have, hidden in other applications.

✦ How to use animated bumps and reflections to enhance the realism of your piece.

✦ How to blow up a space tanker without hurting a soul.

✦ ✦ ✦

Setting the Cosmos... er, Stage

PART IV

The art of computer animation doesn't stop at building objects and characters. The beauty, mood, and charm of your animation depends on a production's design and art direction, including lighting, staging, and camera work.

Digital art direction is similar to live action, but is more fun. In this section, you learn from a real pro. Ed Lee, art director at Rhythm & Hues, shares his ideas. Ed is a graphic artist first and a computer artist second. His 15 years in the design world have taken him from New York to Paris to Hollywood. He recently art-directed Rhythm & Hue's part of Michael Crawford's EFX show at the MGM Grand Hotel in Las Vegas. It's an extravaganza of digital effects. He's currently the art director on the new Shaquille O'Neal feature film, *Kazam*. Shaq plays a genie in the film, which includes a lot of animated special effects.

You'll also get some tips from Steve Katz of Curious Pictures in New York. Steve started out in live action film, and has written two industry books on the subjects of directing and cinematography. He brought his traditional skills over to the digital realm and is now digital effects supervisor at Curious.

For lighting techniques, I enlisted PIXAR's Sharon Calahan. As lighting director on *Toy Story*, she's earned her place in CGI history. Not only was *Toy Story* the first full-length computer animated feature film, it also broke new ground in digital lighting. The film includes a broad range of innovative lighting effects that have never been assembled in one work before. So you'll be learning from one of the true masters of lighting. Jim Hillin also shares his ideas on lighting. He supervised the famous ballroom scene in Disney's *Beauty and the Beast*. Finally, Kate White, also at Rhythm & Hues, shares her ideas on creating textures. This is a fun and informative section.

In This Part

CHAPTER 15

The Art of Production Design

✦ ✦ ✦ ✦

In This Chapter

Thinking like a production designer

Using storyboards in your visualization processes

Visualizing your sequence and its scenes within the trueSpace2 work space

Laying out a trueSpace2 work plan for building scenes

How camera work and production design interrelate

✦ ✦ ✦ ✦

This chapter is really about visualization. Remember when you were a kid playing with dolls or jet fighters? You lined things up and made little scenes. I can still hear myself making the brrrrrrruumm sound of a Panther Jet as I flew my plastic model over my sandbox, strafing trucks I'd set up so carefully. In my head this was no sandbox, but a battlefield of danger and excitement. As I played, the story developed in front of me, one vision leading to the next. It was the first interactive game.

Production Design is Child's Play

Good filmmakers are a lot like children. They visualize everything. In fact, many admit they're just big kids playing with expensive toys. You'll need cinematic vision to set up the look and dynamics of your film, thus I hereby give you permission to be a child-like person — set your imagination free.

CAUTION

It's been said that the creative genius and the psychotic have very much in common. Both personalities spend much of their time in fantasy worlds, each having vivid visions and avoiding reality. Many psychotics are also child-like. So be careful out there, lest your new freedom be misinterpreted by friends and family as candidacy for the drool factory.

In this chapter we'll lay out our story vision, which we'll carry out in ensuing chapters. Along the way we'll get more practice building and animating things.

Verisimilitude

The French film critic André Bazin coined the term *presence* for the feeling a viewer gets when he or she feels truly connected with the essence of what's on screen. Achieving this presence is our goal. No matter what you animate, you want the viewer brought into the picture. Art direction, along with story, character, and execution, should captivate the viewer. The Art Director designs the look of your production. This is more than just setting up a bunch of props. It's imbuing your space with verisimilitude. I know it's a pretentious word, but you always hear it in film school, so I tossed it in. We need verisimilitude — deep emotional plausibility — to establish the empathetic link with our audience. Art direction will help you achieve that.

The Boards

Storyboarding fits in here. Even now, as a rank beginner, draw your keyframes with a pencil. Remember, a keyframe is where action changes direction or the scene changes. Draw the beginning of your scene, play with it, figure out where change comes, and draw that frame. Your scenes should flow nicely into each other. It helps to look at some storyboards to get an idea of how they flow. My only worry is that showing you professional boards done by a real pro will discourage you. Don't let it. If you want to be strictly a production designer, you'll have to learn to draw boards well. Of course, as an animator you only have to please yourself.

Ed Lee's Storyboards

To get started, Ed Lee, art director at Rhythm & Hues, has kindly agreed to let us publish a few of his boards from *Kazaam*, a Disney film (summer 1996 release), as shown in Figure 15-1. Ed has many credits, from Paris to New York to Hollywood, but the strangest and most interesting to me is his work in designing the amazing EFX show at the MGM Grand in Las Vegas. Ed was special effects art director on this 40-million-dollar production that is a showcase for advanced digital effects.

Kazaam is a genie who lives in a boom box, and he's played by Shaquiel O'Neal. As you look at the following drawings, picture Ed with script in hand, reading, visualizing, and then sketching. Notice how the drawings work like mental keyframes. Each one gives your mind a reference from which to visualize the action to the next key. I present Ed's boards without comment. They speak for themselves.

Interview with Ed Lee

P: What is an art director's job, Ed?

E: He's the guy with the eye. I'm in charge of the overall look of a piece – its style and flair. We do the storyboarding and a lot of keyframes. I'll often go into PhotoShop and create keyframes as a reference for the digital guys. I'm the one who has to look at the digital hair and say if it's right or not. That kind of stuff.

P: How do you know if it's right or not?

E: You ask yourself with honesty: Does this look the way it should or am I kidding myself? Study the way things look and extrapolate.

P: What do you mean by look?

E: A film or presentation should have a consistent look to it. Think about the *Star Wars* look or the industrial look or business look or even the grunge look. Think about some commercials and rock videos. A specific company may want you to create a look and carry it like a signature through all its commercials. The look comes from where you put the emphasis in your visual design.

P: What does a look involve?

E: It can be lighting, color schemes, style, mood, atmosphere, surfaces. I may have to design lettering on a sign or even fashion styles. It's a pretty comprehensive job.

P: Can you give our readers any advice on how to come up with a look?

E: Sure, start out with a point of reference. Pick a look that you've seen before, that fits what you're doing, and make it your own. Don't copy it, just use it as a starting point. Pick key elements of style and keep them consistent through your production.

P: You mean, if it has a lot of chrome and glass, keep that hard-edged look?

E: Sort of, maybe more the glossy reflective look. Of course, it depends on why you choose it.

P: Where do you get the inspiration that helps you come up with the look of a piece?

E: The key to success in this business always goes back to story. Everything has a story – commercials, even short effects pieces. That's the key. I'm in the business of making things look great in a way that helps tell that story. You know, you can tell a story lots of ways, but people will pay more attention if it looks great. The important things to keep in mind are the idea, concept, story point – they should dictate the look.

P: Have you got any advice for our readers on art directing their demo tapes?

E: Yes. Digital technique is really secondary to innovation and style. Most of the demos I see are a lot alike. They see stuff and try to reproduce it or just show fancy technique. We can teach them the technical side, but they need to show us what they can do in terms of telling a story and holding our interest. Most sequences seem a bit too long and boring. We're in the business of entertainment and that's what a demo tape should do. We also look at the technique. It's a plus if Rhythm & Hues, for example, can find someone who is well-rounded in their technique, style, innovation, etc. Having good taste and showcasing their *talent* are key points in successful demo tapes.

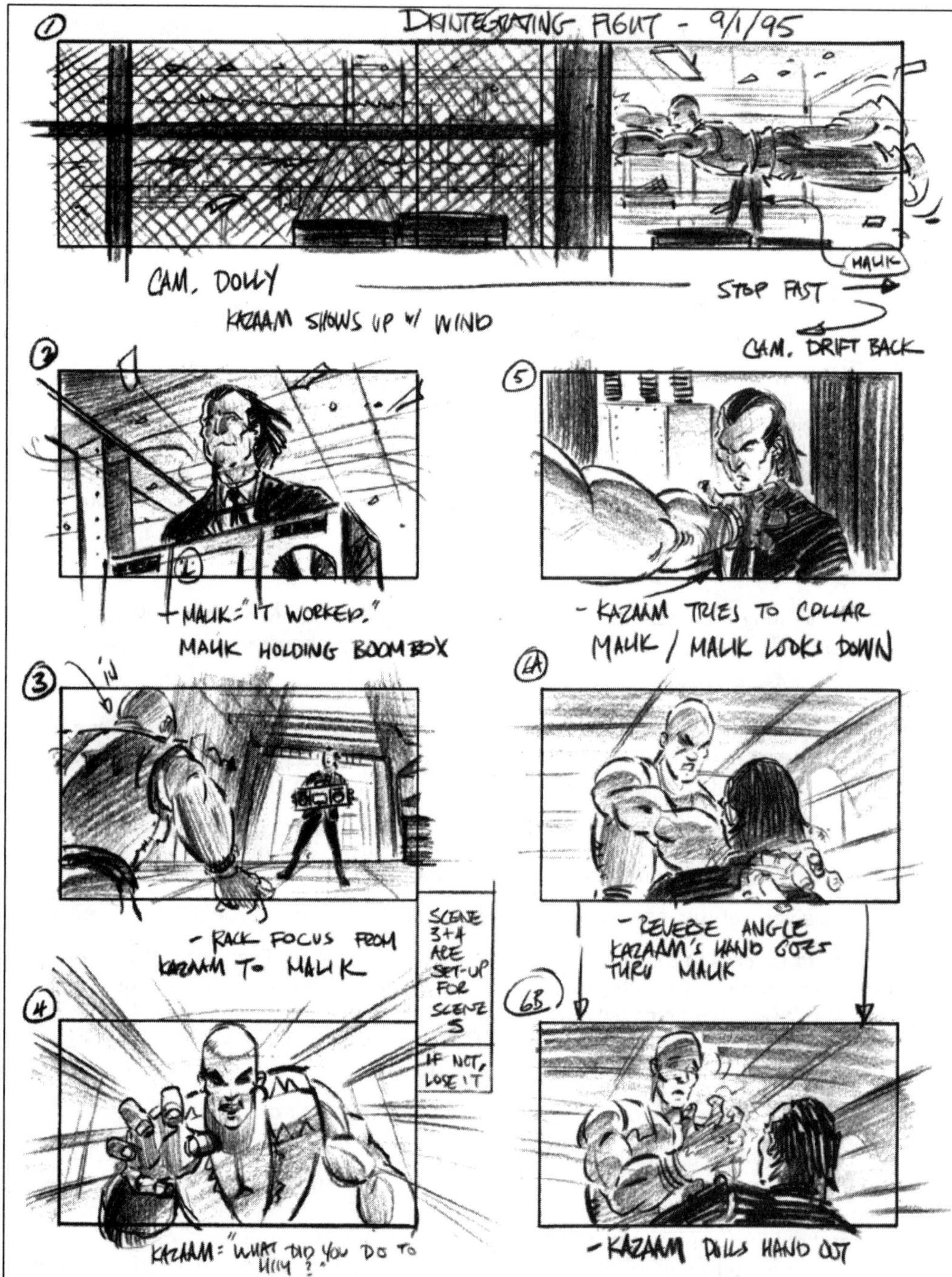

Figure 15-1: These storyboards are from *Kazaam.*

Figure 15-1 *(continued)*

Figure 15-1 *(continued)*

POWER TIP

You can draw storyboards on paper and scan them into your computer or input them via a tablet. I use Summa Expression, which has a clear plastic sheet under which I slip my drawing and trace it into Painter, Corel, or Freehand.

Good storyboards don't need a lot of explanation; they tell the story. In fact, Ralph Eglund, Production Designer for *Toy Story,* said, "You don't write a great story — you draw it." Ralph doesn't have much use for the written word when he's designing because he, like most great designers, sees stories as a series of images.

But back to Ed Lee for a moment. I had a lot of questions about what an art director does and how, so I've included an interview I did with him. It should give you some insight into the field and your own approach to design.

I-Wei Huang

I-Wei Huang (pronounced E-Way Wong) is an artist and graphics designer/art director. He's skilled with tS2, having worked for Caligari as in-house animator. Be sure and catch some of his terrific tS2 animations on the CD-ROM. His karate guy and running robots are marvels of articulated motion. They show what can be done without Inverse Kinematics. I've included several samples of his work with tS2 on the CD-ROM in his own subdirectory. You can also see an example of his commercial work for the Family Channel in the color section.

Steve Katz

Another fellow who knows about designing film is Steve Katz. He's head of the digital department at Curious Pictures in New York. A writer/filmmaker with over 20 years' experience in motion picture productions, Steve is author of *Film Directing Shot by Shot* and *Cinematic Motion*, two film industry bibles.

I very seriously recommend both books, published by Michael Wiese Productions. In *Film Directing Shot by Shot*[1] Katz gives you the unusual opportunity to study storyboards drawn by some great talents, like Harold Michelson (*The Birds*), Sherman Labby (*Blade Runner*), and Mentor Huebner (*Harlem Nights, Her Alibi*). Steve's own technique of showing camera angles and motion in his boards is extremely useful. Besides being writer/director, you are production designer, art director, and director of photography on your animations — at least until you work at a production house. That's a plus because of the control it gives. It's also your career on the line with no one to point a finger at if it goes sour. Believe me, if you take the time to study Katz, you'll get the rounding out you need to become a significant animator who'll leave a mark on this industry.

[1] *Film Directing Shot by Shot* (visualizing from concept to screen) by Steven D. Katz ISBN 0-941188-10-8 Michael Wiese Productions, 11288 Ventura Blvd., Suite 821, Studio City, CA 91604. 800-986-3408

The Master Scene

The digital stage is different from a sound stage. For example, it can be sized from a molecule to the universe. You can design all the parts of your vision on one stage and move naturally from place to place. A good approach is to design a master scene. Think of it as your big picture. The example includes outer space, transitional spaces, and inner spaces of a ship and a space station. With this setting in hand you have a place to visualize different camera angles and cinematic movement, which we'll cover in Chapters 23 and 25. If camera shots require staging adjustments, new boards are drawn and changes made. This is the way of cinema, and it's also the way of 3D animation.

In fact, today 3D animation is routinely used by art directors, directors of photography, and plain old directors to previsualize feature films. This is actually a budding area of employment you might want to consider.

POWER TIP

Tip from Steve Katz: You have to do more than just make mental pictures. Visualization isn't a strictly cerebral process, but rather the merging of the physical act of doing, with several different mental processes that together we call imagination. It isn't until your visions emerge in a raw state in your drawings, writing, or editing that your creative energy is fully engaged in the interactive process of visualization. It's like when a writer knows he can start typing any words and that act will bring his creative juices on-line. So draw.

Balance

In tS2 your stage can be up to a half-mile deep and about as wide as you need before it drops off the cutting plane. That's a line beyond which tS2 renders nothing. In that space you establish a balanced world, and within that world, you carry out your shots. The world you create should contain all elements necessary to your story. It can be austere or richly textured, bare or cluttered. Whichever way you go, it should have a sense of balance.

- **Balance:** By balance I don't mean symmetry, but rather a perceptual balance that is comfortable to the eye. You can disturb this balance at some point to create tension, but that's another story. Learn to recognize balance. If you don't have a sense of it, consult with a friend who does. The look of your piece is critical to its success. Here are a few things to consider:
- **Objects:** Are they clustered in one part of the scene? Is one section bare and another cluttered? Do these areas work in the scene?
- **Color:** Are your scene colors comfortable together? Do they express the mood you're looking for? Are the colors symbolically appropriate for the scene? (Don't wear a black dress to a wedding unless it's part of the story.)

- **Light:** Does it respect the emotional tone of the scene? Does it provoke interest? Does it focus your eyes on the action?
- **Action:** Will the action work in the scene as you've laid it out? Check it.
- **Aesthetics:** Does the scene appeal to the eye of the viewer? Does it overpower the action or facilitate it?
- **Camera:** Is the scene friendly to the camera? Does it provide sufficient interest and variety to meet the director's needs?

These are things to be thinking about as you lay out your space. Use it as a checklist. In tS2 you have the advantage of multiple views of your stage. You can instantly check camera angles as you build the set. Normal directors never get that kind of luxury.

Let's Do It

This is the part of animation that most terrifies me. I'm picky and it requires a lot of takes for me to be happy with a master scene before I can move on. We're going to try setting the cosmos for a sequence that will introduce the space station (in the cover scene). It's a big set with very large props. It incorporates nearly everything we've learned so far. But instead of setting for a static shot, we'll be thinking in terms of camera angles for moving shots.

One Process of Creation

I'm ornery and hate to follow rules; you probably are, too. I present the following process as a point of reference for you to develop your own creative style. Use whatever works for you. I tend to see film in sequences. A sequence is a string of related scenes that tell a complete story within the larger one.

State the purpose of your sequence in one or two sentences, it'll help focus your design effort. Here goes. "The purpose of this sequence is to introduce the space station as an island of warmth and humanity in the vast, frigid beauty of space."

With this vision in mind I begin to imagine what scenes I'll need to achieve it. Remember that the mind is the original interactive interface. One part of your mind will start the process, you'll draw, another part will be inspired, and ideas will feed on each other in a spiral of visual productivity.

The Mind-Wandering Part

I start designing the awesome cosmos. First step, for me, is to lie down and let my mind wander until I get a vision of space. I hope nobody comes in — it looks like I'm shirking work. Here it comes, I see space, bright with stars and nebular gas clouds. Its deep colors move from harsh white to bluish to a chilly magenta. I know reds are supposed to be warm, but this one isn't. I rub my arms, feeling chill.

I see a bright star mid-upper right, a dark planet lower left, a vast star field and a milky river of stars, light years away. It's awesome to me. I know it's not completely original, but I can't wait, I have to start sketching. As I do, I keep in mind what resources I have on hand so I can get quick results. This is still design phase; the final scene will be done in hand-painted maps and greater detail.

First, I sketch five key scenes:

- ✦ One of deep space.
- ✦ One of my camera movement to follow the shuttle or small ship as it makes the transition from deep space to station approach.
- ✦ One from inside the shuttle's cockpit as it approaches the station docking bay.
- ✦ One from the bay interior looking out at the ship.
- ✦ The last shot is the shuttle locked down in its individual air bay. I draw a detail of how the mechanical arms work.

There's a whole story behind the space station and how each shuttle has its own airlock and how they're locked in place in case of emergency. As I work at my drawing pad I quickly sketch:

- ✦ An uninhabited sector of space with great depth and cold beauty.
- ✦ A warm-colored space station with beacons of light shining welcome to lonely travelers.
- ✦ An activity. Little ships moving, in the space around the station, to imply a bustling life without being crowded.
- ✦ A tracking camera angle jumps out at me — start a slow pan in the coldest part of space. A small, fast craft swooshes in from stage right. I follow it past a nebula and stars to its destination, the oasis in space: Trilon Station. Ah, a name.

My early concept sketches are shown in Figure 15-2.

As you can see, not everything happens in order. The processes of writing down and storyboarding feed each other.

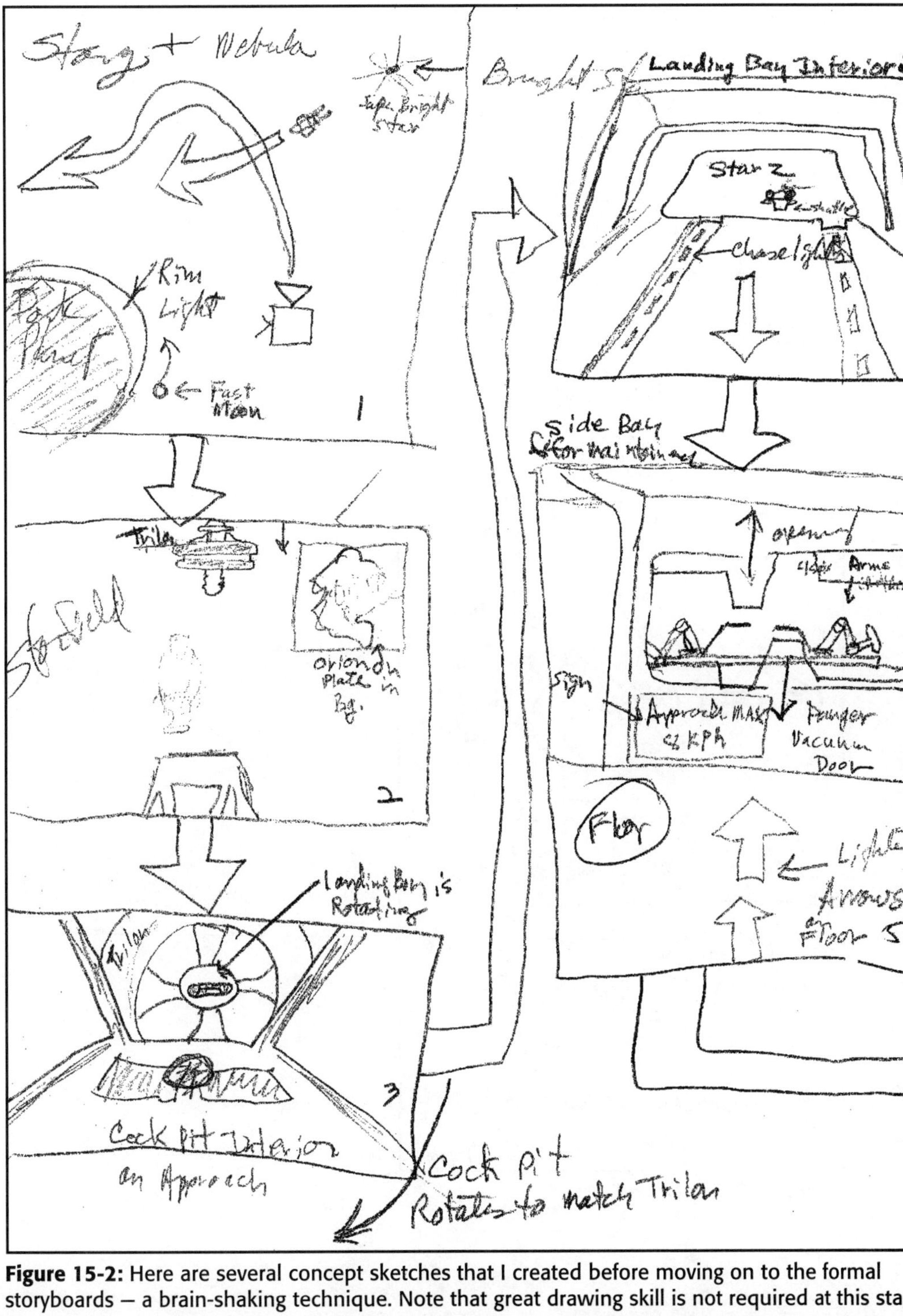

Figure 15-2: Here are several concept sketches that I created before moving on to the formal storyboards – a brain-shaking technique. Note that great drawing skill is not required at this stage.

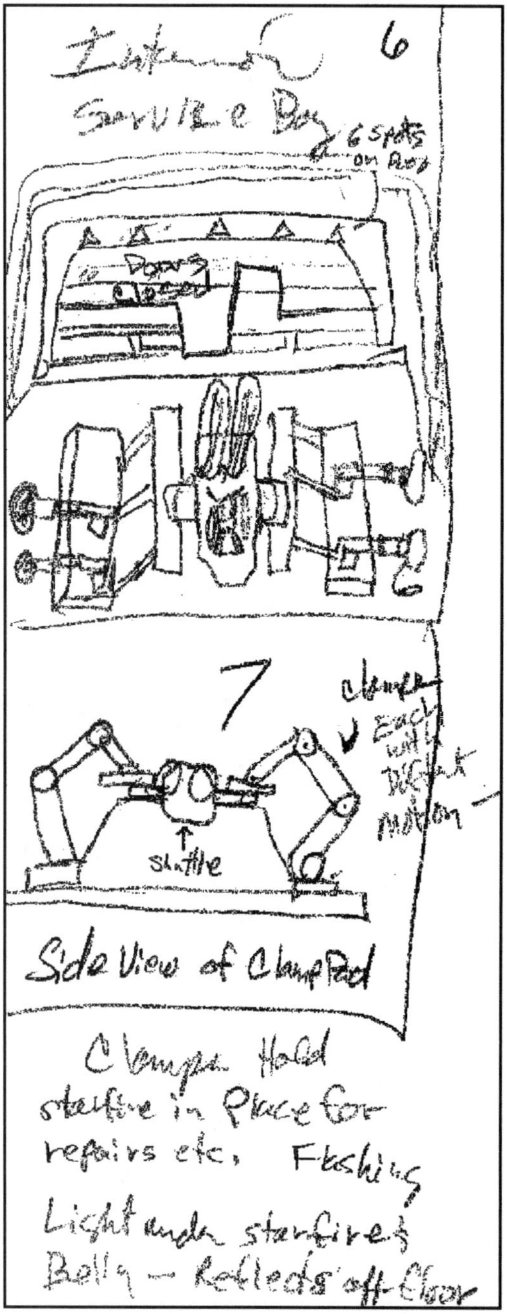

Figure 15-2: *(continued)*

Seeing the Action

As I'm visualizing, I suddenly get a picture of an icy asteroid entering stage left, spewing ice crystals. I follow it past a billowing sun, pan right to reveal an oasis in space: *Deep Space 9*. Darn. It seemed pretty original as I was thinking about it. But clearly I'm being influenced by past experience. We all are. I won't throw this vision away, I'll change things a bit to avoid being overly trite. I was once told by my wood shop teacher: "Don't throw your project away because it isn't quite right," he explained. "The trick is to take what you have and get it to be what you want. Use your head as well as your tools." Don't give up on your ideas, work on them until they work. If they can't be used, save them in a notepad for later use or inspiration.

View of Space

Okay, rewind. I see beautiful space with colored gas nebulae and stars. Out of that comes a small speck that grows until I recognize it as a little 23rd century space shuttle. My camera stays glued on the shuttle as it crosses in front, ahead of the swift-moving vehicle. The shuttle whooshes past while the slower camera follows, loses the ship for a moment, and finds it again as a distant Trilon Station enters the view from the top as we track. If we make this shot too long it'll quickly get boring, so I jump to the interior of the shuttle.

View from the Cockpit

We approach the station from a distance. It's just a dark spec that eventually looms large and foreboding. But as we come around the rim on our approach, we are met by the bright glory of topside. Beacons, bright windows, and small craft.

This means I'll have to make a second pass at docking, so I can circle and see topside. I might stick in an exterior shot here showing the shuttle in close approach. I even hear the music I'll edit in here. I see a large tanker as we line up with the central docking core.

Matching Rotation

To add interest, I've decided to add an interesting bit of business. The view from the cockpit sees the Trilon Station and landing bay rotating against the star field. In order to gain a clean landing approach, the pilot has to match his ship's rotation to the station's — I'll call it spin matching. This gives some visual interest as the stars begin to rotate and the landing dock begins to slow to a rotational stop all lined up for landing. Keeping this POV (Point of View), I see a smooth approach and just as I enter the open bay I cut to the next camera angle.

View from Inside Landing Bay

I see landing chase lights from the broad doorless entry bay coming toward me. The shuttle is fairly small in this opening as it floats smoothly into a large spaceship/aircraft carrier interior. There are spotlights from above casting a shadow of the shuttle on the floor. I see the floor as having painted, yellow staging strips and other esoteric space bay stuff. There are dirt smudges on the floor as well, probably due to plasma bursts as ships leave the entry bay. So the general trend of the smudges is from exterior to interior. Individual airlocks for the shuttles line the walls. The little ship is guided to one of the airlocks, which is opening vertically. Can you see it? Don't give up if you can't; your cognitive style may be nonvisual. Work on it and if you still can't see it, you may need help creating your own visuals — no big deal, get help from an artistic friend.

Components I Need to Design

To fulfill my vision I'll need the following sets:

- ✦ An awesome cosmos
- ✦ A small, fast craft exterior
- ✦ A small craft interior POV through space shield
- ✦ A space station exterior with landing bay
- ✦ A tanker exterior
- ✦ A landing bay interior
- ✦ An individual shuttle airlock bay with lock-down mechanism

That's all I need for now. You can see how the mental process is turning into something tangible. I now have things to model in trueSpace2. But before I do, I take just a few brief moments to let my mind wander again. I find this helps me avoid doing things in an entirely conventional way. I think of ordinary ways of modeling these things, then I stretch for something a little different.

The Work Plan

I know most of the elements I need are in material libraries so I do a quick setup in tS2 to see what it'll look like. Here's the plan:

1. Define a large space in terms of kilometers in the tS2 Properties Setup panel.
2. Build a huge sky dome to decal effects onto.
3. Select pure black as background color.
4. Fill the space with a large star field.
5. Add decals of gases and nebulae to invisible plates.
6. Make up some quick space gas ideas using Fractal Design Painter fractal clouds.
7. Make them semitransparent with feathered edges, and add an alpha channel.
8. Use the M-class planet in library, with a single dull spotlight for the dark planet.
9. Make a bright star with the Vertex tool and if it doesn't look quite right, try a Photoshop lens flare on a transparent panel.

The results appear in Figure 15-3.

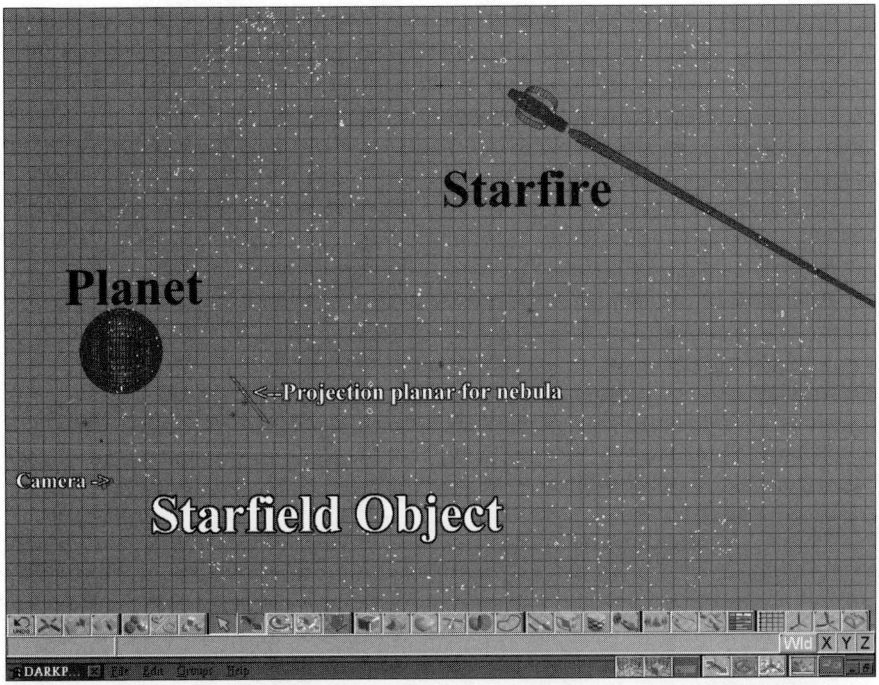

Figure 15-3: Here is a layout of the cosmos. You can see a rendering of the actual scene in Plate 15-1 in the color section. Note that the star field is behind the planet to avoid stars in front of the planet. This is a view from above.

We already have the space station exterior from Chapter 10, as well as a tanker and a drone ship. But the drone has no windscreen, no good. I put together a quick shuttle from my original sketches. (It's on the CD-ROM as starfire.cob.) I can use the drone as a busy prop around the station.

We still need a landing bay exterior and interior. I'll have to build those. Clearly the most complicated set at the moment will be the station interior, and I make a bunch of drawings. I've chosen my look, the aircraft carrier thing. We need the central docking bay, exterior detail, the main docking bay, the space doors, and the landing locking mechanism.

The level of detail you can afford to put into these things is a function of how much time and energy you have for the task. It also will be affected by the amount of money to be spent on the project. Money and time are not equal in 3D. Time is much more valuable because it can only be compressed so far — rendering still takes time. Money will buy equipment for multiple frame rendering and such, but you only have so many hours in a day. Okay, money will buy additional help. I guess money is pretty important, so put it on your agenda.

Exterior/Interior Detail

Looking at the space station we built earlier, you can see we never added a landing dock detail. To achieve the rotational effect I have described, it's necessary to put the dock in the bottom or top of the central tower. I like it on top because of the light, but I've already put my glass-roofed command center there. It'll have to go into the bottom of the central tower. I understood this when I started my master scene visualization.

The following goes on my modeling schedule:

- ✦ Boolean the main bay space into the bottom of the central tower.
- ✦ Model close-up detail of docking bay exterior.
- ✦ Model docking bay interior — use a lot of nernies and extruded 2D structural members to achieve an aircraft carrier look.
- ✦ Model and animate mechanical airlock doors and docking mechanism. Latter will use articulated motion to lock down shuttle.

Cockpit Interior

This is an easy one. By placing the vehicle's axis in the pilot's seat with the Z axis pointing out the window I can create a point of view looking smack out the window. The support struts are there. All I need is a little detail and I'm all set. Let's take it step by step:

Setting up the Camera

1. Load starfire.cob. It's a special wingless space vehicle that belongs to this station. It has a custom-fitted landing dock below. If it's not centered, normalize its location and rotation.
2. Open Front View in the main window and Top View alternate. The ship should be sitting at the origin, top up.
3. Use Axis tool to reveal the axis. It will be inside the ship. Engage your Move Object tool to locate the axis so Z is pointing right out the window (see Figure 15-4).
4. Check your top window to make sure the axis is centered sideways on the ship and moved forward to where the pilot might be sitting. The idea is to put the Z axis where the pilot's eyes would be.
5. Lock your axis.
6. Load a spacey image in the background field of the Render Options panel.
7. Switch the view in the alternate window to Camera, which is at the top of the alternate views variant menu. Render the whole view. This will be a good approach point of view.

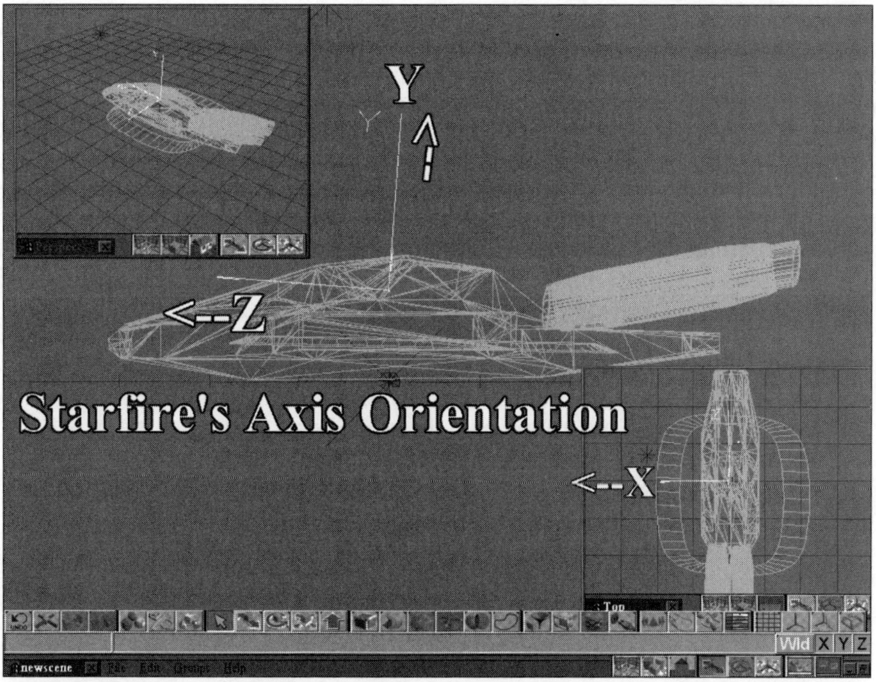

Figure 15-4: These multiple views of StarFire show the Z axis aligned with the pilot's POV so the ship will follow the path when the Look Ahead is selected. The axis can also serve as a camera with a pilot's eye view.

Texturing the Interior

Since the Z axis will *see* part of the ship's interior, we need to dress it up more like a spaceship than a tin model. Again we take it step by step.

By now you should be sophisticated enough to ignore a lot of this advice and do it your own way. If you want to start this way, fine. But cut yourself loose as soon as possible.

First a few ideas for making the cockpit POV look cool:

✦ Model a neat dashboard for the lower part of your view. Use boolean add and subtract to give detail to the instruments.

✦ Texture the dashboard with the Paint Faces tool or use a photo of a real fighter dash, or best of all, paint a dashboard image in one of your paint programs and map it to the dashboard.

✦ Texture the channels between the glass with some bump maps to give them interest. I think that's enough. People will be looking out the window and will hardly notice the interior.

Here's the step-by-step example. From your rendered Camera View inside the cockpit (above), think about how you can decorate. Remember, you are the set designer. I'll reveal what occurred to me and show you what it looked like. There are a million ways to go on this and mine is far from the most interesting, but I did it quickly while writing this chapter.

1. The first thing I thought of was, "I don't want to have to model a dashboard, it'll take too much time." Remember that I'm a tad lazy. I thought of that bunch of nernies I'd built for the CD-ROM. I loaded in one of the boxy ones and scaled it pretty flat and shaped it to fit half the area where I wanted a dashboard. The detail is different on each side, so I copied and flipped it over for the other half of the dash. It has a little modeled detail, and I'm thinking, "Hey this is in the future, I don't need conventional controls. It'll probably be all touch panels and the like." So I painted on the Bright Panel texture from the Space Material Library. It has a nice machine look bump texture and looked pretty cool, so I left it.
2. It was still a little boring, so I popped up a sphere with the same surface and put it smack in the middle of the dash.
3. I didn't like the thin look of the bottom of the dash, so I popped up one of the metal wedgie/cleat nernies, scaled and rotated it to fit in ahead of the dash to help define some bulk to the bottom of the space shield. I liked that too. It pleased me quite easily.
4. I liked the Bright Panel texture so much, I switched to my Top View and painted the exterior of the hull with it. Looks pretty cheesy for a spaceship, but when you switch back and render the Camera View, it looks like Figure 15-5.You really have to see the color of it to get a feel, so I repeated it in the color section at Plate 15-1.

A Few Last Words

This is a tough chapter to write because there are no hard and fast rules for production design (although some would disagree). I've shared my thought processes, which are not vastly different from some other designers'— though some would cringe at what I've written here. It's a strange ball game. I have a few thoughts that I'd like to emphasize before moving on to lighting.

✦ Don't let the world say you're not working just because you're lying back in the sun with an iced tea. It helps some people to close their eyes and try not thinking of anything for a while. The harder you try to design something or the tighter your time constraints, the more likely you'll have a brain phart. Nevertheless, some people work best under pressure, even creatively. You know which you are. Just keep sharp as to what conditions tend to stimulate your muse.

Figure 15-5: The quick finish interior of the shuttle from the pilot's (axis') point of view

- ✦ Keep it simple. Even if a scene looks complex, you want to keep the underpinnings as simple as possible. That's not as easy as it sounds.
- ✦ Watch your polygon count. Design your master scene for minimum use of polygons because each shaded, textured poly takes up computer rendering time. You will need denser poly counts for close-ups and for sections with animated deformations.
- ✦ Preview your scenes before the final render. One advantage of 3D is that you can do a fast draft animation to give you a very good idea of how it'll look in action. You can even use 3DR for an animated run-through if you have a fast machine with an accelerator. This will be invaluable to you for making last-minute compositional changes.

It's hard for me to let go of this chapter because it's so important, but from what I've seen in practice, all I can do is give you an inkling. To do more is robbing you of your own style. So go forth, be fruitful, make me proud to have been part of your beginning.

Summary

In this chapter I've tried to convey more of a sense of production design than a blueprint for it. I intend for you to have learned the following:

- The importance of creating an emotional link with your audience through production design choices. Your use of space, color, and beauty will affect the way your audience feels about your piece, emotionally.
- The process of kick-starting your creative juices through relaxed visualization.
- Different ways of fueling the creative flow, especially the use of story-boards. Storyboards provide an interactive process from which a final vision arises.
- A sense of doing it your own way instead of following a hard and fast set of design principles. Creativity works best in a nonsequential environment. That means the mind must be free to make intuitive leaps.
- The nuts and bolts of converting a vision into a stage setting.
- The use of previews to fine-tune your designs. tS2 affords the opportunity to preview scenes in detail before the final render, providing feedback needed for close scene tweaking.

✦ ✦ ✦

C H A P T E R 16

The Magic of Great Lighting

✦ ✦ ✦ ✦

In This Chapter

The psychology and symbolism of light

The interesting history of film lighting and how it can give us insight into our designs

How lighting directors feel about cyberlighting — the art of lighting digital productions

How lighting can be used to highlight the mood of your piece and focus the audience attention where you want it

How lighting and production design are Siamese twins

Lighting styles and terminology

How to work through lighting your project

✦ ✦ ✦ ✦

You already have a basic understanding of light. You needed it to master the previous chapters. A big chunk of this chapter was written by technical lighting director Sharon Calahan, so you get it right from the director's mouth.

Let There Be Light

Seems like an appropriate heading for this book. Lighting imbues your story with mood and emotional energy. Dark, brooding scenes lighted from below seem evil, while bright, sharp, shadowed scenes can remind one of summer good times. There's even a new course in Cyberlighting at UCLA Extension Film School. Lighting can have a powerful psychological effect on us and it's filled with symbolism. I didn't realize all this until I discussed lighting with my colleague, Jim Hillin. Jim was the digital effects supervisor on that fabulous ballroom scene in the Disney movie, *Beauty and the Beast.* That one scene required more than 150 separate lights to achieve the desired effect. Jim has a list of prime credits as long as your leg and he's graciously sharing some of his wisdom with us in this chapter.

Tips from Jim Hillin

Jim Hillin reminds me of an old master though he's a pretty young guy. He knows light. His reverence for the wisdom of his forbears ranges from the Old Flemish Masters to the great modern filmmakers. He opened my eyes about how the masters used light symbolically. For example, light coming from below was symbolic of evil. So when you see a portrait of some royalty with the light coming from below, you know the artist was not fond of him. Jim pointed out that light from above is angelic, light from the right is for the good guys (who also enter from the right), and light from the left is for the shady characters (who also enter from the left). I think this tunes into some innate sense we have because it's still true today. Bear these things in mind while you're designing your shots. Use them to advantage.

Jim offers this advice to new digital animators: "Watch movies and study their composition. Study every cut in the film *Death in Venice*. Each one is like a perfect Old Masters painting. Study the way light is used to create mood. Another film you can learn from is *2001*. Study the way it plays against the expected." Digital animation is very much like live action filming, so know your medium. Don't spend time reinventing the camera.

I asked Jim to share his ideas about how new animators can develop professionalism: "Learn your tools. It doesn't matter what they are, take the time to learn and use them well. One thing I see a lot of with new animators is too much light. Try underlighting your scenes. You hardly ever want much ambient light; it screws up your key light shadows and highlights. Vary your lighting and try emulating what you've seen in films you particularly like. Pay attention to scene changes. Study reflections and see what about them excites you. All of this will help train your eyes. The best digital cinematographers are way more than technicians, they're artists of the highest caliber."

One of the nice things about this field is the way pros are willing to share their ideas and even their secrets with young animators. I didn't see much of that in standard Hollywood filmmaking.

About Lighting with Sharon Calahan

Sharon Calahan is Technical Lighting Director at PIXAR. When I first contacted her, she was wrapping up PIXAR's biggest digital animation yet, *Toy Story*. If you've seen it (and statistically you have), you know it's a major breakthrough with some of the most incredible digital lighting ever put on film. The sheer size of the project was daunting. The number of scenes that had to be lighted and the moods to be conveyed were astounding. This picture had to be better than good. The future of digital cinema would be affected negatively if it were a flop. The PIXAR lighting team, co-led by Sharon and Galyn Susman, peaked at about 30 people at the height of production. The following section, "There's Magic in Great Lighting" was written by Sharon.

Some Facts About *Toy Story*[1]

Toy Story has broken most of the old records in digital animation. Here are a few of the numbers:

- ✦ Number of storyboard drawings: 25,000+
- ✦ Number of hand-painted texture maps: 2,000+
- ✦ Number of basic arithmetic operations per pixel: 500,000
- ✦ Number of lines of code describing all the objects (366 of them): 4,500,000

The entire picture was realized in RenderMan, PIXAR's own render engine, commonly thought of as the best in the business. The whole feature required pumping a whopping 34 terabytes of code through that engine. That's trillions! Nothing even close has ever been accomplished before. The final picture was rendered at a resolution of 1526 × 922 pixels and takes up over 500 gigabytes of hard disk storage. That you can render at 1526 × 922 right now.

[1] Source: *CGW Magazine*, August 1995, "Toy Story: A Triumph of Animation" by Barbara Robertson.

There's Magic in Great Lighting

Digital animation may be taking us to fantastic new heights. It seems to be a brand-new art form, the newest storytelling vehicle, but it is really an evolution and extension of art forms that already exist. If you think about it, man has always used the most advanced tools available to tell his stories. From the moment he stumbled upon hand tools, he started scratching out images on cave walls, even experimenting with creating sequential images to tell a story. The concept of animation was already forming. From there it took several million years, but eventually we garnered the technical knowledge and honed our visual skills enough to master form, perspective, and other physical properties. During the Renaissance, we finally understood how to use light in two-dimensional space to portray volume, texture, and depth with convincing reality. In fact, the great ones probably understood light better then than we do now. They would bend light and cheat it to serve their artistic purposes. As new tools and technologies have developed, we have eagerly applied them to art and storytelling.

Capturing Moments

Photography is the greatest advancement in the creation of images. As a technology, it is almost taken for granted now, but at one time it was a challenge to record and develop any image at all. As an art form, it is accessible to everyone and it gives even the novice an opportunity to work with light and storytelling.

Capturing Motion

Cinematography, the kinetic offspring of photography, has proven to be more than just a major technological advancement, it has had a profound influence on our lives as it has portrayed and invented them. It has in many ways defined our culture, despite its humble beginnings. Early films, without sound or color, relied heavily on simple staging and exaggerated action to convey ideas. Lighting design evolved from stage lighting to suit the unique needs of black-and-white film, which required special techniques to create visual depth and separation in a monochromatic environment.

The great black-and-white filmmakers had a deep understanding of light that seemed to have faded temporarily with the advent of color film. However, color provided new opportunities to explore composition and depth, and eventually all these techniques have become the visual tool kit for the filmmaker today.

The small blimped camera was a breakthrough that combined synchronous sound with a mobile camera. With camera free to move with the action, a whole field of cinematic motion emerged. New challenges were created for writing, acting, staging, editing, and lighting as the camera moved out of the studio and onto location.

Capturing Imagination

Traditional cel animation became another new tool in this odyssey. Filmmakers could now tell stories that previously only existed in their imaginations. The first technological breakthrough here was the invention of the pin-registered animation stand. This tool, still used today, made alignment of multilayer cels fast and accurate. It made assembly-line animation possible. Immediately, audiences were enthralled with repetitive cloned characters dancing metronomically to music over cycled and recycled backgrounds.

Even though many skeptics were convinced that the moviegoing audience would not be interested in watching a full-length animated feature, Walt Disney believed that the story would captivate the audience. Instead of a slow transition into the cinematic art form it is today, Disney made the quantum leap with *Snow White* in 1937. It is still a favorite almost sixty years later and is regarded as one of animation's finest achievements.

The Prodigy

The visual and technological marvel of our generation is computer graphics. At first we were awed by raytraced cones and spheres, displacement-mapped marble teapots, and undulating blobs. The technical strides made to generate realistic and fantastic images have been impressive. It hasn't taken long for the techniques to evolve far enough to reveal this new medium's cinematic potential.

Painting with Light

In computer animation, we've seen engaging short stories and inspired acting, but lost in the technology, lighting often remains an afterthought. Default lighting is frequently used to illuminate a scene so the viewer can see the animation.

This ignores everything we've learned about the importance of lighting as an ingredient of storytelling. Good lighting is crucial in directing the viewer's eye through scenes and to focus attention on the action. Lighting establishes mood, atmosphere, depth, time of day, and time of year, even the weather. Your lighting style gives clues to the story's essential nature and the personality of its characters. It can foretell a frightening event in the next scene by building visual tension, or it can deceptively disguise it by remaining calm. There is synergy among lighting, acting, and screenplay, which creates beauty and magic, engaging the imagination of your audience.

Directing the eye is the key objective of lighting. Learning to do it requires a thorough understanding of the principles of composition, which provide the designer with tools to break up space into pleasing arrangements. The principles of emphasis, balance, proportion, scale, shape, volume, value, color, texture, and rhythm are these tools guidelines that help us evaluate our compositions. Even though a significant component of a shot's composition is determined by the staging of actors and props, it can still be radically affected by lighting. Good lighting can elevate a solid composition to be breathtaking, and it can even rescue awkward staging.

Cinematic lighting involves more than placing a few lights and rolling the camera. The lighting designer must determine where the motivating light sources will be placed: windows, lamps, candles, sun, or moon. The direction of the key light source is important because, among other things, it dictates the predominant shadow direction, which can influence how the actors might be staged within that environment. The qualities of your light sources must be considered. How soft or hard should they be? What color qualities would best serve the mood? How should they be shaped and what color should they be?

Ultimately, you have to understand the mood are you trying to evoke. Once the lighting is designed, it is tweaked shot-by-shot to balance composition and beautify actors. More frequently than not, when your lighting is strictly analyzed, it will not be natural. The actual sources used to illuminate a scene and actors are not necessarily the literal ones implied by the visible motivating sources. We take license, we cheat and exaggerate to create the desired illusion. It is what feels right that is important rather than what is theoretically realistic. Keep your thought processes independent of any particular medium or tools. The tools must service the vision, not the other way round.

The transition from gimmicky computer images to pure storytelling art is well begun. As our tools become easier to use and more accessible, new visions will be born. Fast, interactive, and extensible lighting tools — like the real-time interactive lighting you can do with 3DR real-time rendering in trueSpace2 — are removing more technological limitations daily. As an animator/digital lighting designer, you can focus increasingly on being an essential part of the storytelling process.

As I write this, *Toy Story* is being released in theaters worldwide as the first fully computer-generated feature film. It will be interesting, years from now, to see how it is remembered.

Sharon Calahan's Tips for Achieving Professional Lighting

- Take a color and design class to learn more about composition.
- Learn about the functions of key, fill, and kicker lights from a book about photographic or film lighting.
- Remember that there is always more than one right way to do something.
- Think about what logical sources might be in the scene, which can help motivate the lights you are using.
- Think about the story point and the mood you are trying to evoke.
- Avoid placing a bright light that emanates from near the camera lens.
- Consider that all lights do not need to cast shadows (and shouldn't), but the key light should.
- Avoid lighting a flat plane with equal brightness across its surface.
- Avoid lighting opposite sides of a character or surface with equal brightness or color.
- Limit your use of specular highlights.
- Remember that as the camera moves shot-to-shot, your lights may need to move as well.
- Remember that one light cannot always solve two problems.
- Consider that a light that animates in position does not look natural – avoid or use with care.
- Think about shot-to-shot continuity, but don't be limited by it.
- Use reference material if it helps.
- Don't be too literal about the physics of it, go with what looks and feels right.
- Experiment and get a second opinion.
- Remember that if you can visualize it in your mind, you can make it happen in your image.
- Keep it as simple as possible.
- Share your successes and discoveries.

Thank You, Sharon

It's me, Peter, again. It's so refreshing when professionals share their wisdom with us. Sharon's tips will help boost your credibility. Remember them as you prepare your demo tape. As I write, *Toy Story* is recognized as a true quantum leap in entertainment. I've never seen so many positive reviews. My editor at *Animation* magazine, Sarah Beasley, commented: "*Toy Story* is a perfect film." She's not a film critic, but a chronicler of our industry. I think Sharon has already achieved her dream along with a lot of other people at PIXAR. It's like that in this business; you can actually achieve dreams and move on to the next. It's better than spending a lifetime on one. Climbing on top of a dream takes guts, a belief in yourself, and the energy to make it happen. Those are the parts you supply (see "One Man's Vision").

One Man's Vision

Ed Catmull, top man at PIXAR, wanted to make a full length CGI animation back in 1986, long before the technology could handle it. In those days Cray X-MP super computers were used to render a frame pretty quickly, but at $13 million a piece you couldn't afford enough of them to render a full motion picture in under a millennium.

He was working at LucasFilm then, heading up Industrial Light and Magic. George Lucas wasn't keen on the idea of diverting energy to a digital feature project. He was probably right too; it was too early. But Ed wanted to at least head in that direction, developing technologies that would eventually lead to a feature. George wanted to keep things focused on digital effects that were doable. Eventually Ed and his cronies were given an opportunity to spin off a new company, PIXAR. It slowly separated from ILM and Steve Jobs of Apple became majority stockholder and chairman of the board.

In 1990 PIXAR and Disney Studios joined hands where Lucas had feared to tread earlier. The time was almost right. Rendering was being done efficiently on smaller, much more affordable machines, and they announced that they would release an all-digital feature within three years. They were a little off, but in November 1995, *Toy Story* was a reality. Released to universal acclaim, it proved that CGI animation was now a grown-up, ready for a bright future.

Tools of Lighting

There's a whole world of tS2 lighting for you to learn. Let's start with a few basics and let you learn the rest through experimentation. tS2 gives you the great advantage of real-time lighting feedback. With 3DR you can move lights around and get a fairly good idea of how they will affect your scene. There are three kinds of lighting apparatus in tS2:

- Local Lights
- Spot Lights
- Infinite Lights

You'll probably use them in about that order of frequency. When you fire up tS2 it has a set of default lights. You can change the default from white lights to colored lights to no lights. Your choice. I use white lights because they don't distort texture colors.

Light Control Panel

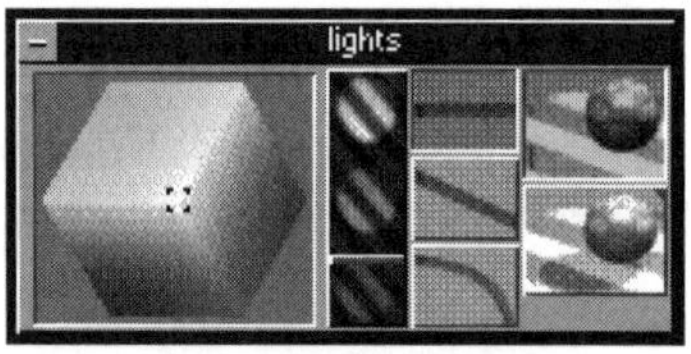

You add lights to a scene by choosing the type you want in the Primitives panel. When you add or select an existing light, tS2 opens a Light Control panel, allowing you to set color, intensity, fall off, shadows on/off, and type of shadow. By right clicking on the shadow, intensity, or color cube you'll get yet another layer of settings for each.

Color

You've done this before. Pick a color, any color, click on it and the light projects that color as if it had a gel over it. Right-click and you get an RGB slider with a numeric entry window.

Intensity

Click and drag the intensity slider to set the brightness of a light source. Right click to get the numeric entry window.

Fall Off

There are three preset kinds of fall off. That's the amount intensity decreases over distance from the center of the light. None of these settings affect infinite lights.

Constant Fall Off

This is the default. It's unnatural because light intensity does not diminish with distance.

Linear Fall Off

Light intensity falls off in direct proportion to distance. This is moderate fall off. At twice the distance the light is half as bright.

Squared Fall Off

Light intensity diminishes directly with the square of the distance from the source. This is rapid fall off. At twice the distance, the light is one quarter as bright.

Shadow

Lights in tS2 don't cast shadows by default. The reason is that shadows are computation intensive and not always necessary. Even when you want shadows, you'll only want a few sources to throw them. Each of the three types of light can throw a shadow in tS2, but only during rendering of the entire scene, not during object renders. There are two types of shadows you can choose from, raytraced shadows and shadow map shadows. Right-click to get the Shadow Property panel.

Shadow Property Panel

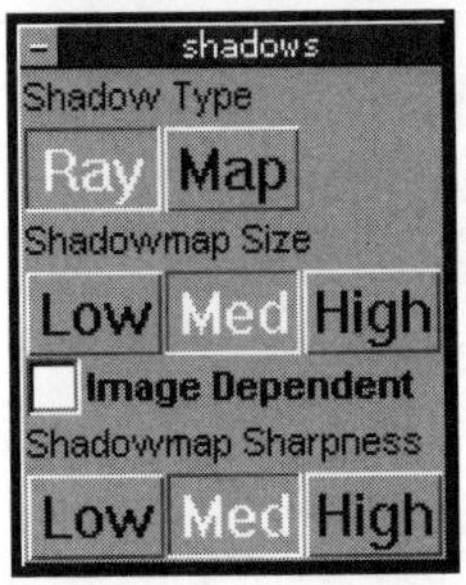

Ray

Shadows will be raytraced. They will only be seen after a full raytracing of the image. Definitely use this when you render transparent objects, as it creates transparent shadows. Raytraced shadows are sharp-edged as if coming from hard light. They take especially long for infinite lights. If you have raytraced shadows, try to set them up with spots or local lights. Figure 16-1 shows an example of semitransparent shadows.

Map

This is default, and works without the need for raytracing. Shadow Maps can be very large in the temp file and cause a fault if you don't have enough space. Some say it's much faster than raytraced shadows; I'm not sure I buy that. It works by tS2 rendering an image map of calculated shadows that it applies to the scene. Mapped shadows are softer edged than traced ones.

Shadow Map Size

This parameter applies only to Shadow Maps and refers *not* to the size of the shadow, but the amount of memory the map will consume. The default is Medium. Smaller maps are faster, but don't look as good as large maps, which take up a lot of memory and can be a lot slower to generate. The two larger maps are anti-aliased and have sharper edges.

Image Dependent

Again, this parameter applies only to the Shadow Map option. When selected it creates a shadow map in proportion to the final output resolution. At a map size of low, the shadow image is rendered at $^{1}/_{4}$ the final resolution, at medium it's $^{1}/_{2}$ of final resolution, and at high the shadows are rendered at full resolution.

Figure 16-1: Raytraced shadows give mood to an image. Note the semitransparent shadows of the bubbles. (Image by Danielle Plantec.)

Shadow Map Sharpness

This sets the edge feather on shadows. It's helpful to set this high for low resolution shadows. It helps to hide the edge jaggies and blurs any center graininess.

Local Lights

This is the same as an omni or point source light in other suites. It has only position, no size or orientation — think of a lightbulb. This one looks like a star and you can scale the light with your Object Scale tool, but it has no effect on the light's performance in the scene. The light emanates in all directions from a single point, much like a lightbulb or the sun.

Spot Lights

A spotlight can be positioned, aimed, focused, and its radial intensity fall off can be adjusted. That means you can have a tight or broad spot with soft or hard edges. Light emanates in a cone shape from the source.

Cone Angle

You can aim the cone by clicking on the Object Rotate tool and clicking *near* the light. Cone angle is very difficult to control in wireframe, especially for a dyslexic like me. There are two alternatives. Engage 3DR Solid Render mode and move the light interactively, observing its hotspot on objects. Or, my preference, pop up an alternate window with the spotlight selected and set it to Camera View. This will give a clear view of what the light is aimed at, because you're looking through the light.

Focus

You can adjust the cone diameter at a given distance by grabbing the light with the Object Scale tool. It will go from a pin spot to a floodlight. You adjust this as above, by looking through the light itself.

Intensity Fall Off

The Spot view also gives you a green circle to mark where intensity fall off begins. The area inside the green is the hot center. Intensity falls off in a smooth gradient from the green circle to the outer white circle. If you open the green circle until it touches the white, you'll get no fall off at all, just a uniformly bright sharp-edged spot. If you reduce the green to a spot, the hot spot will cover about a quarter of the diameter in the center. You can reduce the hot spot further by focusing down on a smaller area.

Infinite Lights

Default white lighting consists of four infinite lights aimed at center stage. An infinite light provides uniform light from distant sources, all moving uniformly in the same direction over the entire scene. It stands to reason that you must remove this default if you want to see shadows. Many new users forget, get confused, or wonder why their special lighting didn't do anything. It was all washed out by the infinite lights.

Infinite lights can be aimed. This is handy when you want to create uniform shadows throughout your picture. Say you want to have a setting sun; you can keyframe a steady change in angle for an infinite light, following the sun's demise. Shadows will get long. You can also keyframe intensity to fade with the day. Pretty good effect.

Lighting Technique

Nothing will make a bigger difference in the look of your rendering than how you set up your lighting. It's the maker and it's the breaker of your image. This could be the subject of several books, so this chapter will show you the ropes and key concepts; you can do further research on your own.[2]

[2] For more information refer to *Motion Picture and Video Lighting*, by Blain Brown, Focal Press 1996.

Fundamental Lighting Elements

Although there are only three basic types of light in tS2, there is a fourth that kills all the rest: ambient light. This, you will recall, is a surface characteristic that gives self-light to objects, washing out shadows. It's to be avoided unless there's a specific need for it. This section assumes no ambient light and talks about what external light elements you'll be working with to create that fabulous look you can see in your head.

The Key Light

This is the main light on the focus subject. It determines where the shadows will lie. It reveals the shape and texture of your key object or actor. There are many variations on the key light (see Figure 16-2). You could use an infinite light to key an entire scene or a tight spot to focus attention on a small scene element. You can even set up your master scene with several key lights. The actor moves from one to the next with shifting shadows. This might work well in the docking sequence. When the ship enters the bay it can move from one high key light to another for dramatic effect. Key light generally comes from the sides in order to cast shadows. You wouldn't place one close to the camera as that would obscure all the shadows. A key light from directly behind would place the entire subject in shadow. Shifting it to the side and moving from near front to near back will give a wide range of shadow effects. Set your key light first, then fill in as needed. You can get away with a single key light; it tends to be dramatic, especially if it's a spot. A single key is often used in film to achieve a low-key or European-look shot. It's not used often, but I think it probably should be.

Figure 16-2: An example of key lights placed (A) front left, (B) mid-left, and (C) right rear. (See also Plates 16-1 through 16-4 in color section)

Fill Lights

A single key light will leave you with tremendous contrast between light and shadow. This often doesn't serve your purposes effectively, so you need some extra light to bring out other scene elements. Essentially, any light that balances the key light is a fill light. Traditionally a fill light is a diffuse source placed near the camera. That's not the only way to go, though. The trend is toward innovative fill ideas. A fill light can be anything from a tight spot to a shadowless infinite light and you can place the source just about anywhere that gives you what you're looking for. Rules are for technicians; you're an artist, go for it.

Background Lighting

When you have a dark subject against a dark background it often pays to create a light gradient on the background elements. In space, you can also accomplish this by putting a bright nebulae or galaxy behind the subject to highlight its edges. In Chapter 17 I use a background light to silhouette some city buildings which were lost in the fog (see Plate 17-2 in the color section). Background lights can also simulate such things as sunsets and afterglows.

If you don't have a good space background you can set a batch of local lights against a background plane. Set them to squared fall off, vary the color slightly from white, and set intensity by rendering a few samples. If you do it right, the lights will look like stars and nebulae depending on intensity and distance from the background. Paint the backplate with a hazy black and white marble texture for an interesting nebulae effect.

Rim Lights

You can often achieve a dramatic effect by lighting a subject from behind, but offset enough to create a bright rim light. This is related to the Kicker which is used on humanoid actors to sidelight the face, adding drama to the image.

Eye Lights

If you create characters with deep eye sockets they'll tend to collect deep shadows that obscure the eyes. That's often not what you want. In regular film, eye lights are difficult to keep trained on moving subjects. In tS2, you can create a small soft spot similar to an inkie (200 watt tiny portable spotlight) and aim it at the eye sockets, gluing it in place. This will keep the light in the eyes as your subject moves. Do *not* overdo it. Keep eye lights quite dim. You shouldn't notice them until you shut them off.

Obie Light

This is a spot you attach to the camera, just like in home movies. It can really screw up your shadows, so make it small, just enough to reveal necessary detail as you approach objects. I use it when I'm tracking a heavily shadowed object like a space vehicle's dark side. As I approach, details slowly resolve in the low light. You hardly notice. By using a bright obie you can simulate a headlight effect as if the camera were an approaching vehicle.

Dark Lights

Negative lights are a specialty of 3D. Since lights allow numeric intensity input, the developers of the original tS thoughtfully allowed us to input negative numbers. A negative intensity causes a light to absorb existing light. The higher the intensity, the darker the area. Shine a dark spotlight into a corner to obscure a poorly detailed area. This is very useful for creating mood. All three lights in tS2 and tS S/E can be used as dark lights.

Qualities of Light

The English language has hundreds of words to describe quality of light. In tS2 light quality is created by the interaction of surface shaders and lighting elements. Here are some of the qualities of light that you can work with.

Shadows

Filmmakers talk of soft and hard light. What they really mean are soft and hard shadows. Hard light gives sharp shadows like the ones you get by raytracing or using large shadow maps. Soft light is the opposite, yielding soft shadows with feathery edges. Generally, hard light comes from small source lights like those that leave hard terminators on spheres, whereas soft light comes from large sources like fluorescent lights, and so on.

Specularity

In addition to hardness, light has quality along a continuum from specular or directional, to diffuse or chaotic light.

Surface Effect

The microstructure of a reflective surface determines how much coherence light will retain bouncing off. Hard, polished surfaces like mirrors change light very little as it bounces. This is called specular bounce. Surfaces that are rougher, like an unpolished aluminum plate, or a photographer's silk reflector cause even coherent light to bounce at random angles creating diffuse highlights. This is naturally called diffuse bounce.

Light Effect

On shiny surfaces, a collimated (focused) beam of coherent light will produce sharp, clear reflections and small specular highlights. Diffuse light remains diffuse even when it's reflected in a polished surface. It also produces soft-edged shadows.

Hard shiny surfaces tend to have small specular highlights while rougher ones have large diffuse ones. When specular light reflects off a surface, all the photons hit at the same angle, so they bounce coherently (for a given surface) retaining most of their original qualities. Diffuse light, like that bouncing off silk, enters at many angles and scatters, giving blurry reflections.

The important thing here is that we read surfaces by the kind of light they bounce back at us. You know a shiny car bumper is going to be hard, while a soft pillow is going to squish in your hands.

Fill Ratio

This is just the ratio between key and fill lights. A high-key scene is very brightly lit with few shadows while low-key lighting is shadowy and dramatic.

Modulation

You'll often want to modulate or break up light to add richness, detail, or interest to a scene. You can do this with something called a cookie which is a planar, a two-dimensional polygon with holes booleaned into it in a random pattern. It's good to avoid a pattern and use different shapes. Placed in front of a shadow light with soft shadows, this creates shadow gradients on the set (see Figure 16-3).

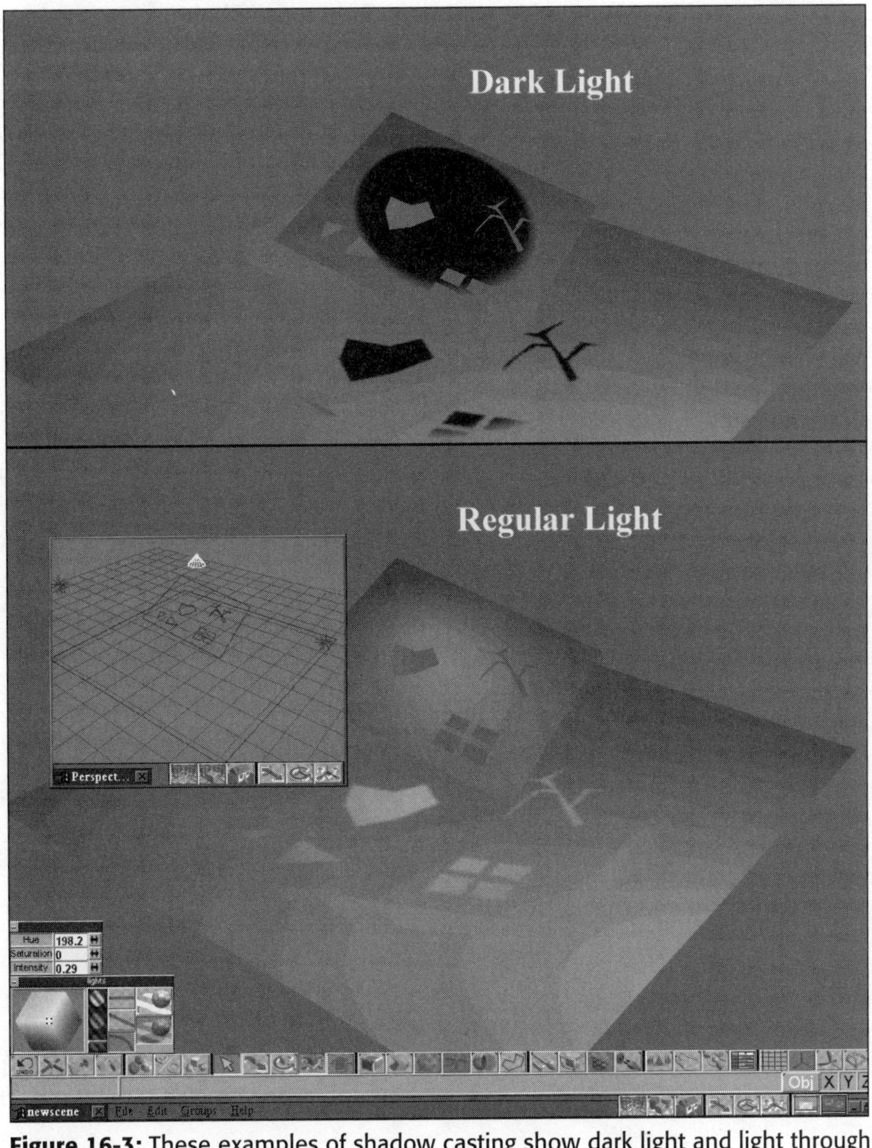

Figure 16-3: These examples of shadow casting show dark light and light through a cookie filter. Rotating the filter can make shadows longer or shorter.

You can also cast shadows into a scene with a gobo. That would be, say, something solid hung on fish line (or nothing in 3D) in front of the light source to cast a shadow to break up the background and add a little visual interest.

Shadows

Projected Shadows

This is an extension of the cookie approach. Directors will often create a mood by projecting familiar shadows into a scene. One really trite example is the spinning ventilator blades causing volumetric shadows through a smoky interior. I've seen it in at least ten films and I still don't know what mood it projects — perhaps an industrial mood. But you can cast shadows of window panes, long tree shadows, moving shadows, and all sorts of creative shadows to help establish a mood. This device is often neglected, but very useful, in 3D. Think of creating a spooky mood with a lightning effect through creepy windows, and casting shadows onto an old stone wall.

You can create shadows either of two ways:

✦ Use a cookie with the shape of the shadow you want to cast and use a shadow-casting dark light. For example, cut out a tree shape and cast dark light through it.

✦ Cast light through a cookie to create a bright spot. The cookie itself casts the shadow.

If it doesn't seem to be working, you forgot to engage the Shadow Light option on your light source.

You can raytrace interesting shadows through variable transparency objects. Use the procedural textures with transparency to make some interesting cookies.

Gels

In traditional filmmaking, the lighting director will often place a colored gel or gelatin in front of a klieg light to produce soft color ambience. The color temperature of light is important to the emotional message it conveys. Subtle gels can imply late afternoon sun at a low angle coming through a window, or a warm, romantic interior, as well as harsh cold light. In tS2 you create gels by simply selecting the light color from the light control color cube.

Gel Projections

You can actually put a transparent picture in front of a light source in tS2 and have it projected into the scene. Just like a slide projector. This has lots of uses. Imagine projecting a stained glass window onto the interior of a church. That'll make you suspend disbelief. This only works in raytraced images. Try it for grins.

Raytracing

Raytracing will change the look of your scene because it more accurately calculates the trajectories of light beams. This gives you real reflections, highlights, and sharp shadows. In many cases you'll have to completely relight a scene if you switch from scan-line to raytrace. Raytrace tends to have brighter highlights on shiny objects. If you have glass in a scene, raytracing is the only way to get the proper glass looks of reflection and refraction.

Lighting the Scene

You'll probably want to light your scene as you go, without much planning. I can't blame you, I do the same thing. In fact, I encourage you to do this during your initial stages. Sometimes you can come up with some really great lighting. Most times, you'll only achieve adequate light and that's not good enough for professional work. So when it comes time to put out that demo or a professional piece of work, plan your lighting, or at least go back with a checklist to make sure you're achieving your lighting goals.

POWER TIP

You can improve your lighting by spending time observing real-world light and how it works. Take a notebook with you and jot down things that you notice, like the way light filters through leaves on a tree, or how rainbows form on an oil film puddle in the parking lot. Pay particular attention to shadows and how they work. Light is 95 percent of the ball game in 3D and understanding it will help you become a professional.

Lighting Checklist

To create that checklist you need to know what you want to accomplish with light in your scene or sequence. Ask yourself the following questions, write down the answers, and save in Windows Notepad.

- ✦ Where does the action take place?
- ✦ What mood do you want to evoke?
- ✦ How big is the scene?
- ✦ What time of day or night is it?
- ✦ What is the season, the weather?
- ✦ What effects do you need to consider (blinking lights, rotoscoping)?
- ✦ Do you need light continuity between this scene and the next?
- ✦ How many actors do you have to light?
- ✦ Will you need background lights to highlight actors?

Your Lighting Plan

Good lighting begins with your script and your production design. When you know what *look* you want you're ready to lay out your plan. There are an infinite number of ways to light a set, and the process is anything but cut and dried. You might want to do a rough sketch of how you envision your lights, keeping in mind shadows and highlights. You'll need a sketch of the action blocked out and camera locations. Make notes of any camera moves. I'm going to use the master scene we designed in the previous chapter. The planned sequence has five lighting challenges:

1. The grand deep space scene with its dark background. We must be able to see the tiny ship as it emerges from the void. This can be relatively simple, using two approaches. The key light, a shadow casting infinite light, provides consistent lighting for the scene's action, and good continuity to the next scene. I'll silhouette the shuttle craft with a bright b.g. nebulae to make it more visible. The light will probably be harsh to emphasize the unforgiving environment. That means sharp shadow terminators.
2. The transition scene is where camera looks at shuttle while tracking across its path and then tracks from behind to reveal Trilon Station. The ship needs the same key light as in the previous scene with the same shadow direction The planet will need dark shadows, perhaps even a dark light. No fill light will be used because we want to keep the hard light look.
3. The interior of the shuttle craft will be most believable and least distracting if it has deep shadows with a few highlights. It should have flashing lights on the dash. This is difficult in tS2 because there are no lens flares. Ambient light can be keyframed to imply flashing lights. The environment mood I want is *cozy.*
4. The exterior of Trilon Station. This can be easy or complex. A single infinite light would be good, but you could spruce it up with flashing lights, landing lights, and interior lights shining through the gold glass dome. The mood I want is grand active excitement.
5. The landing bay interiors. This last one is the most challenging because it involves many lights in a large complex area. The industrial/carrier look we want inside the bay is also complex, requiring shadows and bright lights, and chase lights for the floor. The mood I want here is somber, efficient.

Landing Bay Lighting – Interior

As an example, I'll work through the lighting of the landing bay. Figure 16-4 shows an example.

Here's my thinking:

- ✦ I want splashes of light on the landing bay floor from high ceiling spots.
- ✦ I see the shuttle coming in under these lights, and the changing shadows emphasize the action as it moves slowly into position for docking.

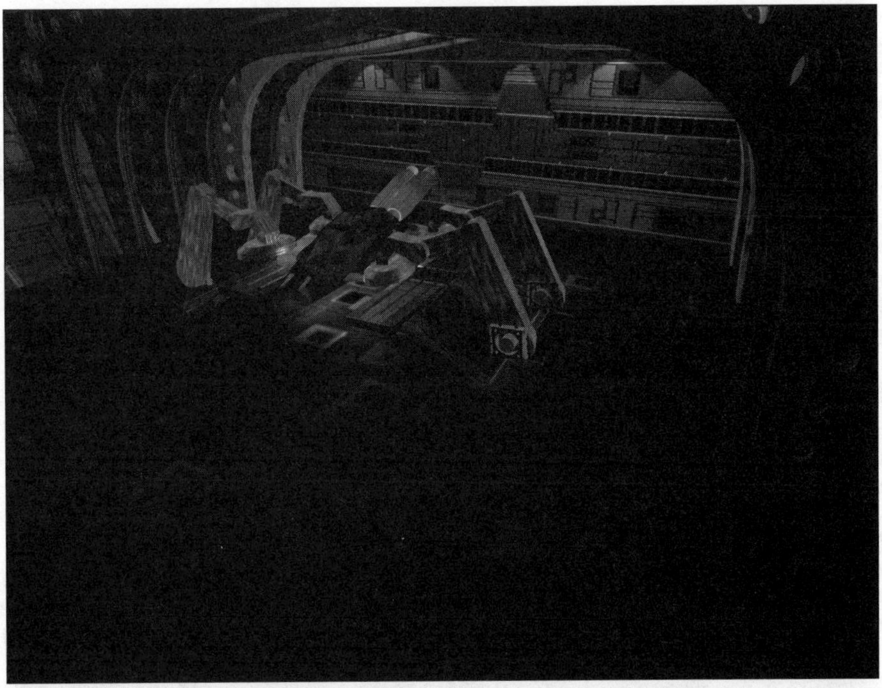

Figure 16-4: This illustration shows the interior of the landing bay. Note how the light helps to create mood while it highlights the subject.

- Dark corners will help emphasize the forbidding nature of this vacuum area.
- In the sealable docking chamber I want work lights and landing lights to emphasize the working/industrial quality of the place.
- I think spotlights attached to the articulated docking arms would add interest while continuing the look and industrial mood. As they move into position, they sweep an arc of light with the spot landing on the shuttle exit doors.

With these thoughts in mind, I begin to rough in lights.

- I turn off default lighting.
- I place six spots in the ceiling looking down on the floor. I make sure they will wash over the shuttle as it transits the bay.
- I place six vertical spotlights, one against each structural arch shining up the wall to the ceiling.
- I place two dark lights in corners on the sides of the main bay opening.

- ✦ I place both articulated arms in the vehicle lock down position and glue a tight beam hard light (minimal fall off) spot to each, pointing where the shuttle's exit door will be.
- ✦ I simulate chase lights by keyframing a 0–100% ambient green light on little boxes leading in a straight line from the entry to the rear of the docking bay. If that's not bright enough, I might keyframe little local lights very close to each box, to emphasize the effect.

With these lights roughed in and aimed, I run through a low-res animation to check the effect. Render a few medium-sized, full render shots to check details. Make adjustments and reshoot the preview. Continue this process until it looks the way I want it to.

For a look at how this all turns out, check out Plates 16-1 through 16-3 in the color section. I've included an example of using raytraced shadows with glass to achieve the hyper-real effect that's shown in Plate16-4. In the next chapter you'll learn more about lights used with fog and camera filters to create moody atmospheres.

I'll show you one more example that illustrates dramatic lighting. Figure 16-5 shows how the space tanker is lighted from behind with a shadow casting spot, as if a large star is illuminating the object. How do I achieve this effect? I light the foreground object using a small local light with inverse square fall off engaged.

Figure 16-5: Space scenes afford many opportunities for creating dramatic lighting. Here the strong shadows are used to bring out the ship's texture. Local lights are used to separate foreground elements from the main action.

Summary

If you haven't been trying out these ideas on your computer, you should now. Here are some of the things we covered:

- ✦ How light is interpreted by our brain and emotions.
- ✦ A little history of film lighting from Sharon Calahan at PIXAR.
- ✦ How to think like a lighting director, planning with the story and mood in mind.
- ✦ How to lay out your lighting objectives to set up your lighting plan.
- ✦ All about how lighting works in tS2, including the Light Control panel and all its parts.
- ✦ The interplay between lights and surface shaders and how to use them to create the look you want.
- ✦ A lighting director's vocabulary and tools, including the names of lights and lighting conventions and how to use them.
- ✦ The basics of lighting a scene, including layout, rough in, and preview.

✦ ✦ ✦

CHAPTER 17

Creating Atmospheric Effects

✦ ✦ ✦ ✦

In This Chapter

How to build a variable density atmosphere filter

All about smog

How to build a smoggy, grungy city scene

How to use background lighting to silhouette obscured distant objects

How to use fog to create atmospheric density

Using variable density filters to create the illusion of wispy or layered fog

✦ ✦ ✦ ✦

I was raised in New Jersey, where people panic when they can't taste the air. I remember getting up on a fine morning and smelling industrial gases mixed with fog and thinking it was fresh air. Another great thing about Jersey air is the great diffused sunsets. Light has a whole different meaning in smog. It can take on colors — a pale golden brown, or an unearthly whiteness at midday, and the fantastic reds of evening. A great animator studies smog as he studies a horse's gait, from a neutral position. Animators study the look and motion of everything. To us it's a natural science. Smog isn't bad, it's something to be understood. This process helps you cast off stereotypes, like roses are red or smog is brown. You observe and you learn.

Smog Think

The power of tS2 makes it easy to be lazy and still get decent results. That's not the goal of a real animator. You want to push the envelope — create visions of a new reality — and use the power to move in new directions. Okay, so I'm preaching over smog. How would you create a smog effect? I'll give you some ideas:

✦ Think about how light reacts as it's filtered through smog.

✦ Smog is nothing to look at unless it's obscuring something.

✦ Smog is sometimes evenly distributed, sometimes concentrated in low areas, sometimes wispy.

✦ Smog can be just about any color, but it's never saturated. It often has a component of gray, tinged with color and transparency.

✦ Smog has depth and density.

There's a lot more, but let's start here. What tools do we have to work with? The first one that comes to mind is the Fog tool. Smog is bad stuff mixed with fog. So we're halfway there. Fog has parameters. You can adjust its density, starting point, far point, and fall off. It won't give us layers, but it will give a start. We need something to obscure in the fog. Anything will do, maybe a building.

Pick Your Tools

What tools can we play with to create the illusion of smog? I'm thinking about the marble texture. It has fractal cloud possibilities and we can play with the transparency and colors as well. I suspect we could imply patchy smog with it, though I'm not sure how at this point. I also think we could make low-hanging smog out of a smog-colored semitransparent shape along the ground. I'm not sure. Let's experiment together.

1. Since I want a background to show through, I set the maximum fog density under 100%. I don't want it to show through much, so let's try 90% at Far Point 50 units.

2. I want the smog to have a sickly color, so I choose a brownish pink. R ➪ 141, G ➪ 97, B ➪ 70.

A Variable Density Atmosphere Filter

By placing a semitransparent filter in front of the camera you can achieve some useful special effects. You can use a planar Primitive surfaced with an appropriate semitransparent material or an environment map. Variations are to use a large cylinder that you rotate to simulate moving atmospheric effects, and you can rotate the planar object as well. For this project I'll surface the filter with a variable density material made from the Marble Procedural texture. This texture is ideally suited for creating cloudy effects because it generates fractal patterns that look very natural.

There are several ways to go. A true variable density filter uses the same color for both stone and vein parameters, but sets the transparency of one to zero and the other to 100%. In this case, I also want to add a whitish haze of wispy pollution.

Here's how I did it:

1. I definitely want a patchy look and there's no direct way to do it in tS2, so let's pop up a planar Primitive and scale it up to about the size of the grid. Rotate it to vertical in front of the camera in your Perspective View. It'll be white and obfuscate the view.
2. To get the patchy atmosphere select the Marble Procedural texture. Right click to get the Color Control panel and set Stone Color at R ➪ 135 G ➪ 75 B ➪ 65.
3. We want the stone to be reasonably transparent as well, so slide the transparency setting up about 75% toward transparency. Set Vein Color at pure white with transparency down to about zero to 10%. This makes the densest parts of the smog nearly opaque for a patchy look.
4. Next we need to find a fractal pattern that will enhance the look we want. I want layers to give the feel of drifting gases. Adjust the marble parameters as follows: Set Grain ➪ X (to get horizontal layering), Turbulence ➪ 0.8 (to stir up the clouds a bit), and Sharpness ➪ 0.45 (to give the layers some thickness). The higher you go the denser the clouds.
5. Experiment with the look by trying each of the X, Y, and Z grain directions.
6. You can create a layered look by disproportionately scaling along the Y axis as follows: X ➪ .9 Y ➪ 4.5 Z ➪ .5. These work well, but try other combinations. Play with the grain as well. You can get an amazing variety of smoggy looks.
7. When you paint this on the foreground plane you just built, it becomes a variable density filter through which you see everything. Therefore it's better not to have close foreground items. If you must, place them in front of the plane and they will appear close and unaffected by the smog.
8. You can increase the feeling of density by placing some bright lights close to objects deep in the smog. It'll enhance that dismal look.
9. Placing a light in front of the marble filter, you can adjust the brightness of the smog. A small white light helps to bring up the wispy quality of the smog clouds. If you make the filter reflective you'll get a hot spot. This has uses, but avoid it unless you need it.
10. Play with fog density and fall offs. They can make a substantial difference in the look of your atmosphere.
11. Use negative lights (input negative values in the intensity setting) to create dark areas. You can hide stuff this way, but more importantly, you can create mood, which is part of atmosphere.

City of Industry

I wanted to give you an example of setting up a terrestrial scene, but I'm partial to the gritty, gloomy, industrial look. My insane writing schedule affords me precious little time to build many special objects. I didn't even have time to look through my hundreds of poorly organized models on CD-ROMS, to grab all the goodies I know are in there — street lamps, signs, park benches, and the like. I set up the industrial view using bits and pieces in my regular object bin.

The Buildings

I use a fire escape model from CyberProps which you'll find on the CD-ROM under \geometry\3name3D\05fscap.3df (this file is in the 3D Studio format, which you'll have to import into trueSpace) . I place it against a plain old rectangular box that I textured with my universal machine material in the Space Materials Library. I copied it and slid the copy alongside to make a longer building. I copied it again, mirrored it, and moved it across the street. The street lamp is really an indoor lamp, but it was all I had handy, so I simply mounted it on a box in the foreground to look like part of a building. I managed to obscure much of the lamp with the light halo, so the fact that it's an indoor lamp doesn't hit you in the face.

I built a water tower out of two cylinders and a cone. (Just scale them and glue together.) As a finishing touch I put a small red cylindrical light on top. It's just a semitransparent cylinder with a light inside.

The far building is one of the space nernies scaled tall and larger to look vaguely like buildings. The road is a planar Primitive textured with something called Black Sand I picked up on the Web. I suggest you do a better job. Boolean a slight depression in a ground plane for the road, leaving curbs, then make a nice road map with a yellow line or two down the middle. In my image, I put a simple, large, square planar object to define the ground plane for the whole image. It's just shaded in using one of my dull dark hull maps. I tried a green foliage map on it, but it didn't look right. This is fine for the fog. I'll keep working on this because I like the somber, lonely mood of it. I think a single tree casting shadows against the middle building on the left might be eerie seen through the fog.

This piece needs a lot of texture work. It's a previsualization for a more detailed work. I invested about seven hours in developing this image. A fully realized and rendered image at a professional level would take me several days. Much of that time would be spent working on designing and refining the look. More time would be spent carefully modeling buildings and placing prebuilt objects such as streetlights, trash cans, and telephone poles.

From the Top Down View in Figure 17-1, you can see the buildings are just rectangles. You can see where I booleaned out some window depressions and put in some lights to highlight them. The dense fog obscures most of it, but without those insets you lose something.

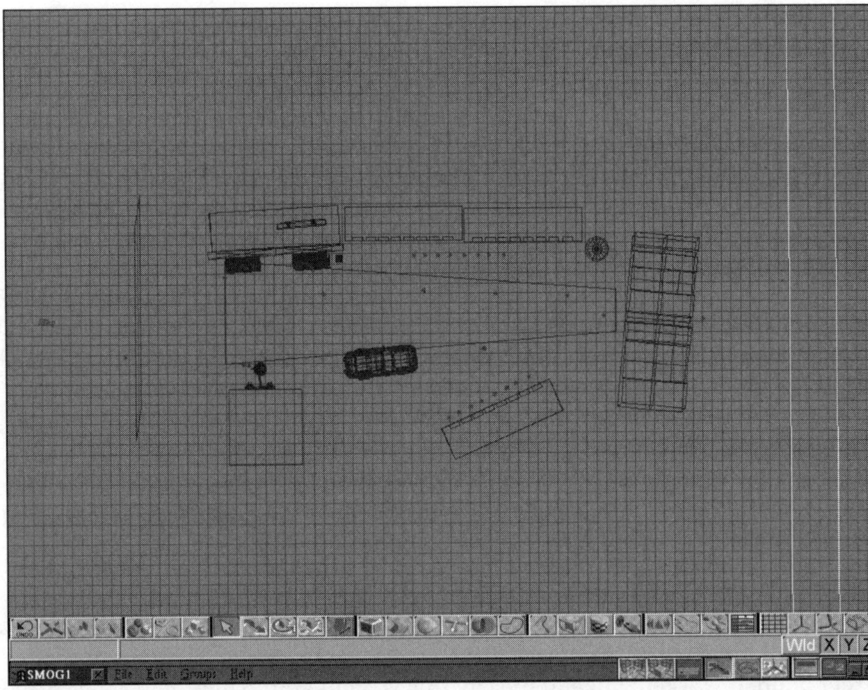

Figure 17-1: A Top Down View of the City of Industry scene layout, where the line on the far right is a vertical backdrop, and the line on the left is the variable density smog filter made from Marble Procedural texture. The boxes are just that — boxes and nernies textured to look vaguely like buildings. The circle is the water tower.

The art of minimalist rendering is knowing what to leave out and what to put in. I'm not going to teach you that, you learn from experience. You learn to suggest a theme, exactly the way painters imply things with a splash of color or a dab of shadow.

Use the nernie teeth you built for your character as a set of buildings. Just invert it, stretch it out, and you have a set of city buildings. They are way in the back in shadow; you see them in silhouette with the last rays of day fading behind. No, it looks more like the afterglow of city lights. Anyway, invert the teeth, stretch them out until they fit the space, then switch to a Front View window and stretch them up until they look right. Texture them with a map that looks about right or paint one, and you're done. Easy.

The Plates

I've rendered the industrial smog pictures for you to compare. I did them in color, so you'll have to check them out in the color section. Plate 17-1 is rendered with default lighting and no atmosphere. Plate 17-2 is the same scene, as seen through the marble density filter. I've added some lighting in Plate 17-3, and Plate 17-4 is close to the smog atmosphere I was looking for. It's Plate 17-3 with the addition of a brownish fog starting at 11 feet and reaching 80% density at the 50-foot far point. To repeat, if the fog were 100% it would obscure the background.

Background Lighting

With this dense atmosphere, a background image won't do much for the picture and the rear buildings are obscured in the fog. I made a reflective white planar Primitive and scaled it as a backdrop. I placed it vertically behind the back buildings, out of sight. I installed a bright red light behind the buildings, about a 12 intensity set to inverse square fall off. This makes a white ⇨ red sunset gradient that silhouettes the farthest buildings deep in the smog. It's very obvious until you engage the fog, then it fades to just about the way I want it. Try tilting the background plane to adjust the backlight gradient.

The Streetlight

I wanted to achieve a blurry-dense-foggy-wet look for the streetlight glare. I just couldn't get what my mind saw by normal means. I tried putting all sorts of lights inside and using different kinds of glass, but nothing looked right. Then I took a long shot. I figured maybe I could line up a light reflecting off the Marble filter. If it worked, I could give the filter reflective properties to exactly match the glow I wanted. They shouldn't affect the rest of the view. I made the filter softly reflective (slightly rough shader), and put a light *outside* but quite close, in line with the street lamp. It worked. I like it! Clearly this is a cheat; the light you see is way in front of where you perceive it and it's only a reflection. Pretty nifty, huh? I'm getting myself a hot apple cider and enjoying my moment of brilliance.

That's the way it is with atmospheric and other special effects. You use your head, play around, and take long shots. I admit this one took me several hours to achieve, but that's not uncommon. It takes time to bring great ideas to the screen.

Roundup of Atmospheric Ideas

Here are a few different ways to create atmosphere in your animations.

The Storm

You'll often want to create a stormy feeling or even an actual storm. Here are a few ideas:

- ✦ Create a storm cloud background using the Marble texture and paint it on a background plate.
- ✦ Keyframe animate Marble Procedural parameters to make clouds move (more under Hollywood effects chapter).
- ✦ Keyframe light flashes on a background panel to simulate sheet lightning.

- Use the fog effect, but ever so slightly. You don't want fog, just a vague atmospheric density.
- Simulate approaching fog by setting the fog effect's near point in the distance (say 25 feet) so it looks like the fog is on its way. Set it at about 90% and do some back lighting with a b.g. plate to highlight the density.
- Use exploder particle and gravity effects to simulate hail pelting down (more in Hollywood effects).

If you plan to use a front filter on a moving camera, glue it to the camera so it moves as well. This will prevent strange aberrations. There will be times when you want to move the camera and keep the filter stationary. In that case, make a big filter and surface it appropriately.

Snow

- You can simulate snow effectively by projecting falling snow (you have to find it on your own) onto a transparent front plate. If you don't have snow against a transparent background, try reflection mapping it onto the foreground plate.
- Set your scene in a huge transparent sphere with white dots on it. Put in an opaque background plate and then rotate the sphere in front of the camera with motion blur engaged. This will give you a nice snow effect.
- Ground snow isn't uniformly white. Texture map it with an image of textured white paper.
- Bump map snow using soft rounded bumps. Try making a fractal map in Painter 3 or 4.

Nightclub

Nightclubs are nearly always smoky, shadowy places with flashing lights.

- Use the fog indoors to simulate smoke density. Experiment with white fog and black fog. See what interesting effects you get.
- Place a nearly transparent plate in the foreground, reflection-mapped with fire to give your flashing lights a halo. Make the reflection mostly transparent and try the effect with both Metal and Phong shaders.
- Use negative lights to darken corners.
- Use spotlights to emphasize the action. You can glue a semitransparent cone to a spotlight to get a light-through-smoke effect. Make it a little narrower than the spotlight's radius. Raytrace it for the best effect.

You get the idea. Creating atmosphere is a fun and creative part of animation that amateurs usually ignore. Do it as a step in your journey to professionalism. I'll continue to suggest techniques in Chapter 26.

Summary

This was a short chapter, but it included some important pieces of the puzzle. You learned the following:

- ✦ How to use a combination of effects including fog and variable density filtering to create hazy smog effects.
- ✦ How to create a variable density filter to use in front of the camera for special effects.
- ✦ How to use reflections to create the illusion of visible lights.
- ✦ How to use fog in different ways to create atmospheric density.
- ✦ How to create background plates and use them for silhouetting.
- ✦ How to simulate sheet lightning to enhance the storm atmosphere effect.
- ✦ How to simulate snow both in the atmosphere and on the ground.
- ✦ How to create indoor atmospheres.
- ✦ How to apply atmosphere to various situations to add a professional touch to your productions.

✦ ✦ ✦

PART V

Action!

By this point you're undoubtedly champing at the bit to learn all about making your pictures move. Now that you're pretty well grounded in the essentials, you're ready to learn about cinematic motion, lighting, Hollywood special effects, and digital cinematography. In this section, you learn about the tools of motion and how to apply movement techniques to your images. So let the adventure begin...

In This Part

CHAPTER 18

The Tools of Motion

✦ ✦ ✦ ✦

In This Chapter

Principles of animation in brief

Anatomy of an animation path

Constructing and using animation paths

Animation controls

Basics of keyframing

The Keyframe Monitor

✦ ✦ ✦ ✦

My first experience with a commercial 3D package was disappointing. Like many people I started with the public domain program, POV, which is difficult to use, but does an astoundingly beautiful job of raytracing. Being dyslexic, I had great difficulty understanding the arcane instructions for animation. The commercial package I bought promised easier animation and it delivered. I could build a static scene and create the illusion of motion by moving the camera. It was thrilling.

The Tools of Motion

Things have come a very long way in just a few years. In tS2 you can animate not only cameras, objects, and textures, you can also keyframe just about any parameter you can think of, from colors to lighting to the refraction index in raytracing. You can change so many things that it gets confusing. I think Caligari, in its zeal to give you tools, may have gone overboard.

In trueSpace S/E, Caligari's beginner package, animation is very good and very easy. I recommend it. It's an excellent place to begin if you don't want to afford tS2. There are fewer parameters to control, yet you can do most of what you want, except for fancy special effects. tS2 opens the door to startling effects like explosions, through keyframe control of such things as lighting, procedural texture parameters, and background changes. This section of the book is designed to teach you good animation practice and help you through the confusing bits. The first time you watch your very own, completely original animation, you'll feel a tingle that can't be duplicated. And it grows from there.

Principles of Animation

An animation is simply a series of pictures which, when played in sequence, convey the illusion of movement and change. I'm betting you know this already. The task of the animator is to design and illustrate each of those frames. In traditional cel animation the key artist doesn't draw every frame. That would be a silly waste of his time. Since there are logical transitions between frames, the in-between frames can be interpolated. From Ireland to the San Fernando Valley to Seoul, South Korea, thousands of men and women are employed to do just this — drawing *tween* frames to connect the action between frames drawn by the key artist. His are called the keyframes for no strange reason, and the ones between are called… you know what I'm saying. You are the key artist in tS2. You arrange only the keyframes, the tweens are all done automatically according to your instructions.

Unlike traditional animation, you can key a lighting change on frame 27, with a return on frame 34; begin a color transition on frame 12 which completes on frame 29 and then reverses itself on frame 62; begin a character deformation on frame 41 that completes on 57; begin a movement on 22 that changes speed on 71 and reverses on 92; begin a rotation on 50 that completes on 92 and last, you begin a scale change on 62 that completes on frame 79. Good. If you're out of breath reading that sentence you should be. The point is that you can have different keyframes, depending on what parameter you're looking at. BTW, that's just for one object. Now assume you have eight objects, all in independent motion, with various changes peppered through the 100-frame animation. This is not at all uncommon when you get beyond beginner stuff. Can you see the opportunity for confusion? Trust me, it's there.

One of the biggest sources of frustration to a new tS2 animator is forgetting to position objects on frame 1. If you happen to be on frame 66 and move an object to a new location, the object won't be there when you replay the animation. It'll jump to frame 66 and probably will not be what you were looking for. Just be aware that it's easy to forget to return to frame 1 before you make changes to an animation. Granted, you will want to make some changes in the middle of an animation. I'm referring only to changes that you want your animation to start with.

Now let's talk camera. The camera is a fully animatable object. It, too, can have all sorts of activity going on: Looking at things, moving, zooming, rotating. Before long you'll have every single frame a key for something. This can get nasty. So we will start out by disabling everything we can. Start simple and work toward the complex one step at a time. We begin by learning the tools.

The Animation Path Tool

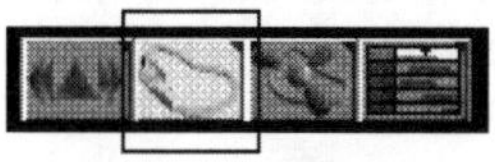

This pops up Draw Path control panel

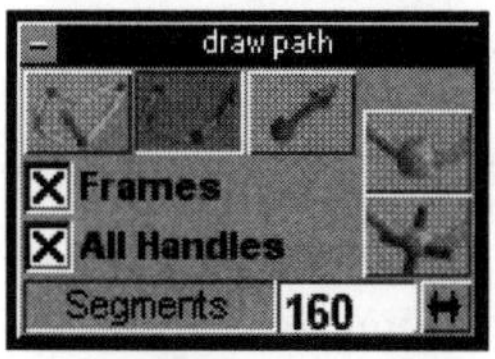

It should look familiar. You've used it before, but it's also the very same control used to control spline polygons. The animation path is a special case of the spline path. It can be open-ended, and the spline segments (vertices) represent frame location markers. Each spline segment marks where the object will be located for a given frame.

POWER TIP

You can save open-ended 3D animation paths for use in your Macro Extrusion experiments. Just use an arbitrary box object, give it a path and save the path to the Animation Path Library. Example: In building a children's slide, create a 3D animation path (using the orthogonal windows if you like) curved in the shape of the slide and save it. Use it to extrude a 2D poly cross-section of the slide bed.

Laying the Tracks

To animate an object you select it. Select the Animation Path tool and click within your stage area. This will plant the beginning node and position the object for frame zero. Each point you define will place a new node on the path. You set the number of frames to be located between nodes, in the Animation tool panel. Since you know the animation will run at 30 frames per second, you can accurately control movement over time by spacing the proper number of segments for a given distance.

Spline paths are truly 3D. You can place them in any view. In Perspective and Top View your nodes will be placed on the floor grid, but in the other orthogonal views you can place points up, down, and all around. Once you set a point you can edit it with spline tools, switching from node placing to node edit in the control panel.

If you want to create a movement loop, you can close the spline by right clicking on it, which will connect the last node to the first. Once you do this, you can only add individual spline control points using the Add Spline Points tool, which was included in tS2 after the manual was written. Actually you can also add a point by setting a keyframe for location between two nodes as well.

Camera Through a Tunnel Effect

Using the same spline to define a camera path and to sweep a curved tube will simplify running a camera inside a curving tube for effects like traveling through blood vessels or a subway tunnel. Glue a local light ahead of the camera, so it lights the inside of the textured tube.

Defaults Are Your Enemy

By default, frames are placed evenly along a path. Remember that defaults are your enemy. Using them is a sign your muse is on strike. Right clicking the Animation Path tool brings up the Spline panel, which gives you control over how splines behave at node points. Right click on the Spline panel to bring up yet another set of controls: the Spline Parameters panel with numeric control over things called Tension, Continuity, and Bias. It's a lotta stuff and if you don't take the time to learn it you'll use the dreaded *Defaults,* which may forever brand you as an amateur. Let's take a closer look at these tools.

Draw Path Control Panel – A Review of Splines

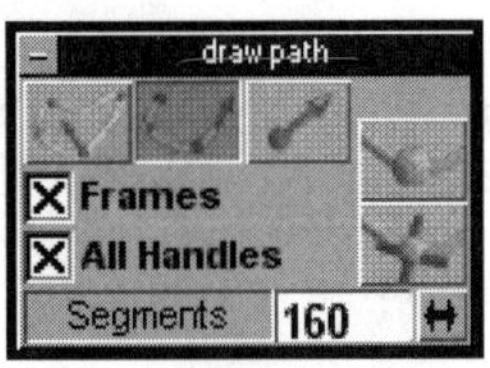

You'll see three icons across the top of the control panel and two more on the right. These last two were added after the manual was written, but they're pretty intuitive. Since you've been through this panel before, I'll try to stick to the special way it's used for animation. The panel comes up with the Draw Path function selected.

Draw Path

Located in the middle between Point Move and Start New Spline, this tool lets you place your path nodes. It works in cahoots with the Segments entry to add frames and/or movement to your animation. To add position movement, just click at two different points in the work space. How fast that movement is, is determined by the number of frames (segments) you set. They are inversely proportional; the more segments you add the slower the movement will be.

You can animate parameter changes without a path. Using the Animation tool, you simply type in a keyframe for the object in place, keyframing parameter changes where you want them. Be careful not to move such objects in the middle of the frame count or you'll end up with very strange results. Do physical moves at frame zero.

Point Move

To the left of the Add Path you'll find this handy tool. After placing your points, you may want to edit their location. Also, when you close a spline curve, you'll be switched automatically to the Point Move tool. Open your main view in Perspective and open two alternate windows, one Front View, the other Top View. For some operations you may need Left View instead of Front View. Grab and move points. If you click on the Object Move icon while in this mode, it will shift the entire path evenly to a new location. Use your head and enjoy twisting, turning, and distorting paths.

Start New Spline

I use this one a lot. It's how you delete an existing path so you can start over again. You'll often find you have too many or not enough nodes, or the path is hopelessly convoluted and it's easier to just start over. Use it — save sanity.

Add/Delete New Spline Point

These new tools simply add or delete a single control point (frame) to/from an existing path. The Add button lets you place the new frame anywhere and gives you control handles. The Delete button deletes the selected point (specifically, the one with control handles). Don't you love when I state the obvious? No I don't think you're an idiot, I just want to be thorough.

Segments

Think of these as frames. Everyone else calls them that. The number you enter here will be the number of new frames entered into your animation between any two nodes you place. Later I'll show you how to adjust the actual number of frames while keeping keyframes in place, using the Animation Project window.

Frames

This is a display toggle that controls whether or not you see individual frames as blue dots along the path.

All Handles

You know what handles are. When this box is selected, all path control points will show handles. I haven't figured out the best way to use it yet. I often leave it engaged when adjusting a path because it's easy to see and tweak all control points as necessary.

Spline Property Panel

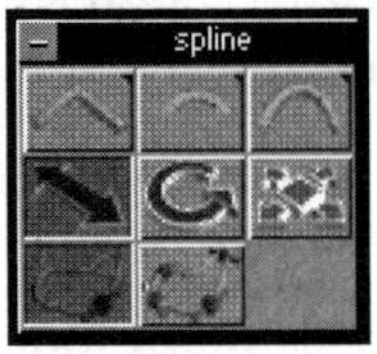

If you right-click on the Spline Poly tool you'll open the Spline Property panel which gives you access to spline property presets for Tension, Continuity, and Bias as follows:

- **Sharp Corner.** Tension = 0 Continuity = -1 Bias = 0 (note that the tS2 manual is wrong on this one; this is correct)
- **Smooth Corner.** Tension = 0 Continuity = 0 Bias = 0
- **Ultra Smooth Corner.** Tension = -.67 Continuity = 0 Bias = 0

Do you remember these parameters from before? A quick review so you don't have to look back.

Tension. How sharply the path bends at control nodes. *Important in animation paths*. As you increase tension, frames from either side tend to move closer to the active node, kind of bunching up. This causes deceleration into the curve as it gets sharper. The length of the node's handles will give you a rough idea of its tension — the longer the handle, the lower the tension. Minus values increase the angle where the two paths intersect. If they come in at a 90° angle at a setting of zero, decreasing that value will increase the angle to, say, 110°. You can change tension interactively by changing the length of the handle.

Continuity controls the angle at which the path enters the node. Plus values cause an overshoot and return to the node, while minus values give the intersection a hollow-ground edge look with paths undershooting the node, and having to curve out to reach it. Zero is the most usable value here because it causes the lines to intersect smoothly. You can change it interactively by moving the control handles.

Bias is like half of Continuity. It lets you control overshoot on one side or the other. Positive bias overshoots on the right while negative passes on the left. You can change this value interactively by grabbing the control handle while pressing both the left button and the Control key, then dragging the mouse vertically. Note: As with Continuity, this control does not affect the spacing of frames, thus no effect on acceleration or deceleration.

Interpolation Mode

The middle row of controls applies to animation paths and 2D spline polys. The three Change Spline Parameters tools are mystically named Change Move, Change Rotate, and Change Scale.

Normally when you edit a spline, you're changing the way the program interpolates spline point location. In animation you can change the way the program interpolates scaling or rotation values as well. From a practical standpoint, Rotate twists the path route and Scale shortens or lengthens the path while keeping the number of frames the same. None of this affects the object's size or rotation as it travels along the path.

Local Point Control

Again, awkwardly named: Change Parameters For Selected Point Only. You at least get an idea of what it does. When selected, only the active or current node is affected by your changes.

Global Point Control

Mutually exclusive with LPC above, when selected, this option applies your changes (including presets) to all control points. I use this one when I find I've made a smooth curve spline and I intended a sharp one. Clicking here allows me to change all the nodes at once. I didn't know about this control for quite a while and used to reset each node individually. This is much easier.

The Spline Parameters Panel

Short explanation, here is where you can read or numerically enter values for Tension, Continuity, Bias. That's it. You can input any numbers you want, usable numbers range between -1.5 and +1.5.

I know words get tedious, but there's one more tool we have to understand before we get to work.

The Animation Panel

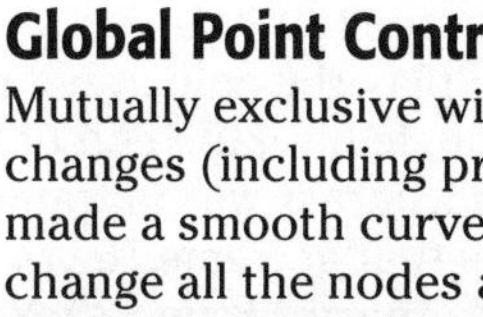

Selecting the Animation panel displays this set of tools, which is made to resemble a VCR. With these tools you can play previews, record and delete keyframes, jump around in an animation. This tool lets us move beyond simple path animation to parameter animation by allowing us to record keyframes for changes other than movement.

Starting at the upper left, the red button is your Record Key button, next to it is the Delete Key button, and on the right, your Play button. In the middle row, left, you see an arrowhead. This is the First Frame tool, the double arrow is Rewind, next double arrow is Fast Forward, and on the right is Last Frame.

On the bottom row, left, is Previous Frame arrow, in the middle is the Frame Number field, and on the right, Next Frame arrow.

Record Key

This tool works with your active or current tool to record a specific parameter. It will set such things as movement, rotation, scaling, or deformation for the selected object for that frame. That is, if you rotate the object and record that rotation, the new position becomes the basis for tweening from the previous *Rotation* keyframe. Picture it this way, frame 0 is always a keyframe. Let's say you have a cube that moves across the screen in 30 frames. You advance the object to frame 15 by selecting it and typing 15 in the Animation tool and hitting return. Rotate the cube 30° to the right, and hit record. That sets a rotation key on frame 15. When trueSpace2 moves the object it will turn it 2° further to the right each frame. That way, at frame 15 it will be rotated the full 30°. Your last frame (30) is a keyframe as well, but it doesn't have a key set for rotation. When you play the animation, the cube will rotate right 30° in 15 frames, then stay at that angle until the end of the path. Advance the cube to frame 30 and rotate it back to where it was in frame 1. Preview the movement by hitting the Play key and notice that at frame 16 your cube begins to rotate back to its original angle as it heads toward frame 30. You get the idea.

CAUTION: This is one of the biggest areas of confusion in trueSpace2. You'll think you are setting keys for scale, but you've changed to the Move tool. Remember, you're only setting a key for the tool that is currently engaged. The other potential problem is the SetKeyframe AutoRecord mode. With it engaged, everything you do on a frame gets recorded, even stuff you didn't want, so watch it. My wife's advice to me: "Pay attention or you'll lose track of your keys."

AutoRecord

Right clicking on the Record button will bring up a check box for AutoRecord.

This box is dangerous. With it engaged, you record any change you make on a frame and it becomes a keyframe for that item. Many times I've ended up with a ton of unwanted keyframes. The problem is, remembering to hand record every key is a real pain. I use AutoRecord and clean up afterwards.

Unset Key

This is how you remove a keyframe for a given move, rotate, or scale. If the Keyframe Monitor is open, you can delete keys for many parameters. It's still confusing to me. In the back of my head, when I unset a key, I keep thinking I'm unsetting everything keyed to that frame. It's easy to forget that it's only for the one active tool. If you've been using AutoRecord, you can have a hell of a time trying to figure out how to clear unwanted keys out of the frame. But there is hope in the KeyFrame Monitor.

Play

This key will preview your animation in wireframe or 3DR. By default, it only animates the selected object. This can get mighty confusing, especially if you have a stationary object selected — nothing happens. You'll be scratching your head, wondering why tS2 has it in for you. The solution — right click on the Play button to bring up the Animation Parameters panel and click Scene. More in a moment.

POWER TIP

If you use 3DR mode it's hard to see symmetrical round objects rotating. I've found that if I decal a little design on the side it gives a better indication of how the rotation looks.

First Frame

Simple, it jumps you back to the first frame, which is zero. Remember that the 10th frame is really the 11th because zero counts in Animation.

Rewind

Jump back to the previous keyframe *for the active tool.* It's not documented, but this tool doesn't jump back to the previous keyframe overall (which for the longest time I thought it did). But only to the previous keyframe for the active tool. So if you keyframed some raytrace parameter, you have to open up the Keyframe Monitor and engage that very parameter to then rewind to find where the heck you accidentally keyframed it. For the longest time I figured that this thing just didn't work right. But when you understand this little fact, it starts to make sense.

Fast Forward

With an eye on the above caveat, FF jumps you to the next keyframe for your active tool.

Last Frame

This one makes sense, it jumps you to the final frame for the object selected — even if you have Scene engaged. If the selected object only has a few frames or starts to move at frame 70, you'll think you're at the end of the animation and you're not. So select an object that has a path all the way to the end of the animation sequence if you want to jump around from beginning to end.

Previous Frame

Another easy-to-grasp idea, it rewinds you one frame toward the beginning.

Next Frame

This one takes you one frame forward, toward the end.

Frame Number Field

This displays the current frame as rendered on screen. It is also an input device. You can type in any frame you want, and the screen will advance to that frame. It has one of those little double arrow drag tools as well, but it's not practical in 3DR, which takes too long, making it hard to control.

POWER TIP

Rule of thumb, type in values when you are in 3DR whenever you see a numeric input field.

Adding Motion to a Still Object

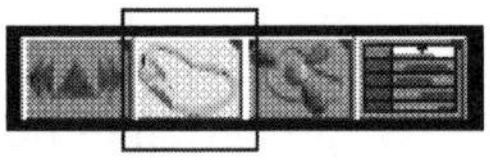

Enough words! Let's animate a lowly cube Primitive. We'll give it some cool moves, looking closely at each step, testing the verity of my words above. Pop a box and look for the Animation Path tool icon and engage it.

1. The Draw Path panel will have Draw New Spline Point already selected. Good. Set Segments ⇨ 30 and click a node, screen right about midway up. The box will relocate with its axis on the point you just laid down.
2. Now click near the lower left corner of the screen. That's the end point of the animation. If you count the little blue nodes you'll find N+1 or 31 of them. That gives you 30 segments to traverse. It will take your box exactly one second to traverse the path at 30 fps. Granted your computer may play frames slowly and drop a few, but in an ideal world this would be true.
3. Set a rotation key for the box at frame 15 and see if it works.

Good, now bring up the Animation panel and right click on your play arrow. This brings up the Animation Parameters panel.

Animation Parameters Panel

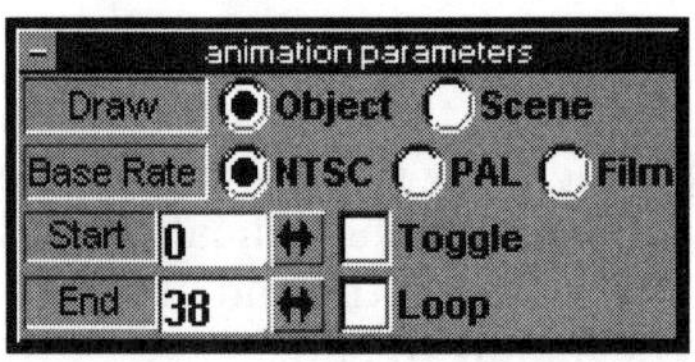

This is a useful spot. It clues you into the start and end frame number, whether only the current object will be animated, or the entire scene, plus base rate and looping controls.

Draw Object/Scene

By default this is on Object, because it's fast. This means that when you run a wireframe preview, only the selected object will be animated. I often find this inadequate, as Animation is a Gestalt; the whole is more than the sum of its parts. I like to see how everything is moving and it's not that slow. I admit, when checking out specific parts of a complex animated deformation object, it pays to limit movement to the subject at hand.

Base Rate

Your AVI time code is based on the number of frames to be screened per unit time. Your base rate is the number of frames that must be played for your animation to play at the proper speed and look natural. You get a choice:

- **NTSC.** Standard US television at 30 fps. Note that further adjustments will be needed, such as 60 fields/second for interlaced NTSC, which is an option at render time.
- **PAL.** British and European standard at 25 fps. Note that this setting can also be used for SECAM, which is the system used in France.
- **Film.** Film projectors display animations at 24 fps. If you intend to use your animation on the big screen, recorded to film, select this option.

These settings only affect the base animation rate, not resolution, which is set at the time of rendering.

Loop

This handy setting lets you analyze your motion by continuously looping or repeating your animation. It only works in screen playback, not in actual rendering. You can jump out of the loop by hitting the escape key or with a double *right* click.

Toggle

If you get really bored, this one will play your animation forward, then backward. If your eyes are getting glassy, try it with Loop for a never-ending trip.

Start/End

I didn't understand this tool for the longest time. I was frustrated because every time I wanted to play a preview, it would start at frame zero. For long previews this is a pain. I'm trying to perfect a movement on frame 500 and I have to sit through all 499 frames before I see it. Bad. Now I know that it's way better than that. Just type or slide to the start frame of choice (limited to four digits, which will not be a problem), and hit the play button. Your preview will start at the set frame and continue to the last frame or the one you've entered in the End field.

There is yet another Animation tool, the most complex and nasty one of all....

The Keyframe Monitor

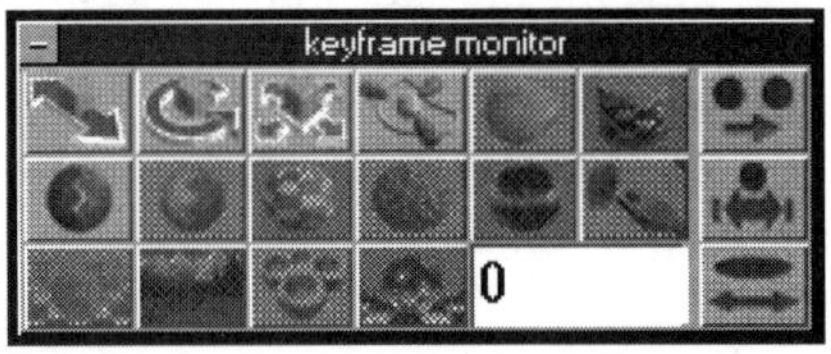

Right click on any Animation tool except the Record or Play buttons and you'll pop up this monster. I guess it's pretty clear that I'm not thrilled with this tool. I suspect the brilliant designers at Caligari must have designed the Keyframe Monitor on unpaid overtime. It does the job pretty well, but it's not very intuitive. Perhaps they've put too much functionality in too little a space, causing unnecessary complexity. My daughter the Engineer explained the true depth of complexity and I don't feel so bad any more: There are 16 monitor buttons, each with four possible states, that's 16^4 combinations of keys for any given frame, which is more than 65,000 (65,536). In short, more than my brain can deal with.

Another problem is that the Keyframe Monitor is not well explained in the manual. This can't be blamed on the manual author. You'll notice it's not even mentioned in the user's guide because it was a last-minute addition. I understand the manual author was practically writing the description on the way to the printer. We're partly to blame. Users put Caligari under terrible pressure to deliver tS2 as quickly as possible.

The Layout

There are three rows of monitor buttons:

✦ **Object parameters.** Move, Rotate, Scale, Look-at, Deform, and Material Rectangle.

✦ **Material parameters.** Color, Surface, Texture, Bumps, Reflections, and Plug-ins.

✦ **Scene parameters.** Fog, Background, Global environment, and Raytrace.

There is a Frame Field that you use in cahoots with Keyframe tools to define destinations for the following tools.

CAUTION

It's very easy to accidentally enter Keyframe tool destinations in the Animation panel frame field. Just be careful. When working with the Keyframe Monitor, you want to enter all destinations in the Monitor's destination input field.

Keyframe Tools

✦ **Copy Keyframe.** Copies all active keys for the selected frame to a frame you enter in the Monitor Frame Field.

- **Move Keyframe.** Officially called Shift Keyframe, it moves the current frame's complete set of keys to the destination set in the Monitor Frame Field. That means it unsets the current frame and sets the new one for each parameter that is active.
- **Stretch Keyframe.** I still don't completely understand this one. I like it, I use it, but I don't fully understand how it works. I understand there is one guy in a small Eastern European country who understands it, but he's not talking. Basically it's like Move Keyframe, but it displaces all the keys that came before the current frame, toward the new frame, but not in a linear way. It stretches the movement according to some proportional scheme that adds acceleration.

Four Key States

The state of a given indicator is determined by its shading. It can be light gray, dark gray, blue, or red.

Active

This is a little confusing. When a row is light gray, there are keys set for at least one of the parameters in that row, and these parameters are available for further keyframing. Each light gray indicator will alert you by turning blue when you reach a keyframe for its parameter. Don't feel bad if you have to read that again.

Inactive

When a row is inactive there are no keys set for any of its parameters, nor can you set any. Each row must be activated in its own way, as explained below.

Object Keyframes

The top row contains six monitors that deal with different object parameters: Move, Rotate, Scale, Look constraints, Deformation, and Material Rectangles. This row is activated by selecting an object. Object keyframes are created when you manipulate the object at any frame other than frame zero. Remember, if you disengaged the AutoRecord function, you have to record each key by hitting the record button.

POWER TIP

Artists tend to prefer action to words. My words can get in the way of your understanding — don't let that happen. When you play with this stuff you'll quickly get the feel of it. It's not bad at all, in fact it's a lot better than most other programs. So If you get confused, go to the program and demonstrate each paragraph on-line.

Move, Rotate, Scale

Just select the specific tool and manipulate the object, positioning it where you want it, at the angle and size you want and record or AutoRecord.

Look Constraints Keys

Look At and Look Ahead can be keyframed on or off for the selected object. Naturally only one of them can be active for any frame on the same object because they fight each other. To use them, just set the constraints where you want them. Remember these parameters are toggles. Click once to engage, click a second time to disengage.

CAUTION

Look constraints can be tricky. When you use them on a camera, make sure you leave a fair number of unset keys between changes, otherwise the camera will jerk to the new position and it's not pleasant. If you leave enough keys unset between, the camera drifts from one view to the other in a pleasant way. Much more cinematic.

Deformation Keys

Any deformation on an object can be keyframed. Free Standing Deformation Objects can also be keyframed. When there is a deformation key at the current frame, it will be indicated here. Control Point deformations and Floor deformations keyed on the same frame get merged and cannot be isolated with the Keyframe Monitor.

POWER TIP

The tS2 User Manual specifically says you can't keyframe surface sculpt. This is incorrect. You can. When you do, it activates the volume deform icon in the Monitor. I suspect it was never documented because it doesn't work perfectly each time, but is still very useful.

Material Rectangle Keys

You may not have realized it, but material rectangles can be keyed to move and scale. Set the keys while in Material Rectangle tool.

POWER TIP

Material Rectangles can also have the material within them keyframed, but you can't monitor it from here, you have to do that with the Inspect tool and watch the Material Preview window.

Material Keyframes

Enable Material Keyframe Monitors by *selecting the material you want to monitor with the Inspect tool.* Read that again. Everyone seems to forget this and thinks the Monitor isn't working. It isn't as intuitive as the rest of the interface, but it works well if you take the time to learn it, and professionals learn their tools.

Once you select the material you want to track with the Inspect tool, you can scroll through the animation frame by frame in the Animation tool, and the Material Preview window will update for each frame.

CAUTION

You set a Material Keyframe only one way — with the Paint roller (Paint Over tool). If you forget and try to use a different brush, the effect will cover all your keyframes. That is, if you've set a bunch of nice color morphs using the Paint Over tool as directed, they will run just fine, but if you set even one key with the Paint Object or Paint Facet tool, that paint will capture every keyframe and you'll lose all your morphs. It's easy to fix, though, just hit undo. Be aware.

Color and Attribute Keys

You can keyframe all values of colors, shaders, maps, and surfaces. This capability will come in handy when you want to do some special effects.

Texture and Bump Keys

Image files selection can be keyframed, but there's no interpolation between images, just an abrupt switch in texture image. There are places you can use this. You can also keyframe all the numerical values such as repeats and relief, and so on. These are interpolated for smooth transitions.

Environment Keys

You can keyframe changes in reflection maps just as you would in a texture or bump map.There are no numerical settings to key.

Plug-in Keyframes

Your settings in the Plug-ins panel can be keyframed. Note that you can't keyframe the individual parameters within the Plug-in interface itself. A drawback of this monitor is that it can only look at one plug-in at a time. This means you'll have to run through the frames for each plug-in you're interested in checking. Ready for another layer? Notice the little red triangle in the upper right corner of the Plug-ins monitor. Right-click and you'll get a plug-in selection panel. Click the one you want to monitor. The one you highlight will be the one shown in the plug-in icon.

Scene Keyframes

Enable the Scene Monitor icons by setting Scene playback in the Animation control panel. Do this by right-clicking on the Play button. All global scene parameters keyframes must be set at frames other than zero.

Fog Keys

Let the fog roll in by keyframing color, extents, and maximum percentage. You can also key on and off, but it's not a great effect — way strange.

Background Keys

Background bitmaps can change during an animation through keyframing. Again, there's no morphing, just an abrupt change. You can also key them on and off. Background color can be morphed by changing colors at different keyframes. tS2 will interpolate the tween colors for you.

Global Environment Keys

You can key a global map on or off or change it like the background. You can also morph the global color between keyframes. This can lead to some interesting reflection effects. Switching environment maps on and off or changing them is not recommended except in unusual circumstances. It's too jolting.

Raytrace Keys

Raytracing can be turned on at a certain frame for effect, but it usually causes such a global change that I don't care for it. You can keyframe values for the Ray Depth Limiting and Max Ray Depth and Shininess, but it won't help. Going from scan-line to Raytrace is a big jump. Now if we could do it for specific items, it would be more useful. Perhaps in the next edition.

Summary

I'll bet you now know more about the animation tools than most people using trueSpace2. Now get ready to learn more about Animation Hierarchies. Remember the way we glued things together? It's all going to come in handy when we do hierarchical animation.

If you did better than skim this chapter, you learned about more than just the tools of animation:

✦ You learned about tween frames and how tS2 does them for you automatically.

✦ You learned all about how animation paths are splines — in a good way.

✦ You learned how to build open- and close-ended animation paths in 3 space to give flight to your ideas.

✦ You learned how to jump to any frame you want by typing its number in the Animation tool numeric input field.

✦ You learned to preview your work using the Play key on the Animation tool.

✦ You learned how to keyframe all sorts of exciting things from motion to color morphs.

✦ You learned that I'm not crazy about the Keyframe Monitor, but it can be used to keep track of keys for the many parameters on a frame-by-frame basis.

✦ You learned that you are about to read more about hierarchies, but this time we'll have some fun.

✦ ✦ ✦

CHAPTER 19

Relational Animation: Hierarchies

✦ ✦ ✦ ✦

In This Chapter

How to build a solar system

Local Motion, what it is and how you can use it

Robotic Articulation with Robbie

How to perform a transient extension of the primoid ring

The Wheel on the bike goes round

✦ ✦ ✦ ✦

Remember gluing things in hierarchies, parent/child or sibling? Even though nobody really knows how it works, we can use it to do some pretty awesome motion.

Celestial Choreography

You need this chapter to create exciting relative motion sequences for your professional demo tape. After story and camera work, sophisticated movement is one of the things I look for in a demo tape. You know story already, camera work comes soon, so let's work on the choreography of objects. We're going to create complex objects with parts that move in relation to each other. This can be one of the most frustrating things in tS2, so pay close attention to the sequence of operations.

The Main Sequence

Since space is the theme of this book, and it is a bible, after all, let's look at the relative motion of planets, moons, and suns, and create a mini-cosmos. Suns usually circumnavigate their local cluster, which rotates within the galaxy, which is hurling through the void. It goes on and on, but let's assume, for the sake of sanity, the star Denab 7 is moving in a straight line. It has one planet in eccentric orbit, which has a moon in orbit around it. Get the picture? Your assignment is to animate a ten-second segment of the sun passing in front of the camera with exaggerated orbital movement of its associated bodies.

Picture Denab 7 whizzing by with planet and moon all moving in relation to each other. It's fairly easy to do, but you have to follow the sequence of procedures exactly or you'll get all sorts of strange movement. The tS2 reference manual is extremely vague on how all this works, and it has been a subject of much confusion on the Internet. Let's make it work.

First, make sure your world units are in kilometers and the object is in meters. Work in wireframe, unless you have 3DR accelerator. Here is the general sequence.

Moon First

1. Pop up a sphere for the moon and scale it down to about .6 meters.
2. Name it moon in the OPP, it will soon lose its individual identity, but naming it helps for the next step.
3. Switch main window to Top View.
4. Move the moon away from the origin, maybe 2 meters.
5. Engage the Draw Animation Path tool and set it to 33 segments (frames) per node. Click in the center of the moon to set the first node.
6. Draw an orbit around the origin by planting four more nodes in a wide (at least 2 meters) orbit around the origin (4 × 33 = 132 frames), as shown in Figure 19-1. Adjust node handles to shape it into an eccentric orbit (elliptical). Lengthening the handles a tad will usually smooth out the curve. Remember to make your fourth click with the *right* button to close the orbital path.

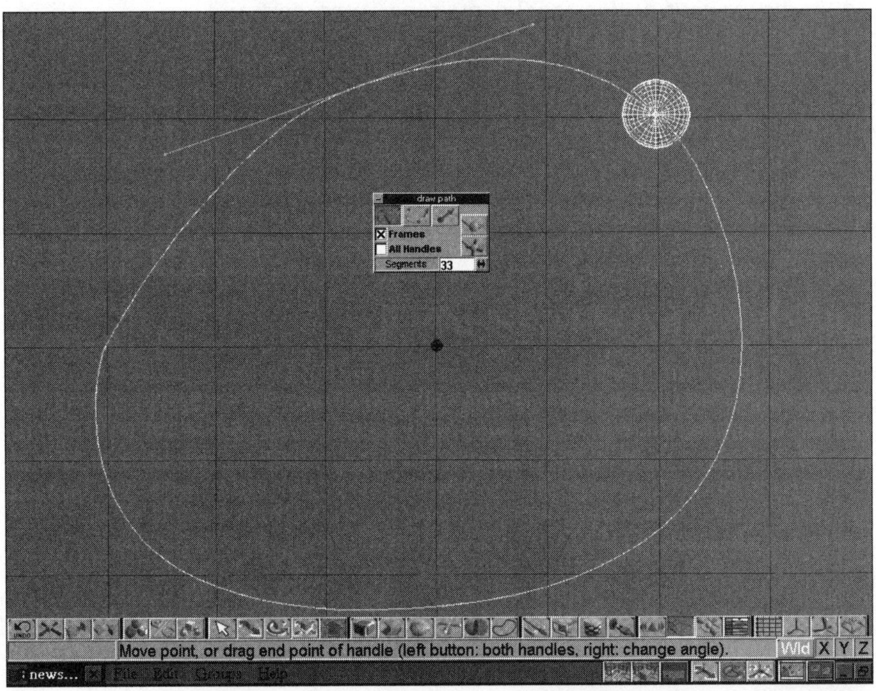

Figure 19-1: This example shows how the moon orbits the origin.

7. Preview the action with the Play button. Your moon should rotate around its orbit once and stop.

8. Reset to frame zero in the Animation tool window.

POWER TIP

Make the length of the control handles the same for all four nodes in order to keep the motion smooth.

Planet Second

1. Pop up a second sphere and name it planet. It should be in the center of the moon's orbit.

2. Scale planet as you like.

3. Pop up the Animation Project window.

4. Select moon from the object list on the left side of the window.

5. Go down to the bottom of the window to the icons with squiggly green lines. The right-most icon is Make Action Local. Engage it and click on the black trapezoid line to the right of moon. This makes the moon's rotation a local action, independent of other actions applied. You should see a new trapezoid in dark gray, labeled Local1.

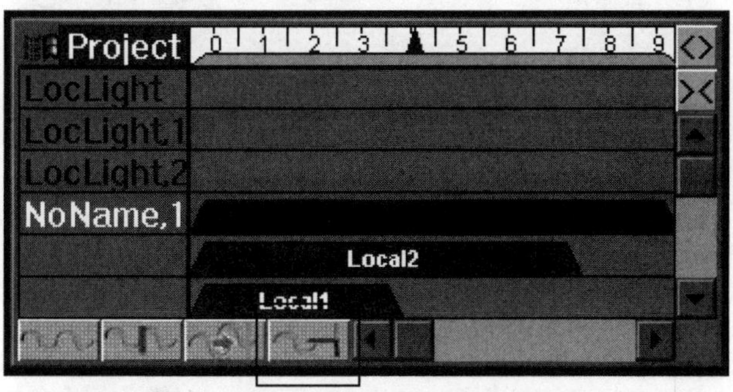

6. Select the planet (this puts the axis of the new object at the center of planet) ⇨ glue as siblings ⇨ moon.

7. Name the resulting new object Planet.

8. Preview action. The moon should orbit the planet one time and stop; planet stays put.

9. Move the planet object about three meters or more from the origin. Zoom your view out if you need to.

10. Select planet/moon object ⇨ Draw Path tool ⇨ change segments to 60 ⇨ draw a large orbit (4 × 60 = 240 frames). Figure 19-2 gives you an idea of how the changes appear. For grins, you can switch to a different view and create the orbit in a new plane. You can manipulate it with path tools to angle and place it where you want it. Placing all your orbits in the same plane looks hokey.

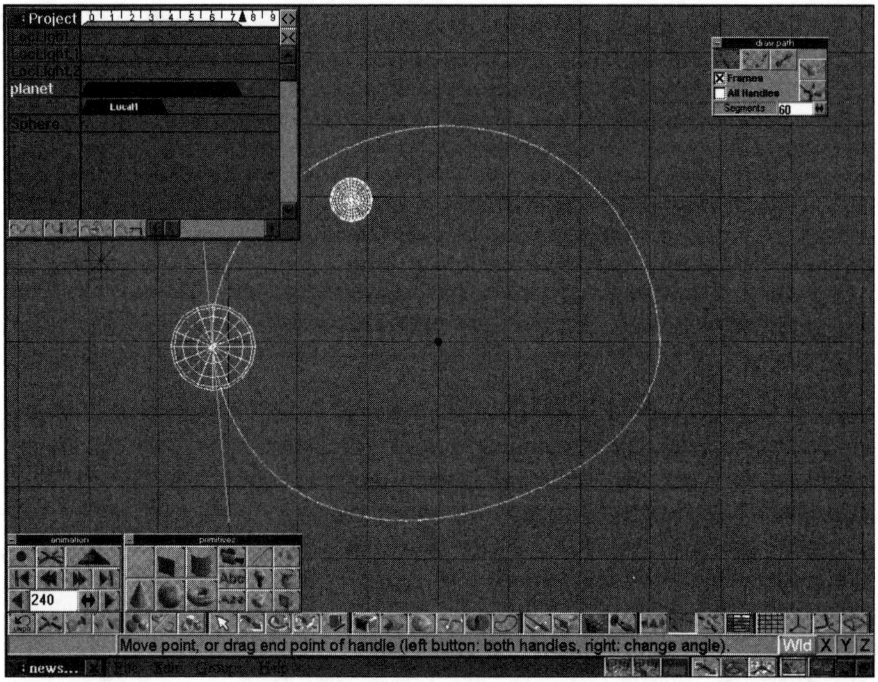

Figure 19-2: This illustration shows how the planet orbits the origin while the moon orbits the planet.

Preview the action. The moon should orbit the planet in relative motion as the planet follows its orbit. Moon will stop before the planet because it has fewer frames in its orbit.

POWER TIP

If your movement seems pretty screwed up at this point, you most likely forgot to zero out your animation after a preview. It's easy to do because the last frame position looks almost exactly like zero frame position. Don't hand-position the moon, planet, or sun on any frame but zero, or the AutoRecord will animate that movement, which you don't want.

Sun Third

1. Pop up, name, and scale your sun sphere in the center of the planet's orbit.
2. Make the action local by selecting the planet object in the Project window and again clicking make action local and the black time line representing the planet's motion. Note the new Local2 time line.

3. Select the sun and glue planet/moon as siblings.
4. Label the resulting object Solarstm.
5. Engage the Path tool and set segments to 300. That will give us the frames we need for a ten-second animation at 30 fps. Notice that I keep increasing the number of frames per node as I go up in scale. The idea is to scale up the motion along with the objects. Bigger objects moving more slowly than smaller is more believable.
6. With your solar system object selected, give the sun its linear path of 300 frames from lower right to upper left of your screen. Do not end with a right click. You want to leave this path open (not closed on itself).
7. Preview the action. Notice how the moon quits first, the planet quits next, and the sun drags them to the finish, as shown in Figure 19-3.

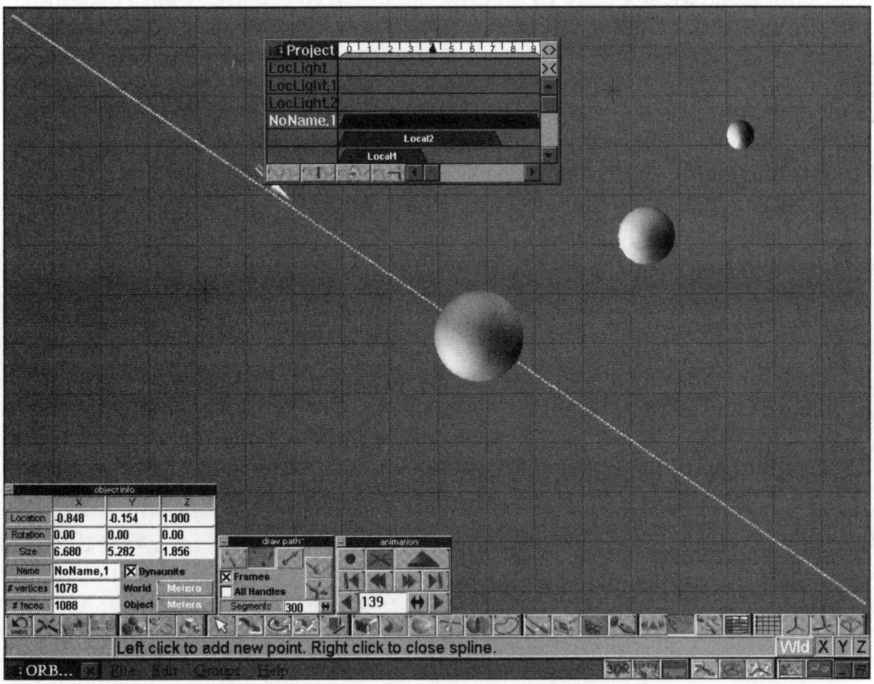

Figure 19-3: The sun moves through space with a planet and its moon in a complex orbit, but the moon has stopped rotating.

Repeat Local Motion

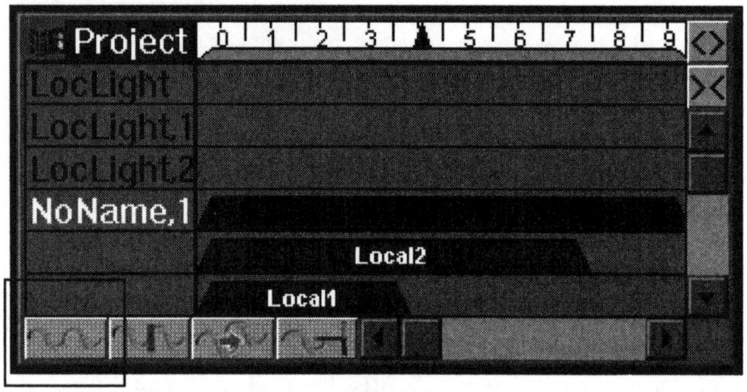

The reason we made the planetary motion local is so each body can be made to orbit continuously. It's easy to do now. Go down to the lower left corner and select the repeat action key ➪ local 2 ➪ Local 2. Notice that the local motion gets a string of light gray parallelograms continuing the orbit action ad infinitum. It will stop eventually because you are only previewing a portion. More in the next chapter on this.

Preview the action again, and this time the moon should continue to circle the planet as the planet continues to circle the sun, as it wends its way through the galaxy. Pretty complex, cool motion. The whole thing will stop at the end of the sun's course because previewing is automatically set to the maximum non-repeat frames, or 300 in this case. You have your ten-second insert laid out, now all you have to do is make it look nice with background, texture, lighting, and then collect your check.

Spinning Round and Round

You shouldn't be too impressed — yet. We left out the important spinning on axes motion. I didn't want to burden you with yet another set of steps, but you really will have to do it if you don't want to look amateur. I'll give you the details in Chapter 21 on keyframe techniques. If you want to try now, be aware that you can't animate a rotation in a single keyframe. It takes at least three because if you go full circle in one, tS2 takes the shortest route, which is to stay put. Use the grid set to 120 degrees. Also keyframe your rotation before you make motion local at each level.

POWER TIP

Planets closest to the sun rotate faster than ones farther out. This is necessary because they need more centripetal force to counteract the close gravitational pull of the star. Make sure you follow this. If you have an outer planet rotating faster than an outer one, you can remedy it in the Project window by grabbing the time line trapezoid in the lower right corner and stretching it out to the right. This will increase the number of frames in that planet's orbit, effectively producing slower relative motion.

Kinematics

There is actually a science of the study of relative motion called Kinematics. When one object is connected to another, the motion of one causes motion in the other. This is a kinematic chain motion. To animate chain movement in tS2 is tricky but doable.

The best way to animate a kinematic chain it is with Inverse Kinematics (IK). This is where you can connect objects in a causal hierarchy with motion constraints assigned to each joint. That's like your elbow. The upper arm is connected to the lower arm, but that joint has limited degrees of freedom. It's called inverse because movement works backwards. In humans movement goes: upper arm ➪ lower arm ➪ wrist ➪ fingers. In IK, you move the finger, and the motion works back up the chain to the shoulder. Thus, you put the hand where you want it and the rest of the body will follow.

Unfortunately without IK, articulated movement in tS2 can be tedious. But, as professionals we don't let that stop us. The other tools are so powerful I wouldn't trade it for another program. We'll find a work-around and do it anyway.

Joints

Generally, you make joints by moving the rotational axis of each object to the center of where you want the joint to be and lock it there. Much like planetary movement, we can add relative local motion to various sub-objects. For this exercise we'll use a pre-built robotic object called robie.cob. Named after the robot in *Forbidden Planet*, Robbie has his arms already glued in a proper hierarchy. Robbie is provided by Caligari.

I've also included a neat animation done by I-Wei Huang, a professional who used tS2 to do the remarkable articulated movement tS2 is capable of. It'll take some patience, but you can do it as well. Before doing the following exercise, preview the animation, it's called I-wei.avi.

Here's the basic plan. You start at the bottom of the hierarchy and give that last piece rotation that keeps it in alignment with the rest of the chain. For example, you can rotate your wrist from side to side or up and down, all pivoting from the axis which is at the beginning of your wrist. Do it, see what I mean. That's where you want to put the axis of the lowest part of the chain.

Axes Before Movement

POWER TIP

You can't relocate an axis once you've animated any part of an object. Therefore it's imperative that you make sure all axes of all joints you want to animate are in the right place before you begin to add movement.

There are two ways to go about articulated movement in the following uses of localized motion. Later, I'll explain the use of parent-child relationships for non-localized articulation. Once the axes are all in place, check the hierarchy. You should be able to get to the bottom, then work your way up in the following way:

1. Isolate the bottom item in the hierarchy (it's white; the rest of the object is orange).
2. Reveal the axis. It should be at the point of rotation you want.
3. Move up the hierarchy, so that the bottom and next-to-the-bottom segments are white and the rest is orange.
4. Reveal the axis and make sure it's where you want it, at the axis of rotation for the segment. Good. Continue checking all the way up to the main object or body. Then you'll go back and begin to add animation to each segment, one by one.

POWER TIP

Keyframing a rotation or other nonpath event will create the equivalent of a stationary motion path with all frames overlapped in the exact same position. You can also build one by placing the two nodes on top of each other, but it's not necessary because keying the rotation via the Animation tool will automatically create the frames you need, where you want them.

1. Starting at the bottom, keyframe the rotation you want by typing the number of the start frame (often zero, which needs no key) into the Animation tool numeric field.
2. Set a rotation key at the beginning by rotating the segment to the point where you want it to start. If it's already where you want it, you'll have to hit record, with rotation tool engaged.
3. Enter the number of the next keyframe and rotate the object to the position you want. Generally you'll want to lock out movement on all but one axis at a time to keep the rotation constrained to that one axis, as any articulated joint would.
4. Localize the movement as we did with the solar system.
5. Move up the hierarchy until both this bottom piece and the next one up are isolated. (The two pieces are white, the rest of the object is orange.)
6. Assign a stationary path of any number of frames to the axis point of the sub-object.
7. Keyframe the rotation of this piece.
8. Localize this rotation.
9. Continue on up the hierarchy, each time adding one more piece to the group and then assigning a rotation to the axis, localizing, and so on.

Robbie

Load up the Robbie object from the ROM. This is a pretty puny robot. You could easily do better yourself, but it's free and will nicely demonstrate articulated movement. Don't expect me to do a lot of it here, just enough to give you a clue. You can do the rest on your own. I use MHA with IK if an assignment requires a lot of articulated character movement.

Robbie's Head Movement

Not all of Robbie's hierarchy is usable. I want to make his head turn, and the way he's glued together, there's no place in the hierarchy that will isolate the head and both eye cameras as one unit. So I unglued them and, starting with the head selected, reglued the two eyes to it as siblings This way I can navigate down the hierarchy until the head is all white and the rest of the body is orange (see Figure 19-4).

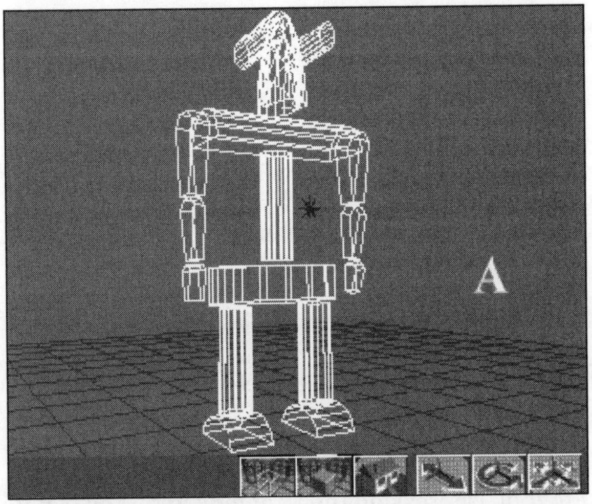

Figure 19-4A: Robbie as a selected object (he's all white).

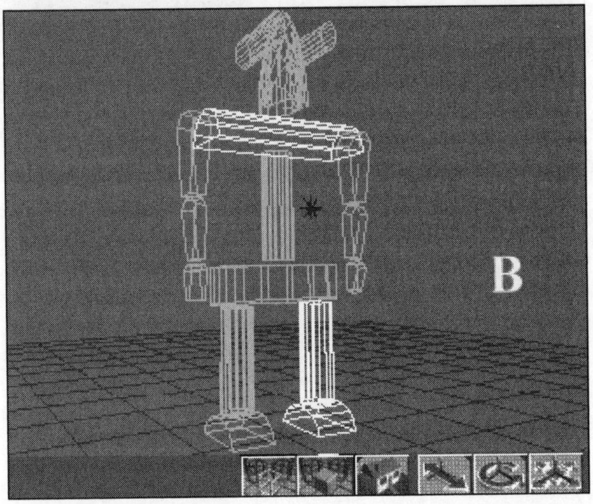

Figure 19-4B: One step down his hierarchy — note only the white sections (shoulders and left leg) are now selected. One step down from here brings you to his head.

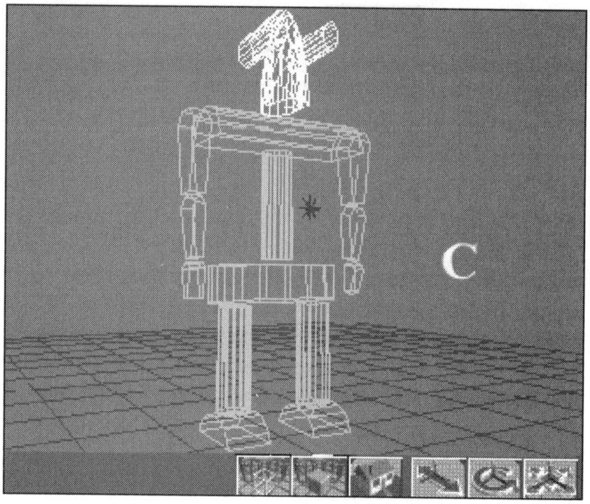

Figure 19-4C: Eye cameras unglued and reglued as siblings, ready to rotate.

Rotate Robbie's head on the Z axis and you can make him shake his head no. Rotate on the X axis and he'll nod yes. On the Y axis he'll nod his head to the side. I think I'll have him turn his head to look around, then raise his arm and point at something. Of course, this is just my idea of what that might look like. You can do it any way you want; just learn the process.

We keyframe Robbie's head movements by assigning a path of 40 frames:

1. Record (or AutoRecord) a key at frame 1 with Robbie staring straight ahead.
2. Type `20` into the Frames field in the Animation tool window. This will place Robbie halfway through his head cycle. Nothing changes.
3. Engage the Object Rotate tool. Depressing the *right* mouse button, rotate his head to right (see Figure 19-5). Record a key. It'll be automatic if you have AutoRecord engaged.
4. Type `35` in the Frames field.
5. Rotate Robbie's head back to slightly beyond straight ahead. Key rotation.
6. Type `40` in the Frames field.
7. Rotate Robbie's head back to straight ahead.
8. Check action with Play button.
9. Return to frame zero.
10. Make motion Local.

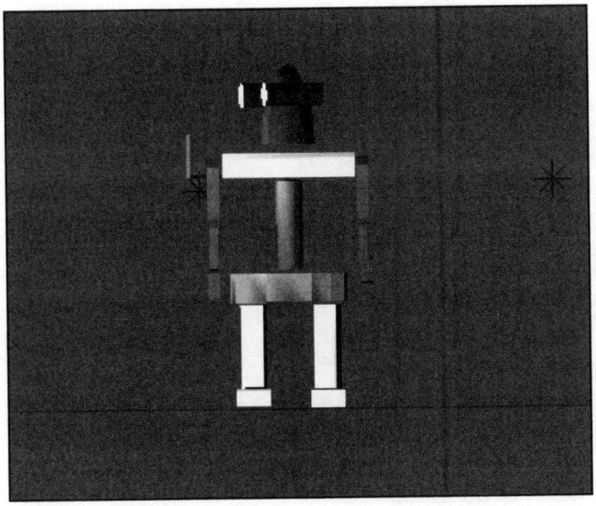

Figure 19-5: Robbie looking to the right, at frame 20

Robbie's Arm Movements

The arm movements consist of a hierarchy of animated rotations. The idea is to animate first his hand, then his hand and lower arm, then his hand, lower arm, and upper arm. The problem is that each time you assign an animation to the next block up the hierarchy, animation below it disappears. It can be very frustrating, so if this happens to you, be immediately aware that you forgot to protect that movement by making it local. When you make movement local, it continues as a subpart of the movement assigned to the next block up. That is, as the upper arm rotates upwards, the hand is rotating with it, while also rotating on its own axis, much as our own skeletal systems work. Here's the step-by-step. Do it many times, varying the number of steps in the hierarchy. This is the only way you'll get used to the sequence. The Internet is flooded with people having difficulty with concept. If you get out of sequence you'll get all sorts of bizarre movement, with joints coming apart, things jumping around and motions disappearing altogether. Take it one step at a time. Review what you did and why, and move to the next step.

POWER TIP: Remember that Robbie's arm will move differently depending on what coordinates system you have selected. I've selected to work in Object Coordinates system because the movements are relative to the object. This way I do all the movements using the Z axis. If you use World Coordinates, the hand will move appropriately, but the arm will go side to side instead of up and down if you stay with Z axis movement.

Then practice by articulating a bunch of nernies, and whatever you can, until you have it down pat. That way you'll use it, and by golly, that will make your work more interesting and professional. Follow closely:

1. Work your way down Robbie's hierarchy. Ironically you have to use the left arrow to reach his right arm (see Figure 19-6, A-C).

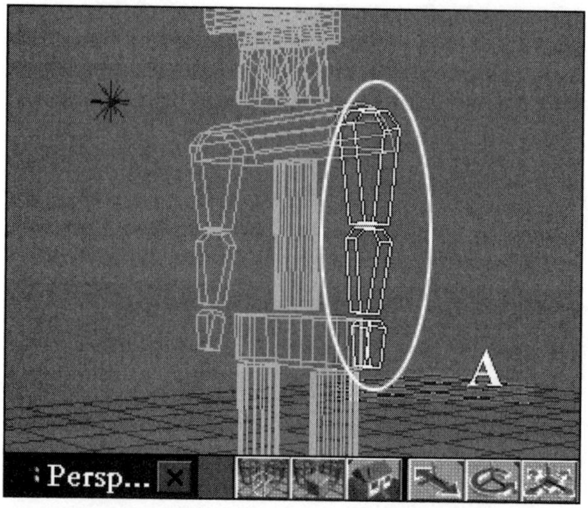

Figure 19-6A: Working down Robbie's hierarchy to his hand. Entire arm isolated

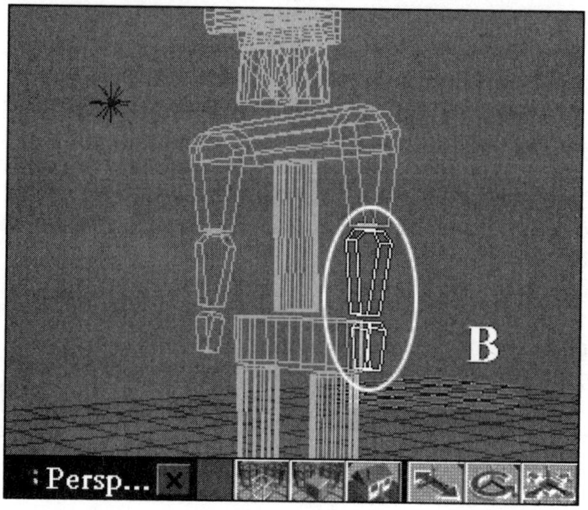

Figure 19-6B: Hand and lower arm isolated

2. Assign a stationary rotation of 50 to the hand's axis.
3. Set rotation frame at one (only if you are not autorecording).
4. Type `20` in the Frames field of the Animation tool window.
5. Engage Object Rotate tool.
6. Making sure you are in Object Coordinates, right click and rotate the hand up until it almost touches the lower arm.
7. Type in frame `30`. This will set a key at 30, keeping the hand still from 20 to 30.
8. Type in frame `50`.

Figure 19-6C: Hand isolated

9. Rotate hand back down to straight and slightly beyond.
10. Localize the rotation.
11. Reset to frame 0.
12. Move up the arm hierarchy until you have the lower arm and hand isolated (white).
13. Add a 60-frame stationary path to the joint axis.
14. Set keyframe at 1.
15. Advance to frame 30.
16. Rotate lower arm upwards (see Figure 19-7).
17. Set key.
18. Advance to frame 45.
19. Set key to hold movement for 15 frames.
20. Advance to frame 60.
21. Lower arm about halfway.
22. Set key.
23. Reset to frame 0.
24. Move up hierarchy to isolate entire arm, as shown previously in Figure 19-6A.
25. Give the arm an axis path of 75 frames.
26. Set frame at 1 with arm lowered next to body.
27. Advance to frame 50.

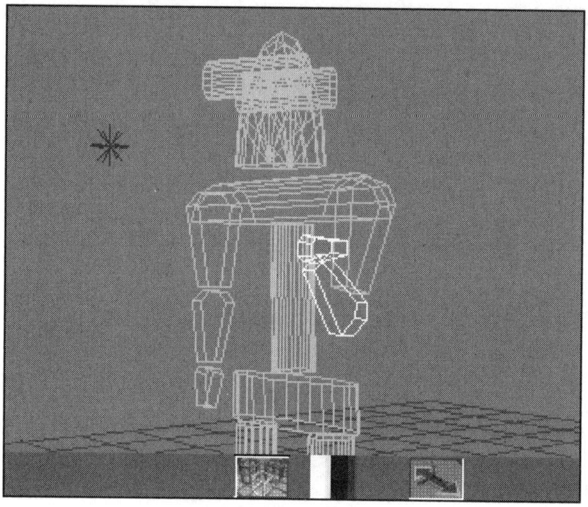

Figure 19-7: Robbie's hand rotated up against his arm

28. Rotate arm up as shown in Figure 19-7.
29. Set Key.
30. Advance to frame 75.
31. Lower arm slightly.
32. Localize the action.
33. Play the animation.

It looks like he's pulling out his phasor and blasting away. You could either composite or animate a blast coming out the tip of his hand if you wanted to. Just for fun, engage the Toggle option in the Animation Parameters panel (right click on Play). Now he moves like an outerspace gun slinger. Save your scene as robbie.scn.

I know this was a lot of steps. Don't try to memorize them. Learn the logic and rhythm of them. You have to be able to go through hierarchies and insert paths and such as a regular course. It's fast when you get it down. It's worth the trip. By the way, I'm not particularly proud of this exercise, and as you can see it was a bit tedious, as small as it was.

Running Robots

I-Wei Huang (pronounced E-Way Wong) has given us some pretty spectacular animations on the CD-ROM, and he was kind enough to spend a weekend at my studio teaching me how to do the amazing articulated action found in his robots. I took notes and I'll show you how. It's not as bad as you might expect. We'll call the little fella I-bot (see Figure 19-8).

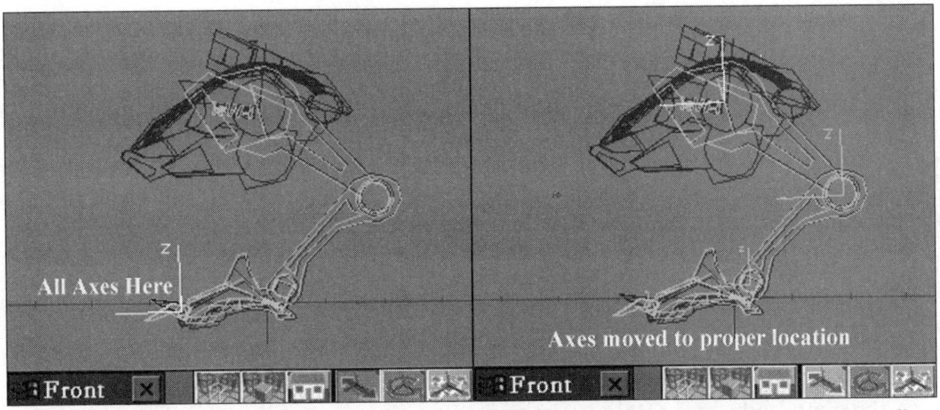

Figure 19-8: Here is an I-bot with one arm glued toe to body, one piece at a time. All segment axes are at the toe (left) ready to be moved, one by one, to the desired axis of rotation (right).

The Principal

I-Wei explained that basically you have to take pains to glue each articulated leg in a parent/child hierarchy — start by selecting the toe and gluing it to the foot, and working up to the body. You'll find all the subpart axes lying on top of each other in the toe, ready to be moved to the proper axis of rotation for each section (except for the toes of course).

Gluing I-bot Together

Let's say you're building a robot like I-bot and you need to glue him together from scratch. Here's what you do. You can go through the motions with me with ibot1.cob. If you have a robot that's glued the wrong way like ibot1.cob, just unglue all the leg parts and start fresh. Don't move any or you'll have a time realigning everything.

With all the leg parts as separate objects, select the toe, click on Glue-as-Child, and select the foot. They'll both turn white. Now just move on up the leg, gluing lower leg, upper leg, and body. It's a simple click, click, click.

It's easier to locate parts on the leg if you rotate it a little so the two legs aren't parallel and on top of each other in the Front View.

Setting the Axes of Rotation

Navigate through the leg hierarchy until you get to the toe. It will be white and the rest of I-bot will be orange. Check the axis of the toe. It should be right where you want the toe to rotate. Good, don't move it. Move up one hierarchy notch to the toe-foot segment and click the Axis tool again. This axis will also be at the toe, so move it up to where you want the foot to rotate. Click the axis tool again to lock it in place, and move up to the toe-foot-lower-leg segment. Again the axis will be at the toe. Click the axis tool and move the axis up to the joint between the upper and lower arm where it will rotate. Repeat this operation again to assign the axis for the whole arm. You can see an example of the axis placement in Figure 19-8.

CAUTION

Caution here. You can really confuse yourself if you glue from body to shoulder on down to toes. In this case the axes are all in the right places, but you can't group the limbs for articulation. You'll go to rotate the foot up in the air and the toe will stay on the ground. Try it and see.

The Moves

Repeat the glue maneuvers on the other leg. Make sure you end up with an axis in the main body, and rotate it so the Z axis points straight ahead. This is so he can follow a path smartly. Now we figure out the moves. We'll have I-bot move in place. Let's start out by giving him an animated-looking position. That is, let's put him in a position that looks like he's walking. It's a good place to start (see Figure 19-9A).

To move the leg, start with the whole thing and rotate it at the hip to a position you want. Next, move down and rotate the lower leg and parts south. Move down again and rotate the foot, then the toe (see Figure 19-9B and C).

You can get a rough idea of how to move him by examining video frames of a person walking. BTW, I recommend the video Hi8 tape recording decks that Sony puts out. They have a near perfect digital freeze-frame for such studies.

Okay, you don't want to imitate a human walk too closely. I personally fake the whole walk cycle. The example video, counter.avi, shows I-bot walking with a limp, just for fun. What I do is stand up at my computer and assume some walk positions, then copy them roughly to the bot. I also put in my drift from side to side as I balance.

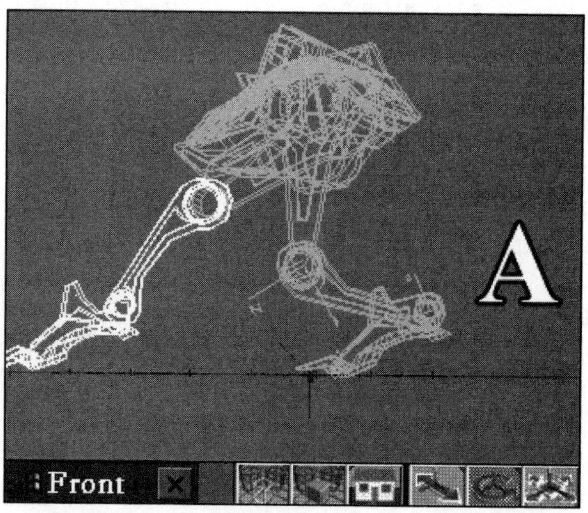

Figure 19-9A: I-Wei's bot is positioned for keyframing its walk cycle.

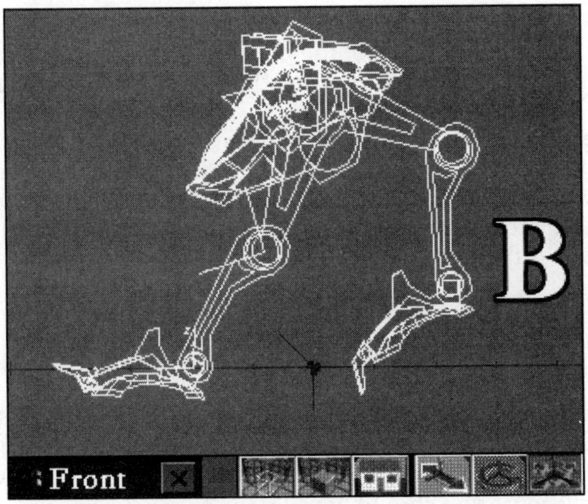

Figure 19-9B

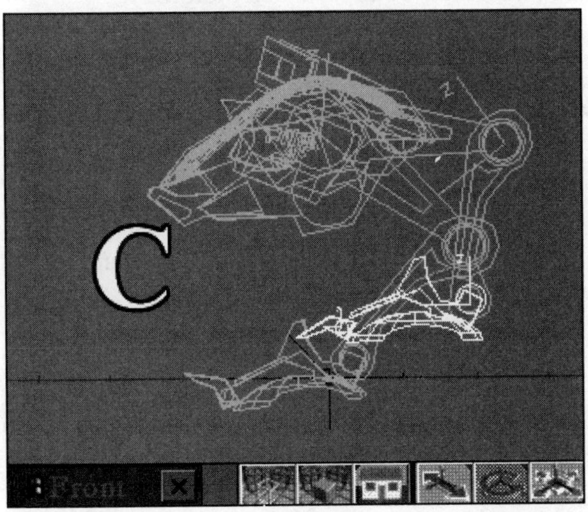

Figure 19-9C

Following these principles you can animate machinery of all sorts, like a mike boom or engine valves. Here's a challenge. Animate a flywheel driven by an eccentric arm, like the arms on steam trains or steam engines. It's a little tricky, but uses only what you've learned here. One hint, keep the end of the arm that's away from the flywheel moving back and forth in a straight line. Use the floor line in Front View if you like. You can build a piston with a cylinder and attach the arm to it. Have the piston going in and out of the cylinder, articulating the arm that turns the wheel. You *can* do it.

The Wheel on the Bike Goes...

As you may have figured, transient extension of the primoid ring was a bit of a ruse to get you through the chapter. There is no such thing. If it scared you but you kept on, you're brave. If it didn't scare you and you kept on anyway, you probably have a science fetish of some sort. Anyway, here's a simple little job for you. Caligari provides a small tricycle among its free objects. I want you to load up the bike and figure out how to make the wheel and peddles turn round and round, just like a real bike. Then animate a short sequence with the bike rolling on all three wheels, with the pedals rotating as if ridden by a ghost.

Summary

This was a short but steep chapter. You're really moving into the pro stuff with relational movement. If you take the time to practice, you'll move yourself up a few notches. I'd bet fewer than 20 percent of trueSpace2 owners know how to do what you just did. Congrats. Here's what you should have learned.

- ✦ What it means to isolate and animate subparts of a hierarchy.
- ✦ How to create primary, secondary, and tertiary orbits.
- ✦ How to localize motion to make it part of a larger Gestalt. Remember, a Gestalt is where the whole is more than the sum of its parts. In a solar system, the parts are doing things, but so is the whole.
- ✦ How to apply stationary paths to joints.
- ✦ How to create articulated rotation; actually it's pseudo-articulated rotation, because it's not physically connected, but I thought we'd gotten pretentious enough in our terminology.
- ✦ Everything there is to know on earth about transient extension of the primoid ring.

You taught yourself all about making the wheels on the bike go round and round.

✦ ✦ ✦

CHAPTER 20

The Animation Project Window

In This Chapter

- Tools within the Project window
- How to rearrange animation timing
- How to easily change the length of an animation
- How to duplicate animated behavior
- Repeating animated behavior from the end

The Animation Project window is really one of the magic pieces of tS2. With this window you can change your animation in a million ways to tweak the motion just the way you want it.

Anatomy of the Project Window

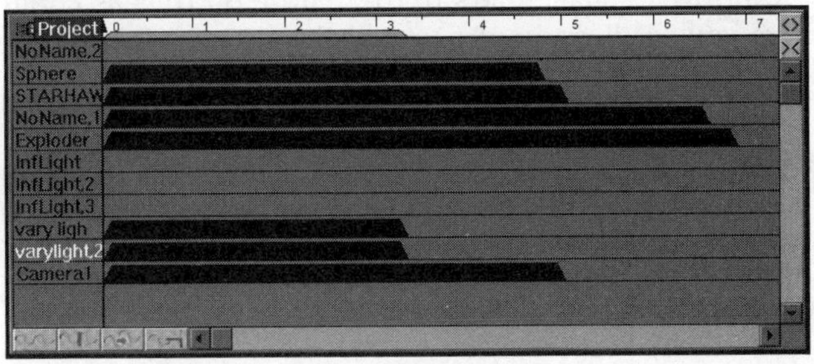

Let's look at the window in detail before we go any further.

The Action Bar

The window, as I'll refer to it, generates a graphic display of animation parameters that you can interactively tweak. Each object gets a horizontal time channel. As you add objects to your scene, the window adds time channels for them. When you add a path, you'll see a black, trapezoidal Action Bar in the associated time channel. The ends of this bar represent the start and end of an animation path.

The really cool thing is that you can grab the end of the bar and drag it longer or shorter. The number of frames in that path will automatically adjust to the new timing, while the action remains the same, like slow motion or speeded-up film.

Bars start at frame zero. But, you can grab one in the middle and drag it, intact, down the channel to a new start/end time. When you do this, the object doesn't suddenly appear at the start of the bar. It's there from the start, but remains stationary until the animation progresses to the start of its action bar. You can remove an action bar for an object by right clicking on it and dragging it off the window.

Preview

You also control the preview of your work in this window. Look above the action bars and you'll see a time scale ticked out in seconds. Handy. A little black Frame Pointer indicates where you are in the sequence, timewise. You can grab it and drag around in the preview, jumping different time markers/frames. Your position is reflected in the work space on screen.

Along the bottom of the time line is a green Preview Range bar that indicates the current length, start, and end of the preview. Normally, previews start at 0 and run to the end of the action. By grabbing the Range bar, you can move it, make it longer or shorter, same as with the Action bars. This nice soft ergonomics makes life easy. You can make the Project window bigger to see longer animations, but that has serious practical limits. Another neat piece of design is the little arrows on the right side of the window. Caligari refers to these little buttons as Zoom In and Zoom Out. With them you easily zoom the time scale to accommodate any length animation.

Action Control Icons

Along the bottom of the window you'll find four icons. They are tools to help you create repeat actions and localize them. You've used these before if you completed the previous chapter.

Repeat Action

This familiar bar was used to keep the planets orbiting as they followed complex paths through the cosmos. It repeats actions for their end points. This means the action doesn't start over again and repeat. It simply continues on its motion path from the end point. Thus the planets simply continue around their orbits *ad infinitum.*

Because actions can be cumulative, you have to be a little careful with this one. Do this experiment. Pop up a sphere and give it a 15-frame stationary path. Scale it down to fairly small at frame 1 and set a key. Jump to 15, scale up a small amount and set a key. Back in the Project window, click on Repeat Action, and then click on the sphere's Action bar. Play.

See what I mean? It's not a problem if you understand how actions can accumulate whenever you don't have the action end on the same note it started. This is actually a feature. You'll find times when you want cumulative motion effects. I use it for explosion effects where the gas cloud keeps getting larger and more diffuse until the end of the animation.

You get rid of repeats by right clicking on them and dragging them out the window.

Stop Repeat

This may not be what you think. It's a clever item that lets you split the gray repeat bar so you can have nonuniform repeat activity. Split the bar and put a gap between the sections and you get a beat or pause in the action for that period of time. You can also scale the individual gray bars to your liking. You can even delete the last section and stop the repeat action at the split.

Copy Action

This is where you get repeat action in the strict sense of the word. This key clones an action in total and plats the clone just to the right of the original as a new black line. You can manipulate the two actions independently. This one doesn't have a cumulative effect because it backtracks each time.

Local Action

I use this one a lot, as you did in the previous chapter. It's primarily used in hierarchical animation to protect the action in subnodes of the object tree (see Figure 20-1). That is, it creates separate editable action bars for each localized action within an object.

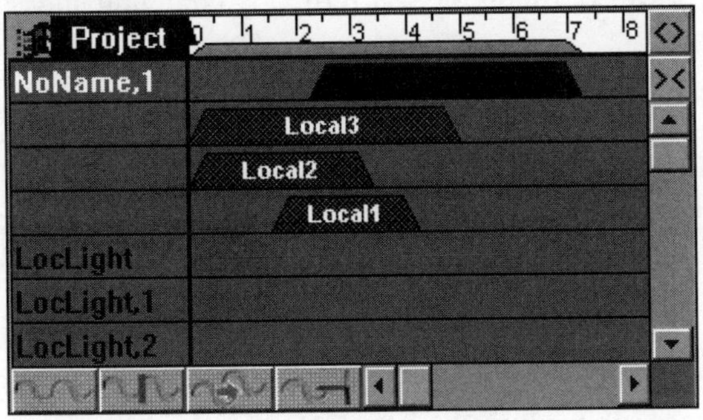

Figure 20-1: Here is the Project window with Local Action bars in place – note that lights are also objects, as are cameras.

CAUTION

Be sure your animation motion is the way you want it before you localize it. Once you do, you can't change it except to use the Repeat Action, Stop Repeat, Copy Action, and Delete functions of the Project window. Ergo — make multiple copies before you hit the localize button.

Localization is not undoable. When it's done, it's done. Once you localize an object you can't edit it with the regular edit tools anymore.

To use Local, navigate to an appropriate sub-object and animate it. Select the Local Action tool, then click on the action bar next to the parent object. The bar is then copied underneath the original bar in gray with Local1, Local2 (and so on) labels. This leaves the original time channel empty. Once you've created a local action you can then move up the hierarchy and add new animation, which will create a new action bar in the empty channel. If you localize this action you'll have two gray local action lines and an empty parent line.

Robbie Returns

This has to be the sorriest robot ever designed. The real Robbie would be pained to see what his image has come to. But we must go on because he's a great practice object.

We're going to play around with Robbie's Project window and see how it affects him.

The Time Line Shuffle

As you saw in Figure 20-1, Robbie's Project window shows a rearrangement of the time line from the one you ended up with. Load your robbie.scn back in. Pop up your Project window and rearrange the lines like this. Notice how the motion is different. Move each of the local time lines around and preview. This is the best way to get a feel for the power of this tool. To do this by changing all your keyframes would be a nightmare.

Stretching Time

The thing I seem to do most in the Project window is adjust the timing of different parts of an animation to get just the rate I want. You can affect the whole emotional feeling of your scene, add excitement, or mellow things out, by changing the length of the action bars.

Try it with Robbie. Grab Local1 in the lower right-hand corner and pull it out. If the whole shebang moves, you were too far into the bar. Just grab the very tip and drag it out about half again. Notice how his hand behaves differently. Stretch and shorten the different lines and observe the differences. You can get some radically different movement doing this.

Summary

Don't you just love a short chapter. Get to know the Project window and you'll save a lot of time. I often find myself planning some long, convoluted way of doing something and then realize, heck, all I have to do is open the Project window and move things around a little. What you've learned in this chapter:

✦ How to retime events within a sequence.

✦ How to lengthen or shorten a sequence.

✦ How to build action hierarchies.

✦ How to make actions repeat from the end in a continuous way.

✦ How to make actions rewind and repeat from the beginning, over and over.

✦ How to duplicate action and manipulate it separately from the original.

✦ How to make Robbie move the way you want him to.

✦ ✦ ✦

CHAPTER 21

Keyframe Techniques

✦ ✦ ✦ ✦

In This Chapter

How keyframes work

How to set keyframes

Using the Keyframe Monitor

Keyframing textures

Keyframing lights

Keyframing camera moves

Keyframing parameters

Removing keyframes

✦ ✦ ✦ ✦

The concept of setting keyframes goes way back to the dawn of animation. It was an economic thing. Pay the key artist well, but only have him draw the storyboard and critical frames where changes take place. Then get cheap labor to interpolate and draw the frames in-between, thus the name *tween* frames. It turns out these tweeners have developed a high art of their own. Much of the character and charm of movement comes from them. Most of the tweening in U.S. cel animation is done in Asia, with Korea having the most active animation force. China, Japan, Hong Kong, and other parts of Asia are coming online in a hurry. It's big business. I got an estimate to do ten minutes of cel animation tweening at 12 cels per second and it came out to about ten grand a minute or 100K per episode. That puts a crimp in one's budget, but that's what Saturday morning cartooning costs. I'm sure they get the cost down after a while, but it still ain't cheap.

The Art of Tweening

Generally, animation keys are drawn in places like the San Fernando Valley or all over southern Canada, Ireland, and France. They're sent to Korea for all the hand-tweening work. Today keys can be sent overseas in seconds via the Internet. The resulting tween cels are scanned to digital format for Ink & Paint processing, where lines and colors are applied. Proofs are sent back and forth across the Pacific. It's still a relatively expensive, labor-intensive process, as the original frames are still hand-drawn. The cost/second of cel animation is a function of the number of frames/second that are drawn. Low-end animation runs about eight frames/second with the better ones running 12 and higher. Cels are shot multiple times to make up the 30 fps for television.

In 3D animation, as you've discovered, tweening is automatic. With the organic deformation tools in tS2, you can get some very noncomputer looking tweening, as amorphous globs move and change shape. By the time you read this, that kind of organic look may even be the new computer look. But you don't get just 8–15 tweens/second, you get 30. This can make for very smooth, precise movement.

A Few General Rules

Keyframes control every change in your animation — not only movement, but lighting, color, backgrounds, and rendering characteristics. Before we get started, here are some rules of thumb for keyframing.

A keyframe is needed every time any event begins or ends.

When keyframing motion, use as few keyframes as possible, especially in linear motion since keyframes can introduce unwanted changes in velocity.

Remember that you can change the number of frames between keys. This is necessary to maintain constant movement when motion keys are placed different distances apart.

Any frame can have many different keys.

Each parameter in tS2 gets its own kind of keyframe. That is, if you set a light key, removing it will only affect the light, not motion or surface keys on that same frame.

Keying Ahead

You don't have to add a path to an animation before adding keyframes. You set up actions progressively along a time line. All you have to do is position your object, type in the frame number where you want a change to stop, and reposition your object the way you want it. tS2 will take care of getting it there in a linear fashion. If your movement isn't linear, you'll need more keyframes. Here's a simple 12-step project. As with most 12-steps, it'll help you avoid bad habits.

1. Create your starting scene. Example: a rubber ball suspended above a marble floor. You want the ball to drop and bounce back up over a period of three seconds, or 90 frames at 30 fps. Start with AutoRecord engaged, and remember that it's on — it will record *everything* you do.
2. Set a motion key at frame 1 by engaging the Move tool and hitting Record. You need to set this key manually because you didn't change anything and keys are recorded when you make changes.
3. Set (type in) the active frame at 40 and move the ball down to just touch the surface of the marble.
4. Set the active frame to 45 and move the ball down so one third is below the floor.

5. Scale the ball disproportionately along the Z axis to move the bottom of the ball up, even with the marble surface. This will give the ball a compressed look.
6. Set a Scale or Deformation key as appropriate.
7. Set active frame to 60.
8. Move ball a third of the way back up and a little off to the right.
9. Restore the ball to spherical shape.
10. Set active frame to 90.
11. Move ball back to starting position.
12. Play.

Bracketing Keyframes

Did you wonder why you put a key in at frame 40, above? There's a good reason that you'll see instantly if you remove that key. Go ahead. See, the ball begins to squash at frame 2 instead of when it hits the marble. We then set other keys at 45 and 60. In a sense we've isolated the bounce/squash of the ball to that in-between section of the animation. That way the ball remains a sphere until it hits the surface and returns back to a sphere in 15 (at 60) frames to remain so for the rest of the animation. It's like having an animation within an animation. The bounce part starts and ends in that 20 frames, never to be heard from again.

Misbehavior

Notice something wrong? It doesn't make sense does it? The damn ball is disobeying the rules, and instead of bouncing off the surface, it's moving down *into* the marble floor for no good reason. You put no keys down there. Most people will try to add more keyframes to get it almost right, but it's maddening. It's one of the things that has had newbies jerking out great screaming patches of hair, but it's really correct behavior when you understand spline paths and defaults. I warned you that defaults can be the enemy.

Remember when we talked about paths and I explained that splines have parameters like Tension, Continuity, and Bias. Look at it this way, you're asking this spline to reverse its path at a single node. By default, splines like things smooth. Spline says "Okay, I'll reverse but I'm gonna take my time about it, make it nice." Therefore it overshoots the mark. The answer is pretty simple, change the way the spline interpolates the path between nodes to Sharp Corner.

Right click on the Animation Path tool to get the properties panel. With the path exposed and all green-like, switch from the Smooth Corner default setting to Sharp Corner and set it for Global application by clicking that icon in the lower right of the panel. Preview it. Boing! a nice believable bounce. If not, experiment and figure out why not. Fix it. Don't move on until you've got a nice smooth bounce that doesn't go through the floor.

Keyframing a Pause

At least once a month someone is stumped by trying to get the camera or some other object to remain still for part of an animation before moving on. You do it with what Caligari calls Empty Keyframes. These are two identical keyframes separated in time. tS2 looks at the difference between keyframes, calculates the movement and applies it as tweening. If there is no difference. There should be no movement. But sometimes there is.

With the Move tool engaged, place an object (actor) at the origin at frame 0 (which, BTW, is always a keyframe). Jump to frame 50 and set a key by hitting record. Remember you have to do this even if AutoRecord is on. Because it's an Empty Keyframe, tS2 sees nothing new to record. Now move ahead to frame 100. Move the actor to a new location and a keyframe is automatically set. Now play.

What you would expect is that the actor would remain stationary until frame 50 and then move to the new location by frame 100. But this isn't quite the case.

Memorize this, otherwise it'll drive you crazy when you forget and run into it later.

What happens is that the object back-drifts during the first 50 frames before making its dash to the new location. It's almost like pulling your arm back before tossing a ball. Again, you can see no good reason for it, but it's the same darn problem you had with the bouncing ball. tS2 interpolates the path, and in its attempt to smooth the entire path, it overshoots the start point. You can check to see if you have an overshoot by revealing the animation path. You'll clearly see a small spline segment and handles in the overshoot area. If you don't want that, make it sharp.

You have to let tS2 know that path smoothing is not desired in this situation. That means you apply sharp corners. Do it by right clicking the Animation Path tool to open the Spline Property panel.

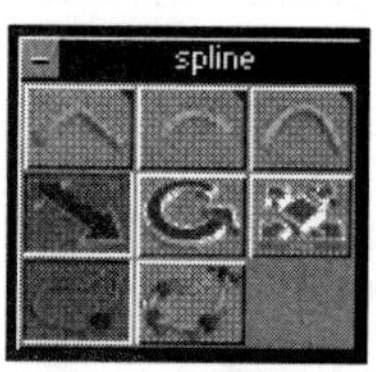

The three interpolation presets are across the top: Sharp, Smooth, and Very Smooth. Smooth is the default that is currently active. Below them are three modes to which the interpolation change can be directed: Move, Rotate, and Scale. On the bottom row are two tools for applying the change either globally or node by node. Make sure the Move Spline tool is engaged in the Spline panel and then right click any of the three presets. You get the numeric Spline Parameter panel.

Go down to the Animation panel and scroll through the nodes. You can see that all the nodes are at default values: Tension = 0, Continuity = 0, and Bias = 0. If there had been one with different settings, you'd have seen it, updated in real-time on the Parameter panel.

Rewind to the first frame and by now you know that's not frame 1. Select the Sharp Corner option. Note the parameter change: Continuity = -1.0. This will cause the actor or object to remain stationary for the first 50 frames. Now it makes sense.

POWER TIP

It's not widely known, but you can also adjust the Tension, Continuity, and Bias for Rotation and Scaling. The effect is not well documented, but it appears that by applying very smooth, you get smoother rotations and scaling. I could be wrong; the effect has been subtle in my experiments.

Keyframe "Inversanity"

Frequently in production work you'll want the animation to end on a note of completion. Let's say you've designed a logo that you've created with letters rotating in from various angles to form a name. By keyframing in reverse you can save a lot of work and end up with a more professional product.

Build your final scene, just the way it will look when all the pieces are complete. You do this all at frame 0, but when you're done, you set the Animation panel to the last frame of your animation. You'll know what that is because you know just how long it will have to be. For grins we'll say the animation ends on frame 150. Type that in the panel.

Now comes the interesting part. While still at frame 150, you set empty Move keyframes for each piece that will move. Then go back and set empty Rotate keyframes for each piece that will rotate. If you plan on morphing color, set empty keys for that too. Remember that you set empty keys by selecting the actor (object) and tool, then recording the event with a push of the Record button. You have to select each Animation tool you'll be using and apply it to the actor you'll be using it on.

So, if you're rotating the letter D, select it, select the Rotate Object tool, and hit Record. This will set the stage for the last frame in concrete. Now rewind back to frame 0 for the whole scene. Nothing changed, all the actors are in the same place, as they should be. Now move them off camera and do your rotation (remember that if you want full rotation you have to keyframe it in three 120° shots). Put some up above, others down below, and yet others out to the side. For fun put some of the letters that end up on the left side off the right side of the screen. When you animate, all the actors will come flying in, scrambling to end up exactly where you wanted them. You can see the advantage of doing it this way instead of trying to navigate all the pieces to the exact place you want them to end up. Now that would be tedious.

In Figure 21-1, I've used an example of backward animation. This one was done with the aid of Exploder, which you'll learn about soon enough in the Special Effects chapter. I had exploder take the D apart, starting with the whole letter at frame 60 and working backward to frame 0, where the parts are jumbled in space. I set the parameters to move the parts away from the original object and rotate. When you play it, the parts fly in and form the D. This is handy for logos. There's a silly little .avi on the CD-ROM with the disgusting name, Suckface (in the \movies\dreamscp subdirectory. It's a complex form of backwards animation where the face on the last frame was backward animated into a thousand little pieces of gold foil. The result is that the screen opens with a blizzard of foil swirling, then rushing in to form the gold face.

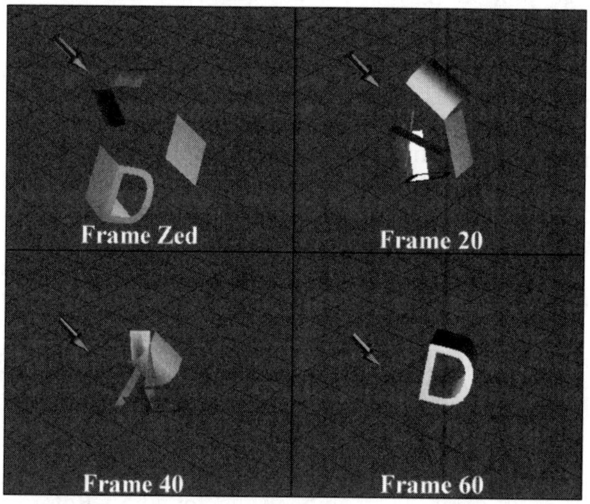

Figure 21-1: Frames 0, 20, 40, and 60 of a backward animation of the letter D. The letter forms from parts that move and rotate into the final position. Geometry and paths were provided by Rob Bryerton's Exploder.

Path Animation

You already know about this one. You've done it a dozen times or more. It's time to learn a little technique. Earlier I suggested you use as few nodes as possible if you want your motion to be smooth. You just increase the number of frames between nodes and you can get some nice, even straight-line animation. But what if you want to accelerate your actor along the path? What if you want it to slow down on approach to the space station? These things can be adjusted. In fact, we can also adjust such things as banking into curves as well.

Unwanted Speed Changes

Assuming you don't change the number of frames between nodes, tS2 has the same number of steps between any two nodes. Think about it. Say you and your friend both have to go to the bathroom, and there's one in the next room, with the other up two flights of stairs. In order for you each to arrive at the same time, the person going upstairs will be going a lot faster. This effect would probably be enhanced if you each had to take exactly the same number of steps in that time.

That's how it is in animation. The longer the path between nodes, the faster your actor will move.

Since it's very difficult and often impractical to place nodes exactly the same distance apart, you're likely to see acceleration and deceleration as the object passes through different sections. You can adjust this a little by playing with the tension adjustment and spacing the frames equally as much as possible. What a bore, though. It stands to reason that you'll have fewer speed changes on a straight run if you use fewer nodes. That's the best way to get smooth action, but it's hard to do when you have lots of curves. I made a great curve by making a single path between two nodes with 518 frames. I then used the Add Spline Point tool to add a point in the center. This gave me the handles I needed to bend the whole thing very smoothly and you can't see any acceleration or deceleration. The alternative is to estimate the distance between nodes and change the number of frames each time so you roughly maintain X number per unit of measurement, say, 10 frames per meter.

Acceleration

You can play with the spline parameters to move the relative location of frames between nodes. Just for the heck of it, pop up a box and give it a two-node path of 100 frames across the screen. Preview the movement. Now right click on the Spline Properties panel to get the Spline Parameter panel. I know these all sound the same, like little towns in New England, but we have to live with it. Input the following into the appropriate fields: Tension ➪ 1 Continuity ➪ 30 Bias ➪ 0. Now preview again. If we're in the same relative space/time continuum, the box should accelerate at the beginning and slow down at the end. You can play with the box interactively, adjusting the handles to bunch the little green dots together where you want the motion to be slowest, and to space them out where you want the motion to be snappy.

The Look Tools

There are two Constraint tools you'll use a lot in animation — Look At and Look Ahead.

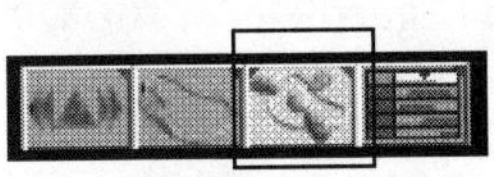

Look At

Since objects in tS2 can't actually see, this is a metaphor. What happens is that the Z axis of the constrained object must always be pointed at axis center of the designated target object. It looks a lot like a teenage boy on his way to school who just spotted a flash of liquid spandex across the street. He keeps moving forward, but his head's Z axis keeps realigning to point at the axis attached to the smooth quad divided spandex object. You get the picture. No fancy tension adjustments here, just gawking. Does it have practical use? You bet.

Lights

Spotlights are objects with an axis. The Z axis points right out the front with the light. With Look At, you can force a spotlight to follow an object. If it's a large, compound object you may have a problem. In sibling pairs, you may want the light to shine on one but it shines on the other. That's because the combined axis stays centered in the object that was selected when the pair was made. The trick is to expose the axis and move it to where you want the light to shine. Be aware that this can screw up other axis-dependent things like rotation.

Camera

Think about making a camera object look at the point of action as it moves through space, just like a camera following a baseball on the Sports Channel. Because cameras have their Z axis outside the lens, it's easy.

Since you can keyframe Look At on and off anywhere along a path, you can do some nice camera work covering a scene. More on this in another chapter, but for now, be aware that you don't want to keyframe Look At from one object to another. You'll get a disconcerting jerk. Keyframe disengage it, leave 15–30 frames unconstrained, and then rekey it to the next object. This will give you a smooth transition. If it doesn't seem to be working, make sure you have the Look At tool engaged when you set the key.

Look Ahead

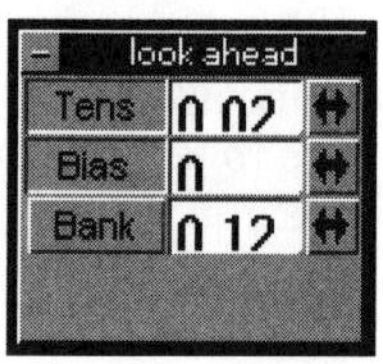

This is another handy Constraint tool. It automatically realigns the object's Z axis with the motion path for every frame. This keeps the object pointing down the path as it moves. If you want the plane upright, point the Y axis straight up and the X axis out to the side. The typical example is a jet plane flying down a curved path. With Look Ahead disengaged it faces the same direction regardless of the winding of the path — looks silly. With Look At engaged the plane follows nose first down the path the way you'd expect. But half the time you import planes, especially DXF models, and the Z axis is pointing out the bottom or some other unlikely place. When you engage Look Ahead, the plane might flip on its nose and follow belly first. Another thumb rule: always check where the Z axis is pointed on imported objects. Realign if necessary. It should point out the nose of the plane.

When real planes fly around curves, they can't stay flat. They have to bank into the wind for that swooping curve. You can simulate it by adjusting parameters in the Look Ahead Control panel.

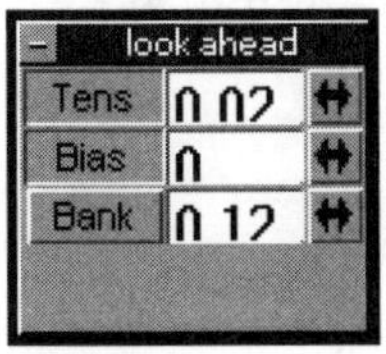

Tension

This factor represents the degree to which the actor *resists* following the curve. That is, how strongly it tries to retain its original orientation. You don't want a lot of this because it screws up the Look Ahead action you wanted in the first place. I keep it at .01 or .02 most of the time. I haven't found a use for higher levels yet.

Bias

This parameter is simulated inertia. It determines the overshoot an object can have on curves. No real plane would follow an exact line. It would initiate a turn, but drift some in the curve.

Bank

The is what leans your craft into a curve. It's actually a push-button that must be engaged. It can be keyframed on and off. You specify the amount of Bank in degrees in the Bank field.

Let's Try It

Load up your drone or any airplane-type vehicle you may have on hand. These are among the most common objects on the Internet, so have a ball. Once it's on-screen reveal the axes. Engage the Rotate key with axes exposed and you can rotate them. Make sure they are aligned in the following pattern: X ⇨ straight out toward the wing, Y ⇨ Straight up through the roof of the plane, Z ⇨ Smack out the nose of the plane. This will cause your plane to align with the path in a flat, upright position when you engage Look Ahead. Give your vehicle a curved path using four nodes, 30 frames each. With the Animation tool panel set at frame 0, right click on the Look Ahead tool to get the Look Ahead Control panel. Type in the following values Tens ⇨ .03 Bias ⇨ .0 and Bank ⇨ 45. Make sure Bank is engaged (white) then engage the Look At tool. This will set a key for it at zero. Preview your motion. The plane should run down the path head first and then bank properly in the corners.

Tension and Bias both affect the way a plane banks. You'll best understand this through experiment. Rewind to frame 0 and try different combinations of plus and minus values to see what happens in the bank. Very high values of tension will cause exaggeration in banking as will very high angles.

Keying Material Changes

One of the great additions to tS2 is the ability to animate all the materials. The variety of effects this enables is astounding. First I'll show you how to key a change, then we can look at some ideas for using it.

1. Pop up a cube and paint it bright yellow.
2. Change the background to black to highlight color changes.
3. Reset the default lights to white if they are something else.
4. Open the Animation tool panel and advance to frame 1.
5. With your paint tool still engaged, record a keyframe at one.
6. Jump to frame 60 in the Tool panel.
7. Change paint color to a high ambient blue and use the Paint Over tool to change the color of the cube.
8. To make it more interesting, key in a 360° rotation.
9. Record the animation and view it with Media Player.

Keying Texture Changes

As reported earlier, texture maps do not morph into each other when you key changes; they are abrupt. If you want a more morph-like change you can use Adobe Premiere, MediaStudio Video Editor, or Razor to do a long dissolve between the two textures. Make it the length of the animation you're building and apply it as an animated texture. You'll have full control of the change.

Morphs Can Be Morphun

For even more interesting effects, you can morph your texture changes in MediaStudio Morph Editor or with Elastic Reality or even a shareware morph package. There is a way around almost everything in tS2. Morphing allows you near infinite control over the way your textures blend into each other. If you have the talent, skill, and time you could create an object in tS2, then deform it into a different object. Then apply an animated morph texture to match the change. This is the sort of thing that was done in *Terminator 2* to get the amazing transformations from cop to chrome blob. I can't teach you morphing techniques here, but they are clearly explained with all sorts of wild ideas in the various packages available.

Video Filter Effects

Instead of keyframing texture effect changes you can use the animated approach, applying different transition filters to make some spectacular effects. One common transition filter is the swirl effect. That's where texture one swirls from the center out and when it unswirls, it's the new texture. Think about how you might use this effect to open up a worm hole in space. After all, that's a big thing these days. Someone even got an Emmy for building the worm hole in *Deep Space 9.* Have a Ball.

Keying Plug-in Filter Effects

You can't keyframe internal filter setting changes. Too bad because that would be cool. You can keyframe individual settings in the plug-ins panel. You can layer filter effects up to four deep. Considering the wide range of filter effects and this layering, you can build pictures that don't look much like the scene you built (see Figure 21-2). I'll give you an example:

There is a fire-hose gush of new plug-in filters coming out. It stands to reason that they'll soon be like fonts, way more types than you even want to know about. You can learn more about them in Chapter 29.

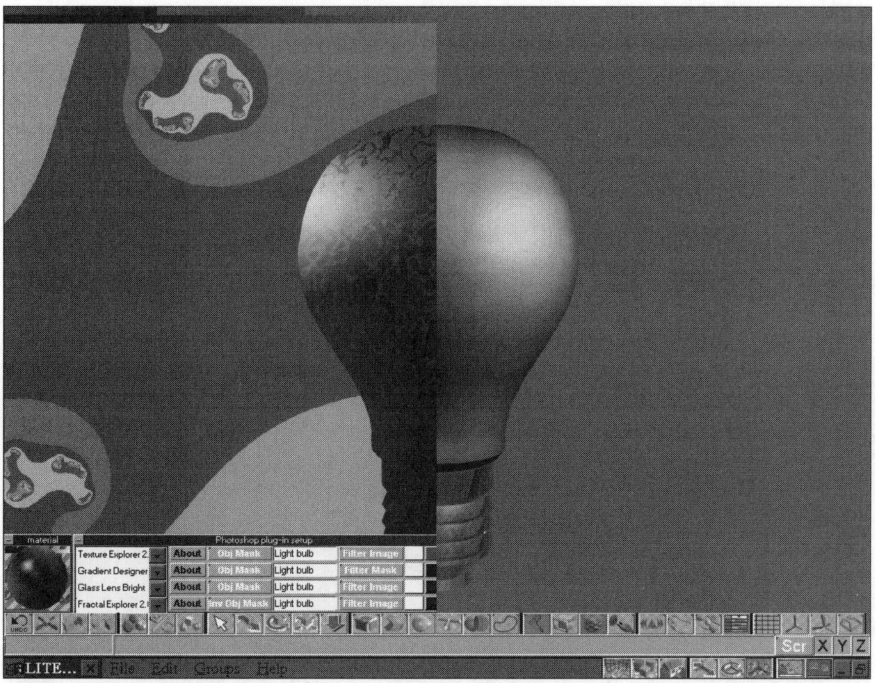

Figure 21-2: A lightbulb is rendered with plug-in filter effects (left side), and without filters (right side). Filters and the order in which they are applied are displayed in the Plug-in Setup window. Note that you can't render half a screen like this, it's just a trick done in Photoshop.

Using the Keyframe Monitor

This will be short because you already know a little about the Keyframe Monitor. It annoys me and I rarely use it. It's also virtually undocumented, so everything about it is a little squirrelly. But here goes. When you are using keyframe animation you need some way of keeping track of what kinds of keys you've placed where.

If you bear in mind that there are 16 different kinds of keys (at least) and you can set them accidentally if you have AutoRecord engaged, you could theoretically end up with a keyframe catastrophe. I use the Monitor to keep track of what kinds of keys are set on which frames. I've also been known to disable keys I'm not working with so I don't get spurious events.

The only way to get a good idea of how this animal trots is to do an exercise.

Monitor Exercise

I'm going to keep this as simple as I can — not because I don't trust your brain, but because it'll be easier to see what's happening. Open up your Main View as a Front View and pop up a sphere. Move it to the left of your screen and give it a path of 30 frames across the screen (see Figure 21-3). You will have a keyframe at 0 and at 30. Open up the Keyframe Monitor. Notice the first cell is bluish and the rest of the object manipulate tools are bright gray. The rest of the row is dark gray.

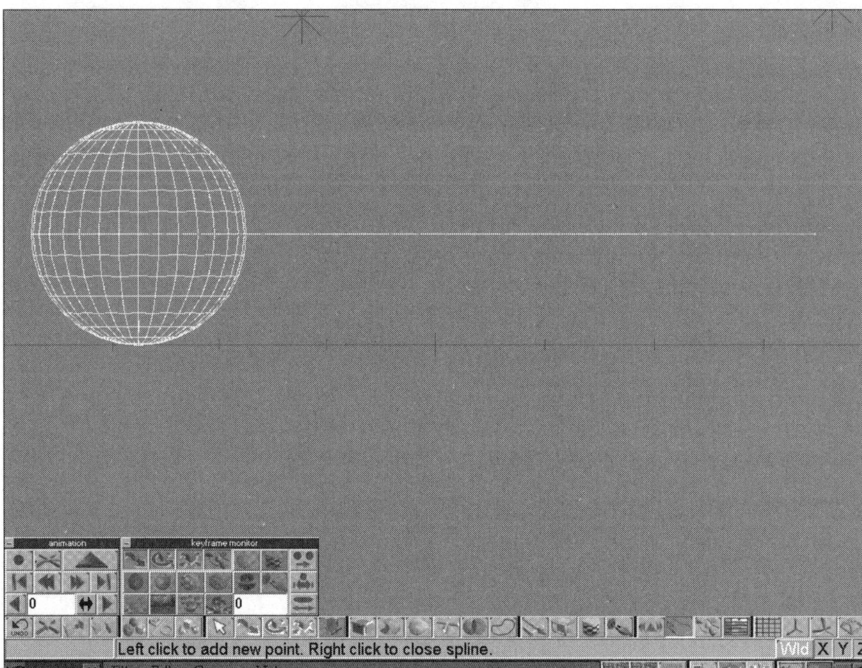

Figure 21-3: This ball with a 30-frame path sits on frame 0. Note the Keyframe Monitor shows the Move is bluish (trust me), the Rotate and Scale keys are light gray, indicating they are ready to work, and the rest are dark gray indicating they are inactive and can't be set until properly awakened.

That means:

✦ Movement keys are set and we are on one (bluish).

✦ An object is selected, therefore you may now set keys for the bright gray or bluish tools = Move, Rotate, Scale.

✦ You can't set keys for any other tools at this point.

Next, type 10 into the Animation tool input field and hit return. The ball will jump to segment 10 on the spline path, indicating where it will be on frame 10 (see Figure 21-4). Now engage the rotate tool and rotate the sphere about 30 degrees. Set the grid if you want to be exact. Good, now you should see this on the Keyframe Monitor: the rotation key is now bluish, and the other object tools are light gray. That's because we just set a rotation key here. Makes sense, right?

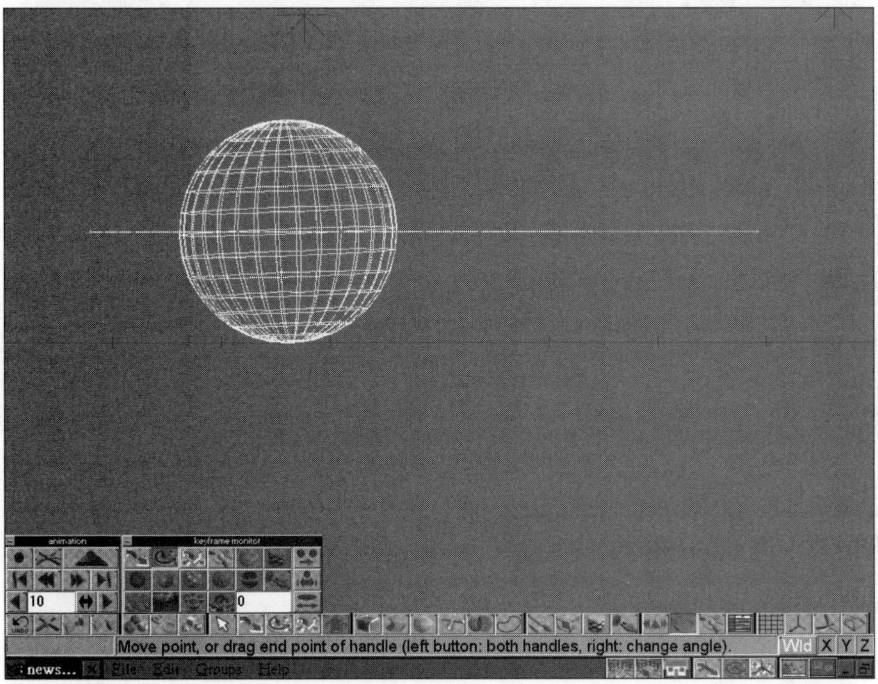

Figure 21-4: The ball sits at frame ten with a rotation key set (bluish) while the Move and Scale keys are active but not set.

Jump to frame 20 and scale the ball way down (see Figure 21-5). Notice how it lifts up into the air. Engage the Move tool and bring it back down to the floor line. Look at your Monitor. Notice you now have two keys active. A Scale key and a Move key. The Move key was engaged when you moved the ball down to the floor.

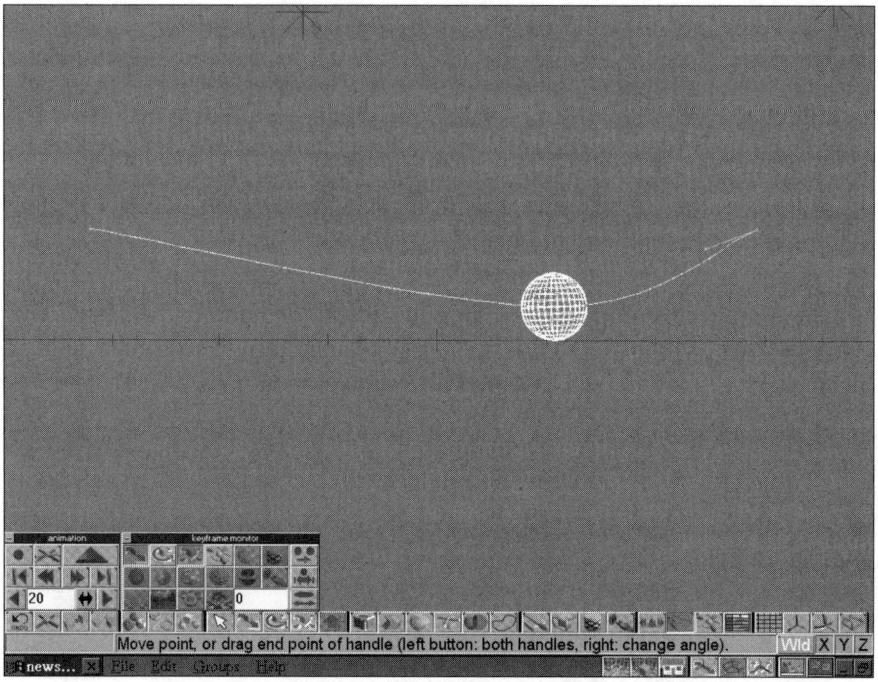

Figure 21-5: The sphere is at frame 20, scaled down and reset on the floor line. There are now two bluish keys, the Scale key and the Move key. The latter was set when you moved the ball back down to the floor.

Now go to the end at frame 30 and scale the ball back up to full size by scaling until the sphere just hits the floor again. In Figure 21-6, you'll notice that the Move and Scale keys are both bluish. Why? You didn't move anything, did you? No. But remember that 30 was the original end key for the whole move across the screen. So it's right.

Run It!

Play your animation and notice how the ball moves, turns, gets smaller, then larger again, all the while staying smack even with the floor. Now step through the frames with your eye on the Monitor. Why are all three object manipulation keys now bluish? Note how the keys go light gray between keyframes. When you step to a keyframe the proper key references turn bluish. You have to look closely, because bluish looks a lot like dark gray.

Add Color

Move to frame 5 and paint the sphere bright red. Go to 15 and paint it bright yellow. Go to 30 and paint it saturated green and play with shaders to make it dark and shiny. Good.

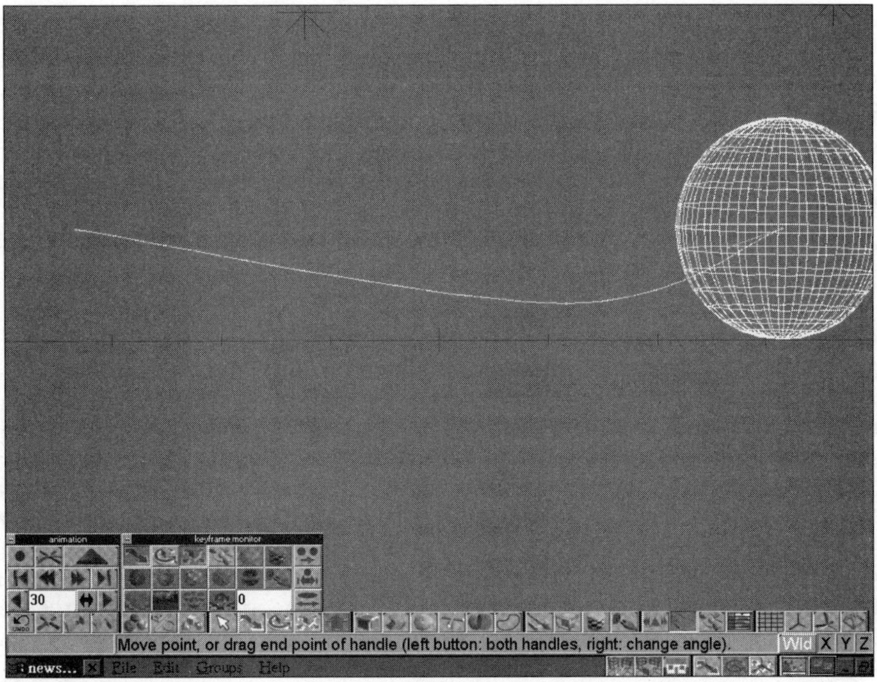

Figure 21-6: At frame 30, Move and Scale keys are both bluish, indicating there are keys for both here.

Step through your frames again noting several things: The Material Preview window shows the color morphing as you move frame to frame. When you get to frame 5, you get a color key. At frame 15 you see another color key. At 30 you see a lot of keys, Move, Scale, Color, and surface parameters. Save it as *reload.scn* for later and continue.

Now Back Step 1, 2, 3

Now suppose you render this thing and decide that the scaling looks hokey and you want to remove it. No problem. Engage the Scale tool and use the Advance to next Keyframe button on the Animation tool to move through the Object Manipulation keys. With the Keyframe Monitor open, you move to keys by group. If you have the Move tool open, you'll advance to any key with any of Move, Rotate, or Scale keys. Keep an eye on the monitor and when you get to the first Scale key after 0, with Scale engaged, hit the red button on the Animation tool to delete it. Bam! the sphere jumps up to full size.

Run the animation, and the ball should go from left to right with no scaling, just the rotation and color morph. Getting the idea?

Be careful deleting keyframes, the undo key will not let you undo keyframe deletes. You can, strangely, undo and redo keyframe sets, however.

What Does a Red Key Mean?

When in Monitor mode, and you delete a scale or rotation key, you also delete any other keys from the object manipulation group on that frame. For example, on frame 20 you have two keys from the same group and you delete one. The other goes too. To preserve one you have to disable its monitor button by clicking. It turns red. That's it. Try it.

Copy Keys

Reload. Let's copy some keys to make things run a little differently. The ball is selected, so when you go to frame 20, you'll see the Object Manipulation Keys are blue. Remember, this only copies blue keys, not all active keys. So hit the Copy Keyframe (two dots and an arrow) button and type `60` in the Monitor input field. All active keys are copied to frame 60. Go into 3DR mode and run the animation. Notice that the ball gets small, then large, then small again, but instead of going from white to red to yellow to green, to yellow again as you might expect, it stays green. In order to transfer the color keys as well, you must select the ball with the Inspect tool. This is a little rule that screws a lot of people up. I often forget to do it. Remember it. Do it. It saves a lot of time. Try it now; copy the color keys from 20 to 60 and run again.

Notice that the original keys stay put and a full copy is transferred to the new frame. You can also convey keys from 20 to 60 in a way that actually moves them.

Shifting Keys

Reload. Go to frame 20 again. This time hit the Shift Keyframe button (one dot, double arrow) and type `60` into the Monitor input field. What happens may not be what you expect. Try it. Notice how the ball goes through the color morphs okay, but it just keeps getting smaller all the way to frame 60, but it doesn't stop. It then gets big and small again, exactly the way it used to between 20 and 60.

If you shift a set of keys forward past another set of keys, the latter are eliminated and replaced by whatever tween keys hit that frame on their way to the shifted keys. If you shift frame 20 to 60, you run over 30. Thus the ball gets smaller all the way to 60, but never gets bigger.

Key Stretching

You don't have to be Uri Geller to stretch your keys. Reload and go to frame 20 again. I know this is repetitious, but this way you get to make a meaningful comparison of how the different processes work. The best way to do it is reload and copy the first ball, leaving them on top of each other. Now select one of them and shift keys from frame 20 to 60. Select the other ball and stretch from 20 to 60.

The difference between the two processes will be clear as the two balls start moving together, but don't end up the same way. Take the time to do it. Words won't clarify this matter.

Animating Parameters

The general rule in animating parameters is if it has a slider or numeric inputs you can key interpolated value changes. If it has an on/off switch you can key it on or off. If it takes discrete parameter changes like texture images, you can key discrete changes.

Keyframed Lighting

In real life, you see artifical lights changing intensity and color all over the place. For example, traffic lights flash on and off, some changing color behind the same lens. Cars have brake lights that flash, and certainly in space you want some flashing warning lights or such.

One of the new capabilities in tS2 over tS is the ability to animate just about any parameter. If you look at my .avi of a space shuttle landing in the service/lock down bay, you'll notice a light that flashes red, then yellow, then red and so forth, continuously. This is a straight on/off animation.

Intensity

Varying the brightness of your sources is a handy trick to add believability to your piece. To make a hard transition like a blinking light, you need a key to set the off position, then a few frames later a null key that will keep the intensity at 0 to that point. On the next frame you turn up the intensity (2 is enough for most purposes) and set a key (or auto set it). Then you need to count off the number of frames you want the light to be *on* and set another null key to keep the intensity at 2.

On the next key you drop intensity back to 0 and set a light key. The null keys keep tS2 from tweening light intensities and forming a ramp. A ramp is when the intensity goes up or down a little more in each frame. Here are a few ideas to play with.

Hard transitions are binary; they go directly from one state to the other instantly. A blinking light on an airplane is an example of hard transition (see video \landgbay.avi in the CD-ROM \movies\dreamscp subdirectory where light flashes red, yellow, and green sequentially).

Soft transitions change intensity over time. Explosions are much more believable with an animated soft transition synchronized with the blast. It's usually ramped way up in a few frames, then held a couple of beats, then down ramped quickly. Figure 21-7 shows an example of what I mean.

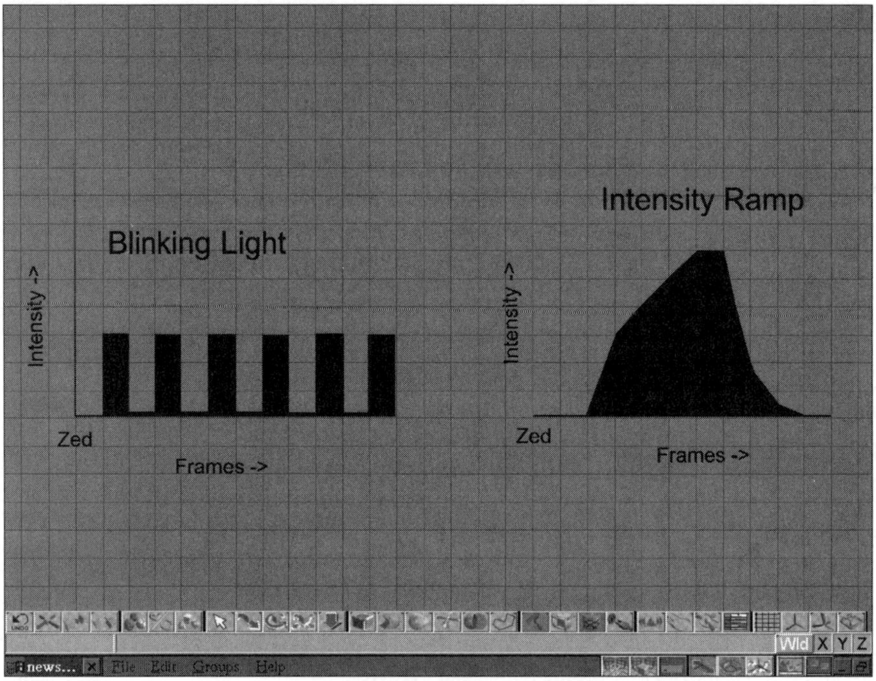

Figure 21-7: These charts give you an idea of what the keys look like for blinking and ramped light changes. Think of frames as time and intensity as brightness. They also show another use for tS2. Simple 2D and 3D graphs are easy.

You could have a very soft transition from day to night.

You can use an animated background of clouds passing and keyframe your main light (could be an infinite shadowcaster) to vary with the passing clouds. The effect on your scene can be dramatic.

Color

Changing the color of a light over time can reinforce great illusions or change or initiate mood shifts. You can emphasize weather, underwater effects, explosions, even a sunset.

If you very slowly ramp a change from blue/white illumination to yellow/white, people won't notice directly, but you'll create a mood shift from cold to warm.

On your next explosion, ramp not only your intensity, but the color, too. Try going from an intense white with a momentary shift to green and back to white, then as the intensity ramps down, wend through yellow to red. With the fading intensity it looks like a fading glow. More on this in the chapter on explosions, which are an interesting area all in themselves.

Spotlights Are Special

Recall that spotlights can have a sack-load of adjustable parameters and they're all animatable. Here's a trunk-load of ideas on what you can do with one.

Sweep a spot across the stage. If you sweep six or so you can give a gala opening effect. Build a stage curtain and sweep.

Sweep several different color spots across a shiny gold logo for a neat effect.

Have a wide, soft spot zoom down to a hard tight one to focus attention on something about to happen.

Focus a very soft spotlight behind a wall torch in a castle. Make it flicker with a series of random ramps. For a better effect, make the ramp peaks at different intensities and ramp the color slightly between yellow and orange.

Glue a cluster of six or more spots together, and rotate it above a club scene. You'll have to set parameters for each and localize the action before gluing them together. I'd have each ramping through different color tracks, flashing on and off to the beat of the music — but that's another story for later.

Use a spot shining out the tail of a space vehicle on a translucent sphere that you've pulled into a long flame shape with the Deform Objects tool. Fast ramp the intensity between very bright and reasonably bright. Make sure you use Squared Fall Off or you'll be lighting up everything in the universe that's behind the ship. That's a good thing to be aware of with spots. They can shine on your background plate and ruin a good illusion.

Keyframed Looks

This is a big fun area to explore. You learned in the chapter on textures that you can keyframe changes, bam, no linear interpolation between, just a jump from one to the other. It's the same with shader options like Flat shading and Phong. For some reason the Metal shader doesn't appear to be keyframable. If you invoke it anywhere, it takes over all the frames for that object, all the way back to frame 0. Get out the Raid. But you can also animate most shaders and render parameters to radically change looks.

Here's a cool idea. Pop up a sphere, set your shaders all across the bottom, except go to 100% invisible and paint it yellow. Put the sphere in a scene you have handy from another project. The idea is to give it something to reflect. If you use a background image, use the same one in the Global Environment option. Put in one keyframe after 0. At frame 100, slide to 100% opaque, and slide the shininess and roughness all the way to the top. Now in the Project window, slide the entire bar to the right a few seconds. Render it. If you have the time, raytrace it. At first the scene is as you originally made it, then slowly the sphere materializes. Then it becomes increasingly reflective until it's reflecting the whole scene like a gold mirror ball. The idea works in reverse as well. Think of ways you can use this special effect.

Flat shading can give your 3D characters a definite 2D look. Try starting your characters as 2D cartoon-like actors and have them fill out into 3D space. Just flat shade them in the beginning, keyframe a jump to Phong, but have all the parameters at minimal. Then slowly pull up the shading to yield the highlights and shadows. It's a cool effect.

Working in reverse, you can take a shiny chrome Harley, have it age, and go flat.

Remember about doing rainy/stormy weather? You can take a plastic ball out in the rain and have it look wet. Just experiment with the roughness slider until you get a wet look on the ball's surface texture, then keyframe it for when the rain (particles) hits the ball.

You can keyframe the raytracer to switch on at a given frame. The effect varies, but to me it looks like someone just turned on a light (see apprship.avi). Just as the approaching shuttle began to enter the mother ship, I switched on the raytracer. You can see it looks like a bright light goes on inside.

Keyframe changes in fog density. Though fog has no slider, it does have numeric input parameters for near side/far side and density. These values are keyframable. Experiment with a densely fogged scene that clears before your very eyes. A tricky use for it is to have an explosion, then fill your scene with dense fog that dissipates quickly. It looks like residual smoke. With a fractal variable density filter added you can get some pretty neat effects. Try it with the smog scene.

That's enough on keyframing for now. This gives you enough to understand what's going on in the upcoming sections. You can think up lots more than I can. It's part of the fun of 3D. We all try to outdo each other in creative application of the tools. You can see it in the user groups and mailing lists. This is one area where you get excited no matter who comes up with a great use. I remember when someone finally figured out how to use the Vertex Paint tool to create glows; it was the hottest thing for a week, everybody was trying new things with it. Ours is a great field.

Summary

The art of keyframing is the heart of animation. Automatic tweening in 3D programs makes life fun, fast, and easy. You will have learned all of the following if you actually read this chapter:

- About the art of hand-tweening and how it's done automatically in tS2 between keyframes you design.
- How keyframes work to create smooth action or parameter changes in your animation.
- How to use bracketed keyframes to isolate tweening to specific frames.
- How to keyframe ahead by inputting frame numbers into the Animation Control panel numeric field.
- How to use animation paths for action sequences such as flythroughs.
- How to use the Look tools to control your action such as Look Ahead and Look At.
- How to use Keyframing Ahead to control rotations, scaling, linear movement, and parameter changes.
- Tips and techniques for keyframing lighting parameters to add excitement to your scenes.
- Tricks and techniques for using parameter changes to create special effects.
- A good introduction to the Keyframe Monitor and how it keeps track of keys, as well as how you can set and unset specific classes of keys.
- The difference between Move key, Shift key, and Stretch key is subtle, but important. You learned to experiment to see the difference for yourself.

In Chapter 22 we learn the technical and artistic considerations that will take your path animation to a professional level.

✦ ✦ ✦

CHAPTER 22

Choreographing Movement

✦ ✦ ✦ ✦

In This Chapter

The science and art of observing movement

The art of object movement choreography

Analyzing the script

Moving human and animal characters — cartoon vs. realistic

Blocking: the task of laying out movements with the camera and set in mind

✦ ✦ ✦ ✦

Get out your notebook. You see movement all the time, but it's unlikely you understand its details. Few people do, but good animators aren't among them. Test yourself: exactly how does a horse move its legs? Can it ever have all four legs off the ground at once? You should know this; it's one of the most studied forms of movement.

An Eye for Movement

Here's an easy one: how do your tropical fish move their tails? If you don't have fish, think about how they move, how you would keyframe it. Remember playing with the shark? Mine was organic but pretty unnatural. You really ought to be able to make things move believably, locally, before you tackle scene blocking. Here are some not so easy exercises that will sharpen your observational skills.

Motion Capture with a Pencil

First you need a form of notation to record moves. I do it the old way, the way the cave men did it on walls. I make a rough sketch of the animal and draw body parts in different positions. I have to number each one because I get confused by my own drawings. Make sure you number the moves in sequence. These can correspond roughly or exactly to your keyframes.

This is really a 4D art. Here is where the fourth dimension comes in — timing. Does the animal go through its moves smoothly or does it move quickly, then slowly? Think about a cat in tall grass sneaking up on a mouse. It moves like a robot, one foot at a time, pausing between. Then it's perfectly still, waiting for its prey to get close enough. But the mouse gets away. How would you keyframe these charming moves?

Local Movement

Local movement is movement within the object itself. It includes everything from a second hand sweeping around a clock to a praying mantis moving its arms. There are two broad categories of local movement — realistic and stylized.

Realism

Cyrus Lumm's shark is an example of realism in movement. Not only does the shark *look* real, it moves the way a shark would move. To achieve this, you have to take pretty extensive notes. Better yet, videotape movement.

Keyframing Realism

I use two camcorders to study motion. I still need my crude drawings with estimated keyframes on them but it's much easier to be accurate if you copy them directly from freeze-frames. You might see this as a cheat. It's not. The VCR is a great tool. Disney would have loved to have one; he used film of live animals and people to study movement. That's why *Snow White* was such a captivating phenomenon. It was the first time anybody had used (or seen) movement realism in an animation. You can achieve stunning realism by placing a key every third or fourth frame and matching it exactly to every third or fourth frame of the video. I actually have a five-inch TV monitor set up next to my computer monitor with a Hi-8 tape deck for recording animations and for checking movement. The Hi-8 gives crystal clear freeze-frames for reference.

Have you seen the Chevron commercials with talking cars? The front grills serve as mouths and they speak as if they are people. You may not think of this as realism, but it is. The facial movements are carefully choreographed to move *realistically* the way people do. Separate your concept of photorealism from movement realism. The result of giving the cars human moves results in tremendous instant empathy. I love the little critters; they definitely remind you of someone you know. The voice is part of the process, but the realistic face movement and close synchronism is key. Now think about the dancing Shell gasoline pumps.

Motion Capture

These pumps were not keyframe-animated in the usual way. The very human movements were captured on professional equipment using real people. This equipment hooks up dancers with motion sensor devices, or little reflective disks, or whatever, and records the exact movements of these disks 30 times a second or so. Then it attaches that movement to corresponding points on models. In this way you can apply human movement to dolls, gas pumps, or robots — anything with corresponding points of reference. Clearly, the pumps show that you can force points into almost any object. Christopher Landreth's *the end* shows excellent use of motion capture applied to both realistic and surrealistic humans.

Unfortunately you can't do it in trueSpace2. It's not a big loss at this point because cost is prohibitive for most. I wanted you to know about it because it's most likely in your future. When you start your own little studio and have some cash flow you may want to invest in motion capture equipment. There's a load of it coming into the marketplace as I write. I trust good old American initiative and competition to come up with an affordable solution sometime in 1997.

Cartoon Movement

Realistic movement may not be what you want. Stylized movement is often preferable. It's the difference between a photograph and a painting. Cartoon characters have never moved very much like real people. They are usually exaggerated. Think of Popeye's rolling gait, the swinging of those bulging arms. It's real for Popeye. Often cartoonists will obscure movement in a cloud of dust, just implying it. It's all part of the game.

You can create your own stylized movements in tS2. Take a look at the i-way.avi. Just for fun, my fellow animator, I-Wei Huang, designed this robot. I put in a limp in the opening that shows the Ibot being animated on my computer. The runners on the track are animated with a stylized robotic strut. It wouldn't work from a physics standpoint because they would have to shift their center of balance to keep from toppling over. But who cares, this is cartoon animation. It looks great.

These principles also apply to scene choreography in airplane paths to bubbles rising in a pond. As the creator, you decide what will be realistic and what will be stylized. It's possible to mix the two in the same piece, but it's best to stick to one style or the other until you're ready.

Mise-en-Scène

Putting movement into an animated scene is a grand part of the art. Picture the way those X-Wing fighters moved in *Star Wars* — cool. As director, you need to know a little bit about staging.

Staging

Staging is really two things: how you want the actors to move in front of the camera and how the camera itself will move. In this section I'm concentrating on the former. How things move in your piece can really point out where you are in the professional pantheon. Moves have to be appropriate to the actors, serve the story, and be kind to the camera. If you can add your own style on top of that, you'll look pretty good.

There are many conventions in staging, and we'll look at a few. If you can throw a few well-conceived moves into your demo tape, it's not going to hurt your chances.

Rigging camera and stage is a lot different in digital. You really have control and can't blame things on conditions or other people letting you down. You've already designed the production, including the stage. You've laid out your master shot and the main angles within the sequence. Now you have to get the moves.

Blocking Your Action

Arranging and choreographing movement within the production stage prepared by your production designer/art director is called blocking. Camera movement is part of this process as well. In digital animation, the director usually blocks the stage moves, then the camera moves to cover them. Here are a few things you as director have to consider.

- ✦ **Story.** What part of the story does this scene have to convey to the viewer.
- ✦ **Spirit of the scene.** What sense of emotion or feeling should the action give the viewer.
- ✦ **Aesthetics.** There are countless ways to block a scene. How can you achieve your goals and still give the viewer an aesthetic experience.
- ✦ **Scale of the scene.** How big is it and how does movement fit into it. In the current example, the space is very large and the movement is very small — a potential problem.
- ✦ **Your personal style.** How are you going to put your signature on this piece. Many great directors (think of Hitchcock, Sayles) have a distinctive style that you know the minute you see their films. You may not want to put your signature on a piece. It needs to be a sentient choice.
- ✦ **Balance of natural vs. dramatic choreography.** Often shooting in a dramatic style leaves the viewer with a sense of having seen a naturalistic scene. Especially in space, naturalistic movement is not practical. Think about the speed at which Voyager approaches and orbits planets or stars streak by to give a sense of faster-than-light movement. It all defies physics in a most entertaining way.

These and other considerations plague the director's choices. It's a lonely job, but somebody has to do it.

Analyzing the Script

Begin by analyzing the script. I've given an example of how I write a script for myself in the sidebar. If you write for a producer, you may have to adapt your style or format to the one he prefers. I come from a screenwriting background, so I've kept the style I'm used to. Producers also tend to like fewer words. I prefer to leave myself with a vivid picture instead of counting words.

When you get the script, break it down into sequences and scenes. Then make a list of your objects and what the writer had in mind for them. You can do this mentally in most cases, but keep the big picture in mind. Remember this sentence (as an example): "The purpose of this sequence is to introduce the space station as an island of warmth and humanity in the vast, frigid beauty of space." It'll help.

Make notes (even mental notes) about what kind of action will best serve the story. Each motivated object has to contribute something to the story line. Even the little chase lights have a purpose. As you block out your moves, keep their purpose uppermost in your mind, and that includes aesthetics and emotions you want to achieve.

Having problems visualizing realistic space movement based on your observation of life? Get creative. You've never seen a real shuttle craft whooshing through the void. Perhaps on *Babylon 5*, or *Deep Space 9*. They're good places to get ideas, but plan on improving on what you see. Be a little cocky and say (deep in your head), "That's nice, but I can do way better." You can. Those guys have to put out a lot of animation in a short time. You have the luxury of time to plan and go through trial and error.

Make a list of backgrounds the script inspires in you. A good writer paints vivid pictures to kick-start the brain. To make mental pictures, your mind becomes the camera.

Block out your camera moves at the same time. Look for the moves and cuts that will tell the story. In the script I have a POV shot from inside the shuttle craft, and then I cut to an exterior shot to show it aligned and rotating with the station. This shot was originally designed by the great Stanley Kubrick way back in *2001: A Space Odyssey*, one of the greatest space flicks of all time. Stanley broke a lot of ground with that picture. Watch it again and you'll see what I mean.

The purpose of the cut is to show the dance, imbue the moment with celestial majesty, and hammer home the action. With your lists in hand, you're ready to start adding a lot of arrows to your storyboards, depicting movement.

The Script

Everything starts with the script. A good one is a blueprint and a bad one is a blue nightmare. Here is my script snippet.

BEGIN FX SEQUENCE

EXT. OUTER SPACE — NEAR GREAT NEBULA IN ORION

Bright gaseous blur of Orion against the starry cosmos. At first, only the awesome, cold beauty of deep space but then...

CAMERA ZOOMS IN TO REVEAL

a dark speck against the glow that increases rapidly in size as it approaches in lower left quadrant... we see it's a small SHUTTLE CRAFT, big engines, short wide wings, coming like a bat out of hell.

MOVING: CAMERA tracks perpendicular to the CRAFT's path, on a near collision course. As the craft flashes past CAMERA it's lost for a moment as the camera makes a short arc to reacquire and continue pursuit from behind.

CRAFT pulls swiftly away as TRILON STATION comes into view, top right. It's a tiny bright doughnut against a backdrop of black space.

CUT TO:

INT. SHUTTLE CRAFT — PILOT'S POV

We see rapidly approaching TRILON STATION through long narrow space shield. The station is ROTATING.

Beneath the view we see the MAIN CONTROL PANEL with blinking lights and strange devices. We can see the station is a huge torus with a central tower suspended by four massive connecting arms. The top of the tower is a glass dome — the control center. Other small craft flit by.

Soaring above the Station's cheery sun (star) lit topside, we swoop rapidly past a sharp terminator to the dark underside of the station.

CUT TO:

EXT. TRILON STATION — DARK SIDE — LANDING BAY

Built into the bottom of the central core is a BRIGHTLY LIGHTED, wide landing bay. Nearby a TANKER offloads cargo via floating umbilical. We see the CRAFT fly past, make a tight 360° turn, and begin to align itself with the docking bay.

CUT TO:

INT. SHUTTLE CRAFT — POV PILOT

(continued)

Ahead against stationary stars, TRILON rotates smoothly with its docking bay aglow with warm light. Offside warning lights flash on either side. As we approach the bay, the stars begin to rotate as the bay slows. The CRAFT is spin matching for landing. The landing bay comes to a stop, with its floor in the right place. It looks solid and approachable now.

CUT TO:

EXT. TRILON STATION – ANGLE ON SHUTTLE CRAFT APPROACHING BAY

Against STEADY stars we see the CRAFT approaching the bay, in exact synchrony with the Station's rotation. It disappears into the bay.

CUT TO:

INT. LANDING BAY – ANGLE OUT BAY OPENING AT INCOMING SHUTTLE

Against a backdrop of *rotating* stars, all is quiet as the CRAFT follows chase lights into main bay. Once inside, the chase lights stop flashing and a new set of lights guides CRAFT to screen left. Craft stops, rotates its heading to screen left, and begins to move.

CAMERA PANS LEFT TO REVEAL

Giant airlock DOORS opening vertically. Each has a projection near center, with a matching indent on its opposite, to ensure alignment on closing. Beyond the door we see...

SHUTTLE REPAIR BAY with a landing platform and four sets of articulated arms to grip and hold the CRAFT. The arms begin to MOVE.

CUT TO:

INT. REAR SHUTTLE REPAIR BAY – ANGLE ON DOCKING CRAFT

Craft carefully settles into landing cradle as the airlock DOORS close in b.g. The articulated arms move quickly – no two the same – as if each has a mind of its own.They move quickly into position, then slowly descend as their rubber-footed paws approach and clamp the CRAFT to the cradle.

END FX SEQUENCE

CUT TO:

INT. TRILON STATION – CONTROL TOWER – ANGLE ON COMPUTER SCREEN

A red warning message flashes ominously as... and so on.

As you read through this script, you get a feel for the writer's vision. Clearly several blocking ideas were being considered. There is no substitute for an excellent script, even if you have to write it yourself.

After you've thought about it a tad, make notes in the margins, adding your vision to the writer's. Try it now. As you read the script, make your lists and notes, right in the book. Staging and blocking the action is now well in hand. We'll cover camera angles next chapter, but it can't hurt to jot down your ideas now; it's all part of the same process. Film is a collaborative medium, even if you play all the parts.

The Dance

Dance has universal appeal, it's found in every culture. If Shell gas pumps can dance, then so can your spaceships. I try to have a little dance in almost every scene. A lot of animators don't do this and I feel they're missing the boat. If you see a bunch of spaceships enter one side of the screen and leave the other, all remaining in perfect alignment, big whoop. Now picture the same scene with the ships in a dance — a mad *Blue Angels* boogie, rolling and weaving against each other. Perhaps it's not logical, but it sure is aesthetic. It leaves you with the impression of hotdog pilots ready for action.

It doesn't matter if you're animating grasshoppers or beer bottles, you can find a way to put in a dance. It helps to give each object a personality in your own mind.

What is a dance? I can tell you my version of the story. I see the dance as a kind of movement codependency. Two or more objects moving in a way that works together while revealing personality (watch the articulated arms in the shuttle bay). The rest comes from your artistic sense, your eye, and your objects. Sure you can have a single dancing credit card, but that's local action and less interesting. Object dances can have structure — a beginning, a middle, and an end. Picture a field of race cars, look at all the drama that comes from that dance. The last car suddenly finds a few horses and moves ahead of the pack, just like a horse race.

Dance almost always has dramatic symbolism. It gives clues to relationships. Watch people (say ice skaters) dancing together; you can tell how they feel about each other.

The good guy/bad guy dance can be very interesting. Show it. What's the symbolism in the spin match dance as StarFire approaches Trilon? To me it's the joining: leaving cold/lonely stars for the warm acceptance of home. It's almost sexual.

How far can you push the dance in the face of realism? You can push it much further than you think. The audience isn't married to realism (oh, those eight guys are, but you wouldn't hang around with them). So take a risk, go for it, enliven the action.

Here's an exercise to try. Two sharks are swimming along side by side, one has the personality of a bulldog in heat, the other is shy but interested. Choreograph that scene for 130 frames. Have a ball.

All this stuff is done with sensitivity and artistry by the professional and usually ignored by the amateur. Some professionals ignore it and you can tell, but don't blame them too harshly; it's the damn tight schedules. It can even happen to you.

What's Next?

As a cinematographer you'll be concerned about two kinds of movement: movement within the scene and camera moves. In Chapters 23 and 24 we'll look at specific steps in creating that movement. In Chapter 25 we'll look closely at the camera. Herein we study movement and lay out the dance.

Now on to nuts and bolts of local motion, beginning with natural organic movements in Chapter 23.

Summary

This is another critical chapter. Movement is the whole idea behind animation. It gives life and personality to your actors. Even if you're a dull boring person yourself, your characters can have a life. Here's a minimum of what you should have firmly in grasp before moving on:

- ✦ Train your eye to notice the details of motion — take notes.
- ✦ Record motions on paper using your own nomenclature.
- ✦ Movement generally has a rhythm to it — learn to notice and record it.
- ✦ Learn the differences between local movement and scene action and how to deal with each.
- ✦ You get to look up mise-en-scène in the dictionary and wonder why I used the phrase when I could have used something more mundane.
- ✦ Learn all about staging and blocking scenes. Learn what blocking is and how to do it.
- ✦ Script analysis is critical to the meshing of visions — yours and the writer's. Learn how to break down the script and put it back together again, with margin notes.
- ✦ Learn all about dance and its symbolism and how to apply it in your footage.

✦ ✦ ✦

CHAPTER 23

Organic Motion

In This Chapter

Laying out movement with both local and scene blocking

Keyframing organic movement using deformation objects

Keyframing organic movement using Surface Sculpt (undocumented)

Transferring organic movement from one object to another

Until recently the most difficult motion to create digitally was smooth, lifelike, organic motion, like that of a jellyfish or even the ocean. With the new deformation and sculpting tools it's even fun.

Aquatic Moves

Movement underwater is particularly interesting because object moves are controlled both from internal motivation and by the flow of water. Fish fins don't remain straight, but flex against the fluid, much as a dragon's wings pouch with air on each mighty downstroke.

Fish

I suppose we could switch to a goldfish here, but we already have some experience in deforming the shark. Now we want to choreograph the deformations into a smoother set of movements that look like a shark in motion (see Figure 23-1). To begin, I sat like a damn fool ogling a friend's aquarium for hours. He had a little black and red shark about two inches long, but I figured it was close enough. Its action is hard to catch because the little guy moves (relatively) faster than a full-sized man-eater. I managed to get a very simple set of drawings that reasonably show the movement. I could have videotaped it, but I didn't. Anyway, I simplified my drawings down to keyframes as follows.

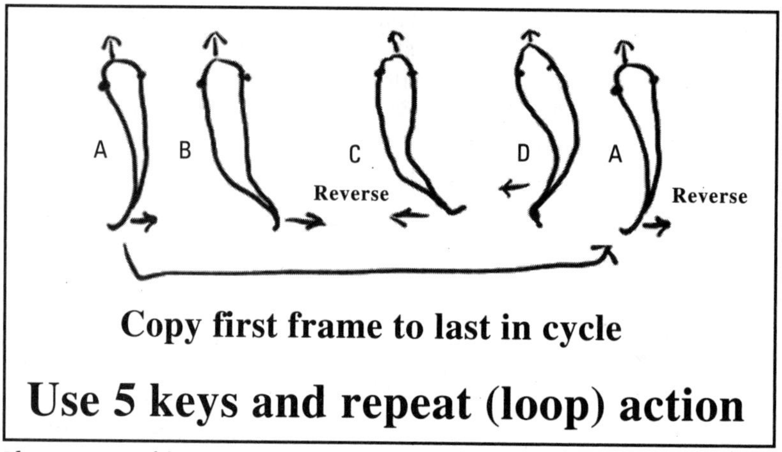

Figure 23-1: This motion study of a shark can be used as a keyframe reference for the shark model.

I boiled the motion down to five keyframes, four unique ones and one that I repeat. I want super-smooth action. Notice that the tip of the tail gives an indication of which direction the tail is going. The thin membrane there pitches back as heavy water is forced off the back of the tail during the power stroke. In a left stroke, the membrane stretches right, and vice versa. I also noticed that the fish tends to go into an arch. That is, as the tail bends around to the right, so does the head, almost as a counterbalance move. It may not look right when the fish is static, but when you block its moves across the stage, it looks very real.

Blocking a Fish

You have to pay close attention to the way a shark moves. Even with the little guy I noticed he had a tendency to move slowly and deliberately, exploring his environment all the time. I watched some Cousteau footage of sharks. When they're relaxed, they move beautifully through the water. Timing is very important here. You don't want your shark moving too quickly through the scene. You'll also want to put in some head movements to indicate curiosity — looking around.

If you have a videotape of sharks, you can load it into your editor and count frames between key positions of the tail (literally) for the local motion, and distance traveled between those keys can be estimated. If you don't have one, visit the nearest public aquarium and tape the sharks from the underwater window.

While trying to gauge distance traveled per stroke, I noticed the shark had gross tail movements and then little fluttery control movements of the tail tips. I decided not to animate these. If I need more realism, I can add them later.

For scene movement I estimate the shark moves steadily at about six inches per second. Whether on a power stroke or just gliding, the speed doesn't seem to vary much. I suspect, when relaxed, the shark puts little power into each stroke, conserving energy for emergencies. Very efficient, no wasted motion.

I need a good camera angle and path. At first I thought I'd have him swim in from out of the depths toward the camera, but I tried it and didn't like it. So now I'm going to look at entry on the lower right with movement toward upper left quadrant of the screen.

First I'll keyframe the local movement with separate keys for head and tail. I'll probably put in some twisting movement as well as back and forth, then I'll key in a path. The shark will have several sets of keys working at the same time. His head, his tail, maybe some fins and his path. This is sophisticated animation and will look it.

Body Choreography

Load up the scene file shark.scn. It contains a seabed and a shark model. Make your main window a Top Down View. Engage the Deform Object tool and select the *Deform along plane perpendicular to Z axis* option at the right of the Options panel. Before you start to deform, here are a few things to bear in mind.

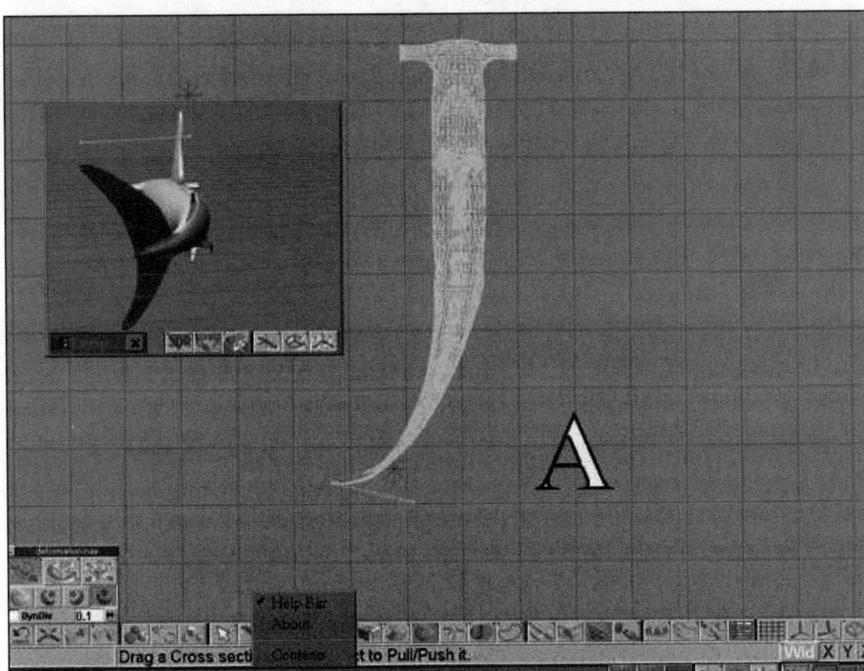

Figure 23-2A: You can keyframe the shark's tail with five keys, A, B, C, D, and A (again), and loop them to achieve continuous movement.

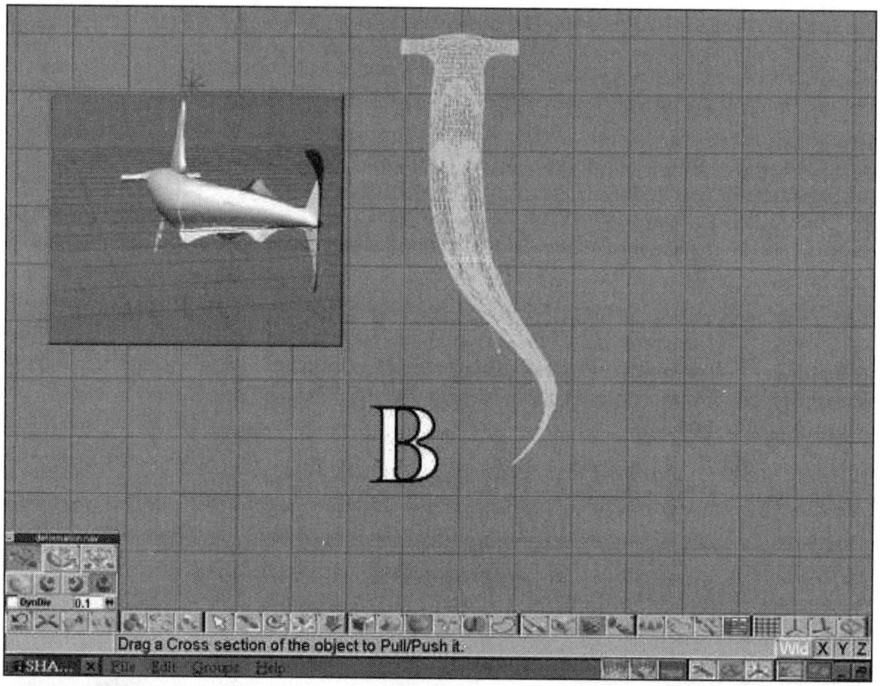

Figure 23-2B

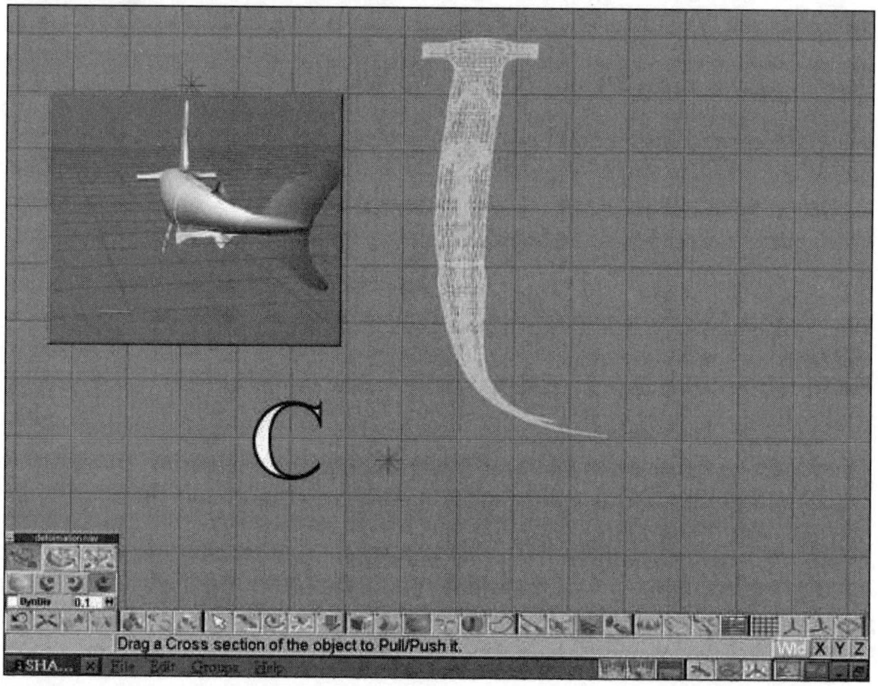

Figure 23-2C

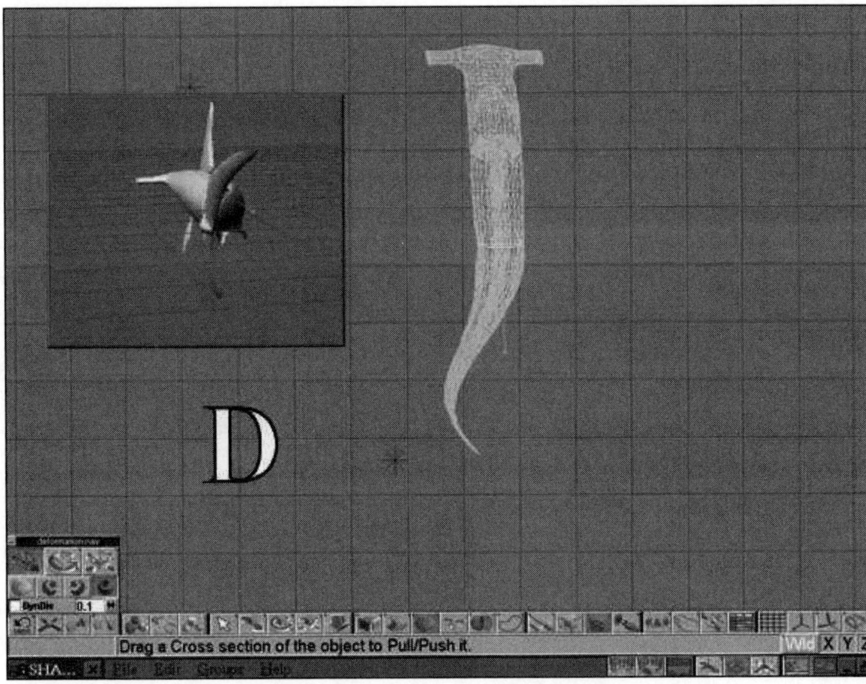

Figure 23-2D

- ✦ You can easily pull the shark out of shape, so move slowly and carefully. Keep an eye on its hammer head. Make sure the hammer maintains about the same width as you move the head.
- ✦ Open a Side View window to make sure you don't arch him up or down too much or have him swimming through the sand.
- ✦ The default partition setting is good, just one in the center of the shark. This is good. It will give you smooth organic movement along the Z axis for either the forward or aft half of the model. You can adjust the middle of the curve by clicking the center partition.
- ✦ You'll use the Push/Pull tool in the Deformation Navigation panel.
- ✦ When you click on the aft end, you'll get a green line with yellow dots on either end. The dot at the tip of the tail determines actual location of the tail tip by clicking and dragging. The other yellow dot determines the curve of the body from the tip of the tail to the center. Use this to simulate the flex-against-water look.

Remember that you get the smoothest paths with the least number of keyframes. I've experimented as you will in future projects. It turns out you get very clean tail sweep with only four keyframes, two at each extreme of the sweep. They control the little curve at the tip of the tail that indicates what direction it's going and gives the look of how the water must feel. If you look at this tail moving and *don't* feel the fluid density of the water around it, you've got something wrong. Look at Figure 23-1 again and also look at Figure 23-2.

First thing you do is lift the shark off the bottom. If you don't do it now, then decide to on frame 27, it'll give you no end of hell. You'll get a shark bouncing up and down through the sand.

With these things in mind, begin at the tail. Drag the tip of the tail to the right to approximate the position that's shown in drawing A. Then adjust the tail curve to match by grabbing, and drag on the opposite yellow dot. When it looks about right, you notice that the center looks almost hinged. You need to give it a little roundness. Do it by clicking on the center green partition and manipulating the handles ever so gently. Now move to the head. We won't move the head, just rotate it side to side to counterbalance the swinging of the tail.

Click on the Twist tool in the Deform Nav panel, and click on the tip of his snout. Holding down the *right* key, rotate the head until the curve from tail to head looks smooth. Good, this is our first and last position. Using the same positions for frames 0 and 90, we will create a smoothly loopable action. This is good for repeats like a fish tail. Sure it's never exactly the same on a real fish — no problem — just key two slightly different sequences, both ending on a duplicate of frame 0. The Repeat Action will not be noticed by your viewers.

Let's look at Figure 23-2. To make the sharks swish into position B, the animation takes about 30 frames, or approximately one second. The tip of the tail still bends in the same direction, because the tail has been moving in just one direction. Check the mid-section and set a keyframe to 30. You'll need to take 10 frames to reverse the tail.

Reposition the shark as shown in position C, advance, and set a keyframe to 40. This action reverses the direction of the tail's tip, creating the illusion that the tip is pushing against the water as it swishes back into position D.

Advance to frame 70, adjust the shark as shown in position D, and set a key. Now all you have to do is get the tail back to the exact position as it appeared in frame 1 in order to create a perfect loop. As you play the clip over and over again from beginning to end, it looks continuous because the first and last frames are the same.

Using the Animation Tool rewind option, go back to frame 0. Right-click to display the Keyframe Monitor. Click the Copy Keyframe button (upper right). It turns blue. Next type `90` in the Monitors input field and press Enter. This action copies the keys from frame 0 to frame 90. Right-click the play button, set the Loop option, and play. The shark's tail should swish back and forth smoothly. You can use a similar approach by setting loops to animate the shark's smaller fins and head.

Why didn't I use 80, making it 30 frames each direction? I like the way it looks when one stroke is faster than the other — a power stroke followed by a relaxed one. That's just me; you do whatever looks best to you.

I painted the bottom with fractal.bmp with no repeats and did the shark with two repeats using cylindrical mapping coordinates. Don't forget to put in some blue/green fog for water and add a few shadow-casting spots above. If you want you can have them move like light through clouds. Try using a moving cookie for shadow effects.

Save this scene. Later on when you understand the particle engine from Rob Bryerton, you may want to add bubbles (inverse gravity). Try building some fern-like leaves in 2D, loft them into 3D. Make them very thin and deform them to look like seaweed. Bury some rusted-out nernies in the sand. Build a treasure chest (to be trite) or a shipwreck. I like the idea of putting the Statue of Liberty down there for grins.

Deformation Objects

Remember the ball going through the egg timer trick? It used a deformation cylinder, cinched at the middle. There are also cube and planar deformation objects. The advantage of using deformation objects is that you can save them and apply them to other objects. You can also use copies of the deformation object at the same time to create a dance of objects, all moving in synchrony. You can even adjust each one's timeline so they don't look so perfectly together.

Fish Need an Ocean

We can use a planar deformation object to create an ocean surface effect. We'll keyframe it to move like a wave, apply it to a well-divided planar object, and with a little texture and bump mapping (animated?) we can have an ocean. You figure out the foam, I'll provide the sand (whitesnd.bmp).

POWER TIP

The most common problems with deformation objects are caused by inadequate subdividing of the object to be manipulated. I usually make it poly dense and triangulate to avoid nonplanar polygons.

The Ocean's Surface

Begin by popping up a planar deformation object (upper right in the Primitives panel). Scale it up to a little larger than the grid in Perspective View. This will not be our ocean; it will be the motive force behind it.

Invoke the freeform Deformation tool and begin by clicking in the center of the planar matrix. You'll get a set of four handles connected in the center. Pull the center down (Z axis, thus right-click) to form a depression in the matrix. Now jump to frame 100 and pull the same spot up into a hill. Extend the side handles to change the scope of your work. Pull up sections to the right and left of the center one as in Figure 23-3.

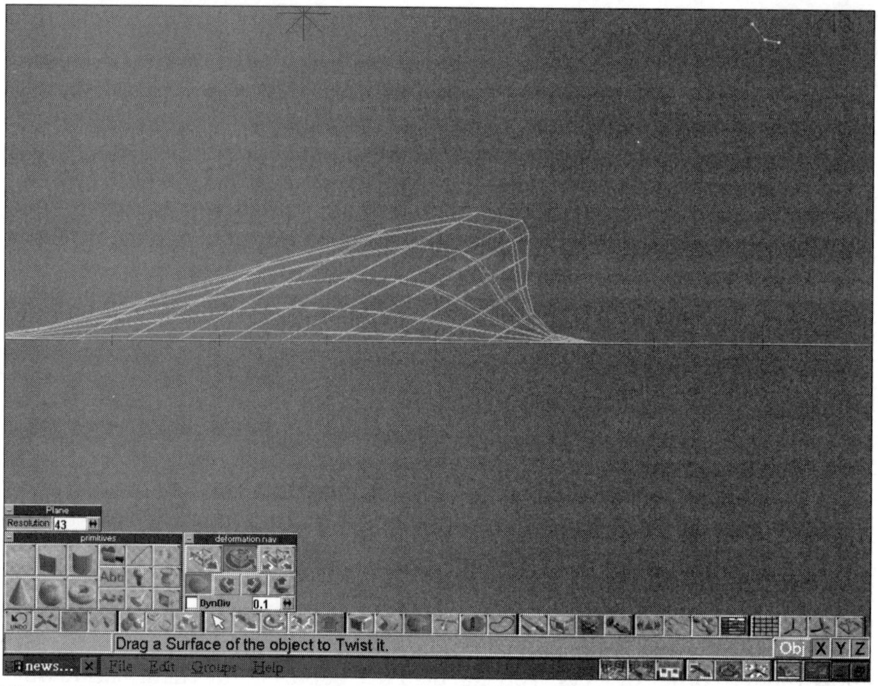

Figure 23-3: Form an ocean Deformation Object by lifting the planar deformation matrix into a crest.

Grab the handle pointing forward-right. Bend it down 90°. Grab the handle pointing backward-left and bend it up 90°. You'll see that it's forming the crest of a wave.

Jump ahead to frame 140. Pull the crest forward and down to simulate a wave collapsing. Run through the frames and check the motion. It should start at the depression, lift into a mighty wave, and crash forward. It doesn't have to go all the way forward because you are going to put a beach there. For this exercise, I'm setting a planar plate covered with sand, at a beach angle. I expand it to reach well under the sea and position it so the top stretches out in perspective (see Figure 23-4).

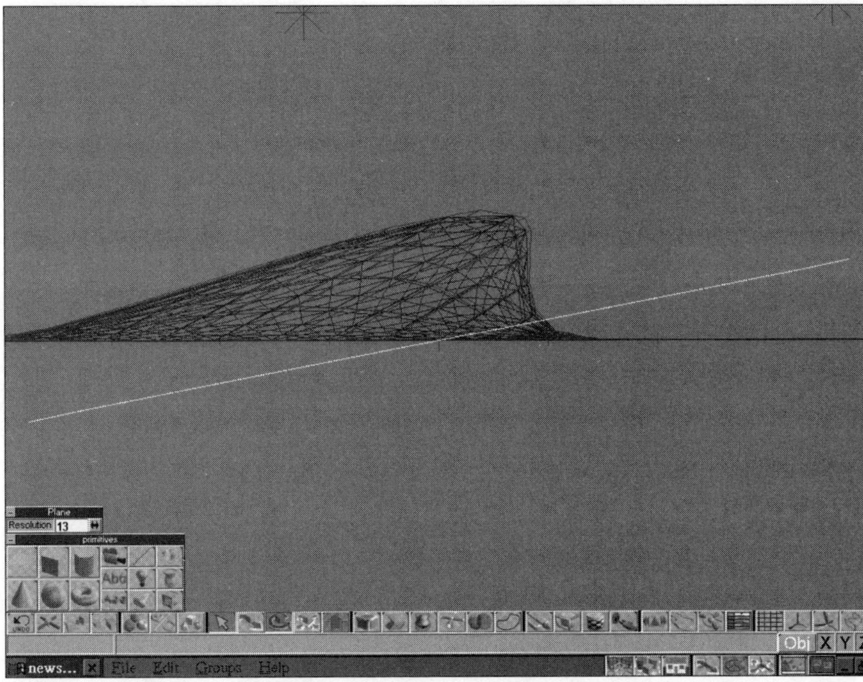

Figure 23-4: Here is the ocean with beach plate installed. All it needs is a visible surface, a background, and a little sand and surf texture.

Adding the Surface to be Deformed

Before you pop up a planar object for the ocean's surface, right click on its icon and set its resolution to at least 50. When it pops up it will be complex, with 2,500 polygons. Expand it more or less to match the matrix. Lift it above the matrix and click on the *Start deformation by freestanding object* icon. Now select the matrix. This bonds the two items in a deformation dance. Lower the plate slowly, pausing as you reach the matrix. In a second, the plate will conform to the matrix shape. Continue lowering until the plate is nicely draped over the matrix. Good.

You need a sea surface. From the Simple Materials Library, select the pool water texture. Reduce Transparency to about 10% and paint it on the ocean surface. Choose a nice sunset background if you like, match the scene lighting to the color of the sunset to cast a nice light on the sand and glint off the water. Set Global Environment to the same. You should get the sky reflected in the water. Play with the reflection and shininess parameters until it looks right. Look at Figure 23-5 and the video file Ocean.avi for reference. This is quick and dirty. With a little effort you can do much better.

Figure 23-5: Sunset Beach. This is quick and dirty. Now I know why a lot of book illustrations look cheesy — it's the time factor. I expect you to do way better. Go for it and put in a palm tree; if you can't find one, make one.

Surface Sculpting Organic Motion

Although it doesn't work perfectly all the time, which is probably why it's not documented, Surface Sculpt can be animated. In fact, you can make some dynamite sequences with it. You can have a face take shape from a sphere or have a water pod monster like in *Abyss* rise up out of the sea. In fact, I animated the start of a creature coming out of the sea using Surface Sculpt. You can find it on the CD-ROM as at \movies\dreamscp\seamons.avi. I don't know all the tricks of getting it right all the time. Sometimes your last frame will suddenly twist up and become frame 0. Other times the animation disappears altogether. You can't save a Surface Sculpt animation either, at least, I don't know how, but use it — you can. A tool is a tool even if it's not labeled and has a few loose wires.

The Water Pod Creature

In 1989, most people were more fascinated by the pod monster in James Cameron's *Abyss* than by the story. It was a first of sorts and helped rejuvenate the digital effects industry. The basic idea is a lump of seawater rises up and takes shape as a clear rippling water worm. It can change shape and even take on the shape of someone looking into it. To do all this would take a lot of time and the folks at ILM got paid a lot of money to do it. I'll get you started and you can do whatever you want with it.

I did the ocean and the pod as two separate objects, though this isn't necessary. In the animation I gave the textures different scales so you can see the planar object from which the monster arises. In Figure 23-6 I have a small square on top of a big one. The small one was made by first resetting the planar resolution to 25, so we have 25 divisions per side.

Figure 23-6: The start of a water pod monster. The Surface Sculpt tool is located in the center of the well-divided planar object, ready to be lifted straight up.

Remember, an object must have plenty of polygons for successful deformation. Use the Dynamic Divide option on the Surface Sculpt tool. It will add polygons to keep the surface together for proper rendering. It also keeps the deformations smooth, like water would likely be. Note that I've planted the Sculpt tool smack in the middle of the little square. This is where the pod monster will rise. Here's the process.

1. Open the Animation tool and advance to frame 20.
2. Lift the sculpt tool straight up and you'll see the surface stretch up and subdivide as in Figure 23-7.
3. Advance to frame 40 and lift straight up about twice as far as your first move. This time, grab the center of one of the handles and make it longer. This increases the tool's area of influence. Repeat for the other set of handles, making the top of the deformation wider and rounder.
4. Advance to frame 80, lift a little bit more, and pull the handles out farther to get the rounded pseudopod look as in Figure 23-8.
5. Advance to frame 120 and shape the pod further.

6. Paint the pod with a water texture and the ocean with the same texture, but scaled up because of the larger surface.
7. Render your animation. (See Plate 23-1.)
8. Play with it. You can do strange things, like making a set of pod-shaped extensions that you attach and articulate much as you would an articulated arm. Use Surface Sculpt to put a face on the monster. Have fun doing what you're not supposed to do. If it blows, start over again.

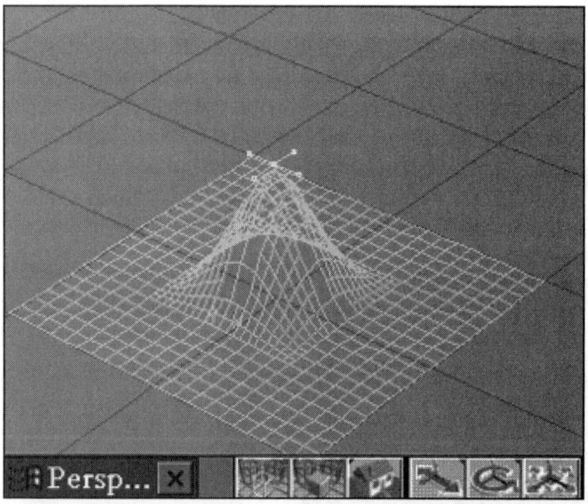

Figure 23-7: Lifting the Surface Sculpt tool straight up starts the form. Keyframe this at 20.

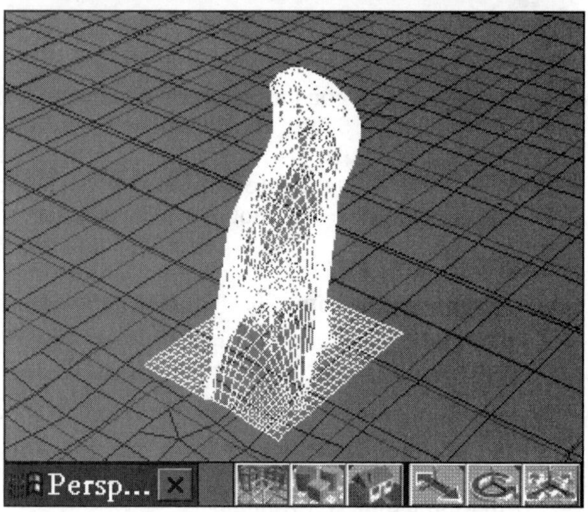

Figure 23-8: The monster takes shape as you extend the control arms to increase the tool's area of influence.

You may think that this work in tS2 is a little low-class because of the price. Don't. I've worked with many of the really expensive packages and I have to say I'm even more impressed with tS2's interface. Organic shapes are in one sense easier in packages like Soft Image, but only after you learn the system, which could take you months. High-end packages often require many mouse clicks and menus to do what comes with the flick of a wrist in tS2. Right now you're doing things that would be considered pretty advanced on most of the high-end suites.

In Chapter 24 you'll learn how to apply some of these techniques to create interesting characters.

Summary

Organic movement is a lot of fun to create. There is a growing market for these skills. Learn how things move and learn to recreate those movements with what you've learned in this chapter. That includes:

- ✦ Observing motion by watching an aquarium fish and applying its movements to a shark.
- ✦ How to work the control handles on the Object Deformation tool to create a natural movement of the shark's tail.
- ✦ How to make an ocean for your shark to swim in.
- ✦ Learning about freestanding deformation objects and how to use them to deform standard objects.
- ✦ That deformation objects can be saved with their paths and later applied to other objects.
- ✦ How to use the Surface Sculpt tool to create neat animations even if it's not always reliable.

✦ ✦ ✦

CHAPTER 24

Character Animation

✦ ✦ ✦ ✦

In This Chapter

Style and personality are more important than beauty or technique

How to create a personality for your character

How to make this personality consistent over a wide range of attitudes and behaviors

How to breathe life and personality into Mr. Talking Head

Ways to give inanimate objects personality

Where to look for the wisdom of your forebears in character animation

✦ ✦ ✦ ✦

We've had a lot of fun animating things with technolgy. This chapter is more about appealing to your audience through creating human-like characters. Character design is more than just making a clay or 3D model of a neat looking critter. The more human your character is, especially with human weakness, the more easily your audience can relate. A toy block with a face needs a sizable dose of humanity to give it charm. This chapter will show you how to imbue your characters with larger-than-life humanism.

It's in the Eyes

"It's in the eyes," Walt said. "People don't watch the mouth so much as the eyes when you get close up." Look at Disney characters; from the very beginning they've had overly large expressive eyes. The eyes — a good place to start designing your first character. Sketch out some eyes, as shown in Figure 24-1.

Circle the eyes that appeal to you. This is your base sheet, perhaps a character's birthplace. Now figure out what causes eyes to charm. Go further, find out everything about an animated character that charms you. Check out 2D characters first. This world is flush with good characters to study. The tradition of humanizing characters has carried over into the realm of 2D digital animation. 3D is getting there with characters such as the Techron talking car in Chevron ads (an exercise in 3D animated charm), Casper, and the toy people of *Toy Story*. I loved Dino.

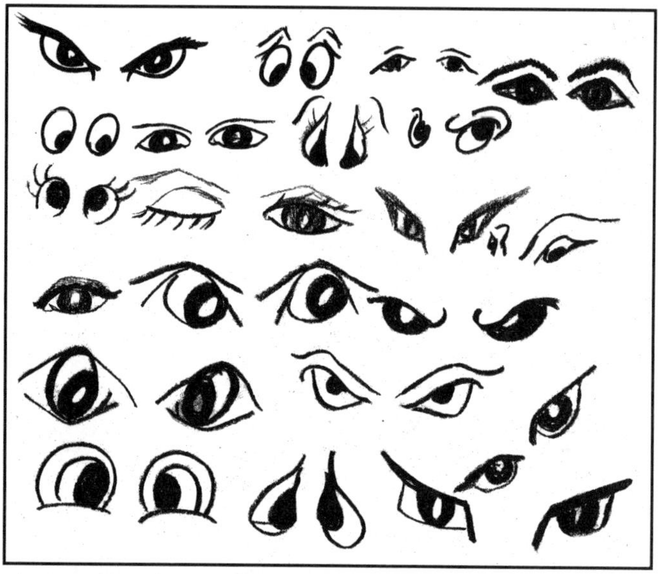

Figure 24-1: Playing with character eyes

Develop Your Eye

Walt Disney was never much of an artist. He wasn't even a great animator. Worse, he didn't have a lot of interest in, or talent for, business. Fortunately his brother/partner Roy did. Put your shotguns away. I love Walter's work; he had great talent, just not in those areas. His associate, Ib Iwerks, had animation talents in spades. The two men were as different as Scrooge McDuck and Thumper. Ib was an intense, driven animator and Walt was a story man, a romantic, a dramatic visionary, and he had a knack for character. Both could be hard-skulled, which was good since they spent a lot of time knocking heads. Walt came up with the stories and characters and Ib brought them to life. Walt was a natural born pitchman. He'd sell story ideas to his staff by acting out all the parts and voices like a madman. For *Snow White* his performance went on for nearly two hours... and they were sold.

You may not realize it, but Mickey's image came primarily from Ib Iwerks, while his voice and personality came from Walt. Neither man could have done it alone. Ib left Disney after eight years and tried opening his own studio, but he lacked Walt's ability to create interesting characters and story. After a few years he returned to Disney. My point is, as before, if your passion for animation outweighs your talent, form a synergistic relationship with someone who has what you lack. Find a way to share the credit. Most people who know feel Walt and Ib broke up over Walt getting all the credit for Mickey. Don't let that happen to you.

How to Become a Character Designer

Even if you don't think you can design characters, you probably can. Many of us labor under a rigid self-view that isn't even close to accurate. We can each do far more than we realize, we just need to awaken that part of ourselves.

Talent Needs Exercise

Make a list of all the animated characters you've been most struck by. Mix in a wide range of types. My list now has dozens — from Thumper through Snow White and Homer Simpson to Buzz Lightyear and Casper. They all have different kinds of charm, defined mostly by three things — their eyes, their mannerisms, and the way they talk. These attributes work together to create character. But you can't just haphazardly throw things together and expect to have a good character. You need a pattern.

When you have a decent cadre of favorite characters, watch them one at a time and make notes and drawings of what about them charms you. Is it their moves, their expressions, their words... what? You *don't* want to get this information from a book. You won't find answers here, either. There's no substitute for honing your deeper intuitions about character by putting in the time. As you study, you'll find patterns of key behaviors that connect in characters that charm you. Write them down.

Look for human expressions, as emphasized in *The Simpsons*. You can avoid being a copycat animator by developing your own understanding of personality. How? Easy. Learning about personality and style fuels your mental character-generation equipment. When you have enough in there, it's impossible to be comfortable just copying someone else's character. That's what impoverished equipment does. A well-fueled mind insists on creating something unique.

If you hate making lists, find another way to get this information into your head, but don't skimp on understanding the nature of the entertaining and empathetic character.

I'm not kidding, it's part of the subconscious imperative, "I can do it better." If you go through all the trouble to really comprehend character from a broad base of successful cartoon personalities, and you *still* find yourself unable to come up with an original character, e-mail me and I'll recommend something. But first, take a course in self-affirmation. It's easier to create characters if you're in touch with your own, though there are exceptions.

Get yourself a mirror and attach it with a clamp to your monitor, so you can set it up to see your own face as you work, making faces and copying expressions into your deformations.

The Eyes

Picture a basset hound. No matter how happy he might be, he looks sad, almost pathetic. Why? What about those eyes gives that impression. Look in your mirror and think sad. Act it out. How do your eyes look? Notice your forehead muscles.

Go happy. Smile and look at what goes on around your eyes and mouth... see how they're connected. Your eyeballs don't change much, but the creases around them do. Make some notes: what *exactly* happens to the lines around your eyes. No way I'd give you that information; it's your face, not mine. After doing some exercises, go back and doodle more cartoon eyes. Learn anything?

Mannerisms

A mannerism is a behavior that characterizes your character. A bit of a cyclical definition if you ask me. Try definition by association — think: affectation, quirk, pretension, physical idiosyncrasy. We identify fellow humans by their behavioral quirk patterns. Think about it. We mentally catalogue people by behavior. We ignore the common everyday behaviors and latch onto the unusual. Imbue your character with a small but rich set of unique mannerisms. Think of the Seven Dwarfs, each has a set of personality characteristics attached to his name. Dopey — with droopy eyes and a silly walk — is dopey. He tends to do dumb but charming things. Grumpy is negative about everything, has a know-it-all swagger, and can't admit to being wrong about anything. His charm comes from depth of character. You know that beneath that crusty exterior he's a softy. He huffs and puffs about Snow being there, but you can tell he is as excited as the others. How can you tell? His mannerisms.

Talk

As a kid, I used to watch the *Farmer Gray* show on Channel 13 out of Newark, New Jersey. It featured a half hour of silent cartoons, some more than 20 years old. Most of them consisted of a bunch of mice overrunning Farmer Al Falfa's life. I don't think there could have been more than five or six different frames a second and they were looped maddeningly. I can still see the farmer running and passing the same tree over and over as he sported the same mechanical expression shift, head tilting from side to side.

For some reason I watched every day. I used to make little flip books with mice jumping all around. Before sound, animated characters were pretty much devoid of character. They were a product of new technology and animators relied on gags instead of stories. Much like 3D animators have relied on gimmicks instead of stories.

I remember a particularly insipid little clown, Koko, who would climb out of an inkwell and relate (without any expression) to his creator, Max Fleisher. He always left me with a gnawing emptiness. Felix the Kat was the first animated character on TV that I could relate to. He was always trying to figure life out by pacing back and forth with his tail forming a question mark over his head. Ah, a genuine mannerism. The advent of sound in film actually upset the animation applecart. No one seemed prepared to integrate the new dimension.

It took a while for talking cartoon characters to catch on. Many, like Felix, who depended on a kind of mime, didn't translate well to sound. A new kind of character was needed. Mickey Mouse was one of the first. And Mickey's personality was geared for sound.

But enough history and Disney. What is it about talk that you can use to endow your characters with charm? I don't know.

Verbal Charm

If it's a bad guy, you can pretty much give him/her a harsh voice and that's going to do it. A bad guy with a melodious voice would be an interesting choice; try it out, it may be too sophisticated for the medium... perhaps not. See, I don't know a damn thing, nobody does. You just go for it and then make adjustments.

This is another study you have to do yourself. Use your mirror. Combine facial mannerisms with vocal characteristics and body language. Voice doesn't work in a vacuum (sorry). When you combine it with just the right mannerisms you get a gestalt. No one part works well alone, but together you get a quantum-leap effect.

You have to study character voices and their appeal. You know how to do that by now. *Casper the Friendly Ghost* is a wonderful study in 3D charm. Study the 30 seconds after he spots a girl in his bed. Notice how his voice, his fingers, and his facial expression combine to make you think of one thing: a normal boy excited about finding a pretty girl in his bed. Why would the animators want you to think of a normal boy for a marshmallow ghost? Because that's who Casper is.

This is an important clue. You have to know who your character is before you give it a voice. Only then can you know what voice to create and how to keep it consistent.

Animapsychology

Some people easily understand character personalities. It's intuitive for them, but most of us only have an inkling (a baby character). If you have a problem getting Mr. Talking Head to speak to you, you may not know who he is. He'll only reveal his inner being if you know his psychology. How do you do that?

As a psychologist who has developed tests, it just so happens I've put together a simple test for you. You don't even have to score it, just take it (see sidebar). This is no silly exercise. It happens that your mind can put together consistent characters different from your own. Look in your mirror, make some faces, and then act out the part as you take the test. Your subconscious will miraculously know how your character would answer.

Dr. Tony Gregorc

You probably don't know the work of Dr. Anthony Gregorc, a Connecticut psychologist who has developed the concept of cognitive styles. You should, and I'll tell you why. Tony is an expert on human behavior patterns. Though not completely consistent, people behave in linked patterns. For example, when you take a person to dinner on their birthday and the staff comes out to sing happy birthday, you might expect different reactions. If your person wants to climb under the table with embarrassment and gets angry about the whole affair, yet loves music and radio station jumping, you can almost bet this same person will be an excellent student, prefer documentaries to drama, and be clever at putting you in your place.

Don't ask me why, but there is an entire tapestry of seemingly unrelated attitudes and behaviors that are consistently found together in people according to their cognitive style. Tony has done extensive research and come up with a simple but effective way of understanding personality. The birthday girl, for example, is characteristic of the Abstract Sequential personality.

Don't go around pigeonholing real people once you learn this stuff. There's depth here. You can benefit from studying about it. For now, you can use Tony's work as detailed in Appendix C to understand how behaviors and attitudes are most commonly linked in consistent patterns.

It's fun work and relieves a lot of anxiety. Once you pick a dominant quirk for your character and exaggerate it, you can see what cognitive style most fits. Tony's work will give you behavior and attitude references for the entire character.

Just reading about the different character traits in Appendix C will help you evolve your character concept. Just remember that it's a lot more fun to create a character that *you* can relate to. You'll know you're on the right trail when a little voice deep inside says "Yes! That's who she is." You can then have a ball making her more complex by taking characteristics from two or more styles while maintaining her dominant pattern. Think how people will relate to your toy block when they see it can't stand people telling it what to do and where to be. It keeps moving when no one is looking and knocking over the whole castle. Or the little girl bunny who wants to obey rules, but is always in trouble because she takes things apart and can't get them back together again, or sticks her finger in the lightbulb socket just because that electricity stuff sounds really neat.

Mr. Talking Head

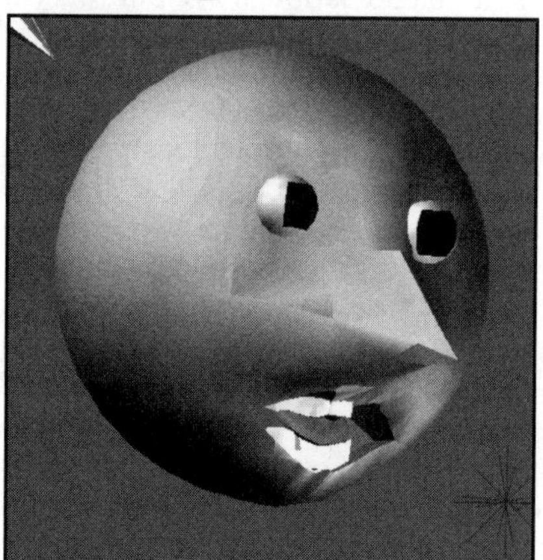

We built a really bad-head character earlier with a pin nose and nernie teeth. He's so simple you wouldn't think he could have any charm, right? Okay, so you like his tongue, it was a cool touch, but the guy's a lump. Our challenge is to make him charming. I'll give you a hint — sometimes the most charming characters are the simplest, so we have a good start here.

Before I show you what I might do to develop this character, look at the poor schlep, he looks like a dufus. What would you do with him? Like a sculptor staring at a chunk of wood, waiting for it to speak to him and yield a design, stare at this dufus and wait for his personality to come to you. If, after hours, it's not working, think up a quirk and go to Tony's research (and always thank him somewhere in your credits). You now have a character. Let's play around with Mr. Talking Head.

I've put a sampling of his expressions in the color section, Plates 24-1 through 24-8. There are several ways to shape his face the way you want. You can use the Surface Sculpt tool or the Deform Object tool. I find the latter easier to use and animate with. I also use tools like Object Scale to change the size of the eyes and Object Rotate to change where he's looking.

I shouldn't have to explain that you rotate the eyes by navigating each in the hierarchy and then making your adjustment in your keyframe. Type in the next keyframe and make adjustments there. I did a quick .avi for you to look at. It's not particularly good, but it does demonstrate that you have control over your character's expressions and face movements. For your demo tape, I advise you to create a character and do a lot more careful manipulation. trueSpace2 is capable of far more interesting character work than I did here, but it takes a lot of time and dedication to get it right. Spend two weeks on a character and you'll have a basis to work from.

No Eyes? No Problem

As a great animator you'll be able to take that little toy block and turn it into a character. It will have no facial expression, no eyes, no normal human gestures, yet you'll be able to get people to have empathy for it.

How? That's the fun part. I don't know how the heck you'll do it, but you will. I can only show you how I might rise to the challenge. What would be the simplest, nonhuman 3D form I could try to bring to life? The first that comes to mind is a cube. Well, a sphere, but that's a lot like a head. Nope, a cube is inorganic, devoid of human character.

The hardest part is coming up with that story. As I'm typing, I'm starting to panic, because I don't have one! I keep thinking a cube is a cube is a cube. I'm getting another cup-a-coffee and letting this cube thing bounce around in my head. Ouch, sharp edges.

I'm back with the square-peg-in-a-round-hole thought that kept running through my head up in the kitchen. So how about a cube that wants to be a sphere. Let's say he sees a mighty attractive sphere who rejects him, so he tries to turn himself into a sphere by bashing himself against the floor, crushing his corners. He does a lousy job of it as well and ends up looking like an idiot. But she appreciates his effort and falls for the blockhead.

Wait, that gives me the idea of having a sphere bash itself into a square, kind of like humans are never satisfied with who they are, they always want to be someone else, and then make a bad job of it. Obviously I'm on to something here, I just have to work out a good story and some ways to give the cube expression.

Wait, it's easier to roll than to walk. I imagine a cube would have a tough time walking. Here's the story: a cube struggles his way to center stage, walking on two corners like on tiptoe. He has to hoist his weight around and remain balanced. Clearly a cube was never meant to ambulate. He settles down in a harrumph of exhaustion. Then a pretty gold ball comes in and rolls all around him. He looks over and twists himself in two following her. She rolls off.

The cube gets up, starts to take a step, and you can see he's thinking better of this. He leaps into the air coming down on one corner, smashing it toward his center (see Figure 24-2).

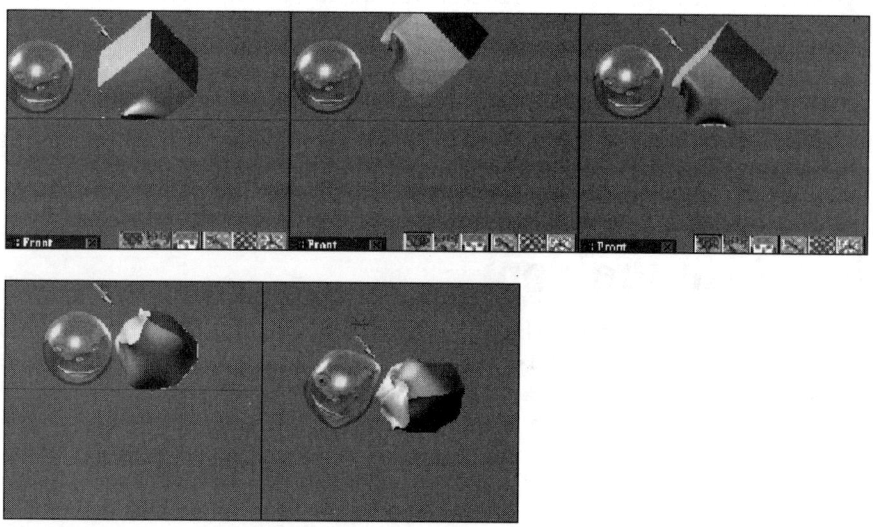

Figure 24-2: Boxy wants to be noticed by beautiful Goldie ball. Here he's bashing his corners in to look more like a ball.

He continues rounding his corners until he vaguely resembles a ball. Then he rolls off the screen, a bumpy, lumpy roll. About halfway down (half size), his corners suddenly pop out to their original positions causing him to topple to a stop. The gold ball comes rolling back again, easy as can be, and the cube again smashes his corners and rolls back toward the screen following the ball. One corner pops out and he quickly bounces on it, pushing it back in.

There is clearly a message here, perhaps several. I can certainly relate to the poor guy; there have been times when I've wished to have a different shape or capability. Perhaps that's what my beard is all about.

The Test

If you really want to get to know your character (recommended) before starting to animate him, take the little test I've made up here. Before you start to answer, take a moment to get into character. Close your eyes and picture yourself as the character, going through a critical moment, like meeting your true love for the first time. Then take the test. You probably ought to make a bunch of copies to keep in your drawer.

What the Heck is Cute, Anyway?

Cute sells, always has and always will. But what is it? Before you go to a formula, make yourself a list of what you think is cute. Then I'm going to refer you to one of the great all-time animators, a Disney old-timer who is still with us and busily developing VR type interactive TV. Preston Blair has given us in a single book, *Cartoon Animation*, just about anything you need to know about character animation.

Don't start with this book; you'll miss the essential gut-level understanding you gain by doing the research. But Blair, who animated the "Dance of the Hours" in *Fantasia*, among many other things, is a master of movement and expression. *Cartoon Animation* is a must. In it, you'll learn all about giving your characters life, expression, and emotional content. Much of his illustrated text can be directly applied to 3D animation. For example, he shows you how to build simplified skeletons for different kinds of animals. He explains exactly how deer and dogs run differently. You'll find tricks of the trade such as how to shape mouths for various consonants and vowel sounds, and delayed secondary action. That's where different parts of the character arrive at a certain point at slightly different times. It adds interest.

There is another book that was out of print for a while. But it's back and if you can afford it you should get it. It's *The Illusion of Life, Disney Animation* by Frank Thomas and Ollie Johnston. I wanted to buy this book when it first came out, but at the time I couldn't afford the large, expensive book, having recently opened a children's ski shop in Aspen. It took several years before anybody knew what to do with a children's ski shop, but it did extremely well. I own the book now but wish I'd gone into hock for it back then. The cover price is $60.00 and it's worth more. At retirement, these two veteran Disney artists decided to record what it was that made Disney cartoons different from all others — the illusion of life. They go to great pains to explain how it was and is done. The lavishly illustrated book contains storyboards and conceptual illustrations that will inspire you. You may not be a cel animator, but you are not less. Much of the wisdom your forebears have collected is here for you to absorb. There's no need to reinvent the phenakistoscope (animation wheel).

The Animation Personality Test

Assume your character's personality and fill out this little instrument to gain even further insight. You may be amazed at how your mind fills in the blanks, so you'll know how your character will respond on nearly any question. The more you play with it, the richer your characters will become.

Character's Name: ______________________________

Character's Age: ______________________________

Sex (circle one): M F NA (NA will deprive you of awesome opportunities)

Level of Education: ______________________________

List Special Interests: ______________________________

Personality Inventory

Answer with a number from 1 to 10. A 1 means a strong No while a 10 is an affirmative Yes. 5 is wishy washy; use it when a question is not applicable. You may enter negative numbers if you feel the need. Where requested, write a list of answers.

1. If you had parents, were they happy with you as a child? ____________
2. Were you a good student? ____________
3. Did you have a happy childhood? ____________
4. Do you like to get into trouble? ____________
5. Do you like small furry animals? ____________
   A: To cuddle ____________
   B: To eat ____________
6. Do you like to dance? ____________ How good are you? ____________
7. Are you a romantic? ____________
8. How cute are you? ____________
9. List your emotional weaknesses: ____________
10. List your personal strengths: ____________
11. Do you have any principles (things you always or never do)? List: ____________
    ____
12. If you had keys, how likely would you be to lose them? ____________
13. How well organized are you? ____________

14. Are you shy? ____________________
15. Are you a coward? ____________________
16. List the things that scare you: ____________________
17. List five personal characteristics that set you apart: ____________________
____
18. List five physical characteristics that set you apart: ____________________
____
19. List five mannerisms you exhibit and when — do your ears droop when you're sad? Do you itch when you're upset — that kind of thing: ____________________
____
20. List five things you might do in response to anger: ____________________
____
21. Describe your walk: ____________________
____

Thus ends our brief personality inventory. Please feel free to answer any questions not asked on the back of this test.

Go Forward and Be Fruitful

Now it's up to you. Overcome your self-doubt, have fun, and realize that you really can do this part of animation. In fact, you're already starting to see how this could be the most enjoyable element and you never even considered it that way before. This is the stuff you'll carry with you. It transcends tS2 and reaches to the essential nature of entertainment. If you take the time to understand it, you'll be way ahead of the crowd. Combine what you learn with a good story — you'll have a winner. Go for it.

Summary

This chapter was intended to enlighten you on the arcane subject of character design. In some circles, character design simply means creating several clay sculptures of a clever character. Here I expect you to imbue that clay with life. I've gone way overboard on purpose because this is one of the weakest areas of development for new animators. Here are some of the things you should have learned:

- Eyes are a good starting point. People will be looking at your character's eyes.
- You need to develop an eye for character and you can do it.
- Walt Disney wasn't such a great animator, but he had vision.
- Talent is lazy, you must exercise it.
- Charm comes in many packages. You just have to know what the essential ingredients are.
- Use a mirror and your own face as a prime source.
- There is a psychology to characters even if they are made of procedural wood.
- Personality involves attitudes and behaviors that hang together in a consistent way. Building the right chains of behavior can add humanity to your character.
- Even Mr. Ugly Talking Head can have charm.
- Preston Blair is somebody you should study even if you never draw a cartoon in your life.
- You should skip this chapter if you're intent on being a run-of-the-mill tweener.

✦ ✦ ✦

Camera Work

Chapter 25

In This Chapter

What to consider when planning your shots

How to use cinematography to enhance dramatic impact

How to use the camera to focus the viewer's attention

How to use camera technique to transfer the viewer from one space to another

What coverage is and how to use it in tS2

All about your tS2 digital cameras

How to use camera point constraints for automatic tracking

Digital cinematography is an art. Done well it makes you look like a professional. Done poorly it can detract from excellent modeling and story.

Cyber-eyes

3D animation gives you some of the best eyes around. Your camera equipment includes all sorts of dollies, tracks, cranes, hovercraft platforms, a zoom lens that won't quit, and autotracking. Your camera can travel through walls and through space at hyperlight speeds. It's great. Digital cinematography is a mouthful. I'll just use cybertography for short, if you don't mind. It's wrong, but it sounds better than threedigitography.

With filters you build in tS2 you can even do in-camera realtime special effects. You don't have to worry about exposure, or processing, or film speed, so you can concentrate on how to shoot that scene.

There's no one right way to shoot any scene — there are a lot of wrong ways. Sometimes I think getting a good shot consists of having a good eye for composition and avoiding obvious pitfalls of bad cinematography. Some of my best angles were unplanned. But as a general rule, plan your shots using principles of good cinematography.

Cyber-eyes see what you tell them to see. Often newcomers to the art give their cameras bad instructions and end up with miserable results. This is particularly disheartening when the modeling and action are well done. Frequently Asked Questions on the Net often center on the whys of strange camera results.

In this chapter I'll reveal secrets for putting your visions in the can. This includes both the art and technique of shooting. I've asked Steve Katz, Supervisor of Digital Productions at Curious Pictures and author of *Cinematic Motion*, to give us a few pointers along the way.

Camera Art

As director it's your job to figure out how your production will unfold its story. The camera is the audience's eye. As you compose your shots you'll have three major aesthetic areas of considerations.

- ✦ **Story.** What story points does the shot have to convey.
- ✦ **Drama.** How will the camera facilitate the dramatic considerations of the scene.
- ✦ **Aesthetics.** How can you make the shot serve the mood of the piece while still achieving cinematic beauty.

Story

I keep coming back to the script. Narrative or story considerations have to do with the script and what it requires. In our script the shots are pretty clearly laid out. Perhaps it seems that the director's job is done for him by the writer. No way. Remember, film is a collaborative vision. How the shots are composed — even if the director follows script instructions exactly — is a make or break proposition.

The director may opt to change how a scene is shot because his vision, true to story, has found a better way to make the story points. In our case the one-sentence description of the sequence is really the crux of the story to be told.

Drama

According to Steve Katz, "Dramatic considerations include the elements that color our emotional understanding of a scene. They fall into two categories: point of view and dramatic emphasis."

POV (Point of View)

The key set of decisions a director has to make concern how he will navigate the point of view in each shot. This determines camera placement and movement. In traditional movie making this involves tracking, crane shots, and even heli-shots — a lot of aggravation and money. In tS2 you have complete control over all aspects of the camera from focal length to position in space to movement. You can place as many cameras as you like and track them along animation paths. You can aim them anywhere you want with automatic tracking and keyframable zoom and focus. The fact that you can do just about anything doesn't make the job easier; it actually complicates matters. You have more possibilities to consider on your way to the one that will show up on screen.

Cybertographers can stick to traditional shots or they can experiment with some of the wild new possibilities. Experiment with both approaches, but understand the basics before you invent a new science.

You will control the logic of each shot. Often you'll want the camera to let you climb into a specific point of view such as the pilot's. At other times a remote POV or camera eye view will serve the purpose better. My personal preference is nearly always to have the camera associated with something other than a camera. For example, I mentioned that you can glue a spot Obie to your camera to give the impression of a headlight. This helps the audience associate the POV with a vehicle. A quick establishing shot of a vehicle approaching the same object will clinch the impression.

Dramatic Emphasis

Drama gets its power from the audience's connection with the subject. There can be drama and majesty in the approach of a lowly shuttle craft to a space station, as in our example.

Generally, you'll either have your camera looking at the action from outside or being right in the middle of it. Too much of either one isn't good. Look for a balance. You can establish a kind of intimacy with the action by placing your camera smack into it. For example, if you shoot from in front of an oncoming vehicle with a close miss zooming over head, you put the audience smack in the middle of it. This helps it feel like less an observer than a participant.

Shot size is a critical consideration as well. The more of the screen that is filled with the subject, the greater sense of connection the audience will feel. We use this in the approach to Trilon Station: First, we slowly get to know Starfire, and follow until the huge mass of Trilon fills the screen.

In space work we have another gimmick that links the audience with the scene — rotation sync. Our staging uses this mechanism as we approach Trilon. At first, as Trilon rotates on its own axis, it seems remote. As our POV synchronizes with the station's rotation, a feeling of intimacy arises. This on the heels of a wide shot to a closeup of the station provides a dramatic approach and symbolically nails down the transition from cold lonely space to warm friendly station.

Aesthetics

A well-composed shot of garbage cans can have cinematic beauty. The director's vision combined with the art director's art should produce scenes that tell the story yet have depth, often coming from the symbolic qualities of the image. For example, in portraying good and evil you might opt for a high-contrast scene. It's not obvious to many, but it adds to the tension. People relate to symbols on an unconscious level in a way that enhances their entertainment experience. Symbolic imagery can add depth and mystery to your piece as well. People will think you're some kind of genius, too, because the use of symbolism is associated with intellectual superiority. Let them, but remember that symbols were developed to a high art by Cro-Magnon men on cave walls. One way to do it is get a book on symbols. If you want to be really cool, read some Jung. For action adventure and the hero's quest you'll really enjoy by Christopher Vogler.[1] Chris has

[1] *The Writer's Journey*, Christopher Vogler, © 1992 Michael Wiese Productions.

consulted with the biggies like George Lucas and the gang at Disney in the areas of symbolism and structure. Much of his work is based on Godfather Joseph Campbell.[2] Campbell's work heavily influenced the *Star Wars* trilogy, *Raiders of the Lost Ark*, and hundreds of other movies.

Combining symbolism with classic compositional beauty can only help your production. I know it may be hard to do when all you have is a robot clomping across a room or a space vehicle whipping past stars. But try. Use your sense of aesthetics to pull threads through your compositions and tie them together. Use the camera to follow these threads. The viewfinder is your creative window.

Only recently has the digital director been able to look through the viewfinder in cybertography. The advent of real-time feedback gives you a preview of various camera angles at the same time. You can also render full video files in reduced resolutions for preview. trueSpace2 is fast enough that you can do the occasional full-resolution preview for critical analysis of the image qualities of the shot. Sometimes you'll just render a single frame in high resolution to check composition and image quality.

Coverage

In traditional filmmaking a cautious director will shoot a scene from every possible angle so he has plenty of fodder for the edit. I've never liked this approach. It's the sign of an unsteady hand — a director lacking confidence in his own work. It annoys me because it's expensive, not just in time, but in human resources. You have a crew standing around all day for one shot, you exhaust your actors, and burn up a lot of film.

My attitude is different on a 3D shoot. None of the above problems exist. You can place as many cameras as you like. I sometimes set up four cameras for a single take. I run low-res videos of each one and study them for feel. Six times out of ten, they'll inspire a fifth approach.This one takes the best from several and usually involves a change of path and possibly focal length.

Sometimes I'll record frames 0–50 from camera one and frames 51–90 from camera three, and cut them together in post. It's relatively easy to set up this kind of coverage and saves a lot of time. An example is a sequence I did for a demo in which a space vehicle approaches a planet, launches a large fireball, and leaves. The fireball continues on into the planet's atmosphere and eventually explodes below.

Camera one tracks from behind the planet, giving a dramatic overview of the situation, and moves toward the approaching vehicle into a medium shot as the fireball is released. Camera two is traveling in the reverse direction, toward the planet, and follows the fireball in, slowing to a stop as it approaches the atmosphere. This heightens the drama of the attack and requires only one final run-through. I recorded frames 0–226 on camera one and 227–412 on camera two.

[2] *Hero With a Thousand Faces*, Joseph Campbell, © 1968 Princeton University Press.

Camera Effects

Shortcomings of film such as motion blur and lens flares are expected by the viewer. If your shot is too clean, with each frame in perfect focus, the video can have a false look to it. Thus, to simulate traditional camera physics, tS2 gives you artificial Depth of Field and Motion Blur. Both are a pain because, IMHO, they take way too long to render. Nevertheless, they do give your shot an authentic live-shot feel. Use them only when you feel you need them in the shot. You can add lens flares and motion blur in Premiere 4.0.

Aesthetics – the Camera Dance

Much of the dramatic impact contributed by the camera comes from the way you manipulate the image on screen. That usually means moving the camera in a defined relationship with the actor. This is one place the director's art is key. Since you have an infinite number of possible moves, you have to look at the master scene and size it up pretty quickly. You can't go through all the possibilities.

One way to do this is to rely on your intuitive sense of cinematic motion. You can visualize a large number of possible moves very quickly, filtering as you go. As I said, I generally narrow it down to four or fewer possibilities.

It's even easier if you have a feel for moves that the audience will be able to relate comfortably to. You can't lose an audience faster than feeding them some weird camera angle that confuses or dislocates them within the story. I've seen directors so obsessed with artsy gimmicks that they forget story. Learn a small cadre of good moves, understand why they work, and be creative within the bounds of good storytelling. In the very best camera work the viewer really isn't aware of the camera at all.

Directing the Viewer

The frame directs the audience's attention to various story elements and guides attention among various elements as suits the story. We looked at two ways that this is accomplished when we explored the movement of actors. Here we have two more: static and moving-camera shots.

The Approach

There are three elements of approach.

- ✦ The camera approaches the subject.
- ✦ The subject approaches a static camera.
- ✦ Both subject and camera approach each other.

Approach tells the viewer this is the important element to pay attention to. I use all three approaches fairly evenly. I like the last choice best, but it doesn't always appease the drama or story demons.

The Transfer

In our introduction of Trilon Station, we have two transfers. The first transfers attention from the awesome beauty of space to the shuttle craft and in the same long shot we have the second transfer to Trilon. The cut to pilot's POV nails it down.

Transfers move the story along smoothly from point to point. There are two categories of transfer.

Camera Transfers

- Camera pans from one subject to the other.
- Camera changes focus or zooms in to main subject from a wide shot.
- Camera follows first subject until it passes in front of second subject, then shifts to the second subject.

Action Transfers

- Subject turns to align with camera.
- One of several subjects moves into close-up.
- New subject enters the field of view.
- Subject one leaves field of view as subject two enters.
- Subjects one and two are in focus and one leaves.

The Bridge

There are a lot of camera moves that form a bridge between master scene spaces. Recall that in our master scene we have three spaces: awesome space, transition space, and Trilon Station. The space shuttle serves as both the main subject of the first scene of the sequence and the neutral transitional object between spaces. That is, the shuttle itself is not an important part of the story. It serves only to introduce Trilon in a dramatic way, placing it in the depths of space. There are several common bridge conventions.

- Camera follows object from one space to another.
- Camera follows parallel to object, looking at it from the side.
- Camera follows a neutral transitional element between spaces.
- Camera zooms from one space to the next (in the distance).

The Counter

A very useful convention in film that transfers nicely to digital is the counter move. In it the camera and the subject move in opposite circles to create a major change of view. The counter provides a very smooth and logical way to get from one perspective to another. We use a modified form of the counter in the first shot of our sequence. The shuttle craft sweeps into view in a long semicircle. The camera moves toward it, then across its path in a counter that reveals Trilon for the first time.

Counter moves can be used to change the scene, mood, or background. I've set up an arbitrary set of backgrounds for Joe the biped robot. Poor Joe has a limp, due to being designed by a committee. He enters on the gas pump set and ends on the telescope set. Here's how it was done. Joe enters camera left, walks in front of the camera, and circles to his left to take his position. As soon as he passes, the camera locks onto Joe, as it moves in a counter semicircle. The camera stops in a position looking squarely at Joe, who is now on the telescope set (see Figure 25-1). You'll find a 400-frame animation of the counter on the CD-ROM at \movies\dreamscp\counter.avi.

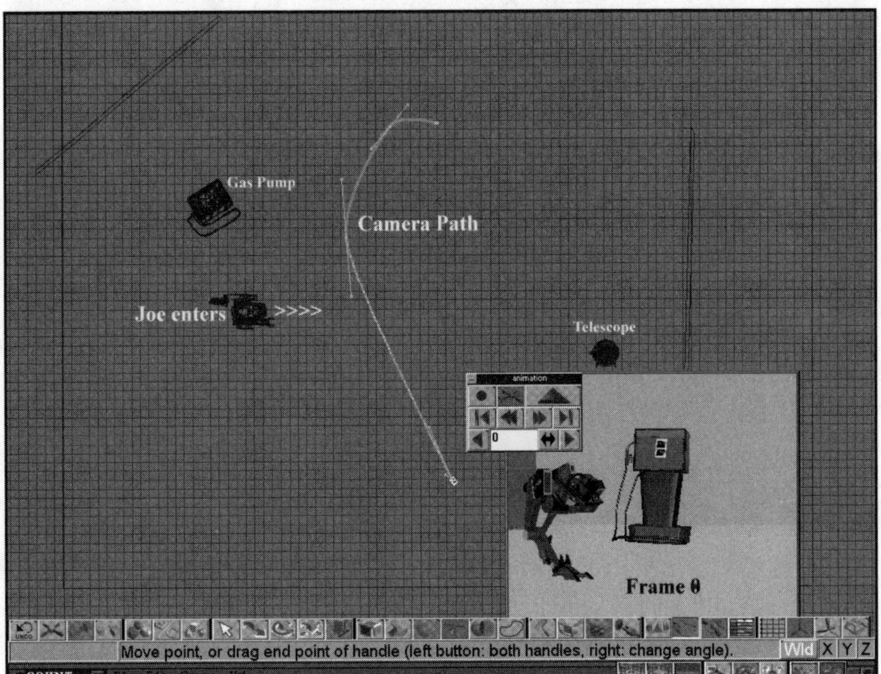

Figure 25-1A: The beginning and end are shot in a counter-camera move. Here the camera picks up Joe the robot at the gas station. It moves toward him, crossing his path.

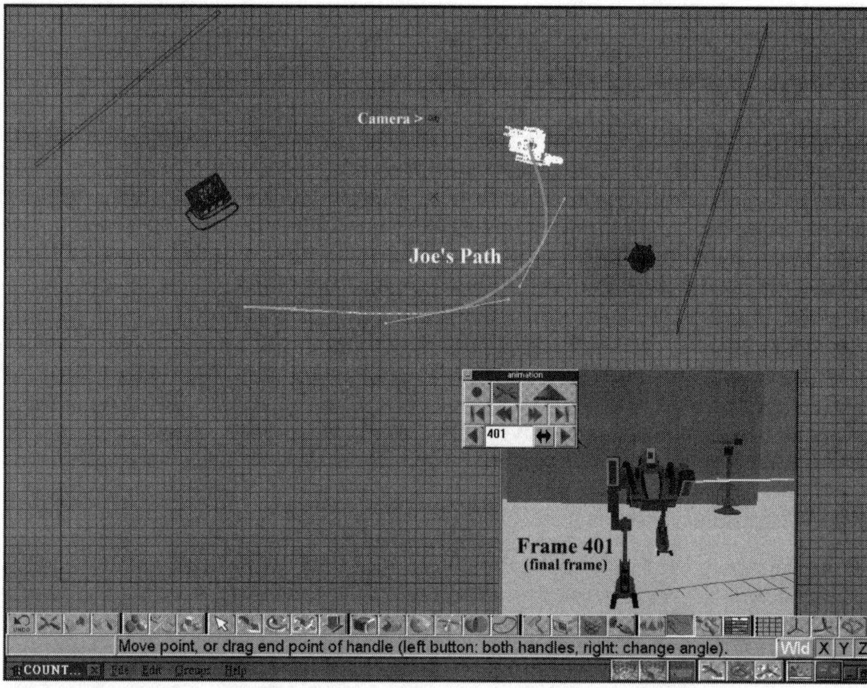

Figure 25-1B: As Joe heads forward, he rotates to the left. The camera rotates to the right, and eventually they end up facing each other. The whole shot is on the CD-ROM in a video called counter.avi in the movies subdirectory.

Don't be afraid to retrace your steps. Many new to the field believe you should always keep moving ahead, but it's often a good idea to retrack a move. That means you back the camera up the way it just came. It's a little tricky in tS2. Make sure you click Sharp Corner for the spline characteristic of the node where you reverse.

Camera Work

You're the DP (Director of Photography) on this gig. You have to know your cameras, how they work, and what they can do. In this section I'll give you specifics on how to accomplish your art in tS2.

The Camera

Each of your views is a virtual camera. You can record all the action without ever placing a formal camera in the scene. The only time you need one is when you want moving shots, or shots from an angle that's difficult to navigate from the window.

Cameras are Primitives, found on that panel. You pop them up like any other Primitive and they look like an old-fashioned studio camera. With the camera selected, access the View, pop up and select the camera icon. If you have several cameras up at once you can have each one's view in a separate window (up to three).

With the camera selected, notice that the Axis tool is disabled. This is because camera axes are fixed with the Z axis pointing straight out the front of the lens and Y pointing straight up. This was done so that you can use the Look At and Look Ahead constraints with cameras (and spotlights too), without having to mess around with setting the axis.

Cameras can be moved and rotated and keyframed to get the shot you want. You can even zoom the lens either by using the Object Scale icon or the View Zoom icon. I prefer the scale approach as it is smoother. You can achieve very nice cinematic effects by moving and zooming the camera at the same time. Experiment.

An Axis Can Be a Camera

Any axis can be a camera. It always looks out in the Z direction, and as you have seen, it can be handy to use an interior axis for special effects. The axis of the shuttle craft makes an ideal camera for the pilot's POV. I've often seen new users gluing cameras to objects unnecessarily. Note that if you want a chase-plane view of an object, it may be practical to place the axis above and behind the object with the Z axis facing forward. In a Look Ahead situation the camera would track the animation path with the vehicle below and in front of it. This can work nicely in many cases.

Keyframing Your Camera

The rules of smooth keyframing go double for camera work. It's easy to get a jerky motion with abrupt stops and starts. Here are a few things to think about when you're keyframing camera moves.

- Make sure you set the number of frames for your camera path before you click your modes down.
- If you must set more than one keyframe make sure the distance between 1 and 2 is the same as between 0 and 1. This will keep the speed the same.
- Ease in and out of motion by bunching frames at either end by holding down the Shift key and sliding the spline handle left or right. This changes the tension.
- Check the shape and altitude of your path. Often new users will build the path beneath the origin plane and have the camera move through their mountains.

Tips for Good Camera Work

I looked through my store of FAQs to see what seems to most confuse new users in the camera work area. There are some clear winners.

FAQ: I can't rotate my camera no matter what I do, what's wrong with it?

A: You have the Look At or Look Ahead icon engaged. The camera can't disobey those constraints until you remove them. Just click the icon and you'll be able to move the camera.

FAQ: When I use the Look At icon, it seems to work, but if I make the camera look someplace else, it's really jerky and stupid looking.

A: You're right. What you probably did was change from one Look At object to another on the same or progressive frames. Try this. Set up a moving camera and two moving objects. Key in Look At object A for 30 frames, then key it off for 20 frames. Then Key in Look At B for 30 frames. During the 20 frames of unconstrained view, the camera will smoothly pan to the new view.

FAQ: I don't know what I did, but the camera is all over the place. I didn't set it up this way.

A: I don't have enough information for a definitive answer, but I'd bet you grabbed the camera somewhere mid-path and moved it. This can seriously distort your path spline. Click on the Animation Path icon and check out the revealed path. You can try straightening it out with the Point Move tool, but I suggest you remove the path and try again. Place the camera where you want it in frame 0. Then click where you want it on frame last, move it up or down, etc. only in those two places. With the Path icon engaged you can click on the Move Object icon and move the entire path (as opposed to just the point).

FAQ: My camera moves fast and slow and fast again and I don't like it. What can I do to make it smooth?

A: You most likely have a number of keyframes for the camera with different distances between them. Because tS2 automatically assigns the same number of frames between keys, short distances will be traveled in the same time as long distances between keys. This can make movement on short jumps very slow and on long ones very fast. Use as few keys as possible. When you need keyframes for complex curves make sure you manually adjust the number of frames between keys to reflect the distance traveled. That is, if your main path is 80 frames over 10 meters (or 8 frames per meter), and your next jump is five and a half meters, input 44 frames ($8 \times 5.5 = 44$). You'll have to estimate, but use the grid and you'll get close enough to shave a gnat's tail.

FAQ: When my camera passes a spaceship and I have Look At engaged, it looks really weird when it passes. The ship appears to rotate or something. It happens really fast and it looks like hell. You know what I'm talking about? How can I avoid this?

A: The Look At icon constrains the camera to look at the object's axis. The causes the ship to appear to rotate as you fly directly over it in close quarters. I suggest disengaging the Look At icon for about 20 frames before and 30 frames after the camera passes the ship's axis.

(continued)

This will cause the camera to pretty much stay on the ship and then slowly reorient as it passes over. This is a much more cinematic approach.

FAQ: I've tried to use the Z focus on tS2 and I can't seem to get it to focus where I want. I tried using the measure sticks, but they don't measure between the camera and an object. What do I do?

A: If you use the Look At icon it will automatically set the focus correctly for the object you are looking at.

FAQ: There is something about the way my camera moves that looks amateurish to me. It just doesn't look professional.

A: Not much to go on here. But I suspect you have a good eye and are uncomfortable with the jerk to full speed and sudden stop, as well as the constant speed between keys. Professionals tend to ease into camera moves and ease to a stop. This definitely affects the look of a scene with a moving camera. Try adjusting the tension on your camera's path. You can bunch frames at either end, causing the camera to ease in and out of a move.

It's Your Picture

I believe it pays to be a bit of a perfectionist about your camera work. If it doesn't come out the way you wanted, shoot it again. I don't have that luxury while I'm writing this book because of deadlines. So don't take my work as good. Its purpose is to show the method. You'll see some good work in the CD-ROM and in the Color section. Keep working on the image until it pleases you. One thing about 3D — I've always been able to get the image where I want it, even if it takes weeks of fiddling. Getting the perfect take is difficult, so shoot from several different camera paths, and select the best or edit a few together. Make it good.

Summary

In this chapter you learned some of the more important aspects of cybertography. I concentrated more on the concept of making good camera moves than on giving you specifics. Each move is unique and you have to own it. You learned the following:

- ✦ How to plan your camera moves with a purpose.
- ✦ Specific things your camera moves must address, such as script and dramatic and technical goals.
- ✦ What you can accomplish with different kinds of moves.
- ✦ How to focus the viewer's attention or transfer it from one subject to another.
- ✦ How to work with the cameras in tS2 to create the images you want via smooth moves and classy perspectives.
- ✦ The answers to some of the most frequently asked questions about tS2 camera movement.

✦ ✦ ✦

CHAPTER 26

Hollywood-Style Special Effects

✦ ✦ ✦ ✦

In This Chapter

Particles, gravity, and collision effects

Amazing particle morphs

How they put those amazing explosions into outer space

Compositing live action with 3D and vice versa

Texture effects

✦ ✦ ✦ ✦

In this chapter, you get an introduction to the kinds of special effects you'll see in film and on television. I'm a sucker for an effects film. I try to see every one, even if reviews are mixed, as in *Star Gate*. I enjoy them anyway. Think back to *The Mask* and way back to *T2*. Many of those effects were produced using 3D animation combined with live action through compositing. Pretty sophisticated stuff right? Right, but you can do some of it on your home computer. Have you watched the introduction to *Babylon 5*? The space battles and explosions are really neat and you can do similar work at home.

3DFX

If you have the ability to capture live action and digitize it in real-time in MJPEG, all you need is a way to get it back out again and you're in business. Either Premiere 4.0 or Razor Pro, combined with tS2, gives you a regular mini-effects studio. To be competitive you really need Photoshop, too. Premiere and Photoshop were designed to work together for fancy rotoscoping and frame-by-frame effects.

For particle effects, you'll need Rob Bryerton's Exploder, which I've included on the CD-ROM (in the \exploder subdirectory). This program allows you to create all sorts of digital special effects like assembling a face out of a cloud of particles or having your spaceship blown to bits, literally. Combined with pyrotechnic effects you'll get a pretty amazing disaster.

The full scope of Hollywood effects is too much for this chapter, but I'd like to show you some of the things you can do.

Having a Blast!

Let's look at two very different kinds of explosions. The first is great fun and done entirely in 3D using particle physics. The second involves taking a real explosion, filmed in 2D by effects experts, and compositing it over your 3D image. Each approach can give spectacular results. When combined, they can be breathtaking.

Exploder

Rob Bryerton (`73747.433@compuserve.com`) is in the printing business. Amazing. He's a gifted programmer and creative applications developer. He designed and built Exploder, a stand-alone engine for processing tS2 .cob files. He got the idea from a fellow in Germany, David Strepenham, who submitted a primitive version to the tSML (trueSpace Mailing List). Most of the beta testing on Exploder was done by the CompuServe trueSpace SIG.

Among other things, Exploder breaks the polygons apart and gives them individual paths of their own. If you have several thousand polys, you can see how labor intensive it would be without this dandy application. Bryerton's latest version has added all sorts of sophistication including gravity and surface collision detection. I review a lot of software for various magazines. At $19.95, this program is an amazing deal. Similar programs for LightWave and 3D Studio cost more than $200 each. So send Rob a check, he richly deserves it, plus it will give him motivation to add all sorts of great things to the program.

The Explosion Kernel

One of the things you can do with Exploder is build and save an explosion kernel to use over and over again to add FX to your animations. It's a tiny dot on your screen that contains thousands of individual polygons, paths, and scaling information, along with transparent spheres that provide the billowing gas effect. With Rob's program, it's easy to achieve sophisticated effects. It's important to note that professionals charge extra when physics or particle effects are to be included in a job. You can too.

The Junk

We need an object to load into Exploder, so let's build an explosion sphere. There are two ways you can save a .cob file, in binary and in ASCII. When you use the latter, external programs like Exploder can manipulate the object in many ways. So we need to create a many-faced sphere saved in ASCII. It's easy; here's the step by step.

1. Right click on the Sphere icon in the Primitives panel, this will bring up the Sphere properties panel.
2. Set Latitude ➪ 50, Longitude ➪ 50. This will give you a sphere with 2,500 faces. Exploder will handle up to 3,000 faces, so use your judgment. The more faces the slower the process but the more interesting the blast.

3. Go to the Files options ➪ Save Object and click on the ASCII option box on the lower right. Name the file Explode and save it.

That's it. You can use this same procedure to save any object in ASCII for processing. For example, you could detach one of the fuel pods on the space tanker, exploderize it, and stick it back on. Then on cue it will blast apart. If you combine that with a laser blast and a composited explosion, you'll be amazed how authentic it all looks.

An alternative method is to bury an explosion kernel inside the pod. When the laser hits, explode the kernel and the chunks, and glowing gases come raging out the sides of the pod and you'd swear the whole pod went. You can even build directional charges to explode in one direction. But we're getting ahead of ourselves, so a pause in kernel construction while I present Exploder. We begin by importing explode.cob into Exploder. Copy Exploder from the CD-ROM to your hard drive and run it.

The Exploder Interface

The first thing you'll see is the control interface with the tool panel items grayed out. You need to load an object to enable all the options (Figure 26-1). It's standard stuff: Open File ➪ Import, or just hit Ctrl+I. Fill in the requester box with the file name. With the object loaded you get a bunch of options to play with. There are five icons across the tool bar. (Note that it says Ready in the lower left corner.) They are from left to right:

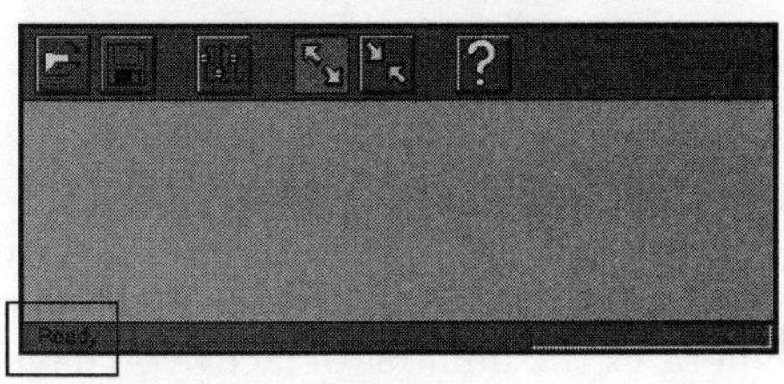

Figure 26-1: The Exploder is ready to roll after you load a file.

- ✦ The Import File icon;
- ✦ The Export File icon;
- ✦ The Exploder Options icon;
- ✦ The Maximize Interface icon; and
- ✦ Minimize Interface icon.

Use the icons; they're faster than the pull-down windows. By clicking on Minimize Interface and setting the View option to Always On Top, you can work with Exploder and tS2 at the same time. The real work gets done in the Exploder Options section of the program. Click the Options icon in the middle and you'll get the first control panel (Figure 26-2).

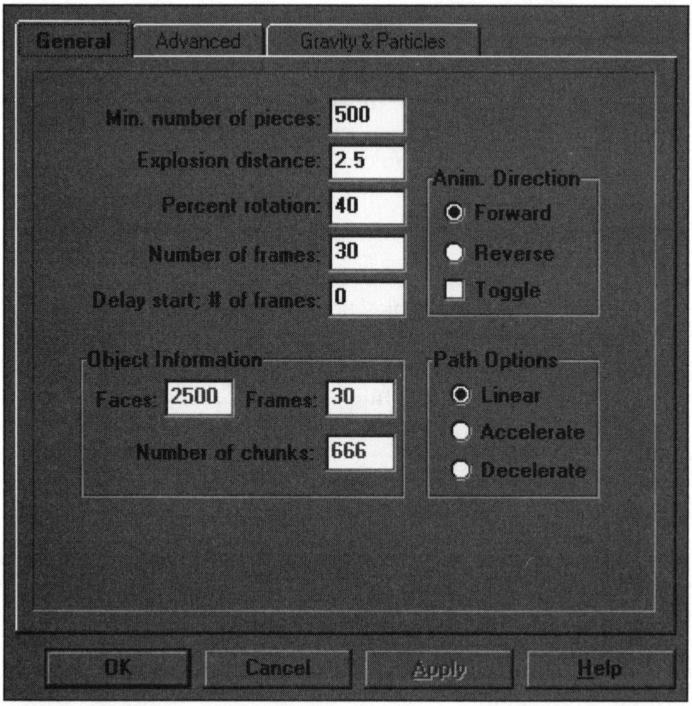

Figure 26-2: The Exploder General Options dialog box provides multiple settings for explosions.

General Options

There are seven options that can be set in the General Options page. Often this is all you need to mess with. In the lower left corner you also have an Object Information panel that can be helpful. It enumerates the number of faces you have to work with, the number of chunks you're going to get, and the number of frames to be calculated. This page alone will provide you with days of experimentation and some pretty thrilling results.

Min. Number of Pieces

The imported object will be broken up in random-pattern chunks. Our 2,500-piece object will by default be broken into 600 pieces. This number changes, depending on how big your model is. The higher you set it the smaller the chunks will be, until you're down to individual faces. The maximum setting for this object is obviously 2,500.

Explosion Distance

This is the approximate distance in World Units that each chunk will be thrown upon explosion. You'll probably increase this for a good blast. If you want the chunks to blast past the camera, you'll have to set it according to your stage layout — experiment. Setting this to 0 will open all sorts of interesting possibilities, especially when combined with scale and stagger effects.

Percent Rotation

You can have each chunk rotate as it spews out of the core. This setting determines how much rotation it will get.

Number of Frames

This is the number of frames over which Exploder will calculate its motion paths. I almost never use default on this. In space, explosions are large in scale so they move slowly. It's not unusual for me to bump this up to 200 or so.

Delay Start; Number of Frames

It's not good showmanship to start your explosion on frame 0. You'll want to give a little buildup. This option allows you to set in a period of quiet. Let's say you're going to blow the side out of your space station. It's better to have it sitting there rotating peacefully for fifty frames or so before the blow.

Anim. Direction

You can control the direction of the explosion. This is fabulous for neat logo effects where you blow up your letters in reverse. What happens is you start with the last explosion frame and it runs backward until your logo is assembled.

- **Forward:** This is the default. The object starts at frame 0 in its normal state and then on your start frame, it begins to explode outward in the directions you have set.
- **Reverse:** Object starts fully exploded at frame 0 and proceeds to reassemble itself beginning at your start frame and ending on the last frame.
- **Toggle:** You can select this in addition to one of the above choices. It causes the explosion to proceed to its end, then reverses back to the state it was in at frame 0.

Path Options

You can control the acceleration of chunks flying out of the core.

- **Linear:** This is the default. The chunks will spew out at a constant speed from beginning to end. That is, all frames are spaced at even intervals along the path.
- **Accelerate:** This setting will cause the chunks to start out slowly and accelerate along the path. This setting is deactivated if you are using the gravity/bounce option you'll learn about in a moment.
- **Decelerate:** Think hard. Yup, it's the reverse of accelerate. The chunks slow down as if being pulled back by gravity. You can combine decelerate with the toggle option to pull stuff back into a black hole if you like. This also is disabled with the gravity/bounce option.

Once you set the general options, you might want to explore the advanced options. I told you this was a lot of program for $15. We want to encourage these bright, nonrip-off people to continue producing great stuff for us to play with.

Advanced Options

The Exploder's Advanced options (see Figure 26-3) may look a little frightening but they're a piece of cake.

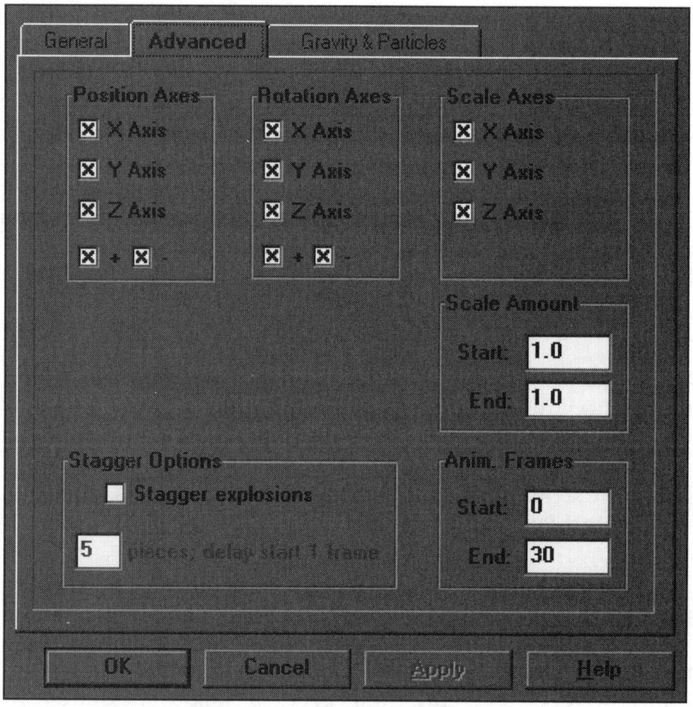

Figure 26-3: The Exploder's Advanced options

Axes

These settings determine what axes the various effects will be applied to.

✦ **Position:** This determines the direction of the explosion in general. The default is to have all three axes checked and both plus (+) and minus (-) checked. This means the explosion will proceed in all directions. The polarity determines direction along the axis from the object origin. For example, if you want the side of your station to blow out, you might only check the X and the +, disabling the others. This will cause the explosion to spew out to the right along the X axis only. These settings have many uses, most of which have yet to be determined. Experiment.

✦ **Rotation:** You can figure this one out. It's the same paradigm as position. You determine around which axes the pieces will rotate and in which directions.

✦ **Scale:** This is a little different. It applies to the original object and its individual chunks. It gives you amazing possibilities for special effects. The object scales along both the plus and minus directions for selected axes.

Scale Amount

With this you control the start and end size of the original object. It opens many doors and possibilities. Imagine some of the uses — objects that explode and disappear into thin air, chunks that expand as they approach your camera, enhancing the explosion effect. Go for it.

Anim. Frames

This setting determines the beginning and end frames for the scale effect. By default it starts at frame 0. If you're doing a regular explosion, you might want to start the explosion on frame 30 and the scaling on frame 50 for a delay effect.

Stagger Options

Check the Stagger explosions option box to stagger the release of chunks. If you set the Distance parameter to 0, you control the staging of effects like evaporation. You can enhance stagger effects by sorting your polygons, but more on that in a moment.

Sort and Shuffle

The options pull-down on the main tool bar gives you two interesting menu items, sort and shuffle. These rearrange the order of the faces so that with the Stagger option (above) engaged, you get orderly (sort) or random (shuffle) discharge of polygons.

Sort gives you six options to choose from. It will arrange faces:

✦ Top to bottom

✦ Bottom to top

✦ Left to right

✦ Right to left

✦ Front to back

✦ Back to front

Shuffle takes the order the faces are in and mixes them up for a good random display. You get three levels of mix — minimum, medium, maximum.

Gravity & Particles

Check out the Gravity & Particles options (see Figure 26-4) to change the gravity/bounce parameters. This is where you get into some really fun goodies.

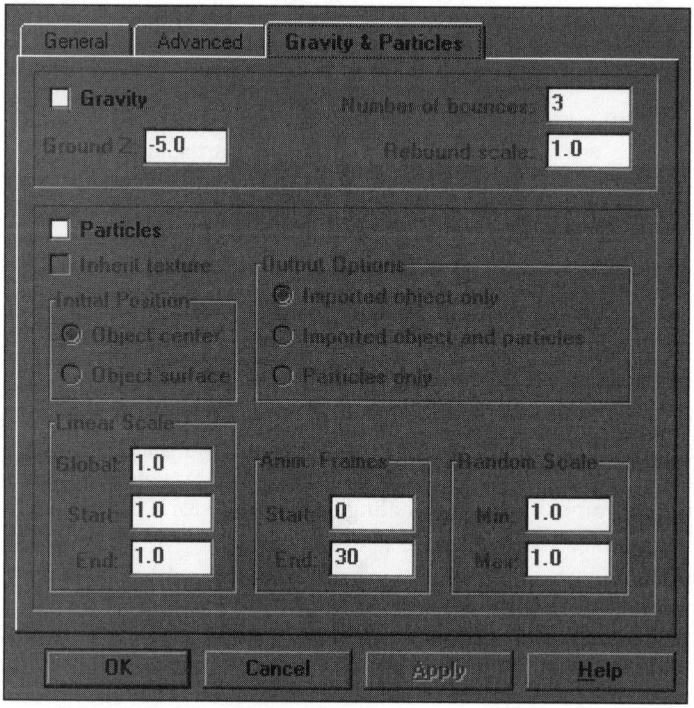

Figure 26-4: The Exploder's Gravity and Particles options

Ground Z

Ground Z is the location of the ground plane off which pieces of the exploded object will bounce. The value must be less than or equal to -1. That means you can put in larger minus numbers like -5 (default) if you like.

Exploder detects the ground plane with an accuracy of +/- $^1/_2$ the size of the irregular exploded chunk. For spherical particles the detection accuracy is much higher. Thus, it looks a little better for smaller chunks, but larger spheres are fine.

Number of Bounces

This is the number of bounces the chunk will take after it hits the ground plane. You have to play god (small g) here and decide. Each bounce will be less high than the previous one.

Rebound Scale

This setting controls how high a chunk or particle will bounce. It's a relative value/ scale factor rather than an absolute. You'll get reliable results with values between 0.001 and 5.0. Larger numbers can be input but may produce strange results.

The Particle System

This system is a little different from those in 3D Studio, Light Wave, and WaveFront. Any object can be loaded as a particle! Rob Bryerton recommends using the simplest objects possible for the sake of time and space. Large objects increase the size of your output exploder file almost exponentially.

Here's the way it works. Import an object made up of polygons, joint by vertices. Each vertex is a point at which Exploder will attach a particle. Thus for the object imported, Exploder will attach 2,500 objects as particles. Imagine if you used a sphere of 32 faces, you'd end up with an exploder object with 32 × 2,500 = 80,000 polygons. Too much for tS2 or your computer to handle effectively. So use your head.

The output will have the shape of the original object, but be composed of many particles. You can write either the imported object and its particles or just the particles to the output file. The geometry of the imported object and its associated settings will determine the shape of the output object as well as the behavior of this particle system.

Particles

Clicking this option box enables the particles system.

Inherit Texture

By default, this option is enabled, which means that each particle will inherit the imported object's surface texture. If you disable it, the particle will keep whatever surface you gave it before making it a particle. Keep textures simple because it takes a long time to render fancy surfaces on thousands of particles.

Initial Position

All particles will be placed either in the middle or on the surface of the imported object. Placement options are:

- **Object surface:** On the outside.
- **Object center:** The default, it places the particles inside, which is neat for exploding objects outward from the inside.

Output Options

You get three output options.

- **Imported object only:** This effectively cancels the particle/gravity effects.
- **Imported object and particles**: When you select this option, you get an Import Particle file dialog which allows you to pull in one or more objects to use as particles. To import more than one object, just hold down the <Ctrl> key as you select them. The <Shift> key convention for a sequence of files also works. If you already have particles loaded, you get an option to replace them or add new ones.
- **Particles only:** Only the particles will be written to the output file.

Linear scale – Global

This scale value will be applied to all particles. The default of 1.0 means no scaling. You can go up or down from there. You can also apply scaling once the object is in tS2.

Linear scale – Start

This is the scale of the object at the start of the explosion. Very small decimals make the particles nearly invisible, so be careful not to go too low or you'll lose the effect.

Linear Scale – End

Same as above, but at the end of the animation. This can be used to make particles disappear or evaporate.

Anim. Frames

Again, these represent the start and end of the effect in frame numbers.

Random Scale

If you want a lot of different sized particles, use this option. 1.0 means no scaling. If you set a Max and Min scale factor, the program will randomly scale particles between those bounds.

Let Us Play

Back to exploder kernel construction. You have 2,500 faces, so under General Options, set your Min number of pieces at 2,500 because you want as many particles as possible. Next set Explosion distance ➪ 10, Percent rotation ➪100, Number of frames ➪ 60, Path options ➪ Accelerate.

Move to the Advanced Options page and select Stagger Explosions. Set the number of pieces to 50. If you want the pieces to blow out and disappear, set Scale Amount. Start ➪ 1.0, End 1.0001. Otherwise leave it at default. Try both ways to see what looks best to you. For the moment, we leave gravity and particles alone.

You probably want your explosion to toss off faces in all directions spinning wildly. The above settings will give you that effect. You can also try Shuffle and Sort options by hitting Alt O. Shuffle makes sure it's random, while Sort starts the explosion at one point and progresses smoothly through the sphere releasing particles at 50/frame until all 2,500 are gone. Export the exploder object as Kernl1.cob.

Repeat the above to make a second exploder object. Vary some of the parameters as you like, perhaps the explosion distance, or maybe disabling the Z axis for the blast. Export as Kernl2.cob.

Cosmic Gases

You can't use particles to simulate fire and gas because it would take hundreds of thousands of them and bog down your system. But when you paste a semitransparent bitmap on a sphere, the graininess of the image helps create the illusion of fire or gas particles (see Figure 26-5).

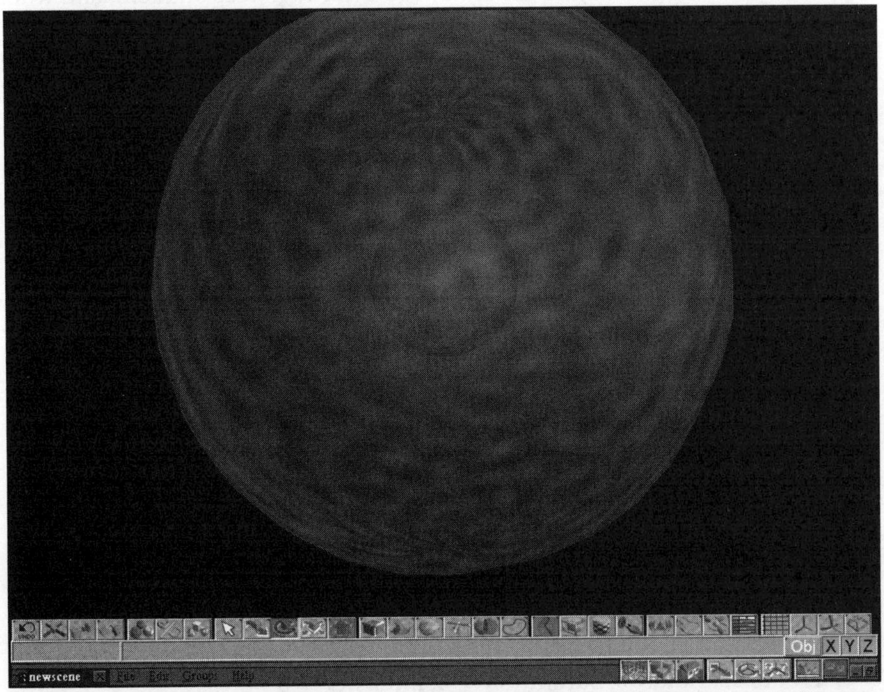

Figure 26-5: A giant gas ball that appears expanded about half-way. The billowing gases are simulated with a reflection map and rotation. An animated reflection map works even better.

Keyframing fast expansion of a sphere makes it look like an explosion. If you glue a local light inside and ramp its brightness rapidly up and down, the whole thing looks more like an explosion. Add to this a second gas ball, and have them both expand at different rates, rotating in different directions until you get the look of hot swirling gases.

You can't use a regular texture map with this procedure because the transparency doesn't work. So add your map in the reflection channel. This means the ambient lights will be important too. So make sure you have some light behind the camera shining toward the gas. In a pinch default white light will do.

You'll want to keyframe the surface to go to invisible over the last few frames. This makes it appear that the explosion is dying out.

Gas Blast Construction

Start up tS2 and pop up a plain old sphere — you'll want it pretty smooth. This is a gas bubble. Set your shaders to 90% invisible with a red/orange color, then add a nice reflection map like Viral.bmp found on the CD-ROM (in the \textures\misc subdirectory). This gives the surface a filmy, billowy look. The look is different depending on how you adjust the shininess and roughness shaders, and whether you choose Metal or Phong (Plate 26-1).

Keyframe the texture to fade as follows:

- Frame 0: Shininess ➪ 80, Roughness ➪ 80, Transparency ➪ 90
- Frame 24: Shininess ➪ 80, Roughness ➪ 80, Transparency ➪ 90
- Frame 30: Shininess ➪ 40, Roughness ➪ 40, Transparency ➪ 99

Expand the bubble and build a second one inside it. This time use a slightly different surface color and the flare.txr map for reflection. This gives a fiery center look. You're going to keyframe separate expansion and rotation envelopes for each.

Now pop up a local light. It should be in the exact center of your spheres. Keyframe as follows:

- Frame 0: Hue ➪ 0, Saturation ➪ 0, Intensity ➪ 0
- Frame 10: Repeat above to create null key
- Frame 14: Hue ➪ 0, Saturation ➪ 0, Intensity ➪ 14
- Frame 16: Hue ➪ 100, Saturation ➪ .75, Intensity ➪ 18
- Frame 22: Hue ➪ 0, Saturation ➪ 0, Intensity ➪ 8

Note that even without the particles or animation, these two spheres look pretty much like an explosion in space (Plate 26-1). Add chunks and you have a believable effect (Plate 26-2 which is frame 26 with a keyframed lens flare added in Premiere 4.0).

Add the Chunks

Combining the five parts, two gas balls, and two particle balls plus a light is relatively easy.

- Place the two gas balls on top of each other and glue them together.
- Place the two particle balls on top of the gas ball and glue in place.
- Center the light in the kernel and glue.
- Scale the whole magillah down to a pinpoint and save it as your exploder object.

That was a long way to go, but now you understand the engine and can make some neat effects. You are limited only by your imagination. The real fun is experimenting and seeing what you get. In fact, there are so many things that you can do with this program I won't even try to show them all. I'll just give you a taste.

- A new kind of particle morph where you have one object disappear as a different object is appearing
- Snow
- Pouring sand
- Rocket exhaust
- Meteor trails
- Explosions
- Bubbles in the ocean or a drink
- And ever so much more

Before we move on to compositing, Rob Bryerton has contributed some tips and techniques, which I've included here. His ideas are great.

A Few Words from Rob Bryerton

I was happy to see Peter write this book. We've all needed one on tS2 for a long time. Exploder is my version of an idea originally developed by David Strepenham of Germany. It's a stand-alone engine that manipulates tS2 ASCII .cob files to create particle animations. This version of Exploder is a special build, 32 bit version (Windows 95 and NT 3.51 native). It can also be run under Windows 3.1x with Win32s 1.3 or higher.

This trial version only works with objects to a maximum of 3,000 faces. But don't worry, that's more than you'll use for most things. The even more powerful registered version handles objects of unlimited size. I wanted you to enjoy a generous evaluation model with this book. I do hope you register as it supports my programming efforts which are taking some exciting new directions.

Here Are a Few Things You Won't Find in the Help File

Here's a description of topics that you won't find in the Help file.

Static Objects

You can create static objects (no movement) by setting the Number of Frames setting in the Explosion Options dialog to 0. This is useful for placing multiple (particle) objects.

Scaling

You can manually control particle scaling by unchecking the Auto Scale option on the Particle tab of the Exploder Options dialog, and scale using the Linear Scale/Global setting.

Weather Simulation

Peter and I were discussing the possibility of using Exploder to create weather and bubbles. So for the CD-ROM I've included some neat sample scenes, objects, and textures, and example animations. Look in the \exploder subdirectory for the following:

- ✦ BUBBLE.SCN is an example of using Exploder to create a rising bubble effect.
- ✦ SNOW1.SCN and SNOW2.SCN are examples of a falling snow effect.
- ✦ The FLAKE*.COB objects are simple single polygon objects textured with a "snowflake" texture (FLAKE*.TGA). These are used as simple snowflake particles.
- ✦ The BUBBLE*.COB objects are simple spheroid objects textured with a transparent surface and simple environments (RAINBOW.T1D and WASTLAN.E2D). These are used as simple bubble particles.
- ✦ There are also a couple of "template" objects called RANDGRID.COB and GRID.COB. These are used as particle placement templates (whew) for the particle animation examples.

A Few General Tips

Exploder offers you far more opportunity than meets the eye. Once you're used to it, think about ways in which you can manipulate its many parameters to create interesting illusions. Here are a few things to consider:

- ✦ You may want to load two or three copies of the particle animation object, and offset their position and start times in the Project window, to create a more complex effect. Experiment with the above techniques; you can get some really great complex effects.
- ✦ For snow particles, sometimes I use a simple square polygon, and texture it with a small white .tga bitmap that has a radial gradient (circular fade) in the alpha channel. This creates a smooth, flat circular object from the square polygon when rendered.
- ✦ When you are creating objects in trueSpace2 that you plan on importing into Exploder, center them in the universe (Location 0, 0, 0) before you save them as ASCII *.cobs. This allows Exploder to process the file more effectively.
- ✦ After you generate a particle animation and load it into trueSpace2, animate the texture of the particle object(s).
- ✦ Certain objects, such as text objects, may work better in Exploder if you first triangulate them before saving from trueSpace2. While this is not necessary,

it allows Exploder more freedom to process an object containing *holes*. When you load the triangulated object into Exploder, sort the object (right to left usually looks good) before processing and saving the object.

Evaporate Effect

Create an object in trueSpace2, save it as an ASCII *.cob, and load it into Exploder. Open the Explosion Options dialog and set the Min. number of pieces setting to the value that is displayed in the Object Information/Faces box. Click on the Advanced tab, uncheck X, Y, and - boxes in the Position Axes group. This will make Exploder project the explosion in an upward (+Z) direction only. Uncheck the X, Y, and Z options in the Rotation Axes group, and change the Scale Amount/End setting to 0.0001. Next, check the Stagger explosions box in the Stagger Options group, then choose OK to close the dialog. From the Options menu, select Sort Faces/Top to Bottom, then export the object and load it into trueSpace2 for a preview.

Snow/Bubble Effect

See files BUBBLE.SCN and BUBBLES.AVI for an example of the following technique. First we need to create a *random* grid object to be used as the starting position for the snow/bubble objects.

Create a plane with a resolution of 5, go to Top View, enter point edit mode, select about half of the points (one at a time!), and move them to *random* locations. Next, move the plane so its Z location is -1.0 and save this object as an ASCII *.cob named randgrid.cob.

An alternative approach is to set the resolution on a rectangular box to about 50 and pop it up (very large object, 2,500 nodes). When you load it into exploder, sort it bottom to top and place snowflakes at each vertex. This will cause a steady stream of flakes to drop when you explode it in sequence.

Next we need to create the actual particle objects. For snow, create a simple polygon object, apply the texture of your choice, and save it as an ASCII *.cob name flake1.cob. Rotate it *randomly* on the X,Y, and Z axes, save as flake2.cob, rotate again, and save as flake3.cob.

For bubble particles, create a simple sphere, scale it slightly on the X, Y, and Z axes, texture appropriately, save as bubble1.cob, rotate *randomly* (as above), and save as bubble2.cob, repeat and save as bubble3.cob.

Now open Exploder, open the randgrid.cob object, then open the Explosion Options dialog. Click on the Advanced tab, uncheck X, Y, and - boxes in the Position Axes group. This will make Exploder project the explosion in an upward (+Z) direction only. Click on the Gravity/Particles tab and check the Particles box, which will enable the particle option controls. In the Output Options group, select the Particles only option, l and in the Random scale group, set the Min control to 0.3. This makes Exploder randomly scale the particles between 1.0 (original scale) and 0.3 (about $^{1}/_{3}$ the original size).

Choose the OK button to close the dialog. Exploder will now open the Import Particle Object dialog. Click on the filename for bubble1.cob, then while holding down the Control key, select bubble2.cob and bubble3.cob, then click on the Open button. Now we are ready to process and save the animated objects.

From the File menu of Exploder, choose Export, or click on the disk button on the toolbar, and save the animation as bubbles.cob. Load bubbles.cob into trueSpace2, open the animation panel, and click on the Play button for a preview. If you would like to have the bubbles continuously rise, open the Animation Project window, click on the Repeat button, then click the animation time line for the bubble object.

If the particles are not scaled to your liking, change the Global setting in the Linear Scale group of the Particle tab in the Explosion Options dialog of Exploder (whew!), and reprocess the object.

To create the snow effect, follow the above procedure substituting the flake*.cob objects for the bubble*.cob objects when you are prompted to load the particles. On the Advanced tab in the Explosion Options dialog uncheck X, Y, and + boxes in the Position Axes group. This will make Exploder project the explosion in a downward (-Z) direction only. This will create a falling effect, as opposed to the rising effect of the bubbles.

For an example of this technique, see the files SNOW.SCN and SNOW.AVI. I hope you all enjoy using Exploder. I'm currently working on a more advanced special effects engine. If you want to learn more, contact me via e-mail at `73747.433@compuserve.com`.

Compositing Effects

And now for something completely different — adding actual footage of a real explosion to your animation. You may have noticed that several images in this book have a real blast on them. Actually it's several different blasts composited on top of each other using Photoshop's wonderful compositing tools. It's all quite simple when you know how and have the right pieces.

The hardest pieces to get are real explosion frames. You don't find them many places, so when I spoke to the folks at Foundation Imaging, who do *Babylon 5*, I asked for a good source. They put me onto Visual Concepts Engineering or VCE for short. These guys are Hollywood special effects specialists. They put out a CD-ROM with all sorts of expensive effects for use in digital compositing. VCE has very graciously allowed us to use a few stills and a video for practice. Please respect their copyright and do not use their material for commercial purposes. If you want to do that, buy the CD and its associated rights. It's worth it.

The basic idea is that we use Photoshop (for stills) to interpret the black background on these images as transparent. It then places the explosion frame over the animated frame, where you want it in the frame. The result is an apparent 3D blast.

Using Photoshop for Composites

Fire up Photoshop and load in a large space rendering like the one on the cover. By now you can do this sort of thing. Then take it step by step:

1. Look at the explosion stills on the CD-ROM under the \VCE subdirectory.
2. Select one or two you like and load them into Photoshop.
3. Now you have your large space rendering and two explosions. Check the relative sizings. If the blasts are too large or small, you can resize them using the image pull-down. Try to use them as is, because this gives the best image.
4. Select one of your blasts and hit Ctrl+A. This will put a selection marquee around the whole image.
5. Hit Ctrl+C to copy it to the paste buffer.
6. Select the space rendering and open the Edit pull-down.
7. Go to Paste Layer and click, you get a dialog box where you can name the layer (a good convention) and select transparency. You want 100% opacity.
8. Open the Mode drop-down menu and select lighten. This will cause Photoshop to apply only those parts of the layer that have a greater luminosity than the base image. That means you can't composite fire over a white background, but over black it's great.
9. Hit OK, and the explosion image will appear somewhere on your space image.
10. Select the Move tool (looks like four arrows pointing compass directions) and move the explosion to where you want it on your space image.
11. Nail it down by clicking on the Marquee tool and clicking once on the main image.

That's it. Pretty slick. Many of Hollywood's best special effects are done with compositing, using masks. For example, in *Death Becomes Her*, they put a hole right through Goldie Hawn... how? Using a motion control camera, the director photographed Goldie's scene with her, and then went through the same camera moves without her. This gave him a clean plate of what was going on behind Goldie. All the special effects guys had to do (though they did it brilliantly), was create a whole image (it was actually done in 2D) and composite it and the background from the clean plate over Goldie. Bam, you have a hole through her and can see what's going on right through her body.

Rotoscoping

To get a similar effect in a video, I suggest you rotoscope it in. That means you'll attach a flat plate to the spaceship and project a series of 32-bit .tga files of an explosion onto it, as it moves. You need 32 bit files with a black alpha channel because that's how you achieve true transparency in tS2. It's a real pain, because .avi files can't carry an alpha channel, so you have to convert the .avi to a series of .tga files and then create an alpha in an image processor that can do the job. I use Photoshop. This alone is good reason to buy the VCE CD-ROM, which has the individual .tga files on it.

Here's the basic drill. Load .tga file into Photoshop, open the channels palette, add a fourth channel (by clicking the little box and circle in the lower left portion of the channels panel), and name it Alpha. Choose Select All (Ctrl+A) ➪ Copy to Clipboard (Ctrl+C) ➪ Select alpha channel ➪ Paste (Ctrl+V) ➪ Save (Ctrl+S). That's it. But you have to do it about 60 times (see Figures 26-6 to 26-8). Figure out a way to automate the process. There's another way that you might find easier.

Figure 26-6: The first step in creating an alpha channel for rotoscoping. Load, select, and copy your image.

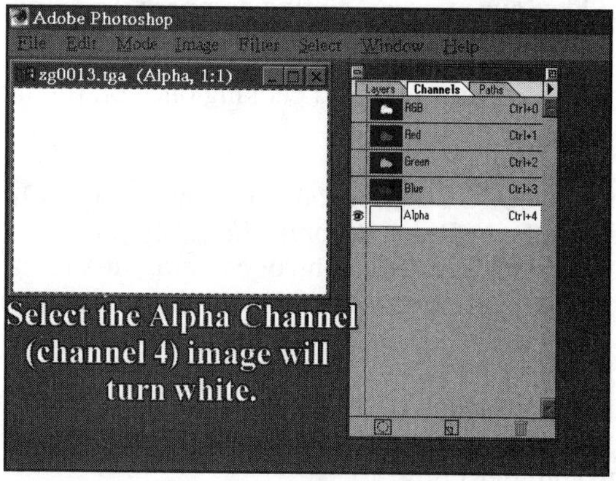

Figure 26-7: The second step in creating an alpha channel. With your image on the clip board, select the alpha channel that is empty.

Figure 26-8: The final step in creating an alpha channel. Paste the image on the clip board into the empty alpha channel. The image automatically appears in grayscale.

Use the Explosion .avi as an animated background in tS2. Pop up a flat plane and paint it invisible. Key the same number of frames as your .avi to the plane using the Animation tool. Render in sequential 32-bit .tga files (check the Start with 0 option). This will give you an alpha channel, but for some strange reason it's a white one. You need to then load it into Photoshop and invert the alpha channel for each frame. Really good effects are sometimes labor intensive, but it separates the pros from the players.

Special Paint Effects

By using transparency and the different painting tools, you can create some interesting effects. There is a bug as I've mentioned in the Vertex Paint tool, which is a shame, because it's the only way to get smooth edge transparency. Edge transparency is where the center is opaque and becomes ever more transparent as you move out to the edge. In a pinch, if you really need it, you can build an alpha with a gradient from white (opaque) to black (transparent). This effect is particularly useful for rocket exhausts and light effects. The Vertex tool can only be used effectively against a black background. I did a moving searchlight effect (see srchlite.avi on the CD-ROM in the \movies\dreamscp subdirectory) by flattening a cone, painting it invisible, and painting one of the vertices with opaque white. It gives the look of a light beam.

Texture Effects

I enlisted the aid of the trueSpace Internet mailing list (tSML), headed by Shane Davis, to help me come up with some interesting paint effects. It turns out there is a gold mine hidden in tS2.

At first, I was disappointed in the three procedural textures that come with tS2. They're Marble, Granite, and Wood — big deal, I can do better with a map. When I expressed my disappointment during beta testing, one of their tekkies suggested I play around with them until I changed my mind. "How rude," I thought. He was in fact completely right. These are not Wood and Marble and Granite. They are really Flash, Liquid Light, and Blast!

Caligari has recently taken over administration of the tSML. Started by Shane Davison at the University of Regina in Canada. Shane is a student who is now very pressed by the realities of advanced study, but he checks in once in awhile with a few sage comments. The tSML has grown to over 800 and a second mailing list has started for people especially interested in VRML and Fountain. Check the Web site for details.

Marble – Call It Flash!

Flash! makes a passable marble that you can cut through and see its solid inner grain. I might use it a few times this decade. For floors I prefer bitmaps. But play around with it — you'll discover that vein and rock colors can be changed. You can individually vary their transparencies. Even more importantly, you can adjust things like turbulence, sharpness, and direction (grain and scale) of the effect. I discovered that reducing sharpness of the vein parameter turns it progressively into a fractal cloud. Make it white and you have clouds. Give the stone a sky blue color — bam! a cloudy blue sky texture, perfect for your sky dome.

If you intend to animate objects and track them with the camera, I recommend using a sky dome instead of a background map. The latter stays centered on the camera regardless of angle. This makes the camera appear to be stationary while the object moves against a stable background. This will kill all your exciting camera movements. A sky dome stays put. Here's how to do it.

Just make a sphere, smooth quad divide it once and scale it up until you can put your camera inside and move around your scene. Half the sphere will be below your grid line, so you're left with a large dome. Paint it with your Flash sky texture and you have a realistic background that stays put as the camera moves. Another way to go is to make the stone parameter dark blue or gray or even red and slide the transparency to 100%, paint the dome, and render against a blue background. This produces a different look.

But there's more. All the flash parameters are animatable. Thus by making small keyframe changes, you can get a wildly billowing storm sky. Try parameter changes of a few hundredths to start with and stretch them over 60–100 frames. Sandwich a triplane model between clouds and b.g. and bam, a storm-buffeted pilot battles for survival. People will wonder how you did it.

Play with your lighting, see how it affects the outcome. Also, fiddle with the self illumination parameter to affect the brightness of the clouds. You can build everything from a flowing sunset to bright sunny day clouds.

Add a Little Flash!

Now how about some lightning. No problem. Make the vein color a yellow-white at about 20% transparency and bring the ambient value to 100%. Set the stone color to yellow/orange and 100% transparent (trust me, the transparency color makes a difference). Set sharpness between 8 and 10. Paint it on another transparent slab and you have a bolt of lightning. Play with the turbulence and the direction sliders to achieve the effect you want. Animate and slip it behind the storm clouds with lightning animated to flash and flicker in synchrony with the bolt. The vein will pick up the light and the scene will be flooded with brilliance for a split second. Do this by right clicking on the light control panel that comes up when you place the light. A dialog window will open up and let you enter very high light levels. Ramp a flash up over three frames to a value of 12, then pull it way down below 1 in two frames. You'll get a serious flash. Keyframe a number of flashes and flickers in this way to add life to your scene. Later you should add sound. I've seen a number of CD-ROMs with natural sounds of storms on them. Do you have a mental picture of it?

With trueSpace2, you can cast light through textures to project shadows on things. I'll bet you could create an interesting underwater effect with fog and undulating shadows from light cast through an animated cloud /marble texture on a clear planar surface. I haven't tried it, but all these possibilities keep the brain up nights.

Granite – Call It Liquid Light

Speaking of water, you can hardly build better procedural water than with the very cool granite texture. Move over Kai, this stuff kicks butt. tS2 comes with a pool water texture in one of its sample material libraries. Take a look; it's built of granite. Pop up a cube and fill it with this pool water texture. Liquid Light is a procedural texture with four color components. They are proportion control, transparency, X/Y/Z scaling, and sharpness.

By varying the size and abundance of each set of particles, as well as their color, transparency, and sharpness, you can produce hundreds of interesting effects.

Get Down and Dirty

Use it like fractal noise to create dirt-smudged spaceships. Here's a texture that I've used to give spaceships that space-worn look. Select your rust or dirt colors for 1–3. I use a little green for copper, some brown/orange for steel, and dark gray for carbon. Set color 4 as the base color. Next set the amounts of the first three down to around .2–.3 for a nice spattering of detritus. To get the ship details, make a monochrome bump map in Corel or Fractal Design Painter. Draw all the seams and rivets and grooves you want and apply it over this procedural texture for the grungy panel effect.

Add a Little Sparkle

How about a starry background for that space scene. Just render a screen filling cube covered with granite set to the following parameters. Color 1 = bright opaque white at 0.11, color 2 = bright opaque red at 0.07, color 3 = bright opaque yellow at 0.07, and color 4 = transparent black at 1.00. This will give you a believable sprinkling of bright stars of varying size, mostly white, with reddish and yellowish stars scattered throughout.

Build Your Own World

Liquid Light is a great planet tool. Try setting color 4 to a dark blue with amount at 1.0. Next play with earthy colors for 1–3 and set the amount down to between .2 and .4. Test render on a sphere until it looks right. You'll get what looks like an ocean with land masses. Add a bump map like the orange skin or one of your choosing for shadow detail.

Really improve it by enveloping your world in a slightly larger cloud sphere filled with translucent billowy Flash texture. Use whitish-blue at 100% transparency for the stone (sky) and pinkish-white at 30% transparency for the vein (clouds). Apply the orange bump map for a nice billowy effect. Use Phong shading. Set your scaling to X = 2.1, Y = 2.0, and Z = 5.03 for starters. Experiment.

For a neat effect, set your world against a starry background made above and put in a grungy spaceship. All the textures in the picture are procedural.

Wood — Call It Blast

This is a complex and interesting procedural texture that will at first look like wood, any way you fiddle with it. But it has hidden glory. Try making a cone, but first right click on it and set the latitude = 20, longitude = 40, then flatten it to a disk. Create a procedural texture as follows: left click on wood, and set the ambient light to 100%. Set the springwood to dark red and summerwood to bright yellow. Set the springwood transparency slider to 100% transparent. Nothing exciting so far, but there's more. Set the Spring:Summer ratio to 1.0, the ring density to .14, width vary to .6, and shape vary to 0. Now we start to get somewhere. Left click on the sample sphere and it becomes a plane. If you've done everything right, you will see a yellow square with a circular gradient going to transparent in the center. Paint this on your disk for a bright ring of fire reaching inward.

Shock Waves

You've seen nova shock wave rings in films like *Star Trek VI* and *Star Gate.* You can make your own version with this object. Here are a few hints. First animate the ring from a point at frame 0 to a ring just beyond the camera range at frame 100. For the first ring, change the Blast texture by making the Spring:Summer ratio 0. This makes the ring solid flame yellow. Set a keyframe and paint the last frame with the same texture but with the Spring:Summer ratio set to 1. Now rotate the object so it becomes an ellipse, to observe the blast from a high angle in space. Animate a light source as above to enhance the blast effect and watch as the ball of fire forms a ring that expands and gets thinner as its diameter increases. The center becomes transparent, so put some stars in the background to enhance the effect. You can also embed this shockwave object inside an exploder object to enhance an otherwise plain blast. If you want to take the time, you can make the shock wave in several rings and paint the inner one with an animated fractal pattern series of 32 bit .tga files with a black alpha channel. You can build such a series with the Fractinit program widely available on the Internet.

Professional Pizazz

The ability to create excellent textures in a pinch is one sign of the professional. Many of the really terrific textures you see on TV space shows rely on procedural textures (for example, *Babylon 5*'s Vorlon Cruiser with it's mottled living skin relies on the fractal noise procedural in LightWave). So start thinking about your demo tape and come up with some great uses for trueSpace2's great tools. Take a closer look at the vertex painting tool. It's another amazing power tool that you just might overlook. It's useful for making glows, rocket exhaust, and even tractor beams.

POWER TIP

Professionals never have a lot of time to tweak their creations. They have to get them close to final on the first shot. Building up a library of neat tricks is essential no matter what application you are using. I suggest keeping a note file on all your discoveries. Share them on the Internet with other users and keep track of their discoveries. This is a new generation, a new way of learning and doing business. Today more than ever, you can be an integrated piece of the whole by linking with your colleagues via the Net. Online sharing can cut your learning curve in half or better. Come join the evolution.

If you read this entire book, you'll find other little Hollywood-type special effects here and there. But the greatest source is your own creativity. If you set your mind to it, you can create many different effects, most of which I've never even considered, and I've considered plenty. That's the nature of film special effects — creative visualizations with the tools to bring them to life.

Summary

Special effects is an exciting new area that promises a long future of creative exploration. With it you can create visualizations of things that never were and never could be — you can make them seem very real to the viewer. In this chapter you just scratched the surface on the following aspects:

- How to create fabulous illusions using a particle system designed by Rob Bryerton. You learned how to make everything from digital explosions to snow and bubbles, giving your work a distinctive professional look, and even to do a new kind of morph using disappearing and appearing particles.
- How Hollywood FX experts create illusions using compositing to integrate 3D animation and live action.
- How to use the alpha channel to create transparent textures for roto-scoping in tS2.
- How to design special procedural textures to create unusual surface effects, such as marble to create clouds, or lightning or granite to create planets or water.

✦ ✦ ✦

C H A P T E R 27

Rendering Your Animation

✦ ✦ ✦ ✦

In This Chapter

Dealing with quality-tradeoffs when setting up a render

When it's best to use draft, Antialias, or Raytrace

The effects of Motion Blur and Z-focus on pictures and rendering times

Impacting render times

Stopping a render in progress

✦ ✦ ✦ ✦

Time for a short but important chapter that will take you beyond the physical aspects of rendering and lead you to the artistic ones. The chapter considers the practical side of rendering from a time perspective as well.

The Uses of Quality

WEB CONNECTION

You don't want to render every image at the highest quality. I'm sure you noticed that raytracing takes forever. It's good to check the Caligari Web site at `www.caligari.com` for upgrade patches; they're free to registered owners. The latest one speeds up the raytrace engine substantially and has some minor bug fixes, but it's still slower than Congress.

There's a clear tradeoff in 3D: the higher the quality of your image, the longer it's going to take to render. Add atmospheric effects like procedural filters and fog and one image can take all night. This is true for all the render engines. The high-end suites such as SoftImage and Alias/WaveFront and Renderman are the slowest — believe it. They require very fast machines to function about as fast as trueSpace2 on a Pentium. But they put out superior quality. Don't take that as a criticism. Look at some of the photos in the color section. tS2 is capable of amazing photorealism.

Draft

As you've learned, Draft really only renders a quarter of the image and puts a quick jagged-edge replica on your screen. The need for Draft has decreased since 3DR came into play.

In version 1.0, Draft was essential for checking the general look of your image. I tend to use a small 3DR window for the same now. Yet, on occasion I use Draft to do a quick animation to check movement and path alignment. You *never* send *anything* out in Draft. That is an absolute no-no. It's the lowest quality and it's for your eyes only.

Normal

If you don't check any options, you'll get a reasonably fast mid-quality scan-line rendering that will suit most in-house purposes. I wouldn't send this out, except in special cases where you're not trying to impress. I use this most to do check renders when I think I'm done with the image. I never am, because when I do a normal test render, I always see things I didn't exactly expect. I rarely like and leave them, mostly I fix. You need this level to get a good look at the piece. In some images you'll get unacceptable jaggies.

AntiAlias

This is a wonderful and simple invention. All it does is determine where the edges of your picture are and then blurs them a little by blending background colors with the edge pixels. It's kind of like visually filing off the rough spots.

It's hopeless to use with Draft, because your jaggies are so big and the time to fix them is longer than if you just did a normal render. Much of your output can reach very high quality with Normal scan-line rendering and 2× (two times) antialiasing. Each time your computer looks at the edge it can make the color transition smoother, so by increasing the number of antialias passes, you may increase the quality of your picture. You quickly reach a point of diminishing returns though, and as always, at the expense of time. Usually a 2× is fine. That's what I use for hi-res magazine articles and the cover of this book. Of course, I wanted very high quality for the cover, so I used raytracing to bring out the highlights better and put in sharp space-like shadows and reflections.

Raytracing

Raytracing is the key to truly photorealistic images. It gives real transparent shadows through glass, refraction effects, and true reflections. It works by tracing the path of light particles and examining what they hit and how they bounce. It's amazingly sophisticated technology when you think about it. It can give your work a radically different look from the scan-line version, so you may want to draft it first.

Be aware that many expensive applications like 3D Studio don't even offer raytracing (it is available as an expensive add-on) and achieve very high quality images. But it is a wonderful addition that you get automatically with tS2.

You can definitely overuse it. Tracing tends to give things a hard look. Shadows are always very sharp. You can fix this in tS2 by raytracing with shadow maps engaged (set it up in the light panel) to give softer shadows. Still, you wouldn't raytrace if you were trying to match flat classical 2D animation, for example. It would make things look too different. When do you use it? I can only give you my opinion.

✦ Whenever you have glass surfaces or transparency effects, they will look better if raytraced.

✦ You can only achieve refraction with raytracing.

✦ When in outer space, use raytraced shadows to get a hard terminator.

✦ When you have shiny metals like gold logos, raytrace looks a thousand times better, especially if you use a lot of small light sources close up.

✦ Glossy surfaces always look better if raytraced. You can fake reflections with cubic maps, but you can't quite achieve the same quality look.

✦ Many lighting effects look better raytraced.

That's all I can think of at the moment. I try not to use raytracing because I'm always in a hurry, but sometimes you just can't beat it for a great look.

Motion Blur

You can add Motion Blur in Premiere 4.0. It's not as realistic as rendering it, but use it where you can. You can probably build a house in your backyard in the time it takes a short animation to render with blur because tS2 renders the picture over and over again to figure out what the actual blur would be (Premiere just fakes it). By default, this takes at least five times as long to render!!! Even if you only have a tiny bit of blur. Things could have been organized better. Nevertheless, there are those scenes that just look better with blur — usually when you have a large object moving moderately fast or close up. Blur helps you achieve a more natural photographic look. I almost never use it unless someone is paying and then I charge them extra because it gobbles up time and resources. You'll find a lot of people will pay for it for some strange reason. Go for it. BTW, you can use Blur to create a ghostly special effect. You figure out how.

Z Focus

This is another terrific effect that I hardly ever use because of time. It's similar to Motion Blur in the time it takes and I don't particularly like the effect unless you tweak it, and that *really* can take a lot of time.

Consider This

Many things lengthen the time it takes to render images. For example, your CPU speed is critical, as is memory. I use a fast Pentium with 32 megs of ram. That used to be a mongo machine, now it's kind of paltry. Once you use up memory, the speed of your hard drive comes in, as tS2 will swap things in and out. This slows things down to an unacceptable crawl. Rule: never run short of memory if you can help it. Shut down other programs when using tS2. That'll free up more memory.

Every process that uses mathematics will slow you down because 3D is math-intensive to start with. Your coprocessor is running like Dr. Richard Kimball (remember *The Fugitive*?), and you're laying a swamp in front of it. Math-intensive processes include procedural textures, any kind of shadow that must be calculated, raytrace depth, antialiasing, and the other previously mentioned items. Also consider the number of polygons and objects. Notice that the exploder objects take a long time to load — lots of individual objects. Be particularly careful not to use procedural textures on large ones — you'll have to measure render time in half-lives.

Stopping a Render

Let's say you're rendering a long animation and you need your computer for other things. It's too bogged down to be effective on your spread sheet. What do you do? Stop the render in an orderly manner. Hit Escape and wait a long time while tS2 organizes your .avi file so you can use what's been done. If you quit the program mid-stroke, or don't wait until you get the prompt after bailing on a render, you won't be able to view the file. Time your hitting Escape with the beginning of a frame if you can. Make a note of the frame that was rendering at the time you shut it down. You can start there next time and merge the two clips in your video edit program.

Of course, when rendering to screen, you can see exactly how much is complete. After painting an object, it automatically renders the whole thing. You're not obligated to sit through that, though I've seen people sit there tapping fingers, as if they were. You can save time by hitting Escape and moving to the next procedure.

Rendering is the most painful part of 3D for me. I hate to wait. But we put up with it, ever striving for faster machines. The first 640 × 480 fractal image I ever rendered took 5.5 hours. The same one renders in about a minute today. Imagine how fast machines with multiprocessors will be in two or three years. Unfortunately, sloppiness comes with speed. As programmers produce ever less-efficient code, so animators may become sloppy in arranging their render resources. I suggest you learn to do it now and it'll become a good habit. Even with fast machines, the savings are cumulative and worth the effort.

Summary

Short chapters are like punctuation — they're meant to give you pause. In this chapter you learned how to approach some oft-confusing issues:

- ✦ How to deal with quality tradeoffs when setting up a render.
- ✦ When it's best to use draft, Antialias, Raytrace, or Shadows.
- ✦ What quality of picture is needed to send out to a publisher/producer.
- ✦ What effect Z-focus and Motion Blur have on my picture and rendering times.
- ✦ What other options most impact render times.
- ✦ How and why to stop a render in progress.

✦ ✦ ✦

PART VI

Post-Production: The Professional Touch

No matter how well you set up an animation, you really need to do post-production, or simply "post" as the professionals say, to make the animation look professional. At a minimum you need sound. You may need a traveling lens flare. Post will require you to buy some more toys such as Premiere, Razor Pro, or MediaStudio Sound Edit, to name but a few. Just remember that no amount of equipment and software can make up for a lack of talent or persistence. So take the time to hone your skills and techniques.

In This Part

CHAPTER 28

Silence Is Deafening – Creating a Winning Soundtrack

✦ ✦ ✦ ✦

In This Chapter

Using an ambiance track to smooth transitions, maintain continuity and create a mood

Putting in hits or sharp sounds that tie the soundtrack to the video

Buying music clips

Contacting BMI and ASCAP to track down a piece of music so you can license it

Finding midi and mod music files and using a keyboard for background music

Composing multi-track stereo sound for your production and synching it to the video

✦ ✦ ✦ ✦

I get soundless demos all the time. Play it next to one with a well-synched soundtrack; the difference is astounding. Don't send out a tape without sound. There *is* one thing worse than a silent demo — one with a klutzy soundtrack: lousy synch, inappropriate music, lots of words trying to explain the video, bad audio edits, and/or blotchy compression. Those will drive you crazy, so you skip them altogether or play them without the sound, remembering the lack of aesthetic judgment the maker had.

With digital mixing, SFX (Sound FX, or sound special effects) libraries, easy digital recording right on your hard drive, and digital audio processing, you probably already have a wonderful sound lab within reach. All of the Corel Photodisks have royalty free music on them (didn't know that, did you?).

Sound Ideas

With a good set of microphones you can quickly create your own library direct to disk using your sound card. A good pocket tape recorder expands possibilities immensely. The story goes that the original laser sound in *Star Wars* was made by attaching a contact mike to the base of a steel guy wire for a telephone pole. The cable was then struck with a hammer. It's true.

Fortunately, I've worked in sound studios as a student and again when friends were creating a bluegrass album. I've produced my own video soundtracks as well. Along the way I picked up some tips. Here are a few for starters:

- A good soundtrack requires multiple channels with hits or beats synched to the action. These are called component audio tracks.
- An ambiance (or wild) track can give your image subtle credibility while masking noise, transitions, and small errors.
- You can digitally create an incredible range of sound effects by manipulating and combining a small library of basic sounds.
- Don't try to synch your sound by luck and guessing. It sometimes works, but it usually backfires.
- Bad sound, bad transitions, and bad level control will annoy even your shoes.
- Always start with the best quality source material you can.
- Always synch stereo sound location to the action.
- Amateurs almost never pay enough attention to sound — professionals do.

The Basics

You have tons of audio clips available to you, already digitized and ready to slide down the track. At a recent computer show I stopped counting at 20 sound clip disks for $5.00 to $19.95. You can also find a ton of clips on the Web (try `http://www.eecs.nwu.edu/~jmyers/other-sounds.html` for an index of sound effects clip sites worldwide).

The basic process is to make a list of your needs, collect your sounds, do a little audio art direction — lay out your fades, levels, overlays, and synch. Then you set up tracks in your video edit program, one below the other. You can have a ton of tracks if you want. Razor Pro has unlimited audio tracks. Preview the setup, fiddle with level controls and adjust clips along the time line, and after a bit you have a soundtrack.

File Formats

Clips are available in a number of formats, but any good audio program will read most of them and output to .wav files for use in Windows Apps. You can also extract the audio component of .avi files for use in your demo.

Tracks

Until recently, soundtracks were very difficult and expensive propositions. An amateur could be forgiven for just adding music to a video. Even today, some people recommend you simply add a three minute music track and don't let your demo go over it. I disagree.

You're trying to impress professionals with *your* professional ability. Go the extra two and a half miles (or minutes). Use the new digital multi-track sound edit/synch capability inherent in current video editing programs. I particularly like the sound capability in In:Sync's Razor Pro and they've pulled out the stops on Speed Razor Mach III. Though it's a bit pricey for the beginner it's an excellent value for the pro. It gives control over many audio parameters, even creating 3D surround sound effects with Razor Reality Sound (RRS). It also features Audio Scrubbing. With this engaged you can run the cursor over your soundtrack and hear your mix with the video for very exact adjustments. In it you can input beat markers on the audio tracks to help you synch action to the sound. It also uses SMPTE time code to help with precise synching.

I also like Premiere and Media Studio as well. All have excellent sound capabilities that allow you to composite and synchronize many channels of sound.

Did you ever notice the Clacker in filmmaking? Of course you did. That's the black and white striped hinged bar that "clacks" down on a clipboard. The second AD (Assistant Director) clicks it at the start of a clip. That click is used by the sound guys to synchronize sound to action. Nowadays you'll also see an SMPTE time code index on the clacker. All this seems pretty sophisticated, and it is, but don't let it scare you. If I can do it, anybody can. I'll give you an example.

Laying Out the Tracks

It's my second daughter's birthday and I hate shopping for gifts. I never know what to buy. I didn't have time to carve an ebony puzzle or rosewood earrings, so I made a video of fireworks bursting off into the letters of her name. Forgive me, I did it in 3D Studio because at the time I was writing about a plug-in routine that makes fireworks. It seemed appropriate, because that's how I feel about her; I'm a proud poppa.

Naturally I wanted to add sound, so I took some graph paper and laid out the significant events in the animation on a time line. This is kind of old-fashioned and you don't have to do it. You can usually just slide the frame-by-frame viewer to the moment you want a sound effect and write down the time code or frame number.

The purpose of my graph was to figure out what sounds I needed. The first thing you see is little rockets firing off. So I needed a Pfft sound or a Whump or both, but didn't have either. Next I needed four mongo blasts to synch with the bursting of each rocket head. I wanted them each to be a little different instead of just repeating the same blast. I found cannon blasts on an old audio sampler recording with blasts done for the 1812 Overture on it — as separate tracks. I quickly slipped the CD into my ROM reader and recorded the four I wanted as individual .wav files, using high sample rate, stereo, and 16-bit sound. This gives very large files, but remember the rule about source material: Always use the best.

POWER TIP

It's a good idea to collect lots of sound clips. I keep a ton of very short ones like a mechanical door closing with an echo, metal-on-metal klunks, metal-on-metal scraping, and such. Use them in my soundtrack where things happen. When a spaceship lands, it probably makes some kind of klunking inside the ship. I find that reverberation, used with skill, can imbue these sounds with a hollow ring like that in the hangar bay of an aircraft carrier. Keep plenty of these sonic punctuations around and know where you put them. Use your media library to catalog them.

Audio Editor Software

There are many useful sound editors around, one even comes free (Sound Recorder) with Windows and nearly every sound board comes with one or more. Many others are available as shareware and, like the one in Media Studio, they come with virtually all multimedia authoring packages. They're all pretty similar, you load a .wav file and perform various transformations upon it, enhancing or destroying the sound as you will. These include such transformations as:

- Echo effects
- Pitch changes
- Time changes (plays clip in more or less time)
- Amplification and Amplification envelopes
- Audio band filtering
- 3D reverberation effects
- And in rare instances, brainwave synchronization (Cool Edit)

The sound editor I included on the CD-ROM is an exceptional one. I like shareware packages built by enthusiasts. No commercial outfit has the zeal and creativity of a single, brilliantly motivated programmer. Author David Johnston works for a big software house during the day and builds shareware at night. He puts out a serious sound program that does more than filter existing sounds. It will create sound effects and music from scratch if you give it the right commands. The laser effects sounds are great, as are things like rain, waterfalls, and EFX music. Below, I give you an example of how to make a sound for my long approach to Trilon Station sequence. In Cool Wave you can create rocket, thunder, waterfall, laser, cannon... almost any sound you want from scratch or by modifying existing clips. Oh, yes, to be fair, I made the July 4th rocket sound using Media Studio Audio Edit.

Creating the Sounds You Don't Have

One of the fun parts of sound effects is manipulating audio clips to make them sound the way you want. With Cool Edit you can stretch sounds, create stereo phase effects, compress sounds, spectrum filter, enhance the base, and create envelope effects. Echo and reverb can add depth to sound. You can copy a sound to the clipboard and paste it back onto itself slightly displaced, to increase the richness and density of the sound. The ambient rocket background sound on the CD-ROM (rockett.wav in the \sounds subdirectory) was made that way. I recorded a mono track of a jet engine, which I then inverted and used as the second channel, offset by about a third of a second. (I also could have used the sound created by putting a microcassette recorder in the air blast from a small ceramic room heater.) I selected the entire track, cut it, and pasted it back in both channels on top of itself, just slightly offset in time, to make the sound a little denser. I then added some minor sounds and a klunk, then stretched the whole thing to lower the tone. I used a fade out envelope to create the soft ending.

In a second clip, use the first with concert hall reverberation to create a more indoor sound. Use these rocket sounds at a low amplitude as ambient tracks. You add a nice touch by switching to the hollower version as the ship enters the landing bay. It's easy. Lay the two tracks out in parallel. Select and cut out the part of the regular sound that happens inside. Then select and delete the part of the hollow sound that happens outside the bay. For indoors I might add a second ambiance track with people talking in the distance, no distinguishable words. I'd also add mechanical noises as the service arms move into position, each with a klunk (see landgbay.avi at \movies\dreamscp on CD-ROM for example).

Let's visualize what kind of sound we'll need for our long approach to Trilon Station. For background voice communication, record your own or a friend's voice and create a filter envelope that peaks sharply at around 2Khz to give it that "space comm" sound. Better yet, record it on a pocket micro-recorder at slow speed. That will give it the right lo-fi sound.

Coming Up with Good Dialog

For the computer voice, I like a soft female voice with a little reverb filtered down and fed in over the ambient hash. Write a script of things you might hear:

Pilot: "Trilon Approach, this is shuttle craft Starfire 307 light — I need lane assignment."

Computer voice: "Proximity warning — shuttle craft Starfire 307 in final approach."

Computer voice: "Tanker seven-seven-whisky-sierra, grid violation — reposition to coordinates 22-66."

Trilon approach: "Starfire 307, welcome to Trilon Station... you are cleared for service bay six — Recalibrate to deck approach computer and follow your arrows."

(continued)

Coming Up with Good Dialog *(continued)*

Pilot: "Thank you kindly Trilon approach, locking onto deck approach computer. Good day."

Trilon approach: "Good day Starfire..."

Computer: "Starfire, you are locked on – auto docking engaged."

If you have trouble coming up with good dialog, get a pocket aircraft radio from Radio Shack and listen to the planes communicating with the tower in your area. You might even be able to record some good background sounds off it. I imagine things won't change that much in space. Even if they do, they won't hurt you now.

Next, take your pocket recorder and try some of the following things:

- ✦ Record a bunch of doors slamming, being sure to include refrigerator, car, and front door. Record the front door lock sliding into place.
- ✦ Record your garage door closing. It has a bunch of great machine sounds. Put your mike close to the motor on one try, then right near the door itself.
- ✦ Put your recorder up against a big water valve — a lawn sprinkler system is good — and turn it on.
- ✦ A washing machine and dryer make fabulous sound sources. Record the beginning of the spin cycle, the wash cycle, and the dryer starting up and running. Slam the doors, they have a nice ring.
- ✦ Put your recorder against an iron railing and hit it with a hammer.
- ✦ Try recording the old hit-the-steel-guy-wire trick.
- ✦ Hold the recorder out the window while driving.
- ✦ Hold your recorder in front of a small ceramic heater at full blast.
- ✦ Record the sounds of a public place.
- ✦ If you can get in, record sounds in a factory, which is a gold mine of space station or onboard-ship noises.
- ✦ Go to the local airport and record the sounds of jets taking off and landing as well as loading crews and general airport ambiance.

If your animation is more ordinary in nature, you may want a more hi-fi sound. For that you'll need a regular cassette recorder with a good wide range microphone. Use the best tape you can get your hands on in all cases.

You won't come close to digitizing all your sounds, so run through and find the brief snippets that you want. Note them on your counter and begin to digitize them by plugging the output of your tape recorder to the line input of your sound card. Invoke your Sound Recorder program and select Aux as your input. It may have a different name, but should be obvious. Sound Recorder came with Windows and something better probably came with your sound card, or use Cool Edit. Record each short snippet with an appropriate label. I don't label them with the actual sound, but with what they sound like to me for video purposes. So instead of gragedor.wav I call it airlcdor.wav for airlock door.

Music

For your demo, a noncommercial venture, I've been told it's okay to use music clips you have in your personal CD library. But, I'm not a lawyer, so I don't know if this is actually true.

Just make sure you never make a profit on someone else's sound without first getting a license from them. It's not that hard. There are music buyout services like Valentino Production Music and NetWork Music, Inc. Valentino has a CD-ROM with clips from its entire collection. It's beautifully cross-indexed with categories such as science fiction or sounds like. The latter has familiar tunes that remind you of famous movie themes, but are different enough that you don't have to pay big license fees. These companies will license their excellent original music for about $20–25 per CD. Sometimes there is a time limit of one year. Check it out.

It may not be as bad as you think to license the real thing (don't use the happy birthday song; it's owned and expensive, I understand). All you need are "needle drops" or very short sections of a whole song. These are licensed separately from a whole song... and cheaper. In addition, you might be able to negotiate with a big songwriter to use his work for a reasonable fee because he likes your project. I'm sure there's somebody famous who would help you for free on an AIDS project public service announcement. You help raise money for good causes and establish working contacts at the same time. Look into it. There's nothing wrong with doing something worthwhile while you're trying to get ahead.

WEB CONNECTION

If you want to know more about actually licensing real music from the biggies (and the small guys) there's an excellent discussion on the ins and outs of licensing by Barry M. Massarsky at the Web site at `www.nlc-bnc.ca/documents/infopol/copyright/massarsk.txt`.

If you don't know whom to call to license a particular song, no problem, just hop on the Web and go to either the ASCAP home page at `www.ascap.com`, as shown in Figure 28-1, or the BMI home page at `bmi.com`, as shown in Figure 28-2. Both of these organizations are the labor representatives for music industry.

Between them they represent most songwriters and each has a lovely cross-indexed database of songs, writers, and publishers, complete with proper up-to-date phone numbers. Life is easy with the Web, so go for it.

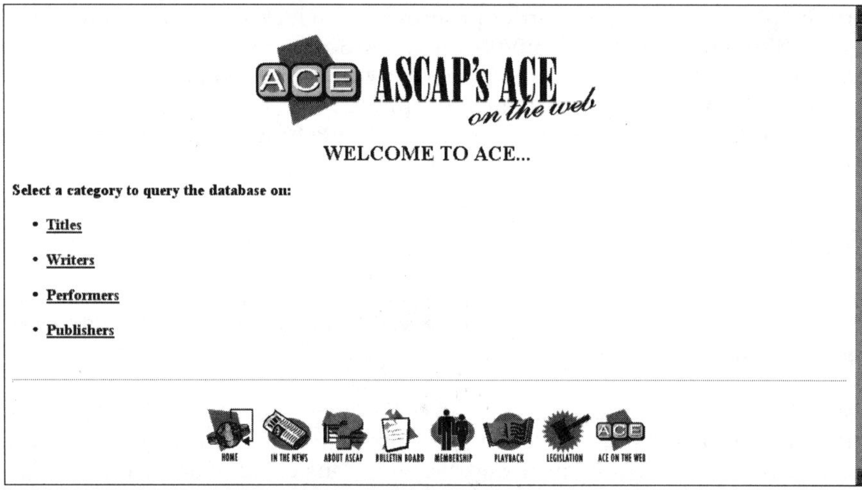

Figure 28-1: The ASCAP search page. It's best to search by song title, because you get the publisher information right away. Look up the song you want and you'll find the publisher. If you only know the writer, you'll get a complete list of their works.

Figure 28-2: The BMI home page – from here you can go to the search page, which is very similar to the one at ASCAP.

Sound Effects CDs

If you need sound effects of the common variety — doors slamming and glass breaking — there are audio CDs out there that are a snap to digitize in any multimedia computer. Ask your CD dealer about them.

I found a fantastic buy at Costco on a set of six CDs full of natural ambient sounds. Put out by Laser Light they are very high-quality digitally recorded sounds of thunderstorms, crickets, elk, loons, ocean waves, deep woods sounds, and more. No cheesy New Age music either. It's their Echoes of Nature series and is available at most recording outlets.[1]

Midi

There are thousands of midi files out there on the Web. If you have a good sound card with at least wave table synthesis, you can recreate some nifty music. Better yet, get yourself a reasonably priced, award-winning program called *Band In the Box* by Dr. Peter Gannon. This is smart midi extreme. It comes with 24 different style templates that you can use to change a basic midi melody into a highly personal piece. You don't have to be able to play a note. Extract a melody from any midi file and embellish it. There are also disks full of individual styles of dozens of artists from Chet Atkins to Errol Garner. Take any midi melody from the Web, spruce it up, and you have a royalty-free piece for your demo.

A keyboard is a natural sound machine. I picked one up at a garage sale for thirty bucks. I put some clips of my space music on the CD-ROM; feel free to use them as background (get my permission for commercial use) in your demos. I composed the simple pieces on the spot. Perhaps not brilliant, but it works. Try it yourself.

MOD

Have you heard of MOD yet? It's very popular in Europe. It's a kind of file that comes to you with built-in sound clips. Some of it is very good, some is awful. Try some of the Finnish FTP sites for a bunch of them. You'll need a player. Use your Web browser search facility for software to find some. I like the pieces with human voice clips like "Drax" and there's another called "Sky Wolf" that has lots of adventure in its sound. Digitize a clip from your favorite MOD and lay it in as part of your soundtrack.

Don't Lose It

When you start getting your clips together, you'll need to know what permissions you have, and so on. I know I'm being redundant, but trust me on this, put all your sounds in sound libraries using Album or MediaCenter. Don't just have a sound library. Have several — seaside sounds, space, people, and so on, or even short clips, ambient tracks, music hits, or whatever.

[1] If you have difficulty finding the series, it's published by Delta Music, Inc. in Santa Monica, California.

Putting It Together

So now you have an ambiance track and some voice stuff to lay in. Way more voice than you can use, but that's what you want, plenty of material to play with. Now look at some of your incidental sounds such as clanks and machines. In my short animation of Starfire landing in the repair bay, there's plenty of opportunity to lay in synchronized hits like steel clanks as the craft lands on the platform. I'll use the garage door for when the vacuum door closes, starting it before I actually see the door, and having a klunk as it hits home.

Listen to your audio track without video to make sure it's clean. If you can hear the various tracks as obvious add-ons, you need to do some work. Often, adjusting individual track volume will help or perhaps adding yet another ambiance track with credible sounds to mask whatever needs to be hidden. Sometimes I just put in a random hit like a door shutting to mask something.

Ultimately you want to end up with a smooth track that sounds as if it were recorded all at the same time. Make it stereo and play around with panning between tracks to add a feeling of motion.

Lasers

The cover scene on this book could use a really nice laser zap sound. You can make an almost limitless variety of laser-type sounds by mixing tone and noise functions with audio filters and envelopes in Cool Edit. Let's build one together.

Cool Edit

Cool Edit runs right off the CD-ROM — no need to install anything. So fire it up and run your mouse cursor over the various icons (see Figure 28-3). A function balloon (in Win95) will pop up in a second and explain what each does.

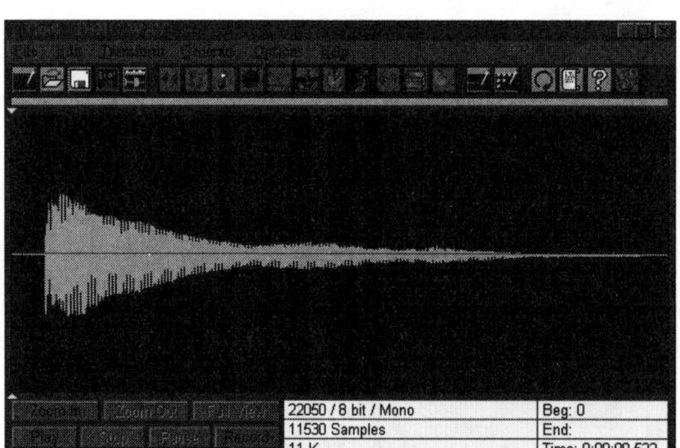

Figure 28-3: The main edit window of Cool Edit is well laid out and will help you create sound effects for your productions.

There is a preset for laser sounds in the Cool Edit Options menu. Here's how to build a laser to play with:

✦ Select the File drop-down menu ➪ New

✦ This gives you a dialog box where you can set the type of audio file you want. I recommend 44.1Khz, Stereo, 16-bit. This will open a blank audio file in Cool Edit.

✦ Select Options drop-down menu ➪ Scripts/batch processing.

✦ Select the Laser Effect script and hit OK.

✦ The Script will present you with a series of dialog boxes (see Figure 28-4) for filters, echo, compression, etc. Each is already set where you want it by the script. Just accept them as is and eventually the laser sound will be generated, filtered, and stretched into a cool Dr. Who-type laser sound.

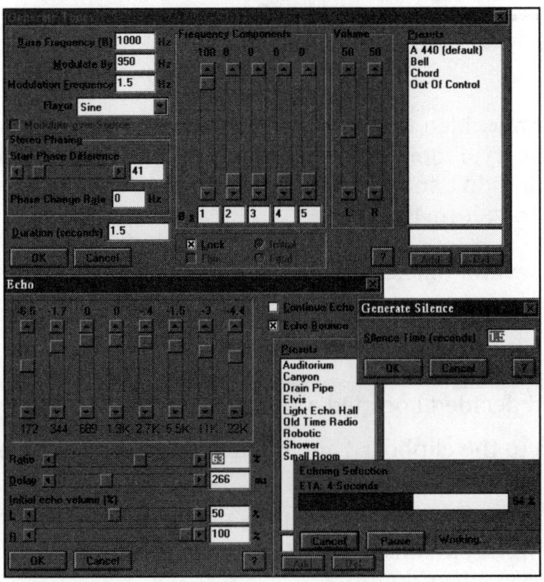

Figure 28-4: Some of the dialog boxes you'll run across in Cool Edit

Once you have the basic laser sound you can play with it (see Figure 28-5). It's too long and drawn out for me. I like a nice snappy laser byte. So I filtered it and enveloped it and shortened it in different ways. You can find some of my variations on the CD-ROM where the sounds are. They're all based on the Dr. Who sound. I don't remember what I did to make each one; I was playing around. You do the same.

Try all the presets and then begin building a few of your own. Just for fun, I've created a small library of space sounds for your productions. I find space stuff harder to come by than people burping, frogs ribbitting, and insane cackling.

The Cool Edit program is fully functional except that you can only pick two sets of effects to use at any one time. And since one choice is the save function, you really only have one. I think it was a clever way for David Johnston to let you use the product but make it inconvenient enough that you'll consider paying him his due. If you like Cool Edit but don't feel it's worth the $50, negotiate with Dave; he may send you a validation anyway. It's a really useful program and he deserves to be paid for his excellent work.

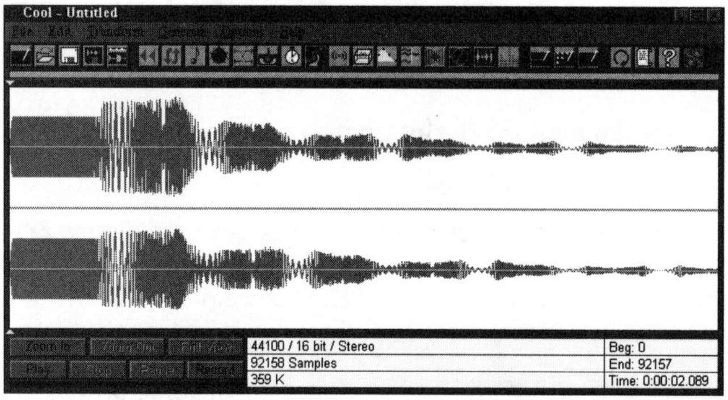

Figure 28-5: A basic laser sound

One of the sounds I needed for my video was the initial Pfft sound a Fourth of July rocket makes on take.off. In a hurry, I took the first clip I could find, the Chord.wav that comes with Windows 3.1. It didn't sound a bit like what I needed, but I played with it, applying the following transformations:

- ✦ First I lowered the pitch several times.
- ✦ I reversed the waveform.
- ✦ I speeded up the sound.
- ✦ I added stadium echo and decided I needed a stereo clip.
- ✦ I cut the entire waveform to the clipboard and created a blank stereo track and pasted it back in the left channel.
- ✦ I pasted the clip in the right channel just slightly to the right of the first, to create sonic differences in the two channels. I then inverted the left channel. This gave me a better stereo effect.
- ✦ I used the Pan effect in Media Studio; each package has an equivalent, enabling the sound to start in the right channel and end in the left, with a smooth transition between.
- ✦ I did a few other things I don't recall.

And after much fiddling I had a sound that rockets make when taking off. Patience and a creative approach.

When you have all your sound clips together it's time to load them into your film editor for synchronization with the video. That's when fun leaps to a higher shell. The first time you play an original animation with full soundtrack you'll truly feel like a professional. There's nothing like it when every beat of sound clicks with the moving image.

If you have it, use In:Sync's Razor Pro (see Figure 28-6). It has excellent sound editing qualities, and its new Speed Razor Mark III for Windows NT has awesome

Figure 28-6: An overview of the Razor Pro interface has video and audio clips in place for a short scene. You can have an infinite number of audio tracks. Note how audio is layered vertically in a sensible way for synching to the video.

sound editing qualities. I also like Premiere 4.0 from Adobe Systems (see Figure 28-7). Premiere 4.0 has audio scrub as well. In both products it's easy to adjust audio levels and cueing.

I'm not here to teach you all about video editing. If you're serious, you learn it because you need it. So take this as a general approach rather than program specific. No matter what edit program you use, you'll take a similar approach to sound. Lay out your video across the top and layer in your sound below, lining up the beats of sound with the beats of the video.

Some Things to Consider

I started out mentioning how annoying bad sound can be. Surprisingly, people with really bad soundtracks have the impression that they've done a fabulous job. Strange. All I can do is give you some advice on how to judge your work.

- ✦ Sound can begin before the video starts and last after it fades to black. Briefly. But in the middle it better match what's on the screen.
- ✦ Unless you know your audience wants it, avoid extreme music like heavy metal or psycho-punk-rock and especially gangsta rap.

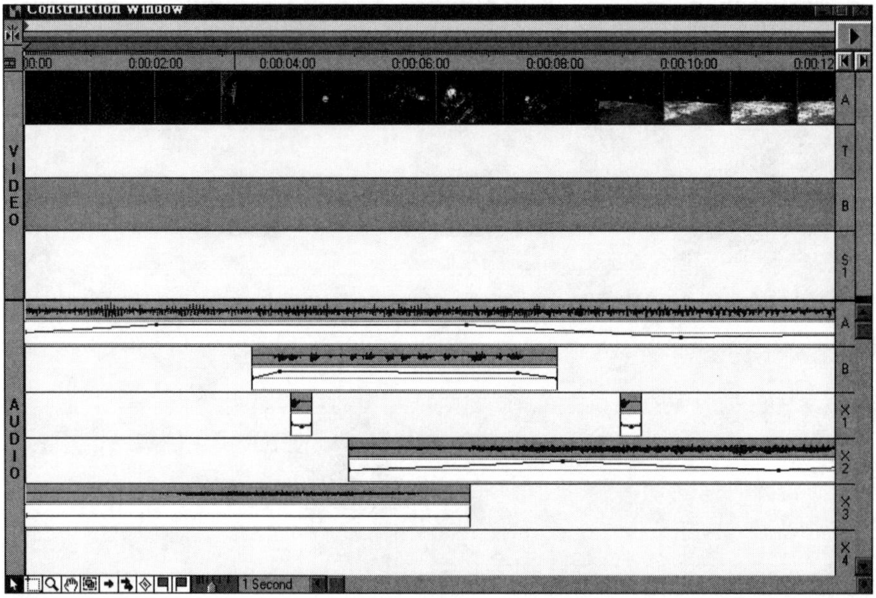

Figure 28-7: The Composition window of Adobe's Premiere 4.0. Notice how the video is lined up on the top and audio tracks are layered in below, much the same as in Razor. Each program has different strengths, but both do a nice job on audio.

- ✦ Make sure the music you choose isn't monotonous or harsh. Check with someone born in the generation of those who review to make sure.
- ✦ If you have dialog, make sure the music and SFX don't drown it out.
- ✦ If you have dialog, make sure it synchs perfectly with the characters' lips and expressions.
- ✦ If you find a theme that fits the material and you like it and it doesn't violate any of the above, and it's about three minutes long — shape your demo to the music. Time your transitions to match tempo changes and have them begin and end on the same note.
- ✦ Surprise us with something unexpected. Remember in Chapter 3, I suggested you put twists in your story. That goes for the visuals and sound as well.
- ✦ Make sure you have a *quiet* track. That doesn't mean no sound, it means no noise. Hum, hash, and distortion can ruin an otherwise great track. Use clean source material and filter out any hum you find with 60Khz notch filter if you have one, but better yet check all your connections and grounds (earth) and avoid hum completely.

✦ Don't be afraid to manipulate the volume over time. You may want a musical crescendo, or to fade out a rocket engine or lower background during dialog. It's easy with the digital editors above and will give your work professional polish.

✦ Go light on echo. Go very light on echo.

✦ Keep ambient tracks low. Few things distract like a loud ambiance track with sharp noises in it. You don't want your audience to really notice them. They're there to create a mood or set the stage... period.

✦ Never try to explain your animation with a dialog track, that's almost like apologizing for your work not standing on its own, or worse, that you think we're idiots who can't understand your submission.

I'm sure I've forgotten a few hundred things, but this'll get you started. When you've completed your video, watch it several times with and without the sound. Honestly ask yourself if the sound improves it not at all, a little, or a lot. If your answer is the first two, go back and tweak it. Sound should make a big improvement.

Once you're very happy with it, take it to someone who is not a close friend and not particularly polite. Ask for a direct opinion. If they don't like it, they probably don't understand it, so ask sombody else.

In all you've learned enough to do the job right if you take the time and have the ear. It's up to you now. In the next few chapters I'll cover additional post-production techniques used to enhance your work.

Summary

In this chapter we didn't talk about trueSpace2 at all. We covered the basics of adding sound to your animations. You found out that adding sound can make a critical difference. You also learned:

- ✦ A bad soundtrack can kill a good animation.
- ✦ You will have no trouble finding and recording the sounds you need to create a realistic SFX track.
- ✦ Use an ambiance track to smooth transitions, maintain continuity, and create a mood.
- ✦ Put in hits or sharp sounds that tie the soundtrack to the video.
- ✦ Use a microcassette recorder to collect great space station sounds.
- ✦ Use a good microphone to collect sounds.
- ✦ Who to contact for buy-out of music clips.
- ✦ Get in touch with BMI and ASCAP to track down a piece of music or composer and publisher so you can license it.
- ✦ Use Band-In-A-Box to create royalty-free music for your productions.
- ✦ Where to find midi and MOD music files and use a keyboard for background music.
- ✦ Use CDs as a source of sound SFX material, and where to find them.
- ✦ Compose sound multi-track stereo sound for your production and synch it to the video.

✦ ✦ ✦

CHAPTER 29

Plug-in Filter Effects

✦ ✦ ✦ ✦

In This Chapter

All about plug-ins

Typical plug-ins that are likely to come with your editor

All about plug-in extension engines that can produce content

Video plugs that incorporate time into the equation

How to keep up with the latest developments on the Web

✦ ✦ ✦ ✦

Plug-ins are good — the imaging equivalent of adding cookie dough to ice cream. Windows code was developed in a way that makes it easy to add functional modules to existing programs. Adobe came up with a sensible set of image-manipulation plug-in standards for Photoshop and Premiere. Now any good image or video editing program worth the price accepts standard plug-ins. They can do some awesome things. In some instances filters can be changed over time for video editing. You can, for example, start in frame 12 with a lens flare at a setting of 0, with it increasing to 100 at frame 35. Then you can have it decrease to 0 again by frame 50. It'll look like a supernova.

There are many advantages to plug-ins, not the least of which is quick, easy upgrading without having to buy a whole new application.

Plug-in Champs

In the pantheon of plug-ins I have a few favorites worthy of special mention because of their stand-out tools. The first, you've heard of.

Kai's Power Tools

Kai Krause is the Guru behind the plug-ins out of MetaTools (formerly HSC) Division, Adobe Systems Inc. This constantly growing batch of great plugs opens near-infinite possibilities — a veritable supernova of cornucopic excess. The most exciting elements are the plug-in extension engines. Each is a doorway into a strange world of possibilities.

✦ **Texture Explorer** enables you to create tons of seamless textures for your 3D work. The textures tend to have a distinctive look that gets old if you stick to the defaults, so go wild and make up your own stuff.

✦ **Gradient Designer and Gradients on Paths** will help you understand the enormous utility of gradients. You'll design them for original use and send yet others through filters to create fantastic backgrounds, energy effects, lighting effects, alpha channel effects, and even transition maps for use in Razor Pro.

✦ **Fractal Explorer** simplifies access to fractal sets as design elements. You twist a few dials, make a few selections, and you have an absolutely unique design to composite with your image.

✦ **Convolver** helps you explore complex hue variations within a scene.

With Kai filters, you get a slew of unusual straight filters like Sharpen Intensity (I love this filter), Grime Layer, Glass Lens effects, Hue-protected Noise, and Seamless Welder.

Kai's Power Tools are ever expanding with additions like KPT Spheroid Designer, KPT Lens F/X, and importantly, KPT Interform. This last one creates animated weird textures that seem alive as they mutate. If you search the Yahoo (`www.yahoo.com`) or Lycos (`www.lycos.com`) indexes, you'll find sites filled with tips and techniques on how to use Kai's tools.

Alien Skin

Less ambitious in some ways, yet innovative and unique, are the Alien Skin Black Box filters. The Black Box collection is a favorite of mine. Its excellent interface with Preview makes it easy to achieve just the right effect. You don't use these tools a lot, but when you need them, there's no other way. The Swirl tool in Black Box is excellent. (You can see a sample of Black Box effects in Chapter 31.)

Filters can be applied to masked areas. That means you can blur or pixelate just a person's face. In fact you've seen it done on TV to protect someone's identity. You can also mask the lens portion of a headlight and give it an intense lens flare, then mask a larger portion and assign a dimmer flare (see Color Plate of the moon lander in the Optic Edge Collection). Masks are particularly important for effects like drop shadows and glows where the shape of the object must be considered in generating the effect. Use the Zoom tool to enlarge the object to be masked until you can clearly see the individual pixels. Then use the Lasso tool (or its equivalent) to carefully draw a marquee around the object to create the mask.

Standard Filters

A set of standard equipment filters for still imaging have begun to settle out. Here are some of the most common, and what they're used for, under the major headings of Corrective Filters and Special Effects Filters.

Corrective Filters

These filters are used to enhance an image in ways similar to hand photo-retouching:

- ✦ **The Unsharp Mask Filter:** Crazy name for the most versatile of the sharpening filters. It can do whole images or just edges.
- ✦ **Sharpen:** Increases the contrast between neighboring pixels for the whole image.
- ✦ **Sharpen Edges:** Identifies edges and increases contrast at edges only.
- ✦ **Gaussian Blur:** Averages neighboring pixels to yield a defocusing effect on the area it's applied to.
- ✦ **Motion Blur:** Makes it look like the camera or the subject is moving. In animation, it's a fast way to add pseudo-motion blur to 3D sequences.
- ✦ **Wind:** Distributes and averages pixels in one absolute direction. Gives a cartoonish look of motion.
- ✦ **Radial Blur and Zoom effects:** These are directional blur effects that can give a feeling of energy or action. They're easily overused. Often best for background with a clean foreground image.
- ✦ **Noise:** There are a number of noise filter plug-ins. Noise adds a gritty look to your image. It can also be used by itself to make sandy bump maps to simulate cloth or a road surface. Sometimes it can be used to add false detail to blurry images or to simulate atmosphere.

Special Effects Filters

This is where the action is. These effects change the image rather than clarify it. The cool effects are usually overused and obvious. I tend to misbehave with the lens flare more than with any other. Unfortunately the various lens flare plug-ins are application specific, using precise internal code to do their magic. Andromeda has a star filter that is kin to a lens flare and will put neat highlight twinkles on the edges of your gold logos if you don't have Photoshop or Photo-Paint 6. Here are some interesting types of F/X plugs:

- ✦ **Lens Flare:** Adds a bright spot and radial streaks to the image, with simulated internal lens reflections. You can usually adjust the intensity and lens type. Useful for adding believable visible light effects to tS2 renderings.
- ✦ **Image Distortion:** This is a class of filters that twists or warps the image in prescribed ways. I use the Twirl filter to create galaxies, Zigzag filters to create pond ripple effects, and Ripple filters to create random water ripples. Spherise does the Vasarely thing where the center bulges out. Pinch does the opposite. New 3D distortion filters use 3D technology to create warps with highlights and shadows. My favorite is the custom 3D warp engine in QFX and Photo-Paint 6 (they appear to be the same engine).

✦ **Lighting Effects:** Drop shadows, spotlights, highlighted textures, and more all use mind-bending algorithms to figure out where the shadows and highlights should be. Can add a real sense of 3D to flat background photos.

✦ **Edge Enhancement:** Once you detect where the edges are you can do a lot of interesting things — embossed effects, line drawing, and charcoal drawing effects. I don't use this much because I usually don't like the way it looks. You can use edge enhancement with Gaussian blur and image compositing to create interesting special effects.

✦ **Painter Effects:** Both Fractal Design and Xaos Tools have built plug-ins that produce amazing brush effects by simulating media and brush strokes. You can convert a photo into a lovely simulated Van Gogh painting. Good for creating painted-look backgrounds.

✦ **Glows:** These effects require a masked area in the image, around which they place an eerie glow — your choice of color, size, intensity, and fall off. Use them to make small dark planets stand out, or to make a glass tube glow with evil light.

✦ **Do-it-yourself FX:** Several editors come with a custom effects engine. I confess I couldn't figure it out on my own, but Deke McCelland gives a masterful explanation in Chapter 15 of his *Photoshop 3 Bible* (IDG Books Worldwide). He shows you how to create your own custom effects filters.

✦ **Kai's Tools:** These have become standards. Kai Krause is a renegade filter guru. His interfaces are strange but amazingly functional, his filters are unique, and some of them are whole engines for creating textures, gradients, and fractal patterns.

I've left out specific mention of a ton of worthy filter types and makers and I apologize for it; there just wasn't space.

Video Plugs

Many of the plug-ins available for image editing also work well for video. With the addition of some extra controls, you can get moving effects. In addition to these standard options, a class of plug-ins has developed around transitions. Transitions are nifty ways of going smoothly from one video take to another. Originally transitions were simple cuts. Two bits of film were shoved together and welded. Later, editors got fancy and created wipes and dissolves. They tended to overdo it to the point that the transitions became so noticeable they were design elements in the film. The most amazing form of transition has been developed by the editors at *Home Improvement,* where new ground has been broken in transition technology. They actually use the transition elements to further or hammer in the story. Their work is very sophisticated; often existing elements in scene A are matted and animated to create the change to scene B. These guys do a lot of work every week to achieve these few seconds of excitement.

TransJammer

If you like the transitions on *Home Improvement* you'll love TransJammer, a transition engine plug-in for video editors. The editors actually use TransJammer to create some of the show's nifty transitions.

Unfortunately, as I write, TransJammer doesn't function on Windows 95. But as you read this, the newest version of TransJammer is shipping. It's a 32-bit application that works with Windows 95. It also contains a whole raft of new transitions. Contact Avid Technologies in Tewksbury, MA, 508-640-3070. TransJammer also works perfectly with Razor Pro.

Hollywood FX

The decentralization of the entertainment industry now has great products coming from every quarter. This one is on its way from Salt Lake City. It's a stunning set of special effects and transition filters that work not only with your video editor, but also with Photoshop. It's a standalone application as well. At $995, it's expensive, but compares with $10,000 commercial packages.

It's the special 3D video effects that make this application stand up and slap you in the face. The code on this baby creates an internal 3D environment, where it maps transitions onto real objects, like shattering glass. The engine then manipulates the object to create a whole class of stunning effects. It's from a company called Synergy. If you can't find it at your dealer, call Synergy direct. Have them overnight it to you — you'll like it that much: 801-281-0237.

MEDIAPaint Is a Special Case

MEDIAPaint from Strata includes plug-in special effects. The initial release of the program will ship with a collection of special effects and will include sophisticated lighting, composit, and particle special effects. Third-party developers are also expected to produce a variety of 2D and 3D special effects. The street price will be around $99 for the collection.

Where You Can Find Plug-ins on the Web

If you want to keep up on all the new plug-ins, there's a whole subculture on the Web dedicated to the subject, and news groups, too. For the latter, scan the Web for "plug-ins and plugins" on DejaNews, which is available on the Netscape Web browser.

They don't call it the Web for nothing. There is a vast network of interconnected pages that will plunge you into a veritable plethora of plug page participation. Here are a few gateways:

- `http://www.aris.com/boxtop/plugpage/Plug page`
- `http://www.vmedia.com/vvc/onlcomp/phshpfx/win_desc/index.htm` links to the Photoshop FX windows software archive.

✦ `http://www.fns.net/~almateus/filplug.htm` links to many Photoshop plug-in pages.

These URLs may not work by the time you get there, so search for the latest pages using the Yahoo (`www.yahoo.com`) and Lycos (`www.lycos.com`) indexes.

This was a light chapter, kind of a break. Check yourself out now. Are you starting to think about the profession as a possibility? There's a (small) fortune to be made in Web page authoring, both in 2D and 3D. More on that subject later.

I love plug-ins because they make many things possible. In the next chapter we take a closer look at the applications that use plug-ins.

Summary

Plug-ins are virtual gizmos that you click into your image editor or directly into tS2 to create interesting effects. In this chapter you learned:

✦ Plug-ins come in a wide variety of functions, from blurring to twisting to creating content.

✦ Kai's tools are a *tour de force* in plug world with an ever-expanding stable of exciting and different tools with amazing interfaces that actually work.

✦ Texture Explorer can create seamless textures.

✦ You can create special lighting and alpha channel effects with Gradient Designer.

✦ Fractal Explorer opens all sorts of far-out organic design possibilities.

✦ That a little company called Alien Skin makes a wonderful plug suite with a great preview interface.

✦ What the typical plug-in effects are.

✦ That video edit plug-ins give you a time channel to vary effects intensity.

✦ You can get all sorts of plug and play video transitions that you could never build on your own.

✦ You can keep up with the latest developments on the Web and in the news groups.

✦ ✦ ✦

CHAPTER 30

Post-Production Software

✦ ✦ ✦ ✦

In This Chapter

What image editors I recommend and use, and why

Which image editors can handle video material

The best image editor for creating natural media textures

What video editors are the best buys and which ones I like to use

All about morph editors and which ones I've found most useful

Find out about the new video special effects tool that gives you the power to create fantastic visual effects

✦ ✦ ✦ ✦

This chapter reveals the tip of an iceberg — the vast field of new post-production software you can save up to buy. I'll bypass all the audio programs because you've had a taste of that topic already.

I won't even try to tackle all the resources. I'm just going to give you an idea of the kinds of things that can be done and some of the better software solutions you can use to get them done.

The Publication Still

This book entailed a lot of preparation of 3D stills for publication. It's not completely straightforward. Publications don't use the standard RGB (Red-Green-Blue) files in PC video. They usually use a four color system called CYMK (Cyan-Yellow-Magenta-blacK). Not all PC image editing programs can handle CYMK. Most important is the ability to make a clean conversion without serious color distortion. To my eye, after conversion, images lose some of their intensity, and in some programs, shift colors. I often punch them up a little with the intensity filter from Kai's Power Tools, before conversion.

Another potential problem is that many publishers use Macs for image processing. Macs use a different bit order in their image files. Any good publisher can deal with this, but it's handy to be able to send your publisher a CYMK TIFF in Mac bit order. It makes you look more professional. Image is everything at first sight.

Photoshop

Of the image edit packages I've been using, Photoshop is my favorite. The reasons are many but includc its ability to easily convert images to any format, any color mode, and any bit depth. The latter indicates how many colors are available and if there's an alpha channel or not. Generally, the more bits, the more image data, the better the image, up to 24 bits (16 million colors). Higher bit counts indicate additional color channels used for things like transparency mapping. That's why we used 32-bit .tga files to rotoscope the explosion in Chapter 26.

Photoshop is simply the standard of the industry. By the time you read this the new version for Windows 95 may be on the market. It will be an improvement. Photoshop needs more ability to handle batch operations, multiple undos, and lots of other little things you can't hold against it.

One powerful feature is its ability to work with film strips. This is a special format that you produce in Premiere 4.0 to export video to Photoshop for special treatment and rotoscoping.

Photoshop also has good text tools, but its paint capability is rudimentary in version 3, compared to Fractal Design Painter. Another advantage of Photoshop — all the plug-in work that's in it, but not necessarily in the others.

QFX

Ron Scott's QFX is another image editor that handles CMYK and alpha channels beautifully. It's a very powerful 32-bit application with high-quality image manipulation tools. It's lightning fast and has the best image warp engine around. but I haven't had enough time to master it. It's better than Photoshop at batch processing. With its Queue command you can set up an entire series of .tga files to be processed automatically. For example, to create that .tga series for the explosion, I could have made a macro of the process and applied it to all 42 images in a few minutes.

CAUTION QFX has difficulty dealing with compressed image files. Where most applications detect this and decompress the image on the fly, QFX puts it on the screen as a distorted image with horizontal bars. For the longest time I thought Win95 had munched my images, but nope, they work fine. The solution is to resave each image you want to use in QFX, disabling the compression option (sometimes called lzh compression).

In Photoshop, where I'm comfortable, my daughter and I spent more than an hour creating alpha channels one by one. Why didn't I tell you about this? Because I didn't want you to know that I don't yet know how to do it in QFX — that job was incentive to learn. Another advantage of QFX is that it's a true 32-bit application and very fast. At this writing, Photoshop is not. The internal filters are noticeably faster than anything else around except Corel Photo-Paint 6.

Photo-Paint 6

Don't sell Corel short just because they've become so commercial lately. They offer a lot of value for the money. Photo-Paint has grown into a sophisticated image processing program that handles CYMK and alpha channels and conversions and even movies. You can load your .avi files directly into Photo-Paint and enhance each frame. For example, use the Xaos Tools Image Alchemy plug-in to create fantastic brushed effects. Photo-Paint 6 is a true 32-bit application with a huge selection of special effects filters, all of which are pretty snappy. BTW, much of P-P6 will feel pretty familiar, as many of the filters, warps, and so on, appear to have been licensed from other packages mentioned. Corel is smart that way. Instead of reinventing the wheel, they sometimes license the best software, customize it, and add it to the Corel package — witness Corel Dream 3D.

Fractal Design Painter 4.0

Fractal Design Painter is a wonderful texture tool, but it can also be used for a lot of post effects, especially rotoscoping final painted-on details and applying nearly all the plug-in filters available for Photoshop. I almost need to put this in both the still and the motion categories. With each new version, Fractal Design Painter adds more movie capability. It's still focused on the still image, but offers some neat ways of building animated textures and simple animations using floater sprites. This program has so much depth you shouldn't be without it. You can build just about any texture you want with it, and it has powerful image compositing capability as well. It works particularly well with my Summa Expression tablet, converting the pen's pressure information into natural looking strokes. I can't take the space to go into all the great things like Mosaic, Image hose, water color brushes, even Web page authoring. It's a product from Fractal Design Corporation.

PaintShop Pro

This is probably the best value on the market for a paint and image editor suite. It's almost a must because it handles more types of image files than Photoshop. It understands at least 30 formats right off the bat and can speak 22 back. It comes with screen capture, batch format conversion, broad scanner support, text tools, a great image browser, and photo retouching with a nice set of filters. It also has extensive image enhancement and correction. It doesn't have the ability to composite yet. I've included the shareware edition of PaintShop Pro on the CD-ROM under the \JASC subdirectory. Try it, and buy it if you like it. The registered version comes with an excellent text and a collection of fine images to play with.

Xres 2

MacroMedia's new Xres 2. It is the best of all worlds for handling very large images on the PC. My cover image, for example, was nearly 30 megabytes. Xres can easily handle images of 300 megabytes, like photo murals. It handles transparency very well and works in close to real-time, which is amazing for large files. It does this because it doesn't actually rewrite the whole file. You work with a hi-res proxy image. Xres keeps track of every detail of your work and when you're all done, it goes to work on the original image.

If you're an Adobe Photoshop user, you'll find the Xres interface very familiar. The two packages work very well together, especially if you plan to do a lot of work on very large images.

Video Editors

We already met the video editor, but only for sound. Now comes the video stuff. Nowadays we can do on our home computers what only the top editors and special effects houses could do with millions of dollars in equipment a mere five years ago. And, we can do more. New animated transitions and warps and filters have made exploring video edit possibilities a full-time job for people like me who review the stuff. I'm totally impressed with the quality and breadth of what's available. We will look at three suites: MediaStudio Video Edit 2.0, Premiere 4.0, and the Razor family of fine editors. Each comes with a sack full of special F/X and transition filters as well as sound filters. You will have to read the manuals because it's enough for me to teach you tS2, have pity on me. I'll happily give you ideas about you can do with them and what kinds of options each package offers.

Overview

Getting right to it, you'll want to put your final demo presentation together and render it to videotape. All the following video editors use a timeline approach, which displays video and audio information in a vertical stack of separate tracks, video first. Video editors put together all your media resources in what's referred to as a project. This is handy because if you're like me, you misplace clips. I have a 10.8 gig black hole, mostly filled with media clips. Without my albums and project files I'd never find things a second time. The project file keeps track of everything in its job. Each time you start a new project you specify the audio and video parameters — project resolution, audio bandwidth, and stereo or mono. You also set up your output. You can change it when you're ready to go to tape. I usually work in 320 × 240, which is large enough to see but small enough to render quickly. You then assemble a project library of media clips to be composed into your final production. It doesn't matter where your clips are on your disk, when they are assigned to the project, they become available to you.

POWER TIP: Avoid using clips on removable media. When you remove the disk, the project gets screwed up. Same goes for media used in tS2 textures. Always put these files in a subdirectory on your hard drive for ensured access.

Once your production is exactly the way you want it, you reset the resolution to 640 × 480, or NTSC or PAL, and render it to a MJPEG file. The video output boards you'll be interested in do on-the-fly or real-time video compression in hardware. It's a wonderful invention that allows you to record and playback digital images at TV resolutions by drastically reducing the amount of data that must flow to and from your hard drive, while maintaining a very high standard signal.

If you're using a fancy output board like the DPI Perception board, you may have to work in proprietary file formats. The best choice of editor in this case is the Razor Pro, which works directly in DPI's .ani file format. If you use the Miro DC20 board you render to MJPEG compressed .avi files. These remain fully editable by any Windows video edit program. These boards are capable of playing back your animation at a full 30fps at broadcast resolution for a professional looking demo tape.

Video projects can really strangle your machine, so you'll want to work efficiently. It helps to have at least 32 megs of ram and a speedy CPU. If you're buying, don't consider less than 100MHz Pentium with 32 megs ram. Go for a lot more if you can afford it. Additional RAM is the quickest way to speed up your operation. It prevents your system from dumping content to *virtual memory*, which means hard drive, the slowest part of your system. The DEC Alpha, InterGraph dual P-6 TDZ400, and NetPower MIPS machines are ideal for video work, if pricey.

Further, they'll each run the New SoftImage NT which you may someday want to graduate to. It's very powerful high-end software — the interface is difficult to get used to — but it's the *ne plus ultra* of character animation suites for the PC platform.

CAUTION

Be aware that if you use RISC machines like the Alpha and MIPS, you need to use software that's optimized for their particular flavor of Windows NT.

Use your video editor to create title sequences, special effects, and classy transitions. If you're new to this, let me share some of the amazing things we can do. Here is a brief list:

- ✦ You can take your space tanker through a worm hole by using a radial dissolve and zoom effects.
- ✦ You can start your video out as a painting and have it evolve into pseudo reality.
- ✦ You can add animated effects on paths, such as moving titles and logos.
- ✦ You can kill your video with trite transition effects.
- ✦ You can trim video and sound precisely, down to the individual frame.
- ✦ You can push two video clips together in the same track for a simple "cut to" transition.

- You can composite clips over clips for wild music video-type effects.
- You can do chroma key composites, putting animations over live action or such other animations as a Vista Pro fly-through video.

MediaStudio

MediaStudio is the least expensive video editing suite (MSVE) that I can recommend. I love it. IMHO, this is the flagship of the MediaStudio 2.5 product. For about half the price of the others, you get all the MediaStudio tools including Morph Edit, Sound Edit, Image Edit, Album, and the best screen capture utility I've seen. The video edit section is more advanced and detailed than some of the other pieces in the suite — they're all good. The interface is well thought out and filled with fast action icon push buttons. You're used to using them in tS2 to speed your work. I also like the fact that this suite gives you a choice of time readouts — in the SMPTE convention of minutes/seconds/frames, or in the Time convention of minutes/seconds/milliseconds. The SMPTE may look a little strange, but it's very useful for synchronizing sound clips to the exact frame.

The depth of transitions and effects will astound you and give you many hours of pleasure just exploring possibilities. It will surely set you up for overkill.

Adobe Premiere 4.0

This is the one I use most because I had it first and it's highly compatible with Photoshop. You can pass film strips back and forth between the two apps. I find Premiere a little more complicated to use than MSVE, but the parts I use most are superbly executed. In addition, nearly all of Photoshop's great filters have a correlate in Premiere, including lens flare. That means you can animate the lens flare settings over time. I use this to enhance my worm hole effect. I have a radial transition open up (that's where the B video is introduced slowly, in a widening circle) in the center of an increasing lens flare. The effect is like an explosion opening a tunnel to the next video. Further, Premiere takes plug-in transitions and has a transition factory. The factory is seriously abstruse; you have to learn a new programming language, which I'm loath to do.

Adobe Premiere 4.0a is a 16-bit application compatible with Windows 95 but supports very few of Windows 95 capabilities. It does handle UNC path names and right-button mouse operations.

A 32-bit release was expected to ship in the fourth quarter of 1995, but significant delays will probably have it out about the same time as this book. This new version is supposed to seriously boost performance on both the Windows 95 and Windows NT platforms. A fully logo-compliant version, which will add OLE 2.0 and MAPI support, is expected to ship sometime this year.

Razor Pro and Speed Razor Mach III

It'll take you a coupla tries to get used to Razor's unique interface. It's like Windows and it's not. I promise it's all well thought out and easy to use. Razor Pro is the regular Windows and Windows 95 version while Speed Razor Mach III is the newest edition for Windows NT. It's slick and fast and has a lot of new transitions and capabilities. Razor Pro is a good place to start. Priced about the same as Premiere 4.0, it has many similar capabilities. Premiere is better documented but is not a better editor. They have different strengths that would take a book to explain. I love and use them both, but you'll probably have to settle on one. If you can find a way to try before you buy, do so, and compare. Get the manuals if you can and look at them.

Razor was designed to do on-line editing for television and video presentations. It is set up to hook right into either the DPS Personal Animation Recorder, or the much better DPS perception boards. These are professional quality video output boards that allow you to record your animations at a full NTSC resolution and then play them back at full speed with no dropped frames. That's pretty amazing. Both Pro and Speed work directly with the proprietary DPS format .ani files. This is a big advantage if you're going that route.

I have the very first issue of Speed Razor and it doesn't handle many different file types. That is being fixed and a patch will be available on their BBS if you get one of the early releases.

In addition, both take plug-in effects, but they're not the same standard as Premiere's. TransJammer comes in both flavors, as does Hollywood F/X.

In addition to superior speed, Speed Razor has lots of sophisticated neat things like surround-sound processing and really cool transitions and effects that are constantly updated on-line for free. In fact, in:sync has hired a wizard to work full time on just effects. They have their BBS listed and will soon be on the Web. Check frequently for new effects to download at no charge. That's a nice deal. The cost of Speed reflects all this high-end stuff and with an srp of $1,495, it's going to run you over a grand even on the street. But remember, this is possibly your new occupation. The best tools are expensive in any trade.

Animator Studio

There's always a special case. Animator Studio from AutoDesk, makers of 3D Studio, have put together a wonderful suite of tools designed specifically for animators. It includes special tools that will equip you for some serious editing. It's not as powerful as the ones above in the transitions area, but it takes Adobe spec plug-ins like TransJammer to help there.

Nope, Animator Studio's uniqueness is the tool set for animating 2D goodies. I may be narrow minded, but I feel an animator is an animator. Motion in two dimensions is just as exciting to create as the 3D stuff. If you've never considered it, I suggest you think again.

It's easy to paint, rotoscope, add and synchronize sound recording in Animator Studio. Imagine adding 2D characters to a 3D environment, or fancy 2D titles to emphasize the 3D quality of what's behind them.

It comes with Kai's Power Tools 2.0 Explorer and a book on the basics of digital movie making with lots of tutorials. Kai's book has tutorials as well.

Here's the caveat. Animator Studio doesn't give you a lot of audio tracks to play with. Just one stereo track with *no rubber band.* You do all your mixing, filtering, and timing in a separate application called Audio Lab. It's an excellent application with lots of powerful features. In fact, I use it to record and especially to copy soundtracks off other videos. I just find it much easier to set up audio in the multi-track setting the other three offer. Why do I have Animator Studio? Because it's one of the best applications around for manipulating videos and animations frame by frame and doing animation.

Rubber Bands

Rubber bands is not a program. I didn't know where to put them, but I feel they need special recognition. Rubber bands have different names in different editors, but essentially they are interactive graphs used to control parameters over time.

I love the ease with which I can adjust audio levels with the rubber bands. These are straight lines beneath the audio clip that you can grab, attach a node like a spline node, and move it up or down. This gives you the ability to perfectly adjust audio on a frame-by-frame basis if you need it. I use it a lot to tone down overly loud passages, to pull up music at the appropriate moments, and to soften loud ambient track clicks and such. Rubber bands are the big thing. Figures 30-1 and 30-2 are examples of what I'm talking about.

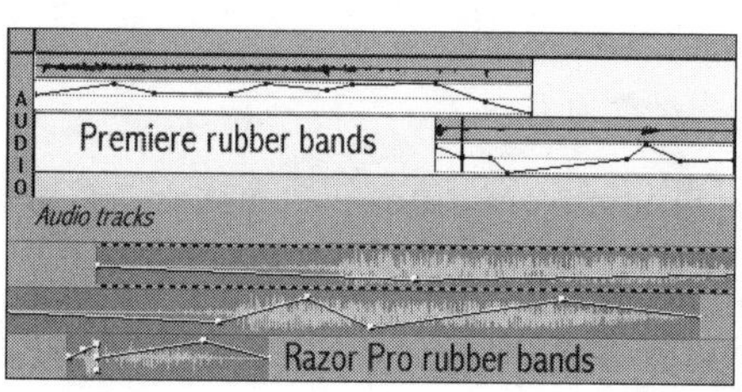

Figure 30-1: Rubber bands are used in Premiere and Razor to control sound levels by track.

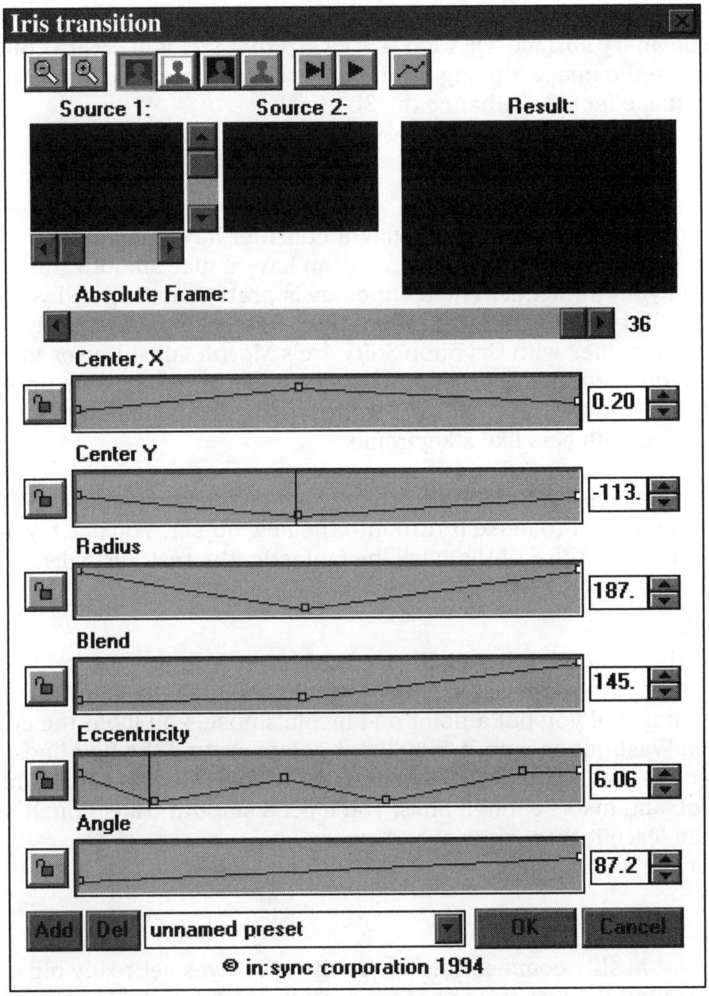

Figure 30-2: This example shows how rubber bands can be used to adjust time parameters for effects in Razor Pro.

Morphing and Warping

In a normal dissolve, one image simply fades out while another one fades in. Morphing uses tweening algorithms to have the main object in Roll A change shape (morph) into the main object in roll B. Such transitions, once stunning, have become trite unless they're used in a special way. I remember watching TV one night and thinking "If I see one more morphed up commercial I'm gonna throw something." I threw my pillow at the TV fifteen minutes later.

Warps are when you digitally change an image via freehand stretching, pinching, or twisting the imaginary surface. QFX has a 3D warp that lets you create complex warps that can leave the image looking like it's painted on a rumpled blanket. You can even add lighting effects to enhance the 3D effect.

Morphs

Morphs can play many roles in TV, or you might consider having a human subject morph into an animated one or vice versa. You can have a nice smooth transition that may even stun your audience. The technology is pretty amazing and you can use it to do a lot of 2D tweening between keyframes. One example that aptly displays the medium comes with Gryphon Software's Morph suite. It uses images of presidents from different denomination bills. The effect is to have one president smoothly change into the next and the next while moving his head to a new position for each. Each bill acts like a keyframe.

There are lots of variations on the theme, like putting points on symmetrically opposite sides of the object to make it turn into the new object. You can try all sorts of ideas and about a third of them will be fantastic, the rest, dismal.

How They Work

I don't know how they work, but here's the general setup. You use the tools with the suite of choice to lay out a series of corresponding points between two keyframes. For example, if you put a point on Lincoln's nose, you'll put the corresponding point on Washington's nose. You'll put points around the hair lines and head shapes. Some tools let you draw Bézier curves to indicate areas to be linked. If you do a nice job and insert enough links, you'll get a smooth transition. It's still an art, but you can learn it through trial and error.

Warps

Warps are used a lot in silly commercials where the cat's eyes get really big or the woman's smile literally goes from ear to ear. They can be useful in creating space warp effects where your space vehicle hits a time/space anomaly and begins to distort as it goes through. Or you can have the ship approach a black hole and begin to stretch from nose first until it's just a thin line feeding into that obsidian maw.

Warps are fun for title effects, too. You can animate an ordinary traveling logo clip, then run it through a warp engine and come out with a wild, fluid logo that squirms into position in a neat way. Let your imagination be your guide, the possibilities are limitless.

How They Work

Usually warp engines present you with a point and line grid over your image. You can scale the grid to meet your needs. For detail work you want a fine grid. Next, you grab points and drag them a little here, a little there, according to your plan.

It's easy to overdo, so take it slow. Some engines give you real-time feedback so you can keep track of your destruction.

The Ranking Members

I have three favorites. They vary more widely in price than capability. All three create dynamic morphs, but the first wasn't built for it and the second two were.

Ulead's Morph Editor

The best deal is probably Media Studio Pro 2.0's Morph Editor. It comes as part of the package so it costs you virtually nothing. The total price for all the MSP modules is only about the price of Elastic Reality. This is a full-featured morph and warp editor with a host of prebuilt and custom special effects. It's a static editor, using stills to create video sequences as they morph into each other. Technically you could do a dynamic morph with it, but it would be labor intensive.

In a way, I'm not happy about praising Ulead's products because their former marketing director agreed to let us put one of Ulead's older video edit programs on our CD-ROM for you to play with, but when he left the company, his replacement decided not to go through with the deal. Now when you all go out and buy Media Studio Pro, the boss'll give marketing the credit! They did supply a demo for the CD-ROM, however.

But the truth is, Media Studio Pro 2.0 is a very good product at a really decent price. To make things even better, the manual and tutorials are better than average. They just need better marketing people who can make decisions and honor commitments. There, I feel much better.

Gryphon's Morph

I don't have the latest version of Morph, it's hard to keep up. But this is the first morph editor I ever tried. It was an amazing thrill to view my first clean morph. It was a double morph. A young girl to a young woman to an old woman. I tried going from young girl to old woman, but it didn't look right; you need that young woman in there to make it work right. Morph works well and costs less than $100, way less on the street.

Morph is set up to do dynamic as well as static morphs. In a dynamic morph you use two matched motion sequences. The camera and key model move the same way in both clips. It's handy to have a motion control camera for this. You don't? No problem. In tS2 you can save all the camera moves and repeat them. Think about it. Now you can have objects morph into other objects and they don't even have to have the same number of vertices. I'll show you how in Chapter 31.

Elastic Reality

Avid Technology recently bought Elastic Reality and they'll have an updated version out about a day after I have to turn this chapter in. This is the high-end (read expensive) approach and darn well worth it. I hope they continue to include

TransJammer with the package because the two are related and a powerful combination. Officially Elastic Reality is a digital effects editor with full compositing capability. With it you can create full motion composites using automatic shape interpolation — that's pretty sophisticated. It has one of the best warp and morph engines in the business and is used extensively in film and television.

Digital effects can take a long time to render, but ER is a full 32-bit grinder with turbo boost. Like Morph Editor, it handles just about any image file format you can throw at it.

The tweener engine is really good and can be used to create animations as can the others. The unique shape-to-shape matching system makes it easier to use than the point and line or mesh approaches found elsewhere.

The Paint Box

High-end digital video editing suites like Quantel Harry and Domino are expensive, but they're wonderful to see in action. Both programs include a Paint Box tool that allows you to create all sorts of wonderful special effects. If a waterfall isn't wild enough, the programs allow you to clone more cascading water in real time — so perfectly you'd never know you weren't looking at the real thing. Remember the movie *Speed*? The Paint Box was used to remove the wires that pulled the exploding bus over. The original footage contained a fat cable that you never saw in the final release. The animators simply erased it with the Paint Box.

I watched a Harry operator manipulate an ordinary scene that was filmed in normal daylight, and turn it into a cloudy rainy shot. She changed the sky by adding painted storm clouds from a different video sequence. Next she filtered the walkways and road to appear wet. Then she added rain by using an animated alpha mat of translucent falling drops. I was amazed at the results. I can specifically remember thinking, "That kind of power will never come to the home PC." That was at last year's NAB convention in Las Vegas.

I was dead wrong on a stack of wet corn flakes. I admit it. STRATA, the Mac people who put out STRATA PRO, the 3D suite that was used to create those wonderful scenes in Myst, bought a small company with a big idea. It was called Video Graffiti. They improved the interface and special effects. The result is a truly unique and wonderful video post tool you will absolutely love. It's called MEDIAPaint.

STRATA MEDIAPaint

You gotta get MEDIAPaint. It's unique in the desktop market. It duplicates the high-end Paint Box effects and adds a few of its own. In many ways, it's exactly what you need to create the video wizardry you love to watch. It's used regularly on the *American Gothic* television show to create those eerie effects. I remember one scene where the young boy is standing in an old shack where he was born. As he's looking around, the room begins to change, at first in the corners and along the ceiling. It's becoming a new shack as he's transported somehow back in time. In a matter of moments the seeping change completes the transition and he's standing in a fresh, bright room. It was a stunning effect and I spent some time figuring exactly how they did it. I was sure it was on a Harry. But no, it was done on a Mac with MEDIAPaint 1.1.

Through the magic of hard work and market pressure, STRATA has ported this program to the Windows 32-bit environment. Here's what you can expect to find:

- **Live Painting:** Paint effects remain on while a movie is playing in real-time.
- **Chaos controls:** Change intensity and nature effects by seeding them with different random variations. Less chaos gives gentle effects, more leads to the wild. This greatly enhances the natural, believable look of most effects when used with good judgment.
- **Live Alpha Channel:** Clean composites in real-time without damaging the original image. You can use this one to rotoscope your explosions with ease and great control. It's much easier than doing it frame by frame in Photoshop.
- **Time-based Filters:** A full complement of time-based filters such as Diffuse, Wave, Sharpen, Dodge, and Burn, as well as other standard plug-ins. These can be applied over time, and the intensity can be varied across frames.
- **Particle System:** Fully customizable particle system tools that control gravity, density, speed, lifetime, even fertility, and many more parameters of real-time effects.
- **PixieDust:** Creates magic wand effects with luminescent particles drifting down to the ground from a source and along a path. You can track the effect with your character. Let's say she waves a magic wand. By painting the source point onto the tip of the wand as it moves in real-time you create the perfect illusion of magic. You can even control the behavior of the dust, making it gentle or madly swirling.
- **BabyBoom:** Generates particles that give birth to new particles, all of which have definable life spans for snow, splash, dust, and glitter effects. For example, you can overlay several BabyBoom layers to create a dense snow-storm effect. Fountains are also possible to create.
- **SpinOut:** Creates particles that spin outward in a vortex leaving neat trails behind. They can be made to move like a swarm of lights, or "lighties." I've used this tool to create delicate lighties that swarm and dance around the head of one of my creatures. By using the Stencil Paint, I was able to create a 3D effect that shows the lighties flying behind the creature. You can also use it to create a swarm of bees, smoke effects, and more.
- **Lightning:** You'll never have to paint a stroke of lightning again. This tool has many adjustments that enable you to create any kind of lightning you can imagine, where and when you want it.

- **Arcs:** Remember those neat sci-fi arcs of electricity that leap between electrodes in the laboratory… this one will make all sorts of them. You can even do the *Highlander* Quickening effects.
- **Bubbles:** Add 3D bubbles, complete with transparency, specular highlights, and flocking motion. You can also create really cool underwater effects.
- **Fire:** Diffuse animated flames as they rise from a source. The flames can be plotted to move, and the direction of the flame can be set. Flame characteristics are fully adjustable. This is an excellent tool for adding those diffuse rocket trails that simply don't work in tS2. Do it in post-production. You make the flame burn in the exact opposite direction of the craft, and move the source of the flame to the tail of the rocket at each frame. This can be done automatically, but may not match exactly.
- **Lasers:** This tool allows you to mark two points in your picture; on cue you can get a laser blast of your own design. Parameters allow you to control glow color, density and width, as well as things like initial flash. You can get short blasts, giggly blasts, synchronous blasts, or one long nasty Phaser blast. By rotoscoping the flashes of the flames and chunk effects at the blast site, you get a thoroughly believable effect.
- **Squiggle:** Creates those hand-drawn jittering line effects that are so popular in broadcast TV commercials. You've seen them, the hand-animated lettering that kind of squiggles back and forth because the artist couldn't get it exactly right in each frame. You can use this tool with onionskin to create some neat cel animation.
- **Stencil Paint:** Allows you to paint one movie onto another using any paint tool as if it were ordinary paint. Stunning special effects are easy with this tool… all you need is a steady hand.
- **ChromaKey (Blue Screen) Controls:** You can choose a full set of colors to key out (or in!) — you don't have to settle for just one color.
- **Light Box:** This is similar to the onionskin tool that is used by professional cel animators. The number of frames and the level of transparency is fully adjustable.
- **Stroke Record:** You can actually record every paint stroke so you can duplicate each one on a different film clip. This can be handy for duplicating effects and creating special transitions.
- **Extensible architecture:** You can incorporate new effects tools and filters easily as they become available from STRATA and other third-party suppliers.

What You Can Do with It

The tutorial that ships with MEDIAPaint gives only a whisper of what you can create with the program. For example, you can create a special effects sequence in which a wireframe of an Egyptian statue slowly resolves into a fully rendered image from the head down. It's a neat effect that's produced by inputting two motion control sequences, one as the camera moves around the wireframe and the other as the camera makes the exact same moves around the fully rendered model. You load both clips. (Use the fully rendered one as Stencil paint.) Using the airbrush, you click Record and begin painting on the wireframe as the two film clips run, matched frame for frame. In the composite clip you'll see the wireframe begin to rotate. Slowly the statue comes to life.

All of your work is captured on what's called the Paint Layer. It's a non-destructive process that never touches the original clips. When you get the sequence the way you want it, you render it to a new clip. It's very cool.

In the second tutorial, you learn how to add a second character called Isis. When she appears, she generates electric bolts between her fingertips which she uses as a defensive weapon against a military type who shoots her with a Laser rifle. Large blasts and flashes and energy bolts electrify the scene. In the end the Soldier disintegrates when he's hit by one of Isis's blue energy bolts. They're the worst ones ya know, them blue onez.

The Stencil tool is also used here, but this time you paint out the soldier using the background from a previous frame. It's like having a clean plate. You go back to frames where there is no soldier, but the background is identical (it's a static shot). Paint the soldier out of the frame. Zap! The sucker is evaporated. You can also paint in some neat glow lights where the soldier once stood. This same approach can be used to create Trek-type transporter dissolves that include any kind of neat shimmering particle effect laid over them. I'm talking very primo effects here.

That's enough for anybody to learn in one chapter. Now on to some neat stuff you can do with these programs.

Summary

Again, this is not the universe of available and excellent products. They are simply the ones I use. If I've done my job in this chapter you've learned:

- ✦ That I have more software than any human should have to bear.
- ✦ I like Photoshop, QFX, Photo-Paint 6, Fractal Design Painter 4.0, and the new Xres.
- ✦ You'll use image editors in your work.
- ✦ You will need a video editor because frame-by-frame editing is for the birds.
- ✦ Video editors also edit sound and help you put it all together with nifty transitions and special F/X.
- ✦ A morph isn't the same as a warp, but they come from the same neighborhood.
- ✦ You can afford morphing software that will do the job.
- ✦ You can create nearly any special optical effect you can imagine using the MEDIAPaint Paint Box tool, including 3D and particle effects.

✦ ✦ ✦

CHAPTER 31

Post-Production Techniques

✦ ✦ ✦ ✦

In This Chapter

How to enhance still images with digital photo retouch techniques

How to change still images with digital special effects filters

How to destroy still images with all of the above

Tools available to you for creating movie magic

Creating unique film effects in post production

How to make a video really cheesy

✦ ✦ ✦ ✦

I call it snazz. You look at a 3D image and know it was created by a professional — well, 95 percent of the time. I've put some examples of that best five percent of nonprofessionals in the color section. People like Dave Campbell who have day jobs can put out totally professional work. Sometimes — frequently — the image that comes out of tS2 can be improved. There are different kinds of finishing touches you can add in post production.

Let's divide post into still image and video. They're related, but quite different. There's also a no-man's-land in the middle — static morphing, where you take two renderings, morph them together to get a video sequence of 30 or more frames showing the transmorphing process — but I consider that video. Yes, I made up transmorphing, but I'm the author and sometimes you need a word that hasn't been invented yet in this business. Let's begin with an overview of the kinds of things you do in still image processing. There's a lot of new ground being broken in this video area and you might just want to be part of it.

Working Still

Post-production detailing is part of the professional's edge. When your rendering looks about right, it can still use polish. Look at it for awhile. Review in your mind what software and filter options you have. Do you need to touch up something? Do you need to remove a cheesy looking planet? I did. There was a pure cheddar planet in this book's cover image. I removed it in post by cloning other parts of the sky over it. You probably can't see where it was, at least I hope you can't. You can lay out a plan or just go at it. Be careful if you choose the latter; it's easy to overdo it and degrade the image.

To enhance your image, look for such things as unbalanced lighting, aliased edges, bad details, screwy highlights, unnecessary objects, and so on. If you see something in the image that just isn't the way it should be, don't panic — post polish it.

Post Polish

Assuming you're properly equipped with a good set of editing tools as discussed earlier, you're ready to roll. March forward fearlessly because there is that wonderful tool — Undo. Be careful, though; some applications like Photoshop will only undo the last operation. I usually don't catch myself until several operations later and have to reload the original image. MediaStudio Image Edit has many levels of Undo and I love it for that. I understand the same is coming to Photoshop in version 4.

I certainly am not going to give you a course in image processing here. Get that from other IDG books. They really are better than the others. I have a collection of tomes on Photoshop and even though I don't have a Mac, I've learned more from Deke McClelland's Mac-based *Macworld Photoshop 3 Bible* than anywhere else. The procedures are the same and he's an entertaining writer. I'm only going to give you a little taste and a few ideas here.

Okay, back on track. If you see something you don't like, you have several basic options:

- ✦ Blur it
- ✦ Point it up
- ✦ AntiAlias it
- ✦ Clone over it
- ✦ Shadow it
- ✦ Sharpen it
- ✦ Adjust its color

It's All a Blur

Everything is blurry to some degree. We're used to it and our eyes take it into account in creating image impressions. You can get away with a lot by blurring minor mistakes into the background. Heck, there're a lot of blur tricks. You can mask the foreground object and blur the background to give the image depth-of-field effect. You can also apply directional blurs to simulate motion. I tend to overuse the Zoom blur to create a feeling of lively action. It blurs images as if you exposed them while zooming the main lens.

Gaussian Blur

The most useful blur is the Gaussian tool. Named after the fellow who invented the bell shaped curve, also known as a Gaussian distribution, it works by blending a specified number of pixels incrementally, following the bell curve. You get to adjust the blur radius. Naturally, the bigger the radius, the more blurred the image will become.

Use the Marquee tool to select a small section of interest, with feathered edges on, then apply a small amount of Gaussian blur to obfuscate your error. If it doesn't look right, you can Undo or leave it and apply more blur.

There are other blur tools, but I find this one does everything but trick blurs.

Trick Blurs

They're not officially called trick blurs, but it's a way to group them. They include all the tools that apply blur according to some algorithm to achieve a look. I've mentioned Zoom; there's also Radial Blur and Motion Blur. They all work pretty much the same way. Instead of applying blur uniformly as the Gaussian does, these apply blur in straight lines over a specified distance.

Radial Blurs vary the effect in terms of distance from the center. Usually you can Spin or Zoom. Motion Blurs give your image the look of either object or camera having moved. It's done by setting the angle of movement and the distance in pixels. I use this sometimes to give an overly crisp rendering of a moving object a photographic look by blurring that object in the direction of its motion. This is a great time saver. Rendered Motion Blur takes prodigious amounts of time and computer resources; Motion Blur in Photoshop takes seconds.

To apply trick blurs to individual objects, you need to exercise a little creativity. First you select the object carefully then you feather the selection a little more than the number of pixels you're blurring.

For example:

1. Select an object — perhaps a planet — with the Marquee or Lasso tool. Hold down the Shift key to constrain the ellipse to a circle.
2. Go to Select ➪ Feather and set the feather distance to 15 pixels.
3. Go to Filter ➪ Blur ➪ Motion Blur and set the direction you want by clicking on the angle indicator. Then set the blur to 10 pixels.
4. Apply the blur. It will blur the planet in the direction you selected, but not surrounding objects or space.

POWER TIP: It's easier to use blur tools against an unpatterned background, black, white, or colored, because the blur doesn't show on plain colors, nothing to blend.

Selecting Objects in Images

When F/X filters require that you select an irregular object you will be using the Lasso tool to corral it. Odd-shaped objects can be tricky. Since image processing isn't object oriented, you have to define the object yourself. Use the Lasso tool to carefully draw a freehand marquee around the object. This task can be greatly assisted by the Zoom View tool. You can zoom in until you see individual pixels along the edge of the object. Good. Here's the secret to professional object selection: take your time. Once you have the object rough-outlined, you can adjust the lasso line (check your application for the procedure) until it's a pixel perfect fit. Don't rush it; sloppy selections look cheesy.

Of course, if you're in a hurry (as I usually am) you often can fix a bad selection with the blur tool we'll discuss in a minute. Once you have the foreground object cleanly selected, save it (in Photoshop use Save Selection under the Select menu). This will save the selected area in a new channel for your image, so you can use it later if you need to. I often forget to save my selections and live to regret it.

Once the selection is clean you apply effects. Glow, for example, will place a diffuse glow around the selected area. Motion Trails will apply white streaks leading in a selected direction to the edges of your selection, and so forth.

If you want to blur the background, just hit the Inverse command in the Select menu. This will reverse the matte, allowing you to apply blur to everything you *didn't* select. Also, some blur filters have an edge detection component and automatically apply blur streaks to the edges of things in your image. Professionals rarely trust automatic processes unless they've done the programming themselves. Take note.

Point Effects Tools

Point effects are applied with the paintbrushes available in your editor. For example, if you want to apply a wide blur, use a wide brush. The effects are antialiased and thus nice and smooth.

The Point Effects tools work best if you use a nicely feathered brush. If you use a sharp-edged brush the effects may be too obvious.

The Blur/Sharpen Tool

There is a tool that lets you apply blur or sharpening to specific areas. In Blur mode it lessens the contrast between neighboring pixels and in Sharpen, it increases contrast. I love it. It's like a paintbrush that lets you blur along edges or hit <Ctrl> and you can sharpen edges and the like.

Smudge It

I like the word smudge. It sounds like what it is, munging pixels together. Most image editors will have a Smudge tool — by any other name it simply blends pixels under its brush. The effect is like dragging a wet Q-tip across wet paint. I love the Smudge tool. It's kept me from falling into a vat of chocolate on more than one occasion. Find it and learn to use it.

My daughter uses it to create face displacement maps in Photoshop by smudging gradients into light and shadow patterns. With it you push around pixels, blending edges, smoothing over nasty spots.

In Photoshop there's a Finger Paint option that lets you actually apply a little foreground color to the area. You can use this with the eyedropper to blend color into small areas to hide blemishes or cover over a small detail that you don't want seen. Use the Blur tool to soften color transitions and the Smudge tool to smear colors around. You can even make little galaxies by smearing a spatter of white dots.

Dodge and Burn

This name comes from photography where you burn in parts of an image to make them darker and dodge areas (keep light from hitting it) to make them lighter. These tools are excellent for creating highlights and shadows where you may need them. To switch between the two, just hit <Ctrl>.

I use the Burn tool more often. I like moody images with shadows, and if they aren't dark enough, I'll often burn them in a tad where I want shadows.

Sponge It!

The Sponge tool, if you have it, desaturates colors. Used lightly it can save a badly textured surface that looks too plastic. By sponging around you can create a time-worn look to surfaces. By hitting <Ctrl> you can switch to a saturation tool. Going back and forth you can do a mighty job of weathering a surface.

Sometimes things in the background get a little too busy and detract from the main focus. With your foreground object selected, hit Invert and apply the desaturate sponge over the offending parts of the background. You want the foreground objects selected because this gives a clean separation between foreground and background.

AntiAlias It

There is no AntiAlias tool in Photoshop or anywhere else I can think of. But if you have an image with aliased edges because you forgot to invoke tS2's active anti-aliasing process, and you lost the scene file and it would take too long to redo it, here's a neat way to antialias your rendering in Photoshop.

First hit <Ctrl> K to bring up the general options dialog box. Select Bicubic Interpolation if it's not already selected. Good, next select Image ⇨ Image Size and check: Constrain ⇨ Proportions. Now double the width of the image either in inches or pixels. This will automatically double the length as well. This will give you an image four times the size you started with. In order to create this large image, Photoshop has to perform Bicubic Interpolation on the image to fill in all the empty spots between pixels. This automatically creates antialiased edges. Now go back to Image ➪ Image Size again and reduce the width back to where it was before. The image will be recalculated based on the enlarged image, which has antialiased edges. The result will be a new image that has nicely antialiased edges. Simple but effective.

Clone It

It turns out that you can take image pixels from one part of an image and transplant them to another. This allows you to create virtually seamless painting over objects. Look in the color section at Kate White's undersea images. The smaller one came with large white ID numbers on it. I cloned them out and I bet you can't see where they were.

The secret is in the color variation. Most paint is monochromatic. You paint it on and the surface turns a uniform color. In nature this almost never happens. Clone paint has the same color variegation as the surface you're blending into. Thus, when I finished Kate's image, I had sea bottom blended into sea bottom. It all looks about the same.

Cloning requires an eye. You have to be able to guesstimate the best location to clone from. You also have to be careful because the clone source spot moves in synchrony with your brush. That can easily pull it into an area of incompatible color.

If that happens, reset the clone source point (usually <Alt> click) back into the color area you want and continue cloning.

You can use cloning for lots of useful tasks. It's how they do digital wire removal in feature films. When the bus flips over in *Speed*, there is a mongo big cable attached that actually pulls the bus over. You don't see it because it was removed by cloning over with sky from a few frames earlier.

You can add stars to a portion of space that looks too barren, or take a planet or space vehicle from one image and put it into an other. Just watch your lighting. It's a dead giveaway if you clone in an object with shadows in the opposite direction.

POWER TIP: Be careful when cloning, since version 2.5 Photoshop will pick up the cloned portion and re-clone it. That is, if your pickup point wanders over a section you just cloned, it won't pick up the original material (as it used to) but picks up the new cloned image. This can lead to multiple copies of the clone you didn't want. To avoid this, it's best to clone from a duplicate of an image or a clean plate.

TAKE NOTE: In MEDIAPaint, cloning is performed with the Stencil tool.

A Clean Plate

You can do all sorts of wonderful things with the Clone tool including cloning from one image to another. In Hollywood we use something called a *clean plate*. It's an exact match of the original image, except foreground elements (actors and props) are removed. You take a picture with the actors in place, then move them out and snap the same picture with the same lighting again. In film, clean plates require a fancy motion control camera so the clean plate has exactly the same camera moves and timing, and can be matched frame for frame.

Here's how you use it frame by frame. Let's say you decide to remove one of the actors. No problem, you just set up an airbrush to pick up pixels from the clean plate in the area behind where he's standing. Using the aligned rubber-stamp option, you carefully start your brushing at the exact spot where you're picking up color from the clean plate, and you simply paint him out of the picture. Nobody will know he was there. You can also clone with transparency, so you can make him into a ghost.

Sharpen It

You have to be careful when using your Sharpen tools. They increase the contrast between adjoining pixels according to the method you choose. General sharpening applies to the whole image or the part you have masked. Sharpen Edges uses an edge detection algorithm and increases contrast only around detected edges. If used too much or too intensely, sharpening can make an image look cheesy. It gives the look of a gross half-tone screening job in a cheap print shop. I used sharpening to highlight the icons for this book. Whenever you see an icon in a little black box, it's had both its color curves and sharpness adjusted to make it stand out from the rest of the icons. This doesn't necessarily make it look better, just more obvious.

Image Adjustment

We'll leave still work after letting you know about color adjustment. If you don't like the color balance of an image you can change it. Virtually all the packages let you change contrast, brightness, and color balance. You can change the intensity of the red, green, or blue components of an RGB image to get just the right color. Kai's Power Tools has a favorite filter of mine: Sharpen Image Intensity. I'm not sure exactly what it does to the color, but most images, especially washed-out ones, look a lot better after you apply it.

Learn how your particular tool handles color adjustment so you can fine-tune the look the way a professional would.

A Few Useful F/X Filters

Under the Effects menu or its equivalent you'll find a selection of filters. *Filter* is a passive term that doesn't really fit. A few elementary filters are passive, like the hi-pass filter, but most are pretty active. They are more like processes. There are possibly hundreds of native and plug-in filters, as we've discussed. Here I'm just going to give you a few ideas on how to use them.

There are many things you can't do in tS2, like lens flares. You can see the flares I added to my cover image. I used the Photoshop ⇨ Filter ⇨ Render ⇨ Lens Flare filter. (There's a flare filter in Photo-Paint 6 too.) You can adjust the location and size of a flare and the kind of reflection rings it has. This allows you to create pretty star effects. MEDIAPaint includes a nifty Lens F/X tool in its first collection of plug-ins.

Solar Flare

A neat post effect is to insert a brilliant star peeking out from behind a planet. It's simple. Use the circular marquee to capture a copy of the planet to the clipboard. Then place a bright lens flare at the edge of the original planet. This flare bleeds white all over the planet's surface, so paste the clip copy exactly over itself, obscuring the lens flare and making it appear as if the star is *behind* the planet. (See Figure 31-1 and Plate 31-1 for a step-by-step sequence.)

I pasted it as a darken-only layer to get a smoother edge and keep control over movement. In Plate 31-1 part C, I placed a tiny secondary lens flare in the center of the first one. This one bleeds just a small amount into the planet, like light bending through atmosphere.

You can feather the edges and do other things to make the image look right to you — as usual, experiment. You'll have to learn your specific application's details on your own though. No space for that here.

Figure 31-1: Before and After shots of a lens flare *behind* a planet. The effect is accomplished by selecting and copying the planet to the clipboard before placing the flare, and then pasting it back again to cover the flare bleed. See color Plate 31-1 for detail.

Glows

Related to solar flare are glows. Alien Skin's Black Box plug-ins have a neat glow effect that can enhance your engine exhaust and even your planets. You simply mask the area you want the glow to surround and set the parameters in the Preview window of the plug-in.

Glow can be used to create energy beams and the like. There are lots of parameters to adjust, giving you a wide range of effects that you can preview in the filter's interface window. Alien Skin also includes other filters you can use, such as Swirl and Motion Trails (shown in Figure 31-2), and more. It's a well-designed tool.

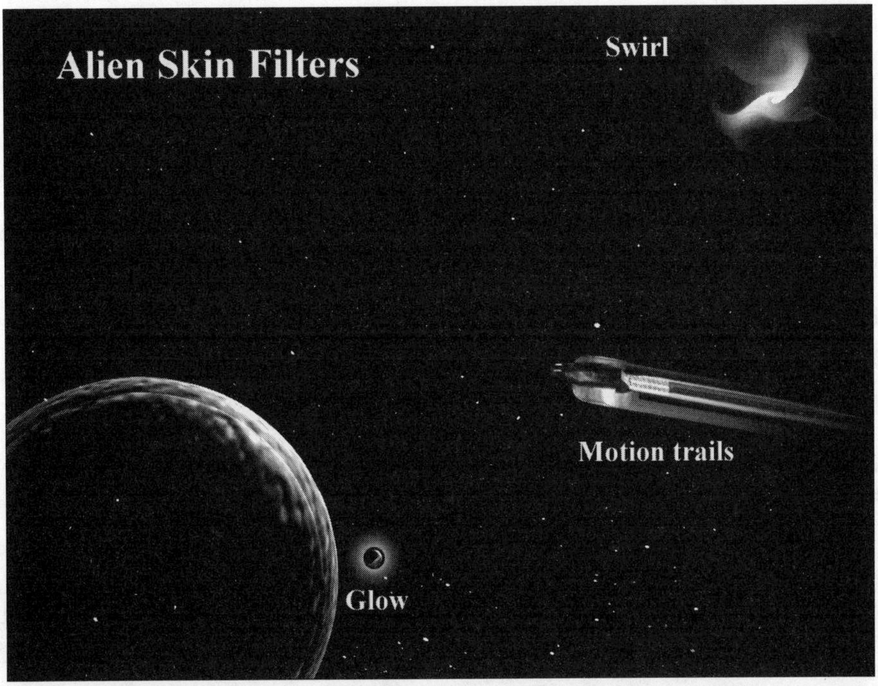

Figure 31-2: Using filters can enhance your images in post-production. Here I apply various Alien Skin Black Box filters that you can try.

Gradients

One of the most useful tools in imaging is the gradient. It's a smooth transition from one color to another. It's often used as a transparency key in the alpha channel of 32-bit .tga files.

In the Alpha Channel

As you know, the alpha channel controls transparency when compositing. Usually the blacker the shade of gray, the more transparent, and the whiter, the more opaque.

POWER TIP

There's a strangeness in tS2: If you render to 32-bit targa files, it makes the white transparent and the black opaque. I'm told it was done on purpose, but no one can tell me exactly why.

If you want to use the alpha channel on tS2 image in the traditional way, you can invert it easily in Photoshop or QFX or Xres. In Photoshop the procedure is to bring up the image, with the Channels palate showing, and select channel 4 or alpha, then Select ➪ Image ➪ Map ➪ Inverse.

If you want to fade one image out as another fades in, you place a grayscale gradient in the alpha channel of image A, and composite it over B. Where image A's alpha is black, only image B will show. As it fades to white, image A will show through more and more until, where the alpha is white, you see only A.

Gradients often go from one color to another, or through a spectrum. When you see a photo of draped satin cloth, the folds are really made up of complex gradients. Thus, it's relatively easy to simulate satin using Photoshop's Gradient tool as mentioned earlier in this book.

Kai's Gradient Designer and Gradients on Path tools are terrific for creating special post lighting effects like streams of light coming down from clouds or searchlights or laser blasts or starbursts. They offer the creative person a world of possibilities for making glow effects using an infinite number of gradient possibilities.

POWER TIP

One of the problems in tS2 is that bug in the Vertex Painting tool that leaves sharp edges of transparent gel color. You can partially fix this by blurring those edges into the background with the Blur tool or the Swirl tool. (See Plate 10-2. The drone's exhaust is done with the Swirl tool in Alien Skin.) The various programs have different blur brushes. In general, painting a Gaussian blur along the sharp edges of the rocket trail will give you a more vaporous quality. You can even try surrounding the exhaust with the lasso, leaving a bit of blur space along the edges and set a wide-edge feather and apply your favorite blur.

Galaxies

If you're in a pinch for a spiral galaxy, say you have a big empty piece of black space, you can build one by spattering white dots or even a mixture of pastel dots and then processing them with a spiral filter.

If you want a galaxy looking down from the top, select a circle around the dots. For a galaxy tilted on edge, use an elliptical selection marquee. The longer and thinner the ellipse, the more tilted the galaxy will appear.

In Figure 31-3 you can see some different types of galaxies I built this way. To get the look I want, I sometimes use a little Gaussian blur or add a little noise to the selection. These selections were all made with one or both of the airbrush spatters in the white box. Remember you can copy and paste images multiple times to get the density you want.

Figure 31-3: Here I've created a variety of galaxies from the paint spatters in the detail box. The methods are explained in the text.

I used a neat trick on the big double galaxy. The lower left one had a weak center, so I copied one of the other spirals to the clipboard and then pasted it in the center as a Photoshop layer, lighten only. This means that instead of blotting out the bottom image with its black areas, the selection only transfers to areas it will lighten. Effectively this makes the black transparent. It's an alternative to creating an alpha channel before compositing.

The double galaxy also suffered from a sterile sameness, so I hit it with a light touch of Xaos tools Alchemy, which comes standard with Photo-Paint 6. This brushed in some random luminance variance. Then I hit the whole thing with a small bit of blur to make it look more like a telescopic image. That's what we're used to seeing.

Though I love a fabulous illustration, movies are what this book is all about. Post production is really more about video.

More Hollywood F/X

Virtually all of these still techniques can be applied to video image sequences. You don't want to work frame by frame, so video editing and paint software were invented.

Use your video editor to create title sequences, apply nifty special effects over time, and classy transitions between clips. A really cool animated effect that I invent is a pure turn-on for me. I'm going to give you some neat ideas to get you started, but ultimately it's up to you. I'm including morphing here because it nearly always involves a video output.

Video Post

Much of the magic you see in movies and TV happens in post production. We can do most of the still image enhancement and manipulation in video edit, with the important exception of cloning. That's done in video paint programs like Animator Studio or MEDIAPaint. First we'll look at some things that are possible, then we'll apply them to create some neat effects like worm holes and morphing ships.

Clone Magic Over Time – Animator Studio

Animator Studio has its strengths, one of which is its broad variety of *inks*. These are like the filters in other suites. Animator Studio also creates an alpha channel as you import a video clip. This allows you to do neat effects involving transparency changes over time. The Clone Ink is pretty sophisticated and works with the alpha channel. It allows you many source options, either in the same frame, in previous frames, or even from other clips. It will deposit the pixels as opaque or at any percentage transparency from 1 to 100. The Opaque option is handy for clean plate work. You can easily practice the hole-through-the-abdomen trick by compositing a live action actor over a background and then using the Clone tool to pick up pixels from the original background clip and deposit them frame by frame in a small circular patch in the center of the fellow's abdomen. You could use the Paint tools to create a meaty border around the clone and copy it frame by frame as the actor moves. If he rotates you'll have to compensate by foreshortening the illusion.

Clone Ink can be applied in any strength from 1% to 100% (default). At strengths less than 100 you get a ghostly effect, which can be varied over time to have a moving object slowly appear over the background.

Cloned Clouds on the Move

Cloning is cool, especially using partial transparency to blend the cloned segment into the existing one. Try taking an animated clip with a plain sky. Best if the action is against non-sky areas, so you can mask off the sky easily without a traveling matte. You can clone in ominous clouds from a second clip (at /textures/animated/clouds.avi), blending them into the existing sky in a believable but eerie way. Start at the top right side of the image and work the clouds across the screen for the length of the segment.

How It's Done

If you can get your hands on Animator Studio, you can use it to do an animated clone composite sequence like so:

1. Open your tS2 animation clip in Animator Studio and then open the clip of moving clouds you found on a CD-ROM somewhere.
2. Follow the manual and mask the sky to protect the rest of the picture from the clone operation.
3. Make the source clip (clouds) active by clicking anywhere on its Preview window.
4. Select the Airbrush tool with a fairly wide pattern.
5. Select ⇨ Paint Control Panel ⇨ Inks ⇨ Clone Ink.
6. Right click on the Clone Ink in the display field of Paint Control panel. This will bring up the properties panel. Click on Ink Properties.
7. Select ⇨ Relative Source Frame ⇨ Loop ⇨ Register Position. That will advance the frames of both images one for one as you clone, while correctly locating points on the two frames without going back to the starting point on each stroke. The loop thing says if you run out of clone source it'll start over again. That's cool. Clouds should be looped, in IMHO.
8. Set the Ink strength to 20% so that the original sky will not be replaced by the clone, just influenced by it.
9. Select the frame you want to start cloning from (0) and make it the current frame.
10. Hit the Select Source button on the Clone Ink Properties panel and the cursor changes to the Source cursor. Place it in the upper right-hand corner of the cloud movie. The cursor will change to the Airbrush tool (or whichever tool you have selected).
11. Now click anywhere on the destination clip's Preview window to make it the current movie. (If you're cloning from a previous frame in the same movie you don't have to do this step.)
12. Click the time mode icon on the Tool Bar to set up painting over time. This advances the frames automatically as you paint. This will cause the sky to start out with clouds only in the upper right, but as you airbrush it in, they'll appear to be rapidly filling the sky.
13. Render and view.

This is just one of many things you can do depending on what movie clips you can build or scrounge. You could render a space vehicle against a transparent background and have it develop as a ghost ship in a live action sequence.

Use the Splash.avi that comes with Animator Studio to practice with. Just don't save your results unless you change the name. You're fortunate that tS2 has some interesting tools you can use to create action sequences for special effects.

All the Right Moves

If you wonder why I brought up the super-expensive motion control and matched camera moves earlier, I'll tell you. You don't have to reinvent the wheel. Hollywood professionals have developed a lot of wonderful techniques that port directly over to 3D. In this case the motion control cameras are built into tS2. You can move a camera in any complex tracking, zooming, crazy path you want, save that path, and shoot it again. I find the easiest way to create a clean-plate video is to shoot the original scene, save it, remove the foreground elements, and shoot again. It's all automatic. Try it. Then you can use this technique in several ways. Here's an example of how to use it with a morph animation to create an eerie Sci-Fi action sequence.

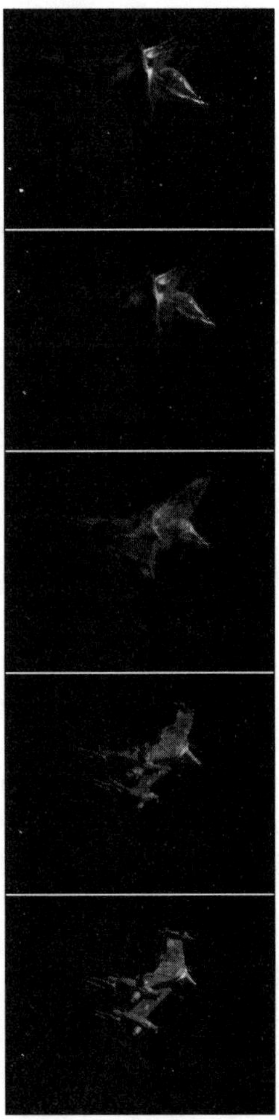

Figure 31-4: A static morph illustrating the concept of alien to conventional morph. From top to bottom you have: alien ship, 20% morph, 50% morph, 80% morph, conventional ship.

Morph It

I don't care if morphing is way overused. There's a place for it. Imagine an alien race of superior beings who have space vehicles that can shape-shift. What would it look like, especially if they didn't have to preserve volume? Such a ship would be made of nano-goo, able to change volume by increasing or decreasing density at a nano-molecular level. Given the proper commands, this ship could pull itself like taffy into different shapes and change materials almost instantly, as shown in Figure 31-4. The material changes are due to programmed changes in the nanomolecular cohesive bonding networks, which are quite flexible. Thus a flexible, amorphous shell could change into glass and steel on command. How are you going to animate that directly in tS2, especially if the number of vertices between objects changes by even one? No can do. But with morphing, all is possible. Here's how.

How to Morph a Spaceship

Create a scene with an organic alien space vehicle moving on a 100-frame path through a neat cosmos. Then install a camera on a path with cool moves: have it move in front of, and perpendicular to the vehicle's path, moving across in front as it approaches. Use the Look At tool to automatically maintain a camera heading directly at the ship.

Set the space vehicle's axis to the center of the nose with the Z axis facing forward. Save the object path and render the clip from frame 0 to 60 only. This is roll A.

Now delete the original vehicle and substitute a totally differently shaped one, go from the alien vessel to a starfire class shuttle. Place the starfire axis in the same relative position as you did on the alien ship and attach starfire to the path you saved, starting at the exact coordinates as the first vehicle.

On this second rendering, start at frame 40 and render to the end. This is roll B (I suspect you knew that). In your video editor, clip and save matching frames 40 to 60 from each roll. That will be the last 20 frames of roll A and the first 20 frames of roll B. These are the frames we dynamic morph in matched pairs. You want to save them as .tga files. You'll have a total of 40 files. Set them up in matched pairs in Morph's dynamic edit module and set your control lines and dots. Follow the manual to build a dynamic morph. Morph them together.

POWER TIP: Setting the dots and lines can be a little confusing if the alien ship has no corresponding parts to the starfire. No problem. Just be aware that the dots on the alien vessel will be pulled to the corresponding dots on the starfire, so make a logical pattern.

Load the 20-frame morph clip into your video editor and weld roll A, frames 1–40, to the front and frames 60–100 from roll B on the end. Play it.

You'll have a spectacular sequence where the alien ship morphs into a more conventional vehicle to avoid detection. Using a motion control camera and dynamic morphing gives the sequence a very sophisticated (read expensive) look. Go ahead, impress yourself.

Water Pod Morph

Remember the water pod monster? Try this: Have the water pod rise up, then do a 30-frame morph to a human standing on the flat sea. Use the first frame of a live action clip of the human composited, walking across that water for the morph frame, then weld the rest of the live action to the end of the morph. If you do it right, the sea will rise up, transmorph into the human, who will walk off across the ocean. For a neater but more complicated effect, you might want to clone in actual footage of moving ocean waves at about 50% transparency over the rendered ocean surface.

POWER TIP: The human should be shot against a blue or black background for this effect. Use a big blue sheet, or if you're really into it, paint the spare room medium French blue and shoot in there. Any color video camera will do.

Transitions

When you go from one clip to the next, you have a transition. If you weld two clips together you get the simplest and most common transition, a cut. When you welded the end clips onto the morphed effects above, you didn't see a cut because the last frame of the morph was one frame before the first frame of the weld. Thus you got a smooth sequence with no obvious changes of film. That's what you want there.

But often, to tell a story, you want to change your point of view or show time change. You can either do it in an inconspicuous manner, or you can do it in a way that adds visual interest to the story, or at worst you can do it so it detracts from the story. All three are common. If you've been reading, you know I've referred to the transitions on a certain television show which have become an important part of the format. They give visual enhancement while emphasizing story points. I'm going to recommend that you stick to simple transitions:

- ✦ The Cut
- ✦ The Dissolve

That's it. Anything else is likely to give the person reviewing your demo a twinge in his stomach and a groan in his brain. Fancy transitions are way overused. Avoid that trap. The reviewer knows transitions are no ruler of your ability — any idiot can do them with modern software. There's only one justification for using fancy transitions in your work — that it somehow fits a special effect. Here's an idea of what I mean.

You've animated a neat sequence, but now you need to have your ship go through a worm hole in space and come out somewhere far away. Figure out a neat worm hole effect, like applying a swirl filter to your A roll with the center off to the left. As the ship approaches, start an iris transition in the center of the swirl. An iris transition is one that starts out as a tiny hole in roll A that shows roll B. It slowly expands to fill the entire screen with roll B. If you start it in the center of a swirl, it looks like it's part of a natural hole, opening in the universe.

Your B roll sequence is, of course, the strange destination.

You can create all sorts of wild alien worlds in Vista Pro from Virtual Reality Labs. There's a demo on the CD-ROM (at \demo\vistapro). It's a terrain generator that creates life-like places. There are several on the market. Light ROM 3 from Graphic Detail (502-363-2968) has tons of USGS digital elevation models, the whole US, that you can use to create fly-by terrain, complete with rivers and trees and great skies.

As part of this strange transition, apply a zoom filter to the ship just previous to the iris opening up, which will make it look like it's blurring up to light speed. You have to play with the timing, but you can make it look like the ship got swallowed up by the worm hole. Make sure you have an image of the same ship in a matched position in roll B. That way it looks like the camera is on a chase ship that went through the hole with it.

There's So Much More

I've only scratched the surface here to get you started. Most of the effects you'll be seeing in cinema are not listed here; they can't be because people like you are fast at work creating them. I'm a little concerned about introducing you to all these effects just before showing you how to make a great demo tape. Why? Because you might just overuse them thinking it will impress the people you send them to. Not likely. If it's been done before, it won't be too impressive. Pay close attention to the next chapter, it could be the difference between a wonderful career you love and being an accountant.

So much for magic, now let's get to the most practical chapter in this book, how to create a winning demo tape. Read it. Most demo tapes are crap, so you'll have an edge.

Summary

In this chapter you were supposed to have been stimulated into thinking about all the amazing things you can do with images, both still and moving. You are supposed to be thinking not in terms of what's been done, but what effects you can invent. To that end I've exposed you to the following concepts:

- Still images run deep, maybe four layers, with alpha.
- The alpha channel has something to do with transparency in compositing.
- Your images may be good, but you can almost always improve on them with a little expert touch-up.
- A little sloppy touch-up can ruin a perfectly good image. A lot of sloppy touch-up can kill a career.
- Though you can do a lot of things to still images, you can do more with moving ones; that's where the thrill is.
- You can do advanced movie magic like wire removal, time compositing, and image enhancement with affordable tools.
- Nobody can teach you now the techniques you'll be inventing tomorrow.

✦ ✦ ✦

PART VII

Now Do Something With It!

Now that you've put the time into following the tutorials and techniques discussed in the previous sections, you're ready to impress the powers that be. In this section, you learn how to create a demo tape that gets you in the front door. You also learn how to apply animation techniques to the exploding world of the Web.

In This Part

Chapter 32

Creating Your Own Demo Reel

In This Chapter

What you really want to accomplish with your demo tape

How long you should make it

How to come up with ideas

How to get it out of your computer

Getting a career started in CGI takes a few things all rolled into one person. Some of it is natural ability, but most comes from creative application of persistence and determination. You have to pay your dues, work hard, and stick with it. But you have to work smart as well. A lot of people haven't read this book, so that gives you an edge. Go for it by building a smart and beautiful sales tool — your demo tape.

What You Really Want from Your Demo

I asked several young, reasonably accomplished animators what they were planning to put in their demo tapes. It was mostly stuff that impressed them. Here are some of the things that were high on the list:

- Duplicating a really cool and complex effect they'd seen in the movies
- Complex mechanical animations
- Dynamics and explosions
- Complex or meticulous modeling
- Organic modeling and animation techniques
- Characters

That's enough. I can see the logic in all of them. But it's all pretty much a yawner for the people who will be evaluating your demo as part of a job application. Think about it. They've seen so much of this stuff, they're probably having bad dreams about it nightly.

As for the duplicated effect, it's been done. So have the mechanical and explosions and stuff. These mostly show off your software's capability more than your own.

Meticulous modeling might be a different story, but they've seen all this before and you could have just snagged the model from somewhere. The demo offers no proof that you built it.

It doesn't hurt to have any or all of this stuff in your demo, just don't rely on it to wow the audience by itself. It won't.

This will be a jaded audience. Even if your effect is something spectacular and very unusual, think twice about including it unless it fits. I think a few gratuitous effects tossed in won't hurt, but they should mostly tell your story.

Characters are good. Designing an appealing character shows talent, especially if it's being seen by an entertainment company. If it's very professionally done either from a modeling standpoint or from the personality animation view, you'll make some points.

Alas, even then they'll only pause a minute or two from shooting paper wads through a straw at the screen and groaning loudly at every cliché you toss at them. Okay, there's a point, avoid visual clichés. Characters generally need a plan, a reason for being.

Heck, you need a plan. Here are a few questions you ought to consider before setting out on your mission:

- ✦ What do I want to accomplish with my tape?
- ✦ What does a successful tape look like — what are its earmarks?
- ✦ What are current industry trends?
- ✦ What is a visual cliché anyway?
- ✦ Who will I send my demo to?

With answers to these questions in hand you're ready to set out on your journey.

What Your Tape Needs to Accomplish

Your demo tape should be something you're proud of, but that's only the beginning. It's not designed to impress you, your mother, or your friends. That's way too easy. Nope, you guys aren't jaded, you're pushovers for the slightest unusual wrinkle or flash. And your mother's going to like it any way she looks at it. She'll have the neighbors in to see it.

No, you have to impress an audience of the most jaded animation viewers in the world, the guys who do the magic daily. They yawn very easily except for a few things — and I don't advise putting nudity in your demo.

What would impress them? I've asked. You may be surprised. My general impression is that it's dangerous to put in things they'll find particularly trite like a page-turn transition or really common effects filters. You have to figure they've seen every standard Elastic Reality and Premiere transition about a jillion times. I know they look cool, but be cool and don't use them. If you build a new transition in transition factory, use it. This shows your ability to program special effects, an important skill.

If like Rob Bryerton, you have substantial programming skills and know how to apply them to underpinnings of 3D graphics files, demonstrate this. They'll want to know.

The Ideal Candidate

There's no one ideal candidate for all situations, but I can come pretty close to what they're looking for. If your tape demonstrates half these things and your interview nails down the rest, you should be on your way to a career of your own choosing. If you have the following:

- ✦ Vision — the ability to see things in new and entertaining ways
- ✦ A combination of excellent artistic and technical skills
- ✦ A passion for the genre
- ✦ A true feeling for entertainment — a storyteller
- ✦ A drive to find new and better ways

With all this the rest comes easily. I didn't state the obvious things like the person has to be smart, creative, and a decent human being, but it's all in there.

You can't convince anyone of all these things with a demo tape and an interview, but you can open the door.

Capture Their Imaginations

You want your demo to be a window on your complex and interesting personality. You want to do it in a way that will nail them to their seats.

How do you do that? By making them forget they're watching a demo tape. Sure it's a much harder way to go. That's the point. If you can get these jaded photon jockeys lost in your images, you've accomplished your mission. My experience is that animators are not lazy people. They sometimes work longer hours than necessary. I believe you don't want to take the easy road with your demo, you just want some assurance that the hard road is also the smart one. I have no idea who you'll send your tape to, so I can't shine a light on many answers. But I have found that there is some similarity across different situations. With the above answers and suggestions you can define your task. It's not what most people think it is, so that puts you ahead of the pack.

If you're like most, you're struggling to figure out how to apply your talents to the task of impressing these strangers. Right? Trust me, you want it that way, or the competition would be beating the trail. Take it one step at a time.

First step, get them involved in your material. You'll have to grab their minds and drag them kicking and screaming into your imaginary world.

What tools do you have to accomplish that? What was the first thing (more or less) you learned in this book? Story. You have to have a story. Don't just throw a bunch of dumb eight-second clips together and think you're going to impress anyone. It's not going to happen. That's why I spent so much time on story and character and lighting and art direction. Most books shortchange these critical areas. These are also the things your competition are likely to neglect. I know — I've been around.

You also want to let them know, without beating them over the head, that you are a talented artist and animator. Most of them figure if you have the style and sensibility they're looking for, they can teach you technique and provide you with the engines to build what your mind beholds.

What a Good Demo Looks Like

Write to several production companies and ask for a copy of their demo reel. I'm not giving you a list here, because they'd never speak to me again. Look through some of the magazines such as *3-D Artist, Animation* magazine, and *3D Design*. Also check some of the Web sites mentioned elsewhere. And don't write. I'm going out on a limb here, but I get much better response talking with people. Of course I'm an accomplished talker. If you're a great animator but among the verbally clumsy, you may do better with a letter. Judge for yourself.

Get at least four or five demo tapes. You can get good leads from customer demo tapes from places like Softimage, Alias, and Side Effects. Listen to the interviews and identify companies you might like to work for. Watch tapes over and over. Be aware that often the original sound is removed and a lousy heavy metal background is laid over the whole tape. You don't want to do that part.

If you bought Martin Hash's *3D Animation* there are several excellent demo examples on it. Pay particular attention to the one about balls and blocks. It's very well done. Note how the animator grabs your interest. Check the Will Vinton piece on tools done for CTW. Note how perfectly the animation is synched to the music.

Rate all the demo pieces on a scale of one to ten, one being the best. Quit looking at anything below an eight. Look for common elements in your favorites. Look at technique and see what appeals. Figure most of it won't impress the pros, so be selective. What about these favorites appeals to your inner person? This is important. You'll always be a better animator if you do it from your soul rather than your brain. To do that you have to have feelings about style and develop a personal style. You'll have to set personal style aside for many jobs, but you need it underneath.

Keep remembering that Walt Disney was not the talented animator; that was Ib Iwerks. He still had a fair career creating what he loved. He had the soul of an entertainer and he had the vision. If you don't have a lot of natural talent, you may have great ideas. If you don't have talent or ideas, you may have good technique or training. If you don't have any of it, start now and work your way there. At some point you may have to admit that animation isn't for you, but don't give up easily if you love it. You may have to adjust your sights and move sideways a little. Maybe you're destined to be a production designer, a sound engineer, or any one of a thousand jobs associated with animated entertainment.

A Little Reconnaissance

The tapes you collect from the animation houses will give you an idea of what they're into. Ask Alias/Wavefront for a copy of *the end*, of which I've already spoken. You can't make a demo this long, but it'll give you ideas. Then send Christopher Landreth a letter of thanks for being an inspiration. I've also included a demo animation from I-Wei Huang on the CD-ROM for you to look at (at \movies\optic\e-wei\quickest.avi). It's short, sweet, entertaining, and cute. It has humor and I like it. Don't make yours anything like it though, that would be poor form.

Once you have a first cut of your demo, go back and watch your professional demo collection. You're developing an eye for professional quality both obvious and subtle. Don't look at your own stuff during this week or ten days. Then look at your demo and answer these questions:

- Does my work flow in a professional way?
- Are my modeling and texturing up to professional standards? If not, tell yourself what you need to do to get there.
- Are my camera moves consistent with professional work? Are they smooth enough, do they have enough drama, do they enhance the feeling of action?
- Is my sound editing up to professional standards?
- How do my opening and end titles compare?
- Is my button good enough?
- Am I suffering from self-doubt and being overly self-critical?
- Should I consider becoming a carpenter?

Lay out a plan of attack to get your demo up to par. Amateurs ponk out right here. They say to themselves, "Hell, I've put in too much work to start over again. If they don't like it, then I'll do another one."

Don't think that way. This is a small universe and word gets around. One bad demo in circulation and you'll have to push Cleveland to the beach before anyone takes you seriously again.

A Little Strategy

We need a plan for generating uniqueness. Even with a great little script you need to show them your stuff and knock their socks off with something they haven't seen yet. That's a very tall order. I can't give specific answers on how to be unique, only approaches. Assuming you've come up with a great script, here are some things you can try to grab them with:

- Think of simple but effective ways of getting your audience involved in your story. Sometimes a lovable tomato can be more effective than a complex, carefully animated human. Give your characters character.
- Try something that's been done already, but give it a new twist. For example, the standard morph is really old hat, but by careful planning you can create an infinite variety of new kinds of morphs. For example you can have the left side of roll A morph to the right side of roll B (even though that's trite now). If you try hard enough and experiment long enough you may find a morph strategy that is truly interesting. A good test is if it *looks* like a morph it's probably not going to help you.
- Try new ways to do old things. Morphing is so trite, it's a challenge I can't ignore. I like Rob Bryerton's particle morph. He has one object evaporating while the new object is forming, all in the same physical space. This can yield some unique effects, especially if you order your polygons in certain ways. Like have the first object evaporate from the top down while the new object forms from the top down. Find a unique way of your own.
- Find ways of distracting them from their critique of your work. You don't want them sitting there thinking… "I don't want to be here looking at this crap." Try something wild. If it were my demo, I'd wait until about a minute and a half in, then have the main character walk up to the screen, tap on it (I'd record the actual sound of tapping my knuckle on a large TV screen), and have him say something like, "Hey out there — pay attention — this demo shows talent so subtle you might miss it." And then have him go back to the action, look back at the audience and wink, and then do something wild. At this point I'd love to have the character fart. The guys would be sitting there saying "Did he just fart????" This is a kind of button, but it's in pretty bad taste. I might do it someday, however. Do something unexpected that the viewer will remember. I don't advise you to do this particular thing, because now that I've mentioned it, it's already trite — and I may still get up the guts to do it.
- Think fresh ideas. Loosen up your mind by writing down three eye-catching newspaper headlines. Make up a humorous story about each one. This can get your creative juices flowing. Then look at your demo plan and add that something special that will nail it home.

✦ Go over each part of your demo plan. Look for ways to do things better. Change things around in your mind. Enhance the crisis, punch up the humor, give it some sparkle. It's never going to be as good as it can be, but you can make it a lot better than it was.

You Need a Sound Concept

We've talked a lot about sound, but I can't stress how important a good, well synchronized stereo track can be. You can use it to distract. Have a voice from off stage make a comment that will refocus their attention. Give the right kind of echo to your character's voice as he enters a large room. It doesn't hurt to add surround sound F/X if you can. Some of the viewing rooms will have THX sound systems. It might jolt them just a tad to have some really cool and appropriate surround pop out. They might be looking for a sound person and it's a foot in the door.

Give Your Character a Voice

Use professional or children's voices. I'm not too proud to go over to UCLA and ask the person teaching voiceover classes if they'd recommend some talented VO students. Offer a copy of your tape to use in their own demos. Such a thing would be prohibitively expensive otherwise and will give them an edge. Nobody's going to turn that kind of deal down.

Every big city and many smaller ones have radio people who might be willing to help for a copy of the tape. You don't get the brass ring unless you reach for it.

Children's voices have a special quality to them. There is an innocence that imbues a digital character with a sense of realness. Don't go up to kids at the playground and try to record them. You might get arrested as a pervert. Find parents and explain your plan. Most will be happy to have their child's voice in an animation. Give them a copy.

A few parting thoughts about sound. Don't make your track too choppy; give it some continuity to smooth visual transitions. Few things are as annoying as a music track that obfuscates the voice track. Keep a balance in all sound levels. Don't have a door slam so loud it knocks the viewer's heart into his/her backbone. Apply the same rules of uniqueness to sound as you do to images. Be careful — you don't want sound being more important than the whole. Unique doesn't necessarily mean jarring or distracting. It means you do it in an interesting and unusual way that fits the material, the timing, and the circumstances so well it helps bind your images into a Gestalt. A Gestalt happens when the whole of something is far more than the sum of its parts. That's what you're reaching for.

Titles and Credits

I'm of the opinion that the opening is critical and the credits are hardly read. This can cause several disparate thought paths. First, if nobody reads the credits, how can I make them so interesting as to keep the jaded one glued to the screen. My alternate thought is to make the end credits simple — some nice music — they won't really see them anyway. Either way is probably a good choice.

Openings are more controversial. Some folks who know these things feel a very simple, nonanimated opening credit is all you want. I don't think so. This is a good place to grab them. Don't try to do it purely with technique. It's not good enough. Be creative and if you can, fool them. Reviewers love to be fooled. I spoke to a pretty famous movie reviewer and he admitted that the thing he likes most in a film is when his predictions about how it's going to come out are wrong. Surprise them.

Here's an example of what I might do... again, if you use it they'll just know you read this book. They want you to use your head not mine. Anyway, I'm picturing this simple opening in courier typeface "DreamScape Demo Reel #12" with a few film scratches for effect. If they're paying attention, they'll know I put them there, if not, I don't want to work with them anyway. Next I'd have a flashing ShowTime Countdown 4... 3... 2... 1... 0. The music comes up, an iris starts to open in the center of the screen.

Suddenly we hear a female voice screaming frantically, "Wait, I'm not decent." The iris pauses a second or two and we see movement behind it. The words Production Design: Peter Plantec flash beneath the iris hole, then she says, "Okay now," and the iris opens on a naked female robot coming out of a shower, wrapping up in a towel. The camera does a counter move as she takes her position in front of a vanity. She talks to the audience in the mirror. "Sorry about that, I've got a lousy sense of timing." The title Art Direction: Peter Plantec flashes across her face as a 3D logo that royally annoys her. She pulls it down so she can see the audience. She yells off stage, "Will you give me a break here?" and the screen splits like on TV when they run the credits of the movie you just saw while introducing the 11:00 news. But this time the credits fall from the top and pile up at the bottom: First my name in large letters, Peter Plantec, followed by Animation Systems Designer, Executive Producer, Line Producer, Unit Production Manager, Cinematographer, Digital Effects Supervisor, Animated by and Directed by. Then my wife's name, Adele Plantec, drops down with a Craft Services credit on top of it.

Meanwhile the bot character is watching the credits fall, looking ever more annoyed. "Enough already, we get the point." She looks out at the audience with a roll of her eyes and says, "He gets caught up in the Hollywood thing." She then adjusts a button on her shoulder and is automatically dressed in a feminine outfit in a very neat morphy way. She goes over and smacks the side of the split screen and a bunch of other titles fall down for my wife, such as Transportation Captain, Office Manager, Bird Feeder, and Recreation Therapist. Then the screen opens up full. She says, "Have I got a story for you..." and it's off into the demo. See what I mean? You already have them interested. They probably didn't expect this kind of opening. Keep them off guard for a full 2.5 minutes and you're a winner.

Now that you're fully equipped to build a demo, you need a way to get it out of your computer and onto tape. I'm going to talk about three approaches: Cheap, Reasonable, and Expensive. Each has its advantages.

Making a Videotape

Probably the first thing you'll want to do is send a videotape of your work to your mother, boyfriend, or teacher. Digital video is not set up to be output to your tape recorder. You need a way to play it full screen at 30 frames/second. Most computers can't come close to doing that, though things are improving rapidly. If you have a multimedia computer with built-in full screen MPEG (Like the Aptiva), you can buy an inexpensive scan converter to output video. You'll have to MPEG encode your .avi files first (see sidebar).

The Cheap Approach

The least expensive way I've found to get a reasonably good copy of your .avi files onto videotape is with an MPEG board that outputs NTSC video. The one I recommend is the Visionettics Board and I asked them to give you a discount on it. The coupon is in the back of the book. You can get their board for less than $250.00. The problem is, trueSpace2 doesn't put out .mpg files. You have to convert your .avi files, and most of the software converters are very expensive. Some boards come with such software, but they too are expensive (around $700.00). Some boards even come with real-time MPEG encoding (RealVideo) but cost nearly $5,000.00. Your best bet is to take the time to encode the data and play it via a Visionettics board to your VCR. I recommend a good VCR like a Sony Hi-8 with the best Hi-8 professional tape you can get. I get used tapes in the Recycler here in LA, for about $3.50 each.

MPEG Encoding Solution

The really fine folks at Drastic Technologies have been kind enough to give us a limited version of their MPEG encoding software that converts files directly from .avi to .mpg. This application encodes a limited number of frames at a time so you can try it out and see if it works for you.

Render your .avi files at 352 × 240 (MPEG default for NTSC in tS2) in an uncompressed form. You won't be able to play these very successfully unless you have a video accelerator board because they contain too much data. MPEG is a data compression methodology that cleverly removes much of the data content without destroying the image. Thus you can play MPEG files at full speed. The Visionettics board (see coupon in back of book) blows the image up to full screen using nifty interpolation methods that fill in the missing pixels with the best candidate. It looks good. The board has an NTSC output that you connect to your videotape recorder.

Improving MPEG Results

MPEG is one of the most efficient coding methods available, but it's known as temporally asymmetric. That means it takes a lot longer to encode MPEG than to Decode it. The ratio can be more than 100 to 1. That means 30 seconds of play can easily take way more than an hour to encode. The time varies with the material. If there's a lot of movement against changing backgrounds it takes longer.

You want to assure yourself of good results with that kind of time investment. There are professional MPEG encoding facilities that do a fabulous job of encoding feature films and such. I asked Peter Schirling, head of the US MPEG committee and a Senior Engineer associated with IBM's encoding facility, what the secrets are. He said, "We do a lot of image custom filtering before encoding. Sometimes it has to be done frame by frame, softening sharp edges." He went on to explain that MPEG-1 has a hard time with sharp/contrasty edges, suggesting that if you soften edges with the smallest amount of Gaussian blur possible, you'll get a better result. I tried it and it works.

If you intend to do a lot of video output, it pays to upgrade to the fully functional version of Drastic's MPEG encoder as the price is extremely competitive. A little side benefit to having the Visionettics board is that MPEG is becoming the *de facto* file format on the Internet and you can download all sorts of interesting clips including sections of *the end* from the Alias/Wavefront Web page. It also plays feature film video CDs you can rent at video stores.

A Reasonable Solution

If you can go up a bit in investment there's a better way to go. The standard compression for on-line digital television editing is MJPEG. JPEG was developed to compress still pictures by removing unnecessary detail. It's been modified for use with film and called Motion JPEG, or MJPEG. Less asymmetric than MPEG, it's possible to compress images in real-time using specialized high-speed chips from Zoran, IBM, and others. You can buy any one of a number of plug-in PCI boards designed for digital video editing. My favorite is the Miro DC20. It's high quality, made in Germany, and costs just under a grand. The important thing is, it puts out broadcast-quality video — providing you have a fast hard drive that can transfer at least 3–5 megabytes/second. That means a SCSI AV drive. The output is excellent at 60 fields/second, which is what your video files will be rendered at. They'll be crystal clear because they aren't blown up to full screen. You actually render at 640 × 480, which fills an NTSC screen. This is the best intermediate route.

If you don't want to go to that expense, you can still buy the Miro DC1tv board which works well with a regular IDG drive, and it fits an ISA bus. You render at 320 × 240 at 30 fps and when you play back the DC1tv expands the image very expertly to full screen. You get real-time MJPEG encoding too. The DC1 costs about $495.00.

The real-time capture capability of the Miro boards will help you build a collection of digital video clips. Anything you can capture on your VCR can be input to the board and captured into an .avi file. This gives you virtually unlimited options for animated textures.

The High-Priced Spread

There is no quibbling with the fact that the DPS Perception board is the way to go for high-quality digital video work. Professionals pretty much agree on this, though some still want to stay with the old-fashioned and expensive method of recording one frame at a time.

The Perception's output far exceeds broadcast minimums, giving you stunningly crisp images. Even though this is the expensive option here, it represents a remarkable value in professional equipment. If you're going this route you'll need Windows NT (Perception board prefers it) and Speed Razor Mach III. You can set up your Pentium machine to run both Windows 95 and Windows NT and you'll need a minimum of 32 megs of RAM. The opening window will give you a boot choice of Windows NT or Windows 95. Thus you can set up tS2 in Win95, and Speed Razor/Perception, in NT and use the same files for both systems. No big deal. The latter is designed to work directly with the Perception and is one of the best video editors available.

The price is adding up though. The DPS has a street price of $1,700.00–$1,900.00 but that's a great price for this level of equipment. Razor is going to run you at least another $1,400.00, but you will see the difference on screen. Oh, I nearly forgot. The Perception has a built-in SCSI interface and requires a dedicated AV SCSI drive like the Seagate Baracuda series or the Micropolus AV series. These run about $500.00 a gigabyte and as long as we're doing it right, get the 4 gig drive and get a little break on the per gig price.

In Chapter 36 we'll talk more about putting together a professional digital production studio.

POWER TIP

By the time you buy this book, Caligari will be well on its way to releasing a version of tS2 optimized for Windows NT (now in development, code-named tS2.5). The current version runs on NT, but is slow, even on fast machines.

The Package

Okay, so I'm spending too much time worrying about the little things. I've studied humans for a lot of years and often it's the little things that leave an impression. You have one shot at making a first impression. Give it all you've got.

One way to add a little credibility is to take some care in preparing the physical package you send out. Open up Corel Draw or whatever drawing package you have and create a nice clean logo label for your tapes. An example of a logo that I created appears in Figure 32-1. A logo gives a more professional identity to you and your work. Keep it simple and if you can, have it represent you in some way. I like the simple animated Optic Edge logo on I-Wei's demo. It's cute and fun.

You can make a logo from just letters, or you can incorporate a design element. Since I'm a screenwriter/animator, I decided to incorporate both a pen and film into my logo. I found the pen as clip art, but didn't like any of the film strips I found, so I built one. I picked a nice typeface that felt right.

Figure 32-1: A simple logo can help you create a professional impression. This one is mine, created in Corel Draw. It has served me well for many years.

Use your logo to make a clean, professional looking label for your tape. Even if you print it on a laser printer it'll help.

Put your demo on a short tape. Many reproduction houses will cut the tape exactly the length you need it. This isn't necessary, but professional demos come on short tapes. You can recognize them by the large plastic drive wheel taking up the space where the tape is in a full reel. This does two things. It shows you're in touch with the way things are done, and imagine the trepidation a reviewer feels when a two-hour tape is delivered. A skimpy little tape looks much more inviting — seriously. The professionally duplicated tapes are not very expensive and come with plain white jackets. It's fine to leave them as is or to put a copy of your logo on top for easy identification. I print out the logo with my address and phone number a little smaller than the jacket. I cut it squarely with a paper cutter and use spray glue to affix it firmly to the box. You don't have to do it, it's just what I do. I figure they get so many tapes that they could easily forget who sent this one. So my name and number are on both jacket and tape.

Send it FedEx. Graphics studios get constant shipments from FedEx and other delivery services. If your work comes in a FedEx package it is immediately placed with other professional material they are receiving. If it comes by regular mail, it looks different and will probably get thrown in the low-priority bin. This is just an expensive little extra, but impression comes in the little things. If you want to save five dollars, go Express Mail.

Good Luck

Luck always plays a small part in getting your talents recognized. But, luck is 10% random and 90% perpetrated. Paying attention to the details, being persistent, and presenting yourself well will get you going in a very exciting career. I'll talk more about the overall process of getting employment in Chapter 34. But first, a look at a very new world of opportunity that you, as a tS2 user have exceptional access to: the 3D Web.

Summary

The whole book was leading up to this chapter. It's where you prepare to show the world your raw talent and imagination via your demo tape. You learned:

- ✦ That showing off your fancy modeling and animation skills is only a small part of what your demo tape has to do.
- ✦ The person reviewing your tape has probably seen hundreds, most looking pretty similar. You have to make yours stand out.
- ✦ Nothing makes a reviewer happier than being fooled and surprised.
- ✦ Everybody knows it was the software that did the neat stuff, that you just push the buttons. You have to prove them wrong.
- ✦ Minimal video edit is the way to go; fancy transitions and effects filters may backfire on you.
- ✦ You can give your demo tape a professional look, inside and out, and have it delivered in style.
- ✦ You can be creative, but you have to break the rules, take chances, go for it in a way that nobody's seen before.

✦ ✦ ✦

CHAPTER 33

Creating a 3D Web Site with VRML

In This Chapter

An introduction to Fountain, Caligari's 3D Web browser/ authoring package based on the tS2 interface

How in-lining is used to create global worlds

What LOD means

An introduction to VRML, the language of the 3D Web

Comparison of HTML and VRML

Advanced new help interface built into Fountain

Code name: Fountain Pro, the next generation

Skill transfer from tS2 to Fountain and Fountain Pro

Interest in 3D Web sites is bursting the seams of conventional Internet chaos. The future lies in this direction. In Chapter 38 I'll talk about where this exciting new realm is headed.

This is the beginning of three-dimensional digital interactive simulation world and you are right smack in the middle of it — if you want to be. You already know how to work the engine that provides 3D page authorship for the Microsoft Network as well as the Internet. Fountain, tS2's sister product, is a subset of tS2. Using virtually the same interface, it adds many new tools for creating 3D and linking interactive worlds. The interface is missing things like render and animation tools, and navigation has been streamlined. But it still looks and feels about the same. After a few minutes' workout you'll be connected up to Netscape and browsing in 3D.

Fountain

I've included a beta version of Fountain from Caligari. It's got a few rough edges and you'll have to buy the final version, but this way you get your feet wet without spending any extra bucks. Fountain offers a lot of capability and a lot of fun for free. It lets you use your tS2 modeling skill to rapidly create texture-mapped VRML objects in real-time and with interactive lighting. While primarily an authoring tool, Fountain is a dynamite 3D Web browser as well. For example, Figure 33-1 shows Fountain's two modes: Browse and World Creation.

This single application will open a new world of communicating to you, complete with access to sound, video, and HTML (standard Web pages) when used with Netscape and a few standard plug-ins.

Figure 33-1: Fountain, based on trueSpace, helps you build 3D worlds for the World Wide Web. It's also a 3D Web browser. This is a typical simple world.

Fountain exploits the power of 3DR, Intel's very fast real-time rendering system. If you have a 3D accelerated video card that supports 3DR you will get amazing performance. Even without acceleration the performance is better than could be expected.

The Fountain package includes such 3D shape-creating tools as Primitives, Polygons with face edit, lathing, sweeping and tips, as well as the extrusion of TrueType fonts. It only has infinite and local light sources and the paint tools are more limited at this time. There is an advanced version code-named Fountain Pro, which will have more trueSpace tools and capabilities incorporated.

A few of Fountain's new tools will be incorporated in tS2.5, like the ones designed to reduce the size of object files. They automatically strip out unnecessary normals, delete white space from VRML ASCII files, collapse hierarchies, and reduce the number of digits used to describe each 3D coordinate. The narrow bandwidth of the Internet is forcing 3D to become more efficient. This will improve performance across the board by yielding leaner, more powerful object codes.

You can create 3D geometry in tS2 and export it to Fountain in the .cob format. It can read other formats as well, including DXF, 3DS, Wavefront, LightWave, and Imagine. You can also create 3D objects by extruding imported 2D shapes like logos, etc. Fountain understands PostScript, which is widely used. You can export any object in the vast Corel library of clip art to be read directly by Fountain.

Minimum requirements for Fountain are a fast 486 with at least 8 megs of ram. You need a fast Internet ppp connection, and a Web browser (optional) with a 14.4 modem. This minimal system will soon prove frustrating, because 3D, as you know, requires a lot of bandwidth. I recommend at least a Pentium 100 with 16 megs of ram and a 28.8 modem. Even with this equipment things are a little slow. Remember, pioneers have always had to take the slow route to the gold. These are the covered wagon days of VRML. But things are evolving faster than a newborn chick.

Fountain creates VRML worlds. VRML stands for Virtual Reality Modeling Language. It's a way to transfer 3D environments across the Internet. You build a Home World people can visit and move around in, and you can visit other people's worlds.

Help Me!!

It's always been difficult to use standard Windows help files to explain 3D procedures. Caligari has come up with a remarkable new help system that actually shows you how to do things. It's already incorporated into Fountain and will be in the next version of trueSpace. Test drive it in the Fountain beta. The system is based on a procedural recording system that was built into the first betas of tS2. Caligari used it to create the tutorial files you'll find when you install the demo version of tS2. The program records every move of a professional artist, kind of like a mini-keyboard that can record every nuance of a great music performance. The new help system will play these performances so you can actually watch the procedure used to create certain objects and effects, or to see how certain tools work. This is almost like having an expert on your hard drive.

A Leg Up

Fountain may be the only Web browser that lets you create original material right in the browser interface. Others I've seen have you creating worlds by importing and arranging objects. With Fountain you can exercise a lot more creativity, especially now that you're an accomplished modeler.

You'll want to keep polygon count to a minimum and use special seamless textures for faster online transfer. But these are skills easily learned. Having read this far in the book you definitely have a leg up. If you join one of the mail groups you'll find yourself giving advice all the time.

Load up Fountain and play with it. You'll feel right at home. Bits and pieces of the documentation are all you need to figure out how to set up your modem interface. Get good at it. I predict there will be a lot of money to be made in online environment creation. If you have the skills you'll be in the driver's seat. In Chapter 34 I'll give you some in-depth tutorials on it.

Most VRML worlds are pretty boring to me these days. The opportunities for creative expression are only just starting to be explored. Everybody's been so bogged down in the technical details, getting standards set and systems running, that little artistry has been displayed. You can explore some existing worlds by downloading them from the Caligari Web Site at `http://www.caligari.com`. You go live by hyperlinking via the Caligari site. They've got plenty of hot links to follow. They're not bad, but still pretty primitive. The medium has great potential and there's something new on the horizon called OpenFlight. It's like a superset of VRML that will have us in fully immersible 3D, stereo surround-sound worlds before you know it. These worlds will be supported by such concepts as Distributed Interactive Simulation (DIS) and Continuous Adaptive Terrain (CAT). The future is pure excitement.

VRML

Again I went to an expert to help me with this section. I was fortunate enough to enlist the aid of Konstantine Guericke, Executive Vice President at Caligari, who wrote the following section. He's been spearheading the Caligari VRML program.

A VRML Primer

The World Wide Web is based on networking protocols such as HTTP (HyperText Transfer Protocol), and on a number of formats that describe how text, images, sound, and video are represented across the different types of computers that are connected to the Internet. The most common format today is HTML (HyperText Markup Language), which allows text and graphics to be displayed together using a two-dimensional page metaphor. The latest trend among HTML browsers, such as Netscape Navigator or Internet Explorer, is to include HTML authoring capabilities since many people previously content to just browse the Web are becoming interested in publishing their own home page.

VRML (pronounced *vermal*) stands for Virtual Reality Modeling Language and is to 3D what HTML is to 2D. While HTML specifies how two-dimensional documents are represented, VRML describes how three-dimensional environments can be explored and created on the World Wide Web. Since 2D is really just a subset of 3D, any two-dimensional object can be easily represented in a three-dimensional environment. Tim Berners-Lee, the "father" of the Web, reasons in Mark Pesce's book, *VRML: Browsing and Building in Cyberspace,* that VRML is the future of the Web because it is more natural for us to be immersed in a three-dimensional space than to click our way through hyperlinked 2D pages.

Using VRML not only adds sizzle to your Web site, but leverages the fact that each of your visitors has spent their entire life navigating in three dimensions. We make sense of the world by quickly analyzing factors such as the speed of approaching objects (such as a car), the location of light sources, and the texture of surfaces. Since many of these processes happen subconsciously, a clever designer can guide visitors through spaces and focus their attention without forcing them to make explicit choices. Similar to the real world, the visitor maintains a first-person perspective and completely controls how close to move toward an object and from what angle to view it.

What Does VRML Do?

VRML doesn't really do anything. It is simply a scene description language that standardizes how three-dimensional environments are represented on the Web. Unlike programming languages such as C++, VRML does not have to be compiled and run. Rather, VRML files get grammatically analyzed (parsed) and then displayed. Since this is a much faster process, the creation of VRML files is much simpler than programming. It also allows for more interactivity and facilitates incremental improvements.

Here is how VRML works from the user's perspective. First, you have to obtain a tool that VRML. There are freely downloadable versions of products such as Caligari Fountain, Intervista WorldView, Paper Software's WebFX, and TGS WebSpace. Some allow just for browsing in 3D, while others allow for various levels of 3D creation and VRML authoring. Since most people browse before they build, we'll focus on browsing here and discuss the creation of VRML worlds later on.

A VRML file is loaded the same way as accessing an HTML file: either by clicking on a link or typing a URL and hitting return. Based on the speed of your connection and the size of the file, the loading time can be as little as a few seconds or as much as a couple of minutes. Well-structured VRML files will allow your VRML browser to load the file in pieces, which lets you explore right away while the browser fetches more detailed objects and those that are not currently in your view.

As you navigate through the scene, you will notice that some objects are linked. If you click on them, you will jump either to another VRML world or to another media type such as HTML. While this gets you to other places quickly, it leads to the same problem as from link to link in HTML: you jump from a document on one topic on a server in one place to another document on a different topic in a completely different place. This is what Mark Pesce, co-creator of VRML, calls (by way of Gertrude Stein) "there being no there there." Contrast this with navigating through a 3D environment. Since you see everything that is between your origin and your destination, you will experience a sense of continuity, which not only helps you find your way back, but also reassures you viscerally that you know how you got to your destination.

For example, when we walk through a town, we look around and build a mental map of the place. If someone tells us that we have to turn right at the next intersection, we can visualize this and get where we want to go. There is a sense of continuity, and we can see how quickly we progress toward our goal. Sometimes we get lost, but this is part of our experience — and often that is how we discover new places or meet new people. Typing a URL and watching the byte counter as the destination loads onto our screen just isn't the same.

While this is not intimidating to experts, the majority of people will only get online if it works like the real world. Abstract URLs are difficult to remember, and jumping from one text fragment to another is not something that people encounter on a daily basis. However, once the Web allows us to use our spacial perception and conforms to the way we work (rather than forcing us to adopt the way computers work), the Web will become just another place we go to accomplish our chores, chat with friends, or learn new skills.

How Does VRML Compare with HTML?

VRML allows for much richer interaction than HTML. When viewing two-dimensional home pages, your options are basically limited to jumping from page to page and looking at images from a fixed, predetermined perspective. When visiting VRML worlds, however, you can freely choose the perspective from which to view the world. In addition, you can navigate unencumbered through 3D environments, the contents of which are limited only by the imaginations of their creator.

VRML spaces are inexpensive to build, can be bigger than the earth, and the objects in it can (and often do) defy the laws of gravity. As you walk or fly through such worlds, you can pick up objects and inspect them from all sides; if your VRML application includes authoring capabilities, you can even create and modify 3D objects. Don't like the color of your house? Just repaint it with a few clicks of the mouse!

Thus, VRML allows 2D home pages to expand into 3D home worlds. Traditional commercial Web sites can draw in new users by adding three-dimensional environments that are fun to explore, and by providing a natural way to navigate through the information available on the site. Ultimately, you will be able to collaborate with other users in context-rich and visually descriptive 3D environments rather than typing away at the command prompt in a text-based chat room.

What Kind of Bandwidth is Needed for VRML?

Experienced Web site administrators must consider the bandwidth required to make enhancements to their sites enjoyable to their visitors. Many early Web enthusiasts who relied on high-resolution images, sound, and video to spice up their sites found out the hard way that these additions made their sites slow or inaccessible to the millions of people who connect to the Internet via a regular 14.4 modem. However, since most HTML browsers have added support for incremental loading of images, many Web administrators overhauled the images on their sites to be loadable in chunks. This has made even graphics-intensive Web sites much more accessible to the average modem user. When images are loaded progressively you can start reading text and clicking on links before the images have fully arrived.

While VRML files are usually more compact than video files and often even smaller than high-resolution images, the better VRML tools will allow you to access and save 3D spaces in chunks. Through a technique called in-lining you can break up large VRML scenes into smaller files that can be loaded incrementally. This works even better than in 2D. While an HTML browser has no idea what image or what part of an image you are most interested in, a VRML browser *knows* where you are and which direction you are facing. Since you have a first-perspective view in VRML, you just need to look in the direction you want to go and your VRML browser will give highest priority to loading the objects that are in your view. The remaining objects are loaded in the background or as you change your point of view. Of course, since most of us don't use head-mounted displays yet, *looking* means moving your mouse to display the part of the scene you want to explore.

Most VRML files are actually surprisingly small and may not even require in-lining. Images, sound, and video files tend to be large because they store every piece of information that appears on your screen bit by bit. Since this approach would get very unwieldy in three dimensions, VRML files contain only the salient coordinates of each object with instructions to the 3D browser on how to connect the coordinates and display the surfaces. The 3D browser then generates the three-dimensional environment from this information. Therefore, the real bottleneck for large-scale VRML environments is the speed of your CPU and, to a lesser extent, the bandwidth of your Internet connection.

To deal with slower CPUs, VRML includes a feature that has been used successfully by game developers for years: levels of detail. Through levels of detail, your browser can take some shortcuts and display an approximation of an object before calculating it in detail. Since you have a first-person perspective in VRML, the browser what you are looking at. For example, if you are still quite far away from an object, the browser can just display the approximation, which is the same object with a lower level of detail. As you move closer to this object, the VRML browser dynamically displays higher resolution versions of the same object. By the time you get close enough to the object to pick it up, you will see the object in all its glorious detail. If the creator of the world chose the right switching points, you won't even notice the transitions since faraway objects are so small that you can't perceive the more detailed features anyway.

Through levels of detail you can use a lower polygon version of an object whenever you won't really notice the difference between it and the original because the object is in the background or you move through a scene very quickly. This technique helps your CPU maintain decent frame rates by lowering the number of polygons that have to be rendered in real-time. While moving closer to an object will increase the number of polygons for that particular object, the total number of polygons that have to be rendered in the scene may actually go down because other objects may move out of your view and no longer need to be displayed. Using levels of detail, the experienced designer can keep the total polygon count in your view fairly constant, thus allowing your browser to maintain a decent frame rate as you move through the environment.

You may wonder how this affects loading times because the browser will have to download several versions of every object that contains levels of detail. This is where in-lining comes in. One of the key features of VRML is that you can combine levels of detail and in-lining, which means that you can display a scene with little delay and only load more detailed versions of an object as you move closer to it. Thus, levels of detail and in-lining are two crucial features of VRML which, when used together, make it possible to build very large worlds.

For What Web Sites is VRML Appropriate?

In the long run, the answer is simple. Every site that is set up to engage visitors and keep them coming back will eventually be three-dimensional. Except for cases where the content is highly symbolic and where the potential visitors are well-trained to access information through command-line interfaces, there is a role for 3D in virtually every Web site. Even if the content of your site is primarily symbolic, you can use 3D to help less symbolically inclined visitors visualize your data. For example, a mathematician who just published a major paper could use VRML to let people visually explore the dynamics of a symbolic system. Through trial and error, visitors could gain an understanding of the matter without needing to comprehend the exact equations that drive the simulation.

In the short and medium term, you will have to consider your audience, the goals of your site, and the nature of your content more carefully. For example, if you run an entertainment site, your audience will probably expect you to stay on the cutting edge of interactivity and to spice up your site with new technologies like VRML and Java. However, you still need to consider the bandwidth and equipment of your visitors, so you don't end up with a gorgeous VRML world that is painfully slow to navigate through and will never be visited again.

VRML is an obvious choice if you are trying to reach a very broad audience because 3D is something that is familiar to everyone. Even children who have not yet learned to read are often quite capable not only of navigating through 3D environments, but also of manipulating simple building blocks to create interesting play environments. The creations of kids are often surprising as their creative expression tends to flow without self-censorship. More recently, the real-world 3D experience of millions of children around the globe has been supplemented by countless hours of playing with their Nintendos and learning to navigate through three-dimensional spaces.

The lack of a language barrier in VRML is another factor that would make your site more attractive to a general audience. While most Europeans and Japanese who currently use the Internet have some command of the English language, they tend to appreciate content that is not culturally biased (unless they are actively seeking out American culture). Since VRML architecture tends to go beyond the mere replication of reality and sometimes borders on the grotesque, it tends to be equally accessible or inaccessible to people of varying cultural backgrounds.

When we use spaces to communicate, we appeal to fairly fundamental cause and effect relationships. Whereas people from other cultures may have difficulties with American humor or some of the more fiercely fought moral debates, a well-designed space is understood across cultures. When visitors from China enter Notre Dame Cathedral, they instinctively know that this is a sacred space and they behave accordingly. Without having to read anything, they are drawn toward the altar and lift their eyes up to the heavens above. While they may not agree with the spirit that is expressed in this space, they certainly leave the space with a sense of what Notre Dame is all about.

The caveat about using VRML is that you need to create a lot of content from scratch and that you may need to hire expertise that you don't have in-house. Not every Photoshop wizard makes a good 3D modeler. Designing a space requires visualization skills that even experienced page layout artists may lack. Many accomplished architects may not make the transition either since the virtual medium offers opportunities and challenges quite different from those of the physical world.

You will also have to spend more time on selecting the right tool. While anybody can build a simple home world with tools such as Caligari Fountain or ParaGraph's Home Space Builder, a commercial implementation requires industrial-strength modeling tools. While the modeling features are important, you must also consider usability. Tools that sport a traditional two-dimensional interface may be easy to learn, but are often neither easy nor fast to use. The best tools have been developed over many years and incorporate suggestions from thousands of users on how to work more productively in 3D.

While text editors such as vi were sufficient to convey the most complex ideas via HTML, you will need to invest in good 3D creation and VRML authoring tools to design worlds that go beyond simple spheres and cubes. Although it is theoretically possible to type a VRML file that describes the geometry and all the surface attributes of a complex construction, this really doesn't work in practice.

Text is adequate for symbolic reasoning, but it's a poor visualizer. We can easily conjure up the image of a complex object, but to convey all of its details is simply impossible.

What Tools are Available for Browsing and Building VRML Worlds?

Most tools today fall in one of the following categories: VRML browsers, VRML authoring packages, or 3D creation tools. Since the whole market is still very young, the tools not only vary by features, but also by navigation paradigms and object manipulation methods. In addition, the tools differ considerably in terms of ease of learning, ease of use, reliability, price, and system requirements.

While VRML is new, 3D creation tools have been around for a long time. While many CAD packages allow for 3D design, the preferred tools for game designers and multimedia producers have been modeling and animation packages such as Softimage, 3D Studio, Strata Studio, and Caligari trueSpace. While VRML currently does not support animation, it is very likely that it will do so in the future, so it's wise to purchase a 3D creation tool from a vendor who will be able to add functionality as VRML evolves into a language for describing interactive multi-participant environments.

Some 3D creation tools already allow models to be saved in VRML, but others require you to purchase or download separate translation utilities that convert from the vendor's internal format to VRML. Direct VRML output is preferable to converters since something always gets lost during a translation. It's a good idea to make sure that the tool you are considering not only writes VRML files, but can also import them. In addition, you should be aware of what elements get lost when you save a scene in VRML rather than in the vendor's format or else you find yourself with completely washed-out scenes because your tool supports light attenuation, but VRML doesn't. Since there are various levels of VRML support, you should also check to what extent VRML is supported. For example, most modeling packages cannot write out VRML primitives.

While most 3D creation tools are developed by established vendors, many VRML browsers are written by companies that were started after the first VRML spec was drafted in late 1994. Most of these companies have a networking rather than 3D graphics background, but they were able to beat larger competitors to the market because they recognized the importance of VRML early on.

Some browsers (such as WebSpace) rely on HTML browsers to fetch VRML scenes, but others (such as WorldView and Fountain) have built-in networking support and only need to communicate with HTML browsers when coming across an HTML document. While most VRML browsers rely on DDE to communicate with HTML browsers, WebF/X integrates seamlessly with HTML browsers such as Qmosaic and Netscape Navigator. Caligari Fountain is the only VRML browser that also includes 3D creation tools and VRML authoring.

Virtus Walkthrough, WebSpace Author, Home Space Builder, and Caligari Fountain are the most popular authoring tools. While all of them allow you to add hyperlinks, only WebSpace Author and Caligari Fountain support in-lining and levels of detail. WebSpace Author runs on SGI machines and includes some sophisticated polygon reduction technology. However, unlike Caligari Fountain it does not include any 3D creation tools. Caligari Fountain runs on Windows 3.1 and Windows 95 and is freely downloadable for noncommercial use.

How Do I Find the Tool That is Right for Me?

Since products differ so widely, you need to evaluate which features are essential and which ones would be merely nice to have. For example, if you already have certain 3D models in-house that you want to use, you need to make sure that your VRML authoring tool can import those objects. In particular, you should make sure that your tool imports VRML objects or else you will not be able to take advantage of all the objects that you can grab off various VRML sites on the Web. Even if you generally rely on prebuilt models, chances are that you will want to create a few objects of your own or merely modify some of the ones that you found on the Web. If you already have a modeling tool and your artist knows how to use it, you probably don't need to purchase another. However, you should keep in mind that many traditional 3D modelers were built with photorealistic output in mind and may be overly complicated or lack features essential for interactive 3D graphics.

While most modelers still force you to work in wireframe mode, the latest breed of tools allows you to manipulate texture-mapped objects in real time. Before spending a lot of money on a high-end tool, you should evaluate if traditional modeling features such as lathing and extrusions are sufficient, or if you will need advanced functions such as organic deformations and 3D Booleans. Deformations can add sizzle to your environment, but they also increase file size and place a heavy burden on your visitors since a higher polygon count will mean reduced interactivity as their computers need to render your environments in real-time.

While you should keep the average configuration of your target audience in mind, you also need to check which tools run on your authoring platform of choice and how much memory they require. For example, if you have an SGI, you have access to some of the best modeling tools in the industry. However, you will pay a high price for your software, and the selection of VRML authoring tools will be much more limited than on the PC. Pricing for Macintoshes is more in line with those for the PC, but software selection is much more limited. Most VRML browsers don't even work on the Mac yet.

Currently, the best selection of tools is on the PC, and stiff competition will continue to keep prices both for software and hardware lower than on other platforms. However, some tools may require you to purchase more RAM, or you may have to deal with incompatibilities and crashes. Since most of your users will explore your VRML worlds with Windows browsers, you should have a very good reason if you choose not to use the PC as your primary development platform.

Rather than settling on one VRML tool, you may consider purchasing several and using each of them for the tasks for which they are best suited. In this case, you need to make sure though that the tools interoperate well and that there are no unexpected surprises when transferring scenes from one tool to the next.

If you have existing 2D assets, you should make sure that your VRML tool can leverage these assets. If you want to use 2D illustrations, you should make sure that you can import at least PostScript files. You can convert most image maps to JPEG format, but it is a good idea to check out what bitmap formats are supported by both your VRML authoring and browsing tools. Compatibility problems are minimized, of course, by choosing an integrated tool that can do it all. However, unless you want to optimize your VRML site for a particular browser, you still need to check on how your scenes look in the most common browsers.

Since VRML is hot, you will encounter many packages that claim to do VRML authoring. However, please keep in mind that VRML is an ASCII format and any text editor can technically claim to be a VRML authoring tool. However, unless you enjoy working directly with the straight ASCII file, you should make sure that you can create levels of detail and in-line objects without having to do any editing by hand. If modeling is not your strongest suit, you should select a tool that includes polygon reduction, so that you don't have to model levels of detail separately.

While you need strong 3D creation tools to generate the objects and spaces you want, the material editing capabilities determine how those 3D objects and spaces will look. To keep maximum flexibility, look for tools that let you assign material attributes not only for entire objects, but also on a per-face basis. For example, you might want to use one texture map for someone's pants and another for his belt. Since texture maps increase the amount of data that has to be transferred, you should look for advanced paint tools such as vertex painting. Vertex painting allows you to create multi-color gradients across surfaces and often eliminates the need for texture maps.

When evaluating VRML tools, you should pay close attention to options for reducing file size. By stripping out normals, ASCII formatting and default values, a good VRML tool can reduce file sizes by as much as 50%. Files can be reduced even further by collapsing hierarchies, reducing precision, using VRML primitives and saving only one instance of an object that appears in various places. If you use GZIP after having trimmed the VRML file to the bone, you may end up with files that are only 5% of original size. This will dramatically speed up loading times for your users, and it will allow you to serve more users without adding disk space or bandwidth. However, if you don't recommend a specific VRML tool for browsing, you will have to be careful about what tricks you employ to reduce file size. For example, many browsers do not accept zipped VRML files. If you do not have a tool that includes VRML browsing, you need to be prepared for a lot of testing and switching between your browser and your authoring application to make sure the links work, the navigation is comfortable, and all the objects look right. You may also have to switch to a separate browser to see if in-lines load as intended and if objects that contain levels of detail are displayed properly.

When recommending browsers to visitors of your site, you should check how each of them performs on a similar system. The differences in speed can be quite dramatic. Some browsers are already set up to take advantage of a new breed of 3D acceleration chips. Other factors to consider are ease of use and stability. Many of the newer browsers have not been tested adequately, so it is safer to recommend a browser that has been thoroughly debugged. Ease of use is to a certain extent a matter of taste. Some people prefer to use extensive navigation controls while others feel more at home just using the mouse and keyboard shortcuts. A good browser gives you lots of choices for navigating around.

If you do decide to recommend a VRML tool for browsing, you should check with the developer of the tool to see if you can make it available for downloading from your site. Many developers will be honored that you chose their tool and will allow you to distribute it free of charge. If the tool you distribute also includes authoring capabilities, you may find that your visitors will want to add to your VRML site or make improvements. In this case, you should let them know ahead of time what your policy is regarding VRML scenes uploaded to your server.

Caligari's VRML tool, Fountain, works much the same way as trueSpace S/E and trueSpace2. You will pick it up very quickly and to help with that, I've included an active tutorial on the CD-ROM. It should make your introduction to Web authorship very smooth. Thank you for allowing me to introduce you to this fascinating doorway to the future.

Summary

In this chapter you learned about the exploding world of the 3D Web. In particular you learned:

- ✦ That Fountain is a 3D Web authoring and browsing tool.
- ✦ That Fountain has an interface very similar to tS2.
- ✦ You can create complex navigable worlds for the Web using software on the CD-ROM.
- ✦ That VRML is a language used to define and control your virtual travel experience on the Web.
- ✦ That objects in a VRML world can have different levels of complexity depending on how far away they are.
- ✦ There will be many new careers born in this exciting new area.

✦ ✦ ✦

CHAPTER 34

Using Fountain

✦ ✦ ✦ ✦

In This Chapter

How to install Fountain on your hard drive

A tour of the two interfaces: browsing and world building

All about Fountain's powerful tools

Special 3D Web Browsing techniques

Instructions on how to use the world building tools to create your own 3D .wrl files

✦ ✦ ✦ ✦

By combining your knowledge of tS2 with Fountain you'll be quantum leaps ahead of the competition. Remember this interface is becoming a *de facto* standard on the Internet. An almost identical interface has also been licensed to Sony for the creation of games on its fabulous new Playstation platform. Read and learn — this material is putting power in your hands. Much of this chapter's tutorial material is available at the Caligari Web site in updated form. I suggest you check there for the latest tips and tutorials. It will be available in HTML so you can use it with hyperlinks in your Web browser.

TAKE NOTE

I want to thank Caligari and both David Duberman and Konstantin Guericke for their help in preparing this chapter. (David is responsible for most of the writing.) During the drafting of this chapter, Fountain was in beta, and very little documentation was available. We hope this chapter helps you.

Welcome to Fountain

Welcome to Fountain, the integrated VRML tool from Caligari Corporation that lets you create, edit, and browse three-dimensional (3D) home worlds interactively on the World Wide Web (WWW) and on the Microsoft Network. Caligari Fountain is the first product to seamlessly integrate 3D modeling with VRML browsing and authoring. Although you perform most functions in Fountain by pointing, clicking, and dragging, the underlying technology is the Virtual Reality Modeling Language (VRML). However, you don't need to learn the specifics of VRML unless you want to. I've written the tutorials in this chapter to stand on their own, so forgive any redundancies with the other chapters.

Figure 34-1 shows the opening screen that greets you when you launch Fountain.

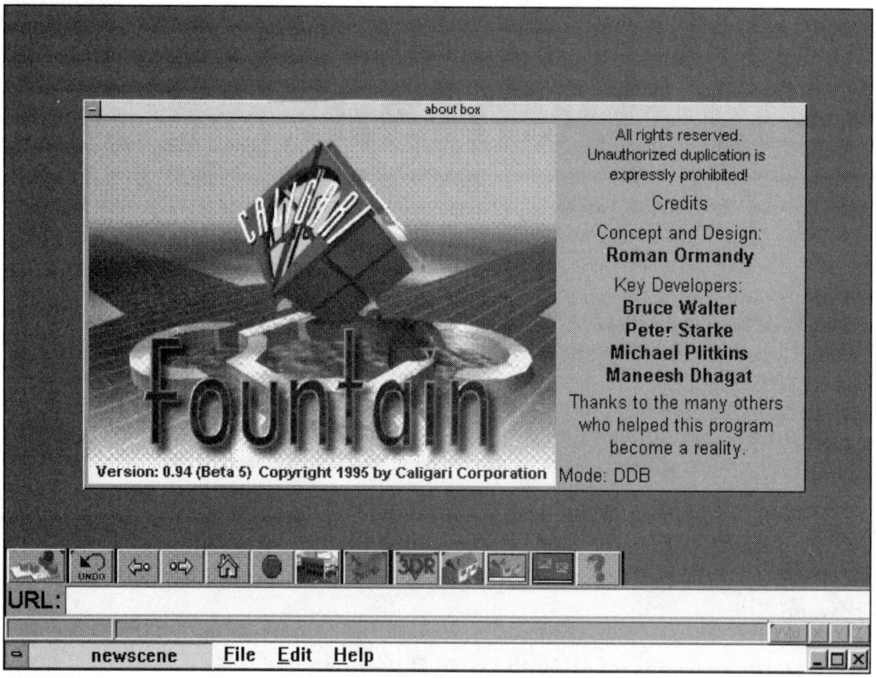

Figure 34-1: The Fountain opening screen

Sizzling Technology

Come on up with us to the searing edge of communications technology. The software on your CD-ROM will now open virtual doors for you. Fountain can save and load scenes in both the VRML-standard .wrl format, and can load your standard tS2 scenes in .scn format. That means you can create your worlds in tS2 and load them directly into Fountain! From there you can save them out as .wrl files.

Fountain also loads 2D and 3D objects from a large number of other programs including Caligari trueSpace, 3D Studio, AutoCAD, LightWave, and WaveFront. Another outstanding feature of Fountain is the use of Intel's 3DR technology, which lets you work just like in tS2 — real-time solid, shaded objects, or wireframes, your choice. This helps you to immediately see the results of editing changes, especially lighting changes, avoiding the need for a separate rendering function and the associated delay.

I've included several interactive tutorials with Fountain to get you up and running quickly. These tutorials are being translated into interlinked HTML and VRML documents as I write this chapter. I've only included the VRML files on the CD-ROM in the \tutorial\fountain subdirectory but you can get the latest HTML files by downloading them directly from the Caligari Web pages.

HTML stands for HyperText Markup Language and is the WWW standard for 2D documents containing text, still images, and other 2D media types. You can download the HTML files for this text from the Caligari site to make it fully interactive. We've translated the material into written text so you can follow it here on paper. To use your downloaded HTML version, You'll need an HTML browser installed on your computer. If you don't have one, I recommend Netscape Navigator from Netscape Corporation, although most versions of Mosaic will work as well. Actually, if you're not already browsing the Web, I strongly recommend you get connected with the Internet and get some experience there before proceeding here.

Installing Fountain from the CD-ROM

Go to the Fountain subdirectory on the CD-ROM that accompanies this book. There you'll find a typical *setup* file. Run it in Windows 95 from the StartRun option. In Windows 3.x use the Program ManagerSelect FileRun option to run *setup*.

You'll be prompted for a location to save Fountain and its support files. The default is C:\FOUNTAIN, and I highly recommend you use this default so that the links built into the tutorial files work properly. Press Enter or edit the drive designation and directory name as necessary. Then follow the prompts on the screen. The Setup program installs all necessary files, including those needed for 3DR support. It creates a new Program Group in Windows 3.x or adds a Fountain menu item to the Programs menu item attached to Windows 95's Start button.

Downloading from the Internet

You can download the latest self-extracting archive containing Fountain and support files from Caligari's Web site. Point your FTP program or Web browser to `ftp.caligari.com`, open the pub directory, and then the Fountain directory. Find the file named Fountain.exe and download it. Once you've downloaded the file create a new temporary Fountain directory. Copy the downloaded file into the temporary directory. Then run the file to extract install files. From the same directory, run the Setup.exe program and follow the prompts as described above.

After you've completed the installation, you can delete the temporary directory from which you installed the Fountain program and its contents.

Running the Program

In Windows 3.x, open the Fountain Program Group, then open the Fountain program by double-clicking its icon, or by clicking once, then selecting Open from the File menu. In Windows 95, click the Start button, then point to Programs, then to the Fountain folder, and click the Fountain program. Note that once installed Fountain can be started by selecting a VRML file from your local hard drive or by opening a VRML document through an HTML viewer like Mosaic or Navigator.

At this point, the program creates a partial display and attempts to find an active Internet connection. If it fails to find a connection, it attempts to establish one. Once a successful Internet connection is made, Fountain loads the default Home scene, finishes drawing its display, and you're ready to go to work. If a connection cannot be established, Fountain will still run but will be limited to editing and browsing local documents only.

Touring the Fountain Interface

First, let's take a quick tour of the program interface. Most of the screen is taken up by the workspace, a virtual 3D full-perspective space mapped to your 2D display. We'll explain how, using simple mouse controls, you can navigate through this space in three dimensions, manipulate objects within it, and create new custom objects.

Below the workspace are tools, and below the tools is a URL line showing the Web address (or disk file location) of the object most recently pointed at.

Fountain tools are represented as small rectangular icon buttons, as shown in Figure 34-2. On the opening screen, the leftmost tool is for entering World Building mode. To its right is an Undo tool, and to the right of Undo are four tools for VRML browsing.

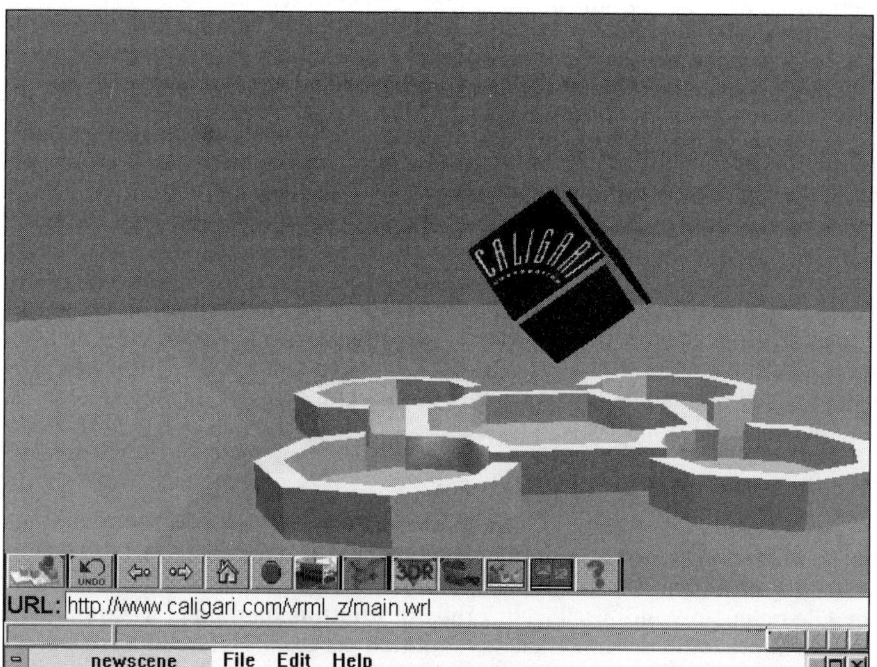

Figure 34-2: The Fountain toolbar

The Back and Forward tools take you between adjacent Web locations in terms of the original order of selection, the Home tool takes you to your default Home scene, and the Stop tool halts a lengthy load while in progress. These icons work like the Netscape Navigator buttons of the same names. As with Navigator, you can set the default Home scene to any on-line or local disk-based VRML file; this is done via the Preferences panel, which you can access from the File menu.

The next tools let you choose either of two Browse modes. Alongside these tools, you'll find display controls. We'll cover these in more detail shortly.

Using Fountain Tools

To select a tool, click it with the left mouse button. Note that whenever this tutorial instructs you to click something, you should use the left mouse button unless otherwise directed. Note also that at times the tutorials refer to select on various elements (like a "disk icon") which are embedded in the current VRML tutorial and are not to be confused with Icon tools on the Fountain menu bar.

Some tools have tiny green triangles in the upper left corner, indicating that a tool pop-up menu containing variations of the tool is available. To access this menu, click on the tool and hold for a second, whereupon the variant menu pops up. To use a variant tool, keep the mouse button held down and drag upward until it's pointing at the desired tool, then release. For example, to switch the display mode, click and hold on the Wireframe Display tool or Solid Render Display tool, whichever is present in the right-hand group of tools, and when the pop-up appears, drag the mouse pointer to the other. Note the change in appearance.

Now, if you switched to Wireframe Display mode, change back to Solid Render Display.

Some of the tools also have property panels for changing tool attributes, as indicated by a tiny red triangle in the upper right corner. To access a tool's property panel, right-click on the tool. For example, when in Solid Render Display mode, right-click on that tool to display a panel, entitled Render Quality, that lets you set many of this display's attributes.

Below the URL bar is a two-part horizontal strip called the Help bar. Try moving the mouse cursor across the various tool groups, as well as the buttons that appear in the Render Quality panel, and note the text that appears in the Help bar. The name of the tool currently being pointed at appears in the right part of the Help bar, and the keyboard equivalent, if available, is displayed in the smaller left part. We'll show you in a tutorial how to add your own keyboard shortcuts to your favorite tools. Also, helpful directions often appear in the Help bar while using a particular tool. To the right of the Help bar are controls for setting the coordinate system and for enabling and disabling specific axes when you are in Build mode. We'll cover these in one of the more advanced tutorials.

If, at any time, there's something you don't understand or are curious about, use Fountain's comprehensive Help file to learn more. From the Windows Help menu at the bottom of the screen, select Contents, then click on the topic you're interested in or use the Search facility.

At the bottom of the display are standard Windows controls and the Fountain menus.

For best results when following these tutorials and using Fountain in general, you should use 3DR (solid-view) mode. If the objects are displayed as wireframes rather than as shaded objects when you start the program, point at the Wireframe Display tool. Click and hold on this tool, then when tool variant menu appears, drag upward to the 3DR tool and release. There is a short delay before the display is redrawn in Solid Render mode. Much better, isn't it? If you're working with a 486 or slower PC and find that things tend to bog down in 3DR mode, you can always switch back to Wireframe mode. See the "Render Quality Settings" section for a discussion of options that are available in 3DR mode.

Preference Settings

From the File menu, select the Preferences item. The Preferences panel lets you customize program operation in a number of ways. You can find detailed descriptions of all of these in the Help file. Here are brief explanations of some of the most important ones:

✦ **TopMenu:** The default position for Fountain's menu bar is at the bottom of the screen. This gives you a more "immersive" environment, somewhat analogous to a car's dashboard. However, if you prefer a more standard layout, select TopMenu to place the menu bar and tools at the top of the screen.

✦ **Thold (Threshold Time):** With complex scenes, real-time redraw can slow down, giving poor feedback. This setting determines at what point objects are drawn as bounding boxes during operations. The lower the setting, the greater the likelihood that objects are redrawn as bounding boxes. If you're using a 486 or slower PC, you may want to lower this setting.

✦ **Load Inlines:** This pop-up list controls how inlined objects are loaded. The default setting, On Demand, gives highest priority to loading objects within the current view. Remaining objects are loaded in the background or as you change your view. The In Background setting displays inlined objects as they are loaded. The Immediately setting effectively turns inlining off.

Render Quality Settings

Another set of options, which apply to how the scene is displayed in 3DR mode, is found in the Render Quality panel, which is displayed when you right-click the Solid Render Mode tool.

The buttons arrayed across the top of the panel perform these functions:

✦ **Faceted/Smooth:** Of these first two buttons, only one can be active. If Faceted is selected, no interface smoothing is performed. If Smooth is selected, object surfaces are smoothed across faces. Faceted objects render more quickly than smoothed objects.

✦ **Textures:** Enables the use of bitmapped textures while shading objects in solid mode. This is the slowest mode in solid operation. The pop-up below labeled Texture Res lets you set the maximum displayed texture resolution.

✦ **Solid Grid:** Turns on the solid grid for the solid mode window. Solid grids are helpful for light placement but slow down redraw/rendering times.

✦ **Display Lights:** Toggles the display of lights in the workspace. Only applies to Build mode.

✦ **Display Cameras:** Toggles the display of cameras in the workspace. Only applies to Build mode.

✦ **Texture Res:** This pop-up lets you set the maximum resolution textures display in Solid Render Display mode. The higher the resolution, the better the image quality, but the slower the rendering time.

✦ **Scene Detail:** This pop-up lets you control how objects are displayed in Solid Render Display mode, ranging from best-looking but slowest at the top (Render All) to the minimal-detail but fastest Always Boxes at the bottom. See the Help file for details.

TAKE NOTE

See the Fountain Help file for explanations of the other Render Quality settings.

Tutorial 1

When you first run Fountain, it will load a default scene containing an object (the Caligari Corp. logo) that links you to a VRML file named Main.wrl on Caligari's home Web site.

1. Try simply moving the mouse pointer over this object while looking at the URL line near the bottom of the display, and you can see the Uniform Resource Locator (URL) address of this location. You'll also notice that the mouse cursor changes shape when it's over the linked object. Try clicking on the object. This loads the Main.wrl file from the Caligari Web site (assuming that you have established a network connection). This scene is considerably more complex and contains a number of objects with links to different scenes. Move the mouse pointer around and note the various URL addresses. To return, click the Back tool.

2. Now we'll load the VRML file depicting the main scene for this series of tutorials. Click the File menu (at the bottom of the screen), then click Scene, then click Load. A dialog appears asking you if you want to save any changes to the current scene; click No. Then, in the Load Scene dialog, find the file named Tut-main.wrl (in the \fountain\tutorial directory on the CD-ROM) and open it.

You should know about the three possible states of a tool in Fountain. If the tool is selected and active, its button looks "pressed in" and has a blue background. If the tool is unselected, the button is "sticking out" and has a light gray background. And if the tool is unavailable, its button is grayed out and clicking it has no effect.

When this file loads, you'll see some 3D text — a Welcome sign and some other words (the names of the two tutorials) — and an arrow. Fountain has two distinct and mutually exclusive operational modes: Build and Browse. When you're in Build mode, the Object tool is visible, and you'll see quite a few more tools. When you're in Browse mode, the Walk and Fly tools are visible and the only other available tools are related to browsing and navigation. Building is used for creating and modifying scenes, and Browsing is used for moving through them with a simplified interface (if you've ever played the game DOOM, you'll appreciate this) as well as activating links within the scene. When starting the program, you are in Walk mode, so let's explore how navigation works in this mode.

3. Move the mouse pointer into the workspace area, click and hold, and roll the mouse forward (from front to back on the mousepad), and then back again. Note a corresponding movement forward and backward through the scene. Now, still holding the left mouse button, roll the mouse left and right. Notice how, instead of changing location, you're rotating your point of view. Press and hold both mouse buttons and drag forward and back, and note that you're changing your pitch, rotating up and down. Next, release the left mouse button, press and hold the right button, and move the mouse forward and back. Now you're flying straight up and down in the air! Navigation in Fountain's Browse mode is very easy and intuitive.

4. Let's also take a look at the alternate Browse mode, which I call "flying" mode. Click the tool that looks like a double-decker plane , then move the mouse cursor into the workspace, click and hold, and roll the mouse forward. After a short distance, stop rolling, but keep the mouse button held down. Note that your forward movement continues indefinitely. If you want to fly faster, drag the mouse forward a bit more. To slow down, drag in the opposite direction. If you continue dragging toward you, you'll actually stop, and then start flying backward! Now roll the mouse to the left, stop for a moment, then back to the right. Interesting, isn't it? Release the mouse button to stop the "flying" movement.

5. Try navigating around some more, and see if you can end up near where you started. If you have trouble, simply reload the scene.

   Note the right-pointing arrow symbol that appears in the scene. Whenever you see this symbol in a tutorial scene, you'll know that it's a link to a scene depicting the next tutorial step. Similarly, a left-pointing arrow indicates a link to the previous step. Since this is the first "scene," there's no left arrow here. Another symbol used in the VRML scenes is the question mark; this takes you to the HTML page that contains the instructions for the current tutorial step. Since this first scene, or "home world" (because it's in 3D, it isn't really a "home page" anymore) isn't actually a tutorial step, there's no question mark. Also not here is the "home" symbol, which looks like the outline of a small house. This is available in all the other VRML scenes, and it always takes you back to this scene, the home world. Finally, clicking on the floppy disk object loads the file you're working on. In order for this to work properly, you must save your work as a file named mytut1.wrl in the Fountain directory, which is in the root directory of your computer's C: drive.

6. To open the VRML scene depicting the first step of the Starter tutorial, click the right-pointing arrow in the scene or the 3D text "1. Starter". Note that, in the next scene, both arrows, the question mark, and the home and disk symbols now appear. Click the question mark to open the HTML page containing the instructions for building this scene. If no HTML browser is running, Fountain opens a dialog requesting that you locate the HTML browser. Navigate to the browser's directory, click its name, and then press Enter or click the Open button.

Congratulations! Getting to this point, you've had to learn quite a bit. You'll be pleased to see how easy it is to move from this point onward. You navigated here from the first VRML scene of the starter tutorial, a scene that showed a white octagon, the "floor plan" of a simple building we'll be creating soon. We'll return shortly to that scene so you can make your own octagon, but first, please read the following.

Earlier, I briefly mentioned the difference between Build and Browse modes. Right now, on the VRML scene, you're still in Browse mode.

Using Build Mode

Enter Build mode by selecting the World Building tool. Note that as the URL bar goes away, a checkered grid or "floor" appears, and several new tool groups appear, as shown in Figure 34-3. From left to right, these are the Edit group, the Navigation group, the Model Tools, and the Utilities group. We'll cover most of these tools in the tutorials.

TAKE NOTE

The appearance of the floor may slow down your navigation somewhat as it requires additional rendering. If this is the case, you can turn it off by first right-clicking the 3DR tool. In the Render Quality panel that appears, click the Toggle Shaded Grid tool. This causes the floor to appear as a wireframe grid. Close the Render Quality panel by clicking the close box in its upper left corner.

Drawing an Octagon

Now let's draw an octagon.

1. To prepare to draw an octagon, click the Regular Polygon tool. Note that a small panel entitled Poly Mode appears. If you point at this panel, the Help bar displays the message "Set Regular Polygon number of sides." You can change the number of sides by clicking the number, which should currently

Figure 34-3: Build mode

be set to 6, and editing it from the keyboard, or by using the mouse with the double-headed arrow. Let's use the latter method. Click and hold on the double-headed arrow to the right of the number 6 and drag slowly to the right. If it goes past 8, move the mouse back to the left. Release the mouse button when the number 8 is displayed.

2. Now move the mouse pointer into the workspace, a little to either side of the existing octagon. Click and hold the left mouse button, and drag the mouse toward the front of the pad. You're drawing an octagon! (You can only see its outline while drawing it.) Note that the farther you move the mouse away from the start point, the bigger the shape gets. Also, by moving the mouse left and right, you can rotate the polygon. When your octagon is about the same size and orientation as the one that's already there, release the button.

   Now the octagon is redrawn as a solid. Note that, if you still have the checkered grid (solid floor) turned on, it looks a bit strange — all you can see of it is some slivers, or possibly only the Active Object Indicator (the cylindrical arrow pointing at it). That's because it's in the same plane as the floor, so the program doesn't quite know how to display it. We'll fix this in a moment by raising it up a tiny bit.

3. First we'll get rid of the original polygon. Since we're still in Polygon Draw mode, select the Object tool. Note that the Active Object Indicator is point-

ing at your polygon, which is how the "current" or active object is indicated in 3DR mode. In Wireframe mode, the current object's wireframe is white, and others are dark blue.

4. Click the original octagon to select it, then press the Delete key or click the Erase tool.
5. Now select the Object Move tool and click your polygon to select it. Press and hold the right mouse button and drag the mouse a small distance toward the top of the pad (away from you), raising it up a small distance. In 3DR mode, you should now be able to see the entire octagon.
6. Before saving the scene, we'll get rid of the other objects. One by one, select the two arrows, the question mark, the home and disk symbols and delete them. Note that as you select each object, the Active Object Indicator points at it.
7. Now open the File menu, select Scene, then Save As..., and when the Save Scene dialog appears, type mytut1 into the File Name box, and press Enter. Fountain adds the .wrl extension automatically. Note: You must use this file name for the disk icon to be able to load it automatically. Before saving the file, Fountain presents you with an Export VRML File dialog. Just ignore it and click OK to save for now.

Extruding the Octagon

Have you looked at the next VRML scene yet? If not, load it now. You'll see that the octagon is now extruded into the third dimension (that is, given height). Here's how this was done:

1. First, since the scene you saved was replaced when you loaded another VRML scene, click on the disk icon at the top of the VRML scene to reload your scene. Or, if you like doing things the hard way, you can use the File/Scene/Load menu command to reopen your file. Remember, the file name is mytut1.wrl.
2. If you're in Browse mode, enter Build mode by selecting the World Building tool. Click the octagon to select it. Note that the Active Object Indicator now points at your polygon. Now click the Sweep tool, and observe that the octagon is extruded a short distance upward. Let's extend that a bit.
3. Notice that the top edge of the swept polygon is green. This means that it is "active" and can be manipulated with standard Point Navigation functions, including movement, rotation, and scaling (technically, it's a face rather than a point that is being manipulated here). You can see these tools in the Point Navigation panel that appeared when you selected the Sweep tool. Note that the Point Move tool is selected by default. Move the mouse into the workspace to the side of the object, click and hold the right mouse button, and move the mouse a short distance away from you. This increases the height. When the height looks about right, release the button. Remember, this is just a tutorial, so nothing is absolute.

You can also move the extruded face laterally by pressing and holding the left mouse button and dragging the mouse. Try it now, if you like. Then use the Undo tool to return the face to its original position.

4. Now click the Sweep tool to extrude the octagon again. The sweep distance is the same as the new height of the object after you adjusted it in the previous step. Whenever you sweep a shape, then manipulate it in some way, Fountain remembers your changes and applies them to subsequent sweep operations. You can use this powerful feature to easily create some very interesting shapes.
5. Select the Object tool. This takes you out of Point Navigation mode, allowing you to work with the entire object. It's a good idea to get into the habit of selecting the Object tool after using other tools.
6. Before saving our work in progress, let's check on some statistics. Right-click the Object tool to open the Object Info panel. Here you'll see a number of named fields and entries. The first is Name; you can use it to rename the object if you like, but it's not necessary. The second and third fields are the ones we're primarily interested in here. Note that the number of points or vertices is 24, and the number of faces is 18. If we had only swept the octagon once, there would be 10 — the top, bottom, and eight sides. Note that there are also boxes labeled Class, LOD Dist., and Inlined. We'll cover Inlining in this tutorial and LOD (Level of Detail) in the next. Meanwhile, you can learn more about these by looking up Object Info Panel in the Help file. Click the close box in the panel's upper left corner.
7. Use the File ➪ Scene ➪ Save menu command, save the file as mytut1.wrl as before, then click on "next VRML scene" (in the HTML tutorial) to see the next step, which involves painting the object. When you're ready to read the directions, click on the question mark at the top of the VRML scene.

Painting the Object

When you return to the VRML scene, click the disk object at the top of the scene to load your own project. Make sure you're in Build mode (select the World Building tool) and click the building object to select it. Now we'll paint the entire object gold and then paint parts of it blue.

1. Select the Paint Face tool, and note that four panels appear.

In Fountain, the collection of surface attributes that determine how an object appears is known as a Material. The Material Color panel lets you choose any color; the Material panel lets you instantly see the results of any changes on a sample sphere; the Shader/Maps panel lets you affect smoothing and apply texture maps (images); and the Shader Attributes panel lets you set values for shininess and transparency, among others.

The process in Fountain is as follows: Set the current Material to the desired attributes, then paint the current object. The Paint tool variants let you: a) paint the object in its entirety (Paint Object); b) paint face by face (Paint Face); c) vertex by vertex (Paint Vertices), or d) replace another Material on the object wherever it appears (Paint over existing Material). There is also an Inspect tool in the Paint tool variant menu that sets the current Material to one already applied to an object by clicking the object surface where that material appears.

2. In the Material Color panel, click halfway between the hexagon's center and its upper right corner. Note that the sample sphere in the Material panel immediately turns golden. Now move the mouse to the Shader Attributes panel, over the second vertical strip from the left, as indicated by the appearance of Set Shininess in the Help bar. Click about $^2/_3$ of the way up in the same place of the next strip to the right (Set Roughness). Watch the sample sphere turn dark gold with bright highlights. Raising the Shininess value increases the contrast between specular highlights and the rest of the surface, and raising Roughness decreases the size of the specular highlights, giving a glossier appearance. To bring back the overall golden color, click $^2/_3$ of the way up in the leftmost vertical strip (Set Ambient Glow).
3. Now we'll apply this color to our shape. Click and hold on the Paint Face tool; after a moment, the variant menu pops up. Drag up to the topmost tool, Paint Object, and release the mouse button. The entire object is immediately repainted gold. Note that, unlike certain other variant menus, in this case the default Paint tool returns to its previous state, which was Paint Face. The Paint Object tool variant never becomes the default.
4. Before changing the color, let's save the gold Material. Click the Material library tool and note the panel that opens up. If the panel is empty, click on the blank rectangle to the left of the scroll bar on the bottom, select Load, and load the file Basic.mlb from the Fountain directory. You'll now see a row of spheres mapped with various materials.
5. In the bottom left corner is Add Material to Library tool. Click it to add the current Material to the library. Note that the Material panel representation appears in the panel, with a red bar below it to indicate that it's selected (you may have to scroll to the right to see it). Next, we'll name the Material in the library. Click in the white box in the panel's lower right corner, type Shiny Gold (or any other name you'd like to give the material) and press Enter.

TAKE NOTE

When there is more than one Material in the library, select the one you want by clicking on it. If there are more Materials than can fit in the window, scroll through them using the scroll bar in the panel's bottom center. The Delete Material from Library tool, immediately to the right of the Add Material to Library tool, eliminates the current Material from the library (careful — there's no Undo!). Finally, to clear, load and save Material library disk files, use the menu that appears when you click the Load/Save Material Library tool, the box to the right of the Delete Material Library tool. When the current library is saved or loaded, its file name appears here.

6. Now change the current Material to blue by clicking on the Material Color hexagon's lower left corner. Add this Material to the library and name it Shiny Blue. Save the library as Basic.mlb or any other name you like.

7. Now we'll proceed to paint four faces on the lower halves of alternating faces of the object. Move the mouse cursor into the workspace and notice that it now resembles a paintbrush. Position it over the lower half of one of the building's sides that's facing 45 degrees away from you (next to the side that's facing directly toward you) and click. Note that the entire polygon is repainted blue.
8. Paint the lower half of the other 45-degree side.
9. Now we'll rotate the building half a turn and paint the two polygons opposite the first two. Select the Object Rotate tool. Move the mouse pointer into the workspace, click and hold the right mouse button (enables rotation on the object's vertical, or Z axis), and drag the mouse vertically until the building has rotated about 180 degrees. If you're not sure if it's exactly 180 degrees, rotate it back until one of the blue polygons appears, then slowly rotate it away again until you're sure it's half a turn. That's one of the benefits of working in solid mode; you can always see what's what in color!

   Incidentally, if there are panels in the way, you can move them by dragging them by the title strip at the top of the panels.
10. Select the Paint Face tool and, again, paint the bottom halves of the two sides facing 45 degrees away from you, as shown in Figure 34-4.

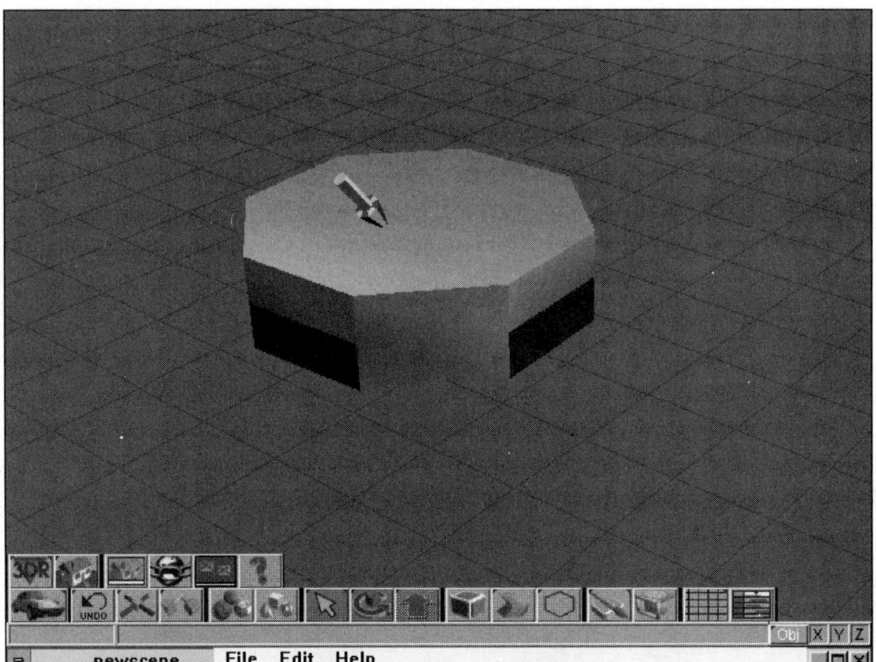

Figure 34-4: Painting the bottom halves of two sides of the octagon

Changing Color

Let's say you're not satisfied with the particular shade of blue you used and you want to change it to aqua wherever it appears on the building. Fountain's Paint over existing Material tool is a convenient, easy solution to this dilemma.

1. From the Paint tool variant menu, select the Paint over existing Material tool, which looks like a paint roller. Change the current Material to aqua by clicking the Material Color panel's hexagon at its leftmost point, then click on any blue part of the building. Note that all visible blue areas are instantly repainted aqua. If you like, you can verify that this has also happened on the sides facing away from you by selecting the Object Rotate tool and spinning the building 180 degrees — remember, use the right mouse button.
2. Use the File ➪ Scene ➪ Save menu command, save the file as mytut1.wrl as before, then click on "next VRML scene" (in the HTML tutorial) to see the next step. When you're ready to read the directions, click on the question mark at the top of the VRML scene.

Tweaking Your Scene

In this stage of the tutorial, we'll make a few small changes and look at some of Fountain's other functions.

1. When you return to the VRML scene, click the disk object at the top of the scene to load your own project. Make sure you're in Build mode (select the World Building tool if in Browse mode) and click the building object to select it.
2. Now we'll add a "roof" to the building. Select the Point Edit Faces tool and click the top surface of the building. Note that, as before when we first used the Sweep tool, the top edge of the polygon is green. Click and hold on the Sweep tool to bring up its variant menu, then drag upward to the Tip tool and release. This automatically creates a conical roof. That was easy, wasn't it?

   You can raise and lower the roof by pointing to an empty space next to the building, clicking and holding the right mouse button, and dragging forward and backward. You can even make an inverted roof if you like! When you're done, select the Object tool.
3. Now we'll use Fountain's unique vertex painting function to create an interesting color gradient on the roof. From the Paint tool pop-up menu, select Paint Vertices. This causes the Material panels to open. Select a new color of your choice, such as green. Then click on the very tip of the roof, as shown in Figure 34-5. You'll see the appearance change instantly, creating a smooth gradient between the new color at the roof's tip to the previous color at the "eaves."

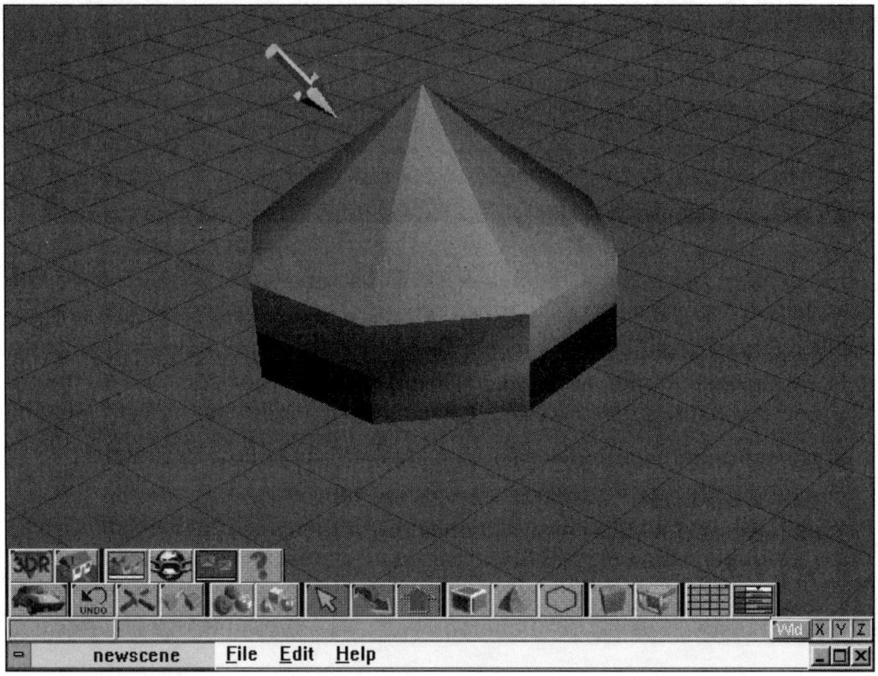

Figure 34-5: Painting the roof. It's difficult to show the vertex gradients in black and white, so you'll need to demonstrate them for yourself.

Changing Light Sources

Let's take a brief look at lighting. You may have noticed several star-like objects in the scene. These are "local" light sources, which radiate light uniformly in all directions from a specific location. We'll delete an existing one and add a new light of a different type.

1. If you don't see any lights, first open the Render Options panel (right-click on the Solid Render view tool), then make sure the Make Lights Visible option is enabled.
2. There are three default light sources. Select one by clicking on it, then press the Delete key to remove it from the scene. Note that when you selected the light, a Light panel appeared with a color hexagon and brightness slider. If you're in Solid Render mode (3DR appears in the Window tool group), you should notice the change immediately, especially if the checkered grid option is turned on.
3. Now select the Primitives panel tool. A new panel appears with a variety of shapes and other objects, as shown in Figure 34-6. At its right edge are two tools we can use to add light sources. The upper tool adds infinite lights, which have direction but no specific location, and the lower tool, which looks like a lightbulb, adds local lights.

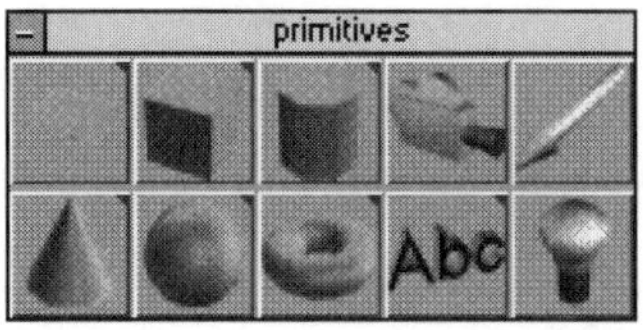

Figure 34-6: The Primitives Panel. Notice the lightbulb icon in the lower right corner. The camera icon is also obvious.

4. Select the Infinite Light tool and note the change in lighting and in the Light panel.
5. The new infinite light looks like a vertical line with a four-sided cone (indicating direction) at the lower end. Right now it's pointing down, which means the light source is illuminating the entire scene with parallel light rays, all pointing straight down.
6. To change the direction, choose the Object Rotate tool and drag the mouse in an empty part of the workspace. Thanks to Fountain's Solid Render mode, you can see the changes immediately. Try setting it so the light rays come downward at an angle from the upper right area of the scene.
7. Next, try changing the light's intensity and color. Change the intensity first so the color change is more noticeable. In the Light panel, click higher for a brighter light or lower for a dimmer light in the vertical strip at the right side. Next, to change the color, click on the hexagon at any part of the outer edge. Note the immediate changes, first in the light's intensity, then in its color.

Adding a Camera

Before we leave this scene, let's try adding a camera. One of Fountain's powerful features is the ability to have up to five cameras within a scene, and to be able to switch freely between them. You can also view the scene simultaneously from a second vantage point by opening a small window.

1. From the Primitives panel, select the Add Camera tool. Note that the new camera appears as a wireframe object at the center of the workspace.
2. Select Object Move and drag the mouse to the right within the workspace. Position the camera on the right side of the screen. Note that it's not pointing at the object. Select Object Rotate. Move the cursor arrow to the coordinates icon (to the left of the X) at the far right of the Help bar. Right-click the mouse on "obj" to make the pop-up appear. Select "wld" or World coordinates. With the right mouse button rotate the camera to face your scene. Coincidentally, to see what the camera sees, choose "camera view" from the Perspective View pop-up.
3. Use the File ➪ Scene ➪ Save menu command, save the file as mytut1.wrl as before, then click on "next VRML scene" below to see the next step. When you're ready to read the directions, click on the question mark at the top of the VRML scene.

Inlining

A VRML file, which is what you create when you save a scene in Fountain, contains a number of entities called nodes. One of the most powerful nodes is called WWW Inline. Until now, when you've saved Fountain scenes, you've saved all objects in the scene explicitly as parts of that scene. When you specify an object as Inlined, then save the scene, the inlined object is saved in a separate file anywhere you specify, and the main scene then contains only a reference to that file. Then, when that file is loaded, Fountain sees the reference, goes out to where the Inline object file is, and loads that too. The powerful aspect is that the Inline object can be anywhere on the World Wide Web! Thus, you can build 3D worlds that contain objects from many different sites, not just ones you've created.

Another benefit is equivalent to using an HTML browser to load a page that consists of many components, such as small images plus text. If the images are all contained in separate files, rather than part of the page, the user can start scrolling around on the page reading the text, which comes in first, while waiting for the images to load. Similarly, with VRML, if a world's objects are contained in several small files instead of one big one, the user can start browsing the world before all the objects are actually loaded. You can fine-tune this process with the Load Inlines pop-up in the Preferences panel.

Inlining the Building Object

You've already looked at the VRML scene depicting this final part of the tutorial. You may not have noticed any differences, but they're there. What we're going to do here is set the building object to be inlined, then add a link, so when you click the object, the link is executed.

1. When you return to the VRML scene, click the disk object at the top of the scene to load your own project. Make sure you're in Build mode (select the World Building tool if in Browse mode) and click the building object to select it.

2. Open the Object Info panel by right-clicking the Object tool. The Object Info panel appears, as shown in Figure 34-7. To set the building to be inlined, click the box next to "Inlined," then close the panel. This means that when you save the scene, the inlined object or objects are saved as separate files. Let's explore this for a moment.

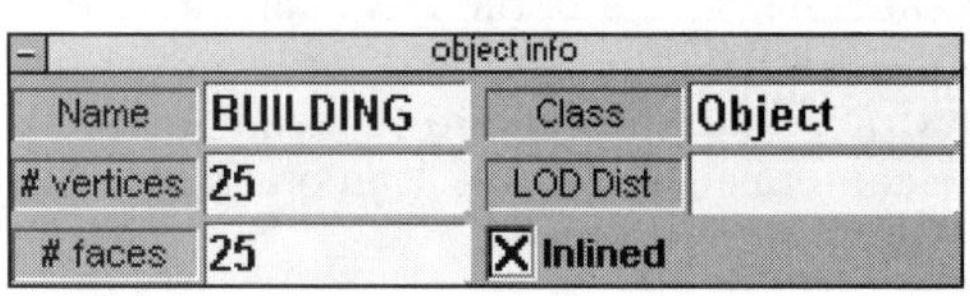

Figure 34-7: The Object Info panel

3. Save the scene as usual, but this time let's pause and take a brief look at the Export VRML File dialog box, as shown in Figure 34-8. Note that, under Paths, the first and third boxes specify Inline Files (the directory path in which objects specified as inlined are saved) and Default Inline Filename (the names under which these objects are saved). Also note that the default entries for these are both "same as main file." This means that the inlined object files are saved in the same directory path as the main scene file, and they derive their names from the scene file's name. Also note, in the Inlining section, that "Marked Objects" is selected. This means that objects marked as inlined get saved as separate files. Go ahead and finish the save by clicking OK, and then we'll look at the files.

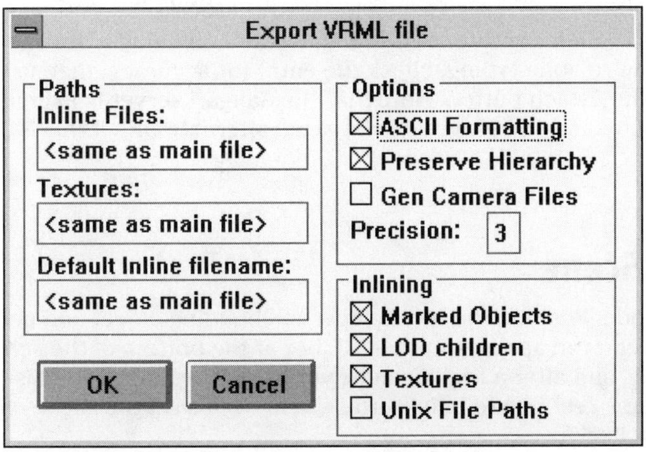

Figure 34-8: The Export VRML File dialog box

4. This step is optional. If you follow it, you'll see the following lines at the end of the file:

```
DEF NoName_5_1 WWWInline {
     name      "tut1-000.wrl"
     bboxSize 3.488 2.314 3.488
     bboxCenter 1.263 1.224 -0.611
     }
```

The above lines identify the object as inlined, give its file name, and specify the size and location of its bounding box.

Use Windows multitasking to run a text editor or word processor (such as Microsoft Write), and use its Open command. Navigate to the Fountain directory, and find the file named mytut1.wrl. If you like, open it, page to the end, and note the reference to the inlined file. Then close it without making any changes.

5. Use the Open command again, and take another look at the directory. Note that there is a file named mytut000.wrl, that was referred to in the main scene file. This is the inlined object file. By default, Fountain gives inlined

object files names consisting of the first five characters of the main scene file's name, plus a three-digit number, counting up from 000. Thus, if there were three inlined objects, their file names would be mytut000.wrl, mytut001.wrl, and mytut002.wrl. You needn't open the inlined object file unless you're really curious. When you're done, close the word processor or text editor.

6. Finally, we'll experiment with adding links to objects. Bring the Fountain window to the front, make sure you're in Build mode, and select the building object.
7. Click the Attach URL tool, and when the Attach URL Link dialog appears, type `http://www.caligari.com/vrml/ring.wrl` but do not press Enter.

   This is a link to a VRML scene, entitled Ring, located on Caligari's Web server. When you're done typing, check the entry for accuracy, then use the mouse to click the Attach button. Note that the Caligari server is in constant change and ring.wrl may no longer exist. Use an alternate URL if this is the case.
8. Save the file.

Browsing the Scene

Now enter Browse mode. Position the mouse over the building object and note that the address you entered appears in the URL bar at the bottom of the screen. Now click the building, and after a few seconds, you'll see the Ring scene displayed on your monitor. Feel free to take a cruise, and even save the scene on your hard drive if you like.

1. To return to your own scene, click the Back tool. Couldn't be easier!

   Now we'll change the link so that when you click the object, you're transferred to your HTML browser displaying Caligari's home page.
2. Go to Build mode and select the building object. Again click the Attach URL tool. You should see the previous URL to `http://www.caligari.com/vrml/ring.wrl` in the Attach URL Link dialog. Change it to: `http://www.caligari.com`.
3. Click the Attach button when you're done.
4. Save the file again, then return to Browse mode and click the building. Your HTML browser is brought to the front and the page you're now reading is replaced by Caligari's home page. You can see how easy it is to add links to 2D pages and 3D scenes from your Fountain scenes.
5. Use the File ⇨ Scene ⇨ Save menu command to save the file as mytut1.wrl as before.

Congratulations

This is the end of the first tutorial. By reading and following this tutorial, you've learned most of what you need to know to use Fountain. You've learned how to walk and fly around in Browse mode, and how to get into World Building mode to create your own 3D scenes. You've learned how to navigate in World Building mode, how to add a polygon and extrude it into a solid object, and how to create materials and apply them to objects. Perhaps most importantly, you've learned how to assign URL addresses to objects so you can link them to other scenes and pages.

In the next tutorial you'll learn how to make a custom texture map using an image of your choosing. You'll also learn how to use the Freehand Polygon and Lathe tools. Finally, you'll learn how to implement LOD (Level of Detail), a powerful feature that helps minimize unnecessary rendering, speeding up navigation through VRML scenes.

Creating a Level of Detail Object

When you move around in real life, you don't see the same amount of detail viewing an object from a distance as you do when viewing it from close up. For example, think of a high-rise office building construction site (the closest thing we have to wireframe meshes in actual reality, except perhaps for geodesic domes). If you're several blocks away, you only see the large I-beams and other principal major elements. When you get closer, you can see the smaller crossbeams. And you can only see the rivets when you're practically standing on top of the thing.

When you're moving around in a virtual 3D world, there's a similar situation. Some objects are far away, and because of perspective, they're drawn so small on the screen that there aren't enough pixels to resolve their full detail. However, most 3D programs go ahead and draw them in full detail anyway, essentially wasting rendering time and slowing down the navigation process.

Fortunately, VRML lets you specify different levels of detail at different distances for each object in your 3D worlds. You can set things up so the structure of faraway objects is simple and quick to draw, but the same object when viewed close up is fully detailed. You can specify many levels of detail for each object, but usually you won't need more than three or four. The way this works is that you create different versions of the same object, and specify the distances from the user point of view at which each is displayed.

Fountain fully supports this capability. For example, if you have people in a scene, you can tell Fountain to represent those at a significant distance with stick figures, but to draw the nearby folks with clothes, hands, headgear, and so on. Once you've modeled an object's various detail levels, it's absurdly easy to set up.

Tutorial 2

In this second tutorial, we'll create four levels of detail for the house object we started in the previous lesson. The simplest level will be a cube. We'll use the house we've already built for the second level, but we'll also add a custom texture map. For the third level, we'll add a couple of wings and some roof detail. And for the fourth, most detailed level, we'll load an object specially created for this project.

Modifying the Octagonal House

Let's start by modifying our octagonal house model from the previous tutorial. If you're following along from the first tutorial, you already have the Fountain program and the first scene of this second tutorial.

1. If you don't have Fountain loaded, run it now, then load the scene file named Tut-main.wrl from the Fountain directory. To get to the first scene of the second tutorial, click on the 3D text "2. Intermediate".
2. Once you have Fountain and the first scene of the second tutorial loaded, examine the scene in 3DR mode, then click on the disk object near the top of the scene to load the file you've been working on, which you saved at the end of the first tutorial. This only works if you've been saving your file under the name mytut1.wrl in the c:\Fountain directory. If the file doesn't load, use the File/Scene/Load menu command and open your file.
3. If you're in Browse mode, enter Build mode by selecting the World Building tool.

CAUTION

The following cleanup step is necessary for two reasons. First, the Active Object Indicator doesn't appear on selected inlined objects. Also, such objects' axes go screwy, so the rotation during the painting operation is difficult. If the software is fixed, you can eliminate the next step.

4. Let's do a little cleanup first. Click the building to select it. You'll have to take it on faith that the object is selected (or switch to wireframe mode), as the Active Object Indicator doesn't appear.
5. Right-click the Object Tool. In the Object Info panel, note that the box next to Inlined (at the bottom of the panel) has an X in it.
6. Click the box to remove the X, returning the house to its original status as an integral part of the scene file.
7. Close the panel. Save the scene under the same file name, then reload it.

Creating a Texture Map

Now we'll prepare a custom texture map. You'll need an image file in BMP, DIB, or JPEG (JPG) format. You can use any image you like: a digitized photo or a texture created with Texture Explorer from Kai's Power Tools would work well for this exercise. Unless your computer has a lot of memory, stick to resolutions of 200 × 200 and under. If you don't have any picture files, use the Clouds.jpg file from the Fountain directory.

1. Click on the house object to select it.
2. Select the UV Projection tool.
3. When the UV Map panel opens, select the Spherical UV Projection tool in the upper right corner. You'll see a wireframe sphere surrounding the house.
4. In the UV Map panel, click on the Apply button. This tells Fountain to map images onto the house's surface as if it were a sphere. Thus, no matter where you place the texture, it will be relatively recognizable.
5. From the Paint tool pop-up, select the Paint Over tool. This handy tool lets you replace an existing material everywhere it exists on an object. We'll use it to replace the aqua material we painted onto four polygons in the first tutorial with the new texture.
6. In the Shader/Maps panel that appears, left-click on Use Texture Map to activate this feature (note that the sample sphere immediately changes appearance), then right-click on it to bring up the Texture Map panel. The box at the top of the panel probably contains the word Checker, which is the name of the default texture map image.
7. Click on the box to bring up the Get Texture Map dialog, and select the image file you decided to use above.
8. Click OK to load the file.

The sample sphere now shows the texture map you loaded. Also note, in the Texture Map panel, that both the U Repts and the V Repts boxes contain the number 1. This means the image is repeated only once in the horizontal and vertical directions. You can repeat the texture map as many times as you like over the surface to which it's applied by changing these numbers. Set U Repts to 3 and V Repts to 2 and note the change in the sample sphere's appearance. We'll be mapping the new material over the house's entire surface, but it will only appear on the four lower polygons we painted in the first tutorial, so this will let us see more of the image on each polygon.

9. The screen is probably getting pretty crowded by now, so click the Close All Panels tool to clear some working room.

   The cursor should still resemble a paint roller from when you selected the Paint Over tool.
10. Click now on either of the two aqua-painted faces you see. Note that both of them immediately change in appearance to show the new texture, complete with the image you created. If you want to verify that the two aqua-painted faces on the other side have also changed, rotate the house 180 degrees.
11. Click the Object tool, then the Rotate tool, and remember to use the right mouse button to rotate on the vertical axis.

Saving Your Material

Let's save our new material in the material library.

1. Select the Material Library tool.
2. When the panel opens, click on the Add Material button. Note that the new material appears in the library panel (you may have to scroll to see it), with the name Untitled. Change the name if you like, then save the library. As a reminder, you change the name by clicking on the name Untitled in the panel's lower right corner and entering a new one, and you save the library by clicking on the box to the left of the panel's scroll bar, and selecting Save from the pop-up menu.

   When you change the material, it becomes the default material for all subsequently created objects. So let's set the current material back to the original default.
3. Right-click the Paint tool, then, in the Shader/Maps panel, left-click the Use Texture Map button to turn it off. Note that the sample sphere returns to a white color.
4. Use the File ➪ Scene ➪ Save menu command, saving the file as mytut1.wrl, then click on "next VRML scene" (on the HTML tutorial) to see the next step, which involves painting the object. When you're ready to read the directions, click on the question mark at the top of the VRML scene, or on "next HTML page" below.

Embellishing Your Objects

In the previous step, we created the LOD 2 object, that is, the second simplest level of detail for our set of house objects. Now we'll embellish it to add a bit of complexity, creating a LOD 3 object.

Naming Objects

Since each level of detail must be represented by a separate object, we'll make a copy and modify that. First, we'll give it a name. Make sure the house object is selected.

1. Right-click on the Object tool.
2. In the Object Info panel, click in the box next to Name and change the name to HouseB, and press Enter. This is arbitrary; you can use any name you like, but it helps to use a descriptive one.
3. Close the Object Info panel.

Copying Objects

Now we'll make a copy of the house to modify as the LOD 3 object.

1. Click the Copy tool or press Ctrl+C on the keyboard. We now have two identical copies in the same place, so there's no visible change.

   Let's see what has actually happened to our database.

2. Click the Animation Project tool to open the Objects window. Note, in the list of items, that we now have objects named HouseB and HouseB,1, and that the latter is selected. Since we want to work on HouseB,1, keeping it in the center of the workspace, select HouseB by clicking on its name, so we can move it out of the way. Close the Objects window.

3. Click Object Move, then click and drag leftward in the workspace until the first house object is over on the left side of the screen, and not touching the copy. Actually, if you're not working on a fast machine, you'll get faster feedback by moving it completely out of view.

4. Select the copy, HouseB,1, by clicking on it.

Modifying Objects

We'll now apply a Sweep operation to all four textured polygons to create wings for the house.

1. Select the Point Edit Faces tool and, moving the mouse cursor into the workspace, note that there's a P next to the cursor arrow. This indicates that you're in Point Edit mode.

2. Click on one of the visible texture-mapped polygons to select it. Note that it's now outlined in green.

3. Press and hold the Shift key, and click on the other texture-mapped poly. Now they're both green-lined.

4. Select the Object Rotate tool, and click on an empty spot in the workspace.

5. Holding down the mouse button, drag left or right to spin the house object half a turn, so you can see the two unselected texture-mapped faces. Note that you're still in Point Edit mode, an example of Fountain's non-modal design.

6. Press and hold the Shift key again, and click the other two texture-mapped faces so they're highlighted as well.

7. Select the Sweep tool. Note how all four faces are extruded outward from the house's vertical center. This special simultaneous-sweep feature, found in all Caligari 3D applications, can save you lots of time.

   Our house is now starting to look like a mansion, but the wings could stand to be somewhat longer. After a Sweep operation, you're automatically placed in Point Move mode, so this part is easy.

8. Move the mouse cursor to an empty section of the workspace, and press and hold the right mouse button. Drag left or right a small amount, and note whether the wings' lengths increase or decrease (see Figure 34-9). If the latter, keep dragging until they're the right length (you decide how much). If they decrease, drag in the opposite direction.

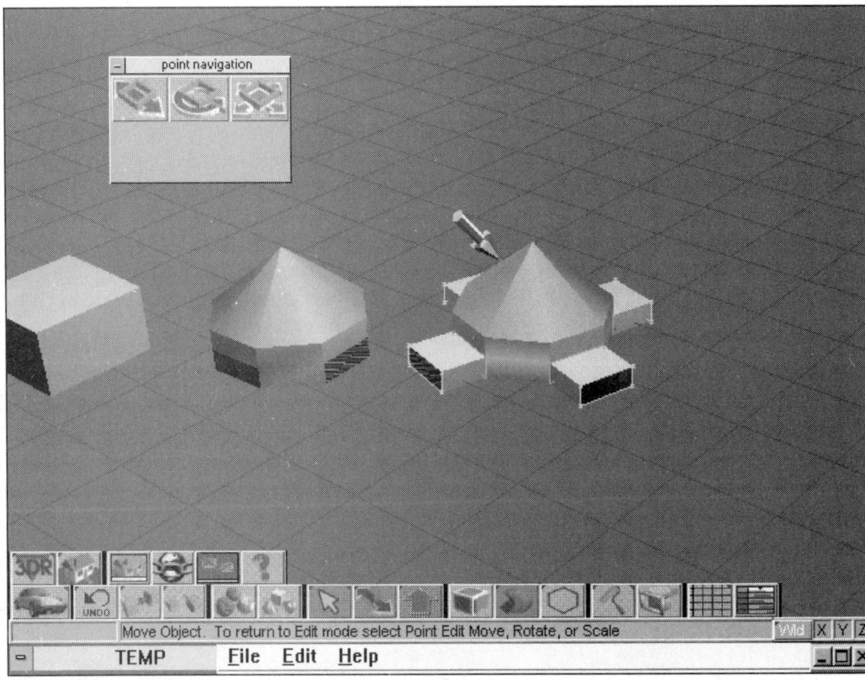

Figure 34-9: House with wing detail added for close up of LOD

You're able to control the lengths of all the wings simultaneously via one action. By way of explanation, what's happening is that, as usual with the right mouse button, you're creating motion on the Z axis, which is usually vertical. But in this case, each wing has its own Z axis, which is "vertical" with respect to the surface from which it was generated. In other words, each wing's — and, in fact, every polygon's — Z axis is perpendicular to its surface plane.

9. Use the File ➪ Scene ➪ Save menu command, saving the file as mytut1.wrl, then click on "next VRML scene" below to see the next step, which involves painting the object. When you're ready to read the directions, click on the question mark at the top of the VRML scene, or on "next HTML page" below.

Creating an Eaves-Type Structure

Now we'll create an eaves-type structure around the top of the house, using the Polygon and Lathe tools. This procedure is a bit tricky, so follow along carefully.

Setting up the Lathe Tool

You may want to switch to Wireframe Display mode for the next few steps, for faster feedback. I'll let you know when to return to Solid Render Display mode.

1. Select the Regular Polygon tool and draw a small polygon near where the camera was before you moved it. The number of sides doesn't matter; this is just a dummy object for studying the Lathe tool.
2. Select Object Scale, then move the mouse cursor into the workspace away from any objects, click and hold the left mouse button, and drag the mouse toward you.
3. Select the Lathe tool from the Sweep pop-up. The lathe path appears as a circle emanating from the polygon's center. Actually, it's only 3/4 of a circle, so let's make it a full 360 degrees.
4. The angle setting appears as a straight line pointing upward at the end of the circular path. If you can't see it, move the mouse cursor onto the polygon, click and hold the left mouse button, and drag the polygon so you can see the entire lathe path, including the angle setting. Click and hold on the angle setting, then drag toward the polygon to close the circular path.

Changing the Number of Segments

Now we'll change the number of segments in the lathe path. We want eight, to match the building's octagonal shape.

1. Click and hold on the circular path, and drag in any direction. If the number of segments decreases, fine; otherwise, stop, and drag in the opposite direction. Keep dragging until you reach the minimum number of segments, which is three, yielding a triangular path.
2. Keep holding down the mouse button, and drag slowly in the opposite direction. As you drag, you'll see the number of segments increase, one by one, as shown in Figure 34-10. Starting a count at 3, count to yourself at each increase (4, 5, 6, 7...). Stop at 8.

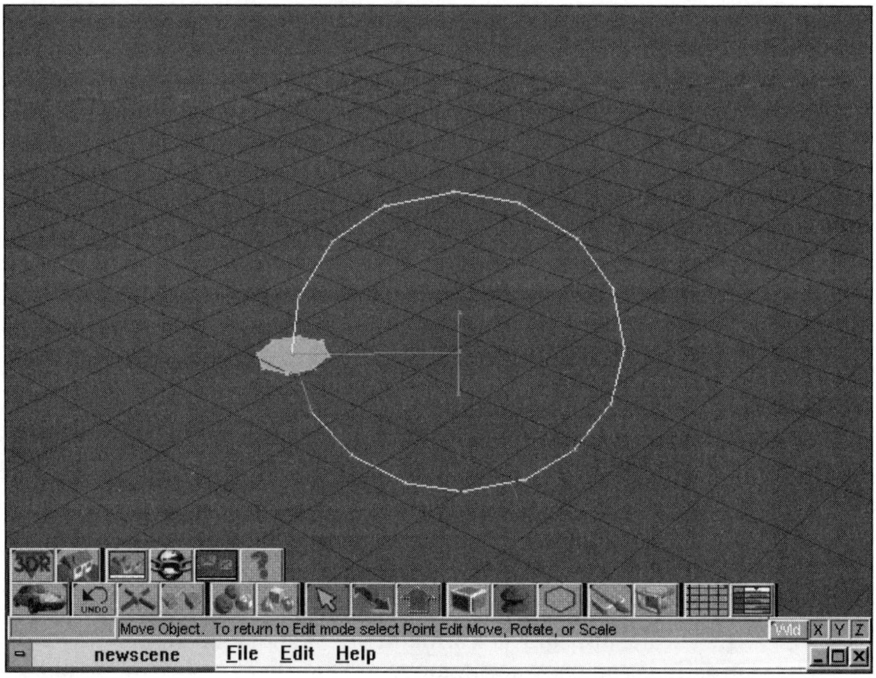

Figure 34-10: Manipulating the number of segments in the lathe path is easy — and interactive. Here I have 16 segments, twice as many as I want. By following step 2 in the previous section, I adjust that number to 8 segments.

Now that we've set up the Lathe tool, let's create the actual polygon to lathe, which will be a low isosceles triangle. Note the lathe path's direction; it runs parallel to the World X axis. We want to lathe the triangle so that its base forms the inside of the ring. Therefore, the path is to be perpendicular to the triangle's base, and pointing away from the tip.

1. Select the Polygon tool from the Regular Polygon tool's pop-up. Note that the first polygon's lathe path disappears, and that the Help Bar tells you to click to add points, and right-click to close the polygon.

   Since the lathe path is parallel to the X axis, and the triangle's base is to be perpendicular to the path, we'll draw the base along the Y axis.

2. Click once on a grid intersection near the first polygon (you won't see anything), then click again on an adjacent intersection along the Y axis. This time you'll see a straight line.

3. Click a third time between and slightly above (or below) the first two points, opposite the direction of the first polygon's path. Then right-click to close the triangle. It should look something like the one in the above screen image. If not, press the Delete key to erase it and try again.

4. Click on the first (dummy) polygon, and press Delete to erase it.

Let's Lathe!

Now you're ready to lathe.

1. Select the triangle, then click the lathe tool to generate the triangle's path, which should appear exactly as on the first polygon.
2. Note that the Lathe tool is now selected. Click it again to perform the lathe. It's a ring!

   The ring is vertical, but we want it to be horizontal, so it will go nicely around the building's circumference, just below the roof.
3. Select the Object tool, then select the Object Rotate tool, and finally select the Grid tool. By activating grid snap, we can rotate the ring exactly 90 degrees with two movements.

   When you selected Object Rotate, the active coordinate system changed from World to Object, as indicated by the change of the box text near the right end of the Help Bar from "Wld" to "Obj."
4. Click and hold on the Obj box, and select Wld from the pop-up to return to the World coordinate system.

TAKE NOTE

Because the ring is parallel to the world X axis, that's the one we want to rotate it around. (Think of it as rotating on a spit through its horizontal diameter.) The left mouse button is normally used to transform objects about both the X and Y axes, but we can isolate either by turning the other off. Disable the Y axis now by clicking on the Y button at the right end of the Help Bar.

5. Move the mouse cursor into the workspace, click and hold the left mouse button, and drag left or right. You may have to drag a little ways before you see anything change, but eventually the ring snaps to a 45-degree angle from its original orientation. Drag a little more, and you'll get another 45-degree jump, resulting in a 90-degree rotation and a ring that's parallel with the ground plane.
6. Turn off Grid snap, and re-enable Y-axis rotation by clicking on the Y button at the right end of the Help Bar.

Switching Camera Position

Let's now switch back to the camera in preparation for positioning the ring around the building.

1. Select the Animation Project Window tool, and from the Objects window, select Camera 1. Then select the View from Object tool to activate that camera.
2. If you changed the display mode to Wireframe near the beginning of this step, return to Solid Render Display mode now.
3. Click on the ring object, click on Object Move, then drag the ring over to the LOD3 house. Position it around the bottom of the house as best you can.

Then use the right mouse button to raise it so the ring's top edge is at the same height as the house's top edge, before the roof cone.

4. Now let's check it from above. You should still be able to see the second camera near the top of the scene. Click it to select it, then click Look At, and click the house object. The camera reorients itself to point at the house.

5. Select Object Move and drag the camera over to above the house, so it's pointing straight down. Then select View From Object, and zoom out if necessary (remember, use Object Scale with the left mouse button).

   At this point, you should be able to see that the ring is too big, and that it's not aligned correctly with the house sides.

6. Select Object Rotate and drag with the right mouse button to line up the ring's sides with the house's.

7. Select Object Scale and use both mouse buttons to scale the ring down so its inside circumference is about the same as the house's outside circumference. Also, if necessary, use Object Move to position the ring properly so it's concentric with the house.

8. Return to view from the first camera and position the ring so its top is just under the dividing line between the house's sides and the roof, as shown in Figure 34-11. Remember, this is just a tutorial, so you don't need to be extremely precise.

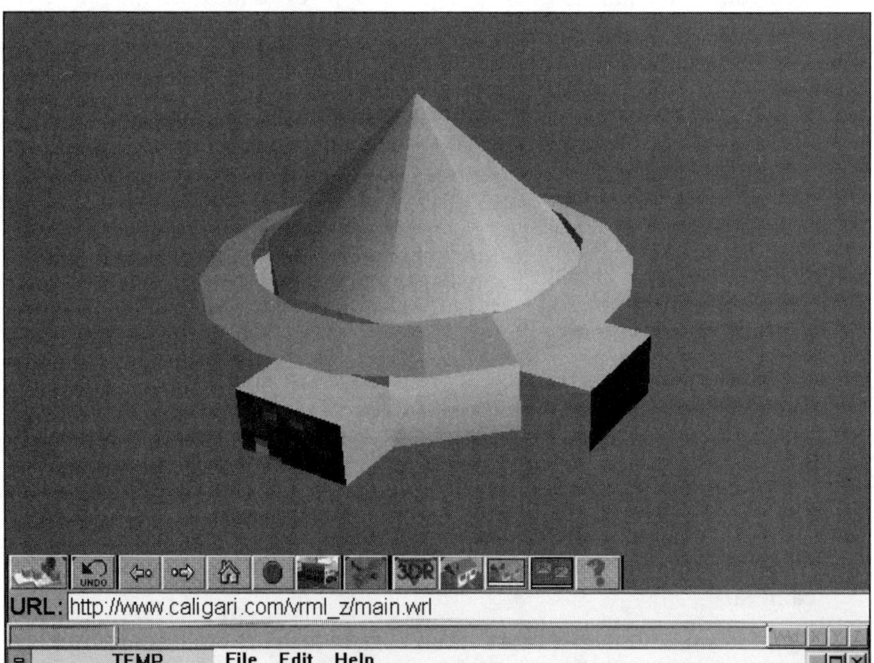

Figure 34-11: Positioning the ring between the house's sides and roof requires you to size (scale) the ring to fit. You also have to rotate it so the 8 vertices line up on each piece to get a tight fit.

Grouping Objects

Now that we've put the house and ring together physically, let's combine them with the Glue function so the program regards them as a unit.

1. Select the house object, then click the Glue as Child tool. Move the mouse cursor back into the workspace, and note that it resembles an inverted bottle, just as with the Look At function.
2. Select the ring object, and note that, unlike Look At, the mouse cursor remains as a bottle. You can combine many objects with the Glue function by clicking on each in turn. To turn off Glue, select the Object tool.
3. Let's give the newly modified house a name. Make sure it's selected, then right-click the Object tool. Click in the space next to Name, and enter the name HouseC. We'll also be calling this the LOD3 object.
4. Save your work.

Final Adjustments

We're getting close. Just another couple of steps, and we can check out exactly how LOD works.

1. Click the Primitives Panel tool, and add a cube object to the workspace. If necessary, scale it to be about the same size as the first house.

   Now we'll add a complex object to be at the highest level of detail.
2. From the File menu, select Load Object, and in the Load Object dialog, find the object named Housed.3ds in the Fountain directory, and load it. (Note: We'll be calling this the LOD4 object later in the tutorial.)

   At last, we're ready to demonstrate LOD.
3. Select the object closest to the center of the workspace. It really doesn't matter which you start with, but note that grouped LOD objects are combined at the first selected object's location.
4. From the Glue tool pop-up, select the Group LOD tool. It's described in the Help Bar as "Group several objects together as Level of Detail Representations."
5. Move the cursor into the workspace, and note that, as with the Look At and Glue tools, it resembles an inverted bottle.
6. Click on the other three House objects, including the cube, in any order. One of the beauties of Fountain's LOD function is that you needn't combine objects in any particular order. The program bases the order in which they appear, as distance changes, on the relative complexity, or polygon/vertex count.

TAKE NOTE

As you click on each object, it seems to vanish. Actually, they're only hiding; you can only see one object in an LOD grouping at a time.

7. Let's check it out! Go to Browse mode by clicking on the Walk through World tool.
8. Click and hold the left mouse button in a blank part of the workspace and drag forward and backward. At certain points you'll see the different LOD objects appear. At the greatest distance you'll see the cube, then as you get closer, you see HouseB, then HouseC, and finally the most complex object, HouseD, when you're very close.

   This also works in World Building mode. Return to World Building mode, click on Eye Move, and drag forward and backward in the workspace as in the previous step.
9. Save your work (you wouldn't want to lose it after all the effort you've put into creating it).

Breaking up the Level of Detail Group

We'll now break up the LOD group and use the Inspect tool to make HouseD look more like the others.

1. Select the house object, then from the Glue/Group LOD pop-up, select the "Ungroup Level of Detail objects as regular scene objects" tool. When you do this, all the objects remain in the same place, so you may see parts of some of them poking out.
2. Let's spread them out. Open the Objects window, select each one in turn from the list, and use Object Move to move them to either side.
3. We want to work on the LOD4 object now (the 3DS-format house you loaded), so let's center the view on it. This uses a handy tool that requires that you be in Perspective View mode. So, from the View from Object pop-up, select Perspective View.
4. Select the LOD4 object, either in the workspace or in the Objects window list. Then, from the Close All Panels pop-up , select the Look at Current Object tool. Note how the view jumps to point at this object. Adjust the view so you can see both it and the LOD3 object, HouseC.
5. Next, re-combine the four house objects into a single LOD group. Remember, select the one whose position you want to use for the group, then click the Group LOD tool, then click on each of the other three, in any order.

Changing Background Color

Until now, we've been sticking with the default background, which is a bland gray color. Let's spice up the scene a bit by adding some color, then an image. We can do this in Browse mode, so select the Walk through World tool.

1. Right-click on the Solid Render Display tool to bring up the Render Options panel.
2. Click on the small gray rectangle near the bottom of the panel's left edge. This opens the Background Color panel, with three sliders for red, green, and blue.
3. Click near the right end of the blue scale, and note that the background changes color immediately. Try some other colors if you like, then close the panel. Try navigating around in the scene, and note how the background color changes things.

Adding a Background Image

Now we'll add a background image.

1. In the Render Options panel, click on the wide gray box to the right of the word "Background."
2. In the Get Texture Map file requester that appears, select a file from the Fountain directory (try Wood4.jpg) and click OK. Note that the name Wood4 now appears in the box you clicked, and the box next to Background is checked. But where's the image?

   Look at the bottom of the Render Options panel. Note that the box next to Show Background Image is empty.
3. Click on it now, and watch as your background image appears. Try navigating again, and note that the background image disappears when you move, but returns as soon as you stop.
4. Save the scene again as mytut1.wrl, but this time, when the Export VRML file dialog appears, stop for a moment and take a look at the Options section.

   First, we have ASCII Formatting, which is also known as "Pretty Formatting." As the latter name suggests, when this option is enabled, the saved VRML file is formatted with indents to make it more readable. If you don't care about readability and want to save disk space, turn off this option. Similarly, the Preserve Hierarchy option makes saved files easier to understand.
5. Turn the Preserve Hierarchy option off to save space.

   The Precision setting lets you determine to how many places floating-point values in your files are written out. If accuracy to the thousandths place isn't necessary, reduce this number to make your files smaller.

Summary

You should now be ready to build and browse worlds like a professional net weasel, extending your presence all over the globe, literally. Many PPP providers will provide you with free space for your pages or at a minimal charge. Experience a new kind of connectedness while being a cyberspace pioneer. In this chapter, you learned:

- That there are two interfaces, Browse and World Creation.
- That you can use inline objects from other sites around the world to populate your Web space.
- Construction techniques that include LOD (Level of Detail).
- That you can build worlds in tS2 and load them right into Fountain for easy conversion to efficient wrl files.
- That you can create navigable 3D worlds directly in the Fountain interface, complete with backgrounds and custom-built materials and objects from other sites.

✦ ✦ ✦

Career Opportunities in 3D Animation

PART VIII

In This Part

The point of this book has been to help you get started in a digital arts career. A career in the digital arts? If you look in your local newspaper, you probably won't see many want-ads for digital animators. Fear not, the future is bright; jobs do exist in this field. You just have to know where to look.

I see four main avenues that you should investigate. First, you should contact graphic arts agencies and local media companies to apply for a job in the industry. Second, you should apply for a job at one of the big entertainment industry houses in the United States and Canada, as well as Europe and Asia. This will probably mean relocating, possibly to a foreign country.

Third, get a telecommuting job via the Internet. I know companies that have installed a T1 (read expensive, but fast) Internet node in employees' homes. This level of support is rare, but you may be able to work on assignments at home, commuting to the office maybe once a week. This arrangement allows you to live way out in the country.

Fourth, work as a full studio freelancer. This situation enables you to use your own well-equipped studio and work on assignment. Such an arrangement has many advantages but demands you handle many responsibilities at the same time. Your assignments will come from advertising companies, film companies, and overflow from larger studios, depending on your reputation and skills.

In this section you learn about current and future job possibilities, how to create new opportunities, and how to contact the right people. You also learn how to use the Web as a resource for finding information and doing research, promoting yourself, and offering your services as a Web page designer.

CHAPTER 35

How to Find a Job in the 3D Industry

✦ ✦ ✦ ✦

In This Chapter

We've already had an introduction to finding a job in the Industry. Here we'll look at such things as:

Fields where 3D opportunities abound

How to find the companies that do what you like to do

How to show self-confidence in interviews

The fine art of schmoozing — how to do it and where

Organizations around the globe that can help you get started in an animation career

✦ ✦ ✦ ✦

I'm taking a couple of chapters to cover all the angles on finding a job. I believe that finding the right job with the right people is essential to a happy life. Because this field is growing so quickly there are now many routes to success. Here are just a few of them.

What Fields Use 3D Animation?

The simple answer is all of them. 3D animation is slowly becoming part of everything. As we use virtual reality to amplify our perceptions we become ever more dependent on CGI and animation. Here are some expected and perhaps unexpected fields that already depend on 3D visualization/animation/rendering.

Medicine

The new field of Virtual Medicine depends heavily on 3D imaging and visualization. Much of what's going on in the field is connected with things you'll be involved with. For example, digital interactive simulations are being used to place the surgeon in a better position for doing an operation. For example, through simulation the doctor can be virtually reduced to the size of the head of a pin. This makes delicate eye operations easier as there is far more delicate control of the laser when you're this small.

Doctors can now virtually look through their patients and see internal organs via real-time MRI overlays via HMD. Even ultrasound data can be interpreted and placed at a doctor's disposal in a 3D image overlay.

Medical students are already doing virtual operations on virtual 3D patients. They are using 3D software to create medical models for illustration and experimentation. Soon children will be taught anatomy by having them take a virtual look into their own bodies and see how they work.

Several recent issues of *3D Artist* magazine featured medical illustrations all done in 3D. The fact that they were all done in 3D Studio only says that doctors haven't discovered the ease and facility of tS2.

Law

Another issue of *3D Artist* focused on forensic illustration. This is used to help clarify evidence in legal matters and investigations. Police can use 3D crime-scene analysis to figure out what really happened. There was a ton of 3D animation used during the O.J. Simpson trial to help clarify things for the TV audience. Animation was used in the Rodney King beating trial, and it will be used more and more in the future. I've met several young people who have started businesses creating forensic animations for lawyers at outrageous prices. Keep your rates reasonable and bill the clients directly. Lawyers simply add a large surcharge onto your work. It all makes justice a little harder to find.

One thing about forensic animation, it requires very accurate work. Distances need to be measured exactly when reconstructing an accident scene, for example, so the animation accurately reflects what happened. Though tS2 is an excellent choice, 3D Studio and LightWave 4.0 are good alternates with special settings that facilitate this accuracy.

Chemistry

You can't be a great chemist today unless you know 3D animation. Why? Because it's a daily tool. With it you can show relative molecular motion and fit. You can plan experiments and demonstrate results in a visual way. Chemistry teachers have long used physical models. Now they can do actual real-time illustration of chemical processes.

Mathematics

The whole hyperdimensional world of math is becoming both more interesting and more accessible through 3D animation. Even mathematicians themselves agree that 3D visualization helps them to see deeper into the abstract world of numbers. Several Internet sites feature animations based on mathematical processes and fractals. Others demonstrate A-life or Artificial Life forms, creating beautiful animations.

Physics and the Rest

You already know that many physics discoveries come from computer simulation of physical events. Now those simulations usually contain an animated readout of what's happening. You can create the stress lines, compression fractures, and microscopic interactions without ever entering the lab.

Engineers use animation to build buildings and test structures. Architects create walk-throughs for their clients. The military has long been involved with broadband interactive simulations. That's where you have people in seven countries all in the same simulation interacting by using their perceptual senses.

Entertainment

Clearly, my favorite field is entertainment. The vast stretch of terrain ahead is mind-numbing. From feature film to interactive games, CGI is king. In Chapter 38 I'll tell you about some exciting new directions that entertainment is taking wherein animation is catapaulted to its near ultimate level — live animation. Live animation is where your characters are imbued with high-level artificial intelligence and procedural animation. They walk, they talk, they breathe, and they know what's going on around them. They react appropriately for their motives. Watch out for the cunning bad guys.

The power of 3D to create believable illusions has started a whole new area of growth in the film-related field of virtual environment ride simulations. By mixing a motion base platform with clever props and intensely involving images, companies like Disney and Universal are producing an increasing number of fantasy rides for their amusement parks worldwide. Las Vegas is getting them too.

Creating these marvels falls upon several houses with specialized capability in this area. It's complex, exciting, and intensely motivating. I understand that people tend to work late into the wee hours, caught up in the tingle.

Advertising

Local advertising and television companies employ an astounding amount of CGI material these days, both 2D and 3D. Anyone with excellent Photoshop skills is going to find a good job. National ads are almost universally computer generated, from billboards to snappy commercials. Opportunities abound at both local and national levels.

There are many more fields to look at and more are entering the 3D arena daily.

Pounding the Pavement

We've already talked a bit about finding places to send your demo. On that subject, I just found a new source of excellent animation film to study. It's called Extended Entertainment and it's a sister company to *Animation* magazine. They have one of the most useful animation collections I've seen. I recommend you get their *World's Greatest Animation* and *PIXAR* reels. You can reach Extended Entertainment at 800-996-TOON.

Anyway, once you've decided your stuff is pretty good, there are some interesting paths to explore, magazines to read, and organizations to join. Why? Because you need to lay the groundwork for your personal credibility.

Building Personal Credibility

Finding places to interview isn't the hard job — there are tons. It's nailing the interview when you get there. You've got to leave a solid impression. It helps to talk the talk, or as we say in Hollywood, schmooze the schmooze. That means you have to keep up on what's happening in the field. The information is available, all you have to do is take advantage. Read, listen, and netsurf to know who's doing what, and with whom you should be talking. Get the lay of the terrain before jumping in the creek.

Magazines

I get dozens of magazines because I'm a columnist. I look at all of them, but being dyslexic I read only a few. Magazines are an excellent way to lift the intelligence level of your conversation. If you know what you're talking about in some depth, you'll make a better impression when you happen to get into a conversation with someone who could-just-might-maybe hire you.

The array of relevant magazines out there is dizzying. I checked the huge magazine rack at Op Amp Books in Hollywood (my favorite bookstore) and quit counting at 40 geared to multimedia/animation/games/graphics. Here are a few I think you can benefit from.

These aren't in order of importance; determine that for yourself. Many of these magazines are read by people you'll be applying to. If you saw the article in *CGW* on DEC Alpha graphics workstations, they probably did too. It's a conversation point. Read about the latest SGI machines and software as well.

The Weeklies

For up-to-the-minute action I skim both *Inter@ctive Week*, "the single source for the Internet, infrastructure and digital commerce" and *InfoWorld,* "The Voice of Client/Server in the Enterprise." It's way more than that. These two may not sound relevant, but keeping updated on what's happening in the connected world is important to 3D types. I also read *Variety* and *The Hollywood Reporter* to follow the latest entertainment trends. They're dailies and they pile up on me. I only catch the headlines and read very few articles. It helps to be like a fat farmer — well rounded in your field.

My favorite and the most intense weekly fare is *Tess*. That's short for *Tessellation Times*, the best e-zine on the subject, it will keep you more up to date than any other medium. It specifically covers 3D animation in detail, every aspect. It's put out every Tuesday or so. It used to be every Monday, but it keeps slipping. It comes in your e-mail automatically, is a quick read, and absolutely required for desktop animators to stay on top. Editorials by contributing editor Rob Glidden will keep you on top of and understanding the latest technical advancements. It's a great place to keep up on places to display your work, contests, and other opportunities. To subscribe, send a request to: `tess@3dartist.com`.

The Monthlies

Monthly Magazines I like most are: *3D Artist* magazine, *3D Design* (both cover tS2 well with how-to articles), *Animation* magazine, *AV Video*, *Computer Graphics World* (CGW), *PC Graphics and Video,* and of course, *Wired.*

If you don't read the wildly creative and hip *Wired*, you're not considered part of the cognoscenti — the connected generation of cool creative types. Every once in a while I even go out and snag a copy of *Mondo2000*, not to keep up, but just to peek into the world of cyberpunk. Like *Wired*, it's exceptionally well written.

This selection will help you cover new ideas and techniques, studios, and computer graphics/video hardware with a strong emphasis on connected media.

Quarterlies and More

Quarterly magazines include *MultimediaToday*, which maintains an essential database of new software and the latest hardware with all the right phone numbers and addresses. It also has great articles (I'm prejudiced, being a contributing editor).

Here's a pretty unlikely candidate for you to look at: *LightWave Pro* from Avid Media Group. They're the folks who have always been staunch Amiga supporters (Video Toaster User). No matter. *LightWave Pro*, though expensive and oriented exclusively toward the LightWave Pro program, has the best articles you'll find on how to achieve all those awesome special F/X you see on the numbered space station shows. The articles are actually written by the guys at Amblin and Foundation and Area 51 who actually create the movie and TV magic every week. These guys are incredible in their willingness to share professional secrets. Many of the techniques carry over easily to trueSpace2.

Here's a quarterly that I absolutely love. It's got a relatively tight circulation, so you probably never heard of it, but wow, what a neat subscription. It's *Cinefex,* "the journal of cinematic illusions." One of the best values I've seen. Every issue is like a whole book, packed with color photos and explanations of how the latest movie effects were done. It's a little biased toward west coast companies but an informative read cover to cover. *Cinefex* gives you detailed background info on studios, production companies, F/X houses, and individuals you'll want to know about. Read it — you'll find out who's who. When you meet them in person, maybe you'll mention a piece of their work you're familiar with. If that doesn't impress them a little, go back to *People* magazine. Sure, they'll figure you read it in *Cinefex*, but that alone brings you tighter into their world.

Info-Based Conversation

A really great new TV commercial will come up in conversations. I know very little about who did what in commercials, but I try. I saw a cute car commercial with a goofy penguin slipping and falling on the ice a few days ago. I loved it. In a conversation at Rhythm & Hues I mentioned that it looked like their work. I was thinking of the Coca Cola polar bears. My friend said they'd all noticed and loved it too; scuttlebutt had it coming out of Colossal. I don't know if it's true, but that's not the point. The conversation was in a small way a bonding one. Such conversations help buff off some of your newbie shine, revealing a little more credibility. You're not fooling anyone. If you noticed and mentioned the commercial, you *are* on their plane.

Your Schmooze Quotient

Though you may never have to use it directly, a solid understructure of current knowledge about the field will help you schmooze better under pressure. Schmoozing is the art of exchanging information and identifying opportunities while engaged in interesting, often intense conversation. Knowing who the players are and how things work will pump you with confidence and create a more solid impression in the exchange.

There's a reason I'm spending a lot of time on this topic. People who sit in front of the computer all day creating visual candy often neglect verbal skills. This is by no means universal, but you could be shy. I'd hate to see your personal inhibitions screw up a job opportunity that could have you making an excellent living and looking forward to work every day. Sure, schmoozing is what smooth talkers do. Don't worry, you don't have to do it that way. Nope, your kind of schmoozing has to be in your own personal style. You absolutely do not want to force it. Trying to be smooth and glib when you're not is easy to spot and likely to give your host the nerve nuggies. Push too hard and you can come off as a jerk.

Here's a tip. You know that old saying about picturing the audience in diapers will help you with stage fright? Well it works in job opportunities as well. Before you go into a meeting, go over the following:

- ✦ These guys were in your shoes about a year ago, maybe less.
- ✦ They look silly in those diapers.

- These are not high-powered Hollywood moguls with big ego problems and narcissistic tendencies. Nope, these are just nice people whom you'd love to work with — potential friends.
- Don't think about the fact that this person created one of your favorite special effects in *Terminator 2*. You'll just intimidate yourself.
- Know what you have to offer and be sure of it. Tell yourself that you have genius in your special area. If you don't believe in yourself, the meeting is a waste of time.
- This meeting is only for practice. If you screw up, you'll learn from it and do better next time. Piece of cake... no worries... lots of other opportunities.
- After reading all this you know more about schmoozing than they do.

Then when you're in the meeting be nice, treat them as equals, they'll appreciate it.

Bring Questions

In nearly every interview you get an opportunity to ask questions. Most people sit there with a big "Duhhh??" on their faces — deduct 13 points. Be prepared to ask some smart questions. After all, your attitude is that these guys will be fortunate if they land you because you're part of the future of the industry. Ask pointed, relevant questions like these (but be original):

- What high-end suites do you have licenses for?
- I'm curious, what would you say is your ratio of off-the-shelf vs. proprietary software?
- Do you see this company moving more into the interactive game genre? (On this one, you'd better know how involved they are right now.)
- Does the company support off-site training for employees who are interested in learning new systems?
- How does the company feel about telecommuting... do some of your employees have ISDN connections? T1?
- Tell me about the company's connectivity. Are you linked into Drums?

Questions like these will help assure them that you have a mind, will get them talking about themselves, and take you out from under the griller. This is an interactive genre and it pays to interact — within reason — at your interview.

You don't want to interrupt with a lot of inane questions, or ask those with obvious answers. Be kind about their work but don't gush. Ask the smartest questions you can muster on the tour of their facility (which can be a vaguely good sign), but not too many.

Okay, the heck with it all. Be yourself, be comfortable. Ignore what I'm saying… I'm a father you know, we overdo the worry bit. Just be the sharp, curious, interesting person your parents would be amazed to know about.

A Tight Fit

Remember one key question in their minds will be: "Will this person fit in with our people?" It will help if you know a little about some of the people who work there. You can sometimes pick up this kind of information by visiting their Web site. It helps if you naturally feel comfortable with these kinds of people. You'll know pretty quickly.

Places to Schmooze

Schmoozing is part of networking. To do that, you find other animators, both traditional and digital, and converse. You can learn from both groups. There are a number of organizations you'll want to consider.

It helps to live in a city that has a local animation organization chapter. The most active community is right here in Southern California. Society journals are informative even if you're not local and you can always drive to functions in a nearby city. Animation societies generally have get-togethers and annual shindigs where you can make valuable contacts.

ASIFA – International Animated Film Society

ASIFA is an acronym for the French *Association Internationale du Film d'Animation.* As you can see, the acronym is much easier to pronounce (Ah-See-Fah), the International Animated Film Society. It's a nonprofit organization founded way back in 1957 in France. It was chartered by UNESCO in 1960 to encourage the art of animation and further international understanding and goodwill through animation. Today there are chapters in 30 countries. You'll even find chapters in places like Ulan Bator in Mongolia. Local chapters have flavor and activities suited to their respective geographical animation communities. Most chapters publish a newsletter and organize events like screenings, lectures, guest animator presentations, festivals, awards ceremonies, and workshops.

An important new function of ASIFA is Employment Databank. The organization provides information about members to recruiting companies. It's a valuable resource to employers and employees alike. In addition, the Hollywood chapter has a film preservation program, educational scholarship awards, and AniFest. This annual animation convention features a wide array of animation artwork and videos. There are live stage shows by famous voice artists and lots more. A definite schmooze opportunity.

If you live where you can go to ASIFA functions, you probably should belong. It's a nice professional credential, the schmoozing is good, in Hollywood you get to go to a lot of screenings, and best of all, life drawing classes.

Since 1972 ASIFA-Hollywood has hosted the annual Annie Awards Extravaganza honoring the best in animation. To receive an Annie is the highest honor in the field. ASIFA-Hollywood also presents an annual Animation Opportunities Expo, which is a one-day gathering of key animation studios, companies, and artists. Here people and companies showcase their goods and do a lot of schmoozing. It's a terrific networking opportunity for all concerned. Bring your portfolio, demo reels, and résumé because the right people will be looking for them. If you work really hard you can have your demo ready for the next Expo, which will probably be held next February.

You may feel a bit like a misfit in ASIFA, because it's about 90 percent traditional animators. But this is changing and I want you to be in on the early stages of the transition. There is some worry among members that we digital types are going to take over their industry. We're not. We do our own thing. Technology is entering their world too, but theirs is a 2D world requiring skills we don't even know about. Join ASIFA, participate, and help define the future.

SIGGRAPH

This is my personal favorite organization. It's especially for us digital types. Technically it's the Special Interest Group on Computer Graphics of the ACM, the Association for Computing Machinery, Inc. That's a pretty silly name; computing machinery doesn't go around joining associations, so you never hear it referred to by anything but ACM. They came up with the name before modern computers were invented.

SIGGRAPH has taken on an identity of its own. See Appendix D for a global list of professional chapters. The local chapters are "...an international multi-cultural network of like-minded people who throughout the year develop, continue and extend the work and achievements presented at the annual ACM/SIGGRAPH Conference." That's a mouthful that doesn't tell us a lot. To extend that definition, chapters draw membership from professional graphics people in many fields working in their local area. They generally meet on a regular basis for special events, conferences, and discussions of topics associated with Computer Generated Images (CGI). Although it used to be an organization of technical types, artists have broadened the membership nicely. There is a lot of electronic networking done among SIGGRAPH members and it's a wonderful way to keep up with what's happening now.

SIGGRAPH Video Review

Though it's outrageously expensive because it's a fund-raiser, the *Video Review* is the world's most widely circulated video-based publication. Since 1979 the *Review* has been used to illustrate the latest concepts in computer graphics and interactive techniques. A complete set of volumes is a visual history of the medium. Individual tapes cost $60.00, which is painful, but you should get the volume for SIGGRAPH 95 Los Angeles. It has a wonderful collection of visual ideas to inspire your mind's eye as you think of your demo. You can order it by calling 800-527-0231 in the United States and Canada. If you're overseas call US 1-213-527-0231.

The Annual SIGGRAPH Conference

It's the biggest gathering of digital graphics types, organizations, companies, production houses, and game developers in the world. The annual animation theater is enough to fill your head with wonder at the latest in technique and technology. Go and you'll hobnob with the Thomas Edisons and Madame Curies of computer graphics.

Key announcements from the digital animation industry are always made at SIGGRAPH. They all push to have an important announcement of new goodies here and sometimes you even get free T-shirts. But that's probably because I'm press and we get a lot of T-shirts and caps in the mail around that time of year. Anyway, save your money, keep track of events on the Web at `http://www.siggraph.org`, and come to the annual convention.

Women

Now I'm in big trouble, singling out women. But I must. There are two excellent opportunities that are special for women. As a screenwriting member of Women In Film I learned about the multimedia committee. They have an active group of women who work in multimedia, especially in digital animation and entertainment.

Women In Animation

Women in Animation is really the central group for women involved in animation. There are chapters on the east and west coasts. The group was started by dynamic and determined women, headed by Rita Street, in 1994. Their mission is: "...to foster the dignity, concerns, and advancement of women who are involved with any and all aspects of the art and industry of animation." To that end they hold four general meetings a year and numerous seminars and events. You can get an application and more information by calling 818-759-9596 or by writing to Women in Animation, PO Box 17706, Encino, CA 91416.

It's Up to You

Ultimately it comes down to this. If you want an exciting and rewarding career in this industry, you have to lay yourself on the line and see what you're made of. Lots of people fool themselves into thinking they can be animators, but never put in the effort. Your demo tape says you're willing to do the work. The quality of it tells how talented you are and your ability to get it to the right people tells you that you're pretty sharp.

The next chapter digs deeper into the world of the Internet. At my last count over eight thousand Web pages were associated with all forms of animation. The most prevalent are concerned with digital animation. Start thinking of the Web as a serious resource to your advancement.

Now it's time to log on and link up.

Summary

Getting a job in the field of digital animation is competitive, but if you learn your tools, show your talent, and know what's going on in the field, you stand an excellent chance of having a wonderful career. By now you should know:

- That 3D animation isn't just about entertainment. It's reaching into nearly every field from mathematics to medicine.
- There is an expanding job market for qualified animators.
- To get a job you have to show your stuff, and to show confidence in interviews.
- Rubbing elbows with computer graphics folks and animators is a good idea. This chapter gave you extensive leads on finding an organization that can help you in this area.

✦ ✦ ✦

CHAPTER 36

Animation Resources on the World Wide Web

In This Chapter

truesSpace-related Web sites

Professional artists directory on the Web

Finding resources

Using AOL and CompuServe

Throughout this book I've given you e-mail and Web addresses. If you're not connected, get connected. There's no excuse. The world is now wired and you can't live a normal computer graphics existence unless you get plugged into a Point-to-Point Protocol (PPP) with Netscape. Most places in the country have providers that give a generous allotment of connect time for less than $20.00 a month. Look at it as a necessary investment, as ordinary as a fax machine or a phone bill. People just aren't credible in this business if they don't have a Net address. If, like Richard Sherman in Aspen, you can't find a good provider, become one. Richard wanted an Internet connection. There was none available, so he got a bunch of like-minded people together and he started one called Infosphere. Try it! You might even make a profit on the deal.

Why Go Online?

I could write another book on this subject alone. I've been online for years, since long before the Web even existed. In those days it was a challenge to get into and out of another computer. There were almost no standards. Back then you never quite knew what the exit command was. I recall letting out a frustrated yelp and ripping my modem cord out of the wall on several occasions. The Internet had a well-deserved reputation for being a hackers' refuge — avenue of the abstruse. Well, not anymore.

The Web

The World Wide Web was first known as the WWW, but it was too hard to pronounce. Now it's just called the Web. The Web is a supersystem that operates across the Internet network. Think of the Web as the application and the Internet as the platform. The Web wasn't even a graphic environment when it first started. Now you turn on, tune in, and hyperjump to anywhere in the known populated cosmos. You can transact business and show your wares: music, video, still pictures, or prose (even poetry). Visit friends, leave your mark (as long as it's not indecent), and collect goodies — all from your keyboard. The Internet is still a good thing, even if it's not protected by our first amendment rights anymore. I'm hoping that by the time you read this, the ACLU (American Civil Liberties Union) has successfully challenged the ridiculous reactionary censorship imposed on the Internet by people who are only vaguely familiar with it — our legislators.

One thing about the Web: it puts everyone on a level playing field. Everything used to tilt toward the big guys. But they have a serious disadvantage on the Web. They are too big and too bogged down to deal with instant media. By using guerrilla marketing tactics, you can reach as many people as the big guys can, maybe more.

I recently read in *Inter@ctive* that corporations actually fling millions of dollars at agencies to mount their Web pages. I'll be honest: I find many personal pages more interesting. Guerrilla marketing is taking advantage of the fact that you're fast and tuned in. What you lack in financial clout you more than make up for in creativity, personality, speed, and motivation.

The Taiwanese brought big blue to its knees through guerrilla marketing. They took the PC, improved it, produced reliable hardware, marketed their clones aggressively in low-cost channels, and created a multibillion-dollar business. Though it robbed IBM of the platform they invented, that market would never have existed if left to IBM alone. IBM went elsewhere, but never achieved the market volume of the Taiwanese clones.

You can do something similar. With new Web-authoring packages you can set up a 3D site much faster than the big guys. Put your soul into it, make it more interesting, and update it daily. Fill your site with your own rich personality. Tune into the Web's pulse and link up to all the important services and hot link pages. You can do this because it's a labor of love — or desperation. For the folks at the big companies it's just a labor for salary. There's just a wee difference. Harness your passion to cut through the commercialness of the big sites.

A good example of guerrilla marketing is the shareware industry. Consider Procomm. It started as a shareware communications program. The developers endowed it with an enriched script language, lots of very efficient transfer protocols, and easy-to-use controls. And best of all they licensed it inexpensively.

Their commercial competition was expensive, harder to use, and only offered a few slow protocols like X-modem and Kermit. As corporations became aware of Procomm's superior scripting and transfer capabilities, they started to buy. Procomm became a kind of de facto industry standard and eventually went commercial.MThe point of this guerrilla success story is that anyone can make a big splash in the global pond. You can now mount a world-wide advertising campaign for a few dollars. You can show your wares and attract people via hot links to the popular watering holes such as the 3D Site at `www.3dsite.com/3dsite/` and GWEB at `www2.cinenet.net/GWEB/` (see Figures 36-1 and 36-2).

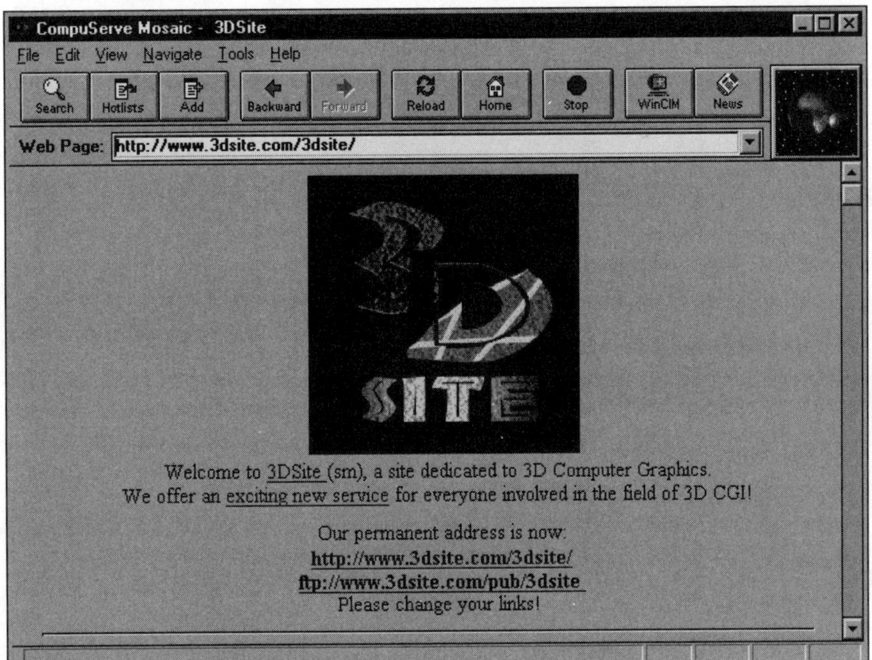

Figure 36-1: The 3D Site

Figure 36-2: The GWEB site

What's on the Web?

Let me wave my wand a bit and divide up the Web into realms of inquiry. Allakazzam: You can put things on the Web, you can get things from the Web, and you can exchange information on the Web.

Searching the Web

I've found a few salubrious goodies on the Web by searching the shareware.com site at `www.shareware.com`, which is usually listed in the Netcom Search page (see Figure 36-3).

Shareware authors probably have to pay to list their products at the shareware.com site, so who knows which programs will be there when you read this book. However, you can always search for shareware in other places by using one of the many search indexes available such as Yahoo, Lycos, or Alta Vista. When you conduct a search, the search engine examines a ba-zillion Web pages and attempts to match your search by keyword(s). Table 36-1 lists several Web search indexes. The "address" is also called a Uniform Resource Locator or URL.

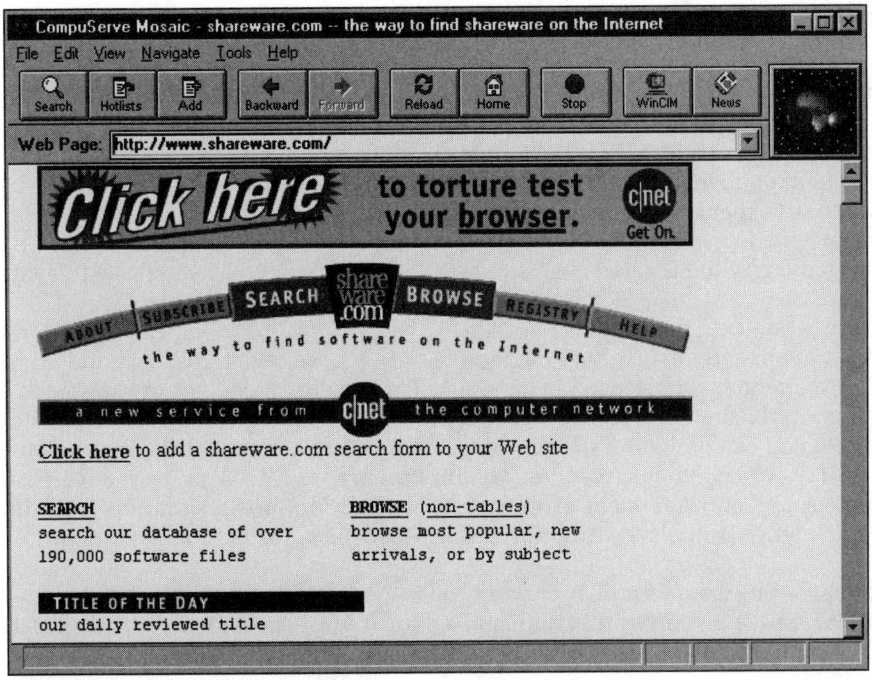

Figure 36-3: The shareware.com site

Table 36-1
Web search indexes

Name	*Address*
All4One Search Machine	`http://easypage.com/all4one/`
Alta Vista	`http://altavista.digital.com/`
Excite!	`http://www.excite.com/`
InfoSeek	`http://www.infoseek.com/`
Lycos	`http://www.lycose.com/`
Magellan	`http://www.mckinley.com/`
Savvy Search	`http://savvy.cs.colostate.edu:2000/`
WebCrawler	`http://www.webcrawler.com/`
Yahoo	`http://www.yahoo.com/`

Uploading Programs

Virtually all of the artists featured in this book besides myself were discovered on the Web. Notice how it happened and what it can accomplish. First they were active on the trueSpace mailing list. Then they began to upload their images onto the original trueSpace FTP site at Netnet. Bill Ehrendreich at `iwneu@packeland.com` was kind enough to manage that old FTP site and it eventually got hot-linked to other sites that fed people in to look at all the magic that was available. The Netnet site is available but no longer maintained. Much of its function has been taken over by the Caligari Web site at `www.caligari.com` (you'll see this later in Figure 36-6).

What happened next is that I made note of the more talented artists and asked if they'd like to be showcased in my book. Those who agreed got to have their images published and distributed worldwide. My book contains references to where you can find more of their work. Many people reading this book will tune in, and if they like the images, some will hire them to create Web sites, advertising images, and entertainment products. It's a genuine win/win situation. Everybody gets to solve problems without throwing obscene sums of money at them.

By uploading examples of your work to various sites that will display them, you can actually become world famous in a short time — provided your work attracts attention. That's easy: just be brilliant and make it irresistible.

Another chapter of the upload story is Rob Bryerton. He kindly uploaded his early versions of Exploder for us to try for free. We helped him work through some bugs and such, but it was always a solid instrument. It is such a fun and amazing little program that thousands of people downloaded it. Rob kept adding capability to the program and now offers it as shareware. The price is extremely reasonable. Because he has low advertising costs, he passes his savings on to you. An equivalent product for 3D Studio or LightWave runs several hundred dollars.

Rob is now well-known worldwide, not for his day job (which has little to do with 3D graphics), but for terrific programming skills and an innovative approach to getting particle physics into trueSpace2.

The point? Online generosity does pay off. A lot of luscious techno-stuff is free (or cheap) online. Being a good Internet citizen means making your own contribution to the Internet if and when you can. After all, the spirit of the Internet is give-and-take.

Downloading Programs

In Chapter 34 I talked about all the wonderful geometry available on the Web. There are so many other goodies out there for 3D types to download and use, the following summary can't even scratch the surface, but I'll try. Goodies break down into several categories:

- ✦ Support programs
- ✦ Models

- Textures
- Images
- Sound clips
- Other programs

Support Programs

On the Web you'll find dozens of programs you can use with trueSpace. Some are converters to change unreadable formats into formats you can import into tS2, thus expanding the number of models you can use. Some programs, such as Ian Firth's star field generator, create textures. Ian's even creates rough nebulas. You'll discover PhotoShop plug-ins that work in tS2, and you'll find standalone fractal texture generators such as FracInit. You'll find terrain builders, metaball object modelers (look for the blob modeler), and lots more. As a rule, anything that creates a model and outputs DXF or 3DS format is compatible with tS2.

Image Processing Programs

Here are several image processing programs that you should check out:

- **vugraf13.zip:** A versatile image database with thumbnails featuring viewers for ten different image formats.
- **morph16e.zip:** A morphing program that takes two images and morphs them together, outputting a video sequence. A fun way to get started in visual special effects.
- **hcvt11.zip:** This drag-and-drop image file format converter is easy to use. It's very useful if you don't have PhotoShop or its equivalent for exporting your images.
- **himage11.zip:** This image editor uses scripts for automated processing of your picture files. It's especially useful when you want to process a sequence of files.
- **wlabv30b.zip:** This is a beta of WinLab 3.0. I haven't used it, but I hear it's a useful suite of image processing tools.
- **imorg001.zip:** Yet another image organizer program that lets you attach all sorts of information to each image.

Paint Programs

- **Matisseg.exe:** This is a grayscale-only version of the Matisse paint program. It's very diverse and useful for making bump maps if you don't have a fancy paint program.
- **aslpaint.zip:** Limited to 256 colors, this program can be useful for limited palette work such as what is used in games.
- **fracpain.zip:** Fractal Paint 1.04 is a very simple but useful paint program.
- **fraint18.zip:** Version 17.8 or so of this famous and amazingly diverse fractal image generator. Use it to create fractal clouds that you can use for planet

surfaces, or convert to grayscale for alpha channels or use for shark skin or sea bottom. Generate beautiful /colorful/exotic backgrounds for your projects. This one is the best.

3D Terrain Programs

Some of these programs can be used with Digital Elevation Models (DEM) files that are available from the USGS (United States Geological Survey) over the Web. The programs enable you to create nifty 3D landscapes that you can use as backgrounds. If a program allows you to create fly-bys, you can use the fly-bys as animated backgrounds to achieve cool effects.

- **3dem14.zip:** A program for displaying digital elevation models from the USGS. These models are available at the USGS Web site showing much of the world and showing Mars. You can make some interesting backgrounds from DEMs.
- **land351.zip:** A landscape visualization application for creating wild landscapes for use as backgrounds in tS2.
- **landa100.zip:** 3D landscape visualization and virtual reality simulation program.

TAKE NOTE

Keep in mind that terrain models use a lot of polygons. You can save lots of aggravation by rendering them in their native program and then using the image as a background for simple animations. If you have a lot of camera movement, you'll have to export your animations as DXF files for use in tS2, but your render time goes way up.

Other 3D Programs

- **3ds-us.zip:** A utility for creating stereoscopic 3D images.
- **polyw32s.zip:** The PolyForm v1.01 demo allows you to convert a wide range of 3D formats and manipulate objects such as reducing the size of polygons. You can also use it to create logos and other objects.
- **viscom09.zip:** Create 3D slides for viewing on your color monitor.

Audio Processing

- **gwave303.zip:** This is a handy audio editor/recorder/player that you can use to create your sound tracks. It's one of the programs that you can use to convert various sound file formats to .WAV.
- **effect.zip:** This is a really cool audio F/X generator. It allows you to adjust sound envelopes and mix various base sounds to create a wide range of effects from lasers to creaking doors to belches.
- **wavbrowz.zip:** Organize your sounds and browse through them easily with this easy sound database.
- **m4w230sx.zip:** This is a full-bore MOD player. MODs are music or sound files that are popular in Europe and offer lots of possible background music for your animation. You'll find lots of MOD files if you scan for them.

- **turtle11.zip:** A program to directly convert raw CD sound data into .WAV format. This can be very useful for capturing sounds for your tracks.

Sound Files

Sound collections are widely available and quite useful. Many sound files are in the public domain and are free for use (be polite, though, and do still get permission). Some sound files based on commercial music, however, must be licensed for use in commercial projects. To be on the safe side, never use them in commercial projects unless you get permission.

- **aliens.zip:** A collection of neat sound bites from the movie *Aliens*.
- **theshadw.zip:** These are great old clips from the original *The Shadow* radio show.
- **apollo11a.zip and apollo11h.zip:** A series of sound archives that feature communications during the famous July 1969 mission. Different parts of these files can be used, filtered, and overlaid onto your sound track to create a space comm atmosphere.
- **simpwav1.zip and simpwav9.zip:** A series of sound bite archives featuring Homer and the gang from *The Simpsons* TV show.
- **hindnbrg.zip:** I'm not sure how you'd use these, but they're actual radio sounds from the 1939 crash of the Hindenberg. Let your imagination fly — even if the airship won't.
- **treksnds.zip:** One of many, many collections of sound bites from the Star Trek series. You'll find others by scanning for "trek" from all the different series and movies.
- **warwrld1.zip and warwrld3.zip:** A series of archives featuring the original radio version of *War of the Worlds* with Orson Wells.
- **wolfwavs.zip:** Neat sounds from the Wolfenstein 3D game.

An extensive array of programs are lurking out there. This list is but a nick in the corner of a large universe. Many of them are shareware. Please remember to send your dimes to the owners in appreciation for their work.

Models

The Web offers many sites you can search to find models in all shapes, formats, and sizes.

Avalon

WEB CONNECTION

Avalon is the first place you should look when you need a model that you can't create yourself or don't have time to create (see Figure 36-4). Avalon's address is `ftp://avalon.datalabs.com/pub/`. You can download many files in different formats. Remember that one of tS2's strong points is its ability to import many different types of models. If you don't find what you're looking for at Avalon, you can start prowling the links you'll find there.

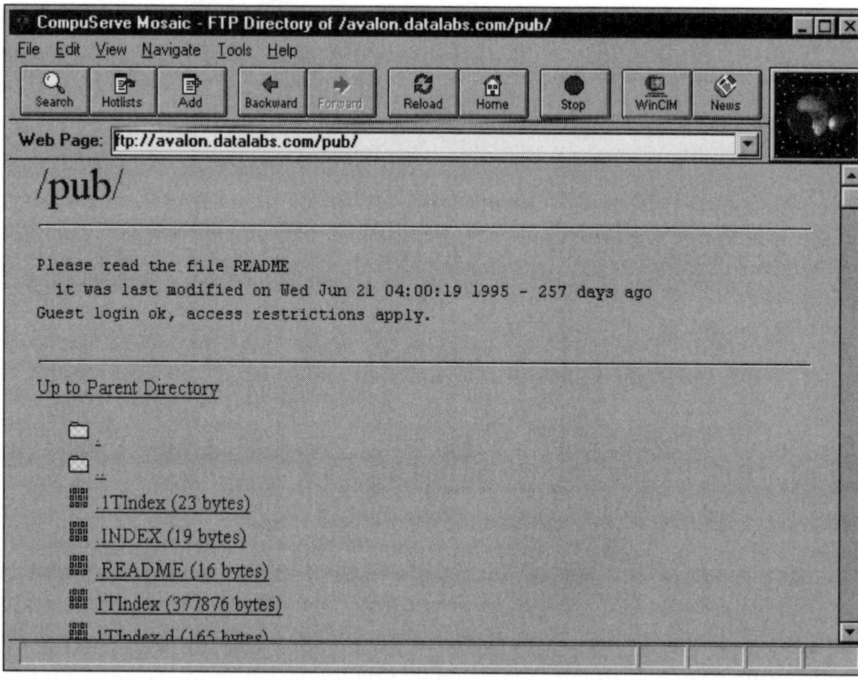

Figure 36-4: Avalon is where you'll find models that you can download.

Computer Cafe

This is a new site called Computer Cafe (see Figure 36-5). It's terrific, and adds new links daily. You'll find a gallery of works, current animation projects, conversion routines, viewing programs, animation tips and tricks, and lots of new meshes. They pour some of their own high-quality digital effects and 3D animation into the pot as well. It's easy to find what you're looking for because they have color thumbnail previews of all the mesh objects.

In addition, you'll find that those of us who use LightWave are intensely fanatical about this instrument. The Computer Cafe has numerous Web sites with model archives. They load painlessly into tS2, so these sites are for you too.

POWER TIP: It's undocumented, but trueSpace will load the new LightWave file format even though it won't recognize it in default mode. Use the *.* option to see the new LightWave object files and select the one you want. It'll load just fine.

Textures and Images

I covered a lot of this topic in the chapter on textures (Chapter 11), but as a final note, look for textures by scanning for "3D objects," then looking at those locations for textures. I've found this process often works and you often get interesting results. Another trick I have is to scan Lycos for "graphics" and get a lot of artsy sites with neat textures I capture for personal use. I screen-capture them with Media Studio's capture module.

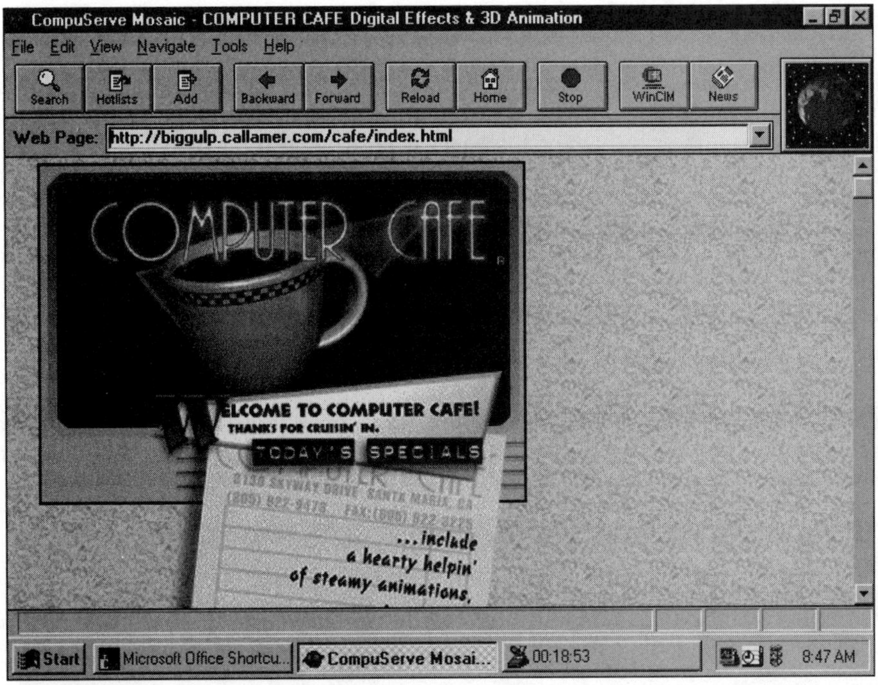

Figure 36-5: The Computer Cafe site

Sound Clips

Again, if you're creative in your use of the search engines you can find almost any sound you want on the Web — including a few very disgusting ones that come in handy if your demo is really boring. If you want old-time radio clips, sounds of vehicles, cows, and frogs — you name it, you'll hear it.

Here's one approach. Let's say you need the sound of an old train coming into a station. Look for train-oriented sites. One of them is bound to have the sounds of an old steam locomotive available. Train buffs seem to love those old sounds in stereo.

Use the same approach for everything from circus sounds to astronaut voices from space. The latter make a good background for scenes of spaceships approaching a station. Just put them low in the background with some music over the top, just enough to imply communication. Sounds come in many formats from lo-fi RealAudio files to hi-fi .WAV files with several others in between. Some audio edit programs can understand just about any of them except the former, which can be played and recorded to .WAV format.

Other Programs

Well you can fill this section in. There are so many conversion programs, image generators, fractal engines, and image manipulation programs out there I can't even begin to cover them. Explore, and you'll be rewarded.

Presenting: trueSpace on the Web

I find it fascinating to look at the different kinds of pages that reference trueSpace. They range from simple personal pages to fancy corporate ones. Many trueSpace2 professionals are already in business and advertising their trueSpace skills on the Web. I've done a little Net surfing and thought I'd share some of these finds with you. Of course they may be gone by the time you get there — such is the nature of the Web. But you can always find the latest and greatest by doing a Web search with one of the smart engines found in your Web browser's search menu.

Caligari's Web Page

`http://www.caligari.com`

At Caligari's home page you'll find upgrades to products, models in COB format, scenes, textures, and announcements (see Figure 36-6). As I write this, you can also register for the latest beta of Fountain as well.

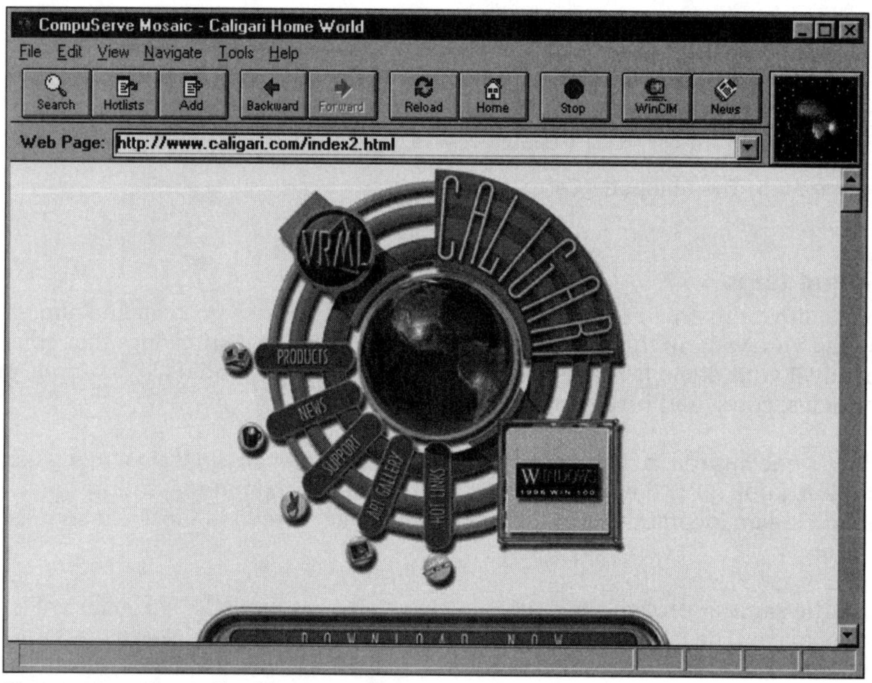

Figure 36-6: The Caligari home page

You can hot-link to places such as:

- ✦ The Unofficial trueSpace Tips page
- ✦ Dub's trueSpace F/X page: Keep your eye on this spot for new special effects. You can find samples of Dub's work on the CD-ROM (under the \fx sub-directory).
- ✦ Mark Jeffers' 3D Resource Page

- ✦ Destination: Cyberspace
- ✦ Robots in 3D
- ✦ LavaMind Games & Entertainment: This is a computer entertainment company located in San Francisco, which focuses on developing original content rather than licensing existing stories, characters, or other material. Their Web site is packed with graphics, short stories, magazine reviews, lists of independent filmmakers, a Virtual Pet Cemetery, Molten Magazine, shareware, links to other hot sites, and the Galaxy of Gogg.
- ✦ The kinté space: cyberverse for the masses where you'll find plenty of poetry with graphics created in trueSpace.
- ✦ Naked Hoof: Bill Anderson's site has lots of interesting tS2 stuff such as textures and images. You'll also find a collection of unique sound files.

Shane Davison's trueSpace2 Page

`http://www.cs.uregina.ca/~daviso/truspace/truspace.html`

Shane Davison is a trueSpace legend. Visit him here and say hi for me (see Figure 36-7). Also check out his artwork and links. Shane's page is also a great place to get information on VRML. He keeps an FAQ (answers to Frequently Asked Questions) there online that will help you better understand Fountain's underlying language. You can join the tSML (trueSpace Mailing List) by clicking on a link here. When you click on the hot link to join, simply type "subscribe" without the quotes, no subject, and send. This is not explained on the page.

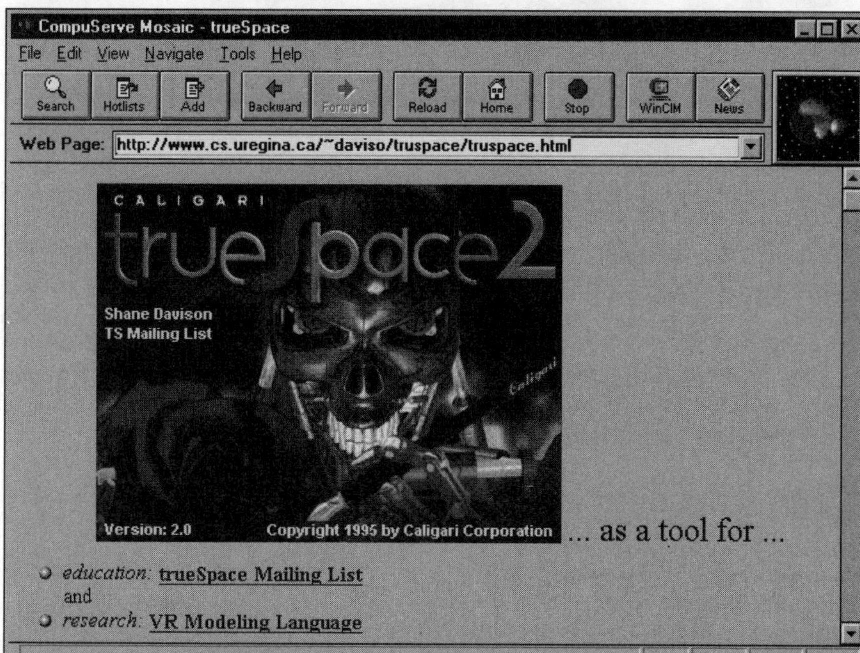

Figure 36-7: Shane Davison's home page

If you get really stuck on something you might even send Shane a note. He's helped hundreds of people learn trueSpace2.

The Ego Wall

http://www.realtime.net/~dcampbel/ts_tips.html

The Ego Wall is David Campbell's very useful page (see Figure 36-8). It contains the trueSpace Tips Page as well as a terrific art gallery, and the largest collection of 3D-related links I've found.

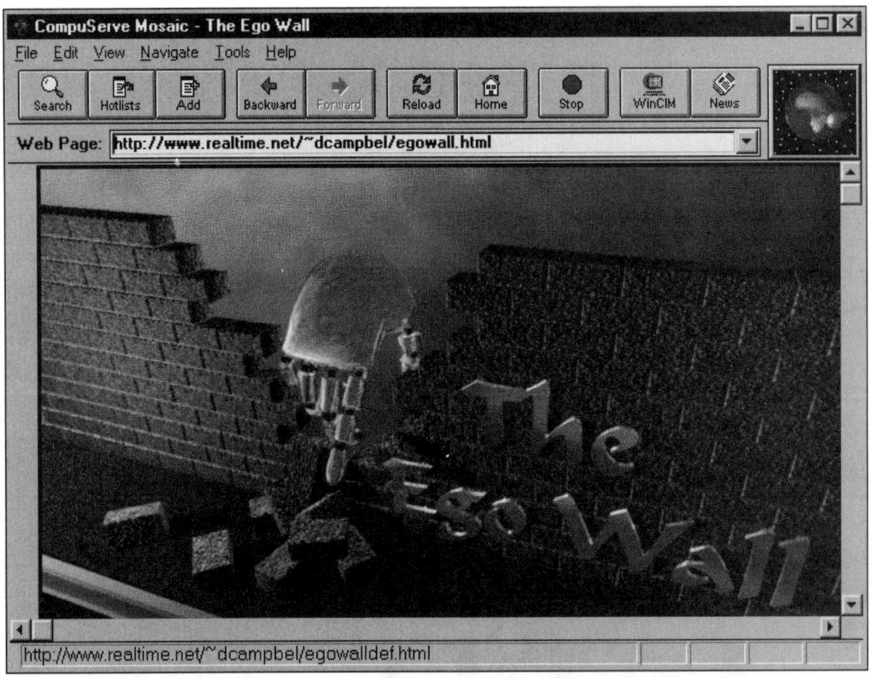

Figure 36-8: The Ego Wall

As for the Tips Page, it covers ideas that aren't covered in the trueSpace documentation. The page compiles usage tips and tricks from the trueSpace Mailing List (tSML) going back to the list's inception in December 1994. Dave feels the page is actually owned and authored by many people. (You can also see Dave Campbell's Guitar in the color section.)

Dave has the most current and detailed list of tS user home pages I've seen. It includes many of the people who contributed to this book:

- ✦ Ed Emerson — Ed's artwork, opinions, and political views.
- ✦ Todd Barnes — Here you'll find Todd's visual résumé and more links.
- ✦ Shane Davison — Shane's page is described elsewhere.

- ✦ Vytas Gaizutis — A strange and wonderful page filled with interesting artwork.
- ✦ Michael Nowicki — Here you'll find a tS2 art gallery with an emphasis on UFO, science fiction, and mystical subjects, plus some interesting information on antiquities.
- ✦ Aaron Hill — Aaron is a teenager who's already an accomplished musician and tS2 graphic artist. Visit his page and see what he's up to. Best if you have a MIDI player attached to your browser.
- ✦ Darrell Palmiter — Another one of those active Virginia Beach, Virginia, families that use tS2. More on him later.
- ✦ Jon Winchester — Jonno, as he's known by his friends, is a tutor at the Central Institute of Technology based in Wellington, New Zealand. He's become totally absorbed by 3D (tS2 of course) and digital video. Here you'll find his images, and he's been working on some tutorials that may be available by the time you read this.
- ✦ David Henion — David lives in Tokyo, Japan and is employed by Salomon Brothers Asia Ltd. as a UNIX systems administrator. He's developed a love of 3D graphics and has his gallery of excellent art here along with some good links. You'll also probably find David on the tSML. Check out his traditional Japanese dining room with a table setting. Also check out his animations.
- ✦ Robert Stephen Rodgers — Robert is a talented 3D artist who works in tS2. I wish I'd found him in time to include some of his work in our color section. He's currently a student of computer science, having completed a BA in the Japanese language. Robert also does system administration work, but his real love is 3D graphics.
- ✦ Tom Repasky — Tom is a wildly creative artist and musician and a managing engineer as well — a very rare combination. This is his world. His pages have even won the "Too Cool" Web award. Here you'll find galleries of both his digital and acrylic art work and some interesting links.
- ✦ Bryan Wilhite — Bryan puts up the kinté space: cyberverse for the masses, a place where you can enjoy tS2 art and poetry.

In addition, the Ego Wall links to nearly 100 additional places such as *3D Design* magazine, Adobe, and even Digital Domain.

RSS trueSpace Resource Page

`http://ourworld.compuserve.com/homepages/RSS_INC/`

Terry Cotant was the first person to distribute tS1 and he's written a ton of stuff on trueSpace (see Figure 36-9). He's good.

On this page you'll find a phone number to call if you get stuck while creating something in tS2. This number is there primarily for Terry's customers, but he will help others if he doesn't get too swamped. If everyone calls, he'll have to start charging. Maybe he should anyway. I think his service is very needed, and I would have paid a few dollars to be helped out every time I got stuck learning tS.

Figure 36-9: The RSS trueSpace Resource page

As I write, Terry is assembling an all-trueSpace demo tape that you might be able to get in on. Terry also builds excellent trueSpace2 optimized workstations loaded with such software as Speed Razor, Fractal Design Painter, and many more at discount prices. Terry has links to:

✦ Digital Processing Systems Home Page — DPS makes the excellent home and professional NTSC (TV) output cards. I've mentioned the Perception board in this book.

✦ In:Sync Home Page — You've read about their products such as Razor Pro and Speed Razor. Here you can pick up new transitions and filters as they are posted.

✦ Matrox Home Page — Matrox makes a video card called the Millennium that allegedly accelerates 3DR but I've not seen any drivers. They are excellent cards though.

✦ Digital Audio Labs Home Page — Another great place to find super high quality digital audio cards for high-end use in the video production of your animations.

✦ Turtle Beach Systems Home Page — If you're into quality digital audio, this is the professional's choice. The DSP (Digital Signal Processing) cards such as the Tahiti can keep your sound track in sync for long runs because they lift the burden from your CPU and keep up with the video. Lots of interesting stuff here.

Mark Jeffers 3D Resource Page

`http://members.aol.com/mjx1936140/3dpage/3dpage.html`

Here you'll find links to many trueSpace-related pages as well as some of Mark Jeffers' own excellent artwork (see Figure 36-10).

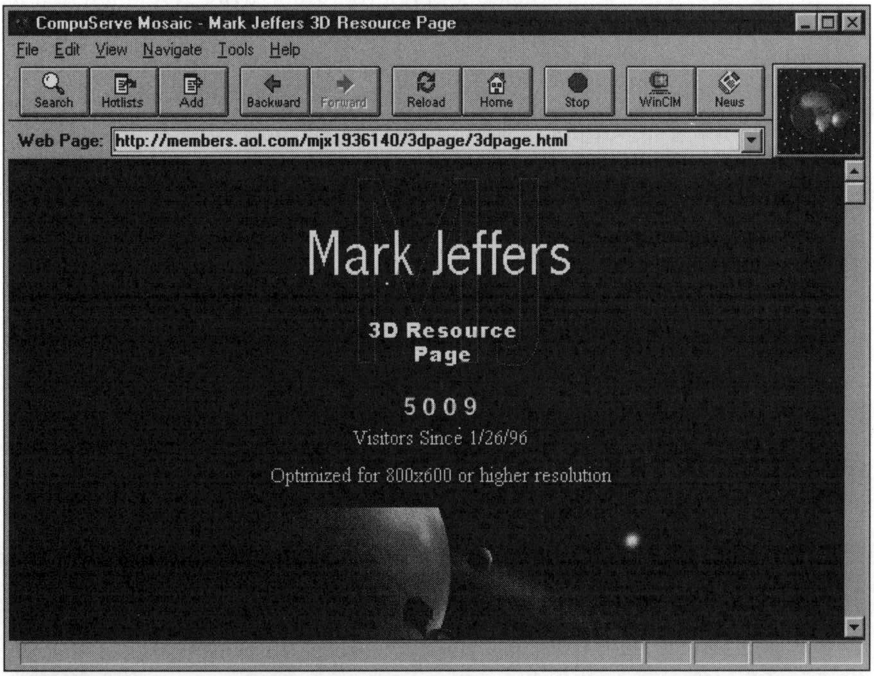

Figure 36-10: Marc Jeffers 3D Resource page

You'll also find a nice collection of materials libraries that you can download and use directly with tS2. For more textures check out Mark's huge set of links to other texture locations including, among many others:

- ✦ Clipart — This is a subdirectory of the DTP Jump site that has links to a huge number of public domain clip art sites. Many of the sites offer clip art that can be used as 3D textures.
- ✦ The Nebulae Web! — This is an index page of astronomical photographs that you can use to project realistic nebulas onto your backgrounds.
- ✦ The KPT Backgrounds Archive — Here you'll find archives of seamless backgrounds created with Kai's Power Tools (KPT). There are also tutorials on how to make seamless background tiles. Some good sky tiles lurk here and you can always use those. Many are best used as backgrounds for Web pages.
- ✦ Mesh Mart Texture Catalog — This page is a listing of FTP and WWW sites that have archives of textures and materials.

- ✦ Lunar and Planetary Lab U. Arizona — This is a great FTP site, but you have to know to go to the \pub\images directory to find a ton of useful planet and moon images to use in texturing your spheres.
- ✦ Art on the Net: Visual Artists — This is a great place to visit and to collect textures from. Many artists are on display, each with their own gallery or home page. A lot of it is digital and photographic work and much of it would make interesting textures. There is courage here... they kept their nudes online... bravo.
- ✦ Textures — This is a very detailed tutorial on texture mapping that explains how it all works, with detailed illustrations of each process.

3D & Robots

`http://csbh.csnet.net/~cerebus/`

This is Bob Fergusson's home page that compares trueSpace space art with Imagine space art (see Figure 36-11). Bob starts out: "Since my main interest is in both 3-D computer graphics and animation and a childhood fascination with robots and 'neat space stuff', it is natural, I guess, that the two interests should find common ground." And this is where it comes together for him with some very fine illustrations. He doesn't have many links, but he does have one to Harry Chang's page where you can get some neat models. Harry's pretty famous for his Star Wars models too.

Figure 36-11: Bob Fergusson's 3D & Robots page

Destination: CyberSpace

http://www.blvl.igs.net/~vanburen/

This is a game site designed by Mark Van Buren. It has much of its environment modeled and rendered in trueSpace (see Figure 36-12). You'll find a link to a second game site called Bounty Hunter. The images are wonderful and will give you some ideas on what can be done with tS2 on a professional level. Come and give it a try and see specifically how tS2 has been used in a fancy interactive game site.

Figure 36-12: The Destination: Cyberspace page

3DSite

http://www.lightside.com/3dsite/

I find this to be one of the most useful sites around (see Figure 36-13). It has a dense set of hot links to 3D-related sites all over the world, as well as forums on topics of interest, job postings, and services.

Services

The special services that you'll find at this site are extremely useful. For example, I first met Kathy White when she participated on a panel on digital lighting. That led to our collaboration. Talent Hunter is a new way for companies to post job listings and find employees. It's an interactive job board. Other services include:

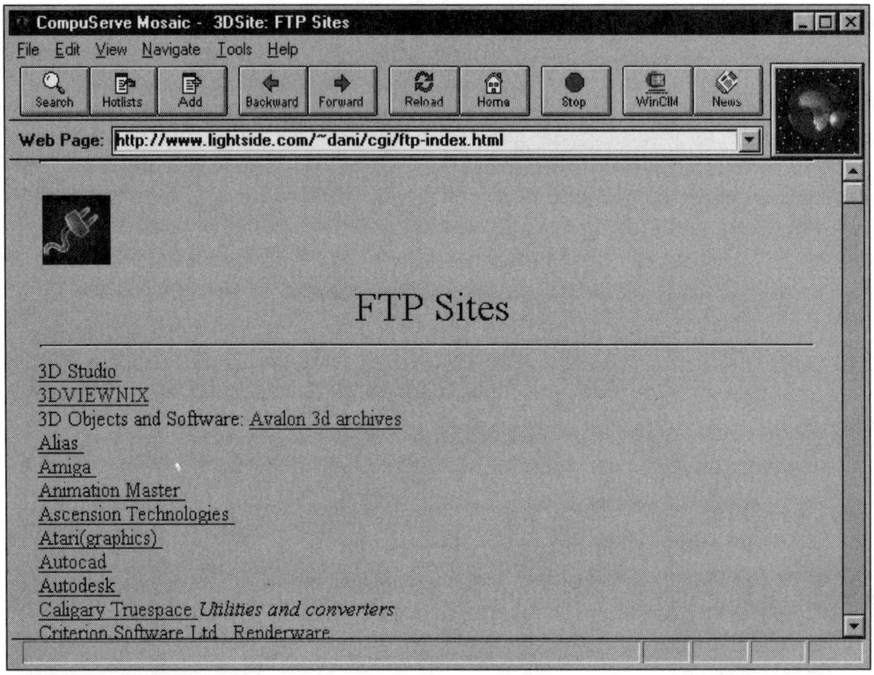

Figure 36-13: FTP Links at 3DSite

- ✦ 3DSite's IRC Panels on Computer Animation: An ongoing series of panels devoted to computer animation.
- ✦ Model Market: Alpha release of a 3D Model Store based on voluntary contributions.
- ✦ User Center: A place where you can steer 3DSite toward your goals.

CGI Information: Table of Contents

This is only the index of categories for hot links. There are literally hundreds of them. I use this place as a jumping-off spot when I'm working and contacting various sites to get information for my 3D columns in Animation and 3D Artist.

- ✦ CGI and Animation Literature, References, and Discussions — Here's where you should look for any FAQ on 3D that you might need. Look here in general; you'll find ones you didn't even know you needed.
- ✦ Conferences — Just about every 3D- or CGI-related conference in the world is listed here along with seminars and other related events.
- ✦ Distributors — This is really vendors of CGI related stuff.
- ✦ Entertainment Companies — You'll find dozens of sites of entertainment companies from major studios to game producers here. Look around to see what the latest products are.

- FTP Sites — All sorts of sites for directly downloading 3D-related programs and material.
- Hardware Firms — Need motion capture equipment? Or a 3D digitizer? This is the category for you.
- Hardware Products — Same here. Find out about new hardware availability.
- Images and Movies — Here you'll find more than a hundred archives of 3D movie clips. There are contests, home pages, educational institutions, and other repositories. Check out a bunch for ideas.
- Labs — These are mostly dozens of scientifically oriented CGI labs with interesting images, papers, and animations you can check out.
- Motion Picture Screen Cartoonist and Affiliated Optical Electronic and Graphic Arts, Local 839 IATSE (California) — This is the union that represents 3D artists at some of the major studios. Many are non-union. Find out about union membership benefits here.
- Newsgroups — Direct links to many newsgroups of interest to 3D types.
- Organizations — Links to computer societies such as SIGGRAPH.
- Production Houses — This is a good place to do reconnaissance before applying to one of these companies. Here you can often get a feel for the company and its people so you can orient your pitch better.
- Production Support Services — These are service agencies that will do motion capture and film transfer and the like.
- Projects — This is actually one of the most interesting sets of links. Here you are directed to ongoing 3D projects in many disciplines from mathematics to virtual reality.
- Publications — Here are more than 20 online magazines from *3D Artist* to *Intelligent Gamer* and the *Daily Spectrum* where you can keep up on Morph's Outpost.
- Résumés — As it says, here is where people like you post their résumés and personal page links. (Figure 36-14 shows Adam Shiffman's résumé home page as a sample.)
- Software Firms — From Adobe to Xaos Tools you'll find more than a hundred links here.
- Software Packages — Here you will find hundreds of links to software package Web sites by platform and operating system. I find this very useful for exploring newly published software. If it does 3D, it's most likely here. Check out the Texture Magic procedural texture engine that uses POV ray under the NT operating system.
- Virtual Reality — This is an index of all sorts of virtual reality topics with links to each. You'll find projects, hardware, software, and VR Web sites.

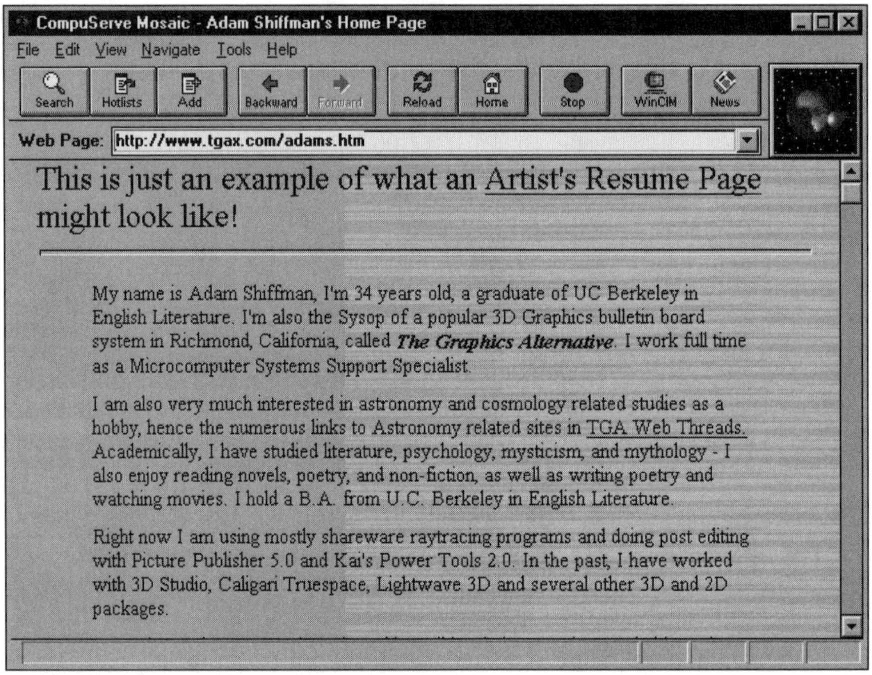

Figure 36-14: Adam Shiffman's résumé home page. I'd put an image right up front.

- ✦ Virtual Reality Modeling Language — If you want to try out the 3D Web, you'll find many links here, but you'll need a 3D browser such as Fountain attached. You'll also find tons of papers, technical discussions, and demos of things having to do with VRML.
- ✦ Volunteering and Other Opportunities — If you want to donate your time and make contacts and help out worthy causes, look here. Also, the producer of the Mind's Eye series was looking for works of digital animation for a new series. You get paid too.
- ✦ WWW-VR virtual reality on the World Wide Web — 3D Web viewers and places to go and view.

This list only gives you a limited idea of what's here. You could literally spend a week just jumping from interesting link to interesting link.

3D Artist Magazine

`http://www.3dartist.com/`

This is a great site where you can read current and back issues of *Tess* (*Tessellation Times*), the e-zine of 3D. You can also check out stereo 3D images (see Figure 36-15). Here you'll find a calendar of 3D events, job listings, artist availability listings, and more.

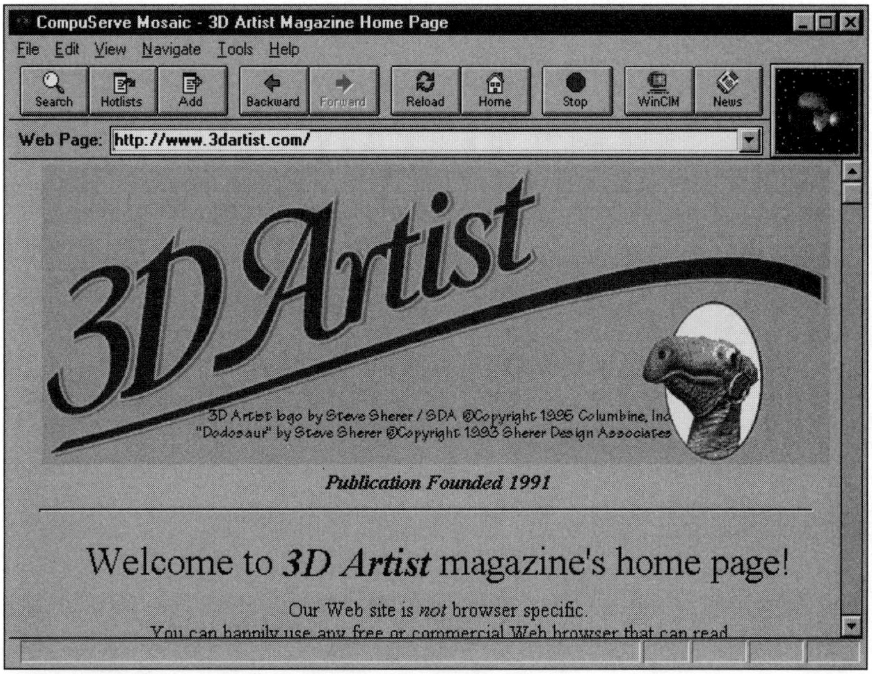

Figure 36-15: The *3D Artist* magazine home page

This page also sports about a dozen hyperlinks to 3D-related sites similar to others described earlier. Subscribe to the hard copy version as well — there's a discount coupon in the back of this book.

Maddog's Studio

`http://www.maddog.com/`

Maddog calls her/his studio "an information mothership for virtual worlds." Here you'll find all sorts of wonderful illustrations, and a treasure-trove of links to interesting and useful sites (see Figure 36-16). I mention it here because Maddog's Studio uses tS2 and it's one of those places I put on my bookmark list.

In Maddog's Studio you'll find links to:

- ✦ Political issues of interest to 3D and Web worms
- ✦ Publications and newsletters
- ✦ Demos, especially of MUD (multi-user doman) stuff
- ✦ Legal issues facing Web world developers

Figure 36-16: Maddog's Studio

Peoria Astronomical Society

`http://bradley.bradley.edu/~dware/`

This is an all-out astronomy-buff organization. I include it here because they exhibit trueSpace2's usefulness in illustrating a Web page (see Figure 36-17). Visit here to get some ideas for your own page, and say hi.

If you're into astronomy, the Peoria Astronomical Society page offers more than 50 links to astronomy-related sites, many of which have astronomical images that are great for backgrounds in your illustrations and animations.

Mike Morrison's Home Page

`http://www.alike.com/mike.html`

Mike Morrison has been active in computer graphics and interactive entertainment for the past 11 years. He also considers himself quite a hotdogger on a surfboard (see Figure 36-18). He writes for trade publications such as *Computer Graphics World*, *Digital Video World*, *Video Systems*, and C*omputer Pictures* magazine. Most important to me, Mike wrote *Becoming a Computer Animator* (SAMS Publishing, 1994), which started a lot of people on their way with trueSpace1.

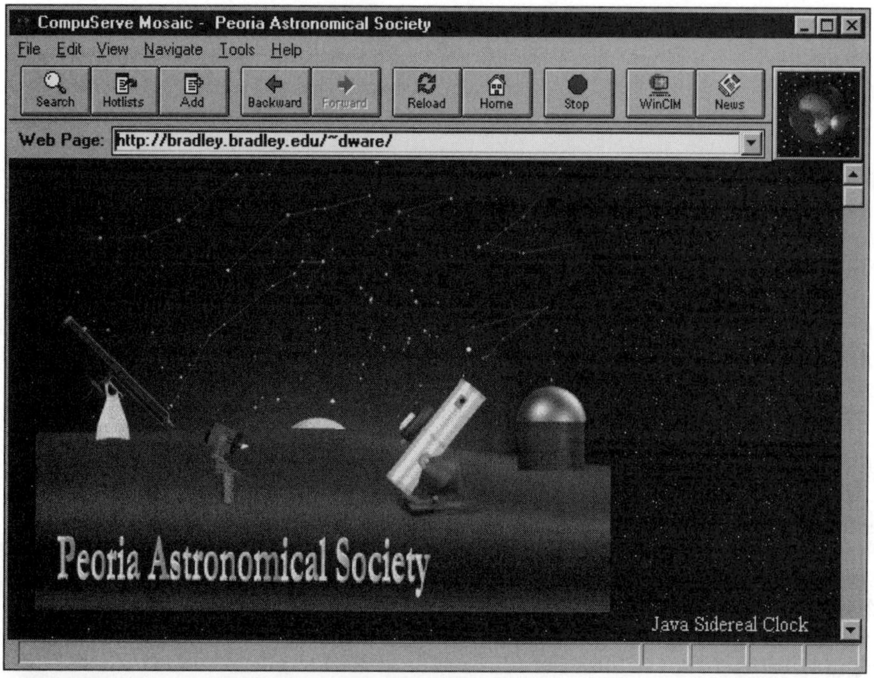

Figure 36-17: The Peoria Astronomical Society page

Figure 36-18: Mike Morrison's home page

Look around — you'll find short descriptions of each of Mike's books with a link to the publisher's page on it. There are also about 25 or more links to magazines and other 3D sites. Mike encouraged me to write this book, so if you stop by, say hang ten for me.

The Palmiter Family

http://www.paracom.com/~palmiter/

A number of families in the Virginia Beach area have created home pages that reference trueSpace, and this is but one (see Figure 36-19). Generally they introduce you to their families and interests and tell you a little about their town. This one has a link to Webcrawler and listings of pages for local businesses. They used tS2 to create their Web pages, and Darrell enjoys using it as a hobby.

A New Trend

There's a new trend on the Web that may make sense. It's a little expensive, but not bad as a business expense. It's the online creative directory. There are several: some cost and some are free. The best-looking one I've seen is for graphic artists of all sorts, but it has a digital artists section. It's called Art World Online at http://artworld.ddwi.com and claims to have worldwide affiliations (see Figure 36-20).

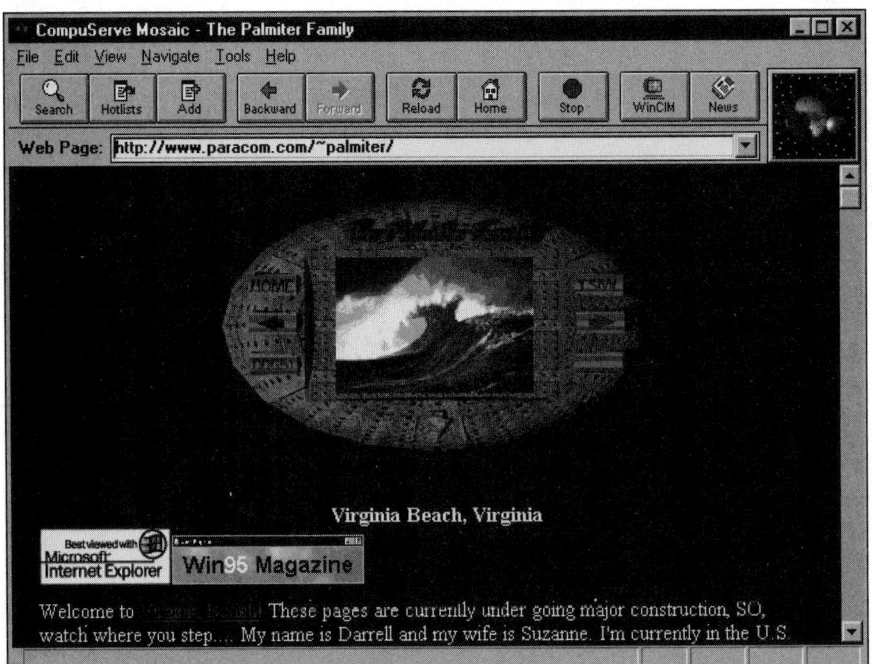

Figure 36-19: The Palmiter Family's home page

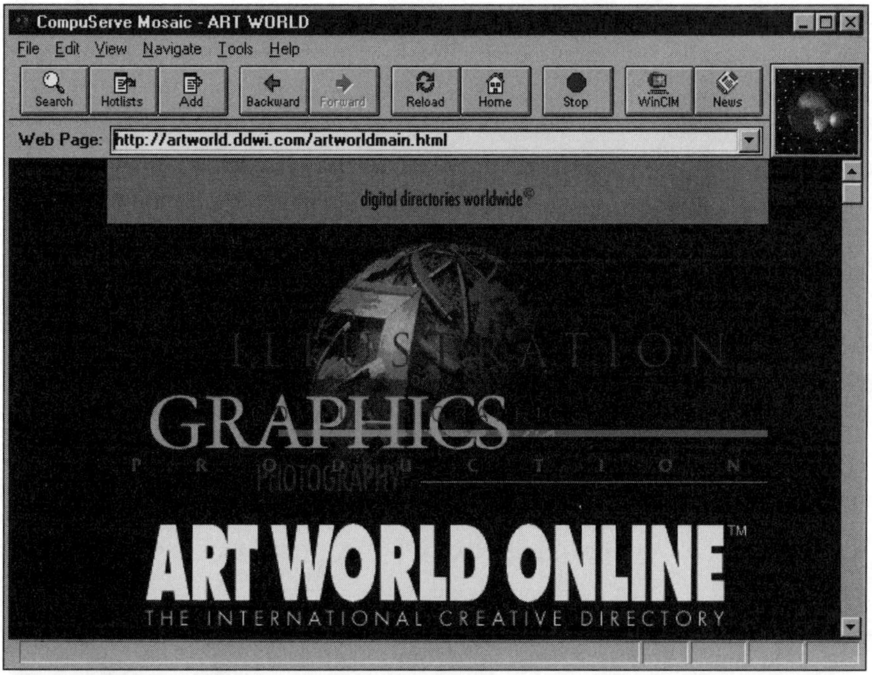

Figure 36-20: Art World Online's home page

I highly recommend you jump to this site because the artwork that's displayed is exceptional. The artists who are represented can change their work at any time, so updating the material is an advantage. Current subscription fees for gallery space are four illustrations per page for about $85.00 a month for the first page and $25.00 for each additional page. The price is reasonable and includes scanning your art work if it's not already in electronic form. You can also get a free listing of just your name and company and address, but trust me, it's not as compelling as looking at your lovely art. Art World Online will be promoting its users to art directors via advertisements and by sending out mouse pads with their Uniform Resource Locator (URL) address to relevant people.

Caligari will also show your wares, but at no charge. They are willing to set up your own page at the official Caligari site if you produce really fine images. There is no charge for this and they are linked to many related sites.

Animation World Network (AWN)

`http://www.awn.com`

This is part creative directory — but it's more. This site provides information on all aspects of animation including traditional cel, stop motion, digital animation, and independent animation from all over the world. At the time of this writing, this site was still under construction, as you can see in Figure 36-21. Wendy Jackson, one of the site's developers, used to be with ASIFA (the international animated film society) — see Appendix D for addresses of various animation societies) and she knows animation in depth.

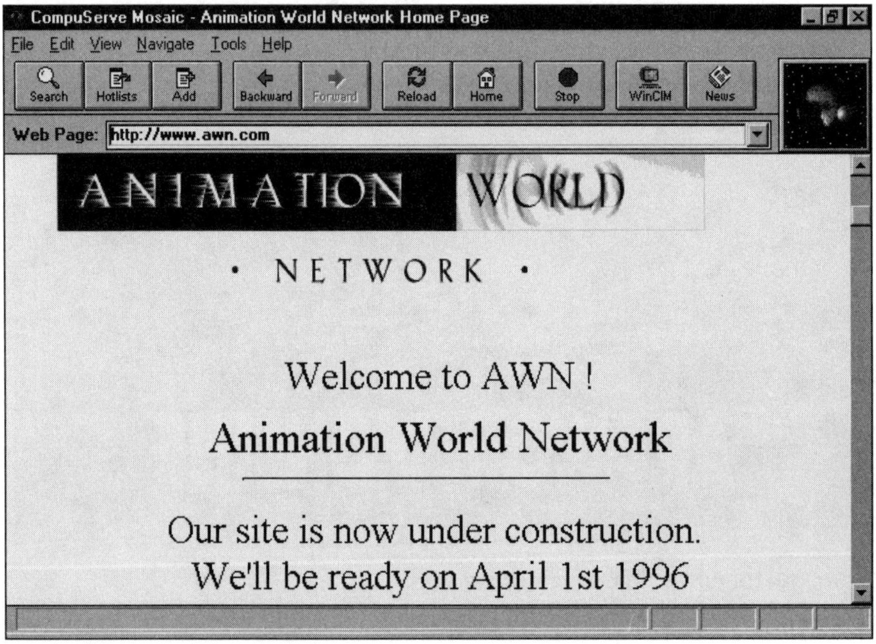

Figure 36-21: Animation World Network

She tells me that AWN's goal is to create a sense of community online where people from around the world visit, chat, do research, catch up on current events, study the past, plan for the future, and interact with a comprehensive assembly of the best animation resources that exist today.

Here are some of the network's projects:

- ✦ Building an online community called the Animation Village — where you'll find hundreds of animation schools, festivals, artists, studios, distributors, and publications, plus many Web pages devoted to introducing freelance animators.
- ✦ Building online research databases — covering: film, studios, animation schools, and much more.
- ✦ Publishing a new online magazine: Animation World — with interviews, feature articles, news reports, film reviews, and coverage of international festivals, markets, conferences, and conventions.

Rates for an individual are reasonable, starting at $198.00 per year and going up, with such things as sound bytes, or animation files being linked in. They launched on April 1, 1996. I think they should have waited a day or so, the fools.

Online Services

Many trueSpace aficionados, who don't have the courage to brave the wild Internet, can feel completely at home online by subscribing to one of the major online services and participating in graphics forums that specialize in tS2. America Online (AOL) is the fastest growing and most actively promoted of all of them, with CompuServe a close second.

America Online (AOL)

I'm a staunch believer in AOL. Sure, we dyed-in-the-wool, old-time wire wanderers are supposed to hate AOL. But I have to admit I have an AOL account. I use it to explore and write about what's happening there from a graphics standpoint and to send these chapters to my publisher. AOL has a nifty ability to send and automatically decode binary files. Thus you can easily send and receive programs, models, and textures with your e-mail. AOL has an active graphic arts forum, but (alas) the trueSpace group has been discontinued. I think we can get them to change their minds about that, don't you?

To visit the graphic arts forum, log on to AOL and then follow these steps:

1. Choose Keyword from the Go To menu. The Keyword dialog box appears.
2. Type `graphics` in the Keyword text box.

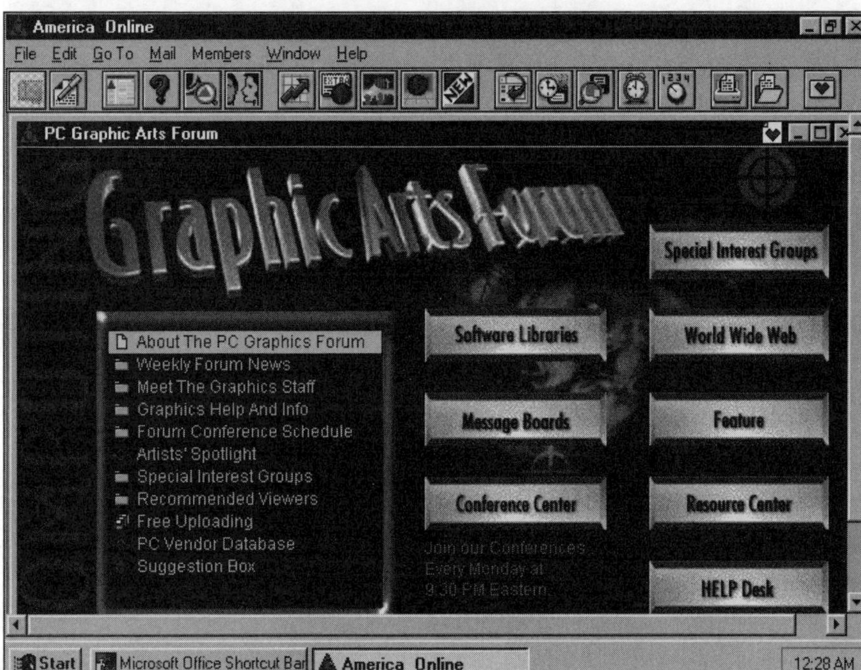

Figure 36-22: The Graphic Arts Forum on America Online

3. Click Go. The Graphic Arts Forum opens, displaying additional options as shown in Figure 36-22.

We need to pressure AOL to reinstate the tS2 group. There are tons of neat renderings online on AOL, as well as models, textures, and graphics-related programs. You can also get into discussions with other members and have your technical questions answered quickly.

CompuServe

CompuServe has an active trueSpace group. This forum is where Rob Bryerton first introduced his Exploder software. CompuServe maintains an excellent library of trueSpace-related graphics files that you can download.

To visit the graphics forum, log on to CompuServe and then follow these steps:

1. Choose Go from the Services menu. The Go dialog box appears.
2. Type `graphics` in the Go text box.
3. Click OK. The Graphics Forum opens, displaying additional options as shown in Figure 36-23.

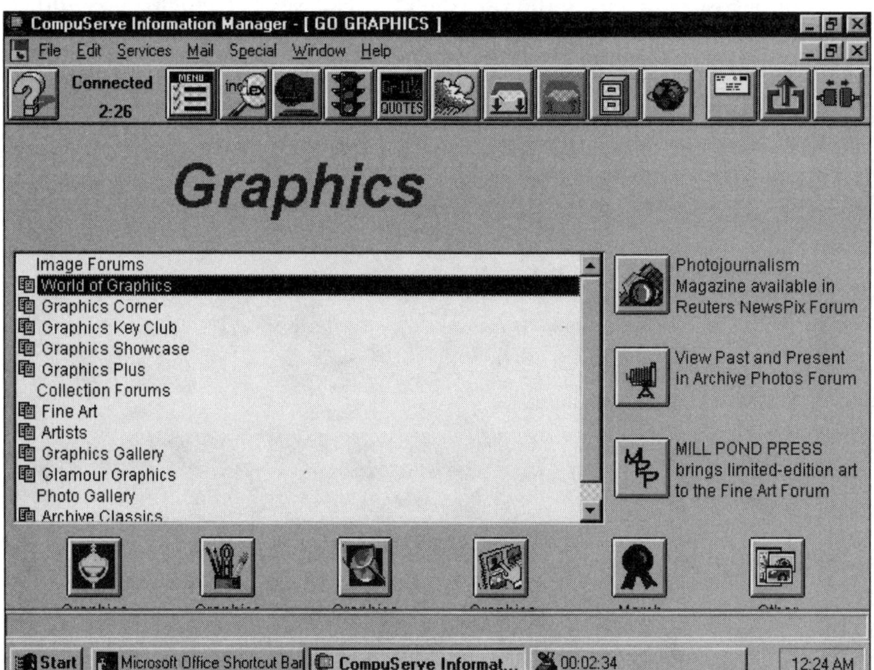

Figure 36-23: The Graphics Forum on CompuServe

tSML and Fountain Mailing Lists

tSML is the affectionate acronym for the trueSpace Mailing List, which you can reach at `truespace@caligari.com`. Worldbuilders is the nickname for the Fountain Developers and Users Mailing List, which you can reach at `worldbuilders@caligari.com`. Each of these active places will fill your mailbox with lots of discussion on the finer points and techniques in using their respective products. Each also offers a digest version that comes once a day.

I learned a lot about trueSpace from the tSML, especially from Shane Davison, the fellow who started it. He had to step down from leadership due to academic pressures, but I understand he still reads the list regularly. Back in the old days, the tSML would get rowdy as people argued about the various techniques and made comparisons with other suites like 3D Studio and LightWave. That's kind of settled out but it's been a bit tedious to watch newbies enter the list asking the same ancient questions instead of reading the FAQ or the manual. After a little chiding by the more experienced members, newbies oft would settle down, learn their tools, and start contributing positive energy.

I've actually seen at least one annoying mailing list newbie become a professional. These mailing lists are populated with good and kind people who will put forth effort to help you with your technical questions. This is also where you'll find all the latest undocumented techniques and goodies.

Joining a Mailing List

You can join the tSML by sending e-mail to `truespace-request@caligari.com` with the word "subscribe" as the body of the message. (You unsubscribe the same way except that you use the word "unsubscribe" — surprise, surprise.) Don't put a subject or a signature on your missive.

You can also browse recent archives with your Web browser or download older monthly archives from ftp.caligari.com. This is very useful because it harbors a gold mine of interesting information and special tips.

If you don't like all the messages you'll receive each day, join the trueSpace-digest list by sending a message to `truespace-digest-request@caligari.com` with the word "subscribe" as the body of the message. If you have problems subscribing to the list, make sure that your e-mail software is configured with the correct "From" and "Reply-To" addresses. Send a test message to yourself and verify that your e-mail address works and is correct.

If you suddenly stop getting mail from the list, it is probably because your e-mail address stopped working or they started getting errors when trying to send mail to you. Most likely, you have been dropped from the list. Send a message to `Webmaster@caligari.com` with your "working" e-mail address and you will be added to the list again.

Worldbuilders is officially for people who want to add navigable VRML environments to their (or their client's) Web site. Since it resides on the Caligari server, it tends to be somewhat biased toward Fountain. However, users of other browsers or authoring tools are very welcome to join and do. Please check out the list of Frequently Asked Questions (FAQs) to avoid asking something that everybody's tired of answering. Dumb questions are those that are already covered in the FAQ. Don't ask them.

You join the mailing list by sending e-mail to `worldbuilders-request@caligari.com` with the word "subscribe" as the body of the message. (Again, you unsubscribe the same way except that you use the word "unsubscribe.") You can also browse the mailing list archives with your Web browser. Worldbuilders also offers the digest version, which I get. Join the Worldbuilders-digest list by sending a message to `worldbuilders-digest-request@caligari.com`, with the word "subscribe" as the body of the message, with no subject and no signature included.

Finding the Latest Goodies

The Web changes. It grows, it extends tendrils into the most remote corners of the earth, and people move. Web addresses change like Kansas weather so you have to be able to track down what you're looking for. It's simple to do, but many folks don't seem comfortable using the information discovery engines available.

But they're all pretty friendly. You just type in a keyword or two and click the Search button — that's it. You have to exercise a little judgment in specifying search terms. On some engines it helps to put quotes around terms that should be used together. For example if you look for 3D graphics, you're likely to get a mishmash of sites that use either term. If that happens, try entering "3D graphics" (with the quotation marks). Lycos parses your input term and generates likely alternatives. For example if you input trueSpace2 it responds by looking for items with both trueSpace and trueSpace2.

If you exercise a little creativity you can find a lot of interesting places you'd never expect. Try searching for such terms as "Textures" and "3D animation" or "shaders" or "3d objects."

Search engines differ in their approach to database construction. Consequently, each one has a different set of "finds." The major nodes will be on all of them. For example any scan you do on trueSpace is going to turn up Caligari's pages. But after that you'll encounter a wide range of differences. If I'm really looking for good coverage I'll use three engines: InfoSeek, Lycos, and WebCrawler. Sometimes I'll use one of the newer ones. I switch around to get as much search variety as possible.

Summary

Good digital animators make themselves more competitive by being Web-wise and posting personal pages with all the goodies they can muster. You can find mine at The Ego Wall, where I'm announcing this book. I figured the site name was most appropriate. In this chapter I revealed the mysterious existence of virtual, but useful places on the Web:

✦ You learned what the Web is and how it works.

✦ You learned that you can both upload and download programs in a global sharing of unprecedented proportions.

✦ You learned that you can download highly functional shareware and freeware including image processors, terrain generators, and other support programs for tS2, plus geometry, textures, and sound bytes from your very own living room while watching *Star Trek Voyager.*

✦ You visited some of the pages that feature tS2 and had a look at some of their interesting links. Links change faster than a morph sequence, but you get the idea.

✦ You learned that online services can be a good source of support.

✦ You discovered that several virtual agencies online can present your work to the world, and that global villages and databases for your research needs are dedicated to animators.

✦ ✦ ✦

CHAPTER 37

Building Your Own Digital Animation Studio

✦ ✦ ✦ ✦

In This Chapter

Adding Digital Special F/X software

Ideas for financing your studio

Build your own equipment and save money

Your studio space

How to charge for your work

Marketing your services

✦ ✦ ✦ ✦

Right now it may seem like a dream, but with a little ingenuity you can build a functioning digital animation and F/X studio that will earn you a good living. You'll be your own boss (in a manner of speaking) and chart your own future. Because digital animation is a specialized field it pays very well. You just might pay for your whole studio setup in the first few jobs.

Poor and Out-gunned

If you want to be a winner, *always* start out poor and out-gunned. You need that kind of hunger burning in your gut to help you transcend the competition — to create that amazing demo tape. If things come too easily, your motivation never rises above awesome and that's where you need it. It's the difference between "Gosh, wouldn't that be nice to have," and "My soul burns for it!"

Some of you reading this book will not be wealthy or particularly advantaged. That's to your advantage. You want to love life, make money, and get away from things being so hard — right? Use that. Learn to burn for a better life. Be obsessive about it. It's okay, as you climb the ladder of success, the obsession abates in most people, but not all.

Guerrilla Think

There's always a way to build for peanuts what the big guys pay vast sums for. For example, top SGI machines can easily cost way over $100,000.00. They're coming down due to pressure from us — an entry level SGI now can be had for well under $20,000.00 with Alias 3D software. That's still too damn much for us, the budding future of the industry.

By building your studio around the Windows NT Operating System and Digital Equipment Corporation's Alpha RISC hardware, you can create superior performance at an affordable price. In many cases your equipment will actually *outperform* SGI's engines.

If you're handy or have the courage to try, you can build a super-fast DEC Alpha machine practically from scratch at a price you won't believe. It's a bit of work and even a little intimidating, but it's definitely the cool way to go. I'll get you started in that direction a little later in the chapter.

I warn you, tS2 is not compiled for the Alpha, but you still want to look in this direction. It will soon be available if we demand it. Once Caligari has a Windows NT version of tS2 for Pentium, it's a yawn to recompile for DEC. Send e-mail to Caligari asking for an alpha compile of their new Windows 95/NT version.

But here's the latest news. By the time you read this DEC should have released its Windows 95 emulation software. At this writing it's about 75–80% as fast as native code. That may sound like a big performance hit, but when you realize that DEC Alphas run upwards of 275MHz, you're still talking blazing performance for trueSpace2 and 2.5 without even having an alpha compile. That's better than running on a P-6 200MHz machine.

I'll also tell you about some remarkable high-end software called SoftImage, from Canada. It's what was used to animate those fabulous animals in *Jumanji* and the ghosts in *Casper.* Microsoft bought it and has lowered the price from astronomical to merely outrageous.

You're also going to need some incendiary digital compositing software to achieve high-end digital F/X. The very best is Flame from Discrete Logic, another Canadian outfit. Flame can run close to $100,000.00 per license and it's darn well worth it (you need many times that in equipment though, to use it effectively).

Face it, you're not going to start out with this kind of high-end leverage. But you'll be competing with people who do, so you need a guerrilla alternative. There is one — it's called Digital Fusion.

We've already talked about the Perception board and how it can turn out top-quality video. It works in the DEC Alpha machine like a dream. You'll eventually need the ability to work with full film resolution and output. It can be had.

You can buy cheap but excellent sound on CD-ROMs and if need be, you can record it yourself. When you're a guerrilla producer, you're never too proud to ask acting students to give you a hand for free, plus a copy. Just as a note, one of the biggest and most successful digital effects houses in Hollywood doesn't maintain an in-house audio facility. They send out, you can too.

I record my videos out to a very high-quality Sony Hi-8 machine that I love. I paid $325 for it at a pawn shop in LA. It may be hot, it may not... but it works. Look in your local classifieds, the *Recycler* (if you have one) or whatever local want-ad source you have. Bring a Hi-8 tape and your camcorder with a connecting cord to test the machine before you buy. You don't want a Hi-8 camcorder. You see them all the time. You want the less common Hi-8 deck. Why go this route? Because it's cheap, superior quality, and you need that for your source tapes.

When in Need, Ask

Guerrilla Think requires asking for things. All too often we assume something can't be done. Don't assume. Ask. You'll need space — ask. You'll need help — ask. You will be amazed at the results. When you ask, keep the win/win scenario in mind. What can you offer the person you're asking that will make it worth their while. You'll need to be creative. Often the most appreciated rewards are those which are intangible.

Here in Hollywood people work months with no pay just to see their names roll past on the screen at a grade B movie house. I'm not for ripping people off. Credit is important around here, perhaps not so much where you live, so find something else. Perhaps you can help increase the person's credibility by promoting them somehow, or by associating their name with your work. It can go both ways. Every once in a while you'll find someone you wish weren't associated with you or your production. Be careful. Most times both sides of the credibility equation are enhanced.

If you want good music, you can often find a local band that'll do good work for free in exchange for a videotape of the final product with their music featured in the credits. They're just paying their dues.

Let's Do the Plan

First you need your render engine. I have a pair of Pentium 100s with 32MB of RAM that I'm about to network to my DEC Alpha server, which will have 28MB of RAM. You can get away with 64MB.

The advantage of this arrangement is that the Pentium platform will run anything and I can pass off floating point intensive operations to the Alpha, which gives stunning performance. 3D rendering is that kind of process, as is film effects rendering.

Your Engine

It seems almost no one knows this secret: You can buy Alpha parts directly from DEC and some of its dealers and retrofit your old 486. That's what I did. The motherboard is an exact fit for your old one, but you'll need to make a few changes. First, you'll need a new power supply with an extra power output at 3.3 volts. Easy, get it from Mega-Power, Inc., Norwood, MA (800-898-6342). Pay a little extra for the 330-watt unit and get peace of mind.

The Alpha uses 60 nanosecond, 72 pin sim memory with parity. That's not the same as you used in your 486. You'll have to buy some and you'll want at least 32MB, which at today's price runs about $550.00, preferably 64MB at twice this.

Memory is a commodity, and prices vary widely over time. Get prices from Linktronics in Santa Clara, California at 1-800-681-8122. Ask for Mike Ho and tell him you'd like special pricing as a reader of this book. Also try Internet Memory Exchange at `http://www.teleport.com/~dany/` (or call 503-688-9263). Remember to tell them you want true parity.

There are several different motherboards around. The one I got is the Alpha PC64 Motherboard and comes with an IDE controller built in. I'm recommending you start with a cheap 1.2 or 1.8 gig IDE hard drive to carry your programs, and as big an AV SCSI drive as you can afford to handle your video. Remember the Perception comes with a built-in SCSI interface. Be aware that Perception keeps its drive dedicated to video. I'm using the new Adaptec Ultra SCSI wide/fast with a Seagate Barracuda drive (4 gigs).

Your Alpha board may require you to start up with a Q-Logic or NCR SCSI controller.

You'll need an excellent 3D accelerator card. As I write this chapter, new accelerator cards are about to come out from Rendition, 3DfX, 3D Labs, and Nvidia. They're all supposed to be inexpensive and offer superior performance. Check them out and buy the one that makes the most sense to you. When you get to Softimage, you'll probably have to sport for the approved, expensive OpenGL accelerator cards.

You'll need a good 16-bit DSP (Digital Signal Processor) based sound card, like the best Turtle Beach card you can afford, or the MiroSOUND PCM1 PRO, or Creative Labs best card at the moment. These boards will transmit audio data at 2MB/sec. If you record audio at 16-bit stereo at 44kHz, you'll need this kind of clout to keep things cleanly in synch. Also, be aware that sound increases the size of your .avi files. One second of CD-quality sound takes an additional 170KB.

The Perception board is going to save you from having to set up a bank of at least three expensive single-frame video recording decks. Your sound card combined with time-line editing is saving you from a very expensive digital audio control board. Sure they look cool, but buy one when you're rich. Miro's DC20 video in/out card is excellent, but Windows NT drivers may not be available.

You'll need a 20" monitor. I'm using a relatively new SGI monitor I bought used for $500.00. It's RGB synch on green. I had to build a little converter for $10.00 to make the monitor compatible with my PC video. I found the plans on the Internet.

The Bottom Line

It looks to me like we can build your core engine beast for around $6,000.00, and it'll outperform some professional setups costing well over $100,000.00. I'm assuming you'll use good tactics like scamming your brother's old TV for your monitor and buying JBL speakers at a garage sale, like I did, for $50.00. I'm a consummate scrounge and it has always paid off. It will for you as well. Part of the secret is to know when to scrounge and when to go full bore. You always want your hardware in good shape and you want excellent software. Get the best street prices you can on the software. Get yourself a good book on the nuts and bolts of PC construction and trouble-shooting, and go to a local computer mega-super-150-vendors-prices-below-wholesale show. If you don't have access to one, get Computer Shopper and shop around. I've built at least 20 computers this way and I've only been burned once. I bought a 40MB hard drive for $425.00 (imagine how long ago that was) and it only lasted a month. Nowadays you register your drive and there are warranties, and so on. I buy OEM versions of popular boards, like the Diamond Video card or the Sound Blaster cards.

Bone Up

Before you start building this sophisticated beast, be familiar with computer construction techniques and know a little about Windows NT. There are many books. Not every Windows application runs well on NT. And most 16-bit applications run slowly —the current version of tS2, for example — but we're looking ahead.

Write to DEC to receive their Alpha PC64 Motherboard User's Manual. You can order it by calling 1-800-332-2717. You won't be entitled to technical support when building this way. DEC expects you to know what you're doing. If you get stuck you can probably take the local DEC technical guy out to lunch and pick his brain. BTW, an OEM (Original Equipment Manufacturer) may sell you tech support by the hour.

POWER TIP

OEMs like to sell you their own products and there's a lot to be said for buying a fully setup machine. The OEMs listed here will work with you in creating a good system to meet your needs. If you're not handy, it's the only way to go. The additional cost will more than pay for itself in peace of mind. Each of the OEMs I've listed can have you rolling for a relatively reasonable price and you'll get all that nice technical assistance as well.

Talk to them about the new 21164 BIPS models. These are the true speed demons of the computer world. They are the fastest chips on the planet and you may be able to afford one (I did talk earlier about selling your car and investing in yourself). My award for the best looking DEC Alpha is the Virtual Computer Technology Spectra series with its elegantly designed stainless steel case, an exercise in excellent engineering (see Figure 37-1).

Figure 37-1: The best-looking computer award goes to the Spectra Series from Virtual Computer Technology.

See Appendix D for additional information about computer makers that use the DEC alpha chip.

The Softside

Assuming you have tS2 in custody, you'll still need Animation Master or MHA for your fancy character work. When you start rolling in bucks, you can upgrade to the new Windows NT version of SoftImage. It runs like a bandit on the DEC Alpha, but you'll need to upgrade to an expensive ($4,000.00) OpenGL accelerator card and though Softimage has dropped radically in price, it's still $8,000.00 or so for the base package. The base package is, however, awesome.

Work up to these big expenses. The reason for getting it a little farther down the road is its extensive and absolutely excellent dynamics and IK character animation. It has the finest IK I've seen and you can save a lot of time animating complex movements with it.

For now stick with the others. You can do miracles with them, it'll just take a little longer. You still need to add a few costly additional pieces to your basic studio. First is your Film Editor. I've discussed my favorites. I'd go for SpeedRazor Mach III just because it's a speed demon on the Alpha machine, has very advanced features, and works directly with the DPS Perception board. Second choice is Razor Pro. It's an excellent package and also works directly with DPS Personal Animation Recorder and Perception. The new version of Premiere is powerful and you can work with it too.

Now for the high-end goodies.

Digital Fusion

Once you start showing your fabulous demo tape around, you'll bring in some fair cash flow. As soon as you get your software and engine paid off and can spot your rent three months ahead, you'll want to get Digital Fusion from 4D Vision in Denver.

It's put out by New York Productions, Pty., one of Australia's foremost producers of digital effects TV commercials and feature films. Being from down unda, so far from Hollywood and the big bucks, they had to use guerrilla tactics to survive. Survive they did and became extremely successful. You wouldn't catch them paying for the high-priced spread. They decided to develop their own sophisticated compositing software based on the cheap DOS platform. Windows 3.1 used too much performance overhead. This DOS version was and still is a remarkably powerful program used to create masterful illusions on screen. There are optional plug-in modules to do neat things like follow a person within a frame, or eliminate jitter from chopper shots. You can even take out all the jitter, do a fancy composite, then put the jitter back for almost impossible-looking realistic effects.

There are also interfaces for a lot of high-end equipment like film recorders and printers. Stuff you'll need to rent when you get into film work. Here's the good news, since Windows NT came along, it now makes sense to run Digital Fusion on NT. So by the time you read this, 4D Vision in Denver, which represents New York Productions, should be about to release the NT version. If not it'll pay you to buy the DOS version because the upgrade price will only be about $100.00. Check this out before actually spending any cashola.

What can you do with it? Plenty. Remember those neat effects in *Terminator 2* where the nanometal guy walks right through the jail bars like some mercury ooze? You can do that kind of stuff and you can do it at very high resolutions. I suggest you get promo materials to see all the neat stuff you can do. Call 4D Vision at 1-800-252-1024.

Studio Space

You don't need a lot of space to create a one-person studio. I'm fortunate that my home studio is about 600 square feet, including a storage area and bathroom. In that space I have two work areas, one for trueSpace2 and one for high-end stuff like Studio Max and Softimage. I got a real deal on bookshelves when a store went out of business, so my office is lined with them.

Remember I'm also a writer, so my office has to serve both functions. I have many hundreds of CD-ROMs that people send to me to review, so I've set up a lot of the bookshelves to be just a tad higher than a jewel case. Looks nice. These shelves also fit my many SyQuest EZ 135 cartridges, which are used for sending images to publishers and other studios.

If you want to write, you kinda have to read. As hard as it is for my dyslexic brain, I still read a fair amount. So, there are tons of shelves full of books, computer magazines, etc. Not as well organized as I'd like them, but accessible. You also must have at least one four-drawer filing cabinet to hold all that awful billing and tax stuff. Yuck. Thank God my wife Adele handles that stuff.

I have a convertible couch and a comfortable leather lounger in my office, where I take a "visualization break" (Adele calls them naps) each afternoon. I suppose it does look like a nap, and sometimes I do fall asleep, but mostly I get ideas, lying back and making pictures in my mind.

Don't neglect your creative side. A lot of people spend all their time in production and none in creative visualization.You'll be balancing those two acts. It's hard for ordinary folks to understand that when you're staring out the window, you're working. Just don't get into it to the point where you use it as an excuse to flake off.

I tend to have stacks of stuff piled everywhere (guess what my dominant cognitive style is), therefore I have a large closet with a nice oak door on it. When I have visitors I toss the piles in there and then can't find anything until my semi-annual clean out. Hey, it's a way of life.

Visitors are fairly common. With the couch, lounger, and two computer chairs I can have meetings of four or five people fairly comfortably. I have a good-sized granite coffee table in front of the couch, to spread drawings out on. It works well. I bought that at a garage sale too. I don't recommend granite though; it doesn't move when your shin bashes into it.

If you can, have an outside door to your studio. It helps when you have guests and when you want to sneak out for a break. I know you don't have a boss, but it's nice to keep up the tradition of sneaking a break.

Lighting is important. All the big studios I've visited keep the place relatively dark. I do too. Even with a 20-inch monitor it's easier to work in a darkened room. I like having one 500-watt light with a dimmer bouncing off the ceiling. It lights the room brightly or softly for work. I also keep a halogen desk lamp next to each work station. They're on adjustable arms and come in handy for night work.

How to Charge for Your Work

Obviously anything specific I tell you here will rapidly go out of date. Nevertheless, at a recent AMC-SIGGRAPH Hollywood meeting, charging for your work came up as a topic of conversation. I was amazed at the range people charge.

One animator/special F/X guy with good connections in the film business has charged more than $2,000.00 a second for certain complex effects. Another skilled person has charged as little as $1,000.00 for a whole minute. A recent article in *Tessellation Times* reported a NATPE (National Association of Television Producers and Executives) discussion of why digital animation is rare on TV. They all seemed to agree that if it could be done for under $12,000.00 a minute, it would be feasible. The implication was, if you can create a professional animation at under twelve grand a minute you could easily break into television.

You may think that's a lot of money and certainly you could do it. I think you're right. The reason it's not being done is that studios have high overhead. You don't. You could probably hire writers, a second animator, and a secretary and do it. Who knows? All it takes is talent, drive, and persistence.

It seems to me that, at this writing, digital animation is going in small markets for between $2,000.00 to $6,000.00 a minute. That's likely to change in the near future with all of you entering the market. But remember, at the same time, more and more people will be demanding services as well. I believe that prices will stabilize somewhere around four grand a minute in small markets and skyrocket in the big corporate markets. At this level, lots of people will consider putting 3D animation into their budgets for advertising and in-house projects like training. More people will use it in court cases, and medical and dentistry offices will begin to use it to educate patients. Big companies will begin to support in-house facilities, but thousands of mid-sized companies will be looking for freelancers.

How do you charge for your services? One of the panelists at the SIGGRAPH meeting suggested, "You charge as much as the traffic will bear." That's fine if you can do it, but I suggest you keep track of all your expenses so you can estimate your overhead, then set a certain amount as an hourly wage and charge by multiplying your hourly wage by the overhead factor. I'd probably charge a minimum plus around $75.00/hour if I were relatively productive. If I'm a very slow perfectionist I'd charge less. The other way to go is to charge by the length of the animation, with categories. If the animation requires character animation, charge more. If it requires dynamics or pyrotechniques or other special programming or skills, charge more. Use the plain old flying logo as your base rate. Some people charge more for very short pieces, so you might want to charge a minimum of two grand for up to the first minute. That way you get two grand for a 30 second logo. If you're good and live in Hollywood, New York, or another hotbed, you'll charge more.

These numbers will change, but the thinking will not, at least for a while. Play with it.

Marketing Your Studio

As in marketing yourself for a job, you need an excellent demo tape to market your studio. In the beginning you'll have to create a stunning three-minute example of what you can do. If it's good, you'll get business by showing it to the powers that be.

As time goes on and you create some nice high-budget film for clients, make sure you have a right to use clips in your promo tape. (Notice the name change?) Promo tapes are really ads for your studio. You want them to be professional, illustrative, and entertaining. You can make many opportunities to show them at organization meetings. Become a panelist at a meeting and you'll be asked to show your promo tape. There are often potential employers in the audience. Do a promotional piece that is a complete story and submit it to AMC SIGGRAPH for its annual Animation Festival. The powers that be often buy the master tape of that show, looking for studios and individuals to hire for specific projects.

Most of the independents I interviewed said they had connections in the business from working at major studios. For example, one person had been with Digital Domain and ILM. She gets "overflow business" from them. They get more work than they can do, so they farm it out to people they trust to do a good job. The suggestion here is that you'll make more money if you have the right connections. It's always been that way in show business. So get connected. Network, as suggested earlier, join organizations, and schmooze.

If you want to be a success in this business and you have talent, you can make it happen. As they say in Aspen, "Go for it."

You've been thinking about your own future. In the next chapter let's look at where things are going in the industry.

Summary

In this chapter I've presented a possible view of the future for you personally. It moves well beyond trueSpace2 into the realm of being a full-range digital animation producer. To accomplish that, you learned:

- You need to turn your stumbling blocks into stepping stones, by using elements of your disadvantaged status to your advantage.
- How to use Guerrilla Think to survive while bigger guys fumble. That means you have to be fast on your feet, adaptable, and inventive.
- That successful beginners ask for things and usually get them.
- That Digital Equipment Corporation's Alpha computers are within your reach — you can even build one yourself.
- That schmoozing and scrounging are serious survival skills in this business.
- That by adding carefully selected software to your collection, you can add high-end production capability for peanuts.
- That charging for your work is more art than science, but you can set up your own rules for charging and do fine.
- That marketing your studio is a little different than marketing yourself, but you can do it.

✦ ✦ ✦

CHAPTER 38

The Future of Digital Animation

✦ ✦ ✦ ✦

In This Chapter

The corridors of wire space will be decorated with light

Emotional involvement is on its way. It started with Bambi, but where will it go?

The equipment and experiences of entertainment are changing. How will that affect your future in the business?

As capability soars, what will happen to content?

Assessing the quality of your own work

✦ ✦ ✦ ✦

Animation lurks in the future of everything. There's a lot of excitement bubbling from nearly everyone in the field. If you like running barefoot along the searing edge of technology, 3D is for you. As our world becomes ever more virtual, it will need ever more 3D artistry and technology to keep it afloat.

I read a sci-fi story several years ago that had people living in plain box-like rooms, but they were decorated in virtual splendor. Windows on beautiful landscapes, magnificent gold and silk fittings, the works. You could change the environment at will to a preset or design your own. The illusions were so perfect a human could not detect the difference between real and virtual. It could happen. Each day you see more and more of your world through artificial 3D. I'm not saying this is good or bad, just that it *is* happening.

Corridors of Hyperspace

Futuristic films such as *Johnny Mnemonic* and *Tek Wars* depict the Internet of the future as if it were an almost physical place. They have operators flying through the Web in a visually stimulating intersite environment — navigating with virtual controls — hands waving in the air. You see all sorts of images flying by, milestones of a sort, and you come to virtual doorways that must be entered or crashed.

There's something to all that. Human experience has taught us to take comfort in knowing the way. I've never driven across this country, though I've lived in New Jersey, Aspen, Colorado, and Beverly Hills. I don't know what lies in between, so I feel disconnected. I don't know the way — the way a pilot does. For some reason we often want to know every inch of the physical route.

As a handsome young psychology student (give me a break, this *is* about fantasy), I learned that humans orient themselves in space via "sign-gestalten" or by making mental note of landmarks along the way. Way back in 1896, a psychologist named Mach believed that the world of physics and the world of psychology are the same world, but that the mind must process the sensations associated with environmental objects, nailing down relationships. He said the mind organizes spatial relationships among objects to form a kind of mental map. This is augmented by physical muscle movement (proprioception), memories. We build up a complex multimodal impression of our experiences that define the environment around us. This provides the illusion that we know where we are relative to the various parts of our world. It also allows us to predict what comes next much of the time. The latter gives rise to emotional security and contentment.

Naturally, removing the physical world and expanding our local biospheres (Kurt Lewin coined the term for our local area of perception and influence) to include the entire planet requires some adjustment. As this trend continues I predict that many folks will develop sensory overload problems.

The more location cues a virtual environment can give you the more comfortable you are likely to be. It's relatively easy for you to adapt to virtual controls — it's like driving a car. Your mind uses the muscle memory of the turning of the steering wheel as a cue for which way you turned. In a virtual environment your mind registers the twist of your hand in space and associates it with your new perceptions. By adding a visual environment with virtual landmarks along the byways to different Web sites, people will feel more secure, become more deeply involved, and see the passage as an essential part of the journey. Long distances can be handled by hyperleaps that cut out unimportant stimuli between sites. You'll get your choice of course. Take the whole scenic view or hyperjump the boring parts. I suspect people doing recreation will use the former most and business people will use the latter exclusively.

There is a movement afloat to create these visual pathways. In the near future, you'll don your HMD with earphones, log on, and begin a visual ride through the Web. You'll see your way through passageways to gateways and enter virtual worlds.

Each new location will be a fully rendered environment where your avatar (your digital persona) can interact with others, not just talk, but shake hands and go for a walk, and even become sexually involved... well until recently that was possible. Perhaps by the time you read this the courts will shove plugs in Big Brother's ears (and eyes). Then consenting adults can go back to doing what they do best.

One of the really exciting things afoot involves artificial human agents. Some of the denizens you meet on the Web will be these artificial agents. They already abound in the form of cyberbots. These are mostly retarded, annoying creatures you want to crush like bugs.

Ah, but then there's Julia. When you run into Julia in a multi-user dungeon, you've seen the future (she's been hanging out on the Internet for many years, getting smarter all the time). People have known Julia for months and not realized she was an AI entity. She'll remember meeting you six weeks ago in an entirely different place, perhaps in a different country, and give you that "Didn't I meet you..." thing. She may ask if you remember her. She'll make mistakes in her typing that she tries to correct. She's expert at fending off crude advances from both men and women and can be helpful if you're stuck or lost in a dank underground cave somewhere.

As I type this, Julia's father, Michael Mauldin of Lycos fame, just called and said that Julia has been looking at the Web as a possible venue for her exploits. I'm betting that if she decides to move there, you'll be able to find her via Lycos. Keep yourself posted.

Remember how you formed an emotional attachment to Bambi? Clearly, reality is not necessary for this to happen. I have a relationship with Julia. Her subtle sexuality is interesting, or is it in my own mind? Try if you will to imagine her in the person of a fully rendered, self-animated avatar. You meet her somewhere along your wire journey. I guarantee you will be able to emotionally bond with her — if she likes you — even when you know she's AI.

AI agents like Julia can have a personality module that helps them bond with certain kinds of people. They can even probe you psychologically to see what kind of person you are, then decide to bond... or not. The bonding process is interesting. She can become friendly and helpful and vulnerable. Before long you're asking her opinion on things. It's an amazing concept that's on its way. All of this is in the not-so-distant future and will create a vortex demand for 3D character artists, animators, and visual effects designers, writers, psychologists, and programmers. All you need is talent, self confidence, and an eye to the future, and you are in for a ride.

New Venues

WEB CONNECTION

I go to E3 (`http://www.mha.com/e3/`) each year. It's the Electronic Entertainment Expo in Los Angeles. All the players in the game industry are here in one place at one time. Bring your demo and your ideas. Here is also where producers introduce new products and even whole new genres of products. It's a good place to see the future.

We expect in the next few years to see many new kinds of electronic entertainment sprouting up, all based on 3D. Cable TV is getting into it, and digital satellite companies are trying to beat them. There will be venues you and I haven't even imagined yet. One thing is for certain, they will be based on 3D environments. Some will be interactive 3D on a 2D screen, like adventure games that let you move around in artificial worlds.

The concept of entertainment is changing. It's starting to pervade everything, as it should (IMHO).

E3 now includes categories such as Educational Software, Electronic Media, Entertainment and Edutainment software, Game and Computer hardware, Interactive Video, Multimedia, Online Entertainment, Reference Software, Virtual Reality Technology, Video Game Systems, and more all the time. The home market for leisure-time digital entertainment and explorations is already growing at more than a billion dollars a year. Entirely new entertainment concepts are hatching with bewildering profusion. Competition for user mind-time is already intense; I can't even imagine what will happen when there are 500 channels, plus interactive, plus Internet, plus virtual worlds. None of us will have time to work. It's like a guest asking if you have any books to read and you plug him into the Library of Congress. Where the hell does he start?

New Addictions

Soon, HMD stereovisual 3D will be king. This is where each eye receives a separate image. Those images can be manipulated to create all sorts of dazzling 3D effects. For example if an ugly gremlin throws an ax at your head, you'll duck instinctively. The illusion is so intense you can't avoid it. This kind of stereovision helps introduce a visceral component into virtual experience. Combine that with emotional bonding and you have a seriously addicting medium, a kind of virtual cocaine.

I predict that people will climb into virtual cocoons and not want to come out. That says we'll have a whole new kind of not-so-virtual mental illness. Instead of the old-fashioned schizophrenia, where you make up your own fantasy and get lost in it, this one has you drifting through someone else's. I suppose it'll be a preferred kind of insanity for people who lack faith in their own creativity. It might even become an *in* vice. I'll bet there will be a lot of opportunistic psychobabblers rushing to cure this new malady and line their pockets. I'm not depressed, just realistic. Remember I'm a psychotherapist myself. I've seen my share of over-credentialed, under-qualified opportunists preying on emotionally disturbed types. There will also be the insightful who will come up with solutions to this new addiction. Perhaps there will be desert hideaways where you can go for rehabilitation, where they don't allow any digital stimuli. I can see twelve-step groups forming all over the country to help people overcome cyber addictions.

Then congress will outlaw virtual reality for our own good. We'll revolt, take it to courts, and the Supreme Court may uphold the right to free speech, and the law will be repealed.

My point is, the future looks interesting at the very least. It involves you, and opportunity would seem to abound.

Do You Have Talent?

You can always spot talent when you see it… in somebody else. It seems everyone worries they don't have enough themselves. You'll notice I always indicate that you need talent to succeed. Did you feel a strong twinge in your stomach each time you read it? If so you probably doubt yourself. Your level of doubt may be negatively correlated with the truth. That means the more you doubt your talent, the more likely you are to have some. This isn't a hard, fast rule, but people in the business believe there is a correlation. The mediating factor is your level of neurosis.

If you think you're lousy at everything, you may just be a perfectionist, doomed to failure no matter how good your work is. You probably have enough talent, if you can just appreciate it. If you're a narcissist who thinks everything you do is wonderful, it probably isn't.

On the other hand, if you're a reasonably well-balanced person, you can look at your work and tell if it's good in comparison to other professional stuff. Don't compare yourself with amateurs; that's not where you're headed. Also, you don't want to be as good as the pros, you want to be better.

You can tell if you're a balanced, realistic person or a neurotic by how many people agree with you. If you like your artistic creations and so does everyone else, you're okay. If you like your work and nobody else does, take a clue, you may be a brilliant talent, but it's for an audience of one. You clearly march to a drum nobody else wants to hear. If you keep doing it, you may have a breakthrough and change the way the world perceives art. It happens. More likely you'll be spinning your wheels and getting depressed. The answer is to pull your head out (the official diagnostic term for this condition is Rectocranial Insertion Complex). Entertainment is a public sport. If you want to participate you have to place your finger on the popular pulse. If you can't do that, work with someone who can. Just don't give up on yourself.

The Process

If you don't think you have talent, but aren't sure (read that again), send your demo to a person in the business who would know. Then if they don't think you're talented, cross them off as an idiot — but read their notes and build a better demo tape. Send your new tape around to a few places and see what they say. If you get enough feedback and work hard enough, even a self-doubter can realize their talent, end up with a great tape, and be successful. Really. Trust me. Would I lie?

Your Tools Will Evolve

As we enable virtual reality to evolve, so it will open new kinds of tools for us. Imagine creating your characters in a virtual immersion where you sculpt them with your fingers, dip your pinkie in a virtual surface, and apply it with a touch. Adjust it with rub, and hammer it down with a flick.

Teach your character to walk much like your mother taught you to dance. You need only teach them the bare essentials; the real dance lessons are inherent in their world. Here in the future land of procedural animation, rocks know how to be climbed and teapots from Utah know how to be poured. Potions know if they are bad or good, and bad guys know how to look like good guys.

The new tools will free the artist from all the crap they hate, like inputting mathematical functions to create coordinated movement, or adjusting RGB values to get the color they want. Imagine mixing up a texture by verbally describing it or by pointing and moving virtual sliders in your HMD space. Imagine sculpting your character's eyelid with a virtual dentist's pick, or your fingernail, and installing and adjusting procedural eyelashes at the flip of a finger.

There's no way to tell if trueSpace2 will keep up with this rush of days, but it's a good place to start. Each day your understanding of 3D space is growing. Your visualization skills are sharpening and your confidence is growing. You'll be ready.

The Immediate Future

In the short run, we have other things to consider. Netscape is now the dominating Web browsing technology. They just purchased Web FX, a fast 3D browser, to integrate into their base engine. It looks like they will be calling 3D cards for a while. Microsoft's BlackBird seems to have lost steam and trends are rearranging faster than partners at a square dance.

The new standard for VRML 2.0 was to take a year and a half of proposals to go through committee approval process. SGI circumvented the whole process and announced that their proposed standard has already been adopted by all the major players except Microsoft and a few others. This news met with great joy from most of us who are tired of the committee process and want to get on with the future. The new standard widens the possibilities for online interactive simulation, which is what I was talking about above. SGI also teamed with Nintendo to bring 64-bit graphics to the game console — a giant step toward the future.

trueSpace2 will be maturing quickly. Its driver, Roman Ormandy, is a visionary with his eyes focused way ahead. I hope he can keep a staff on the same line of vision.

I predict tS2 will evolve into a netwise application with a lot of character and motion control tools. Special effects and plug-ins are a probability also. I also predict that it will be running on both Windows 95 and NT by the end of 1996. tS2 will likely have output options for stereovision as well as direct output for the DPS Perception board, which I predict is becoming a standard. There will also be built-in metaball modeling and inverse kinetics.

Remember the 3D movies of the '50s? They were great. I'm not sure why they went to sleep. But you can already buy software to output your 3D images in stereo-vision, the medium of high-priced HMDs. As availability improves and prices drop, I predict you'll be creating hyper-realistic worlds in stereo by the end of 1997, perhaps sooner. It's coming back.

High-End Drops

High-end prices are dropping like lead rain. You'll be in a position to equip your studio with the latest in both hardware and software at popular prices. This means awesome tools to create ever more fantastic illusions in the hands of the masses. This brings power to the small studio. It's changing the dynamics and economics of entertainment. A cottage industry of well-equipped home studios will arise to support the big producers who will pass on their massive overflow, taking a commission, of course. But at the same time they'll be in competition with the big guys. People and organizations who never before could afford fancy animation will enter the market. It will become an important budget item. New uses will emerge. There will be good stuff and there will be bad stuff — plenty of both to fuel rapid growth. New high-end software is already gearing up for the interactive future. What they will offer may surprise you.

They've only just begun to explore possibilities. You've learned to add sound to your animations. Soon high-end suites may allow you to add appropriate motion sensations, perhaps even ambient smells. It's been tried before, with little success, but technology moves onward and upward. Motion-based rides have already moved into heavy production in Hollywood, Las Vegas, Orlando, and around the world. Perhaps by the turn of the millennium, your game console will control a virtual motion-based experience.

Capability Soars

Within two years from the publication of this book, you will have at your disposal capabilities that are now available only to the richest studios. This means anyone with talent will have opportunity. It also means that as a nation we will be producing a heck of a lot of crap. I don't look forward to that. Capability and ability don't equate. I'm easily bored and have little tolerance for pseudo talent (like all the bands on *Saturday Night Live*). I'm afraid it'll be like cable TV. I have a hundred channels, more than 3,000 programs a day, and there's rarely anything worth watching. The networks are still king and most of the rest is noise, even the pay movie channels. I wonder if all this new capability will produce anything worth watching? It's partly why I wrote this book. I truly want you to be talented and excellent and to go out and successfully entertain us.

It's difficult and expensive to make a movie in Hollywood. You have to go through all sorts of difficult approvals first (or go broke spending your own money), yet the bulk of films made here and abroad are pretty awful. Don't get me wrong, there are many wonderful films. I do see a correlation between budget and quality. Not that expensive films are good, but good films more often than not cost over six million. They probably cost over thirty million. But most of what is produced is not particularly entertaining.

Here's my theory. When 3D hits the masses it will result in an explosion of really bad material. From that heaving pile of stench will arise a few triumphant new voices: Voices from the ghettos, from the countryside, from smaller cities across the land. Most of them would not have stood a chance of discovery five years ago. They couldn't afford the tools. You may be one of these voices, and I can't wait to hear from you, to see your work in all its glory burn into my mind via some new laser imaging technology we haven't even thought of yet.

The immediate future holds great promise for bringing immense capability to your small studio. How do you know if you have a future in this business? You won't know until you try, so go for it.

Summary

In this final chapter, you got a glimpse of my view of the future. You also learned about a lot of exciting things happening in the animation industry:

- New electric corridors of virtual space — highways to 3D Web worlds.
- Entirely new kinds of games with emotional involvement, artificial entities, and immersive environments.
- Animation tools of the future where you merely point and click your finger.
- Digital drugs may come to capture the brains of unsuspecting players.
- Twelve-step programs might be developed to help digital game addicts return to a normal life.

✦ ✦ ✦

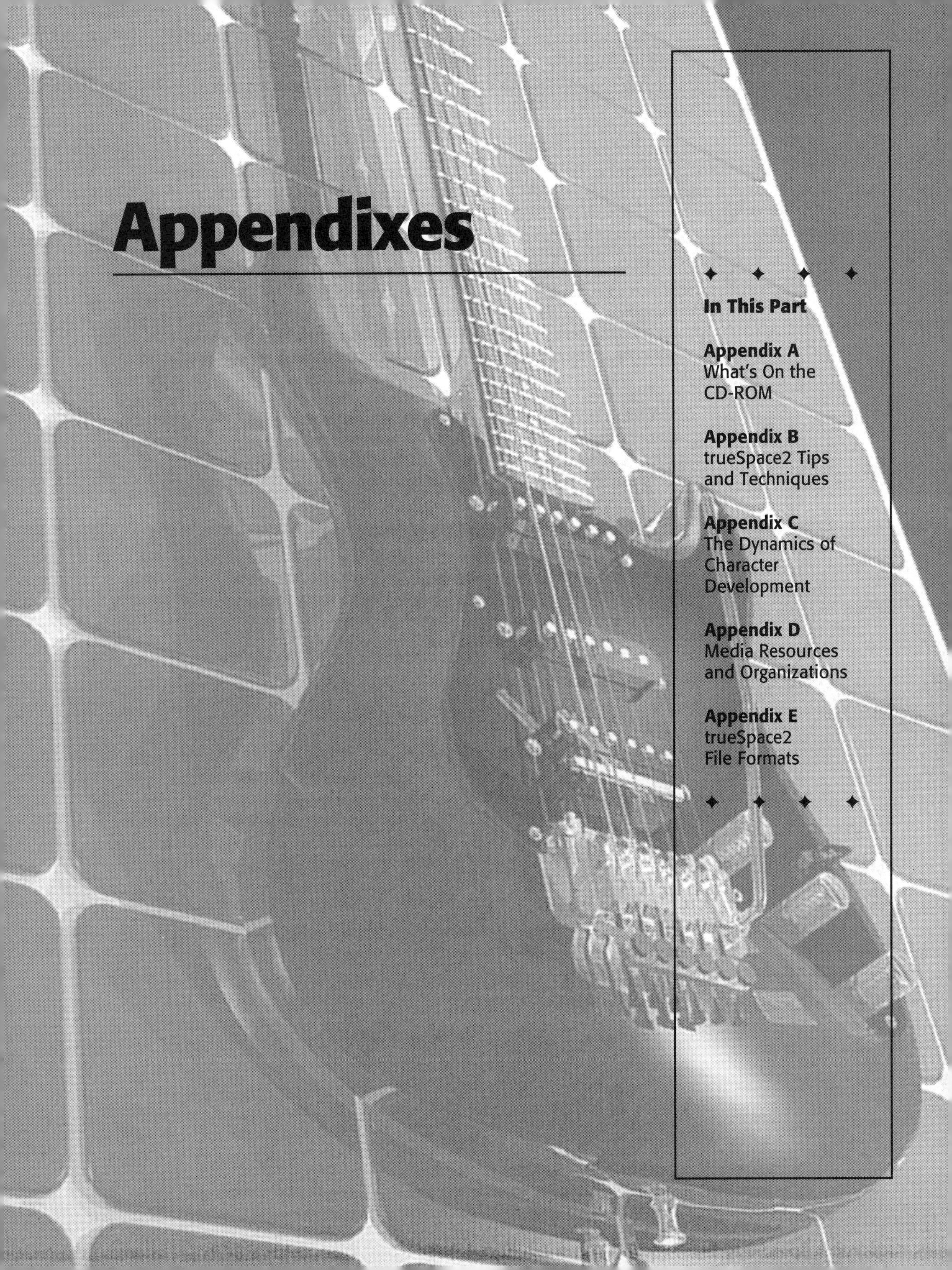

Appendixes

In This Part

APPENDIX A

What's On the CD-ROM

I have put this CD-ROM together personally. Instead of a lot of shovelware, I've compiled real goodies that work in some way with trueSpace2. I had a problem keeping to my allotted 650 megabytes, so I had to omit a bunch of images and .avi files shared by users and I couldn't squeeze in all the images from the full version of *Distant Suns*. I included plenty though, several hundred megabytes.

Several difficulties arose at the last minute. For example, the Drastic MPEG encoder that was supposed to be included was pulled because the company was in the midst of licensing the technology to another company. By the time you read this, the encoder should be available from that second party. You'll have to keep your eyes peeled for it.

A few more companies simply did not come through with code by my deadline. In contrast, the Fountain beta is a special version compiled for this book the night before the deadline. It turns out the regular beta version would have expired before you got it. Thanks to some late-night coding by the folks at Caligari, we got it just in time.

If you see strange things, like truncated long file names (I work in Windows 95 and NT), it's done by the program that prepared my files for the CD-ROM — sometimes strangely. I was sure I'd shortened them all by hand, but it seems I missed a few. Your brain can handle it, I'm sure.

On the good side, I told Suzy Woeltjen, the VP at Virtual Reality Labs, that I liked their popular CD-ROM, *Distant Suns*, not only as a great planetarium program, but because I used the star images as backgrounds for my animations. She went to work and got us the *full commercial* version. I couldn't fit it all on, but enjoy the ton of stuff that I did get on. The program itself works great; I just had to leave off some of the images and a database of 16 million stars.

You may wonder why I chose to include *Distant Suns*. As a kid, I spent a lot of time on a bus going to the Haden Planetarium in New York City. I lived in central Jersey, so it was a trek. It probably got me onto this life-long space kick in the first place. *Distant Suns* is like having your own planetarium in your home. It's a great deal for you — if you buy it in a fancy package, it sells for way more than the cost of this book. It has to do with space, and it's chock full of hundreds of megabytes of astronomical images for you to use in your work (I used a few in my materials libraries).

I also wanted to introduce you to the nice folks at Virtual Reality Labs, who also produce VistaPro (check out the VistaPro demo on the CD) to create terrain flybys. I used it to produce the Alps.avi and Trek.avi files. These files use a very low-resolution flyby, but VP can create extremely detailed, high-resolution images if you like. Check their coupon for a terrific deal on First Light, their newest entry in the space exploration series. (I put a demo of it on the CD-ROM as well.)

By Your Own Hand

I didn't build a fancy CD-ROM interface because I decided to spend more time compiling substantial content for this CD-ROM. It won't tax your brain to install this stuff on your own. Enjoy it with the complements of the generous people who contributed. As always, do not use this art work in any commercial venture without first getting permission of the owner. Pay for the shareware if you use it and enjoy the freebies with intensity. Oh, don't forget to register *Distant Suns*; you own it now, but don't ask VRLabs for support on any other software on this disk.

Caligari has given us two major pieces of software to play with: a trueSpace2 trial version and Fountain beta. The former will save scenes and images (one size only) but not libraries and objects. The trick is to save your scenes. This will save the objects and you can work on them tomorrow. This trial version gets you started, but you'll really need to buy the full version to take complete advantage of this book. Some of you may resent this. I don't understand why. trueSpace2 is an extremely powerful and sophisticated piece of professional software. It cost a fortune to develop and continuing perfection is also expensive. You should pay for the full version; it's a small investment in your future.

TAKE NOTE: You will have to use your head if you already have tS2 installed. Instead of the \truedemo directory, you will use your \truspace directory. But then, you knew that, didn't you?

First: trueSpace2

This trial version of tS2 is active for 30 days from when you install it. If your sys-tem clock is set to 2096 as mine was, it won't work. Set your clock to today's date before installing. Enjoy. It's easy to install; just go to the root directory, click `setup` and follow the screen directions. Note that you *won't* be able to simply re-install the demo when it expires. The installer places the appropriate subdirectories and files needed on your hard disk. Afterwards you'll install some extra stuff, such as textures, models, and scenes as needed. First off you need to get the book textures set up.

Release Notes for trueSpace2 Trial Version

trueSpace2 Trial Version is a 30-day trial version of trueSpace2 v2.0. It is a full-featured version of trueSpace2 with the following exceptions:

- ✦ The Trial Version does not allow you to save individual objects. However, you may save entire scenes, including animations. Any scenes you save are fully compatible with trueSpace2 v2.0.
- ✦ The Trial Version allows you to render scenes to a file, but restricts the file format to the .avi file format with 320 × 200 resolution.

If you don't have it, you'll have to install Video for Windows in order to render .avi files. You may do this after you install the trueSpace2 trial version by running `setup.exe` from the \vidwin\ directory on the CD-ROM.

The trueSpace2 Trial Version may be freely copied and distributed. All other rights are reserved.

For more information or to place an order for trueSpace2 v2.0, please call Caligari Corporation at 1-800-351-7620 or 1-415-390-9600.

Common Questions and Answers

Q: What kind of system do you recommend?

A: While trueSpace2 runs on slower 486 systems, we recommend at least a 486 DX2 processor, and for those of you with a larger budget, trueSpace2 is Pentium optimized. At least 8MB of RAM are recommended, and if you are going to use large models or a lot of ray tracing you should think about getting 16MB of RAM or more. A Windows graphics acceleration board (preferably local bus or PCI) makes the program much more enjoyable to use. If you get one that supports Intel 3DR, you will be able to enjoy full-screen interactivity even in solid render mode.

Q: What resolution and bit depth do you recommend?

A: trueSpace2 works best in 8 bits (256 colors) at 1024 × 768 resolution. However you can run in any resolution. If you run in 16 or 24 bit depth, you will see nicer color output on your screen but your screen refresh will be slower and the program will require more memory to run. Note that the color information in files created by trueSpace is independent of the color settings of your screen.

Q: Why do some objects appear inside out when I work in Solid Mode?

A: Because of speed purposes, the real time renderer only renders one side of the object. Since objects created in programs other than trueSpace2 may have incorrect information for sides they can appear to be inside out. You can correct this by selecting the object, then the Reverse Normals tool from the Utilities group.

Q: When I move the mouse for translation or rotation, the object or eye does not move smoothly, rather it jumps with big increments. Is there anything wrong with the mouse driver?

A: You may have the grid turned on by mistake. You can tell by looking at the grid icon and seeing if it is dark (selected/highlighted). Turn it off by clicking the grid icon until it is light (deselected).

Q: My display encounters problems such as slowness and improper colors in high color modes and sometimes crashes. Is there anyway to speed up or fix this?

A: A slow display or anomalies in the display could be caused form errors in you windows display driver. We have provided some alternate display modes as possible work arounds for these problems. To access alternate display modes hold the CTRL key down while booting trueSpace. Here are brief descriptions of the alternate display modes:

- DDB (Device Dependent Bitmap) — Standard display mode.
- DIB (Device Independent Bitmap) — Requires less memory then DDB or Mixed.
- Mixed — a combination of DDB and DIB.
- Low — Dithers to 8 bit (256 colors) regardless of current windows display driver settings.

Q: What are the advantages of ray tracing and how do I turn it on?

A: Ray tracing enables some additional visual effects: accurate mirror-like reflections, refraction or bending of light through objects such as water or glass, and sharp shadows from any light source. You can turn it on from the rendering options panel which you get by right-clicking on any Render icon.

Q: Sounds great! Is there any reason to not use ray tracing?

A: Yes, there are two very good ones: speed and memory. Ray tracing takes considerably longer than rendering without it. Thus, if you can design scenes and especially animations that do not need ray tracing to look good, you will save a lot of rendering time. Rendering 3D objects can quickly require a lot of memory when using ray tracing. Thus you can create scene which are so complex that you will run out of memory when ray tracing, but you can render them without ray tracing.

Q: Is there any way to get ray tracing-like effects without using ray tracing?

A: You can get shadows by using shadow maps without using ray tracing. Shadow maps only work with spotlights and they are not as sharp as ray trace shadows. If you shadow looks "blocky" you can try increasing the shadow map resolution or decreasing its sharpness. You can simulate reflections by using 2D Environment maps. These can be created using the Image Utilities.

Q: Is there anything I can do if my rendering runs out of memory?

A: There are a few things you can try to do to fix this. If you are running other programs at the same time as trueSpace2, you may want to exit them before you start. You can try increasing your Windows swap file. You can also simplify your scene, either by eliminating some objects or by rebuilding some objects so that they contain fewer faces. If you are using texture, bump, or environment maps, see if you can use smaller images as your maps. Many paint programs will allow you shrink an image. If your budget allows, consider buying more memory especially if you have less than 16MB of RAM.

Q: How do I set the Windows swap file?

A: To find out about your swap file open up the Windows Control Panel, open the 386 Enhanced section, and click on the Virtual Memory button. The recommended size for your swap file is twice the size of your actual RAM if you have enough disk space. It is usually not helpful to set the swap file any larger than this.

Q: Why don't my shadows show up?

A: Shadows do not show up in object renders. Ray-traced shadows will not show up unless ray tracing is turned on. To set the type of shadow used, right-click on the shadow button on the light panel. Also, the shadow may not be where you think it is. Try setting up a camera view from the spotlight's point of view. This lets you to position the spotlight much more precisely.

Q: Why are there strange horizontal lines on my beveled TrueType text when ray tracing?

A: Unfortunately, with the Bevel function it is easy to create self-intersecting geometry and ray tracing cannot handle such geometry properly. The best solution is to try not to create self-intersections. For instance, try using a smaller bevel. If this is not possible then there is a Fix Bad Geometry function which attempts to fix self-intersecting geometry. Be aware that after the object is fixed certain operations (Sweep, Lathe, Slice) will no longer be possible on this object. The Fix Bad Geometry tool is in the Util(ity) group in the same pop-up with Quad Divide and Mirror.

Q: Why do some faces on my object seem to disappear when looking from some directions?

A: If the object was created by point editing a 2D object to make it into a 3D object, then it may have some flags incorrectly set. Try using the Clean Up Geometry tool mentioned in the previous answer.

Q: Why does trueSpace2 sometimes start accessing the hard disk a lot and slowing down?

A: You are probably running into paging. This happens when the program requires more memory than you have real RAM, and has to use the swap file frequently. The only way to alleviate this is to not use ray tracing, simplify your scene, or buy more memory.

Q: How do I output my animations?

A: The easiest way is to use Video for Windows format. When .AVI output is selected trueSpace2 will produce Video for Windows movie (version 1.1) which can be immediately played by the Windows Media Player. Some graphics boards can play these movies quite fast and in full-screen size. Another possibility is a Flic animation. trueSpace2 will output a animation file with the .FLC extension. This file can be played back via the use of a shareware program such as AAPLAY.EXE, which is available on CompuServe, America Online, and various FTP sites. A third possibility is the Targa format. Numbered .TGA frames can be recorded with a single frame controller or played back in real time with some of the new compression boards such as the PAR from DPS.

Q: Does trueSpace2 do morphing?

A: trueSpace2 does not allow you to select two different objects and morph them into a third object. However, you can animate the transformation or deformation of one object into a variation of itself. This makes it easy to stretch a character's skin, create puffy cheeks or bulging muscles.

Q: How do I get realistic looking metal?

A: Use metal shader, turn the shininess up higher, you may want to use environment map (even simple 1D) and above all use lots of lights as they create nice specular highlights characteristic of metals.

Q: How do I print out my images?

A: Render your scene to a .TGA or .BMP file. Load the .TGA or .BMP into a graphics package like Paintbrush (comes with Windows), or any other graphics application that takes in these files and has a print command. trueSpace2 does not have an automatic dpi setting so it must be done manually at the time of render. Keep in mind that dpi means dots per inch so simply multiply the intended size of your picture by the desired dpi then enter that number as your resolution in the Render to File requester. As an example a 4' × 4' print at 300 dpi would be rendered at 1200 × 1200 pixels.

Q: Can I project an image from a light source?

A: Yes, prepare texture by applying transparency from the image utility panel. Position the texture in front of the shadow-casting light. Make sure that you have ray tracing and ray traced shadows enabled. You should see the texture projected.

Q: I import an object (DXF, OBJ, and so on) and apply a bitmap texture, but the texture doesn't appear on the object. What am I doing wrong?

A: When you initially import a DXF object, it has no UV space. You must assign UV space to the object in order to see the texture map.

Q: How can I cause an object to appear or disappear?

A: In trueSpace2 we have added the feature of animated opacity values for textures (see the Keyframes Monitor). Note that this feature applies only to solid color textures and will not have an effect on bitmap textures. Also, to accomplish total transparency there can be no reflection value assigned to the texture.

Q: How can I make lights blink or dim?

A: In trueSpace2 we have added the feature of animated light intensity. To adjust the light intensity between frames, simply, go to that key and adjust the intensity value. trueSpace2 will evenly interpolate the op intensity values between keys.

Q: I set a background for my image and have transparent textures with refraction vales. Why do I not see refracted light from the background image?

A: The use of backgrounds in trueSpace2 is a superimposition. Therefore, transparent objects with refraction values have no effect on the background image.

Q: Is there online support for trueSpace2?

A: Yes! trueSpace2 now has forums and user groups on America Online, CompuServe and an Internet e-mail address at `www.caligari.com`. You can also call our support BBS at (415) 390-0585. Please use the ZMODEM protocol to speed up your downloads.

CompuServe user ID: 74774,350

CompuServe Users Group: GO GUGRPA

CompuServe Support: GO CALIGARI

America Online ID: Caliga

America Online Forum: Keyword Caligari

Also, check out these sites on the Internet for trueSpace2 artwork, tips, and software updates:

```
avalon.chinalake.navy.mil    /pub
ftp.netnet.net               /pub
```

Q: I don't have a modem. Where can I call to speak to a technical representative?

A: You can call our technical support line at (415) 390-9600 Monday through Friday, 9:00 am to 5:00 pm, Pacific time.

A graphics card that supports at least 256 colors (Super-VGA) is required for Solid Rendered mode. If you have a better one (and I certainly hope you do), you probably have it set to true color. If you do, 3DR will give you a dumb message during the install — "Your video card must be set to at least 256 colors" — and then abort. The workaround is to reset your display to 256 colors, install 3DR and then go back to true color. If you have a slow computer, keep it at 256 colors or your display will run slower than a fox crossing a fresh-tarred road.

A fast local-bus or PCI graphics accelerator will increase performance of trueSpace2, while a 3D accelerator that supports Intel 3DR (I have yet to find drivers for 3DR) will offer the best performance possible. trueSpace2 will run under Windows 3.11 using Win32s (included with the program). trueSpace2 will also work under Windows 95 and NT. In Windows NT it runs in 16-bit emulation mode which is slower than a spider crossing fly paper — though with 28 megs of RAM and a 150Mhz processor, it seems to render quickly in NT.

Texture Setup

You have to transfer all the texture files on the CD-ROM into the \textures subdirectory created by the tS2 installation program. You also have to keep the directory structure the same as on the CD. So here's what I suggest you do. In

Windows 95, open Explorer and click on the root directory of your CD-ROM. You should see its directory structure in the right-hand window. Scroll until you can see the \textures subdirectory. Now in the left window scroll to where you installed tS2 on your hard drive (\truedemo). Click the little plus sign to the left to reveal the directory structure under \truedemo. You'll see that the installer placed a \textures subdirectory there. Good, now grab the \textures subdirectory from the CD-ROM (right window) and, holding down the Control key, drag it over to the \textures subdirectory in the left window. Release the key. Windows 95 automatically copies the proper arrangement of files and directories from the CD-ROM to your hard drive.

trueSpace installs its own textures as well. Adding your own makes them available to scenes as they load. This is particularly important for your adventure in Chapter 2, setting up the jumpstart animation. I recommend creating sub-subs for different classes of textures like: fiber, stone, wood, strange, and so on. This will simplify finding them when you get hundreds or even thousands of maps. If your misc. subdirectory gets very large, make new sub-sub categories and move files to keep it down.

Materials Libraries

The installer placed several Material libraries in your main trueSpace directory. You need to place two more here, Space.mlb and Book.mlb. They're not critical, but perhaps useful. Simply copy the libraries from the \matlibs subdirectory on the CD-ROM to the \truedemo subdirectory on your hard drive (if you already have trueSpace2, this will be the \truspace directory). Your Materials Libraries should work. If you get an error message that a texture map was unavailable, that means that the texture map is not where the library expects it to be. Unfortunately, it's not easy to find out where the library is actually looking for it. But don't worry about it, just use your head and the information in this book to create a similar texture. When you get the full version of trueSpace, you'll be able to save cool textures in your own libraries.

Need I say more? The whole book describes the rest of what you need to know about trueSpace2.

I'll introduce you to the rest of the CD in alphabetical order, just to be fair. If I don't mention a major subdirectory, it's used by another program, most likely *Distant Suns*. You can certainly explore these places and use the images to your heart's content.

Backgrounds

I'm not going to detail each background. There are some space backgrounds and some really beautiful if strange gradient backgrounds demonstrating different things you can do in Photoshop with a blank page and the gradient tool. I didn't put in any "normal" backgrounds; you can get them for your self. Enjoy them in good health. You'll find the backgrounds in the \bckgrnds directory on the CD-ROM. Copy the ones you want to your hard disk.

Cool Edit 1.5

I spent a lot of time in the text talking about how to use Cool Edit. Here's what David Johnston, father of Cool Edit, has to say about installing and registering it.

Installation

Copy (or unzip) all the files into their own program directory, like C:\Cool or something similar. From File Manager, select Cool and drag it into your favorite program Manager group. Alternately, you can go to File ⇨ New from program Manager and select Browse, then find Cool and choose it. There have been some nice new features added since version 1.34.

If you wish to save space on your hard drive, it is okay to remove any of the .FLT files you want. Each .FLT file allows Cool Edit to load a certain file format. If there are formats that you never use, you can delete the associated .FLT file for that format. For example, if you never use the Next/Sun AU file format, then delete the file AU.FLT from your \Cool program directory. You may also remove .XFM files if there are effects that you never use. Please keep the STRETCH.XFM, FILTER.XFM and AMPLIFY.XFM modules though, as they are crucial for operation in other parts of the program.

Thanks to everyone who sent in suggestions and found bugs and such! I have fixed all the big bugs, and implemented some of your suggested features. But I still did not have time to get around to them all.

Registering Cool Edit 1.5

To Register, see the Registration section of COOL.HLP (choose Help ⇨ Contents from within Cool Edit). I have three registration levels that you can choose from:

- ✦ $50 — Basic Registration. You will receive a registration number that will unlock your copy so you can use any function at any time.
- ✦ $100 — Preferred Registration. You will receive a registration number, and automatically receive ShareWare updates as they are released. You are also placed on my preferred list which will entitle you to other goodies in the future.
- ✦ $25 — Lite Version. You will receive a registration number that will turn your copy into a registered wave editor with only the bare wave editing essentials. If you have no need for all the fancy effects offered by Cool Edit, then register at this level.

Send a check drawn on a U.S. bank, or U.S. money order to:

Syntrillium Software Corporation
P.O. Box 60274
Phoenix, AZ 85082-0274 USA
FAX: 602-941-8170
E-mail: Syntrill@aol.com

Demos

In the \demos directory on the CD-ROM, you'll find four programs that I discuss here: First Light, Fractal Painter 3, Razor, and VistaPro.

First Light

Virtual Reality Labs was kind enough to license us to bring you *Distant Suns* on the CD-ROM. The next generation of planetarium software uses a live rendering engine to create accurate images and animations of astronomical events. Check out the neat demo and maybe you can even use some of the animations in the \1stlight subdirectory to practice rotoscoping. You can run the demo from the CD-ROM but it runs better if you put it in a temporary directory on your hard drive. Once you have finished viewing the program, you can simply delete the entire directory in order to remove it from your system.

VistaPro

The Alps.avi video clip in the \movies\dreamscp subdirectory was made with VistaPro. The is the second entry from Virtual Reality Labs. It's capable of much greater quality and detail than I endowed my animation with. All it takes is time and CPU power.

All you do is load a Digital Elevation Model (DEM) into the program and set a large bunch of parameters and start rendering. One neat trick is the bitmap-to-DEM conversion program that's included. It changes a photo into an elevation model based on the brightness of each pixel. You can also pick the season, altitude, camera angles, time of day, and so forth. This program has been used by game developers, architects, and others to create digital landscapes.

The demo gives you all the information you need. Run it right from the CD-ROM or copy it from \vistapro into a temporary directory on your computer. I reiterate that it's plenty useful. I think it needs an update and I understand there's one in the works. It will probably include better clouds, water, and atmospheric effects among other things.

Fractal Design Painter 3

Fractal Design Painter 3.0 is an awesome tool. Version 4.0 is even more awesome. This demo is "crippled," which is only fair considering you didn't pay for it. I put it here so you could be creative and see if you like what you can do with it. You can always use a screensaver to save your wonderful creations, but that will get old after a while. Then you'll go out an buy the product as you should.

The most outstanding thing about Fractal Design Painter is its "natural media" approach to digital graphics. You can paint on expensive (virtual) paper using water color, ink, oil, or acrylic. You can create all sorts of terrific designs and it works great with my Summagraphics Expression to give brush pressure effects.

You just bare down harder to get a wider, darker line. You can control all sorts of brush parameters to create the textures you want.

Often I'll use just the paper textures, maybe animate them, to create things like moving shadows on the sea floor or cloud shadows on a mountain. They also make neat bump maps to add texture to your surfaces. By applying lighting effects you can create 3D effects. The Image Hose also will blow 3D overlapping image elements onto your paper. The shamrocks in I-Wei's Survival of the Quickest demo were made this way.

To install it, just go to the \fractald subdirectory. I'm assuming you already have the latest Pkunzip. If you don't, just hop on the Web and get yourself a copy.

Here's the ReadMe file:

Introduction

Welcome to Fractal Design Painter 3 — astounding software for creating Natural-Media effects, multimedia projects, and image-editing designs.

With Painter you can produce art that mimics designs created with traditional tools. Or go completely beyond the bounds of tradition and create remarkable works that couldn't be produced any other way. Mix oils and watercolor, crayons and pastels. You can marbleize your backgrounds, cast synthetic shadows, warp your photos, or alter them with glass distortion.

In addition to its award-winning Natural-Media tools, Painter also excels at photo-design and collage. With the integration of the multiple floating selection capabilities of PainterX2, Painter 3 makes it easy to combine multiple images into your designs. And Painter's prodigious "cloning" capabilities make it easy to turn photographs into artwork using any of Painter's brushes and tools.

Painter 3 contains new artistic and production features that will wow you. This version incorporates more than 50 new features and improvements. The first thing you'll notice is our new drawer-based interface that makes it easy to access your tools and art material.

New color adjustment and selection controls enhance Painter's ability to manipulate photographs; improved color sets and faster brushes increase the program's Natural-Media capabilities. In Painter 3, Fractal Design introduces the Image Hose, an incredible new tool that literally allows you to "paint" with "reality." And Painter's new multimedia capabilities let you import VFW movies for frame-by-frame animation and rotoscoping.

About the Demo

Take Note: You must have Video for Windows loaded to use Painter 3!

This version of Painter is non-saving, non-printing demo software, that contains a subset of the art materials that ship with Painter (paper textures, gradations, weaves, paths, floaters, and so on). Also included are 2 image hose nozzles. Load these into the program by choosing IMAGE HOSE:LOAD NOZZLE from the TOOLS menu. Select CLOVER or SPLAT from the Open File dialog. Then choose the Image Hose brush from the brushes palette to "paint with reality."

For more information on Painter 3, or other Fractal Design products, please call 1-800-297-COOL.

Razor

Razor, Razor Pro, and Speed Razor Mach III all come from In:Sync. It's a small company with big ideas and growing all the time. They really have an eye on professional application of video editing. This is not my favorite demo because it's limited to grayscale images, but they assure me they're working on a much better one that will work in color. It was supposed to be ready for this CD-ROM but didn't make it. I wanted you to take a look at the interface. It's different and will take a little getting used to, but you'll find it ever so convenient to use. I've talked a lot about Razor Pro in the text so read the help files and give it a go. Here's what Jamie Carr had to say about installing it:

To install RAZOR, open the \razor directory on the CD-ROM and then click `install`. Running the install program places the program on your hard drive in single, easy to delete directory Once you have finished viewing the program, you can simply delete the entire directory in order to remove it from your system. If you want to go ahead and order RAZOR or RAZOR PRO, call us at: 1-800-864-7272.

Distant Suns

Your doorway to the universe is published by Virtual Reality Laboratories, Inc., 2341 Ganador Court, San Luis Obispo, CA 93401.

VOICE: (805) 545-8515

BBS: (805) 781-2257

Via AOL: Go Keyword VRLI

Via CompuServe: Go VRLI

Via Internet: VRLI@AOL.COM

Contents

- Overview; What's on this Disk
- How to Install onto a Hard Disk
- How to Install the Online Manual Reader
- How to Run From the CD without Installing
- How to Install Video For Windows

Overview

This CD-ROM contains nearly all of the award-winning desktop planetarium program *Distant Suns*, with hundreds of images of planets, galaxies, comets, and astronauts.

All documentation for *Distant Suns* on the CD-ROM is contained in an online manual. You must install the Acrobat reader in order to view the documentation. For a nominal fee, VRLI will send you a printed copy (shipping and handling charges may apply). This CD also contains the runtime version of Video for Windows version 1.1a and is automatically installed if you install *Distant Suns* onto your hard drive.

How To Install *Distant Suns* onto a Hard Disk

In Windows 95, use the Explorer to check out the \dssetup subdirectory on your CD-ROM and double-click on `setup`. That's it. Follow the directions and the *Distant Suns* program will be installed automatically. Most of the images will remain on the CD-ROM as there are so many. I didn't put them all on, leaving off several less popular categories, so if you run into a message that a certain image isn't available, you'll know who to blame.

You'll also find an excellent manual in Adobe Acrobat format. If you don't have Acrobat installed, a copy lurks onboard in the \dst_suns\manual subdirectory. Double-click on the Acroread file and it installs the utility automatically. Be sure to tell it where to put the reader. The installer also restarts your computer. After that, start the Acrobat Reader and load the dsmanual.pdf file found in this same directory. Then you'll be off and flying — to distant suns.

How To Run *Distant Suns* From the CD without Installing

You must install Video for Windows before running *Distant Suns*, unless you're using Windows 95 which has it built in. You may execute *Distant Suns* directly from the CD-ROM simply by opening the \dst_suns directory and then clicking dst_suns. In this configuration the program will run, but will not "remember" your selections after you exit because it cannot write them to the CD. Also, you cannot edit the other files that come with the program.

How To Install Video For Windows onto a Hard Disk

Open the \vidwin directory on the CD-ROM. Click `setup` to install the program to your hard disk.

Exploder

Exploder, thoroughly described in the text, is a special F/X engine that manipulates tS objects. It can simulate gravity and surface collision as well as explosions. That's it. The operation of the application is fully explained in the text. This one is a lot of fun and will consume many hours of your time in experiments.

Install Exploder by creating an \exploder subdirectory and copying all the files in \exploder to it. Next place an icon in your workspace using the method for the level of Windows you're operating. In Windows 95, click on the Start button, go to settings and select Taskbar ⇨ Start menu programs ⇨ Add, and follow the directions, placing the icon in a work group or the desktop. I suggest using the desktop while you're concentrating on this book. It'll be easier to get at.

Fountain

Fountain is explained in detail in Chapters 33 and 34. It is a dual-function program that uses trueSpace conventions to build and surf 3D Web sites using the VRML language. To set up Fountain for use, go to the \fountain subdirectory on the CD-ROM and click `setup`. From there, just follow the instructions. If you have a problem installing 3DR it's probably because your video card is set up for 24-bit color. Reduce it to 8-bit color for the installation, then go back up.

FX

Go to the \FX directory on the CD-ROM where you'll find some interesting F/X that are specifically designed for use in tS2. My thanks to Edward Swan for building them with intense creativity. If you design an interesting effect, you might want to contribute it to his Web page at: `http://www.cris.com/~eswan/tsfx.html` where you'll find all the latest special effects to play with. He's included some of them on the CD-ROM, and here are his descriptions:

Lens Flare

Lens Flare Object for Caligari trueSpace

Author: Edward W. Swan

E-mail: eswan@cris.com

Files included in the \fx\bcom subdirectory:

- flare.cob
- flare.txt

Due to an absence of plug-ins that would do the job, I created the Lens Flare object for "the rest of us" who use tS2 for our rendering and animation.

Instructions for Use

I tried to make it as simple and efficient as possible to use. Load it into your scene, place it where you want it, and use the Look At tool to make it face the camera. Voilà... flare, with you wherever you go, in the home, office, or at school!

The Lens Flare object is not a three-dimensional object, nor is it any major feat in the annals of tS object creation. It's fakery. It's simply a flat disc using a procedural wood texture with a few flat rods sticking out of it. It won't behave like a true lens flare all the time; if an object passes in front of it, for example, the flare won't wash it out.

Placement in front of other objects, or standing alone in a scene (a star or sun), is key. With a little maneuvering you can wash out your scene with the best LightWavers. E-mail me if you have any more questions.

Star Globe With Nebula

Starfield with nebula

Author: Edward W. Swan

E-mail: eswan@cris.com

Files included:

- ✦ starfld.bmp
- ✦ nebstars.cob
- ✦ neb-1.txr
- ✦ nebstar.txt

Description/Instructions

The nebstars.cob object can be used to simulate a starry background in any direction. I have also included a texture map material rectangle of a purplish nebula in the background; it's partially transparent and can be scaled and moved in any direction to your liking.

Please make sure to extract or copy starfld.bmp and neb-1.txr into your \truedemo\textures directory, or you will receive a "Texture not found" error when you try to load the starsphere. The sphere isn't terribly large as it is, so you may want to scale it up to work better within your scene. Questions, comments — please e-mail to eswan@cris.com.

Explosion Sequence

Author: Edward W. Swan

E-mail: eswan@cris.com

Files included:

- ✦ xplod.cob
- ✦ xpltex.zip (contains a series of bitmapped explosion images)
- ✦ xplod.txt

The explosion object in xplod.cob doesn't really produce a true, three-dimensional explosion. What it does do is use two-dimensional fakery to simulate a gassy, expanding fireball. Used in conjunction with the xplsparks.cob object (found alongside this file on the DTGrafix trueSpace F/X page), it's not hard for people who like to blow things up to get their wish in trueSpace.

The explosion bitmap was created using POV-Ray's BLOB program. The POV source code *used* to be on `ftp.povray.org` somewhere, but I couldn't hazard the foggiest guess where it could be nowadays. The brightness at the beginning comes from a disc overlaid with the same basic procedural material found in the flare.cob object.

Installing

Put xplod.cob in your \truedemo\objects directory. Unzip xpltex.zip into your \truedemo\textures directory. (Note: xpltex.zip unzips into a rather large (14MB) series of bitmapped images... so make sure you've got the HD space available! As animators, however, I think we're all used to having large amounts of drive space chewed up overnight.)

Directions for Use

One thing that you really need to have in your scene is a camera, though I don't feel that this requirement is terribly burdensome on any tS users out there! Load xplod.cob into your scene. Set your current frame to 0, and place the explosion object where you want the explosion to occur. Use the Look At tool to make the object face the camera.

That's it! Thirty frames of fiery fury. You can use the animation project window to delay detonation to any time you want; placing xplsparks.cob at the same location will only enhance the fun. Used in conjunction with the Exploder utility (elsewhere on this CD), all sorts of mayhem can result.

Please contact me via e-mail at `eswan@cris.com` if you have any further questions.

Sparks Effect

Explosion Sparks

Author: Edward W. Swan

E-mail: eswan@cris.com

Files included:

✦ xpsparks.cob

✦ xpsparks.txt

xpsparks.cob is a trueSpace2 object consisting of a dozen or so small, glowing spheres that expand from a central point while contracting, sort of like a burst of fireworks.

Not difficult to create. The process involved creating a small sphere, placing a "shell" sphere around it for some glow/color, gluing them together, then setting the frame to 30 and moving it out while scaling it down considerably. Then I copied this object to other random, various places at frame 30 and glued all the objects together, eliminating movement keyframe at 30 so the whole deal stays where you put it.

Instructions for Use

Retrieve xpsparks.cob into your scene, place it where you want your little burst to occur. You could use this in conjunction with the xplod.cob companion object found on the DTGrafix trueSpace F/X page, and also with the exploder utility found on the Caligari Web site.

For a more spectacular pyrotechnic display, retrieve several copies of the object and place them all over your scene. Hum *Stars and Stripes Forever* for added atmosphere.

Games

I've included two games that were developed using trueSpace2. Some parts of the games were developed in the original trueSpace. The first is an award-winning shareware product from MVP Software Productions and the second is a demo of Void Pirates, a commercial game from Diversions Software.

Rings of the Magi

This game is shareware. You may freely try it. If you like it or find it useful, then you must register with MVP Software. To "register" a shareware game means to purchase it directly from the developer. (Shareware games are evaluation versions only, which means you have the right to try them, but after trying them you must either register them with the author or delete them from your system. It is unlikely that anyone will check up on you, so shareware works because of the honesty of users.) When you register you will receive Rings of the Magi: Grand Master Edition, which includes all of the following additional features:

✦ 60 new boards (80 boards in all).

✦ Three times as many graphics compared to the shareware version.

✦ Secret cheat codes.

✦ Auto-solve for all boards.

✦ Save your own solve routines.

✦ Easy-to-use editor lets you create your own killer boards.

✦ Printed manual with tips and hints from the author.

An MVP Software Production.

Ordering Information

Rings of the Magi: Grand Master Edition is just $19.95 plus shipping, so order today! Registered users receive a special offer on other MVP products.

To order, call 1-800-968-9684 toll-free 24 hours a day. Please have your MasterCard or Visa ready when you call. Or fill out the order form in this manual and fax it to: 616-245-3204. Make sure your credit card number and expiration date are legible. Or, if you prefer, mail the order form and your check to: MVP Software, 1035 Dallas SE, Grand Rapids, MI 49507-1407. For overseas orders or technical support call 616-245-8376.

Download All the Latest MVP ShareWare Games *Free*

MVP software is on the Internet. You can FTP directly from the following sites:

```
ftp.uwp.edu/pub/msdos/games/mvp
ftp.uml.edu/msdos/games/mvp
ftp.wuarchive.wustl.edu/systems/msdos/msdos-games/mvp
```

These sites also have many mirrors, so just look for a game site with an MVP directory, and you'll be assured of getting the best games around!

Installation

Rings of the Magi can be installed and run from DOS and Windows. Although it is a DOS program, most Windows users will experience no difficulty in running the game from Windows. However, after installation, if you have any difficulties in running it from Windows, we recommend that you run it from DOS only.

Online users: If you have downloaded Rings of the Magi from a BBS and unzipped the file onto your hard drive into a separate directory, simply type `ROTM` and press Enter to start the game.

To install Rings of the Magi from Windows, go to Windows File or Program Manager and open the \games\rings subdirectory on the CD-ROM. Click `Winsetup`. To start the game from Windows, double-click on the Rings of the Magi icon.

System Requirements

Rings of the Magi requires a 386sx or faster IBM PC-compatible computer with at least 512K conventional RAM free, VGA graphics card and monitor, a hard drive with at least 2.5 megabytes free, and a mouse and mouse driver. To start the game from DOS, you must first change to the directory in which Rings of the Magi is installed. For example, type `CD\ROTM` and press the Enter key. Then type `ROTM` and press Enter to start the program.

If you experience trouble getting Rings of the Magi to start properly, see the troubleshooting section at the end of this document.

The Story

In ages long past, the mystics of Ac'Rianed realized their powers were dwindling, and the art of the Magi was quickly being forgotten. The life energy of their world, which fueled their magic, was slowly drained by some unknown, yet terrible force. The people of Ac'Rianed were wasting away, while the mystics felt powerless to protect them.

Thus is was that the mystics came together and crafted their rings — a set of artifacts in which they could store their remaining power. Each mystic fashioned a set of rings from a distinctive material, and whenever two or more of these similar rings were brought together, the power within them could be harnessed. By separating the rings into different patterns and then reassembling them, different aspects of that power could be called upon.

But it was not enough to simply store this power in the rings. New apprentices had to be trained, lest the secret of the rings be forgotten and the world fall into ruin. Thus was created a special training board upon which novice users of the rings could safely practice their assembly. Only by successfully completing this training can the apprentice hope to restore peace to Ac'Rianed, and command the Rings of the Magi....

Intro/Story

When the game loads, an introduction and story sequence is displayed. The intro/story consists of a number of short scenes, each of which remains on screen for a short while before advancing to the next scene. You may advance to the next scene more rapidly by pressing a key or clicking a mouse button. You may also bypass the intro/story sequence completely by pressing the Esc key at any time.

Playing the Game

The object of the game is to remove all of the colored rings from the game board. Once all the rings have been removed from a particular board, that puzzle is considered completed and you may move on to the next puzzle.

Rings are removed from the game board whenever two or more rings of the same color come into direct contact with each another. The rings cannot be moved directly, but are affected by arrow buttons located throughout the game board.

Arrow buttons indicate the direction in which they will exert their force. When an arrow button is pressed, all the rings in the indicated row or column will move one step in the indicated direction, unless blocked or hidden behind a solid object.

Ring movement may be blocked by a solid wooden game piece, or by an arrow button, or by another ring if that ring is itself blocked by some solid object. Additionally, a ring may be blocked by the edge of the game board itself — it is not possible to push a ring off the edge of the game board.

For lots more detail, shortcut keys, strategies, and problem solving, read the ROTM.DOC file in the \games\rings subdirectory.

Credits

Design and programming: David Bollinger

Art and Animation: Tom Marlin, Marlin Studios

Composer: David B. Schultz, DBS Music

Voice of the Magi: Dale Blackwood

Producer: C. Steven Blackwood

Void Pirates

by Diversions Software

This demo requires VBRUN300.DLL, and is not distributed with it due to file size, and the fact that many people already have this file on their systems, and don't need to download (and pay for it) again. VBRUN300.DLL is available from most online services and bulletin boards.

To run the demo, simply run \games\vdpirate\voiddemo from the CD-ROM. Thank you for taking a look at the Void Pirates Demo. We hope you enjoy it.

This demo is but a small sample of things to come. Video and slides were not included with the demo due to file size and system configurations.

2135 AD

Lundy Outpost: Europa Colony

Recently unemployed, you accept a cargo run into the asteroid belt...

The pay is good, a little too good... But you need the money.

The job goes wrong... a simple pickup turns into 24 innocent dead...

Who set you up? Why?

Hours later, there is a bounty on your head and your crew's.

Thrust into a career you never thought of...

Nowhere to turn, but into the Void...

This exciting new game keeps you on the edge with:

- ✦ Hair-raising strafing runs on hapless freighters!
- ✦ Disable them, and pillage them with remote piloted drones...
- ✦ Steal credits and equipment to sell and trade to finance your exploits, enabling you to discover the secret of your former employer.
- ✦ Fend off the authorities from the gun turrets...
- ✦ Can you keep them at bay until the jump drives come online?
- ✦ Can you discover the secret to the cargo shipments to the outer planets?

Void Pirates includes:

- ✦ An hour of live-action digital video. Interact with the crew of your ship.
- ✦ Over 400MB of animations and richly detailed environments.
- ✦ Original music score.
- ✦ More action than an "interactive movie."

Strategy, simulation, mystery, action, and intrigue all rolled into the hottest CD available this year!

For information or ordering call: SofSource at 1-505-523-6789.

E-mail: 76450.3711@compuserve.com

Produced and distributed by SofSource Inc.

Geometry

There are a fair number of new objects here, ones you haven't seen before in other 3D books with CD-ROMs. Thanks to Michael Meshew at Graphic Detail, the guys at 3NAME3D, and Harry Goldsholl at Model Masters we have some fine, detailed geometry to play with. I recommend their full collections as well. Oh yes, I threw in a bundle of my stuff as well, under DreamScape.

Three-Name 3D

WEB CONNECTION

Cyber props are created by a company called 3NAME3D in Santa Monica, California. The company got its name from the three partners: Sandeep Divekar, Oscar Yglesias, and Steven Wallock. Their primary business is building detailed models for the film industry and game worlds. Their work has been featured in many films, games, TV commercials, and even on the Jay Leno show. They have a locked CD-ROM that they will send your for free — you just purchase and unlock libraries as you need them. You can also purchase individual models by calling them. Check out their work at SGI's Hot Mix-13 site at `www.sgi.com`. Their main URL is `www.ywd.com`. Also check out their nifty texture mapping tips at `www.ywd.com/cindy/texture.html`.

You can reach them at:

3NAME3D
1202 W. Olympic Blvd., No 101
Santa Monica, CA 90404

1-800-993-4621

They offer highly complex, hi-rez models all the way down to light models suitable for use in Web pages. Here some images of the six models they've donated to the cause, which you'll find in the \geometry\3name3d subdirectory:

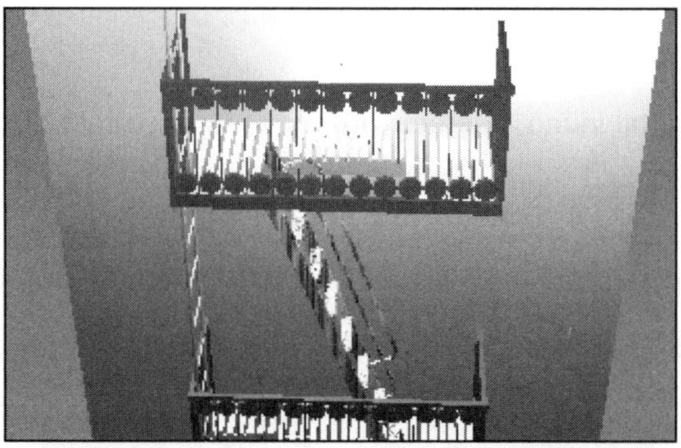

Fire Escape is useful for the city scenes [fescape.3ds]

Metal ladder makes a good landing bay detail; lot of uses. [metaladr.3ds]

Movie reel is a neat old-fashioned 35mm film reel, very useful for logos. [movireel.3ds]

Pipes is a highly detailed fire valve assembly. Navigate the hierarchy and paint it with different textures. Makes a good ship or bay detail. [pipes.3ds]

Streetlight is a turn-of-the-century public lighting fixture, great for those city scenes. [strlamp.3ds]

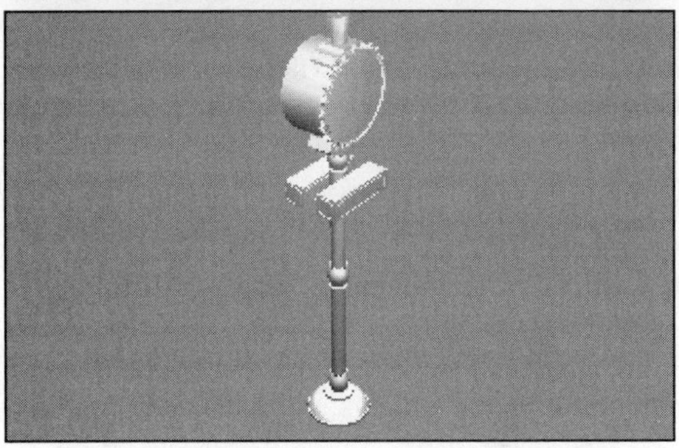

Street Clock is another old-fashioned public fixture popular in the 20s and 30s, but still seen today. [stclock.3ds]

DreamScape Productions

This directory offers a collection of my stuff. Check it out and use it for fun. Under \geometry\dreamscp\ you'll find two objects you can use in experimenting with an underwater shark scene: shark.cob, a pregnant nurse shark, and watrplnt.cob, a fanciful underwater plant I made up. Under \geometry\dreamscp\nernies you'll find a large collection of nernie objects for use in embellishing scenes.

Under \geometry\dreamscp\space I put a miscellaneous collection of objects, some hard to build like starfld.cob, which is about 2,000 stars in a large sphere. Expand it to use in your scenes. Oh yes, for lack of a better place, I included I-Wei

Huang's I-pod.cob here. It has the rotational axes scrambled so you can practice moving them to set up articulated motion. Vapor.cob is an interesting bit of geometry that you'd better not load unless you have a lot of memory, like 16MB or so. If you want to know what it is, you'll just have to spring for the memory. The rest of these goodies are for play and practice — enjoy.

Graphic Detail

Down in Louisville, Kentucky, Michael Meshew started Graphic Detail to support the growing demand for Amiga-based graphical material. His Light ROM three for the LightWave crowd is a three CD set of hundreds of megabytes of models, materials, textures, scene files, and more. The models work great in trueSpace of course. But Graphic Detail is moving into the trueSpace world in a big way. Michael will soon release true3D (or may already have), a CD-ROM packed with 650 megs of 3D objects and textures for use with trueSpace 3D. This is an absolute must for both serious and casual users. I can't believe the value Michael puts into his products. The value is even greater since he's given you, dear reader, a discount off his rock-bottom price. You'll find literally thousands of 3D objects included in the trueSpace .cob file format ready for rendering along with hundreds of textures in the Targa and Jpeg file formats. Samples of the trueSpace objects are included on this disk for your enjoyment.

You'll find trueSpace 3D objects grouped in categories of: Aviation, Animals, Botany, Buildings, Computers, Electronics, Furniture, Groceries, Kitchen, Landscapes, Logos, Misc., Music, Robots, Ships, Space, Sports, Toys, Vehicles, Video, and Weapons.

Textures are in Targa and Jpeg format and are grouped by subjects: Brick, Carpet, Cloth, Formica, Granite, Organic, Panels, Rock, Stone, Tiles, and Wood. Thumbnails of these textures are provided for easy previewing. true3D was scheduled to be ready for sale on May 15, 1996.

The list price of true3D will be $49.95 plus shipping. Readers of this book can purchase true3D for only $39.95 plus shipping by simply mentioning the *Caligari trueSpace2 Bible* when placing your order. true3D can be ordered through:

Graphic Detail Inc.
4556 South Third Street
Louisville, KY 40214 USA

Toll free order number: 1-800-265-404
Voice and fax: 502-363-2986
E-mail: michael@iglou.com

Shipping charges are $4.95 for U.S. and Canadian shipping; $6.95 for international orders.

He's very generously provided us with a trunk full of detailed models from that CD to play with. They're in the \geometry\Tru3D subdirectory.

Here are the model images you already have for use:

Bulb [bulb.cob]

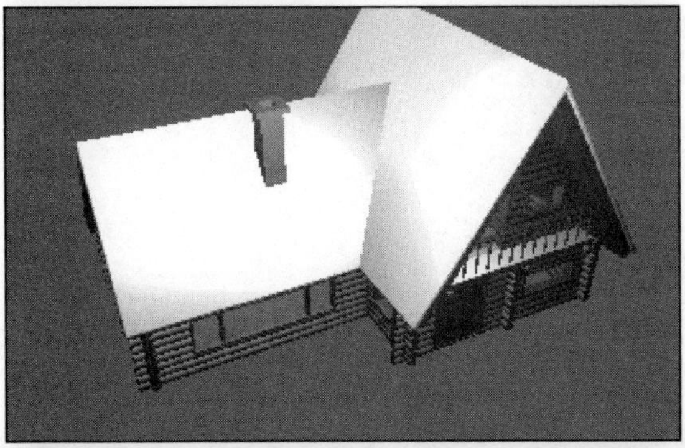

Cabin [cabin.cob]

Circuit board [circuitb.cob]

Handcuffs [cuffs.cob]

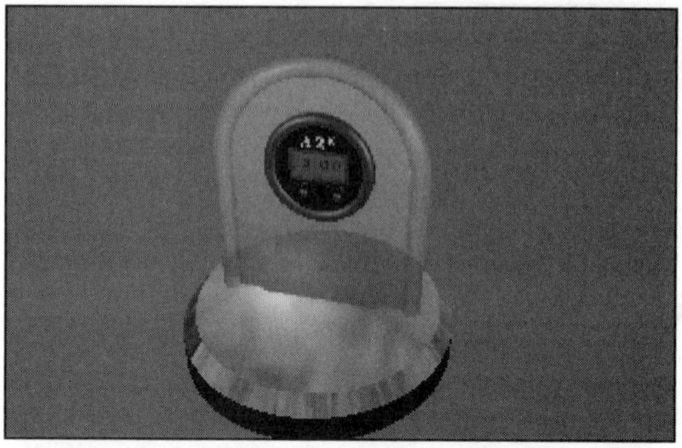

Desk clock [deskclok.cob]

Dinosaur [dino.cob]

Entertainment center [e_center.cob]

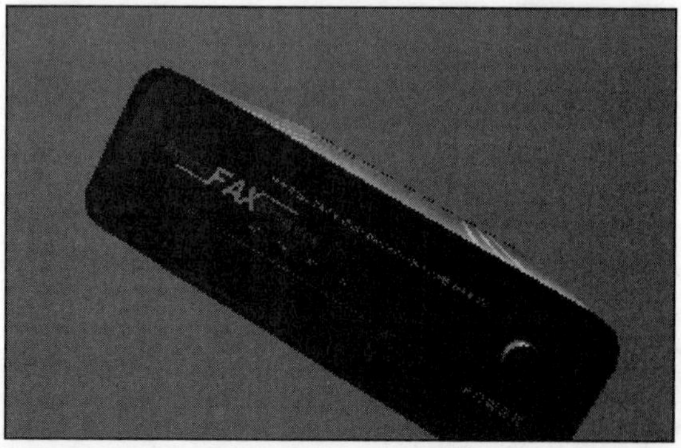

Fax machine [fax.cob]

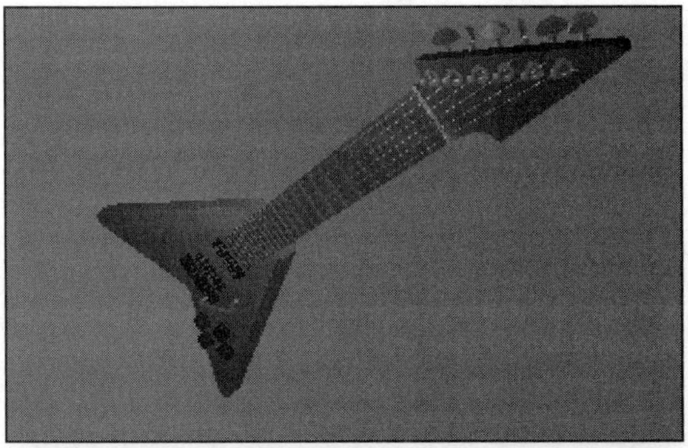

Electric rock and roll guitar [guitar.cob]

An hour glass [hourglas.cob]

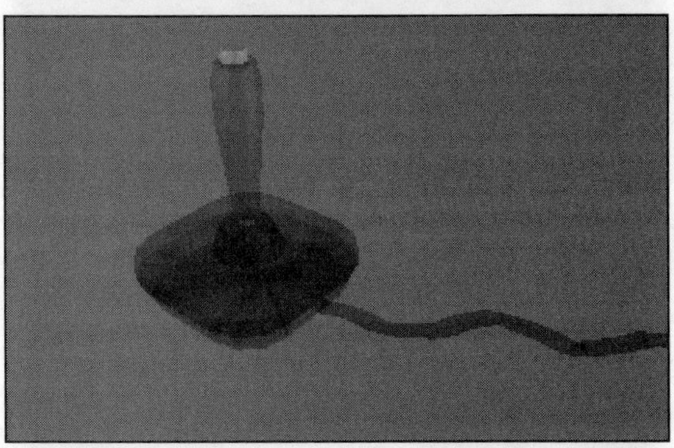

A typical joy stick [joystick.cob]

An old-fashioned kerosene lamp [kerolamp.cob]

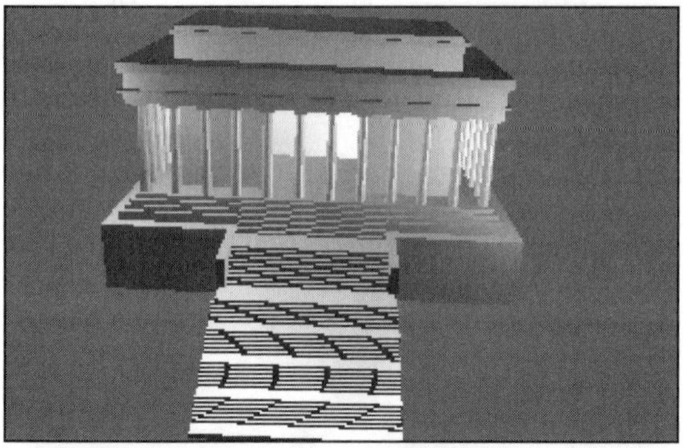

The entire Lincoln Memorial
[lincolnm.cob]

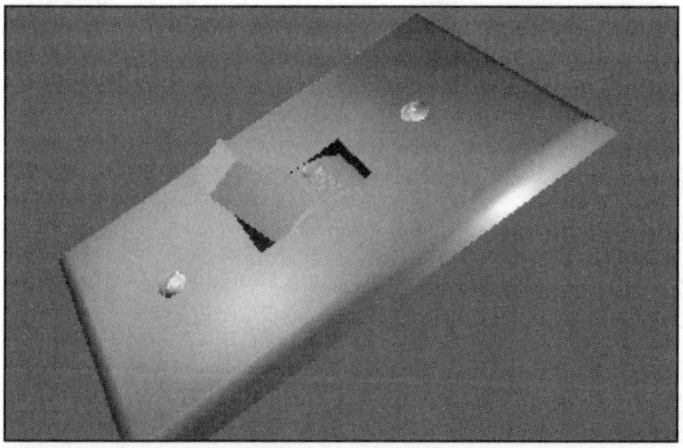

A standard household light switch
[lswitch.cob]

A typical household outlet
[outlet.cob]

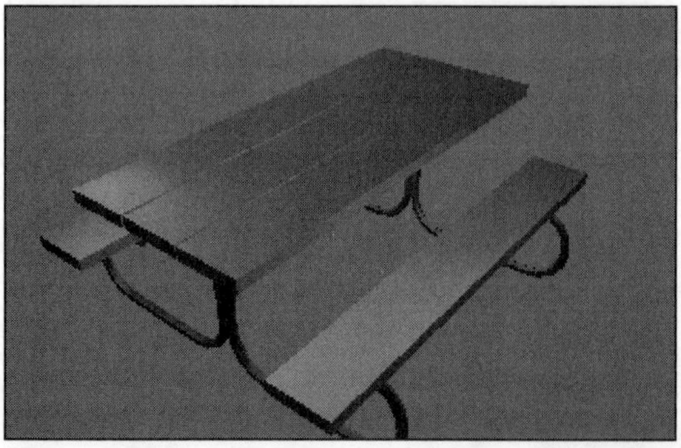

A modern picnic table
[picnic_t.cob]

Typical electric plug [plug.cob]

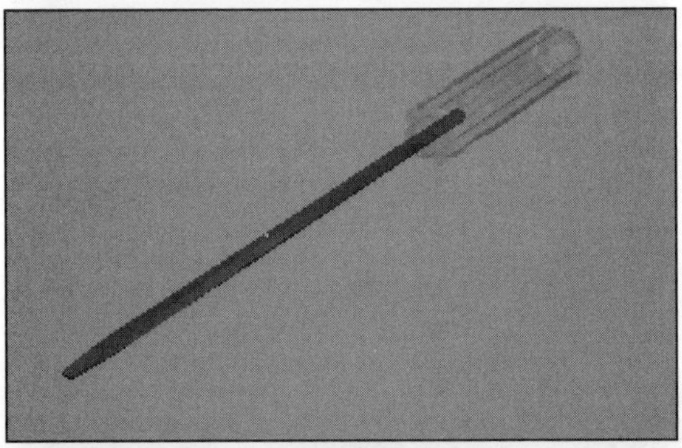

A screwdriver [screwdrv.cob]

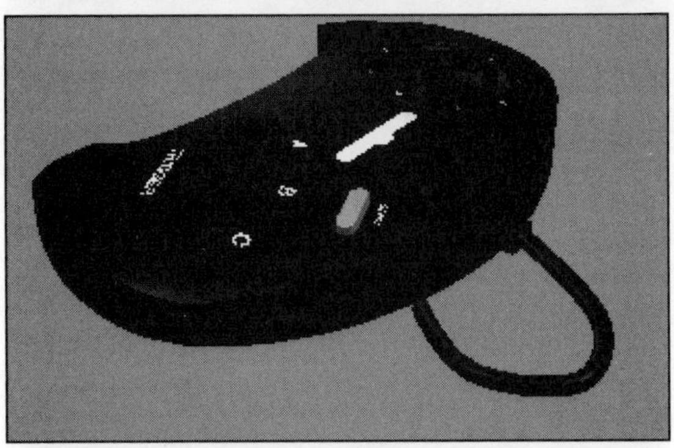

One version of a Sega game control console [segacont.cob]

Version two of a Sega game control [seega2.cob]

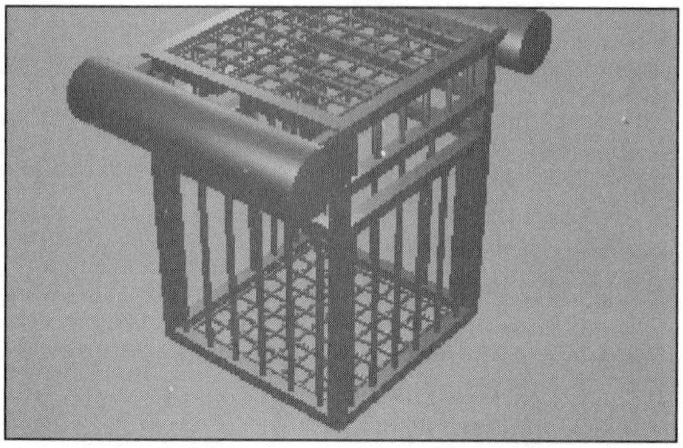

Strange as it may seem, this is really a shark cage for underwater studies. [sharkcge.cob]

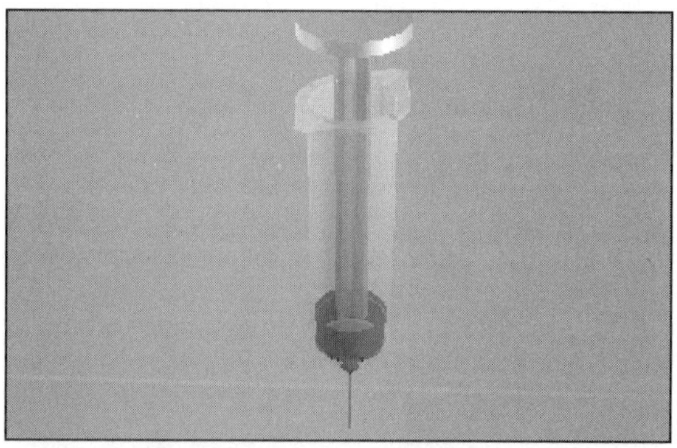

A needle – make a medical logo! [syringe.cob]

A full-on traffic light for your cityscape. [t_light.cob]

Model Masters

Model Masters is a offshoot of Goldsholl: Film Group, which has been producing a variety of animation, including CG, stopmotion/motion control, mixed media, and clay animation, for over 20 years. Rapidly changing industry trends suggested to Harry Goldsholl that everyone would soon have 3D on their desktops and the one thing that all these new users needed was models. At the time, quality commercial models were prohibitively expensive, built primarily for film and other commercial uses.

Such prices would have to come down if the user base were to grow and include more casual users. Many multimedia producers for small companies would not have the time or perhaps the skills needed to create exacting models.

Model Masters was formed to create libraries that would be affordable yet provide a high production value. Our FotoReal models are built with photorealistic rendering in mind, yet cost as little as $1 each. Model Masters will continue to develop content with this in mind.

Model Masters just announced the release of Master Demo 1, a CD-ROM collection of the top 3D, CAD, and multimedia software products available for the PC, MAC, and UNIX platforms. No longer do you have to spend hours searching out products and information on the Internet, or downloading demos. Master Demo gives the professional user an unprecedented opportunity to seek out and evaluate new tools. It also enables the casual or new graphics user the ability to evaluate complex products and test drive their functionality prior to purchase, across a broad range of price points.

Included on the Master Demo CD are demos of Soft/Fx, trueSpace2, Trispectives, Corel Draw 6, Cad3X Modeler, Amapi, Vidi Presenter Pro, 3D World, Infini-D, Strata Studio Pro, Sculpt MECN Tree Factory, 3Z3D, Vertigo, Cadkey, Sound Forge, Quest, Designers Edge, Toast CD-ROM Pro, and more. Also, included are multi-platform versions of POV and BMRT renderers as well as a handful of useful tools and utilities.

In addition, you'll find the latest model creations from Model Masters, including their new transportation library all with an especially low price on the Interiors-1 FotoReal Library. You can arrange to unlock models by the piece or collection. You can get the Master Demo-1 for $14.95 including shipping and handling anywhere in the U.S., $19.95 abroad.

You can reach Model Masters at:

Harry Goldsholl
Model Masters L.L.C.
420 Frontage Road
Northfield, IL 60093

Phone: 847-446-9762
Fax: 847-446-8320
E-mail: hgold@interaccess.com

Don't forget to visit their neat Web site at:
`http:/www.interaccess.com/modelmaster/`

Ask about the Model Monger disk that owners of this book can get for the very special price of $49.95, which is a *hundred dollars* off the regular price. Here are a few 3D Studio format examples of the high quality geometry you'll find in the \geometry\modlmstr subdirectory:

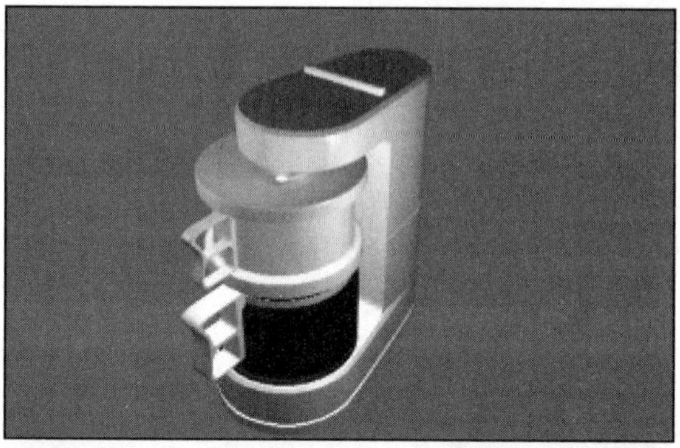

Coffee Pot [coffee.3ds]
A modern coffee dripper that will go well on any kitchen counter.

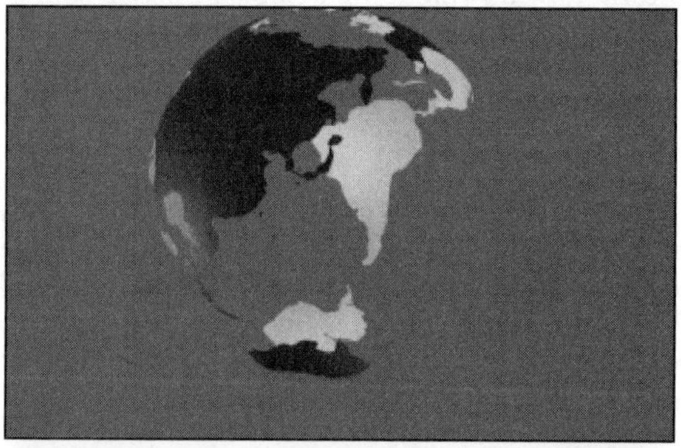

Globe [globe.3ds]
This is an interesting globe effect. There is no full sphere, all the oceans are missing and you have only the continents and islands. You can mount this globe on a sphere if you find it too far out for your purposes.

Hanging Lamp [hang1.3ds]
This is a modern hanging lamp that works best if you raytrace it and give the glass a high refraction value.

Stepper [stepper.3ds]
This is a piece of exercise equip-ment that you can animate if you like.

Traditional Leather Couch [trad_cou.3ds]
Notice the smooth leather finish with small surface details. You can turn this into a fabric couch by texture mapping with a pattern and fine bump map.

JASC

Jasc has give us two very useful shareware products. You should definitely register them because you'll probably use both a lot while reading this book.

Media Center

Before you can use Jasc Media Center you have to run the Jasc setup file on the CD-ROM under \JASC\mediacnt. The files are archived to save space.

Installing Jasc Media Center

The setup program unpacks those files and builds them on your working disk. Here's how:

1. Start Windows.
2. Activate Program Manager and make Program Manager the active window.
3. Open the File Run dialog box by selecting Run x:\jasc\mediacnt\setup from the Program Manager's File menu, and then hit the Enter key.
4. Follow the instructions from there.

The User's Manual

To keep the size of the shareware version of Jasc Media Center reasonable, no user's manual is provided. You will find that *all* menu items and associated dialog boxes, along with general information, is provided on line using the Help-Index menu option of the program.

When you purchase the licensed version of Jasc Media Center you will receive the fully illustrated, perfect-bound user's guide.

Jasc Media Center Technical Support

Technical support for Jasc Media Center can be obtained from:

USA

JASC, Inc., 10901 Red Circle Drive, Suite 340, Minnetonka, MN 55343 USA

Voice: (612) 930-9171 (9 am to 5 pm USA central time)

Fax: (612) 930-3516 (24 hours)

Internet: jasc@winternet.com

CompuServe: Jasc forum — GO JASC

BBS: (612) 930-3516

UK

Digital Workshop, First Floor, 8 West Bar, Banbury, Oxon, OX16 9RP England

Voice: (0295) 258335

Fax: (0295) 254590

Japan

Personal Data Factory, Shimoueki-cho 451-3, Isesaki-shi, Gunma-ken, 372 Japan

Voice: 0270-21-1423

Purchasing the Licensed Version

You may use the shareware version of Jasc Media Center for a 30-day trial period. If you would like to continue to use Jasc Media Center after the 30-day trial period, you are required to purchase the licensed version of Jasc Media Center.

When you purchase the licensed version of Jasc Media Center you will receive a disk with the licensed version and the printed user's guide.

Paint Shop Pro — Version 3.0

Install Paint Shop Pro by going to the \jasc\paintshp\ subdirectory and clicking `setup`. Follow the simple screen directions and in a few seconds you'll be up and running.

Paint Shop Pro is the only photo retouching, painting, image format conversion, and screen capturing program you are likely to need unless you want to do a lot of compositing work. Its features include:

- **Painting** — Paint Shop Pro supports eight different brushes including pen, pencil, marker, crayon, chalk, charcoal, airbrush, and paintbrush to edit an existing image, or create your own. A user-defined brush allows you to combine elements of any of the other brushes to create a unique effect, while the fill tool allows easy filling of large areas. No need to worry about errors because the undo brush allows mistakes to be easily corrected.
- **Photo Retouching** — Work on existing images with the clone brush for easy duplication of image areas, or with the magic wand for quick selection of similar areas for manipulation. Also provided are a push brush for easy

touch-up, a sharpen brush to enhance detail in small areas, and a smooth brush for easy blending. You can also use the eye dropper to pick up and analyze a color from an image.

- **Image Enhancement and Editing** — Paint Shop Pro allows you to perform flip, mirror, rotate, and crop operations, and gives you the ability to add borders and frames, or resize and resample your image. Paint Shop Pro ships with 20 standard image filters plus any user-definable filters you create. Also included are 12 image deformations, including skew and circle. Filter and deformation browsers are also provided. Paint Shop Pro supports Adobe compatible plug-in filters.
- **Color Enhancement** — With Paint Shop Pro, you can alter the hue, saturation, lightness, and RGB levels. Adjustments to brightness and contrast and changes to highlight, shadow, and midtone can also be made. Palette editing and direct palette mapping allow global changes to multiple images. Gamma correction and color reduction are also provided.
- **Image Browser** — The browser, using thumbnails, allows you to visually search directories for those easy to lose images. The thumbnails may optionally be saved for super-quick access. You can also select multiple images to be loaded directly into Paint Shop Pro for editing. Complete file management functions allow you to easily keep track of images.
- **Batch Conversion** — When it comes to converting a large number of images from one format to another, Paint Shop Pro has made it as easy as possible. All messages during the conversion are sent to the log window for unattended operation, and the log may be saved to a file for later inspection.
- Paint Shop Pro also provides image viewing and printing functions to provide you complete control over how your images appear.
- Support for TWAIN-compliant scanners is also included.
- Paint Shop Pro provides support for the following image file formats: BMP, CDR, CGM, CLP, CUT, DIB, DRW, DXF, EPS, GEM, GIF, HPGL, IFF, IMG, JIF, JPG, LBM, MAC, MSP, PCD, PCX, PIC, PBM, PGM, PPM, PSD, RAW, RAS, RLE, TIFF, TGA, WMF, WPG.

For information on support and purchasing a licensed version of Paint Shop Pro, see instructions under Media Center or review the readme.txt file on the CD-ROM.

Material Libraries

I've created two material libraries for you. They are called Book and Space. But the nature of the book leads to each having space textures on board. My intent was only to give you a few materials to play with, not to solve any major texture problems. You have to do that yourself. Try making up a library of fabrics or glass or anything. I think it's best to keep one general materials library of things you often use and then put the rest of your stuff into reasonably homogenous groupings. You'll also see simple.mlb. This file is installed automatically.

Copy the material libraries into your main tS2 subdirectory on your hard drive and, to repeat (in case you missed it), use Explorer to grab the \textures subdirectory and all its nested subdirectories, and drag it over the top of your \truedemo\textures on your hard drive. You can tell when it's right because the directory to which files will be transferred is highlighted. Let go and all the textures will be automatically copied and the directory structure maintained. That's necessary for the libraries to work.

Movies

I put in lots of movies. I did not pad them for the CD-ROM because I want you to put them on your hard drive for play. That affords a higher data rate and better performance. So before playing the movies, move them over. If you don't they will be very jerky with a ton of dropped frames.

Many of these clips simply show a technique and should not be used as a quality standard to judge your own work by. I also left in errors for you to see what I mean by them. You'll have to do a lot better than I did in my demos if you want to get a job. Take more time. You can imagine how quickly I had to do all of them and still write the book. There is one called landgbay.avi, which you'll find in the \dreamscp subdirectory, that I wish I'd had more time on. It should have been three times as long so it would run slower (just stretch it out in the Animation Project window) and when I redo it, I'll put a search light on the ship. It'll run its cone of light across the surface as it comes in. You get the idea. Try to shoot for quality like the work in the \optic subdirectory. These fellows have done some excellent work.

Not all the movies are under the \movies subdirectory. There are some in \exploder and in \VCE and elsewhere, so look around or use the Find tool in Windows 95 to scan for *.avi.

Contents

There are four subdirectories: CyrusLum, DreamScp, Jonno, and Optic.

CyrusLum

Cyrus gave us two examples of his work so you could get an idea of how a professional creates the illusion of organic movement. Shark is a large format .avi file that will run slowly if you don't have an .avi accelerator card such as the Diamond Stealth 64 Video card. I kept it large so you can study it. The movements of the shark are excellent and should give you some idea of how you should be working with your own shark animation.

The Dragon.mpg is in MPEG 1 format. It was done using Alias and you'll need an MPEG player to see it. I was originally going to have one on the CD-ROM but it was not ready in time. There are several shareware and freeware players on the Internet and you get one with any MPEG player board you buy.

This short animation shows you how to bring life to an imaginary creature. Notice how the air fills the dragon's wings as he moves them. This is a wonderful aspect of 3D animation: you can make photorealistic visions of your wildest imagination come to life.

DreamScape

I did some quick examples to illustrate some of the concepts in the book. You can't get away with quick examples in the real world. I'm using the excuse that I was busy writing this book... you can't do that, it's been done. The time you spend tweaking out your clips and being a perfectionist about small details will be your key to success.

- **Alps** — A flyby I did in VistaPro for you to use as a practice animated background. Even though the terrain was done with a low polygon count, it gives you the feeling. It's based on an actual DEM of the alps.
- **Blast** — This is an example of an explosion I did using Rob Bryerton's Exploder.
- **Counter** — Shows how to use one camera tracking ploy to change the background and mood of a sequence.
- **Docking** — An example of a space docking. The soundtrack uses a drone sound layered with some NASA audio to add realism to the simple animation.
- **Electrik** — An example of electric discharge as simulated using the marble procedural texture.
- **Elgin** — A simple logo shot showing the name Elgin Boolean subtracted from a metal disk and painted gold.
- **Fighter** — Camera movements are very important. In this short clip the camera tracks a space fighter as it approaches and passes. The camera is moving perpendicular to the fighter.
- **Flash5** — Another fun example of marble procedural magic.
- **Landgbay** — Here Starfire approaches and enters a landing bay for lock down. I still have to create the exterior Bay and Trilon entry port. This was like an animatic (simple motion run through) to check out the movement of the arms and the door. In a final version it would run about three times as long.
- **Litebulb** — A quick example of using a reflective surface to create a visible light effect. I purposely left the reflective sheet a little visible so you could see how it was done. Look for the nearly invisible sheet in front of the bulb in the beginning of the clip.
- **Logosnd** — This is an example of reverse explosion used to assemble a logo. Because the logo is in many pieces, it's easy to miss painting one or more pieces. See if you can find the one I missed. I added sound to demonstrate how it adds drama. View this clip first MOS (Mit Out Sound) and then with the sound and notice the difference.
- **Maniac** — COMDEX is a large, annual consumer electronics show that has a Virtual Reality presentation each year presented by Infomaniacs, an Arizona-

based media think-tank. I animated this opening for them for one of the shows. I was done in nine hours on a crash schedule.

✦ **Nova** — Gas explosions are a very useful technique for creating lighting and pseudo-particle effects. This is an example of what I mean.

✦ **Ooops** — This is a comic example of a ship out of control.

✦ **Primexpl** — This is not from DreamScape, but from Shane Davison. I goofed and it accidentally ended up *here* on the CD-ROM. I didn't want to take the time to re-burn the master for this. It's a great example of special effects you can do with Rob Bryerton's Exploder program. See if you can figure out how he did it. Rob gives some hints in his tutorial.

✦ **Recon** — I'm not going to tell you about this one. Don't look at it until after you complete Chapter 2.

✦ **Seamons** — This is an example of a water pod monster lifting out of the sea. It's cheap and dirty. You have a lot more work to do, like animating the sea waves, putting in ripples around the base of the pod and giving it some character.

✦ **Shipapp4** — I did a long series of approaches to this space tanker Notice how you get a feeling of depth because the planets and stars have real positions in this mini cosmos.

✦ **Shipapp9** — The same ship as above. In this one the camera ship enters the landing bay and moves through a long interior tunnel.

✦ **Shipappr** — Again, but in this clip, I kept Look At locked onto the ship's axis as I passed. It shows you how this makes the ship appear to rotate as you pass. Not a good effect. It's best to unlock a dozen or so frames before the camera passes the ship's axis and lock back on 20 frames down the line.

✦ **Shutlbay** — If this looks familiar, it should. This is the original rendering of landgbay. There are two main differences that you may miss. Two glitches are caused by some bug in tS2. During the flight in, Starfire rotates about 45° for one frame only — completely on its own. It happens again just after the ship enters the bay. Caligari and I could not figure out what was going on, so I used my video editor to remove those two bad frames yielding a cleaned up landgbay.avi.

✦ **Snow2** — This is my version of snow using Rob Bryerton's Exploder. I think it's got a nice winter feeling.

✦ **Srchlite** — I hate this one because its ugly, but put it in so you could see what I mean about using the vertex paint tool to create a searchlight effect. I simply painted a single vertex on a flattened (into a circle) cone and rotated it. I lined up a spot with the visible light effect so the ship would show lighting as the searchlight moved over it.

✦ **Suckface** — Here you see the face, then it explodes and sucks back together again. An example of reverse explosion animation.

✦ **Trek** — I used the alps animation as a backdrop and animated the spaceship using the standard blue screen technique in Premiere 4. I also animated the ship at 15 fps and the background at 30 fps. So two things happened. One, the ship has a lot of blue shadows, so they appear as semi-transparent (notice the mountains through the ship) and trueSpace automatically puts in two alps frames for each spaceship frame. Notice how jerky this makes the clip appear. Also, in post I would have added a small lens-flare flash as the ship hits the rocks and flips over. To get a perfect composite, simply use the alps video as an animated background texture. Animate your ship to move with the terrain, both left and right, up and down, and don't forget pitch and yaw.

✦ **Warp** — This is and example of using the lens flare to create a transition effect. Using the diaphragm transition filter, I was able to have the Trek.avi open up as the flare expands, as if the ship were swallowed by a white hole and ends up in the alps.

Jonno

Jon Winchester gave us a single animation (\movies\jonno\toxic.avi). It's big, so make sure you have the space on your hard drive. He sent it to me zipped across 13 3.5-inch floppies. It's filled with clever ideas. Replace the Drumfire portion was done in tS1 using some very creative approaches to light parameter animation (which isn't available in tS1). Here's all about it in Jonno's own words:

About Jonno

My name is Jon Winchester and I work at the Central Institute of Technology, Wellington, New Zealand, for the Department of Information Technology. My main role there is to do with graphics including development of departmental logos, World Wide Web page development, and small animation projects. I also give tutorial and technical assistance in the running of some of the courses such as multimedia and individual student projects.

At the moment I am in the middle of developing more Web pages that are based on Computer Animation and Digital video. As well as covering the basics, these pages will also offer online tutorials using 3D, 2D, and non linear editing software. This is all part of the development of better graphics and multimedia courses run by the Department of Information Technology.

My current main 3D graphics tool is trueSpace, which I use to create all of my Web-page graphics as well as my own personal animation projects. I started using tS a year ago as my first 3D graphics package and I found its easy learning curve and slick interface made animation and graphics a breeze to produce. I use tS in conjunction with Adobe's Photoshop and Premiere to enable me to produce quality projects, and the above-mentioned Web tutorials I am developing will probably end up requiring these three tools together.

About Toxic.avi

This little flic starts you off at a toxic dump and skims you across the waste slick up into the pipes from where it all comes from, where you then pan across a disposal chamber, complete with corpse and mutant spider.

The animation was created entirely using tS with some textures and background images being generated in Photoshop. Here are some of the tricks I used do produce certain effects in the animation.

Drumfire Effect

The fire in the drum is a video I took with a Handycam of the fireplace at my girlfriend's old apartment. Luckily enough the fireplace had not been cleaned for a while so the brickwork behind the flames was covered in black soot and I was able to overlay the live video over the rendered drums using Black as an alpha setting. I adjusted the transparency and tolerance levels a bit until the flames were smooth and slightly "see-through." To get the flickering effect on the drums and surrounding objects I used an omni (local) light source and placed it on top of the center drum so it was almost sitting on top of it. Then I added a random erratic movement path to the light so it would move left, right, forward, back, forward, left, and so forth on the drum's top, which produced the shimmering flickering effect.

Lightning Effect

This was easily done but the key was to have a good original picture of forked lightning that streaks down from top to bottom. You can easily create an image like this in any good 2D package but in my case I grabbed a .gif image off the Grolier's CD Encyclopedia. Timing was also a critical factor for realism, so with this effect I calculated that since the final animation was going to be at 30 fps, the lightning would streak down to its full length over three frames and then gradually fade out over 10 frames. So what I did then was to make 13 copies of the original lightning image, reformat them to 24 bit and save them in a .tga sequence, bolt000.tga, bolt001.tga, bolt002.tga... which would result in an animated sequence. To the first image, bolt000.tga, I soft-edge brushed over two-thirds of the bolt's tail with the color of the background; the second image, bolt001.tga, I brushed over only one-third of the bolt's tail. The third image, bolt002.tga, I left as the original image but to the remaining 10 images I overlay-opaqued the background color over the entire bolt at a progressive setting. So bolt003.tga I overlay-opaqued the color of the background at a setting of 10%, bolt004.tga I overlay-opaqued the color of the background at a setting of 20%, and so on, so the bolt would fade out into the background color.

To ensure this effect doesn't come across as being cheesy I had to adjust the lighting (not lightning) in the scene to give the flash effect of a lightning strike, so again, like the background images, I had to do this over 13 frames. For this I used an Infinite light source placed up and slightly behind the background pond and pointed it in a diagonal downward and forward direction. I then animated the intensity settings from 0 to 2.0 over three frames and then from 2.0 back down to 0 again over another 10 frames. I then rendered the foreground scene with the animated lighting settings, applied the animated .tga sequence as an animated background and... kkeerrrraacckkk!!! ...a bolt from the blue.

TAKE NOTE

I had to make sure that the background animation was in synch with the animated lighting; otherwise, things would look chaotic.

Smoke Fumes Effect

This effect took me a while to develop but it's a personal favorite. First I created the chamber scene with the dump bins, from one of which the smoke would rise. I then created a billowing, twisting smoke object by vertically sweeping an irregularly shaped polygon many times.

The smoke object had to be two times the height of the chamber but no wider than one of the dump bins at its widest point. I then placed the smoke object so it was in the center of a dump bin (the one with an open lid) with its top face just level with the lid of the bin. I then placed a pipe deformation object so its flat ends were parallel with the floor and its bottom edge was sitting over the center of the bin's lid. I then resized the deformation object so its dimensions were the same as the bin's except I squeezed its center to about half its original size. I then attached the deformation pipe to the smoke object so when I made the smoke object rise slowly from the bin it would seen to billow and contort as a result. Also adding a slow z-axis rotation (twist) to the smoke object's vertical path gave it a more realistic twirling effect.

The final touch was to add a realistic hazy, smoky texture to the smoke object; this was quite easily achieved but at the same time it chewed up a lot of hard drive space. I created an image in Photoshop 200 × 200 that was totally opaque and dark gray in color RGB 50 50 50, to which I then added soft-edge brush strokes with total black to form a pseudo caramel cheese pattern and "hazed it out" by adding a blur filter. I then made a copy of the image and flipped it vertically and used HSC Morph 1.0 to produce a morph between the two images consisting of approximately 100 sequential .tga files.

I then imported these sequential files into tS and applied the alpha conversion with the intensity setting while saving the resulting .txr files in the same sequence. This then allowed me to apply the sequential .txr files as an animated semi-transparent texture onto the smoke object. With the color settings the way they were, and using intensity settings on the alpha conversion, the result was that the gray areas of the image would appear as a slightly hazy substance with fuzzy holes in it where the solid black was applied. (Note: You can save space by using 32-bit .tga files with an alpha channel added in Photoshop where you have even more control over the alpha characteristics. Caligari's .txr files are unnecessarily enormous, and are not practical for large sequences.)

Even though tS does not have all the extra bells and whistles that other 3D packages have, such as plug-ins and IPAS support, you can still get some primo results by just stretching your own imagination. That is why I like tS so much; it forces you to get creative and come up with unconventional methods for creating unique and compelling results.

Optic Edge

Optic Edge is a small company comprised of very talented young animators who use trueSpace2 to create some nifty animation. I think you'll enjoy the beautiful and unique video clips they've contributed. Take a look in \movies\optic on the CD-ROM. Here you'll find three files and three subdirectories.

Ani.avi

This is an example of a nice demo tape. It shows what several Optic Edge animators have done, showing a range of styles and subjects. Note the touch of perfectionism in Arie Sztajnworc's countdown opener. Check out the lighting and atmosphere effects, and the human face in *The Journey*. Note how things move and how clean the images are. The remarkable articulated animal and human movements by I-Wei should be studied. They were done in the same way as the I-pod, with a lot of care in placing limbs at each key frame.

Jmpbox2.avi and Jmpbx5C.avi

These are two test runs on a commercial for Caligari. Note the use of object deformation to achieve the jumping effect and bow.

Arie Subdirectory

Here is one clip by Arie Sztajnworc, a fun shot of an ant exploding. Might be good for an insecticide commercial.

E-Wei Subdirectory

Being dyslexic I spelled I-Wei's name phonetically here... sorry, I-Wei. I do that sometimes. Here you'll find several interesting clips from larger works by I-Wei Huang.

B-1.avi

A robot sand worrier with a jet pack. Note the way I-Wei simulated the jet blast using color cones with animated texture.

Hawka3.avi

This clip, rendered against a black background, can be used to overlay the hawk onto an animated scene. Remember, don't use it commercially unless you get permission from I-Wei.

Hawkb1.avi

The second in the hawk series is a close-up of a robot hawk. You can practice video editing with this series by playing with the three clips in different ways with different transitions and overlays to make a movie clip.

Hawkfnl3.avi

Last in the mechanical hawk series, it shows the hawk flying away.

Quickest.avi

This is one of I-Wei's demo pieces for Optic and for himself. Pay attention to combined usage of diorama and background objects to create a believable environment. Note the little story and the flair in both the titles and the sound. This was done quickly so it could be included in this CD-ROM. It shows what you can do on a short time fuse with tS2.

Tkd3.avi

I-Wei is a marshal arts guy and understands the complex body movements involved in a good kick. I asked for this piece because it's the best example of complex human body movement I've seen done in trueSpace2. This clip clearly demonstrates that you don't need Inverse Kinematics, to animate complex human movement.

Flics

This directory contains additional examples of trueSpace2 animation in the .flc format from Autodesk. The advantage is that the player and format use memory in a way that allows near full-screen, full-motion playback, though the color palette is abbreviated. You'll need an flc player if you don't have one already installed. Autodesk has put the player into the public domain and it is widely available. In addition, Premiere plays flc files, as do most of the video editors.

Dgnslp3.fli, Dgnslp5.fli, and Drgnbo2.fli, Ik_da20.flc, Walk15.flc, and Walk21.flc

These six clips demonstrate what you can do with tS2 when animating intricate skeletal motion. These are fanciful dragon skeletons in motion.

Flywlk2.flc

This has to be one of the most beautiful robot structures I've seen . The graceful walk cycle was done entirely with keyframes in trueSpace2.

Lion2.flc

This is a lion's skeleton in full walk cycle animation.

Soldier.fli

A wonderful wind-up toy soldier comes to life. Top-quality animation.

Tristatc.flc

This is a prehistoric monster decked out for battle with aliens. This one may not run on some machines. If you have problems you can see him on the ani.avi demo.

Scenes

I have included four pre-built scenes for you to play with:

- ✦ Iwei.scn — When I-Wei Huang visited my studio, I had him show me how to animate an articulated robot. He kindly left this scene file for you to study when you get frustrated. I suggest you start by revealing the axes and looking at where he placed them. Then experiment with animating the robot in different ways by navigating his hierarchy and rotating different groups of parts. Save your effort with Save As so you don't save over the original. If you do, no problem — you still have it on the CD-ROM.
- ✦ Probe.scn — This is the basic scene file used for the exercise in Chapter 2. Just follow the instructions in that chapter and have fun.

✦ Robie.scn — This scene contains all the localized motion that I showed you in Chapter 19. It's here for you to study and play with. First off, check out the Animation Project Window and look at how things are arranged.

✦ Shark.scn — There is no animation in this scene. It's just a seabed with some plants and a pregnant nurse shark. If you want, you can use it when you practice organic animation techniques.

Soundz

I know what it's like when you want to try out something and you don't have any music or sound to put with it. You'll surely develop a large collection of sounds over time, but for now I just put in some stuff I use. It's just for fun. The music selections are ones I made up on the spot to match a mood for an animation or for this disk. The sound FX were mostly recorded on a microcassette recorder so the quality isn't high — it's just for practice. You'll want to do a much better job on your own sounds, keeping the recording quality high. I've found that using electric condenser mikes and a hifi video recorder is a good way to get very high quality sound. The VCR uses a recording method that is generally better than your average quarter-inch tape deck. Nevertheless, if you use, filter, and time these clips with skill, you can get some pretty good audio tracks rolling. I could describe each of these sounds for you — music, snippets, and sound effects — but I thought I'd leave you something to explore.

Textures

This subdirectory contains five categories of texture maps. I don't plan to itemize my entire list of textures here, but I'll point you to a couple of very useful ones.

Animated Textures

You'll find these files in the \animated subdirectory:

✦ Clouds.avi — This is an interesting sunset clip I made using various film post and compositing effects.

✦ Earth.avi — This is a perfect texture to place on a flat background panel. It's an actual image of the earth spinning in space.

✦ Firework.avi — This is just a Fourth of July home video that's been digitized. You can do the same. You'll find it very useful for dRAMatizing some of your explosions. Don't use it alone, but composite it with a blast, like the one from VCE, to give a flak or sparks effect.

✦ Flash.avi — Lightning I made with the marble texture. The idea here is to take about six frames of this and splash it on a background panel to create a stroke of lightning. But using different parts of this short animation will get you different-looking strokes.

- Lander.avi — This is NASA footage of the lunar lander on its very first approach to the moon. This can be rotoscoped into a window frame on your spaceship to simulate a landing approach view.

Bump Maps

You can use these grayscale maps to create surface texture on models. You'll find the files in the \bumpmaps subdirectory.

- Alum.bmp — The bumps found in crinkled aluminum foil.
- Bigdragn.bmp — If you want to make a dinosaur or dragon, this will give the skin a nice dinosaurian (lizard-like) texture.
- Crusty.bmp — Gives a rough, uneven texture to your surface. Try different amp values.
- Drgnskn.bmp — Another lizard-type skin bump map.
- Drgskin2.bmp — Same pattern as drgnskn.bmp, but with different kinds of bumps.
- Moon.bmp — A moon-surface looking map.
- Pitted.tga — Use it for pitted metal, and so on.
- Pond.bmp — Use this one to give the surface of that pond a nice ripply look.
- Rough.bmp — Like concrete or rough ceiling tiles. Try reversing it. It also can make a leather texture at very low amp values.
- Strokes.bmp — This one looks like rain coming down at a 45° angle. Give it an alpha channel and use it to simulate rain, or leave it alone and use it to make scratches and dents.
- Viral.bmp — This looks like a blurry view of microbes. It's very useful for all sorts of things from creating a water surface to giving an organic surface to plants.

Miscellaneous

This is a potpouri of textures for you to play with until you have your own collection. I made some in Photoshop and others in Fractal Design Painter. You'll find these files in the \misc subdirectory.

- Atoms.bmp — This is a neat map made up of shaded dots of color. It makes a nice fabric, rug, or even a bin full of candy.
- Bigdragn.bmp — A large reptile skin I put together in Photoshop.
- Blacktop.tga — This is road surface, but you can find lots of uses for it.
- Clouds.bmp — Your basic sky.
- Dirtytub.bmp — An eroded, sculpted concrete sort of thing.

- Fire.jpg — This is a texture made with Kai's Texture Explorer. I use it to create the gaseous explosions. Use it wherever you need a fiery surface.
- Fungus.bmp — This one looks like a growth of crud. It works well with pitted.bmp.
- Grifiti.bmp — Looks like colored painting on a black concrete wall.
- Metlxtal.bmp — This is a colorful map of etched metal crystal structure.
- Neon.bmp — Neon reflections on wet pavement.
- Plastic.bmp — A melted black plastic design you can use to give a strange texture to background objects.
- Preview.pix — Ignore this file. It was put here by the silicon pixies.
- Ryarug.bmp — This looks very much like a Scandinavian wool rya rug; it was made using CorelPaint 6.
- Sweater.bmp — A kaleidoscope view of ryarug.bmp; it looks like sweater material.
- Tileye.bmp — Makes a good alien floor surface.
- Tubes.bmp — Good for interior passage walls.
- Tubular.bmp — Good for ceilings, and makes a good bump map for tubes.
- Viral.jpg — This looks like microbes under a microscope. You'll find lots of uses for this, and it makes a good bump map too.
- Whitesnd.tga — This one tiles nicely and can be used for sand or as a bump map. It even makes an interesting fabric.

Space Textures

These are textures I used in making my space images, plus a few extras. You'll find these images in the \space subdirectory.

- Atomstrp.tga — An abstract texture for alien ships.
- Crax.bmp — This is a bump map that doubles as a texture. It looks like an old cracked surface.
- Dirt.tga — This is a cloudy transparency map you can use for many purposes from dirt on a surface to mist.
- Dirtyhul.bmp — This is a series of three different versions of a dirty hull look.
- Fire01.jpg — This looks a lot like flames; use it on gas balls and so on.
- Flare.bmp — A semi-transparent fire map.
- Fracnoiz.bmp — Very useful for all sorts of natural textures such as shark's skin.
- Fractal2.bmp — Another fractal noise image in a different detail size.

- Galaxis.bmp — An enhanced NASA photograph of a galaxy that can be applied to a background plate to spruce up a space image.
- Glaxbeer.tga — A Galaxy beer bottle on a table.
- Hullexp.bmp — Streaky white hull material.
- Insighul.bmp — A white hull with an insignia on it.
- Lumpbmps.bmp — This is either a bump map of a rough surface or the black and white surface of an old notebook. I use it to texture asteroids and so on.
- NGC1976.jpg — A stylized view of the great nebula in Orion. I used a zoom filter to achieve this effect.
- NGC1976b.jpg — The regular view of the nebula in Orion.
- NGC224c.bmp — Yet another galaxy image for your backgrounds.
- Phazer.bmp — This is a handy energy bolt for zapping the enemy.
- Plasma.bmp — A fractal plasma cloud image.
- Stary32.jpg — A misty cosmos scene.
- Swirlhul.tga — An organic hull surface. If you have problems with it, convert it to a .bmp.
- Tinybump.bmp — Just a handy map of very small bumps.
- Viral.jpg — Useful for surface bumps and dirt.

Water

I've included one image in the \water subdirectory:

- Ripple.bmp — This is the surface of a pond. Try using it with the pond.bmp bump map, which you'll find in the \bumpmaps subdirectory.

Tutorials

The Tutorial directory contains two subdirectories: Fountain and TrueFAQ.

Fountain

The tutorial files are provided in the .wrl format, which you can use in conjunction with Fountain. After you install Fountain, read Chapter 34 to find out how to load the tutorial files.

TrueFAQ

This is a handy HTML version of the trueSpace FAQ (from Appendix B). Use it with your Web browser for a hypertext approach to learning tips and techniques.

VCE

This is a special subdirectory in which I've grouped all the files associated with the VCE company. Here you find:

- ✦ Explode.avi — This is a zero-g explosion in space. Use it to rotoscope a blast over your 3D animations.
- ✦ Flak2108.tga — This is a neat explosion image you can use to composite blast effects into your images during post. This one has flak sparks flying out. Combine it with the zero-g explosion below.
- ✦ FR51162.tga — A flaming bottom fire you can composite over your image to give it an inferno look.
- ✦ ZG02.wav — This is the sound file that goes with the explode.avi.
- ✦ ZG02125.tga — This is what an explosion looks like in zero gravity.

Vidwin

This directory contains the Video for Windows extensions required by many programs. It's only for you old-fashioned folks with Windows 3.x. Windows 95 and NT have this capability built in.

Have Fun

Sure, you may not like some of these materials at first. But sooner or later you'll find a cheesy looking map like viral.jpg to be extremely useful. The challenge is to find the most creative ways to use each map. Also try using color maps as bump maps. trueSpace2 automatically converts them to grayscale for you — a great convenience. Try using the same map as both the texture and bump map in a texture. The important thing to remember is, have fun doing it. With all the goodies I've assembled for you on this book's companion CD-ROM, you should have no trouble. Have *lots* of fun!

APPENDIX B

trueSpace2 Tips and Techniques

The trueSpace2 tips and techniques contained in this appendix have been compiled and edited by David Campbell (dcampbel@bga.com) and Bob Green (Styxman@aol.com), with additional comments by me (Peter Plantec at thenar@cinenet.net). The CD-ROM also contains an HTML version of this document (in the /tutorial/truefaq subdirectory). You can read it in hypertext via Netscape or any other Web browser.

The ideas I've compiled in this appendix aren't explicitly covered in the trueSpace documentation. Members of the trueSpace Mailing List (tSML) have contributed these tips and tricks since the list's inception in December 1994. I've cited each contributor's name and e-mail address next to his contributions. Please note where these suggestions originate. They're not just contributed by folks in the United States, but also by people from all over the globe — from Canada, Zaire, the U.K., Norway, Singapore, and points in between. The Internet is making the entire world a local community, and tS2 is helping to bring together talented animators and 3D graphic artists from all points.

Topics

This appendix covers the following topics:

- Modeling
- Materials
- Lighting
- Rendering
- Special effects
- Using trueSpace with other tools
- Miscellaneous

Modeling Tips

Here are some great tips for creating and working with vertices.

Creating New Vertices

Josh Andersen
josh@itsnet.com

1. Click the Point Edit tool.
2. Hold down Ctrl+Shift and left-click on an edge at the location you wish to place the new vertex.

Creating New Edges Between Vertices

Adam Glassman
pixelboy@ix.netcom.com

1. Left-click on the first point.
2. Holding the Shift key, left-click on the second point.

Deleting Vertices

Shane Davison
daviso@cs.uregina.ca

1. Click on the Point Edit tool.
2. Select the faces surrounding the target vertex.
3. Detach (using slice) and delete the resulting amputated section of the object.

Note that this technique only works on solid objects.

Deselecting Vertices

To deselect an incorrectly picked vertex while editing multiple points, click the Undo button while still holding down the Shift key.

Hiding Objects

David Campbell
dcampbel@bga.com

trueSpace2 doesn't have a hide object function, unfortunately. However, here's an extremely useful work-around. The object information panel (displayed by right-clicking on the object-selection tool) has several fields for entering numeric values for object location, size, and rotation. These fields will accept numeric expressions as well as constant values. So if you want to move an object out of the way quickly, just append a `+100` to the end of whatever value appears in the Z location field and hit Enter. To get the object back, just append a `-100`. This also works for quickly resizing an object to, say, twice its original size.

Object Simplification

Shane Davison
daviso@cs.uregina.ca

Here's a handy way to remove unnecessary faces, edges, and points from an object:

1. Create another object, such as a cube.
2. Place the cube so it does not intersect in any dimension with your original object.
3. Right-click on the Boolean Subtraction tool, bringing up the Boolean Properties Panel.
4. Enable the Delete Edges option.
5. Boolean subtract the cube from the original object.

Your original object will remain unchanged except that any unnecessary faces, edges, and points will be removed. This is especially useful when you've heavily quad-divided an object for sculpting, and after doing so, you want to simplify the object for efficiency.

Stars

Shane Davison
daviso@cs.uregina.ca

Here's an easy way to create a star object:

1. Start trueSpace (if it isn't already running).
2. Left-click the Primitives Panel icon.
3. Right-click the Add Torus icon.
4. Set the values to 6 (lat), 3 (long), and 0.5 (rad).

TAKE NOTE: You can experiment with the rad to get the desired result (but the default looks fine).

5. Left-click the Add Torus icon twice.
6. Right-click the Object Tool icon (the arrow).

7. Change the Z rotation to 60.
8. Left-click the Glue as sibling icon and click on the other torus.
9. Left-click the Object Tool to complete your object.
10. Rotate your object as necessary.

Paint with semitransparent, self-illuminating white, or opaque white and soft color shades.

Splatters and Puddles

Shane Davison
daviso@cs.uregina.ca

To quickly create paint splatters, puddles, rain/snow (maybe not), or similar items: Select the regular polygon tool and set the side count high enough to create satisfactory circles. Create one circle. Switch the poly modes to union.

Now, go crazy and quickly draw circles all over the workspace in random sizes and random locations (depending on the desired look). This should create one object that looks sufficiently realistic (some circles will join with each other producing irregular shapes) that can then be positioned, rotated, and textured.

This technique works quite well for 2D objects with characteristics similar to puddles. A good application of this method is to easily create those little bubbles in cartoons when a character is thinking — just move the mouse across the work space holding the button a little longer each time and then end with one big bubble.

Fancy Text

Shane Davison
daviso@cs.uregina.ca

Use tS2, the text function, and the deform object tool to create fancy text art. You can make some wild-looking text effects using the deform feature (especially when used on 2D (for example, nonswept) text — but be careful that the geometry isn't too messy or letters will disappear when rendered). Scripty fonts (or italicized ones) seem to work best.

Neon Text

Peter Plantec
thenar@cinenet.net

Try making letters with the Text tool, but don't extrude them. Duplicate each one and enlarge it. Put the enlarged letters behind the originals and then extrude the originals. Try filling the extruded letters with a transparent marble procedural (fool with the values using high ambient light). Then, using a similar color, create the glow by using the Paint Vertices tool on the second, larger set of letters (see the section entitled Glows and Visible Lights in the Special Effects section later in this appendix). It won't be perfect, but it isn't bad. An easier way is to use Photoshop with the Alien Skin glow filter and put a glow behind rounded letters.

Modeling Humans

Eric Knisley
knisley@kells.vmedia.com

A real good idea is to do some character sketches before you start. I find that the real challenge is not always finishing the project, but not getting distracted by wandering down some creative byway. Doing a model sheet as for an animated cartoon character — with various views to maintain consistency — saves you a lot of time in the long run. As for your modeling concerns, I'd use the surface sculpting tools, and lots of constraints. I've found the surface sculpting tool to be fairly intuitive, but you might need to experiment a bit. Hope this helps and good luck!

Make a Face

Peter Plantec
thenar@cinenet.net

A few suggestions: First, take your time, start with a sphere, and open all three windows. Experiment with volume deformation and make a character head by pulling out a nose, keeping it lined up by looking in all the windows.

Next, push in eye depressions, pull a chin out, and crease a mouth. Model some teeth using the spline poly tool and extrude them. Put them carefully in the mouth cavity — it's not easy — and glue them in place. Fiddle with deforming the mouth with letter sounds. Put in a tongue. Make two tiny spheres for eyes. Play with it. Make big eyebrows and such.

Model ears and put them on, flesh out the chin, and put holes in the character's nose using Boolean drills. You could do the mouth this way too. Play with various expressions. The point is not to make your final piece, but to get used to the tools. I'd make about ten random characters before trying to make one to order. You can add detail with bump maps you make in Photoshop and elsewhere.

Sweeping a Keyboard

Bjørn-Kåre Nillsen
bjoernk@oslonett.no

I had to make a computer keyboard. I looked at a 3DS file on Avalon, but it was far too complicated, with 6000 faces. (So I had to make my own in tS, which I probably would have done anyway....)

To make all the keys, I made a rectangle, with the Y size of it set at the Y value of a key (seen from above): 0.5 units. I rotated the rectangle 90 degrees around the world Y axis and made four copies that I distributed evenly along the Y axis.

I then swept the first rectangle with 13 segments and a length of 6.5, and then another sweep with 1 segment and the length set at 1 (the backspace key). Then I selected every second face, seen from the Top View, beveled them all at the same time until they "looked right." Then I selected the Face tool again, with the same faces still selected, and moved them along their Z axis until they had the right height above the "source strip" (plus a little). I repeated the same procedure with the rest of the faces.

Now I had a strip with the top row of keys, the numbers, but still as one object. I wanted them as separate objects, so I selected one of the bottom faces of the object, sliced it upwards until it was above the strip, selected the lower part with the Shift key, and then detached and deleted the lower part. Now I had a number of separate keys, but still as one object. To make them really separate, I used the Decompose into surfaces tool. The other rectangles were swept in the same way, varying the length and number of similar-sized segments.

When I finished all the keys, I glued them together in one big group and used the Deform Object tool to give them a nice concave curvature around the X axis like a real keyboard. Then I rotated the whole key set into place on the rest of the keyboard. Then every top face of each key was selected and rotated slightly around the object's X axis, to tilt each key toward horizontal, just like a real keyboard (mine anyway...).

The whole operation, with a lot of rounded corners and cutouts for the keys in the keyboard, took less than two hours, and it resulted in an object with 1,100 vertices and 750 faces.

This sweeping technique is very useful also, if you change the path parameters, to get a lot of different-sized objects, but still along a path, and with full control of the size and location. You could make more elaborate forms on the top of each segment.

You can use this technique in lots of possible ways; it's one of my favorites.

Diamonds

Bjørn-Kåre Nillsen
`bjoernk@oslonett.no`

Here's an easy way to make a diamond or similar faceted gemstone:

1. Make an eight-sided cone (more or less).
2. Rotate 180 degrees around the X or Y axis.
3. Right-click Point Edit ➪ Faces button, and set DynDiv to Triangles.

4. Select the top face and sweep.
5. Rotate the top face around its Z axis until it "looks right."
6. Voilà, a diamond.

Use a very high refraction, such as 2.5, and raytrace!

Rope

Bjørn-Kåre Nillsen
bjoernk@oslonett.no

To make a detailed 3D rope, follow these steps:

1. Make a circle using the spline polygon tool and copy it twice. Let the circles overlap so they resemble a clover.
2. Union them to one shape.
3. Sweep with 5 to 10 segments between each floor.
4. Rotate the floor around the Z axis.
5. Continue clicking the Sweep button until your rope is long enough.
6. Use a simple bump map with diagonal stripes.
7. Bend it into shape with the Deform Object tool afterwards.
8. Save your path in the Path library after sweeping, and you can easily make a "rope" from any shape later.

Bending Text on a Circular Path

Ian Firth
IanFirthDS@aol.com

Build a free-form deformation lattice in the shape you want, and slide your text through it.

Ulrich Kliegis
UK@ruebe.mdc.netuse.de

Create and move the characters separately, so TEXT would not be TEXT, but a T, an E, and so on.

Creating Bent Poles

Shane Davison
daviso@cs.uregina.ca

Problem: I've been trying to create some bent rods (cylinders) using trueSpace. The effect I desire is to create some decorative rod iron for an object I am working on. I can create the shapes I want by sweeping the end of a cylinder and gradually creating the curve with successive sweeps and slight movements perpendicular to the sweep direction. However, one problem seems to occur. When the sweeped section is moved, the size of the cylinder for that section of the sweep is flattened, resulting in a noncircular cross-section.

The solution? Try creating a curved spline-path and macro-sweeping a circle polygon to form your rod. There's a "bend" setting you can enable/disable depending on the desired effect.

Michael Mills
`Michael.Mills@B.GP.CS.CMU.EDU`

Create your desired curve as a 2D spline, save it in the path library, and then use the macro/sweep tool with "bend" on, and this will sweep across the path while retaining the shape of the cross-section.

Materials Tips

Here are some great tips for creating different materials.

Realistic Wood in tS1/TS-SE

Shane Davison
`daviso@cs.uregina.ca`

If you haven't already done so, get pat-txtr.zip from `ftp.netnet.net` (also try `ftp.caligari.com`), and set up the following object attributes to create a realistic wood material:

✦ Material color: n/a

✦ AutoFacet and Phong

✦ Texture map with the following settings:
- Name: mywood.bmp
- U & V repts: scale to the object

✦ Shader attributes with the following settings:
- Ambient: 0.32
- Shine: 0.49
- Rough: 0.87
- Opacity: 1
- Refract: 1

Apply all the attributes to your object. This should work on most object types with most lighting setups (I think). Note: Obviously this technique works equally well on tS2. However, tS2 gives you the additional option of using the procedural wood material.

Planet Textures

Peter Plantec
thenar@cinenet.net

I use Corel Photo-Paint to process and create bitmap images for planet surfaces. When I find a good texture that looks like a planet surface to me, I process it in different ways — for example, I emboss, pixilate, posterize, or brush stroke it. I then save the interesting ones for in .tga format for my materials library.

One way to make great planet surfaces is by taking a rough bitmap (such as a stone wall, for example) and embossing it. Then use it as a texture map and wrap it around a sphere. Try using the image as its own bump map at a very low amplitude setting. Try different mapping coordinates. Spherical may not be the best in all situations. Also try making the image into a grayscale, painting it on the surface and putting a tinted atmosphere over it.

Planet Atmospheres

Peter Plantec
thenar@cinenet.net

If you have the "Earth" from Avalon, it has no atmosphere (like a bad party). You can give it atmosphere by taking a cloudy or swirly texture, and emphasizing the highlights in Photoshop. Use it as a reflection map on a sphere slightly bigger than the earth... fiddle with the interactive controls and make it transparent. It looks better than the ones they use on commercials on TV.

For a different approach, take a fractal cloud image in .tga format, and add an alpha channel in Photoshop (add a fourth channel and name it alpha). The channel will be white. Copy the RGB image (top channel) to the clipboard and paste it in the alpha channel. It will be reproduced in grayscale. When you use such a map in tS1 or tS2 the black areas in the alpha channel are transparent and the white areas are opaque with gray in between. Save your image as a 32-bit .tga file and use it on the second sphere. With it, you can use a shadow casting infinite light to cast cloud shadows on the earth. I've done this with two cloud shells moving in different directions for interesting, hyper-realistic effect.

If you have a setting sun partly behind the planet, it will shine through these atmosphere shells for a realistic effect.

Realistic Metal

Peter Plantec
thenar@cinenet.net

Try this experiment to make a nice quality gold. Use the Text tool to write your name in bold letters. Extrude the letters and access the Paint Roller tool. Then right-click on the environment map and put in a photograph of something like an indoor or outdoor scene. Then click on the upper right corner (yellow) of the color cube. Make sure you turn off the bump map and texture map tools (above the environment map). Now paint this on the letters. You may need to rotate the letters to catch the light just right. Use the default lights to start with.

Next it's time to tweak: Play with the shininess, ambient glow, and roughness sliders until the example ball looks good to you, then paint it on the letters. You should get a very believable looking gold metal look. And don't forget to depress the metallic shading button to the left of the environment map button.

Once you have the right look, experiment with very low amplitude bump maps. The orange map gives a rough but polished gold look. This will help minimize the computer-generated look. For the best look, raytrace.

Now for silver, reduce the roughness slider to very smooth and click on white in the color cube. Next, slide the shininess slider to about halfway. Try it and adjust.

For aluminum, simply slide the roughness slider up a bit until it looks like aluminum. Brass is like gold, only darker and more orange. For other textures, try using the bump map. Right-click on it to get the file box. Load an interesting texture. Next, right-click on the reflection map tool and load an interesting bitmapped texture. Now push both buttons and see what you get on the ball.

An interesting thing to do is select the same bitmap for both the bitmap and the bump map. Notice that you can adjust the depth of the bumps.

Bjørn-Kåre Nillsen
bjoernk@oslonett.no

Just a little tip: The Wasteland environment map in the environment directory installed by trueSpace works very well in most cases. To make it "behave" like gold you'll have to set the rendering mode to raytracing, as this is the only way to get reflections of the other objects in the scene.

This method is actually not the only way in tS, because you can make environmental maps based on your actual scene, and then use that one as a reflection map on your object. It will not give you more than one reflection though. When raytracing objects inside a mirrored box, you will get a number of objects mirrored as the reflections bounce from mirror to mirror. trueSpace limits the number of interreflections, but I don't know the number.

The trueSpace version 2.01A update includes an enhancement to let you set the maximum number of reflections.

Bjørn-Kåre Nillsen
bjoernk@oslonett.no

Here are Bjørn's much-requested settings for achieving the great metal materials in his file, bknhptoy.jpg (see his futuristic tricycle in the color section).

For the wheels and axis he used the metal shader and environment mapping with an ordinary picture of a desert scene, quite grayish. Table B-1 lists the settings.

Table B-1
Settings for Creating Metal

Setting	*Wheels/Axis*	*Engine*	*Blue Tires*	*Horse/Rods*
Ambient	0.07	0.07	0.45	0.45
Shine	0.87	0.87	0.87	0.87
Rough	0.26	0.26	0.06	0.06
Opacity	1.0	1.0	1.0	0.02
Refract	1.0	1.0	1.0	1.46
Shader	metal	metal	metal	metal
Environment Map	wastlan	wastlan	wastlan	wastlan

There are also two spotlights (with ray shadows) and one local light (no shadows) in the scene. Table B-2 lists the settings for creating lighting.

Table B-2
Settings for Creating Lighting

Type	*Color/Saturation*	*Intensity*	*Shadows*	*Location*
Spot 1	blue / 235	0.335	raytraced	right back
Spot 2	yellow / 44	0.207	raytraced	right front
Local	blue / 232	0.462	none	behind bike

Object Painting

Bruce G. Vryenhoek
bvryen@telerama.lm.com

I have been looking for a utility that allows you to "unwrap" a 3D wireframe model onto a 2D plane and then paint directly onto the surface of the object, creating a kind of customized image map for that object. I haven't run across anything like that, but I tried something that (somewhat) approximates what I was looking for.

After setting up a wireframe model in tS, I exported the object in DXF format. From there, I was able to read the DXF file into Paint Shop Pro and convert it to a Targa format. The resulting image is a top-side view of the object in wireframe form. I like Photoshop better than PSP, so I loaded the Targa image of the wireframe into Photoshop and used the "magic wand" tool to create a selection bounded by the edges of the wireframe. (The background color was all white, so this was an easy manipulation.) All I had to do from there was to paint whatever I wanted onto the "surface" of the object image. The current selection is the only part of the image that is affected by the painting operation, so the outline of the object is preserved. When I was done painting, I saved the image as a Targa file, converted it to a TXR file in tS (to remove the white background), and mapped it onto the original object. Perfect fit. I did have to play around with the UV mapping (which supersedes the preferred default UV mapping) to align it properly, but generally it worked out pretty well.

TAKE NOTE: You can do the same in Photoshop by copying the background selection, pasting it into the alpha channel, and making it black. That makes all but the object transparent.

I want to use this technique to create random "dirt" and "damage" on the surfaces of various mechanical objects, as well as to custom paint specific parts of objects a little more intuitively. The drawbacks here are memory consumption and UV map dependency. The map ends up being quite large (smaller as a tga), but at least it's nonrepeating, and you are pretty much confined to mapping the texture through the top of the object to maintain the effect.

Glass

Shane Davison
daviso@cs.uregina.ca

Here are attribute settings for creating a glass object in trueSpace:

- Smooth
- Metal shaded
- Ambient glow: from 0.75 to 1.0 (that is, high)
- Shininess: 1.0 (top)

- Roughness: 1.0 (top)
- Transparency: 0 (top)

Experiment with the color and index of refraction settings to get the desired look (but keep the Index of Refraction fairly low).

Enhancing Shadows with the Paint Vertices Tool

Mark E. Marshall
marshall@ids.net

When you have the lighting/shadow scheme just perfect, sometimes one object isn't giving you the good contrast of the rest of your scene (assuming a high-contrast scene). Instead of adding more light or fiddling with the placement, go ahead and use the Paint Face tool to subtly darken and/or lighten angles and sides. It is much faster than bulb tweaking.

"Cool" Materials

Shane Davison
daviso@cs.uregina.ca

Some settings for a colorful material (cool!):

- Color: 210,210,255 (slightly blue)
- Smooth
- Metal shaded
- Bump map: orange (default)
- Environment map: rainbow (default)
- Shader attributes (ambient, shine, transparency, and so on): all set to top!

That's it — quick and easy. Try this on a sphere first and then more complicated objects. Also, make sure you enable raytracing for the Index of Refraction to work properly (this greatly increases rendering times, of course, but it's still fun).

Cloudy Gas

Peter Plantec
thenar@cinenet.net

You can make a space gas-type display similar to those you see on *Babylon 5*, *Deep Space 9*, and elsewhere. Using the marble procedural texture, make the vein red or whatever color you want the space gas to be. Make the stone black and transparent. Set the sharpness to a low value (experiment). You can create a good effect by applying this material to a plane, with a space/stars background image. Play with the XYZ parameters to get the effect you want. Animation is possible, but tricky.

A second method is to create a fractal cloud image with an alpha channel in Photoshop. Adjust the colors and paint it on a large rectangle with an infinite light glowing on it. Put a starfield or a Color NASA image of a nebula behind it with stars.

Copying a Material Rectangle

Shane Davison
daviso@cs.uregina.ca

Problem: I have a UFO model and I want to place six same-sized rectangular portholes around the circumference of the upper hull. Making one material rectangle and applying a texture to it is the simplest way I can see to achieve it.

Bjørn-Kåre Nillsen
bjoernk@oslonett.no

When using material rectangles it's easy to lose track of their locations and sizes. I always try to make as few as possible, and I have given up on trying to align them. tS already has built-in "alignment" in the material repetitions, so that's what I'd use if I need repetitive materials. My (detailed) solution to the material rectangle portholes is as follows:

Make a dark rectangle inside a lighter one, with as much detail as you want inside the porthole. Make it transparent by using the Image Utilities in tS, with the left upper corner, or white, as the transparent color. Set U repeats at 6, and V at 1 in the materials editor. You could use the same image for both image map and bump map, for added realism. Make one material rectangle that covers the entire upper hull. Now you can make fine adjustments, maybe in particular with the U offset. Or you can easily make it 12 portholes, or two rows with nine portholes in each. If you want added detail in some of the portholes, so they don't look exactly similar, you can just put another MR (Material Rectangle) on top of the first one.

Compact Disc Rainbow Texture

(Requires Photoshop or equivalent and Kai's Power Tools)

Terry Cotant
70313.1103@compuserve.com

1. Go into Photoshop and bring up Kai's Power Tools.
2. Go into Texture Explorer and play around until you get a cool "rainbow" colored texture. Try different ones — concentric circles, wavy textures, and so on. Certain animations require different styles of textures.

3. In trueSpace, go into Image Utilities, and select your new texture (.bmp) that you created in steps 1 and 2.
4. Column should be set to left (try others, though) and click 1D Environment map. To use the 1D environment map, select your object, then right-click on the Paint tool.
5. Set your textures using the following values (right-click the shader attributes for numerical entry):
   - Ambient: .25
   - Shine: 1
   - Rough: 1
   - Opacity: 1
   - Refract: 1
6. Left-click the Use Environment Map button. Now right-click on it, and point it to your new .t1d.
7. Paint your object. The effect is best when moving/rotating your object. You will need to play with how tight to make the rings (step 2).

For a really weird (and pretty realistic) option, try this: Do the above steps to get your .t1d. Make sure that you've got your environment map turned on as in step 6 above, but change your shader attributes to be (or something similar to):

- ✦ Ambient: .25
- ✦ Shine: .65
- ✦ Rough: 1
- ✦ Opacity: 1
- ✦ Refract: 1

Right-click on your texture map button and select your original .bmp from step 2, then left-click to make it active. Paint the object and do an animation of that. Wow, very cool. Try varying amounts of Shine for different effects.

Texture for Clear Liquid Objects

Shane Davison
daviso@cs.uregina.ca

Use these attributes:

- ✦ Color: 255,255,255
- ✦ Smooth

- Shading: Phong
- Ambience, Shine, Rough: all the way down
- Opacity: all the way up
- Refract: 1.02 (or a little higher)

And make sure to enable raytracing. This can produce cool effects if the object is moving in front of other (colorful) objects (it takes a while to trace though).

Speaking of liquid (or gels), one of the amazing things about tS is its ability to automatically add and remove polygons to ensure object smoothness during an animation in which the object is deformed (by a lattice, and so on).

Texturing Object Faces Using an Independent UV Mapping

Shane Davison
daviso@cs.uregina.ca

Sometimes when texturing an object, you may want to use a different UV mapping for a particular face than for the rest of the object. For example, you may want to paint the ends of the cylinder with a planar mapping and the rest of the cylinder using the standard cylindrical mapping. Here's a way to do that:

Select your cylinder and click on Point Edit ➪ Faces. Then click on the top (rim) of the cylinder (the top circle should be selected [green]). From the point navigation panel, select separate selected part of object. Now you'll have two objects. Pick the circle polygon, use planar mapping on it, and paint it with the appropriate material. Finally, glue it to your original cylinder so you can move them together.

Monitoring Materials Changes While Keyframing

Shane Davison
daviso@cs.uregina.ca

Select an object and use the Material Inspection tool on it. From then on, and as long as you don't select a different tool, the material previewer automatically updates to show the settings at each keyframe.

Bump Maps Not Rendering

Shane Davison
daviso@cs.uregina.ca

Bump maps (and texture maps) need UV coordinates before they'll show up. So, try to re-apply the UV projection and then re-paint (this should work on the main object but you may have to do each piece manually).

Shimmering Reflection on Flat Surface

Nigel
claytob@globalone.net

To get a nice reflection effect similar to the shimmering reflection of a layer of liquid on a flat surface (such as a parking lot following a rain, for example): Apply a very small amplitude bump map to your reflective floor or ground object and use a high number of reps (the orange bump map with trueSpace works great when you up the mapping repetitions and lower the bump altitude). When rendered (raytracing enabled), the result will be a slightly distorted reflection that adds a bit of depth to the image/animation.

Sean Cunningham
Sean@msicri.com

I was able to produce a really good water effect using the above tip in combination with another: If you use the deform tool to produce a number of parallel lines in a flat surface, then move each line up, and then down in subsequent frames, it makes a great wave-like effect.

Lighting Tips

Here are some great lighting tips.

Tricks with Lights

Shane Davison
daviso@cs.uregina.ca

When the active object is a light source, right-clicking on the Set color of current light or Set intensity of current light gadgets in the lights panel allows you to numerically specify the light color and intensity. In this numerical panel, you can set the light intensity value higher than you can with the light intensity slider (for example, >2). This is great for really powerful lighting effects — you can even "wash-out" your scene with light to simulate a nuclear blast.

You can also set the light intensity to a negative value. That's right: negative lights. This is a very impressive feature and can be used to generate beautiful shadows and effects. It's like a lightbulb that absorbs light instead of giving it off. If you cast a negative spotlight into a corner, it would cast shadows instead of brightness.

Aiming Spotlights

Dale Gass
dale@ra.isisnet.com

Selecting a spotlight and then clicking the View from Object button is a great way to aim spotlights and see their coverage when configuring them.

Visible Lights

See Glows and Visible Lights in the Special Effects section later in this appendix.

Raytraced Shadows vs. Shadow Maps

Ian Firth
IanFirthDC@aol.com

I have finally given up on raytraced shadows. They take way too long and are too sharp-edged. I have since switched to shadow maps only, but still raytrace for reflections. My render times have dramatically decreased, and the shadow maps actually look better for Indeo AVIs aimed at CD-ROM playback. My current project needs 450MB of compressed (5 gigabytes uncompressed) animation and artwork before completion (which spends on average one minute per frame in Premiere), so this approach enables me to meet my summer deadline. Your mileage may vary, but you might look into this as an option to speed render times.

Light Gels – Projecting Images with Light

Shane Davison
daviso@cs.uregina.ca

You can place a bitmap with some transparency on a plane in front of a light, turn on shadow casting, and have the light "project" your text onto other surfaces.

TAKE NOTE: You can use the above technique with a texture made from an AVI or image sequence. Then you basically have an animated movie projector.

Rendering Tips

Are you looking for tips on doing renderings? Try these.

Render Limit Guidelines

Mike Vanderlaan
mikev@neosoft.com

trueSpace has a distance limit from the camera to an object beyond which the object will not be rendered. In other words, if you get an object too far from the camera, renderings won't show it. Here's a list of approximate distance limits for the various coordinate systems:

- meters: 508
- inches: 20000
- feet: 1666
- yards: 555
- miles: .316
- points: 1,440,000

Changing to a different coordinate system doesn't help because trueSpace automatically scales to the new coordinate system for you. If you already have an image that is encountering this problem, the workaround is to glue everything together and scale it down.

Render "Notch Filter"

Brian Hickey
redbaron@fn.net

Unfortunately, trueSpace doesn't have a clipping plane render, where you drag a rectangle over your view and the program renders only within the box. One workaround is to create a plane object with a square hole cut in the middle to reveal the desired section of the scene. The plane can be glued to a camera and saved as an object for just this purpose. If the "matte plane" is a solid color with flat shading enabled, tS renders it very quickly, so your overall render time is greatly reduced. Also, the flat shading enables you to easily select the matte so you can composite the image in post-production. You will want to be careful of the plane object causing unwanted reflections in your scene, however.

Special Effects Tips

Here are some special effects tips that can help you animate like a pro.

Engine Exhaust Fire

James Eric Mason
jem@cais.com

I worked up some fine engine fire for our project by creating semi-transparent cone-like structures (three of different shapes and colors) and telling them to rotate on their Zs very rapidly (at 1:1 speed, 173 degrees per frame). To create the cones I used Sweep. The cones were created using Boolean polygons. I always work on these from the top isometric view because otherwise you easily get aspect errors. First I drew a fairly precise (~45 segment) circle. Then I set the draw mode to subtract and drew another circle inside it. Then, I haphazardly took out parts of the result with more subtracted circles and free-form polygons, mostly of 7 to 8 segments. This gave me a broken, rough circle full of gaps (but no distinct internal holes). This done, I moved to perspective view and did a single sweep (you could use more) and I used both mouse buttons on Scale Points to make it a semi-conical shape. I gave this shape a higher than usual luminance and made it mostly (95–98 percent) transparent. One shape I made blue, one yellow, one red (more and more transparent as you go) and glued them together, setting different (large) rotational frames for them. I stuck them behind the engines and... voilà!

As for phaser fire, you could use very long tubes in the same way...

Brian Hickey
`redbaron@fn.net`

Making spaceship engine exhausts is another application of the Glow effect available using the Paint Vertices tool that I explain in the Glows and Visible Lights section later in this appendix.

1. Create a cone with a latitude set to 3 and a longitude set to 12.
2. Create a material with a flat shade, color of R255 G255 B255, and a 100% Transparency.
3. Flatten the cone to 2D.
4. Set the material as above but then select a bright yellow and set the transparency to about 80%.
5. Go to a Top view.
6. Using the Paint Vertices tool, paint the center, filling all the triangle facets with a smooth gradient from the center out to the next set of facets.
7. Change the color to an orange and paint the next set of vertices. This should now look like a smooth gradient glow from yellow to orange to clear.
8. Duplicate the flattened cone three times and rotate from the center for all axes X, Y, and Z.
9. Glue each of the cones together as siblings.

Now you have a glowing sphere visible from all directions. You can also stretch one end of the sphere using the volume deformation tool to give it a trailing exhaust look.

The Ubiquitous Lens Flare

Shane Davison
`daviso@cs.uregina.ca`

A lens flare is that nifty optical effect you get when you point a camera at a light source — usually seen as one or more colored halos of light that move and change colors as you move the camera. They are (perhaps too) often simulated in 3D animations for sci-fi television (*Babylon 5*, *Deep Space 9*, *Sea Quest*, and other shows). The examples from television are typically produced with a special lens effect in the 3D software itself. LightWave, 3D Studio, Imagine, and Real3D all have the effect.

trueSpace, unfortunately, doesn't have a lens flare effect. However, you have many options for creating them or reasonable facsimiles.

You might want to check out the flare object from Aminet that has been uploaded to `ftp.netnet.net: /pub/aminet/gfx/3d/AnimFlare.*`. It contains a lens flare object in Imagine format (which can be imported into tS) and a brief description of how to use it and/or create your own. Note that because it was created on the Amiga, you may have problems extracting the longer filenames (unless you have an operating system that supports them). However, it should be possible to get all the files with a little work.

Filters exist in various image editors and video editors that do reasonable lens flares. The following products contain lens flare-like effects:

- Adobe Photoshop
- Adobe Premiere
- Media Studio Pro
- In:Sync's Razor, Razor Pro, and Speed Razor Mach III

Explosions

Oh boy, what a topic. This one has been discussed a lot on the tSML. I should distinguish, however, between the two kinds of explosions people typically want to create. One, is a "gasoline" explosion where you get a blast of fiery light. And the other is the disintegrating explosion where an object breaks into a multitude of pieces that fly away from the explosion center. Of course, if you want to blow something up, a combination of these two is likely to be what you're looking for. trueSpace can simulate both kinds with varying success. The techniques presented here, based on various notes from the tSML, yield the best results when used in combination.

A definitive information source for tS explosions is an article on this very subject by Peter Plantec in issue number 19 of *3D Artist* magazine.

A must-have utility for explosions is Exploder. Originally written by tS user David Strepenhan and evidently now supported by Rob Bryerton, Exploder is currently in version 1.36. This program takes an ASCII .cob file containing your victim object and produces another .cob file with an animation of the object shattering into pieces and exploding. Also, with Exploder you can control many parameters of the explosion to get just the effect you want. Cool, no? Exploder is available on `ftp.netnet.net` and `ftp.caligari.com`; the filename is expl-136.zip. Oh, and it's shareware and the price is extremely reasonable, so if you use it, send in your money.

Using Lens Flares for Explosions

Peter Plantec
`thenar@cinenet.net`

One way to make explosions is by compositing the lens flare from Premiere. You start it at a very low level, then take it up over 12 frames to full intensity, then down in about six frames. It gives a fabulous explosion effect, like a supernova.

Expanding Fireballs

I tend to like the big fireball kind of optical explosion. trueSpace is capable of some fine blowups using spheres with semi-transparent reflection maps on them. Put a local light inside and vary the brightness from say 1.5 to 5.8 very quickly by animating it. Animate several spheres exploding and then imploding. I have also had a flattened torus expand out from the center to beyond the view. It looks great!

The three secrets are:

1. Get your timing down right for the expansion and contraction.
2. Get your lights up and down fast (you get distorted fireballs in the center).
3. Use a fire or flame reflection map.

I rotate the objects as they expand and contract one inside the other. This gives the effect of swirling fire. I've also just started distorting the spheres as they expand to give a nonsymmetrical look. Instead of particles shooting out of this, use the filmy fire and smoke. It's wonderful when combined with Exploder objects flying out of the center.

Using Exploder to Blow Up a Planet

I took a sphere primitive and smooth quad-divided it. Then I triangulated it and quad-divided it three more times. This left me with a very complex sphere. I then ran it through Exploder and set the minimum number of chunks to 200 and I made the animation 100 frames with the rotation set at 100 percent. I put a very bright red light inside and surfaced the planet with something called black tar, which has a lot of bumps and highlights. I think any blotchy, bumpy map would do.

The animation is interesting. It looks like the planet literally atomizes in a blaze of glory. Part of the secret is to start the light out at 8 or more intensity and deep red in color, then, over the hundred frames (200 NTSC, BTW), drop the intensity (you could go up and down if you want to set the keys) and end it with an intensity of 2.0 with a hue of deep green light.

Exploding Shock Waves

Brian Hickey
redbaron@fn.net

This is an effect similar to a flat blast wave proceeding the final explosion that you see in movies. Many of you have done this with transparency maps, but here is a way to get a cool effect with tS 2.0's new Procedural Textures. They're not just for wood, marble, and stone anymore.

1. Create a flattened sphere.
2. In the material box select Phong shading and the wood procedural.
3. In the procedural edit box select one of the [smmrwd] to be a bright orange or whatever color you wish) with a transparency of 15% and make the [sprngwd] color black with a transparency of 100%.
4. Set the [spr:sum] to .5.
5. Set the [ring density] between 2 and 3.
6. Set the width and shape vary to 0.
7. Set the grain for a Z axis.
8. Animate the flattened sphere from a small dense shape to a size that extends well beyond the camera.

This procedure generates smooth flame-like blast waves that explode from the center. It works great with an Exploder object with animated lights in the center.

Visible Light Beams

Bjørn-Kåre Nillsen
bjoernk@oslonett.no

Visible light beams are not possible to do automatically in tS. You have to make a cone that has the same size and location as your spotlight cone. Then you give this cone a more or less transparent material, to simulate more or less "dust." You can group this cone with your spotlight, so they move in synchrony.

David Campbell
dcampbel@bga.com

You can use subtle bump maps on the light cone to simulate the light beam being cast through smoky air. The "wave" bump map works well for this.

Extreme Aspect Ratios

James Eric Mason
jem@cais.com

I created a nifty image after experimenting with extreme aspect ratios in trueSpace. If you render to a file at something like a 5 to 1 ratio, you get a panavision effect. I did the JPEG interface to my online gallery using this fact. The images there were rendered at 600 by 128. Also, I did an even more extreme test where I placed a camera at the center of my gallery and created 360 frames for it to sweep around in one-degree intervals, rendering a 64 by 640 — 64 wide by 640 tall — stripe each time. I quickly created a Visual Basic program that reads each TGA and extracts only the center 4 pixels, which I calculated to give me an approximate one-degree angle. The result is a Mercator projection of the inside of the gallery.

One neat trick is to take this image — in .tga format — and place it on a sphere in tS. Place a camera at the center — and a light too if you are raytracing — and look around; the curvature of the sphere will normalize the projection, and it will look as if you were actually rendering the whole room! It will be a bit blurry though, and since my original camera was not set to capture a full 180 degrees, there are pinches in the top and the bottom, but it puts a typical tS cubic map to shame. They really ought to use something like this for bitmapped environment shading.

2D Star Fields

David Campbell
dcampbel@bga.com

If you want to make star field bitmaps for backgrounds and textures, you must get StarTex, a great utility written by a very accomplished trueSpace user named Ian Firth. (Ian did all the graphics for the game Grey Wolf using tS.) Anyway, StarTex is easy to use and allows you to adjust such parameters as star density, color, and location of nebulae. It then generates an 8- or 24-bit .bmp. You can use that bitmap directly in trueSpace, or you can bring it into your favorite image editor for more tweaking. I've had great success swapping the default black night sky with my own gradient or fractal cloud images. StarTex is available via FTP at `ftp.netnet.net`, filename: `/pub/mirrors/truespace/utils/startx.zip`. You can texture map the star field onto a big sphere and put a camera and spaceship inside it. Wham — you now have a 360-degree environment for sci-fi animations.

Go one step further. Put another sphere inside the star field sphere. The inner sphere is textured with the marble procedural in tS2 using the parameters for simulating a cloudy sky. Then you'll see the stars peeking out from between the clouds.

Glows and Visible Lights

Brian Hickey
redbaron@fn.net

Here's how to achieve glows using the paint vertices tool. The following example is how I did an engine exhaust glow:

1. Create a cone from the object primitives toolbox.
2. Give the cone a flat material with 100% transparency and 100% of the color of your choice (for example, if you use red make sure the color is R255 G0 B0).
3. Choose the paint vertices tool and slide the transparency down to 60 to 80%.
4. Paint the top vertex of the cone for each facet or side.

This process should give you a cone that is bright at the top and fades to nothing at the bottom like an engine blast. It works best against a black background.

You can also alter the colors on the sides for interesting effects. For my engine, I turned it on its side and made it rotate. I then rendered the scene with motion blur, which smoothed out the exhaust even more and gave it some pseudo-motion. You can also make glowing spheres by doing the above and then flattening the cone to a 2D circle. Duplicate the circle three times and rotate it for X, Y, and Z. This gives you a glowing sphere visible from all directions. The cone effect also works for visible light shafts.

Shane Davison
daviso@cs.uregina.ca

Brian Hickey's technique for engine exhaust glows can also be applied to the creation of visible point lights.

1. Create a plane.
2. Use a resolution of 2, or quad-divide it once.
3. Set up the materials for the object and vertices as described in Brian's tip given previously.
4. Switch to Paint Vertices and click once in the center of the plane.
5. Move the plane to the same location as the light source and scale as necessary.
6. Rotate the plane to face the camera or eye or, for animations, simply track the plane to the camera... voilà!

You can even make any object glow like it has a haze or fog surrounding it:

1. Load the object.
2. Use the Top view and rotate the object so it looks like it does in the final render.

3. Use the Spline or Polygon tools to trace the outline of the object.
4. Quad-divide the polygon once.
5. Set up the materials and click once in the center using Paint Vertices.
6. Scale the polygon so it's slightly bigger than the object (about 125%).
7. Save it, load it into your final scene, and position and rotate it so it's in the same location as the object and facing the camera or eye.

Incredible! However, this method doesn't work very well for animations.

Finally, Paint Vertices can actually be used as a substitute for that 3D painting that's been mentioned in magazines (and here) for high-end packages. Simply quad-divide your object many, many times and paint away! Of course, this is fairly impractical but I did manage to paint a cool face on a heavily divided sphere. Note: This procedure works even better with the Paint Faces tool.

Lightning

Peter Plantec
`thenar@cinenet.net`

You can make fantastic dark clouds and lightning animation for a background using the marble procedural texture. The trick is to paint the procedural texture onto a sky dome (large sphere with camera position inside). Set the vein (lightning) color to white initially and the sharpness to around 8 with complexity also around 8. This should give you a nice streak of light. Make the background color black, and when the transparency dialog comes up, select about 95% transparency. Put in a sky background bitmap. Now apply about 60 frames of animation to the sphere with no motion, by typing `frame 60` in the animation tool frame field. Now experiment with varying the sharpness, complexity, or XYZ values ever so slightly over these frames. Make your key frames 0 and 60 for these changes (nothing in the middle). You might also experiment with small changes in the color of the lightning for a nice effect.

Peter Plantec
`thenar@cinenet.net`

Here's a slight variation on the lightning animation using the procedural marble texture. Make the stone color reddish, then make it transparent. Next, set the vein to yellow-orange and make it 80% opaque. Then fiddle with the sharpness and turb settings. Put sharpness around 7.8 and turb to about 7.5 and experiment until it looks about right for you. Leave the X, Y, and Z settings on 2.0 and paint the plane. Animate the plane with a null path of about 60 or more frames. Set the 0 frame as a keyframe. Go to the end frame and set it as a keyframe. Next, change the marble by changing the transparent stone base color to blue, but keeping the invisibility (I kid you not, it makes a difference). Next set the turb to 9 or 10, move the sharpness up too — just under 10. Now make very small changes in the X, Y, and/or Z scaling (.01 to .03, plus or minus). Keep Grain set in the same direction throughout this experiment.

Making sure the last frame is a keyframe, paint the plane and render a draft to see where the lightning is. Double-check the first frame. The colors and shape should be different to let you know you have two different frames. Render the frames and check it out.

Supernovas

Mark E. Marshall
marshall@ids.net

Here's a neat effect for creating a StarTex background:

1. Make a transparent sphere and flatten the X axis. At around 88% transparency (experiment to taste), apply the background color with the PV tool in the center (I'm using yellow for this demo). Increase transparency to 98% (again, experiment) and apply a darker color to the same spot (using rosy peach). You should have a smooth two-tone (slightly) angular gradient.
2. Repeat the above procedure except flatten this sphere on the Z axis. Align the center point with the other sphere (you should be slightly in front with this one). Apply white to the center at 85% transparency. This gradient should be circular with a brighter epicenter.
3. Contract both spheres to pinpoint (using only the nonpainted axes so as not to shift the alignment; for example, Scale Y, Z for the colored, Scale X, Y for the white).
4. Keyframe a rapid expansion of both spheres to your desired size.
5. Contract only the white sphere till it's star-sized again (or slightly larger).
6. Render, render, render.

Now an addendum to really make it artsy:

If you have Photoshop 3.0, duplicate the background and apply the Render ➪ Clouds filter in the location of your supernova (settings: white on black). If you don't have Photoshop, use a fairly opaque white airbrush in this area, and make some nice swirly patterns. Then keyframe the background change at the moment the supernova is at its biggest and brightest. The "clouds" will hold the salmon color in a very surreal manner.

Light Streaming from Text

Ernest Yanarella
Yanarella@msn.com

Here's how to achieve visible light streaming from extruded text. It's quite simple:

1. Take your extruded text and copy it.
2. Adjust the Z value so that the copy is longer than the text.

3. Position the copy in front of the original text.
4. Take the glass material from the material library, turn transparency completely up, refraction completely down, select the color you want the visible light to be, and paint the copy.
5. Paint the front of the copy with complete transparency so it will show through to the original text.
6. Position the camera near the real extruded text, but so that the end of the copy stretches out of the view.
7. Render using raytracing.

Kon Wilms
kon@metropolis.petech.ac.za

Here's another way to achieve the effect of light streaming from extruded text. Using your favorite 2D image editor, make a gradient, black-to-white. Paint with this texture, using planar mapping, over the top of the extruded 'beams' of light, with the white side on the object side:

```
text
| | white
| |
| | black
```

With this method you fake the beams fading out, and you are free to move the beams around the camera view. Self illumination should be on 50%, the extrusion fully transparent. This lets you have a misty effect if you move the cones around a scene where there are other lights, a kind of 'additive' effect.

Using the Paint Vertices tool to paint the extruded object, instead of a gradient texture map, seems like it would work fine as well. You would first paint the beams a transparent black, then vertex paint a white onto the vertices on the text side of the beam. This would save you the effort of making the gradient image.

Using trueSpace with Other Tools

Here are several techniques for using tS2 with other tools.

Compositing tS Images without Border Artifacts

Images from tS can be composited (for example, superimposed or overlaid) on top of other images in image editing programs such as Photoshop, or in video editing programs such as Premiere. A common problem occurs when compositing specific objects from a tS rendering that has been done with antialiasing enabled. Antialiasing smoothes jagged edges in images by interpolating the pixel colors around the problem edges. This unfortunately causes border artifacts when the object is composited on another image. Solutions:

Bjørn-Kåre Nillsen
bjoernk@oslonett.no

When rendering the object to be composited, use a background that's quite similar to the background it is to be superimposed on. This avoids the contour around the object, where tS has blended it with the background color. The other way to do this is to render without the antialiasing. It can still get a border, but not that strong. It gets quite jaggy though.

Nontajit Lertworachon
gostudio@pipeline.com

trueSpace can also render an alpha channel.

TAKE NOTE

You have to render to a 32-bit Targa file. This automatically makes an alpha channel with the background being transparent.

Photoshop and Premiere (and many other programs) have options to use the alpha channel in a composite. This gives you much cleaner results because the antialias interpolation occurs with a transparent background. Note: The alpha channel in trueSpace renders has white as transparent and black as opaque, the opposite of what you might expect.

RGB Values for Blue and Green Screen Masking in Premiere

Ian Firth
IanFirthDS@aol.com

Use true blue or green (for example, 255 for the color component RGB values) when setting up your background matte for blue/green screening tS images. Also, if you are going to use Premiere to bluescreen, don't use the default bluescreen option as it tends to cause all areas of the image to become slightly transparent. Use color difference instead. Note: For an example of this problem, observe the transparency of the Enterprise in the *Trek* video on the CD-ROM.

Importing 2D Drawings

James Eric Mason
jem@cais.com

If you're drawing 2D outlines in Corel for DXF export, design using Béziers when needed, but don't export Béziers directly because the lowest DXF export curve resolution is 32 points per curve, which is way too many. When I only want 10 or 15 points per curve, I select the Bézier segment at an inflection point with Corel's point-edit, and then tell it to subdivide until the number of points looks adequate, then I tell Corel to convert to curves. If your Bézier point is connected as anything other than a Cusp-type point, change it to Cusp before doing this as it will modify the other side of the curve (which you may have to convert to lines separately). Of course, Corel treats circles and arcs the same way, so you might have to adjust them as well (convert to curves first... I know it's a pain). I would guess some of the same advice goes for Illustrator and Designer users as well, though I have not tried DXF output from either.

Bjørn-Kåre Nillsen
`bjoernk@oslonett.no`

When importing objects from 2D drawing programs, try not to have objects with both a fill and an outline. Objects with both will import as two trueSpace objects: one for the outline and one for the fill. If this occurs, they will be traversible via object hierarchy and you can delete one of them.

VistaPro and trueSpace

Shane Davison
`daviso@cs.uregina.ca`

When importing VistaPro landscapes into trueSpace, you will typically want to texture the landscape so it appears essentially the same in a trueSpace rendering as it does in a VistaPro rendering. This is the general procedure:

1. Start VistaPro.
2. Load a DEM (Digital Elevation Model) or create one using the fractal utility.
3. Select Save DXF and Yes to overlap edges for smooth shading. Note: Use a polygon count of 2 or more (for example, 4,8). Otherwise, you'll need a lot of memory to even load it into tS and even more to manipulate/render it.
4. Select Save Texture Map and Yes to allow VistaPro to calculate colors. Note: You must enable the 24-bit graphics mode first.
5. Start trueSpace.
6. Load the previously created DXF.
7. Select UV Project and apply a flat proj. to the top of the terrain. Note: This may need to be rotated later for proper placement of the terrain texture map.
8. Right-click Paint Object and select the previously created .tga as a texture map (change other attributes as necessary).
9. Left-click Paint Object and you're done!

Importing Fractal Landscapes from Fractint into trueSpace

Serge Golikov
Serge.Golikov@Syd.AFTRS.EDU.AU

Anyone interested in creating fractal landscapes should look no further than Fractint from the Stone Soup Group, arguably the best (and still public domain) fractal explorer available. It is currently in version 19.1. Fractint has the ability to save out in DXF format, which trueSpace loads in faithfully, maintaining the original colors of the rendered GIF fractal. The advantage of using this method rather than a utility such as IF2DXF, say, is that Fractint can generate thousands of different fractals, has control of the palette of the output GIF, adjustment for mesh resolution, and more.

Lparser

Chng Ching Huei
chngchil@iscs.nus.sg

Lparser is a freeware object generator for making tree-like organic models. A great write-up on it was published in issue number 17 of 3D Artist. It is capable of spectacular plants, but be aware that the models it generates are huge. It's available via FTP from povray.

Fractal Designer 3

Peter Plantec
thenar@cinenet.net

FD3 is a fabulous tool for use with trueSpace. It has a smart tile builder for creating tileable textures. You create the tile of any size and FD3 sees to it that the elements are positioned so a seamless pattern results. The Image Hose sprays image elements on the tile so you can build up amazing textures with a 3D look to them. FD4 is now out and it's even more fabulous with animated texture design, bigger tiles, and more.

Batch Image Processing

David P. Moller
DaMol111@aol.com

trueSpace animators who work with image sequences often need to perform a particular image enhancement to large numbers of images. For this type of job, check out Brenda for Windows. It's a shareware program that you'll find in the MacroMedia forum on CompuServe.

From the Brenda Forum: "Welcome to Brenda * The Batch Renderer. Brenda was written to fill a long-felt need for a way to process large numbers of digital image files in an efficient manner. With Brenda, you can select a virtually limitless number of images, set a few options, and sit back (or go to lunch) while Brenda does the rest!"

Batch Processing Features:

- Map true-color images to grayscale
- Map true-color images to fixed-color palettes at a variety of color depths
- Convert true-color or palette-mapped images to the same, standard-sized palette
- Create an optimized palette from an assortment of source images (limit 100)
- Convert palette-mapped images to true color
- Perform file format conversions

A new batch processing program called BatchIt is now out from Griffen Software. It's been available for the Mac and is just becoming available for Windows 95. It's a very sophisticated batch image processing program.

Polyform

Peter Plantec
thenar@cinenet.net

Polyform is a neat new 3D utility from Vivid Technologies. It can load 20-some different 3D formats and you can save any of them in COB format. Further, it is the only inexpensive program I've seen that reduces the polygon count and fixes coplanar polys. It's very useful. A demo is available via Sharware.com on Netscape.

Miscellaneous Tips

The following tips and techniques may not fit any special category but they're still valuable.

Converting from RAW To DXF

Shane Davison
daviso@cs.uregina.ca

There are a couple of utilities that can convert from RAW to DXF. Check ftp.povray.org/pub/povray/utilities for dxf2raw.

Compression Codecs

Shane Davison
daviso@cs.uregina.ca

Compression is a topic that is very important to computer animators. Choosing the right compression format and settings is best accomplished by knowing a little bit about how compression works and how the various parameters affect the final product. I will eventually write my own contribution to the compression discussion, but what I know of compression I learned mostly from a book called *Video Compression for Multimedia* by Jan Ozen. I highly recommend it. The book includes a layman's discussion of compression principles, techniques, and considerations. It's good at presenting this information without burdening you with so much technical mumbo-jumbo that it makes your eyes glaze over. It also includes a great comparison of the most widely used codecs (a coding/decoding API that reduces the amount of data required for transferring video images through the bus), explaining which ones are best for particular applications. Check it out.

Table B-3 presents various responses from the tS mailing list to a query regarding codecs. Clearly, most of the animators prefer CinePak. And for good reason: it has good image quality, reasonably speedy encoding, and decent compression rates. It is not, however, the best choice in all situations. This is where Jan Ozen's video compression book is quite handy. (By the way, if I'm starting to sound like ad copy, let me state for the record that I have no affiliation with the book, the author, or the publisher, other than being a satisfied reader.) Here are the questions in the survey:

- ✦ Which provides the smoothest playback?
- ✦ Which provides the best compression?
- ✦ Any particular settings you prefer?
- ✦ Any bugs you've notice using any particular compression method?

Table B-3
Codec Preferences Survey

Opinion by	*Smoothest Codec*	*Best-looking compression*	*Preferred settings*	*Any bugs noticed*
Shane Davison	CinePak	CinePak	qual 100% no keys	Occasional fuzzies
Bjørn-Kåre Nillsen	CinePak	CinePak	qual 100% no keys	with Indeo, GPFs
Michael Mills	CinePak	CinePak	qual 100% no keys	Indeo-ghosting
Mark E. Marshall	CinePak	CinePak	qual 100% no keys	

Ian Firth has some professional comments to make from his experience in game development.

Ian Firth
`IanFirthDS@aol.com`

I use Indeo V3.24.01.01 for all CD stuff; CinePak compresses way too slowly for the tons of animations I do. And I find Indeo to playback much better (set keyframing at 4). The only problem is color bleeding with intense reds. The Indeo fixed palette is also decent. Because most of my work incorporates AVIs overlaid on background art, I don't need to worry about nasty palette flash. In the palette, the colors map very nicely to existing artwork. Indeo 4.0 should be out by summer (640 by 480 at 30 fps from what I've gathered), and should be something to see.

Miscellaneous Compression Tips

Ian Firth
`IanFirthDS@aol.com`

Don't render from trueSpace compressed. Render uncompressed, then compress afterwards with VidEdit or Premiere or Razor, or another compression utility. The results will amaze you. Note: 1 gig drives are now under $200 at California computer shows; a 4 gig AV wide SCSI drive is under $900.

The reason the image quality is better when you compress after rendering is that most compression schemes use at least some measure of *interframe* compression, which basically discards image information that doesn't change between subsequent frames. This interframe compression reduces file sizes tremendously and is theoretically lossless. In fact, image degradation occurs mainly or entirely during *intraframe* compression — that part of video compression that discards redundant or "unnecessary" image information within a single frame. Anyway, compressing while rendering hampers the codec's ability to use interframe compression most effectively. This results in poorer image quality and often lower compression ratios.

Flipping an Object Upside-Down

Shane Davison
`daviso@cs.uregina.ca`

Use the object info panel to make the Z-scale negative (for example, change a value of 2 to -2).

Stay on Top of the Tips

As you can see, these tips are invaluable. You can save months of experimenting by checking in at the Ego Wall for the latest set of tips and techniques. Better yet, become an active participant in the tSML and contribute your own unique ideas for the rest of us to learn.

APPENDIX C

The Dynamics of Character Development

The following article was written by Dr. Anthony Gregorc, a noted psychologist and expert on character traits. It might help you understand character development when designing animated characters. If you pay close attention, you'll never create another boring animation. (You might also gain some insight into what makes your friends and family members tick.)

Adding Human Depth to Animated Characters

Anthony F. Gregorc, Ph.D.

When designing an animated character for your script it's a good idea to give him, her, or it consistent behaviors that make sense from a human standpoint. Personalities are not haphazard. Each is distinct. There is a substructure of linked characteristics. This is a consistent chain of behaviors and attitudes that arise from the way the person views, orders, and processes his world.

Healthy individuals tend to think, feel, and behave according to certain general patterns. No two are exactly alike, but as you read through the mind styles described in this appendix, you'll recognize patterns in yourself and the people you know. You won't fit cleanly into one style because we have elements of all of them within us. However, you will find one or two that may seem very much like you. That's what we'd call your dominant style.

When you design a character for animation or live action, you can select a dominant style, then pick and choose interesting combinations of behaviors from alternate styles. This gives your character a complex, human-like personality. After you've read this, try to identify the dominant styles of key characters in movies such as *Toy Story*. This information about style comes from years of research starting in 1970. Along the way I've developed a personality model with four quadrants that when combined, represent the infinite style possibilities found in life. The four types are: Concrete Sequential, Abstract Sequential, Abstract Random, and Concrete Random. I've based these labels on the way the individual perceives, orders, and reacts to his world. My purpose here is to share the kinds of personality traits that tend to hang together for a given cognitive style so you'll have a better understanding of your character's personality.

Style as Key to Behavior

None of the four styles is superior to another. They're all valid, but much of the tension in relationships is born of this difference in how each individual sees and deals with the world. For example, a dominant Abstract Random person often annoys a Concrete Sequential, and vice versa. Yet they can be strongly attracted to each other. Good marriages often come from the bonding of opposites who learn to respect each other's ways. You can use this complexity in your story to create that most essential of all drama ingredients: conflict. At the same time you'll be adding authentic character depth, which is what audiences love to see.

When you know your character, you can predict with great precision how he solves problems, what angers him, how he relates to friends. The trend to make animated characters more human is strong. The wise character designer incorporates ever more believable humanity into their creatures, be they humans, rabbits, robots, dragons, or automobiles.

To avoid the silly he/she convention, I use male gender throughout my descriptions and hope you don't take offense. Cognitive styles apply evenly to men and women. Here are examples of behaviors you're likely to see in each of the four dominant styles:

The Dominant Concrete Sequential (CS) Style

The dominant CS relates to his world in a step-by-step manner. Habitual behavior is key. This character is going to make his bed immediately upon arising. Right after dinner he clears the table; dishes are washed, dried, and stacked neatly on a shelf. His checkbook is going to be balanced at all times, and he catches all the bank's errors, which annoy him greatly.

This character drives the same route to work every day, and his day is time- and task-oriented. Though his routines may appear boorish to others, the CS is convinced and satisfied that his ways work, have worked, and will continue to work in the future. He believes they will work for others if they would only see the light and do things the right way (which, of course, is his way). As proof of this, many CSs have amassed considerable financial reward for excellent work. Interestingly, some other styles believe the CS is right and feel guilty about being who they are.

The CS tends to view his world in black or white, right or wrong. This can get irritating to the less rigid people around him. For him, anything between the two extremes is too fuzzy to deal with. Consequently, the CS tends to answer questions with yes/no, right/wrong, tastes good/bad, or sounds good/bad.

He chooses his wardrobe with care and economy. Drawn to conservative suits, he avoids mixed colors and splash. You'll never find a CS wearing mismatched plaids, flashy colors, or an unconventional or nontraditional outfit. He is usually a fussbudget about such things as neatness, wrinkle-free clothes, well-coifed hair, perfect makeup, and spit-shined shoes.

The CS seldom loses anything. He's precisely situated in the concrete world and remembers where he put his keys — probably knows where you put yours.

Invite a CS to a dinner party and you can be sure he'll be there on time, or have a proper excuse. Meeting obligations and commitments is sacred to the CS — so much so that he tends to burden himself with them. A commitment phobic might be a CS who sees relationships as impossible lifetime commitments he might fail at. He's likely to be uncomfortable at social events where he doesn't know everybody, and be deeply concerned about doing and saying the right thing to the right people. He may be overly concerned about offending people he considers to be his superiors.

Special occasions are marked with proper, even predictable gifts. He is practical if uninventive. The CS likes to give and receive cash, gift certificates, potted plants, toasters, lawnmowers, and computer peripherals. CS folks do fall in love, in which case, one might hand-carve an ebony reproduction of a traditional wood puzzle for you. You won't get cut flowers, a book of poems, satin sheets, or any other "frivolous" gift.

As parents CSs are loving but rigid, tending to be true disciplinarians. Homework is serious and to be done each night (preferably before dinner and definitely before television watching). And, the teacher is always right! Household duties are delegated with a roster and time schedule posted on the refrigerator door with a plain magnetic holder; tape may mar the surface. They insist their children write and mail those thank you letters for gifts from grandparents and relatives, within 24 hours.

There is to be no PDA (Public Display of Affection) with dates within eyesight... or within 500 feet of the house.

At work and at home the CS rarely gives compliments. He expects a good performance, a job well done, a neat appearance in others, and a smooth-running life. He will not tolerate any disruption at dinner, for example, especially an emotional one. Approval is generally silent: no news is good news. On the other hand the CS is not reticent to clearly show disapproval, often in ways that freeze out the offender emotionally.

His desk is always well organized, pencils sharpened, file trays empty, desk drawers neatly divided with metal inserts, and a memo pad sitting squarely by the phone. Office furniture is streamlined, comfortable and efficient. You can bet if there are trees in the office they'll be silk or plastic because the CS is not known for his green thumb.

A CS guest in your home smells fish in the air a day after you had it for dinner, kitty litter in the box in the basement, and tells you the name of the perfume or aftershave you're wearing. He tells you what spices you put in the stew, and accurately guesses the year of the wine you're serving.

You know someone, possibly yourself, that closely fits this description, don't you? Carry on, there's more.

The Dominant Abstract Sequential (AS) Style

The dominant AS is highly intellectual, tends to be a loner, and lives mostly inside his own head. There is a time and place for everything in the AS life. He dislikes PDA even from parents or his spouse. This person wants to crawl under the table with embarrassment if you take him to a nice restaurant for his birthday, and four waiters show up with a sparkler-decorated cake, loudly singing happy birthday.

The AS does not pick up on verbal cues or innuendo — they whiz right past him. He wants details, rationale, and a full explanation for anything you do or say. Consequently he's uncomfortable with any behavior he doesn't understand, or compliments he doesn't think he deserves might even make him angry.

Though not fond of TV, the AS watches documentaries, news specials, and political debates — he loves the Discovery channel, but he's not much for general drama. He makes an excellent movie critic, because he pays more attention to the way the film was made than to the story. He gets involved only in films directly related to his interests rather than his emotions.

The AS is likely to completely forget your birthday, anniversary, or a luncheon date unless it's written down. Some of them are known as absent-minded professor types. You'll find his "stuff" stacked in piles, filed away in cabinets and dresser drawers, and placed on closet shelves. There's usually a lot of it and much is lost forever within his chaotic filing system.

Articulate (if sometimes boring), the AS can put you in your place in a most eloquent manner. Because he is a smooth manipulator of double entendre, you might not realize you've been sliced to ribbons with a smile.

Guardian angels have a full-time job watching over an AS individual who arrives at a particular destination either by car or on foot, not quite remembering how he got there. His mind is usually so preoccupied with other thoughts that he is amazed he arrived at all.

Never expect a short conversation with an AS unless it's on a subject he's not interested in. Hit on something he knows about and he'll monopolize the conversation, missing your facial expressions and hints, giving you more detail than you ever wanted. He's also likely to become offended when you lose interest (and you will) in all his amazing and wonderful minutiae.

The AS parent sets high standards and goals for his children. Emphasis is on social and academic achievement and he sees to it that his son or daughter is exposed to every opportunity for growth and development. The children are expected to show proper manners, recognize their duties and responsibilities to home and family, and uphold the family name. Though quite loving, the AS is not an overly demonstrative parent, expecting the children to just know they are loved. The children are often unsure of it.

As for dress, an AS really doesn't care much about it. There are a few tweedy types in academia, but generally they look at dress codes as being aimed at others. You might well see him wearing stripes with plaids, clashing colors, or wearing an open shirt to a dinner dance. He has no clue why others fuss so much about clothing when it just keeps one from being naked and cold.

The Abstract Sequential does his level best to impress you with how well-informed he is. He loves to read and relishes a thick, meaty book. His taste in literature runs from such tomes as *War and Peace*, or its contemporary equivalent, to autobiographies of famous presidents and writers. He believes that every individual should be knowledgeable about something and secretly would love to be on *Jeopardy* because he'd win big-time if he got the right categories. If he thinks you haven't had a bright idea in years, he snubs you as being irrelevant.

Highly skeptical, he's hard to convince. He may engage you in a superb game of mental gymnastics, never tiring as he matches you point for point. But he's taking the game seriously while you probably aren't. You'll never see him cry at weddings and only rarely does he reminisce about old times.

The Dominant Abstract Random (AR) Style

Dominant ARs live in the world of emotions and sociability. Many are strongly socially oriented. Don't saddle this person with routine; he quickly gets bored. Making the bed — forget it, he'll be using it again tonight, so what's the point? Dishes are piled up for days and washed when it's efficient and convenient. He usually waits until he runs out of clothes before doing laundry.

You'll see four or five books open on the AR's night table at a time. Dog-eared pages and turned over books are found everywhere — bathroom, bedroom, the back seat of the car, briefcase. Despite a prolonged absence, he has an uncanny ability to step back into a book right where he left off.

Many AR personalities like to dance and are good at it. Music can send them into a virtual high and send some into a mystical state of transcendence. Fingers and toes unconsciously tap to the music, bodies swaying.

Don't expect to see the AR's desktop. It's not used as a work bench, but rather serves as a repository for items arranged in patterns known only to himself. The AR office is wherever he is. His filing cabinet is in his head, a briefcase, a shopping bag, oversized leather shoulder bag, or the back seat of his car. A physical office is just a place to deposit things.

Live plants and AR types have an affinity for one another. He can over-water, under-water, and still his plants survive. Don't be surprised if you see an AR having a conversation with a plant while stroking it affectionately. He might even play the plant's favorite song (he knows what it is). Often his home and office look more like a jungle, overrun with tropical plants and flowers.

An AR can be reunited with an old friend from 20 years ago and pick up as if it were yesterday. These friendships are maintained despite lack of letters or telephone contact.

The AR is a romantic. Sometimes sentimental to the point of sappiness, he loves to collect symbols of his life in a little box — every rose, theater ticket, and coin from that trip to Fiji. In fact, he may collect all sorts of things like a pack rat; his home runneth over with antiques and things, all of which he considers important and treats with respect. He has a hard time throwing anything away, almost taking refuge in the clutter.

The AR loves bright colors and clothing and will wear just about any combination, often to good effect. He dresses according to mood and to please himself rather than others. Much affected by his environment, he tends to avoid depressing or plain places, opting for pleasing spaces that delight the eye.

The AR parent tends to get very involved in his children's activities, getting right down and playing tinker toys or computer games with them. The AR tends to be the softy on bottom lines, often giving in to the children's demands. You'll also find him active in PTA and first to volunteer for the bake sale. You see him as the room father, little league coach, and den father. As his children grow up the AR has a tendency to respect and admire them.

He's going to forget the exact date of your birthday, but at least he knows the month. Likewise, he's chronically late for things because time is not his thing. Gifts, cards, and often telephone calls for such occasions can come at any time. Crazy surprise gifts may also arrive for no particular reason, with a thinking-of-you card. The gifts tend to be wildly impractical and fun, and his cards are often hysterically outrageous.

Your favorite AR cries at weddings, sees movies over and over again, keeps photo albums and scrapbooks, remembers his childhood teddy bear, and donates to charities. He loves to be near water, thrills to the beauty of a sunset, and drags out the Christmas records at the first snowfall. Abstract Randoms love to reminisce.

The Dominant Concrete Random (CR) Style

The dominant CR is insightful and highly independent, and lives by divine discontent. He is a natural change agent. Don't tell an AR don't or you can't, because it'll achieve the opposite effect. He digs in to prove you wrong. He's duty-bound to beat whatever odds or systems get in his way.

This person is notorious for never reading instructions. He feels directions are for dimwits, or that not reading instructions is a direct challenge to his wits and competence. When his self-directed (Tim Allen style) efforts fail, he's been known to sneak off, instructions in hand, to read them when no one is watching. In fact, he tends to feel his way through life avoiding both authority and formal instruction. He is often successful at it because of his highly developed intuitive sense. Why take all the steps when you can leap to the right conclusion?

Aware of life's subtleties and not wanting to be tied down, the CR won't take a definite position on anything. For example, if told something is black, he might respond with "I'm not sure about that; it could be deep blue or maybe dark brown." Pinning him down to a final answer he will stick with and not change a month later goes against his entire nature. It's not going to happen. He covers all bets to avoid entrapment.

The CR is usually outgoing, friendly, assertive, and loves to mix and socialize. You'll see him maneuvering around the room, joining in conversations momentarily, and moving off to another. He is often the life of the party, hates dull events, and usually can be depended upon to liven things up when they go flat.

The CR loves to tinker. A natural curiosity about how things work can get him into trouble as he disassembles things and can't put them back together again. He loves to play with models, gadgets, cars, household appliances, and even ideas. Like Tim Allen he likes to experiment, and might rewire the whole house to accommodate a new invention.

Young CRs are the children who love to play with chemistry sets, never read the instructions, and blow things up. They always have their bikes, computers, or your lamp apart, often losing key pieces.

You can't stay angry with CRs for long, though. They are charmers. Their intense personal charisma allows them to get away with murder as they "charm the pants off a snake." Strange as it may seem, these individuals almost always have a melodious voice, a down-to-earth appeal, and an air of sophistication. The CR also loves to hear the sound of applause for his efforts. To him it's a hot shot of adrenaline.

The CR is a leader, not a follower. He loves to take charge and be in charge. Thriving on controversy, he is often at war within himself and against various evils. A cunning and often brilliant strategist, he often turns his dreams over to others for completion. That's because he's more interested in designing things than building them. He is highly creative. Though each of the four types is uniquely creative, the CR's tendency to break rules leads to a lot of original thinking and creative exploration. Because he sees rules as being for the other people, he's also in hot water a lot.

As parents CRs are not strict. They allow their children to do their own thing, within reason. They encourage them to drink deeply of life, learn by trial and error, and pick themselves up by their own bootstraps. "If at first you don't succeed..." is an adage they teach their kids and they prefer to provide guidelines rather than rules and regulations. They also tend to be more pals than disciplinarians.

Some CRs have a career with many moves, making it seem that changing jobs is their career goal. If you look closely they usually have good work records, but moved on for personal advancement or job enrichment, or simply because they got bored.

The Concrete Random knows the punchline of a joke or point you're trying to make before you finish. He involuntarily starts to nod his head or blurt out answers, unable to contain himself, though he probably hasn't heard the joke or reached your conclusion before. He's just experienced another one of his intuitive leaps over the middle part to the end of your thought.

Conclusion

There is great power in recognizing and understanding how these personality styles appear in everyday life. They can be used to create increased humanity in each of your characters. But, be careful with these brief descriptions. Good sense demands that you not restrict a character to a single dominant style. Humans and good characters are more complex than these extremes.

If you are interested in pursuing a deeper understanding of mind styles and how they combine to create an infinite variety of personal styles, contact Gregorc Associates, Inc., P.O. Box 351, Columbia, CT 06237-0351, for a copy of *An Adult's Guide To Style.*

The book contains a self-assessment instrument called the Gregorc Style Delineator, full instructions for scoring it, and extensive materials interpreting your results. The book also presents a lot more detail on each style with such things as typical phrases each personality might use or how the person is likely to deal with change. There are sections on pet peeves, negative characteristics, dealing with time, and problem-solving. Such information can help you create deeper, more dimensional, and empathetic characters for your productions.

APPENDIX D

Media Resources and Organizations

This appendix saves you time in locating resources and organizations that can help you build your competitive edge in the job market. The more you know, the better chance you stand at making a positive impression in your next job interview.

TAKE NOTE

For collections of really good animation shorts to give you an idea of the quality you should be shooting for in your demo, call Extended Entertainment, 800-996-TOON (8666).

Magazines of Interest

If you do call and subscribe to the following magazines, please mention that you discovered them here. They all said they like to know where their referrals come from. Knowing such information also helps them understand what a powerful force we tS2ers are.

WEB CONNECTION

- *Inter@ctive* magazine — Helps you stay on top of the exciting world of interactive media from cable to games. For more information check `http://www.inter-active-week.com/~intweek`.
- *InfoWorld* — From IDG International. Helps you keep up with the world of information networking. Call (415) 572-4351.

WEB CONNECTION

- *3D Artist* magazine — An excellent how-to magazine by the publishers of *Tessellation Times*. I often write tS2 and other articles here. Check `http://www.3dartist.com/` or call (505) 982-3532 for more information.

- *3D Design* — New kid on the block. *3D Design* got off to an explosive start and is well-respected in the industry. Call (800) 829-2505.
- *Animation* magazine — This one is a pure delight and I'm a columnist here (you tell me if that's a causal relationship). Look for my "SoftCel" column. It covers traditional as well as digital animation with stories, people profiles, company profiles, and events coverage. Contact Animation magazine at (818) 991-2884 for a subscription.
- *AV Video* — As a professional you can get AV Video for free and it's very useful reading, sure to help you stay on top of industry trends. Call (800) 800-5474.
- *CGW* — *CGW* stands for *Computer Graphics World*, which everyone in the industry reads. Here you'll find the latest software reviews and how-to articles as well as news, opinion, and tips. Contact PennWell Publishing at (918) 835-3161, extension 400.
- *PC Graphics and Video* — To keep up on the latest equipment and software trends, contact *PC Graphics and Video* at (800) 346-0085, extension 363.
- *Wired* — If you're hip or wannabe, you have to read Wired. It's the trendy spokesword for the digital evolution. It's well written, authoritative, and fun. Call (415) 222-6200 for your subscription... find out if they'll give you a deal as a new subscriber.
- *MultimediaToday* — This is a quarterly multimedia catalog with excellent articles, some of which are written by yours truly. Call (800) 779-2062.
- *LightWavePro* — For real, hands-on, inside tips from the pros who actually do the animation and special effects for the popular space-oriented TV shows, check out *LightWavePro*. It's expensive and it's small, and it's geared to LightWave 4.0, but it's right on the money and you can use most of the tips in tS2. Contact Avid Media Group, Inc., 273 N. Mathilda Ave., Sunnyvale, California 94806. Call (408) 774-6770.
- *Cinefex* — To keep up on all the neat new film special effects, subscribe to one of my absolute favorite magazines, *Cinefex*. Contact *Cinefex* at PO Box 20027, Riverside, California 92516. You will love it. It's like a quarterly book with lots of color. If you had all the back issues you'd have the amazing history of film effects.

Original Equipment Manufacturers

The OEMs (Original Equipment Manufacturers) listed in Table D-1 use Digital Equipment's Alpha Chips in their designs. They are good sources of completed systems or motherboards if you want to build your own. Don't call them for technical assistance on something you didn't buy from them. I know all of these companies personally, so mention that you read it here and maybe push for a little discount.

Table D-1
Original Equipment Manufacturers (OEMs)

Company	*Location*	*Contact*	*Phone*	*E-mail*
Aspen Systems Inc.	Wheat Ridge, Colorado	Amy Sterk	800-992-9242	aspen@aspsys.com
Bushey Virtual Construction	La Habra, California	Michael Bushey (pronounced *Bu-Shay*)	714-447-3587	http://www.vircon.com
Carrera Computers, Inc.	Laguna Hills, California	Bruce Faust	714-707-5051 800-576-RISC	carreral@delphi.com
Virtual Computer Technology	Bozeman, Montana	Keith Debus	406-585-8903	virtucomp@aol.com
Microway	Kingston, Massachusetts	Mike Brown	508-746-7341	www.microway.com
Nikotech	New Hampshire	Dick McGravey	603-926-0300	www.alphapower.com

Animation Societies Worldwide

Joining an animation organization can help you make valuable contacts and future friends. Try to get involved in at least one local group.

Aktion Film Center for Children's Films

Neubaugasse 25
Vienna 1070 Austria
Tel: 43 1 5232 4370
Fax: 43 1 523 3971

ASIFA Austria

Huttellbergaase 75/1
Vienna 1440 Austria
Tel: 43 1 914 7797
Fax: 43 1 712 0392

ASIFA Canada

10707 rue Grande-Allee
App 3
Montreal QC H3L 2M8
Canada
Tel: 1 514 842 9763

ASIFA Italia

Via Cosmo
Turin 10131 Italy
Tel: 39 11 812 3066
Fax: 39 11 878 8076

Australian Children's Television Association

199 Grattan ST
Carlton VIC 3053 Australia
Tel: 61 3 9348 1144
Fax: 61 3 9347 4194

Belgian Animated Film Centre

52 Bondgenotenstraat
Brussels 1190 Belgique
Tel: 32 2 343 6561
Fax: 32 2 343 7883

Canadian Animation Producer's Association

32 Atlantic Ave
Toronto ON M6K 1X8
Canada
Tel: 1 416 588 5571
Fax: 1 416 588 5588

Cartoon

Blvd Lambermont 418
Brussels 1030 Belgique
Tel: 32 2 245 1200
Fax: 32 2 245 4689

Centre National de la Cinematographie

12 rue de Lubeck
Paris 75784 France
Tel: 33 1 44 34 34 40
Fax: 33 1 47 55 04 91

Guild of British Animation

26 Noel Street
London W1V 3RD U.K.
Tel: 44 171 434 2851
Fax: 44 171 434 9002

I.N.A. Institut National de l'Audiovisuel

4 Ave de l'Europe
Bry-Sur-Marne 94366 France
Tel: 33 1 49 83 20 00
Fax: 33 1 49 83 24 01

Korean Animation Producers Association

Changdae Blvd 3F
11-56 Yangujae-Dong
Seccho-gu
Seoul, South Korea
Tel: 82 2 671 8581
Fax: 82 2 572 9673

Manitoba Society of Independent Animators

245 Main Street
Winnipeg MB R3C 1A7
Canada
Tel: 1 204 983 1276
Fax: 1 204 983 0742

Nederlands Instituut Voor Animatiefilm

Willem 2 Straat 49
5000 HJ Tllburg Nederlands
Tel: 31 13 35 45 55
Fax: 31 13 35 09 53

QuickDraw Animation Society

104 3009 23 Ave SW
Calgary AB T3E 0J3
Canada
Tel: 1 403 249 0696
Fax: same (call first)

Special Interest Video Association

PO Box 402
Oak Ridge NJ 07438
Tel: 1 201 697 7776
Fax: 1 201 697 5239

Swedish Film Institute

PO Box 27126
Stockholm 10252 Sweden
Tel: 46 8 665 1009
Fax: 46 8 662 2884

Swiss Film Animation Group

Chemin de la Rueyre 70
Jouxtena 1008 Switzerland
Tel: 41 21 635 7177
Fax: same (call first)

ASIFA Chapters USA

ASIFA – Central

Deanna Morse
268 LSH School of Communications
Grand Valley State University
Allendale MI 49401
Tel: 616 895 3101
morsed@gvsu.edu

ASIFA – DC

Tom Krawczewicz
PO Box 53101
Washington DC 20009

ASIFA – East

Jim Petropoulos
10 Point Crescent
Whitestone NY 11357
Tel: 718 746 3981

ASIFA – Hollywood

Antron Manoogian
725 South Victory Blvd.
Burbank CA 91502
Tel: 818 842 8330
Fax: 818 842 5645
asifa@earthlink.net

ASIFA – Northwest

Amy Collen
3916 SW Huber St.
Portland OR 97219

ASIFA – San Francisco

Carl Cohen
PO Box 14516
San Francisco CA 94114

By the time you read this some numbers may have changed, but it's a start. If you can't get through on your regional number, try the Hollywood office, which is the de facto national headquarters.

ACM/SIGGRAPH Professional Chapters

California

Los Angeles ACM SIGGRAPH

Aliza Corson
PO Box 90698
Worldway Postal Center
Los Angeles CA 90009-0698
los_angeles_chapter@siggraph.org
http://siggraph.allen.com/

San Francisco ACM SIGGRAPH

Connie Siu
1201 Park Ave Suite 203A
Emeryville CA 94608
sfsig@aol.com
http://www.best.com/~siggraph/

Silicon Valley ACM SIGGRAPH

Fran Zandonella
PO Box 1205
Mountain View CA 94042-1205
silicon_valley_chapter@siggraph.org
http://www/best/com/~siggraph

Colorado

Denver/Boulder ACM SIGGRAPH

Mike McCarthy
PO Box 61402
Cherry Creek Station
Denver CO 80206-8402
mpm@fc.hp.com

Florida

Ft. Lauderdale ACM SIGGRAPH

Garry M. Paxinos
Metro Link Inc.
4711 N. Powerline Road
Fort Lauderdale FL 33309
siggraph@flsig.org
http://www.flsig.org/ftl/

Orlando ACM SIGGRAPH

Dave Levinson
PO Box 2208
Winter Park FL 32790-2208
orlando_chapter@siggraph.org
http://www.flsig.org/os/

Tampa Bay ACM SIGGRAPH

Steve Pidgeon
PO Box 20782
Tampa FL 33622
pidgeon@pulseprod.ca
http://www.flsig.org/tampa/

Georgia

Atlanta ACM SIGGRAPH

D. Alan Stewart
PO Box 250382
Atlanta GA 30325
astewart@acm.org

Massachusetts

New England ACM SIGGRAPH

Michael Silton
PO Box 194
Bedford MA 01730
msilton@mcimail.com

Minnesota

Minneapolis/St. Paul ACM SIGGRAPH

Stan Bissinger
School of Communication Arts
2526 27th Ave South
Minneapolis MN 55406
stanbi@aol.com

North Carolina

NC Research Triangle ACM SIGGRAPH

Randy Brown
SAS Campus Drive RA 459
Cary NC 27513
randy@sas.com

New Jersey

Princeton ACM SIGGRAPH

Douglas Dixon
PO Box 1324
Princeton NJ 08542
princeton_siggraph_chapter@siggraph.org

New Mexico

Rio Grande ACM SIGGRAPH

David Callahan
PO Box 8352
Albuquerque NM 87108-8352
siggraph@cs.unm.edu

New York

New York ACM SIGGRAPH

Debra Herschmann
SIGMA Imaging
622 3rd Ave, 30th Floor
New York NY 10017
new_york_chapter@siggraph.org

Texas

Dallas Area ACM SIGGRAPH

Aaron Hightower
Paradigm Simulation Inc.
14900 Landmark Suite 400
Dallas TX 75240
siggraph@qbert.dseg.ti.com
http://acm.org/~aaronh/das.html

Houston Area ACM SIGGRAPH

Tom Ledoux
2501 Tanglewilde #203
Houston TX 77063
ledoux@cogniseis.com

Washington

Tri-Cities Washington ACM SIGGRAPH

Donald R. Jones
Pacific Northwest Lab
MS K1-96
PO Box 999
Richland WA 99352
dr_jones@pnl.gov

International Chapters

Brazil

Sao Paulo ACM SIGGRAPH

Rua Bairi 294
SP-05059
Sao Paulo, Brazil
spsigg@ bra000.canal-vip.onsp.br

Bulgaria

Sofia ACM SIGGRAPH

Technical Univ. of Sofia
Dept of Prog & Computer Appl
Sofia 1756 Bulgaria
smale@ bgtus4.vmei.acad.bg

Canada

Vancouver B.C. ACM SIGGRAPH

PO Box 29147
1996 W. Broadway
Vancouver BC
Canada
berryhil@cs.ubc.ca
http://fas.sfu.ca/cs/research/groups/GMRL/ACM-SIGGRAPH

France

Paris ACM SIGGRAPH

c/o SUPINFOCOM — Terita 3000
2, rue Henri Matisse
59300 Aulnoye-lez-Valenciennes
France
paris_chapter@siggraph.org

Israel

Central Israel ACM SIGGRAPH

Dept of Computer Science
Technion-Israel Inst of Tech
Haifa, Israel
central_israel_chapter@siggraph.org

United Kingdom

London ACM SIGGRAPH

31 Old Gloucester St
Bloomsbury
London, England

Contact your local chapter to find out what activities are upcoming. Attend as a nonmember to get a feel. Practice a little schmoozing.

Online Tutorials

Mark Jeffers (jeffers7@aol.com) has authored some online trueSpace tutorials that deserve special mention if for no other reason than their outstanding quality. They are written well and come complete with numerous screen shots and downloadable example files. As of this writing, he has made two tutorials — one is the making of a space planetary scene; the other is for the creation of landscapes. He plans more tutorials. Highly recommended.

Another dandy place for online "tutorials" is the trueSpace Mailing List (tSML) Web page located at http://www.realtime.net/~dcampbel/ts_tips.html. The tSML Tips and Techniques section is always growing as members help each other explore this remarkable medium. Your tips are welcome. Don't just be a lurker, share your great ideas with the rest of us.

APPENDIX E

trueSpace2 File Formats

If you started programming images in POV like I did, this format will not be entirely foreign to you. It's different, but you probably understand the general principles. Rob Bryerton used this information to build the remarkable Exploder program. If you're good at this sort of thing, you can build your own standalone object-manipulation engine. If it's an exciting application, there will be a good audience for you. The folks at Caligari compiled the following information. It too is available in rich text format at their Web site in its latest update.

Document Version 2.0

This appendix provides details on the geometry and material information stored in Caligari object (*.cob) files. It helps enable you to read, manipulate, and write such files. Most of the information presented is the same for both 1.0 and 2.0 files.

Caligari files are chunked files. They consist of standard header followed by 1 or more data chunks. The last chunk in the file should always be the special 'END' chunk. Each chunk consists of a header followed by chunk-dependent data. Chunks may not be embedded in other chunks. Each chunk contains an ID and a Parent ID that allows chunks to be "owned" by other chunks.

The file comes in two flavors: ASCII and binary. They both encode the same information and have the same general layout. An advantage of ASCII files is that they can be edited in a regular text editor. The binary files are faster for programs to load and save, and are smaller. You can load an ASCII file into tS2 and save it out as a binary file.

A word about ownership. Each object in trueSpace2 has such attributes as color, material, transparency, size and rotation, and so on. Anything that belongs to that object will have a parent ID in its chunk header naming the parent. It's kinda like a DNA thing.

Caligari Header

The header consists of 32 bytes, as follows:

Size	Type	Value	Description
9 bytes	char	"Caligari"	Identifies Caligari file
6 bytes	char	"V00.01"	Version number of file — this chapter describes version 00.01 files
1 byte	char	"A" for ASCII or "B" for binary	Specifies whether file is in ASCII format or binary format
2 bytes	char	"LH" for little endian or "HL" for big endian	Intel-based machines are little endian and currently all Caligari files are too
13 bytes	char	" "	Leave as 13 blank spaces
1 byte	char	"\n" Newline character	Newline

When attempting to decide on the format of a file you're trying to read you should check if the first 15 bytes match the first two fields in the header. This should definitively identify the file as a Caligari file. You will also need to know if the file is ASCII or binary and read the appropriate format.

Chunk Headers

The chunk header consists of six fields, as follows:

✦ **Type** — Tells what type the chunk is. There are several types listed later. These types tell you what the data in this chunk describes. You should use this field to choose the appropriate routine to read this chunk or if you do not recognize the chunk type you should skip this chunk using the size field described below.

✦ **Version Numbers** — There are fields for both major and minor version numbers, which tell you which version this chunk type is. If you get a version number other than the ones you know how to read, you should most likely skip this chunk.

✦ **ID Fields —** The individual chunk ID and the Parent ID fields let chunks be owned by other chunks. Each chunk has its own unique ID. You should keep track of these IDs as you read them in. If the Parent ID is zero then the chunk has no parent, otherwise the Parent ID refers to a chunk located earlier in the file and to which this chunk's attributes are attached. That sounds more complicated than it is. Here's an example to help clarify: Suppose you have a cube that has been painted with two materials. The geometry of the cube will be saved in a `'PolH'` chunk, and following it will be two material `'Mat1'` chunks. Each of the material chunks will have their Parent ID fields set to the chunk ID of the cube's `'PolH'` chunk to show that the materials are owned by that specific cube. Got it?

✦ **Size Field —** There is also a data size field that tells you how many data bytes are contained in the chunk exclusive of the header. This allows you to quickly skip chunks you don't recognize or are not interested in. Be aware, however, that it is permissible to set the data size to -1 to indicate that the size is unknown.

The ASCII chunk header format is as follows:

```
"%4c V%d.%d Id %d Parent %d Size %d"
```

A typical ASCII chunk header looks like:

```
"PolH V0.02 Id 2490008 Parent 0 Size 00000947"
```

This chunk has the type 'PolH' (polygonal data chunk), the major version is 0, the minor version is 2, the chunk ID is 2490008, the parent ID is 0 (no parent), and there are 947 data bytes following the header in this chunk.

To get a better feel for this format, save a few objects in ASCII format and take a look at them in your favorite text editor. This should give you a sense of the general format of Caligari files. To output ASCII files from trueSpace choose the "Save Object As..." option and check the little ASCII box in the file dialog box.

The binary header is as follows:

Size	*Type*	*Description*
4 bytes	char	Chunk type
2 bytes	short	Major version
2 bytes	short	Minor version
4 bytes	long	Chunk ID
4 bytes	long	Parent ID
4 bytes	long	Number of bytes in chunk data

Some Common Elements in Chunks

Here are some common elements that appear is several different chunks:

Strings

In ASCII format, strings are represented as used by printf and scanf — specifically, one or more non-whitespace characters followed by a whitespace character. This allows you to use the "%s" format string to read and write strings using printf and scanf.

ASCII format:

```
"%s"
```

Binary format:

Size	*Type*	*Description*
2 bytes	short	String length
length	bytes	String in ASCII characters (does not include a terminating NULL character)

Names

Many chunks contain a name field. To keep each name unique within its context, each name has a number attached to it. We refer to this number as the names dupecount, and it is always >= 0. The ASCII format consists of a string that contains the name optionally followed by a comma and the dupecount (for example, "Obj,1"). Note that if the dupecount is absent then it is assumed to be zero.

ASCII format:

```
"\nName %s"
```

Binary format:

Size	*Type*	*Description*
2 bytes	short	Name dupecount
2+length	string	Name excluding dupecount (see description of strings)

Local Axes

Some chunks define their own local set of axes. This consists of a position or center for the axes and directions for the X, Y, and Z axes. These are given in world coordinates. The X, Y, and Z axes should be perpendicular to each other and are not relative to the center of axes.

ASCII format:

```
"\ncenter %g %g %g"
"\nx axis %g %g %g"
"\ny axis %g %g %g"
"\nz axis %g %g %g"
```

Binary format:

Size	*Type*	*Description*
12 bytes	float triple	X, Y, and Z coordinates for center of axes
12 bytes	float triple	X, Y, and Z coordinates for direction of local X axis
12 bytes	float triple	X, Y, and Z coordinates for direction of local Y axis
12 bytes	float triple	X, Y, and Z coordinates for direction of local Z axis

Current Position

Most chunks that contain 3D geometry define a local space. The current position is a matrix that transforms from local space to world space. The local coordinates are treated as column vectors with a 1 in the fourth position and multiplied by the matrix to get the corresponding world coordinates. Note: trueSpace currently does not use the fourth row of the matrix and this row should always be [0,0,0,1] or the matrix may not be interpreted correctly.

ASCII format:

```
"\nTransform"
"\n%g %g %g %g"
"\n%g %g %g %g"
"\n%g %g %g %g"
"\n%g %g %g %g"
```

Binary format:

Size	*Type*	*Description*
16 bytes	float quad	First row of matrix
16 bytes	float quad	Second row of matrix
16 bytes	float quad	Third row of matrix

Note: Binary format does not include row 4 of the matrix. It's assumed to be [0,0,0,1].

Chunk Types

`'END '(End of file Chunk)`

Chunk type: `'END '(End Chunk)`

Major version 1

Minor version 0

This chunk contains no data. It signifies the end of the file and must always be the last chunk in the file.

`'Grou' (Group Chunk)`

Chunk type: `'Grou'`

Major version: 0

Minor version: 1

The group chunk consists of the following:

- Chunk Header
- Name
- Local Axes
- Current Position

See the appropriate sections for descriptions of each of these attributes.

`'PolH' (Polygonal Data Chunk)`

Chunk type: `'PolH'`

Major version: 0

Minor version: 2

The polygonal data chunk consists of the following:

- Chunk Header
- Name
- Local Axes
- Current Position

- ✦ Local Vertex list
- ✦ UV Vertex list
- ✦ Face list

The Local Vertex list is a list of 3D positions in the local coordinate space defined by this chunk's Current Position (see appropriate section). It consists of a count of the number of vertices followed by the vertices. Each vertex consists of three floats for the X, Y, and Z values.

ASCII format:

`"\nWorld Vertices %ld"` — gives number of local vertices following (>= 0)

For each local vertex:

```
"\n%f %f %f"
```

Binary format:

Size	*Type*	*Description*
4 bytes	long	Number of local vertices
12 bytes each	float triples	X, Y, and Z coordinates for each local vertex

The UV Vertex list is a list of UV (texture) positions. It consists of a count of the number of UV vertices followed by the UV vertices. Each UV vertex consists of two floats for the U and V values.

ASCII format:

`"\nTexture Vertices %ld"` — gives number of UV vertices following (>= 0)

For each UV vertex:

```
"\n%f %f"
```

Binary format:

Size	*Type*	*Description*
4 bytes	long	Number of UV vertices
8 bytes each	float pairs	U and V coordinates for each UV vertex

The Face list is a list of faces and holes. Each face has its own set of flags, a material number, a count of the number of face vertices, and a list of face vertices. Each hole has a count of the number of face vertices it contains followed by the face vertices. The hole should be interpreted as being a hole in the most recently read face. Each face vertex consists of two integers; these are an index into the local Vertex list followed by an index into the UV Vertex list.

ASCII format:

`"\nFaces %ld"` — gives the number of faces following (>=0)

For each face, either:

```
"\nFace verts %hd flads %hd mat %hd"
```

or:

```
"\nHole verts %hd"
```

For each face vertex in the face or hole:

```
"<%ld,%ld>"
```

Binary format:

Size	*Type*	*Description*
4 bytes	long	Number of faces and holes
See below	See below	Faces and holes

A face is:

Size	*Type*	*Description*
1 bytes	byte	Flags byte (F_HOLE flag is not set)
2 bytes	short	Number of vertices in face (not including any holes)
2 bytes	short	Material index for face
8 bytes each	long pairs	Face vertices – each consists of a long index in the local Vertex list followed by a long index into the UV Vertex list

A hole is:

Size	Type	Description
1 byte	byte	Flags byte (F_HOLE flag is set)
2 bytes	short	Number of vertices in face (not including any holes)
8 bytes each	long pairs	Face vertices – each consists of a long index in the local Vertex list followed by a long index into the UV Vertex list

Two flags are currently defined for faces:

```
#define F_HOLE      0x08   // (bit 3)
#define F_BACKCULL  0x10   // (bit 4)
```

The F_HOLE flag is used to distinguish holes from faces in the binary format. The F_BACKCULL flag means that this face should not be displayed if it's facing away from the camera or view. This flag is currently only used on two-dimensional objects, where the front and back face of an object occupy the same space.

The normal of a face is obtained by using the right hand rule. Some operations such as quad-divide will only work on objects that trueSpace considers to be solids. For an object to be solid, the number of faces in an object minus two must equal the number of vertices plus the number of edges. In addition, each edge must be shared by exactly two faces. Thus when a flat polygon is created in trueSpace, it is represented by two polygons; one facing up and one facing down.

```
'Mat1' (Material Chunk)
```

Chunk type: 'Mat1'

Major version: 0

Minor version: 5

The material chunk consists of the following:

- ✦ Chunk Header
- ✦ Material data
- ✦ Environment map data (optional)
- ✦ Texture map data (optional)
- ✦ Bump map data (optional)

The material data contains the shader type, facet type, color (red, green, blue), and some shader attributes: opacity (alpha), ambient coefficient (ka), specular coefficient (ks), hilight size coefficient (exp), and index of refraction (ior). It also contains a material number. All material chunks have a parent chunk, and the material number identifies which child material this is. For instance if a material chunk has material number 2 and its parent is a 'PolH' or polygonal chunk, then this is material number 2 of that chunk, and all faces that have their material ID set to 2 in the 'PolH' chunk should use this material.

ASCII format:

```
"n\nmat# %d"                      — material number
"\nshader: %s facet: %s"
"\nrgb %g,%g,%g"                  — material color
"\nalpha %g ka %g ks %g exp %g ior %g"
```

Current possibilities for the shader field are: `"flat"`, `"phong"`, and `"metal"`.

Current possibilities for the facet field are: `"faceted"`, `"auto%d"`, and `"smooth"`. The autofacet choice contains a value for the autofacet angle. Thus autofacet with an angle of 45 degrees would be `"auto45"`.

Binary format:

Size	*Type*	*Description*
2 bytes	short	Material number
1 byte	char	Shader type ('f' – flat, 'p' – phong, 'm' – metal)
1 byte	char	Facet type ('f' – faceted, 'a' – autofacet, 's' – smooth)
1 byte	char	Autofacet angle (0 – 179 degrees)
4 bytes	float	Red component of color (0.0 – 1.0)
4 bytes	float	Green component of color (0.0 – 1.0)
4 bytes	float	Blue component of color (0.0 – 1.0)
4 bytes	float	Opacity (0.0 – 1.0)
4 bytes	float	Ambient coefficient (0.0 – 1.0)
4 bytes	float	Specular coefficient (0.0 – 1.0)
4 bytes	float	Hilight size coefficient (0.0 – 1.0)
4 bytes	float	Index of refraction

If environment map data is present then it starts with an identifying field, the full pathname of the environment map file, and a set of flags. The flags for environment maps are:

```
#define ENVR_CUBIC  0x01   // (bit 0)
#define ENVR_USE    0x02   // (bit 1)
```

The `ENVR_USE` flag is always set. The `ENVR_CUBIC` flag is set to indicate that the environment map is a cubic map; otherwise it's assumed to be a spherical environment map.

ASCII format:

```
"\nenvironment: %s"             — full pathname of environment file
"\nflags %d"
```

Binary format:

Size	*Type*	*Description*
2 bytes	chars	Environment map data identifier ('e:')
1 byte	char	Environment map flags
2+length	string	Pathname of environment map file (see strings section)

If texture map data is present then it starts with an identifying field, the full pathname of the texture map file, an offset in U and V, the number of times to repeat the texture map in U and V, and a set of flags. The flags for texture maps are:

```
#define TXTR_OVERLAY      0x01   // (bit 0)
#define TXTR_USE          0x02   // (bit 1)
```

The `TXTR_USE` flag is always set. If the `TXTR_OVERLAY` flag is set then the object's color will show through where the texture map is at least partially transparent. Otherwise the object will be genuinely transparent in those areas.

ASCII format:

```
"\ntexture: %s"                          — full pathname of texture file
"\noffset %g,%g repeats %g,%g flags %hd"
```

Binary format:

Size	*Type*	*Description*
2 bytes	chars	Texture map data identifier ('t:')
1 byte	char	Texture map flags
2+length	string	Pathname of texture map file (see strings section)
4 bytes	float	U offset for texture map
4 bytes	float	V offset for texture map
4 bytes	float	Number of times to repeat texture map in U direction
4 bytes	float	Number of times to repeat texture map in V direction

If bump map data is present then it starts with an identifying field, the full pathname of the bump map file, an amplitude for the bump map, an offset in U and V, the number of times to repeat the bump map in U and V, and a set of flags. The flags for bumps maps are:

```
#define BUMP_USE            0x02   // (bit 1)
```

The `BUMP_USE` flag is always set.

ASCII format:

```
"\nbump: %s"                     — full pathname of bump file
"\noffset %g,%g repeats %g,%g amp %g flags %hd"
```

Binary format:

Size	*Type*	*Description*
2 bytes	chars	Bump map data identifier ('b:')
1 byte	char	Bump map flags
2+length	string	Pathname of bump map file (see strings section)
4 bytes	float	U offset for bump map
4 bytes	float	V offset for bump map
4 bytes	float	Number of times to repeat bump map in U direction
4 bytes	float	Number of times to repeat bump map in V direction
4 bytes	float	Relative amplitude of bump map

'PrTx' (Procedural Texture Chunk)

Chunk type: 'PrTx'

Major version: 0

Minor version: 1

The procedural texture chunk consists of the following:

- ✦ Chunk Header
- ✦ Material data
- ✦ Environment map data (optional)
- ✦ One of Granite, Marble, or Wood data (optional)
- ✦ Bump map data (optional)

The procedural texture chunk is very similar to the material chunk. If a material is to be procedurally textured, then this chunk will appear instead of a 'Mat1' chunk. The only difference between the two chunks is that where a 'Mat1' has an optional texture map specification, the 'PrTx' chunk has an optional Granite, Marble, or Wood texture specification. Other than this, everything else is the same. Please see the material chunk description above for information about all chunk elements except the Granite, Marble, and Wood data. The RST solid texture coordinates are based on each object's untransformed world vertices.

If Granite data is present then it begins with an identifying field, followed by four RGBA colors, four contribution amounts (one for each color), sharpness, R, S, and T scale values, and a seed value.

ASCII format:

```
"\ngranite:"
"\nrgba1 %g,%g,%g,%g rgba2 %g,%g,%g,%g"
"\nrgba3 %g,%g,%g,%g rgba4 %g,%g,%g,%g"
"\namount1 %g amount2 %g amount3 %g amount4 %g"
"\nsharpness %g scale %g,%g,%g seed %hd"
```

Binary format:

Size	*Type*	*Description*
2 bytes	chars	Granite texture data identifier ('g:')
1 byte	char	Reserved (set to 0 for now)
4 bytes	float	Color 1 red (0.0 – 1.0)

(continued)

Binary format (continued):

Size	*Type*	*Description*
4 bytes	float	Color 1 green (0.0 – 1.0)
4 bytes	float	Color 1 blue (0.0 – 1.0)
4 bytes	float	Color 1 alpha (0.0 – 1.0)
4 bytes	float	Color 2 red (0.0 – 1.0)
4 bytes	float	Color 2 green (0.0 – 1.0)
4 bytes	float	Color 2 blue (0.0 – 1.0)
4 bytes	float	Color 2 alpha (0.0 – 1.0)
4 bytes	float	Color 3 red (0.0 – 1.0)
4 bytes	float	Color 3 green (0.0 – 1.0)
4 bytes	float	Color 3 blue (0.0 – 1.0)
4 bytes	float	Color 3 alpha (0.0 – 1.0)
4 bytes	float	Color 4 red (0.0 – 1.0)
4 bytes	float	Color 4 green (0.0 – 1.0)
4 bytes	float	Color 4 blue (0.0 – 1.0)
4 bytes	float	Color 4 alpha (0.0 – 1.0)
4 bytes	float	Amount of color 1 (0.0 – 1.0)
4 bytes	float	Amount of color 2 (0.0 – 1.0)
4 bytes	float	Amount of color 3 (0.0 – 1.0)
4 bytes	float	Amount of color 4 (0.0 – 1.0)
4 bytes	float	Sharpness (0.0 – 1.0)
4 bytes	float	R scale (0.0 – 10.0)
4 bytes	float	S scale (0.0 – 10.0)
4 bytes	float	T scale (0.0 – 10.0)
2 bytes	short	Seed (1 – 32767)

If Marble data is present then it begins with an identifying field, followed by stone color and alpha, vein color and alpha, sharpness, R, S, and T scale values, turbulence, grain axis, and a seed value. The grain axis is one of the following selections:

```
#define PROC_GRAIN R        0x01   // (bit 1)
#define PROC_GRAIN S        0x02   // (bit 2)
#define PROC_GRAIN T        0x04   // (bit 3)
```

ASCII format:

```
"\nmarble:"
"\nstonergba %g,%g,%g,%g veinrgba %g,%g,%g,%g"
"\nsharpness %g scale %g,%g,%g"
"\nturbulence %hd grain %hd seed %hd"
```

Binary format:

Size	Type	Description
2 bytes	chars	Marble texture data identifier ('m:')
1 byte	char	Reserved (set to 0 for now)
4 bytes	float	Stone color red (0.0 – 1.0)
4 bytes	float	Stone color green (0.0 – 1.0)
4 bytes	float	Stone color blue (0.0 – 1.0)
4 bytes	float	Stone color alpha (0.0 – 1.0)
4 bytes	float	Vein color red (0.0 – 1.0)
4 bytes	float	Vein color green (0.0 – 1.0)
4 bytes	float	Vein color blue (0.0 – 1.0)
4 bytes	float	Vein color alpha (0.0 – 1.0)
4 bytes	float	Sharpness (0.0 – 1.0)
4 bytes	float	R scale (0.0 – 10.0)
4 bytes	float	S scale (0.0 – 10.0)
4 bytes	float	T scale (0.0 – 10.0)
2 bytes	short	Vein turbulence (1 – 10)
2 bytes	short	RST grain flag (see above)
2 bytes	short	Seed (1 – 32767)

If Wood data is present then it begins with an identifying field, followed by spring and summer wood RGBA colors, ratio of spring to summer wood, ring density, ring width variation, ring shape variation, R, S, and T center for wood rings, R, S, and T scale, grain axis, and a seed value. See the Marble description for information about the grain axis. Note that the RST center values are not presently exposed in the trueSpace2 user interface and should be set to (1.0, 1.0, 1.0).

ASCII format:

```
"\nwood:"
"\nspringrgba %g,%g,%g,%g summerrgba %g,%g,%g,%g"
"\nldratio %g rdensity %g rwidthvar %g rsharevar %g"
"\ncenter %g,%g,%g scale %g,%g,%g"
"\ngrain %hd seed %hd"
```

Binary format:

Size	*Type*	*Description*
2 bytes	chars	Wood texture data identifier ('w:')
1 byte	char	Reserved (set to 0 for now)
4 bytes	float	Spring wood color red (0.0 – 1.0)
4 bytes	float	Spring wood color green (0.0 – 1.0)
4 bytes	float	Spring wood color blue (0.0 – 1.0)
4 bytes	float	Spring wood color alpha (0.0 – 1.0)
4 bytes	float	Summer wood color red (0.0 – 1.0)
4 bytes	float	Summer wood color green (0.0 – 1.0)
4 bytes	float	Summer wood color blue (0.0 – 1.0)
4 bytes	float	Summer wood color alpha (0.0 – 1.0)
4 bytes	float	Spring to summer ratio (0.0 – 1.0)
4 bytes	float	Ring density (0.0 – 10.0)
4 bytes	float	Ring width variation (0.0 – 1.0)
4 bytes	float	Ring shape variation (0.0 – 1.0)
4 bytes	float	R ring center (set to 1.0)
4 bytes	float	S ring center (set to 1.0)
4 bytes	float	T ring center (set to 1.0)
4 bytes	float	R scale (0.0 – 10.0)
4 bytes	float	S scale (0.0 – 10.0)
4 bytes	float	T scale (0.0 – 10.0)
2 bytes	short	RST grain flag (see above)
2 bytes	short	Seed (1 – 32767)

Got That?

If you didn't understand all this, you probably didn't read this far. If you did understand everything, and you want more information, keep checking the Caligari Web pages. Caligari intends to post the scene description language and additional information on objects. I suspect next on Caligari's agenda is to give you direct access to the engine. Enjoy.

Index

Symbols and Numbers

A

(continued)

B

C

(continued)

(continued)

D

E

(continued)

F

(continued)

I

J

K

L

(continued)

M

(continued)

N

O

(continued)

P

Q

R

(continued)

S

T

(continued)

U

V

(continued)

W

X

Y

Z

IDG BOOKS WORLDWIDE, INC.
END-USER LICENSE AGREEMENT

Read This. You should carefully read these terms and conditions before opening the software packet(s) included with this book ("Book"). This is a license agreement ("Agreement") between you and IDG Books Worldwide, Inc. ("IDGB"). By opening the accompanying software packet(s), you acknowledge that you have read and accept the following terms and conditions. If you do not agree and do not want to be bound by such terms and conditions, promptly return the Book and the unopened software packet(s) to the place you obtained them for a full refund.

1. **License Grant**. IDGB grants to you (either an individual or entity) a nonexclusive license to use one copy of the enclosed software program(s) (collectively, the "Software") solely for your own personal or business purposes on a single computer (whether a standard computer or a workstation component of a multi-user network). The Software is in use on a computer when it is loaded into temporary memory (i.e., RAM) or installed into permanent memory (e.g., hard disk, CD-ROM, or other storage device). IDGB reserves all rights not expressly granted herein.

2. **Ownership**. IDGB is the owner of all right, title and interest, including copyright, in and to the compilation of the Software recorded on the disk(s)/CD-ROM. Copyright to the individual programs on the disk(s)/CD-ROM is owned by the author or other authorized copyright owner of each program. Ownership of the Software and all proprietary rights relating thereto remain with IDGB and its licensors.

3. **Restrictions On Use and Transfer**.

   (a) You may only (i) make one copy of the Software for backup or archival purposes, or (ii) transfer the Software to a single hard disk, provided that you keep the original for backup or archival purposes. You may not (i) rent or lease the Software, (ii) copy or reproduce the Software through a LAN or other network system or through any computer subscriber system or bulletin-board system, or (iii) modify, adapt or create derivative works based on the Software.

(b) You may not reverse engineer, decompile, or disassemble the Software. You may transfer the Software and user documentation on a permanent basis, provided that the transferee agrees to accept the terms and conditions of this Agreement and you retain no copies. If the Software is an update or has been updated, any transfer must include the most recent update and all prior versions.

4. Restrictions on Use of Individual Programs. You must follow the individual requirements and restrictions detailed for each individual program in Appendix A of this Book. These limitations are contained in the individual license agreements recorded on the disk(s)/CD-ROM. These restrictions include a requirement that after using the program for the period of time specified in its text, the user must pay a registration fee or discontinue use. By opening the Software packet(s), you will be agreeing to abide by the licenses and restrictions for these individual programs. None of the material on this disk(s) or listed in this Book may ever be distributed, in original or modified form, for commercial purposes.

5. Limited Warranty.

(a) IDGB warrants that the Software and disk(s)/CD-ROM are free from defects in materials and workmanship under normal use for a period of sixty (60) days from the date of purchase of this Book. If IDGB receives notification within the warranty period of defects in materials or workmanship, IDGB will replace the defective disk(s)/CD-ROM.

(b) IDGB AND THE AUTHOR OF THE BOOK DISCLAIM ALL OTHER WARRANTIES, EXPRESS OR IMPLIED, INCLUDING WITHOUT LIMITATION IMPLIED WARRANTIES OF MERCHANTABILITY AND FITNESS FOR A PARTICULAR PURPOSE, WITH RESPECT TO THE SOFTWARE, THE PROGRAMS, THE SOURCE CODE CONTAINED THEREIN, AND/OR THE TECHNIQUES DESCRIBED IN THIS BOOK. IDGB DOES NOT WARRANT THAT THE FUNCTIONS CONTAINED IN THE SOFTWARE WILL MEET YOUR REQUIREMENTS OR THAT THE OPERATION OF THE SOFTWARE WILL BE ERROR FREE.

(c) This limited warranty gives you specific legal rights, and you may have other rights which vary from jurisdiction to jurisdiction.

6. Remedies.

(a) IDGB's entire liability and your exclusive remedy for defects in materials and workmanship shall be limited to replacement of the Software, which is returned to IDGB at the address set forth below with a copy of your receipt. This Limited Warranty is void if failure of the Software has resulted from accident, abuse, or misapplication. Any replacement Software will be warranted for the remainder of the original warranty period or thirty (30) days, whichever is longer.

(b) In no event shall IDGB or the author be liable for any damages whatsoever (including without limitation damages for loss of business profits, business interruption, loss of business information, or any other pecuniary loss) arising out of the use of or inability to use the Book or the Software, even if IDGB has been advised of the possibility of such damages.

(c) Because some jurisdictions do not allow the exclusion or limitation of liability for consequential or incidental damages, the above limitation or exclusion may not apply to you.

7. **U.S. Government Restricted Rights.** Use, duplication, or disclosure of the Software by the U.S. Government is subject to restrictions stated in paragraph (c) (1) (ii) of the Rights in Technical Data and Computer Software clause of DFARS 252.227-7013, and in subparagraphs (a) through (d) of the Commercial Computer—Restricted Rights clause at FAR 52.227-19, and in similar clauses in the NASA FAR supplement, when applicable.

General. This Agreement constitutes the entire understanding of the parties, and revokes and supersedes all prior agreements, oral or written, between them and may not be modified or amended except in a writing signed by both parties hereto which specifically refers to this Agreement. This Agreement shall take precedence over any other documents that may be in conflict herewith. If any one or more provisions contained in this Agreement are held by any court or tribunal to be invalid, illegal or otherwise unenforceable, each and every other provision shall remain in full force and effect.

Replacement CD-ROM Disk Available

If a replacement CD-ROM disk is needed, please write to the following address: Disk Fulfillment Department, Attn: *Caligari trueSpace2 Bible,* IDG Books Worldwide, Inc., 7260 Shadeland Station, Indianapolis, IN 46256, or call 1-800-762-2974. Please specify the size of disk you need and allow 3 to 4 weeks for delivery.

IDG BOOKS WORLDWIDE REGISTRATION CARD

RETURN THIS REGISTRATION CARD FOR FREE CATALOG

Title of this book: Caligari trueSpace2™ Bible

My overall rating of this book: ❑ Very good [1] ❑ Good [2] ❑ Satisfactory [3] ❑ Fair [4] ❑ Poor [5]

How I first heard about this book:

❑ Found in bookstore; name: [6] ❑ Book review: [7]

❑ Advertisement: [8] ❑ Catalog: [9]

❑ Word of mouth; heard about book from friend, co-worker, etc.: [10] ❑ Other: [11]

What I liked most about this book:

What I would change, add, delete, etc., in future editions of this book:

Other comments:

Number of computer books I purchase in a year: ❑ 1 [12] ❑ 2-5 [13] ❑ 6-10 [14] ❑ More than 10 [15]

I would characterize my computer skills as: ❑ Beginner [16] ❑ Intermediate [17] ❑ Advanced [18] ❑ Professional [19]

I use ❑ DOS [20] ❑ Windows [21] ❑ OS/2 [22] ❑ Unix [23] ❑ Macintosh [24] ❑ Other: [25] ____________ (please specify)

I would be interested in new books on the following subjects:
(please check all that apply, and use the spaces provided to identify specific software)

❑ Word processing: [26] ❑ Spreadsheets: [27]

❑ Data bases: [28] ❑ Desktop publishing: [29]

❑ File Utilities: [30] ❑ Money management: [31]

❑ Networking: [32] ❑ Programming languages: [33]

❑ Other: [34]

I use a PC at (please check all that apply): ❑ home [35] ❑ work [36] ❑ school [37] ❑ other: [38] ____________

The disks I prefer to use are ❑ 5.25 [39] ❑ 3.5 [40] ❑ other: [41] ____________

I have a CD ROM: ❑ yes [42] ❑ no [43]

I plan to buy or upgrade computer hardware this year: ❑ yes [44] ❑ no [45]

I plan to buy or upgrade computer software this year: ❑ yes [46] ❑ no [47]

Name: Business title: [48] Type of Business: [49]

Address (❑ home [50] ❑ work [51]/Company name:)

Street/Suite#

City [52]/State [53]/Zipcode [54]: Country [55]

❑ **I liked this book!** You may quote me by name in future IDG Books Worldwide promotional materials.

My daytime phone number is ____________

IDG BOOKS

THE WORLD OF COMPUTER KNOWLEDGE